NEW HORIZONS FOR THE FAMILY

THE MACMILLAN COMPANY
NEW YORK · BOSTON · CHICAGO · DALLAS
ATLANTA · SAN FRANCISCO

MACMILLAN AND CO., Limited
LONDON · BOMBAY · CALCUTTA · MADRAS
MELBOURNE

THE MACMILLAN COMPANY
OF CANADA, Limited
TORONTO

NEW HORIZONS
FOR THE FAMILY

By

UNA BERNARD SAIT, Ph.D.

PROFESSOR OF PHILOSOPHY IN CLAREMONT COLLEGES

NEW YORK
THE MACMILLAN COMPANY
1938

SET UP AND ELECTROTYPED BY T. MOREY & SON

PRINTED IN THE UNITED STATES OF AMERICA

PREFACE

In recent years the study of the family has attracted wide attention and led to the publication of numerous books. So complicated a subject naturally admits of a variety of treatment. History and anthropology, sociology and economics, biology and psychology must all contribute, if we are to achieve adequate understanding of the family. The result is a growing mass of information. It ranges in reliability from objective, but limited studies, employing approved methods of research, to one-sided interpretations of special pleaders. Such a situation is bewildering to students whose interest lies in the realities of family life and who need, above all, to be given understanding of the present significance of the family to the individual and to society. There is, therefore, a definite need for books whose purpose is to provide orientation and perspective, books whose chief endeavor is to develop a broad philosophy of the family.

In *New Horizons for the Family* an attempt is made to discern possibilities for the future suggested by our knowledge of the family in the past and present, and to examine means and methods for the realization of those possibilities which seem most desirable. The first necessity is an analysis of the inter-relationships between family members and of the family with other families and with wider social groups. Family functions and the values inherent in family life are thus disclosed. At the same time it becomes apparent that certain social conditions and attitudes, certain individual habits of mind have obstructed the realization of these values. Other influences have, on the contrary, proved beneficial to family well-being. Herein, then, lies the clue to a remedy for family ills, to a resolution of present conflicts. Specific suggestions may be made for the eradication or modification of adverse influences; other suggestions for the reënforcement and further development of influences which enhance and extend the values of family life and render them more secure. New possibilities for a more satisfying family life are forecast in imagination, ideals which are rooted in actual fact and spring from contemporary need. Guiding principles may be discerned and plans for action formulated, plans susceptible of test and modification in the light of the consequences they effect in dealing with present problems.

A philosophy of the family conceived in this spirit is obviously an application to a special field of the philosophical principles of John Dewey. The writer's indebtedness to his profound and illuminating insight will be apparent throughout this book. Emphasis upon the far-reaching significance of scientific method is central in Dewey's thought. Humanity is now in possession of a new and highly effective method for directing change. New techniques bestow unprecedented control over physical and human energies. But the social implications of scientific method have hitherto been largely overlooked. It is to these social implications that Dewey calls attention; to the imperative need for the use of coöperative experimental intelligence in social affairs.

In experimental method intelligence discovers the principles of its own effective use. Reflective thought may hope to achieve its purposes only where attention is concentrated on specific means and where there is willingness to revise both thought and action in the light of consequences and of the further discovery of relevant data. Symptoms may then be diagnosed in terms of underlying conditions, and causes be dealt with rather than results.

The urgent need to-day is for a scientific spirit in all efforts to influence human nature or to remodel social institutions. Those who, with Dewey, realize this fact, place their chief reliance on education. The most potent means for the reconstruction of social methods and ideals is to be found in the modification of the mental and moral attitudes of individuals. From such a standpoint, moreover, no field offers greater promise than that of education for marriage and family life. Within family life are found the fundamental determinants of the character of the younger generation. But fathers and mothers need adequate preparation if they are to make effective use of their opportunities. While, therefore, the general purpose of this book is to contribute to a philosophy of the family, its specific purpose is educational: to assist in preparation for marriage and family life.

It is hoped that, as a textbook, *New Horizons for the Family* will allow of varied uses. The same subject matter which is of value in education for family life may also be used with advantage in the education of teachers and social workers. While the book is designed to be used as a whole, varying emphases may be laid on different parts in accordance with specific purposes. Bibliographies appended to each chapter provide the means for further and more detailed study wherever this is deemed desirable. A liberal use of quotations serves as an introduction to many of the books included in the bibliographies.

Few references are made to periodical literature and none to contemporary fiction. Both, however, may be used effectively in a study of the family. Newspapers are an indispensable adjunct. Where students become concerned with the effects of social conditions and of current legislation on family life, interest is stimulated in civic and political activity. Added realism may be gained through observation of the proceedings of juvenile, domestic, and divorce courts, and of the work of nursery schools and child-welfare agencies, supplemented, where possible, by some participation in work with children. Even without such aids, there is no lack of strong appeal in a study whose subject matter is relevant to the natural desire of men and women to find happiness in marriage and family life. To education belongs the opportunity of making this vital interest more responsible and more fully intelligent.

UNA BERNARD SAIT

CLAREMONT, CALIF.
May, 1938

CONTENTS

THE MODERN FAMILY

HOME LIFE

INTRODUCTION

CHAPTER I

SOCIAL CHANGE AND THE FAMILY

The Recent Acceleration of Social Change. Half a century has passed since Nietzsche's vivid portrayal of the Western world as adrift and struggling in a "chaos of contradictory valuations." What phrase could even he have found by which to characterize the life of to-day? Conflicts grow no less acute, while confusion increases in the aims and purposes of men.

One source of our present bewilderment is not hard to find: the complexity and rapidity of the social changes in which we are involved. Social changes follow inevitably from alterations in the conditions of human life. Alterations, so radical and so extensive as to amount to a revolution in all aspects of human life, have, as we all know, been brought about by the scientific development of the last three hundred years. Science and the machine are of the very recent past, but already they have led to an acceleration of social change unprecedented in human history.

There has been, it is true, a "progressive shortening in the time-span of social change." [1] Prior to the rise of science, however, its movement was still so slow as to render even more impressive the recency of its acceleration. We are wont to speak of "the stream of history." Could not the metaphor be made more vivid and more true to fact if human history were to be compared to a mighty glacier, advancing irresistibly but imperceptibly for hundreds of thousands of years? Now and then there has been a partial release of some of its waters; only to-day is such liberation widespread. We toss in the grip of a turbulent torrent, bearing with it the debris of past traditions and institutions, and sweeping us on to uncharted seas.

Changes in the external conditions of human life, with accompanying changes in human interests, have had a disrupting effect on social traditions and social institutions. This aspect of the social consequences of the development of science is obvious to all. There remains, however, another aspect not so obvious, realization of which reveals another and more funda-

[1] John Dewey, *Philosophy and Civilization* (Minton, Balch and Company, 1931), pp. 318 *et seq.*

3

mental source of bewilderment. While the world in which we live and work has been transformed by science, our habits of thought and desire, far from keeping pace with these radical alterations, have persisted all but unchanged, clinging stubbornly to traditions and institutions belonging to a pre-scientific age. "It is impossible," says Dewey, "to overstate the mental confusion and the practical disorder which are bound to result when external and physical effects are planned and regulated, while the attitudes of mind upon which the direction of external results depend are left to the medley of chance, tradition, and dogma. . . . In spite, then, of all the record of the past, the great scientific revolution is still to come. It will ensue when men collectively and coöperatively organize their knowledge for application to achieve and make secure social values; when they systematically use scientific procedures for the control of human relationships and the direction of the social effects of our vast technological machinery. Great as have been the social changes of the last century, they are not to be compared with those that will emerge when our faith in scientific method is made manifest in social works." [1]

Intelligence and Morals. Of recent years several books have appeared bearing titles such as *The Manhood of Humanity*, or *Man Comes of Age*. They agree in pointing out that, with the discovery of scientific method, humanity has the opportunity of developing the self-reliance and self-guidance of maturity. *Moral* maturity must be central in this process. Emancipation from the swaddling clothes of custom, from reliance on the authority of tradition and dogma, make possible a more fully *reflective* morality.

Customary morality, on the other hand, is "ethical" or "moral" in the sense of conforming to the *ethos* or *mores* of the group. Human beings naturally live together in social groups and are inevitably involved in a complex network of interrelationships with their fellows. Moral conceptions and processes emerge from the actual conditions of human life. *Mores* based on regard for group welfare give meaning to the "good," while those based on recognition of mutual relationships set standards for what is held to be "right." [2] Customary morality is, however, largely implicit and unconscious in the control it exercises as a stabilizing force.

[1] *Ibid.*, pp. 329–330.
[2] See John Dewey and James H. Tufts, *Ethics* (Henry Holt and Company, rev. ed., 1932), Chapter IV.

While many customs are conducive to the welfare of the group, many others are irrational and even definitely harmful; and all alike tend to inflexibility. Morals as a product of social experience have enduring strength. Sophocles' *Antigone* holds the moral law sacred, "because it is not of to-day or yesterday, but lives forever, and none knows whence it sprang." Beliefs without discernible foundations are hard indeed to undermine. But change is inevitable even in the most stable social groups. Customary morality fails to give adequate guidance where new issues arise, and the emergence of reflective morality is typical of transitional periods "when old institutions break down; when invasions from without and inventions and innovations from within radically alter the course of life." [1]

Greek philosophy was born of one such period of struggle. We live in another, far more critical. As did the Greeks, we realize how precarious is our hold on life's values. Much more fully than did the Greeks, we realize the injustice of the uneven distribution of satisfactions, and the deprivations suffered by the majority of human beings. Our chief advantage, however, lies in the possession of a method for the control of change. Change need no longer appear as chiefly loss, for progress is made possible through the intelligent direction of change. Moral maturity is reached to-day in a philosophy which affirms that "intelligent action is the sole ultimate resource of mankind in every field whatsoever." [2] "Morals, philosophy," Dewey says, "returns to its first love; love of the wisdom that is nurse of good. But it returns to the Socratic principle equipped with a multitude of special methods of inquiry and tests; with an organized mass of knowledge, and with control of the arrangements by which industry, law and education may concentrate upon the problem of the participation by all men and women, up to the capacity of absorption, in all attained values." [3]

Even so, progress must inevitably be slow. There is no short cut, nor, indeed, can we ever be sure of success. Dewey recognizes that it is "a hypothesis rather than a settled fact that extension and transfer of experimental method is generally possible. But like other hypotheses it is to be tried in action, and the future history of mankind is at stake in the trial." [4] A new responsibility is laid upon the men and women of to-day.

[1] *Ibid.*, p. 198.   [2] John Dewey, *The Quest for Certainty* (1929), p. 252.
[3] John Dewey, *The Influence of Darwin on Philosophy and Other Essays in Contemporary Thought* (Henry Holt and Company, 1910), p. 71.
[4] *The Quest for Certainty*, p. 194.

For in a new and highly significant sense the future is dependent upon their thought and action.

The future, growing as it does out of the past, is at all times dependent upon present thought and action. But there are wide variations in the quality of control thus exercised. Those in the grip of outworn custom and tradition will dogmatically insist on the preservation of the codes and social arrangements of the past. "The hard and fast conservative," says Dewey, "is the man who cannot conceive that existing . . . social arrangements are mechanisms for achieving social results. To him, *they* are the results; they are final." [1] One aspect of conservatism is, of course, wholly justifiable: its emphasis upon the conservation of values. But, while existing institutions may have secured such values in the past, to-day they may be inadequate for this purpose. Many people, the majority indeed, simply drift, clinging to the past and avoiding, more or less unconsciously, the responsibilities of the present. They may be genuinely bewildered by the complexity of modern problems, or else they may belong to the commonplace "masses," so strikingly characterized by Ortega y Gasset as "mere buoys that float on the waves," content to be like everybody else and to demand of themselves no "effort towards perfection." [2]

To criticize the conservative is not to uphold the so-called radical. His revolt against existing institutions is apt to be as wholesale and one-sided as is the effort of the conservative to preserve the *status quo*. The identification of the radical with the destructive rebel is, however, a "perversion of language." [3] By rights, the radical should mean one who delves to the *roots* and origins of social arrangements and plans, not for destruction, but for reconstruction.

Our present responsibility is for progress through reconstruction. "What is needed," says Dewey "is intelligent examination of the consequences that are actually effected by inherited institutions and customs, in order that there may be intelligent consideration of the ways in which they are to be intentionally modified in behalf of generation of different consequences." [4]

The Family in Transition. The discussion of the preceding pages has peculiar pertinence to the situation of the family in contemporary society. The family occupies a unique position

---

[1] *Characters and Events* (1929), Vol. II, p. 827.

[2] José Ortega y Gasset, *The Revolt of the Masses* (English translation, 1932), p. 15.

[3] John Dewey, *Human Nature and Conduct* (Henry Holt and Company, 1922), p. 168.

[4] *The Quest for Certainty*, p. 273.

among social institutions. Not only may it lay claim to being the first social institution; it is also the most fundamental. The family, according to MacIver, is "the nuclear organization of the larger society. . . . It influences the whole life of society in a myriad ways, and its changes . . . reverberate through the whole social structure." [1] At the same time every social change, every modification in social attitude or in any other institution of society is bound to have its effect on the family.

Inextricably involved in the recent acceleration of social change, the family has been of necessity profoundly affected thereby. Economic changes, in particular, have revolutionized the conditions of family life. And yet, with the single exception of primarily religious institutions, the family, both in its structure and in its influence, is of all institutions the most conservative. Its religious sanctions have been in some measure responsible. But there are at least two additional reasons for its conservatism. Antedating history and persisting in some form through all social change, the family provides satisfaction for certain fundamental human needs. Embedded in its structure are values to which men cling with tenacious loyalty. Again, the social heritage is transmitted first of all through the family. The ways of thinking and behaving inculcated in the family circle are profoundly influential in their determination of later thought and action and so tend to be preserved with little alteration through succeeding generations. Even more acutely than other institutions, the family thus exhibits the phenomenon of what has been aptly described as "cultural lag." [2] In certain aspects of family life revolutionary changes have taken place; other aspects remain relatively unchanged. Most persistent of all are certain outworn attitudes, and certain traditions no longer relevant to present conditions. In the complex "fabric of relationships" binding together the different aspects of family life "strains" have developed which, unless eased through readjustment, must lead to disruption.

When we of the Western world speak of the family, we mean the monogamous family which traces its descent directly from

[1] From R. M. MacIver, *Society: Its Structure and Changes*, p. 109. Copyright 1931. Reprinted by permission of the publishers, Farrar and Rinehart, Inc.

[2] See F. Stuart Chapin, *Cultural Change* (1928), Chapter X, "The Cultural Lag in the Family"; also, William Fielding Ogburn, *Social Change* (1922), pp. 200–203. The phrase "cultural lag" is suggested by Ogburn to describe the relatively backward development of "adaptive culture," that portion of non-material culture which is most closely related to material culture and which must be adjusted to changes in material culture.

the patriarchal family systems of Rome and of the Teutonic tribes, and which was further defined and developed under the sanctions of the Christian Church. The patriarchal family in its complete development was not only a biological unit, but also the unit of social structure and, more or less fully, the economic, religious, and educational unit as well: a compact, closely knit, and inclusive whole, defining the status of its members, providing for their maintenance and protection and for the transmission of the biological and social heritage to succeeding generations. But, as MacIver points out, "Like that of all other great social agencies the sphere of the family has in the course of evolution become more defined and more limited." [1] Long before the days of the Industrial Revolution the family had begun "to surrender certain of its inclusive functions to other agencies of society." [2] Gradually such agencies, educational, protective, religious, and economic, developed and became specialized to perform the functions they had taken from the family. Within the last hundred years this process, particularly in its economic aspects, has been so greatly accelerated that the family in its patriarchal form has well-nigh disappeared. But, however deeply economic change may affect the form and character of the family, "it does not affect the basic biological facts and the social needs which create the essential functions of the family," [3] those "it is peculiarly fitted to perform and which give it its justification in a world of specialized agencies and institutions." [4] In the great evolutionary process of society "the family has been gradually stripped of functions irrelevant to its peculiar character as a system of more or less enduring social relationships based on the fact of sex." [5] "The process in which irrelevant functions have been stripped from the family has also made clear its essential nature. The peculiar claim of the family is not that it alone fulfils any one function; it is that it alone provides a way of combining and harmonizing certain closely related functions. The functions for which it provides this common basis are at the minimum three in number:

"(1) the perpetuation of the race—this is the broader social aspect, but from the point of view of the partners in marriage it includes the satisfaction of philoprogenitive desires, involving not only procreation but also the care and nurture of the young.

"(2) the more stable satisfaction of the sex instinct.

[1] Op. cit., p. 143. [2] Ibid., p. 123. [3] Ibid., p. 124. [4] Ibid., p. 133. [5] Ibid., p. 124.

"(3) the provision of the home, with its combination of material, cultural, and affectional satisfactions. In a successful family, and in it alone, these functions are so united that each of them reinforces and enriches the satisfaction of the others. Sex becomes not a detached phenomenon but part of a larger partnership of comradeship in work and in life. And the nurture of children is given the setting of the home which, as much experience seems to show, is a far more favorable environment for them than that of the state nursery or other public or private institution. In our modern society the family, denuded of its ancient socio-economic functions, stands (or falls) on its claim to harmonize those needs and satisfactions we have just described." [1]

MacIver's discussion of the family has been quoted at such length for two reasons. In the first place, these passages, far better than any others known to the writer, summarize the evolution and present status of the family in an accurate and illuminating fashion. Secondly, they define the general problem of this book, a fact made more apparent by yet another quotation: "The shedding of irrelevant functions prepares the way for the development of relevant ones." [2] How best then, amid the changes of contemporary society, may the essential functions of the family, and the inherent values of family life, be not only preserved, but assured of fuller and freer development?

The Family in Historical Perspective. Historical perspective is an obvious necessity. The situation and problems of the modern family can only be understood as results of its evolution in adjustment to a changing social environment. History reveals the family enduring through the ages because of its value to the social group as a whole, and to the individuals composing the group. From the social standpoint it combines and harmonizes certain essential functions in a way conducive to social stability; from the individual standpoint it brings the more stable satisfactions of certain fundamental needs. But history reveals at the same time the peculiar susceptibility of the family to extraneous influences, to the pressure of social conditions, and to the forces of custom, tradition, and public opinion. The pattern of family relationships in any society, at any period, is accordingly derived only in part from its own proper functions, and very largely from an inclusive pattern of cultural relationships.

---

[1] *Ibid.*, pp. 133–134. This passage also occurs unchanged in *Society* (1937), pp. 219–220, a revised and enlarged edition of MacIver's earlier book.
[2] *Ibid.*; p. 134.

In consequence of this fact the customs and traditions interwoven into the structure of the family vary widely in value. Some which have been of service in meeting specific needs have outlived their usefulness. Others have always had consequences harmful to family well-being. In the next seven chapters we shall endeavor to supply the historical background necessary to an understanding of the complex influences which have molded the evolution of the family.

The choice of historical background is, of course, to some extent determined by the fact that our central concern is with the family in contemporary America. In tracing the development of the family in Western civilization emphasis is accordingly laid on England and America. In most histories of the family the treatment is by periods. In this book a different method is adopted. The chief influences operative in family life are dealt with, one after another, in successive chapters. Chapters III to VII start, in each case, with a consideration of a certain aspect of the family in primitive groups, and proceed with a discussion of this same aspect in its historical development. It is felt that more is gained than lost by this mode of treatment. In any case, not everything can be said at once. The separation of one influence from others is, of course, no more than relative, a matter of emphasis. The strands in the complex pattern so constantly intertwine with each other that no one aspect of family life can be considered without some reference to others. But, by seeking to unravel first one basic strand and then another, we may reach a clearer understanding of the ways in which the fabric was woven.

Chapter II, *The Basic Trends of Social Change*, provides an underlying framework for succeeding chapters. In brief outline it traces certain aspects of the process of social change which have profoundly influenced the evolution of the family. Some knowledge of these general aspects of social evolution may then be taken for granted in the later discussion. Emphasis is laid on those tendencies which make for reconstruction and new adjustments, and also on those which are definitely conservative in influence.

In Chapter III, *The Family and Social Organization*, a summary and evaluation of the divergent theories of the origin and evolution of the family is followed by a functional analysis of the relation of the family to social structure. Malinowski's characterization of the family as an institution whose central core is to be found in procreation and nurture affords anthro

pological evidence consonant with MacIver's account of the
essential functions of the family. The development of the
family in its relation to social structure is followed only as far
as Rome. Beyond this period it becomes impossible to proceed
without considering the influence of religion. Chapter IV,
accordingly, deals with *The Family and Religion*. A peculiarly
potent influence is exercised on an entire cultural complex by
its religious aspects: the beliefs, traditions, and customs which
have developed as men feel the need to adjust themselves to an
unseen supernatural environment. In this chapter, a preliminary
discussion of the influence of religion on the family and conceptions of sex in pre-Christian days is followed by an account of
the influence of Christianity on the family in Western Europe
and America.

Chapter V considers *The Family and Economics*. Maintenance
is the fundamental human need; and the ways in which this
need is met provide, as it were, a groundwork for all social
institutions. In all ages the division of labor between the sexes
has been a powerful determinant of the family pattern. At the
same time, with the accumulation of property, systems of inheritance have profoundly influenced family life. In this chapter our survey of the economic aspects of family life concludes
with a brief account of the Industrial Revolution and its effect
on the family.

Chapter VI, *The Family and Sex*, begins by considering the
cultural determination of sex differences. Growing boys and
girls in any culture are inexorably shaped to conform to accepted
masculine and feminine rôles. This fact, far more than physiological or temperamental differences, has determined the relations of the sexes. Religious and economic influences, in
particular, have always been decisive in their effect on family
relationships. This effect, moreover, has been more potent in
the case of subordinate and dependent family members—the
children and, very generally, the women. While Chapter VI
accordingly includes a historical survey of the position of women,
Chapters VII and VIII, *The Family and Education*, are devoted
to a consideration of children, and the ways in which prevailing
attitudes have molded their lives. In most cultures, influences
emanating from the irrelevant functions of the family have
distorted and frustrated the performance of its relevant and
essential functions. Accordingly only to-day are we beginning
to realize more fully the supreme significance of the family as an
institution for procreation and nurture. This realization has

been part of an educational development in which emphasis has been shifted from conformity to social patterns to the personality of the child.

The Modern Family. In passing from history to a study of the modern American family we borrow from Ellen Key's prophetic characterization of the twentieth century for the title of Chapter IX, *Education in the Century of the Child.* Throughout our investigation of family problems a central emphasis is placed on the significance of childhood. It is therefore wholly fitting that we should begin by considering the central aims of education. Individual and social welfare depend on the measure in which home and school achieve their educational purposes. A thorough understanding of the principles and procedures of progressive education is of importance in this connection. Chapter X continues with an analysis of *The Reciprocal Functions of Home and School.* Sex education and parent education are recent and promising developments of great importance to men as well as to women. Another recent development of the utmost significance to family life is an increasing tendency towards *The Assumption of Public Responsibility for Child Welfare.* Chapter XI gives a brief account of the three White House Conferences, of the creation and work of the Children's Bureau, and of systems of Mothers' Aid. It concludes with a discussion of measures for safeguarding health in childhood.

It is now realized, however, that a wholesome physical environment is insufficient, in itself, for the nurture of sound human beings. We need a wholesome social environment as well.

Chapter XII, *Children in Need of Special Care and Protection,* discusses child labor, physically and mentally handicapped children, and also those children who, from an enlightened point of view, are now characterized as *socially* handicapped; not only dependent and neglected children, but the illegitimate and even the definitely delinquent. There is growing realization to-day of *The Reciprocal Relations between Child Welfare and Social Welfare,* the subject matter of Chapter XIII. Parents devoted to the interests of their own children are finding themselves led to consider the well-being of other children as well, and to evaluate social arrangements and conditions in terms of their influence on childhood. On the other hand, the very instability of family relationships, in contemporary society, has forced a recognition of the indispensable social services rendered by families which provide stable and happy homes for their children. In this chapter a number of social problems are considered in their relation to child welfare, and family endowment and social insurance are discussed as measures facilitating the performance of family functions.

In Chapter XIV we turn to a consideration of the present status of women. Since the so-called emancipation of women is a very recent development, we trace first *Changes in the Status of Women in England and America*. In Chapter XV we survey the *Occupations of Women in America* to-day, and in Chapter XVI discuss *Conflicting Values in Women's Lives*. The status of women has at all times been more closely related to their family life than has that of men. Accordingly the revolutionary changes which have recently taken place are of profound and far-reaching significance to the family. The whole issue, moreover, is still unsettled and highly controversial. After all, it is not very long since all women were grouped together in common parlance as "the sex," to be divided only into those who were respectable, "virtuous and chaste females," and those who were not, "the fallen"! The former might be subdivided once more into "genteel females" and domestic or extra-domestic drudges. Unenviable indeed was the lot of the genteel female who found no place in "woman's proper sphere" of wife and mother: she might still, of course, exercise the "magic influence" of a "pious female," as sister or daughter. Even to-day, there are many conservatives who ignore the changed conditions under which the modern family must function and insist that "woman's place is in the home." Equally extreme is the attitude of many radical feminists who, without consideration for the welfare of the family or society, still fight for "women's rights," in the name of the ambiguous and abstract principle of the equality of men and women. The large majority of men and women are actually more conservative than they might admit; the men clinging to traditional prejudices, but confused and uneasy; the women restless in their demand for freedom, but unwilling to relinquish the privileges of spoiled dependents and to assume the status of fully responsible human beings. A critical evaluation of the position of women in contemporary society is accordingly of the utmost importance. A chief cause of much marital disharmony is found in conflicting attitudes of husband and wife with regard to their respective rôles in the home and society.

The concluding four chapters of our study of family problems are occupied with the crucial and, in many cases, controversial issues involved in modern marriage. Chapter XVII deals with *Population and Birth Control*, in an endeavor to give a broad social setting to the birth-control movement, and to point out the advantages for the family and for social well-being of intelligent and responsible *voluntary parenthood*. Chapter XVIII, *The Instability of Modern Marriage*, brings us to a consideration of the present unrest in the relations between the sexes. It is hoped that a more balanced perspective may result from the placing of this discussion *subsequent* to our treatment of other aspects of family life. An objective and unemotional attitude is of peculiar importance to us to-day, living as we do in a period of revolt and rebellion from earlier restrictions, when, as Tufts says, "The pendulum is swinging from sex repression to sex obsession." [1]

Chapter XIX, *Marital Adjustments*, first attempts an analysis of tensions typical in marital relationships to-day and then deals with the beginnings now being made in scientific diagnosis and treatment of these difficulties. Of great significance for education is the discovery that attitudes and dispositions, very largely the result of early conditioning, are the underlying causes of most marital disharmony. On the other hand the one most potent means for the facilitation of marital adjustment is what may be called a *socio-psychiatric* attitude on the part of married partners, an objective, emotionally mature understanding of themselves and of one another and of the realities of their mutual relationship.

It is to the deliberate inculcation of attitudes and dispositions favorable to harmonious family relationships that we must look for *The Emergence of a Coöperative Family*, the subject matter of Chapter XX. Education for marriage and family life is indispensable if a democratic family pattern is to emerge more fully from the confusion and conflicts of the present. The stability and solidarity of the family in the past were largely the result of coercion from without, of the pressure of social, economic, and religious forces which have now lost their former power. But bonds such as these are irrelevant to the essential life of the family which is to be found in the personal relationships between the family members. To-day, more than ever before, does it become possible to develop families which achieve enduring stability through their own inherent strength; coöperative families where the relationships between the parents, and between them and their children, are so interwoven as to enrich and reënforce one another.

[1] *America's Social Morality* (1933), pp. 92–93.

Home Life. A first essential of stable and coöperative family life is that men and women should achieve a fuller measure of mutual understanding and sympathy. All lingering traces of sex antagonism, all defensive attitudes must be relinquished. In some of its passing phases the movement for emancipation was, it is true, a movement of women away from men. Fundamentally and in the long run, it means the movement towards common occupations, interests, and ideals. Society has not as yet succeeded in fully liberating and putting to use the inherent capacities of men; far less those of women. Any restriction of women's work, any hard and fast lines of demarcation between men's work and women's work are therefore premature. Actual experiment rather than prejudice and preconception must determine how best women may coöperate with men within the family and in community life. As women come to share more fully in social responsibilities outside the home, we may hope for the development of more realistic attitudes towards many of the problems of contemporary life. Women, whose central preoccupation in all ages has been the care of life, are more prone than men to judge of social arrangements in terms of their effect on human values. Already the influence of intelligent women is apparent in the trend towards a new family pattern. Of particular interest is the fact that in the coöperative family men may be expected to take a far larger share in home life.

In order to give concrete meaning to coöperation in family life, we must supplement our discussion of the relationship between husband and wife with an account of everyday experience in the home. The first two of four chapters on home life, Chapters XXI and XXII, deal with the relation between *Housekeeping and Homemaking*. They include a consideration of the implications of coöperation in financial management, in the various economic aspects of home life, and in the choice of a standard of living. In Chapter XXIII, *Homemaking and the Children*, we consider the home as the environment of childhood and the significance of the learning which results from coöperative family life. Chapter XXIV discusses some additional *Aspects of Family Education.*

New Horizons for the Family. Our study of the family in the past and present is thus brought to a close. What may we hope for the future? In Chapter XXV, in an Epilogue bearing the title of the book, we imagine some of the possibilities which lie hidden in the mists of the future, beyond the new horizons which to-day open for the family. To some this Epilogue may appear too visionary: an incongruous supplementation of pragmatism with mysticism. But, however far imagination has been allowed to take flight, nowhere is there the slightest suggestion that attention should be more than momentarily deflected from the actual concrete needs of the present, or from our responsibility for making intelligent use of present opportunities. Always, it is only the next step forward which is within our present power. We may, however, find fuller courage to take this step through faith in the possibilities of human experience. For "as the essence of courage is to stake one's life upon a possibility, so the essence of faith is to believe that the possibility exists."[1]

[1] William Salter, quoted by William James, *The Will to Believe* (1896), p. 62.

THE FAMILY IN HISTORICAL PERSPECTIVE

CHAPTER II

THE BASIC TRENDS OF SOCIAL CHANGE

THE EVOLUTION OF HUMANITY AS SOCIAL

The Capacity for Mental Response. In his earlier stages of development man was an animal struggling for existence, for self-maintenance and perpetuation of his kind in an environment consisting of the forces of inanimate nature, and of plants, animals, and other men. At first sight he appears as singularly ill-equipped. To what may his increasing mastery be attributed? To the fact that he, alone of all animals, has the capacity for *mental* development in association and communication with his fellow men.

The primary fact in all life is that of the interaction of organism with environment, in the course of which the organism, in adjusting itself to its environment, utilizes the latter for its own needs. Step by step from the lowest living organisms we can trace the stages whereby greater precision and integration of adjustment have been attained, stages which correspond, along the line of evolution leading to man, with the development of the central nervous system and of the cerebral cortex.

In common with many of the higher animals, man is aware not only of his immediate environment, but of stimuli coming from a distance. An interval elapses between stimulus and response in which choice may be made of the most adequate response. Man differs, however, from all other animals in his capacity for response on the basis of his memory of past experiences and his imaginative forecast of the future. He is able, as it were, to abstract himself from his immediate spatial environment, and from the present moment of time, to delay overt action and to *think*, to deliberate on his course of action. Deliberation is unnecessary when response is *direct*, in the form of some acquired skill, some habitual way of acting. But for the human being who remembers, the present acquires *meaning;* it signifies alternative future possibilities. The uncertainty, the problematic quality of the future often forces him to respond *indirectly*, not to things as they immediately are, but to things as signs of the consequences to be expected from alternative modes of response. Response to *meanings* is *mental* response, the first stage in the development of intelligence.

19

Language and the Use of Tools. Long ages must have passed, however, before man's preëminence was in any way assured. The definitely human type developed when descent from trees to the ground became habitual. With upright posture, the hands were freed for other purposes than locomotion, and the development of a larger, heavier brain, supported on an upright spine, became possible. Increase in manual dexterity, accompanied by corresponding change in brain structure, led to the emergence of *the mental*, the lifting of awareness to a new and higher dimension. The rudiments of mental quality are to be found, it is true, among the higher animals.[1] It is probable, however, that continued mental development would not have occurred without language and the regular use of tools. Bergson has suggested that *homo faber* would be a more correct designation for the human species than *homo sapiens*, indicating by this that the use of tools was a primary factor in the development of both language and thought.

Tools may be considered artificial extensions of the human organism. They are devices which make possible a more efficient application of energy. While increasing the power of the organs of the human body, their use demands skill and dexterity. A clenched fist is ineffectual in comparison with the branch of a tree used as a club. With the expenditure of no greater amount of energy, this most primitive of tools increases man's power and widens his range of action.

For our present discussion, however, the more important quality of a tool is the fact that it is a thing used as a means to consequences. A stick used as a tool is no longer primarily a stick, a relatively unnoticed part of the physical environment; it becomes endowed with meaning from the uses to which it may be put; it becomes a club, or, in other situations, a spear or a lever. Mental response, the use of imagination, is implied in the use of tools.

The use of tools in association with other human beings must have played a large part in the development of language. Gestures and sounds are spontaneous ways of behaving, but they may be used as signs, signals to other human beings, in an attempt to influence their behavior. As Malinowski says: "In its primitive uses, language functions as a link in concerted

---

[1] Köhler has shown that chimpanzees are capable of response to meanings. Confronted with the problem of securing a banana out of reach beyond the bars of a cage, a chimpanzee may break a branch from a tree and use it as a tool. *The Mentality of Apes* (2nd ed., 1927).

human activity. . . . "[1] Sounds become language where there is mutual assistance and direction, where at least two human beings participate in a common situation, where there is *co-operative* behavior and *communication* of meaning. A word for a tool would indicate the uses to which it might be put; it would both communicate meaning to others and record meaning for use in the future.

The development of language is the indispensable condition of social and mental development, its symbols being, quite literally, the tools of thought. The spoken sound and, in later times, the written word are significant, not for what they objectively are, but for the uses to which they may be put—the communication, preservation, and transmission of meanings.

The Social Environment. We have assumed that primitive man lived in association with his fellows. Possibly, before what has been called the "taming of fire," human beings may have lived in less close association. Even then, however, the basis of all subsequent association was to be found in the length of human infancy and the consequent relationship between mother and child. This brings us to a consideration of the fact that, pervasive and urgent as are the ever-present stimuli of the physical environment, the *social* environment is of far greater significance for human development.[2] The human infant, physically helpless, is dependent for survival on the nurture of one human being, at least, probably of more. In these earliest social relationships dispositions and habits are formed that largely determine all future activities.

Through biological heredity only the broad patterns of human reactions are laid down. In contrast to the animals, who are provided at birth with a greater number of specific reactions, adjusting them with little or no modification to their environment, the native impulses of human beings are highly flexible, and may become organized in a great variety of ways. The slow maturing of the human brain provides a prolonged period of plasticity and of *learning*, during which impulses are modified and integrated into more or less settled modes of response, more or less definite ways of behaving, into dispositions and

[1] Supplement I, C. L. Ogden and I. A. Richards, *The Meaning of Meaning* (4th ed., 1936), p. 312. See also John Dewey, *Experience and Nature* (2nd ed., 1929), Chapter V.

[2] "The social environment consists," in Dewey's words, "of all the activities of fellow beings that are bound up in the carrying on of the activities of any one of its members." From John Dewey, *Democracy and Education*, 1916, p. 26. By permission of The Macmillan Company, publishers.

habits. For the understanding of social development it is these learned activities that are of primary importance. The impulses of a new-born baby to-day are in all probability much like those of the baby in prehistoric days. The great change that has taken place is in the social environment through which these impulses have been modified. Human evolution is social rather than biological.

SOCIAL CHANGE IN PREHISTORIC SOCIAL GROUPS

Habit, Routine, and the Development of Folkways. A certain amount of routine in life is inevitable; never more so than in the rigorous life led by our remote ancestors in their struggle with the untamed forces of nature. In the first place nature itself exhibits certain definite rhythms, those of the recurring seasons, of day and night, of the phases of the moon. The lives of plants and animals on which man subsists involve certain regular sequences of change. Such rhythms are necessarily reflected in recurring and ordered cycles of human activities through which adjustment is made over and over again to the same types of situations. Long before any accurate systems of time measurement were devised, certain activities must have recurred at regular intervals of time. All such routines tend in the direction of the mechanization of life and the fixity of habit. Habits, being abilities learned in the course of past experience, are not necessarily inflexible. There is a strong tendency, however, for a habit formed in response to a frequently recurring situation to become fixed and limited to the repetition of past action. Over and over again the urgent necessities of life must have forced primitive man to seek satisfaction of his needs in ways that had been successful in the past. Gradually certain expedient ways of doing things came to be selected, ways which afforded greater satisfaction and involved less effort. Along such lines of behavior, skills, habits, and routines developed and became customary. There was formed that body of social usages to which Sumner gave the illuminating name of *folkways*, the customs of the social group, whose pervasive influence on the actions, feelings, and thoughts of its individual members inevitably constrained them to conformity.

The Development of Useful Arts. No wonder that successful modes of adjustment should have been seized upon and conserved as precious. It is impossible to exaggerate the hardships, the utter precariousness of human life in the earliest stages of social development. Living in the forests without fire, without all but the most primitive tools, sticks as clubs, stones as missiles and hammers, human beings must often have been forced to revert to the trees for comparative safety.[1] Man's mastery of fire, celebrated in myth as a superhuman feat, was in actual fact his first great victory over natural forces. Without fire man could never have spread to those cooler regions of the earth's surface where conditions proved most favorable to his advance. Necessity was indeed the mother of the earliest inventions. Where life is too easy, as in certain tropical regions, no notable development of the useful arts has taken place. Where there is too great hardship, as in the Arctic, development is inevitably arrested. Life in temperate regions, with the aid of fire, furnished the happy mean. Conditions were difficult enough to spur to invention, but not so difficult that they did not admit of progressive amelioration. Man had started on the long and arduous path of the development of the useful arts, of inventions, techniques, and skills, through which he gained greater security in his struggle to maintain himself in an environment which to some extent sustained his efforts, but which, on the whole, must still have appeared to him as hostile.

Fire protected him from cold and from savage beasts. No longer was he forced to flee helpless from cave-bear and saber-toothed tiger. At night, the dangers lurking in the darkness were driven beyond the circle of the friendly firelight. Group life was made possible round the common hearth.

Adjustment to the Imaginary Supernatural Environment. Even so, human life was far from secure. The precarious nature of human existence, the frustrations to which human hopes are subject, the uncertainty of the future—these are constant, inescapable, and fundamental characteristics of human life. Humanity has everywhere and at all times been driven to seek security, a fact which is most clearly evident under primitive conditions. Life is insecure for other animals as well as man, even though they are better endowed with natural means of defense. But because our primitive ancestors were capable of mental development, the fear of the unknown and the uncertainty of life must have increasingly dominated their imagination. Palliation of fear and added security were sought through adjustment to the imaginary environment of the supernatural.

[1] See Vivian Meik, *The People of the Leaves* (1931), for an account of a group surviving to-day in the forests of Central India under similar conditions. They have no knowledge of fire, nor of any art but that of weaving leaves to cover the entrances to their holes dug among the roots of trees. Fear of the unaccountable is their nearest approach to religion.

Such illusions are not hard to understand. How natural it would be to feel the darkness alive, not only with real, but with imaginary menace! To the actual and ever-present dangers of suffering and violent death, through cold, starvation, and the attacks of beasts of prey, were added the imaginative terrors of ghosts and demons and of the personified malevolent powers of nature. How natural, too, to conceive of all things as animated, to interpret all phenomena in terms of living forces, since the source of energy most obvious to man is his own living body!

Man must also have early become aware of the part played by "luck" or "chance" in human affairs. In all ages the contrast between good and bad luck has made a profound impression on the imagination. For the unforeseen, the unprepared for, and the inexplicable are frequently decisive in turning the scale. Naturally it is *bad* luck on which attention concentrates. To primitive men it must have seemed an ever-present threat to be explained only by supernatural influences. As the extreme case of the inexplicable, men were confronted with the fact of death. Its inevitability was not understood. Further, in *dreams*, the dead man appeared as still alive. To him was accorded a new form of existence, in which his soul, having passed from his body with his last breath, had become a ghost. But, if men and animals have souls, why should not all other things as well?

In ways such as these arose the belief in the imaginary environment of the supernatural, the realm of ghosts and spirits and of mysterious unearthly powers, to serve as an explanation of all that was inexplicable in ordinary life. Surpassed only by necessity for maintaining his existence would appear man's urgent need for adjustment to the supernatural. The perils of the natural world are never so appalling as are the terrors of the unseen. It appears probable, for instance, that fire, all important as it was for practical purposes, was valued most of all for its efficacy in dealing with ghosts and spirits.[1]

Beneficial and Detrimental Effects of Belief in the Supernatural. It is hard to estimate how far such beliefs have been of service and how far definitely harmful. Some writers, such as Briffault, see in religious belief little that has not been of detriment to human progress. Delicate mechanisms are liable to perverted use; and man's brain is no exception, man being "the only animal that enjoys the privilege of persuading himself that things are, not as they are, but as he would like them to be."[2] True that,

---

[1] W. G. Sumner and A. G. Keller, *The Science of Society* (4 vols., 1927), Vol. I, p. 188.
[2] Robert Briffault, *Rational Evolution* (1930), p. 11.

wherever religious practices have been relied on as a "short-cut" to some desired result, they are potentially harmful. For attention is then diverted from devising the means by which such a result may be actually reached. To-day, with our scientific knowledge of resources and means, such an attitude is inexcusable, although still very prevalent, if not in physical, at least in social and moral matters. In the early stages of human history, however, when man was so much at the mercy of natural forces, any belief that gave him confidence and courage was of genuine practical value. Fear itself, in binding men more closely together in concerted action, was a definitely socializing force. So too, and in a preëminent degree, were the ceremonials which form so large a part of primitive religion.

Imagination has many uses. Not only can it create fear of the supernatural, but it can add interest and enjoyment to life. In moments of temporary escape from the coercive necessity of useful labor, primitive man must have added thrill and excitement to his enjoyment of leisure by telling stories in song, in pantomime, and dance, reliving dramatically his experiences of battle and the chase. Literal accuracy of recollection was unimportant; intensity of emotional appeal was his primary concern. He lived in a world of fancies, of emotionally congenial suggestions springing from his hopes and fears. Uncritical belief is natural to the undisciplined mind. The most striking of such tales would be retold and would pass from generation to generation. The brave deed of some ancestor would be celebrated in legend and myth; or some frequently recurring experience, of vital interest to the group as a whole, would be given a mythical setting and rehearsed in festival and ritual dance. Gradually traditions are built up, forming an "abiding framework of imagination," a "kind of norm to which individual fancy and suggestion conform."[1] Religions, beliefs, rites, and cults became a permanent part of the social heritage.

Rarely, if ever, are the effects of customs, institutions, or beliefs wholly good or wholly evil. Almost always, while originally of some service, they have also had harmful consequences. This is particularly the case when, persisting unchanged of their own inertia, they outlive their usefulness. Of all the traditions and customs of mankind, religious beliefs and usages tend to assume the most inflexible rigidity. One reason for this is obvious. Customs originating in man's adjustment to the physical environment have constantly to meet the test of the

[1] John Dewey, *Reconstruction in Philosophy* (1920), p. 8.

stern realities of life. Failure to adjust to changing conditions means actual disaster, pain, or death. There is no such rigorous check on religious belief. And religion easily becomes dogmatic, with almost unlimited sway over human life, and, as such, is definitely detrimental to human progress.

The Religious Sanction of the Mores. The well-nigh indestructible conservatism of religious beliefs extends, moreover, beyond what at first sight appears to be their proper sphere. But we must remember how every detail of daily life, in hours of toil and hours of leisure, must have been permeated by their influence. One of the chief functions of religion is accordingly to be found in its sanction of the *mores*. In its original Latin usage, this term covered all group customs which were regarded as conducive to the common good and were sanctioned by tradition. Sumner, who introduced the term into sociology, uses it to mean the folkways surrounding some vital interest, folkways that have been practised over a considerable period of time, that are permeated by the conviction that they are essential to human welfare and that their infraction will involve calamity.[1] *Mores* are the *right* ways of doing and believing, the ways having religious sanction. In origin they represent successful adjustments to life: but their endurance depends largely on extraneous factors. The familiar is always valued; it gives a sense of security. Thus emotional bias is always in favor of existing customs. Even more potent among primitive people was the conviction that the dead are custodians of the *mores*. Familiar and ancient usages are *holy;* the novel and strange must be profane. The religious sanction of the *mores* is accordingly expressed largely in the negative form of prohibition, of what has come to be known among anthropologists to-day by the Polynesian word "taboo."

Primitive Education as Conservative. The hold of tradition on successive generations is still further strengthened through education. A social group secures its continued existence only by the education of its immature members, by transmitting to them its habits of doing, thinking, and feeling. There was little need for formal education among primitive groups. The young learned by sharing directly in the activities of their elders. In learning the language of their group, they had already assimilated much of the mental outlook of those about them.

---

[1] In *Folkways* (1906), p. iii, Sumner defines the *mores* as the totality of "popular usages and traditions, when they include a judgment that they are conducive to social welfare and when they exert a coercion on the individual to conform to them, although they are not coördinated by any authority."

New Horizons for the Family

By Una Bernard Sait, Professor of Philosophy, Claremont Colleges. New York, 1938. 772 pp., Cr. 8vo, $4.00d.

This text for courses in the family will interest both men and women and prepare them for marriage and family life as well as for teaching or social work. Its purpose is to provide perspective and a broad philosophy of the family. In addition to presenting the facts about the various aspects of family life, the author has interpreted these facts to give an understanding of both beneficial and adverse influences on the family, and has pointed out new possibilities for increasing both the individual and the social satisfactions to be gained from family life.

The historical background of the family is made especially significant by tracing through separately the developments of each contributing aspect of family life. Notable in the treatment of modern problems is the full, well-rounded material on child care and education; on relationships between child and social welfare; and on the changing status of women. Everyday life in the home is treated in considerably more detail than usual.

Bibliographies appended to each chapter provide the means for further and more detailed study.

A simple, lucid presentation of the relation between consumption and the physical sciences.

ORR
Food, Health, and Income
See page 18.

Through close association with the other members of the social group they still further absorbed its mental attitude and became proficient in its heritage of skill. Education has in all past ages been a potent conservative force, never more so than in primitive society. Generation after generation, the same more or less successful adjustments to the environment, and the same explanations of their imagined significance have been passed on all but unchanged. Tradition most efficiently preserves the past and becomes ever more sacred with increasing age. It is not to be wondered at that for long ages man made almost imperceptible advance. In view of the hardships of his lot and of the rigid hold of tradition we may almost wonder that he made any progress at all.

Typical Methods of Maintenance: Hunting. Slowly, with the gradual development of more effective adjustments to the environment, human society evolved. To understand the factors making for progress, a brief account is necessary of the typical methods of maintenance. If he is to survive, the human being must have water and food, in the form of plant and animal life. Maintenance is man's primary and central occupation; in the earlier stages of social development, all other usages were relative to and derived from the fundamental need for maintenance of the individual and of the group. Social progress was thus primarily due to the invention of methods for obtaining a better and more abundant food supply. Patterns of culture center around the pursuit of typical maintenance occupations, such as hunting, or herding, or agriculture.

Without adequate weapons food must have been gathered in the form of nuts, fruits, seeds, and roots; bird's nests were doubtless robbed of their eggs and some of the smaller animals captured. Human groups must have been small, loosely united, and constantly on the move in search of sustenance. Life was lived from day to day and there can have been little or no opportunity for the development of *foresight*, "one of the most elementary and elemental qualities productive of civilization." [1] With the development of weapons hunters gained increasing mastery over animal life. The food supply became not only more abundant, but of better quality. Skins provided clothing and added facilities for shelter. At the same time skill in the use of weapons enabled each group to hold and defend its own against strange or hostile groups.[2] Numbers increased. Where the use of fire

[1] W. G. Sumner and A. G. Keller, *op. cit.*, Vol. I, p. 52.
[2] The Latin word *hostis* means both stranger and enemy, a significant identification.

made food more easily digestible for children, more and better
nourished children would survive. There would be less wandering, for accessibility to the best hunting grounds would
determine the location of semi-permanent headquarters. Here
capital in the form of weapons, tools, and other possessions
might accumulate as insurance against the insecurities of life.
Increased leisure would give added opportunity for advances
in the useful arts and for the artistic embellishment of life.
Foresight was implied in the very invention of tools and weapons
and was further fostered by the exigencies of the hunt.

   Typical Methods of Maintenance: Herding. Herding, as a
method of maintenance, supervened upon and supplemented
hunting. Man's fundamental achievement in appropriating
natural energies to human uses was his mastery of fire. The
domestication of animals became the means for a further significant appropriation, this time of animal energies. Game may
sometimes have been preserved within certain boundaries.
Many times, also, must the hunters have brought back young
animals to be reared in captivity as pets. Their uses would
soon become evident. Dogs could be trained to hunt, while
sheep, goats, and cattle gave milk and provided reserve supplies
of food in times of famine. As the population grew, wild game
must have become scarce and good hunting grounds harder to
find. Groups which had succeeded in breeding animals in captivity were in possession of a method of maintenance superior
to that of groups dependent on hunting alone. The pastoral
group with its flocks and herds was assured of an abundant and
steady food supply. Milk was now provided in addition to
earlier forms of food, a notable advance in meeting the needs
of children and increasing the population both in numbers
and in quality. Wealth consisted largely in flocks and herds, a
form of capital which multiplied with rapidity.[1] While pastoral
peoples are called nomads by permanently settled agriculturalists, this does not mean that they wander without purpose; it
means definite seasonal migrations in search of more abundant
pasturage. Possessions are moved from winter to summer camping grounds and are thus preserved intact. With these changes
human life became more secure, and there was further cultural
development. Added emphasis, too, was laid on foresight, a
quality far more necessary to a herdsman than to a hunter.

---

   [1] Our word "pecuniary" is derived from the Latin *pecunia* which meant first of
all "property in cattle" (from *pecus*, cattle) and was later extended to mean money
as a measurement of wealth.

Hunting has as its immediate end the satisfaction of allaying hunger. But in the raising of cattle, many intermediate stages must intervene before the cattle serve as food. An ordered series of activities must be undertaken as *means*, if the desired end is finally to be obtained.

Typical Methods of Maintenance: Agriculture. The development of foresight is still further stimulated through agricultural processes. Selection and storage of seed, preparation of the soil, and tillage over a protracted period must all precede the harvest. Among hunting peoples the food supply was supplemented with the products of plant life. Seeds accidentally dropped would take root and germinate. Where this fact was noticed, the first crude attempts at agriculture might follow. But agriculture proper did not become the predominant method of maintenance till far later, after the invention of the plough.

Agricultural people did not by any means abandon the care of flocks and herds; but they were now able to supplement pasturage with the crops they raised on the land where they settled permanently. Private property in land is the mark of an agricultural people, for the tiller must stay with the land he has improved, and naturally desires its ownership in perpetuity. The gains of successive generations thus accumulate in one place and a high degree of culture becomes possible. Tillage is laborious and monotonous work. The work of the herdsman was light in comparison, while hunting was an interesting, immediately rewarding occupation. Accordingly, with the fuller utilization of land through tillage, slavery, which had developed among pastoral peoples, became systematized. Having appropriated physical forces and animal energies to his service, the successful man made greater use of human energies through the enslavement and forced labor of his less successful fellow man. With agriculture as the predominant method of maintenance, conditions were favorable for the rise of the earliest civilizations.

Factors in Social Evolution: Association in Coöperative Groups. Let us summarize the results of our previous discussion through an enumeration of certain factors which are involved in social evolution. Although discussed here in their simplest form among prehistoric and primitive peoples, it is obvious that these same factors have also been operative in the evolution of civilized societies of all degrees of complexity.

Association in coöperative groups is in a great variety of ways a superior form of adjustment. Many in coöperation can do what one cannot; power is augmented. There is added protection against enemies, the food supply is larger, and the group increases its numbers. But at the same time individual effort is economized, particularly where, through division of labor, each plays his or her special rôle. Even a rudimentary degree of specialization necessitates organization. Individuals must sink their differences in order to form a *coherent peace group*, united in its offensive and defensive activities against enemies and the powers of nature. While the liberty of the individual suffers restriction, he gains immeasurably in security. Association further provides the necessary condition for accumulation of culture. What one member of the group learns from experience may be communicated to others that all may benefit by his discovery. And as the social heritage, ever growing, is transmitted from old to young, each generation is the beneficiary of the wisdom and skill accumulated by their ancestors through untold centuries.

Factors in Social Evolution: Appropriation and Utilization of Natural Resources and Energies. Steady advance becomes possible in the appropriation and utilization of natural resources and energies. Fire plays a central rôle in community life; wood, stone, bone, shell, and, much later, metal are fashioned into more and more efficient tools and weapons. Basket-making and pottery develop. Plants and animals furnish food; animal skins are used for clothing and tents. With the domestication of animals there is not only a larger and steadier supply of food, hides, and wool, but animals may be used for the transportation of men and supplies. Finally, through the exploitation of slaves, human energies are appropriated in a way making possible an increasing amount of hard and onerous labor. Each step in advance means greater security through fuller control of natural forces.

Factors in Social Evolution: Accumulation of Capital. Unforeseen emergencies are, however, bound to occur. Drought, flood, pestilence, or famine may threaten the very existence of a group. While unable to cope directly with such disasters, a group has a far greater chance of survival when it has accumulated a store of capital, of *subsistence* capital in the form of food, grain, or cattle, and of *production* capital in the form of tools or weapons. Insurance is provided by capital against the contingencies of the future, be they great or small. Increasing stores of capital are made possible by more permanent dwelling places. Where permanent agricultural settlements develop, land becomes the chief source of wealth. Private property, which had probably at first taken the form of ownership of weapons, and later of cattle, now, with the private ownership of land, reaches a stage of development of crucial importance to the future of humanity.

Factors in Social Evolution: Development of Foresight and Intelligence. Interest in the accumulation of capital means a subordination of the present to the future, it means preparation for future needs and possibilities, envisaged on the basis of past experience. Capital therefore is of peculiar significance in connection with the growth of *foresight*, a quality which, as we have seen, not only becomes more and more necessary at the successive stages of human progress, but is increasingly stimulated by the processes on which this progress depends.[1] Cultural progress, in other words, implies the development of intelligence.

Factors in Social Evolution: Environmental Changes as Necessitating New Adjustments. Our enumeration of factors making for social evolution is obviously incomplete. Successful adjustments, as we have seen, tend to become fixed in custom. It is true, of course, as MacIver points out, that "each new generation is a new beginning. . . . It starts with new energies in an altered world. What has already been done furnishes a basis for its own doing. . . . The greater the social heritage, the greater too the potentiality of change." [2] All the same, so tenacious is the hold of the past that we must explain more fully why any evolution at all took place, what specific alterations in conditions led to new adjustments, and forced change, despite customs and traditions. In the first place some cataclysmic change in the environment, drought, flood, earthquake, forest fire may completely alter the surroundings of a human group. Whether the survivors migrate to new surroundings or whether they remain in the neighborhood of their former home, they must adjust themselves to altered conditions. Climatic changes, though supervening very slowly, must finally have the same effect.

Factors in Social Evolution: Invention as Leading to Variation from Established Usage. Again, there is always the possibility

---

[1] The interesting suggestion is made by Gerald Heard, in *The Source of Civilization* (1935), that the Neolithic culture pattern, the precursor of civilization, "is not the result of a series of colliding discoveries. It is rather a series of discoveries resulting from a new integration of experience, a new insight into the environment and a new extension of outlook over time. These discoveries are all discoveries based on foresight." Pp. 134–135.

[2] From R. M. MacIver, *Society: Its Structure and Changes*, p. 397. Copyright 1931. Reprinted by permission of the publishers, Farrar and Rinehart, Inc.

of changes originating in invention. A variation from established usage is achieved when some individual puts familiar
materials to a new use. The occasion for such a variation must
often have arisen accidentally; but it took inventive talent to
perceive its significance, to be able to view the familiar in altered
perspective. We may well imagine that an accidentally broken
flint revealed possibilities whose perception led to the extensive
use of flint implements and weapons. Perception of the effect
of the grinding of stone against stone might similarly have led
to the use of polished stones. An invention of obvious utility
would have been speedily adopted by the group in which it
originated.

*Factors in Social Evolution: Group Contacts as Tending to the
Selection of Successful Variations and the Diffusion of Culture.*
Most potent of all the influences tending to change has been
contact between groups with differing customs and traditions.[1]
Such contact must often have been violent. Here the group
that was in possession of more successful forms of adjustment
was likely to prevail. Where contact was peaceful, some obviously successful invention would be adopted by allied or friendly
groups.[2] Successful variations were thus selected in the course
of competition between groups, and transmitted to future
generations, not alone in the group of their originators but in
other groups as well.[3] Change in environmental conditions,
invention, and group contact are thus the chief factors in the
breaking of what Bagehot calls "the cake of custom." Where
there is some density of population, where there is travel, trade,
transportation of men and things, where barriers to free intercourse are broken down, there is likely to be widespread diffusion
of culture.

[1] See Robert H. Lowie, *Primitive Society* (1920). Lowie states that: "Cultures
develop mainly through the borrowings due to chance contact" (p. 441). Lowie also
admits independent development, because "there are certain conditions that may
recur in different areas and produce similar results" (p. 432); but the products of
individual development "have a negligible influence on the total course of events"
(p. 433).

[2] While the stranger was originally regarded as an enemy, he *might* be a potential
friend. The word "guest" is akin to *hostis*, and the widespread insistence on the
"duty of hospitality" is significant of the change from exclusive group solidarity
to the development of friendly relationships between groups. The interesting suggestion has been made that fire may have played a large part in the initiation of
friendly contacts between groups. Fire may be given to others without depletion.
A group whose fire was extinct might borrow from strangers and enter into friendly relations with them. W. G. Sumner and A. G. Keller, *The Science of Society*, Vol. I, p. 198.

[3] MacIver points out that a wider range of association between individuals makes
possible the intermixture of more diverse hereditary factors and so increases the
range of potential variation in the succeeding generations. *Op. cit.*, p. 397.

SOCIAL CHANGE IN THE EARLY CIVILIZATIONS

Cities and the Growing Complexity of Governmental and Industrial Organization. Civilization is a "function of numbers in contact,"[1] and, so far as present knowledge goes, seems to have first arisen where environmental conditions were favorable in the fertile river valleys of the warmer temperate regions of the old world, in India, Mesopotamia, and Egypt. Startling discoveries are being made at the present time in the East, enabling archaeologists to penetrate further and further back into the history of the civilizations of the fifth millennium B.C.[2] But there is, as yet, no certain knowledge of the two or three thousand preceding years, during which the earliest civilizations must have come into being. The general processes of social change may, however, be inferred.

On the banks of the Nile and Indus and in the Tigris-Euphrates valley, civilization developed as men learnt to make use of irrigation. Coöperative effort is essential in order to control and direct flood waters by means of canals. In Egypt, for example, regular irrigation was only possible when controlled by a single authority, and centralized power was necessary. Amalgamation of the numerous agricultural settlements must thus have taken place, either through negotiation or conquest. Extended and coöperative peace groups were formed, supporting themselves on the fertile fields surrounding a central storehouse and stronghold, the walled city from which the word civilization is derived. Later such city-states formed more or less stable federations under the leadership of the more powerful among them. Complex forms of organization became necessary, for industrial and commercial and governmental purposes. The earlier social groups had been small and compact, with kinship the natural bond of social union. A direct method whereby larger aggregations of groups could be welded into coherent communities was by means of subjection to the authority of chief, king, or ruling class. Military and religious leaders must usually have been commanding figures, who were able to retain and increase their prestige and political power and to enforce peace and order.

Slavery and Class Inequality. Class inequality is a striking characteristic of early civilization. Prestige and privilege belong to the few holders of power by whom the masses are held in

[1] W. G. Sumner and A. G. Keller, *op. cit.*, p. 14.
[2] See V. Gordon Childe, *New Light on the Most Ancient East* (1934).

subjection. Such an arrangement made possible the complex organization and the cultural achievement of the ancient world. Prior to the introduction of slavery no wholesale form of specialization of labor had existed save sex specialization based on biological differences. Man had reserved for himself the more active and interesting side of life, hunting and military activities. Victory in war now made possible the enslavement and coerced labor of the conquered. With the increasing demand for labor to accomplish the hard monotonous toil necessary in cultivation of the soil, it became to a high degree advantageous for a conqueror to preserve his captives alive: a distinct mitigation of the savagery of warfare, although leading to the oppression and exploitation of subject classes. In this way social differences came for the first time to form the basis of specialization of labor. A superior level of social organization was made possible, and, since all the necessary labor was performed by the conquered, their conquerors were free to engage in the duties of war and government and the development of the arts and sciences.[1]

The Influence of Written Records. While spoken language is a distinctive attainment of human beings as compared with other animals, the use of writing marks the transition from prehistoric to historic times. Written records became possible, first in the form of pictographs and then in a series of transition forms, until, with the invention of the alphabet, written language reached its final form, its symbols now being representative of the sounds of spoken language. Written records have a permanency impossible of achievement through oral tradition. Myths, customs, codes, observances, and rules may now be accurately inscribed and preserved in an authoritative form. Such records must have served as a unifying force in the amalgamation of groups which made civilization possible. Differences in customs having to do with industry would not offer much obstacle to the union of neighboring groups; language differences, unless very slight, would take somewhat longer to overcome; but religious differences would be hard indeed to reconcile. Nevertheless, some form of reconciliation and integration of conflicting beliefs had to be brought about. Written records would have tended to harmonize, as far as possible, divergencies

---

[1] Slavery is perhaps one of the most striking examples of the fact, already noted on page 25, that social arrangements which bring progress at certain stages of human history, may at the same time entail such evils as to become at later stages fatal to the welfare of society.

of tradition, the accepted version being finally preserved in literature that was considered sacred. Written records not only preserved the culture of the past, but in their control of thought exercised an influence even more conservative than that of oral tradition.

The Power of Priests as Interpreters of Sacred Traditions. The scribes, recorders, and interpreters of tradition were the priests, the only learned men of their time. Religion, the most conservative of social forces, now reached even greater heights of power. Tradition, as we have seen, transmits not only the useful and beneficial products of human intelligence, but also the superstitious beliefs and practices resulting from man's age-long effort to adjust himself to the supernatural. Leaders of primitive society, such as the great hunter or war chief, were highly honored; but even more revered and powerful was the *medicine man*, the intermediary between man and the incalculable mysteries surrounding him, the *shaman*, he who is inspired or possessed. Such an individual was supposed to have the aid of spirits; they spoke through his mouth as he prophesied; by their means he could heal disease or bring the rain in time of drought. When ritual became complicated and needed exact knowledge for its interpretation and performance, the shaman, alone being qualified for such an office, became a *priest*.

The priest's unique position gave him opportunity to increase his prerogatives and possessions. Often the priest was at the same time the war chief or the king. In any case, the priests were the ruling class, those holding supreme authority. Leisure too was theirs, part of which they devoted to learning: as the creators and interpreters of sacred literature, they laid the foundations not only of religious orthodoxy and the early cosmogonies, but of the sciences and cosmology. With vast resources in materials and unlimited supplies of forced labor at their command, they built temples and tombs and so were influential in the development of the fine arts. They were the first professional educators, training their successors to the priesthood and instructing the people in orthodox belief and observance of ritual. Always, however, the authority of the priest was exercised to maintain and increase his own power. For holders of power and privilege are necessarily conservative and despotic. Their position is only secure where there is continual subjection of the masses.

Every detail of daily life was regulated by religion. The various social institutions, "the established forms of relation between social beings," [1] developed as they were from the *mores* centering around some major human interest, became at this stage more exactly defined, conformity being authoritatively enforced. The industrial organization with its rigid class distinctions, the forms of property, governmental and military organization, the forms of marriage and the family, and, crowning them all, the sanctions of orthodox religion held successive generations inflexibly to unchanging ways of life.

THE ACCELERATION OF SOCIAL CHANGE IN WESTERN CIVILIZATION

The Greeks and Critical Thought. In the concluding section of this chapter, we must limit ourselves to noting a few factors of outstanding significance in the development of Western civilization. Marked acceleration of social change is very recent, but it was made possible through influences which had their origin among the Greeks, Hebrews, and Romans.

Life on the shores of the Mediterranean offered unusual opportunities for travel, commerce, and the contact and intermingling of cultures. In the case of the Greeks, these stimulating conditions led not only to the development of alert intelligence, but to an escape from the stultifying influence of superstition. With remarkable freedom and boldness of speculation, the earliest Greek philosophers sought to trace the interrelationships of things, in an ordered cosmos of which humanity forms a part. But Greek naturalism did not survive. The attention of the leading philosophers became absorbed in the social changes taking place in Athens. The authority of custom, of tradition, and of the group were challenged by the development of critical intelligence. Socrates, however, doubted and questioned with a constructive aim in view. He hoped to disentangle the moral standards embodied in custom and to place them on a foundation securer far than that of tradition: the foundation of understanding and intelligence. Man's full duty is to know himself, for, said Socrates, enunciating the principle fundamental to an intelligent morality, "the unexamined life is not worthy to be lived by man." But the influence of the greatest of Socrates' successors, Plato and Aristotle, made itself felt, not in fuller intellectual freedom, insistent though they were on the preëminence of *reason*, but rather in the renewal and restatement of their philosophy by the Christian Church in Mediaeval Europe.

[1] R. M. MacIver, *Community* (3rd ed., 1924), p. 155.

And so this first freeing of critical intelligence, in spite of its development of concepts and ideals that have their permanent place in the human heritage, was largely conservative in its results. Science did not develop, because such positive knowledge of nature as had been obtained by experiment lacked prestige and authority. It was in the possession of industrial craftsmen, who occupied the low social status accorded in Greece to all who engaged in manual labor. "It doubtless was this fact in Greece," says Dewey, "which in spite of the keenness of observation, the extraordinary power of logical reasoning, and the great freedom of speculation attained by the Athenian, postponed the general and systematic employment of experimental method." [1] But, after all, "If Greek thinkers did not achieve science, they achieved the idea of science." [2] The Greek ideal was that of the *wise* man, he who through critical thought should find a remedy for human ills; and so they at least pointed to a road open to humanity, which "after two millenia of obscuration and desertion was refound and retaken; its rediscovery marks what we call the modern era." [3]

After one of the most brilliant periods in history, when, in less than three hundred years, lived many of the greatest statesmen, dramatists, sculptors, and philosophers the world has ever known, Athenian civilization decayed. Weakened within by internal dissension and attacked from without by Sparta and Macedon, it finally fell before the growing power of Rome. From this disheartening spectacle some of the best minds turned to introspection. The many-sided influence of Socrates was manifested no longer in grappling with social ills, but in finding a way of escape from life's vicissitudes. How may the wise man preserve his soul unmoved in the midst of uncertainty and peril? Security was sought not so much through religion as through an ethical substitute, a control of emotions to attain to Stoic fortitude, Epicurean imperturbability, or Sceptic indifference.

The Coming of Christianity. Into this troubled world where many sought some saving way of life, ethical or religious, came Christianity. But the original gospel of its founder was destined all too soon to reinterpretation and adjustment to the needs of the period. Socrates' insight into the function of critical intelligence had been too far in advance of the social outlook

[1] John Dewey, *Reconstruction in Philosophy* (1920), p. 13.
[2] John Dewey, *Experience and Nature* (1st ed., 1925), p. 125.
[3] *Ibid.*, p. 127.

of his day; so too was the insight of Christ into human relationships.   In a time of mingling of cultures and of consequent
bitter racial and class antagonisms, he visioned the brotherhood
of all human beings as children of God the Father.   His fundamental ethical principle was the Golden Rule in which was
enunciated the essential worth of every human soul, the right
of every individual to consideration.   Having faith in unspoiled
human nature as manifested in the little child, he was critical
of institutions and the authority of tradition in their control of
human life.   Among the Jews this ethical and spiritual gospel
met with interpretation in terms of the Old Testament.   Its
spread to other peoples was accomplished through its further
intellectual reinterpretation in terms of Greek philosophy.   In
successive church councils the opinion of the majority was
decisive in building the imposing edifice of orthodox dogmatic
theology.[1]   Christians became not so much the followers of
Christ as those who were "true believers," who accepted un-
questioningly the doctrines of the Church.   The living spirit of
early Christianity thus gave place to conformity to standards
of thought, feeling, and behavior imposed from without by the
increasingly powerful Church of Rome.

Rome and the Development of Jurisprudence.   The Romans
were originally a group of farmer-warriors, surrounded by hostile neighbors.   In time, partly by conquest, partly by treaty
and agreement, a political federation was built up under the
leadership of Rome, which, before long, became strong enough
to defeat its leading commercial rival, Carthage.   Once started
on a career of conquest and organization of conquered territories, the Roman legions moved on with invincible power,
until the boundaries of the Empire extended from Britain
to India.   The Romans were possessed of remarkable talents
for administration and government.   Stern and industrious,
they were from the first embued with a strong sense of
civic duty.   Customary law was handed down from father to
son in patrician families till codified in the fifth century B.C.
in the Law of the Twelve Tables.   Class distinctions were
strongly marked in Rome, but as the Roman rule extended
there came about at the same time a leveling of barriers between
peoples of differing races and cultures.   The development not
only of governmental organization but of an adequate system

[1] The derivation of *dogma* is instructive.   It meant originally an affirmation of
personal conviction, and was the substantive form corresponding to a Greek phrase
meaning "it seems to me."

of jurisprudence became a necessity. The combination of great wealth with political power had by this time to some extent undermined the rugged virtues which had underlain the strength of Rome in its early period. But it was this same spirit which, finding a new expression through Stoic philosophy, now perfected Rome's most enduring contribution to civilization. The practical genius of the Romans had enabled them to build cities, roads, and aqueducts to provide a material embodiment for their vast empire. Only ruins of these now remain, but Roman jurisprudence, formulated to weld together subject peoples under the *Pax Romana*, endures to this day as the basis for most of the legal systems of Europe. Roman law was the work of successive praetors and jurisconsults. From Stoic philosophy and the interpretation given it by Cicero and Seneca, they derived the concept of *justice* as grounded in a rational and universal law of nature, and as the rightful test of governmental institutions.[1]

The Barbarian Invasions and the Predominance of the Mediaeval Church. The conquest of Rome by hordes of Teutonic barbarians brought about one of the most marked retrogressions in the history of civilization. Western Europe was for centuries the scene of strife and disorder. The accumulated culture of the past was all but swept away. All forms of production and industry were ruined, and the West fell back into the economic life of primitive peoples. Bands of armed brigands roamed abroad. The great Roman roads fell into disrepair, bridges collapsed. Travel and trade thus became all but impossible. By the year 600 no more than one-twentieth of the population of Rome survived amongst its ruins. Those who had escaped death by the sword perished of hunger or disease. Seldom has there been a time of such utter insecurity of human life, such dire misery and want. In the absence of any central authority, land and dominion over the masses were seized by those who had power, the successful barbarian chieftains and the Roman Church. Thus were laid the foundations for the development of the feudal system. The Roman Church, sole surviving heir of Greco-Roman civilization, alone preserved both its stable and orderly internal government and its traditional authority. It must be admitted that, by allying itself with barbarian conquerors, it countenanced the most appalling cruelties. Wholesale conversions were made at the sword's point, and Chris-

---

[1] Compare the well-known saying of Terence: *Homo sum; nihil humanum a me alienum puto.*

tianity was for the most part a superficial veneer on Teutonic barbarism. Yet, even so, the Church was the chief instrument in the gradual bringing of order out of chaos.

Some remnants of the learning of the ancients had been pre- served in isolated monasteries such as those in far-off Ireland. In monasteries, too, manual labor was enjoined, workshops were developed, and methods of cultivation improved. Again, in insisting on the right of sanctuary and attempting to limit vengeance, the Church helped to secure more peaceful condi- tions; while, through its charitable work, it sought to alleviate the misery of the masses. For these unfortunates, amidst the insecurity of a life where cruelty and oppression were universal, hunger and disease an ever-present threat, and fear of the super- natural a waking nightmare, the hope of eternal happiness in heaven offered them by the Church must often have been the sole alleviation of earthly life. Life on earth was to be accepted as the time of trial preparatory to the life to come. On this hypothesis, treated, however, not as hypothetical, but as abso- lutely certain, was based the authoritative hold of the Church over human thought and action. Out of the ruins of ancient civilization arose a new civilization. "Feudalism and the ideals of universal empire and universal church had bound together the various peoples of Europe in a rigorous hierarchy which imposed order on the confusion of barbarism." [1] Under the all-embracing sway of the Mediaeval Church, a magnificent and seemingly stable synthesis of human thought and activity was reached in the thirteenth century, the century which saw the completion of most of the great Gothic cathedrals and the perfecting of the Scholastic system of theology.

The Renaissance. But already, for more than two centuries, influences had been at work which were to destroy the pre- dominance of the ecclesiastical system. The great cathedrals, begun during the period of the crusades, owed their completion to the class opposed to feudalism, the wealthy city burghers. There had been a gradual reconstruction of towns going on for centuries, some on the sites of the old Roman cities, others near fortresses or monasteries, but not till about 1300 did the citizen class reach a position of established power. The growing importance of cities and of the commercial class had been due in large part to the development of trade in the eleventh and twelfth centuries. In the course of successive crusades, methods

[1] E. M. Hulme, *The Renaissance, the Protestant Revolution and the Catholic Ref- ormation in Continental Europe* (1st ed., 1914), p. 61.

for the transportation of troops and the carrying of supplies had been developed that were of the utmost benefit to commerce. Commercial intercourse with the East was further stimulated by the growing demand for imported luxuries, for cottons, silks, sugar, spices, perfumes, jewels, and glassware. Intermingling of cultures provided the conditions for progress. The Arabs, who in the seventh and eighth centuries had swept over Northern Africa into Spain, were not finally dislodged from Western Europe for seven hundred years. Possessed of a culture far in advance of their European neighbors, their influence was revolutionary. Epoch-making inventions were introduced into Europe by the Arabs: the arabic numeral system, derived from the Hindus, made possible the development of modern mathematics; the magnetic needle led to the discovery of distant lands, including the New World, and brought about a vast extension of commerce; gunpowder, by rendering obsolete the mediaeval castle and the armored knight, revolutionized methods of warfare. Paper too, introduced from Asia by the Arabs to take the place of the costly parchment, became, with the invention of printing in the fifteenth century, the means for a rapid multiplication of books. Spoken language and written language each marked humanity's rise to new levels; so, too, did the development of printing: the most potent means as yet devised for dispelling ignorance and disseminating ideas.

The rise of separate nations and of vernacular languages and literatures were other influences, in addition to those already enumerated, tending to break up the feudal system and the hold of the Roman Church. Released from the spell of ecclesiastical ideals, men began to turn with eager interest and appreciation to the world about them. The rediscovery of classical manuscripts, brought to Italian cities after the fall of Constantinople in 1453, reënforced this tendency. But, while the recovered knowledge of the literature and life of the ancient Greeks and Romans powerfully stimulated and permanently enriched European culture, it also led to a new form of tradition, "classicism," an insistence on the authority of the past that was definitely retrogressive in its influence.

The Development of Science and Francis Bacon as Forerunner of the Modern Spirit. We have as yet barely mentioned science, the most revolutionary of all influences leading Western European culture definitely away from the past and on toward the modern age. An experimental and inventive tendency had begun to manifest itself during the thirteenth century in Europe.

The properties of lenses were discovered, and, before long, by means of telescopes and microscopes, human powers of observation were vastly extended. Mathematics, astronomy, and physics came first. Modern mathematics, taking its rise in the work of such men as Descartes, Leibniz, and Newton, makes possible a statement of natural events in their quantitative aspects, and so gives that understanding of mechanical structure which alone may secure control. In his substitution of experimental method for mere observation of nature, Galileo pointed out the only sure road to a knowledge of natural laws. He was enabled, through his controlled observations, to verify the hypothesis of Copernicus that the earth, the home of man, could no longer be regarded as the center of the universe. It is hard for us to-day to realize how subversive of hitherto accepted ideas the new world view must have appeared. The Empyrean, heaven where God dwelt, vanished from actual space, while man could no longer feel securely at home in this vast and bewildering universe.

While contributing little to the actual growth of the sciences the work of Francis Bacon is significant from another point of view. He stands preëminent as the forerunner of the spirit of modern life, as possessing a more adequate appreciation of the social possibilities inherent in a scientific control of nature. He uses the word "progressive" in the modern sense; it was he, again, who first distinguished between "ancient" and "modern" times. He insisted on a break from the past and its useless learning; the human mind must free itself from error and prejudice and seek to follow the genuine method of the sciences. "Knowledge is power," its true aim being human progress ever renewed through a human control of events.

The New Individualism. A growing sense of the importance of the individual had permeated, partly as cause, partly as effect, the many changes marking the transition to the modern age. It is only through the individual in any age that new inventions, new art, new thought come into the world. This was true even when the individual was all but submerged in the primitive group. In the ancient world, although the importance of individuality was recognized, the individual was regarded objectively as part of the order of nature. In the hierarchical order of mediaeval times, man was not so much an individual as a member of the varying groups to which he belonged.

Now, however, all was altered. An insistence on the function of the individual as the agent of progress became a keynote of the modern age. The religious liberty of the individual was insisted upon by the Protestant reformers, while his political liberty was affirmed through revolts against despotic power, and through insistence on the natural rights of man, and on the ideals of liberty, equality, and fraternity. The new views of nature, moreover, led to a transformation of the individual *soul* of earlier Christian theory into the *conscious self* set in opposition to a universe conceived in mechanical terms. This over-dualistic point of view, distorting, by its statement in mutually exclusive terms, the reality of man's unique position within natural events, has led to all the difficulties of philosophic materialism and subjectivism. It has also reënforced an over-individualistic, *laissez-faire* attitude in the world of affairs, which, whatever may have been its services to economic progress, has to-day become a grave menace to social amelioration. Individualism laid a needed emphasis on the pivotal position of the individual in thought and in action. In its extremer forms, however, it obscures the fact that man never lives to himself alone, isolated from his relationship to society. Now, more than ever before, must the individual, without relinquishing his hard-won freedom of thought, realize his position in a social order vaster and more complex than any the world has hitherto known.

The Machine Age. The factors which have made for social change in the past are operative to-day and to a hitherto unparalleled degree. Hence the recent and rapid acceleration of social change. Foremost comes the factor of invention. The modern age is preëminently the age of science and of the machine. Invention follows invention with startling rapidity, for discovery is a function, not only of the individual brain, but of the social environment which stimulates and facilitates discovery. Each new invention leads to others. So radical and complex and widespread are the changes being effected in both the physical and social environments, that we are as yet unaware of their full import. Possibilities for good and possibilities for evil, always present where there is change, are to-day intensified to an unlimited degree.

Let us note first the revolutionary changes effected by the machine in agriculture and in industry. Civilization in the past was the product of local conditions and dependent on the ability of a small number of men to command the labor and resources of others. Now, in its appropriation and utilization of natural resources, the modern age relies less and less on animal power and man power, and becomes dependent on its vastly augmented control of the inanimate forces of nature. Human power is multiplied in a constantly increasing ratio by the machine which enables it to harness mechanical, chemical, and electrical power and to manipulate them for human purposes.

One result has been a tremendous increase in commodities. Never before have there been such reserves of capital in the form both of money and of goods. Such conditions, as always, have raised the level of human well-being and led to an increase in population. Not only are there many more people in the world to-day, but by means of the machine they have been brought into closer relationship with one another. The changes brought about by the machine in agriculture and industry are no more revolutionary in their effects than are those in transportation and communication. The stage coach has been superseded by the steam engine and the sailing ship by the steamer, and transportation by air is now in process of rapid development. The widespread dissemination of information and ideas, begun by printing, may now take place directly and far more rapidly, by means of the telegraph and the radio. One part of the world can no longer be considered in complete isolation from any other; the whole is linked together by bonds of association incredibly complicated and far-reaching. The crucial problems of social welfare are thus perforce international.

In the development of Western Europe and the world-wide extension of European power and influence, the usual processes of conflict have been manifest: the subjection of the weaker and continued friction among the stronger. But, under present conditions, war has become so disastrous to all concerned that the desirability of the organization of the whole world into a peace group has become obvious. Unfortunately, as Robinson says, "It has fallen out that just when the world was becoming effectively cosmopolitan in its economic interdependence, its scientific research and its exchange of books and art, the ancient tribal insolence has been developed on a stupendous scale." [1] Nationalism, at one time a distinctly beneficial force in its promotion of social unity and public spirit within the nation, has become detrimental to human welfare in its stimulation of rivalry and hatred between the nations. There is urgent need for broader conceptions of human welfare which shall extend beyond the nation, as in the past they have been extended beyond the family and the clan.

[1] James Harvey Robinson, *The Mind in the Making* (1921), p. 167.

A stage in human history has been reached when ruthless conflict between groups can have only destructive consequences. This is true not only of conflict between nations, but of conflict between classes, between the privileged few and the exploited masses. New forms of association, new social arrangements are urgently needed. While individualism in social affairs must be superseded as more effective coöperative methods are devised, in thought and in judgment, individualism must not only be retained but intensified. Not only is there as always the tendency to rely on the past, and to think along fixed lines, a condition of mind well termed *psychosclerosis*, but there are other very real obstacles to the independent use of intelligence, inherent in the closeness of contact between human beings and the ease with which communication now takes place. For prejudice and emotion are contagious, and misinformation is easier of communication than actual fact. Congestion of population in cities, the centers of manufacture, commerce, and finance, has enormously increased the danger of the domination of society by the mob mind. Nor are the so-called educated by any means exempt. Ortega y Gasset, in his *Revolt of the Masses*, deplores what he calls the "barbarism of specialization," the fact that those qualified in some narrow field too often speak with authority in fields where they have no special knowledge.

The problems confronting humanity seem overwhelming. But we must remember that only very recently have we added to our knowledge and control of physical forces some understanding of social forces and of the mechanisms underlying human life. The life sciences developed last. Less than eighty years have passed since the formulation of the theory of organic evolution, a theory revolutionizing our whole conception of human life, and giving insight into the unity of all life and into its processes of development. We are aware not only of change, but of some of the methods of change. Human aspirations are at last in a position to understand some of the basic conditions of their realization. Confusing as may be the results of such a rapid and widespread breaking down of the barriers to change, hitherto undreamed of opportunities are ours. Human welfare and the greater security and extension of human values may now be won by the intelligent direction given to change.

CHAPTER III

THE FAMILY AND SOCIAL ORGANIZATION

THE DEVELOPMENT OF SOCIAL ANTHROPOLOGY

Difficulties Attending the Study of the Family among Primitive Peoples. Archaeological research supplies us with a reliable account of the early development of *material* culture. Tools, weapons, the bones of men and animals have been excavated from the many-layered deposits on the floors of caves or in the beds of lakes and rivers. A study of these remains of human life and activity, found in the successive layers of such deposits, correlated with geological information as to age of the strata of the earth's surface, has enabled archaeology to reconstruct the periods of prehistoric culture with a high degree of accuracy. Such was the evidence on which we relied in Chapter II for our outline of social change in prehistoric society. In a study of the family, on the other hand, archaeology can render but slight assistance. The physical characteristics of early men, women, and children at certain stages are known. We know what weapons they hunted with and what animals they slew. We can infer much as to primitive industry from their tools. Certain definite ideas about death are attested to by methods of ceremonial burial, and primitive art gives us further clues as to religious beliefs. Indirectly such materials may help us to picture the life of the family in early times, but of *direct* evidence there is none.

It is of importance, moreover, that we should have some understanding of the earliest forms of the family. In the earliest stages of social evolution, mental and social patterns were formed which were to determine the future development of society and which underlie our present mental and social organization. Under such circumstances we are forced to turn to the study, by scientifically trained investigators, of the living representatives of primitive mankind. We cannot, of course, assume that the customs of such peoples to-day are identical with those of their prehistoric ancestors. As Briffault points out, "No existing society or race is, except in a relative sense, primitive; all have behind them a past exactly as long as our own." [1]

---

[1] From Robert Briffault, *The Mothers* (3 vols., 1927), Vol. I, p. 79. By permission of The Macmillan Company, publishers.

Nevertheless, the findings and conclusions of social anthropology furnish the most reliable basis available for inferences as to the family in prehistoric groups.

There is, it is true, one other line of approach. Since the time of Darwin it has been recognized that knowledge of the family among animals, and above all among the anthropoid apes, might furnish us with certain clues as to the earliest forms of the human family. Needless to say, analogies between animal life, based so largely on instinct, and human life, which is human because it is social and modified by culture, must be drawn with the utmost caution. While, therefore, zoölogy may be of some assistance, our main reliance must be on anthropology. Here, too, difficulties are encountered on every side. The greater part of the earth's surface is inhabited by innumerable tribes of uncivilized peoples. In Europe, alone of the continents, savages are no longer to be found. Adjusting themselves to all varieties of climate and physical environment from the Arctic to the equatorial tropics, uncivilized peoples have developed a bewildering variety of customs and beliefs. Certain practices and ideas are, it is true, of such widespread occurrence that a certain amount of generalization has been possible. It must be borne in mind, however, that few, if any, generalizations apply universally, there being many exceptions to even the most prevalent customs. There is danger, moreover, of misinterpretation. The whole pattern of a culture must be understood if the observed facts are to be accurately apprehended. The difficulties in the way of ascertaining the facts, and of their interpretation, are well evidenced by the conflicting theories of anthropologists as to family and marriage customs. It is obvious that the reports of untrained observers, such as travelers, traders, and missionaries could scarcely be expected to yield wholly reliable evidence, biased as most of them have been in their interpretation by racial prejudice or preconceived religious ideas. But even the scientific observer has his own form of bias, and is far too often partially blinded by theoretical preconceptions. As Malinowski says, savages "are being constantly used as pawns in controversy and props in hypotheses, rather than as living beings and the subjects of a living science. The institutions of the native races of to-day, instead of being used as material for sociological study, as a basis for scientific induction, are regarded as 'survivals' of past stages and indices of vanished historical periods." [1] Hasty inferences as to the earliest forms

[1] Bronislaw Malinowski, *Parenthood—The Basis of Social Structure*, in V. F. Calver-

of the family thus militate against unprejudiced observation of the institution of the family as found among uncivilized peoples to-day.

Earlier Interpretations of Native Customs in Terms of the Patriarchal Theory. Social anthropology may be said to have originated in the intelligent interest taken by the Jesuit Fathers in the New World. With the expansion of European civilization during the seventeenth and eighteenth centuries, travelers and missionaries came increasingly in contact with native peoples. Unparalleled as was their opportunity, these early observers of native customs were, of course, wholly lacking in scientific technique. Moreover, in those days, when the concept of organic evolution was unknown, the origin of the human race was believed to have been due to special creation and the primitive state of mankind to have been one of moral perfection, which meant, Briffault remarks, "that it accorded with the moral standards recognized in European societies." [1] The first systematic book on social anthropology was Father Lafitau's *Mœurs des Sauvages Ameriquains comparées aux mœurs des premiers temps* (1724), where it was argued that marriage, though "shameful," is necessary for the procreation of the human species and has always been "regarded by all peoples as a thing sacred and solemn." [2] Another reverend father, recording, in the middle of the seventeenth century, his observations on the Guanches of the Canary Islands, "not only states that they married but one wife, but is also at much pains to demonstrate that no less could be expected of them, since polygamy is 'contrary to the nature of man and woman' and can exist only as a detestable aberration introduced into the world by 'the depraved sect of Mahomet'!" [3] The same writer felt polyandry to be an even greater abomination, for "was not woman formed out of the rib of man?" [3]

While such an attitude rendered much misapprehension inevitable, we cannot discard these early ethnographical reports as wholly lacking in value. They were free at least from the sophistication introduced by anthropological speculation. Indeed, while admitting an over-zealous attention to what were considered the more admirable aspects of native custom, much of the information given us as to the individual family with its emphasis on motherhood as a universal human unit is, Mali-

ton and S. D. Schmalhausen (editors), *The New Generation* (The Macaulay Company, 1930), p. 116.

[1] *Op. cit.*, Vol. II, p. 9.　　　[2] *Ibid.*, pp. 13, 14.　　　[3] *Ibid.*, p. 286.

nowski considers, of unquestionable value. Nothing, in fact, was discovered, before the second half of the nineteenth century, seriously to upset the view in acceptance up to that time, that mankind had lived from the beginning in the typical patriarchal family.

Such a view, deriving as it did in part from the Bible, was incorporated in Christian theology. In part, too, it was an inheritance from classical antiquity. So deeply imbedded was the patriarchal form of the family in European social tradition that the Encyclopedists found in it a natural institution, suited to the natural man. Later students of Indo-European linguistics and institutions gave definite scientific form to the patriarchal theory whose chief upholder was Sir Henry Maine. In *Ancient Law*, published in 1861, Maine sets forth his reasons for believing that the patriarchal family, represented in typical form by the family in Ancient Rome, was the earliest form of the family, the form from which all others have been derived.

The Discovery and Interpretation of Evidence Contradictory to the Patriarchal Theory. The year 1861 also saw the publication of *Mutterrecht*, a book in which its author, Bachofen, set forth a somewhat fanciful theory in total opposition to the patriarchal theory. Anthropological evidence was accumulating, and it seemed that certain aspects of savage life were incompatible with the patriarchal theory. Reinterpretation was necessary. Like Maine's ancient peoples, the majority of native tribes were found to be divided into "gentes," "clans," or "sibs," groups larger than the family, which yet preserve the character of kinship groups.[1] But Maine's picture is incomplete. Sometimes a tribe is divided into halves or moieties, and usually such a division is accompanied by the strict prohibition of marrying within the moiety. *Exogamy*, the law of marriage outside a prescribed group, in this case the moiety, combined with the *endogamous* prescription of marriage within the tribe, results in closely knitting the moieties into the whole, since every individual family must necessarily consist of both elements. In some tribes further bisection takes place, and there are four or eight clans with corresponding marriage regulations. And then again there are tribes where the number of clans is odd, and exogamic rules cannot be derived from the principle of bisection.

[1] Lowie, in adopting the term "sib," points out (*Primitive Society*, 1920, p. iii) that most American anthropologists use the term "clans" only for mother-sibs, while they use the term "gentes" for father-sibs. British anthropologists include both in the term "clan." British usage is followed here unless otherwise indicated

The members of a clan treat each other as kindred, tracing descent from a common ancestor, and acting together on certain occasions as though they were of one blood. Indeed, in some societies, these larger kinship groups are far more prominent than the individual family. There are, for instance, communities where the mother, with her children, lives in the communal house and is only visited by her husband at night, his time being spent in a men's clubhouse. In these cases, however, the husband and father still has indispensable functions. He must be married to the woman if their children are to have full legal status in the tribe; he has certain economic duties and must often act as the representative of his wife and children on ceremonial occasions.

Such a situation as the above is more likely to be found where *mother-right*, or the *matrilineal* principle, prevails.[1] Here, indeed, is a feature of many primitive societies wholly at variance with the patriarchal theory. For, in primitive society, descent is by no means always *patrilineal*, as it is where the family is *patriarchal*. The father is not always recognized as of primary importance in determining descent, nor has he always the right to hand over his possessions and privileges to his son. In many societies the mother is the parent through whom descent is counted and her brother is the male head of the family, exercising authority over, and at the same time being bound by obligations to, his sister's children. This relationship between a man and his sister's son is usually spoken of as the *avunculate*. The father even here, however, is not without marital and paternal influence. Anthropologists speak of the "bilateral" principle of counting descent, to describe the fact that the kinship relationships within the family are never wholly obliterated, even when the "unilateral" principle of counting descent, only through *either* the father *or* the mother, operative in the formation of clans, appears to receive the greater emphasis.

Most puzzling of all was Morgan's discovery, made in the course of his field study of certain American Indian tribes, of what is known as the "classificatory" system of kinship nomenclature. This means the widely prevalent practice of extending family terms—such as father, mother, brother, and sister, to

---

[1] This system is also referred to as the *metronymic* system in contrast to the *patronymic* system; reference being, in this case, to the family name. Marriage is *matrilocal* where the husband joins his bride and lives among her people. It is *patrilocal* where she leaves her own family to live among his kindred.

certain definite classes of more distant relatives and clansmen. For certain other relatives entirely new terms are devised which are also applied, not to one, but to several people. This is no mere linguistic usage, for a definite set of mutual obligations unites the individual with, for example, all those whom he calls "father." These latter, again, are a well-defined social class acting as a group on certain specified occasions: in economic coöperation, or as a legal unit, or at tribal ceremonies. It appeared at first sight as though group relationships were thus substituted for the individual relationships of the family, an interpretation strengthened by certain strange marriage customs entirely at variance with patriarchal marriage, either monogynic or polygynic. Certain tribes, for instance, were found to practice polyandry, and in some cases a woman married a man and his younger brothers, a practice known as *fraternal polyandry*.

The first result of these new discoveries was to render the patriarchal theory untenable. The patriarchal family, far from being the universal or original type of early family, was recognized as in all probability a comparatively recent development. *Patrilineal* families exist in primitive society, but the typical *patriarchal* family was found to develop usually only within more advanced forms of social organization.

It was perhaps to be expected that speculation should swing first of all to the opposite extreme in Bachofen's famous theory of the matriarchate. This Swiss jurist pictured our earliest ancestors as living in a state of sexual promiscuity. Marriage was unknown and fatherhood unrecognized, and children belonged to the group. Aided by their brothers, their natural male protectors, women were the founders and rulers of the earliest societies.[1]

Despite the fact that there are instances of uncivilized women possessing unusual property rights or playing prominent parts in public life, anthropologists are well-nigh unanimous in discarding the theory of the *matriarchate* in its literal sense. Not so, however, the allied hypotheses of primitive promiscuity, sex-communism, and group-marriage. Indeed, until recently, by far the greater number of anthropologists have been agreed that sexual intercourse was originally without regulation and that individual marriage and the family are the product of a

---

[1] For a summary of Bachofen's speculations see C. E. Howard, *A History of Matrimonial Institutions* (3 vols., 1904), Vol. I, pp. 40–43. The first three chapters of this volume are devoted to a survey of the development of anthropological theories of the family.

gradual development through a series of stages. Great diversity
of opinion has existed, however, as to the character and order of
the stages whereby more permanent sex relationships came into
being. Such theories appeared, at first sight, to have adequate
support. While, apart from the unverified reports of travelers,
there was no evidence that any existing savage tribes lived in a
state of sex-communism, many puzzling customs, such as the
great variety of standardized sexual liberties, seemed readily
explained if looked upon as survivals of a long past stage of
promiscuity. Such a theory served also to explain Morgan's
discovery of classificatory nomenclature. Morgan's attack on
the patriarchal theory, coming almost simultaneously with
Bachofen's, was more formidable.[1] For Morgan based his theories on his own first-hand acquaintance with natives and their
language. His study of the Iroquois, where women have
an unusually influential position, and his etymological discoveries gave what seemed to him decisive clues to the early
evolution of society. Being influenced by the newly enunciated
Darwinian theory, Morgan sought to outline a complete scheme
for the evolution of marriage, assuming throughout that there
must exist an invariable series of stages from the lowest stage
of promiscuity up to the highest stage of monogamy. Group-
marriage was supposed by him to follow promiscuity, the clan
or exogamous group appearing at this stage as the domestic
institution, and accordingly as the unit of social organization.
According to him the archaic clan must always have been
matrilineal since paternity was uncertain. Far later, with the
accumulation of property and greater certainty of fatherhood,
antagonism arose against a system which excluded the owner's
children from inheriting his goods. In many tribes a transition
must then have taken place from matrilineal to patrilineal
rules of descent and inheritance.

Such very briefly is Morgan's theory of the stages of family
development, as set forth, in 1877, in his *Ancient Society, or
Researches in the Lines of Human Progress from Savagery,
through Barbarism to Civilization*. Though differing from Morgan
in the details of his reconstruction, McLennan in *Primitive
Marriage* (1886) is in substantial agreement with Morgan's
main hypothesis.[2] To these three men, Bachofen, Morgan, and
McLennan, is due the credit for having revolutionized social
anthropology in the latter half of the nineteenth century.

[1] For a summary of Morgan's views, see Howard, *op. cit.*, pp. 65–70.
[2] For a summary of McLennan's views, see Howard, *op. cit.*, pp. 75–88.

Following, or giving them at least partial support, came a number of notable investigators. Among the more recent are Sumner, Rivers, Keller, Durkheim, Hartland, and Briffault. A maternal system is postulated by most of these men as having everywhere preceded the paternal, and since mother-right and father-right are treated as mutually exclusive alternative systems, any society exhibiting features of both is supposed to be in a stage of transition and to preserve in the form of survivals traces of the matrilineal stage through which it has passed. However, as Lowie points out, "only if we accept as an axiom Tylor's and Morgan's belief in uniform laws of social evolution . . . is every difference at once invested with sequential significance." He further warns that "the extensive spread of cultural traits by borrowing is bound to play havoc with any hypothetical tendency of communities to traverse certain stages in fixed succession." [1] It is true, of course, that the highest civilizations are predominantly patrilineal, but so also are some of the lowest cultures known. Matrilineal cultures fall between these two extremes.

Westermarck and Other Opponents of Matriarchal Theories. In his notable work, *The History of Human Marriage*, Westermarck, a leading opponent of matriarchal theories, devotes the greater part of the first volume to a criticism of the hypothesis of promiscuity.[2] Pointing to the fact that there are no actually authenticated instances of savages living in a state of promiscuity, he argues that, even if such instances were known, this would not furnish proof of an original state of promiscuity. Customs which seemingly point to an earlier stage of promiscuity admit of other and more satisfactory explanations. He agrees with the other opponents of group-marriage that such a theory cannot be reconciled with the supreme importance of individual motherhood and of the family. Descent on the paternal or maternal side does not mean that the other side of the family is ignored. It is not in any way necessary to believe that mother-right and father-right represent stages of development; rather may they be explained as due in large measure to social conditions. Central to Westermarck's attack on the hypothesis of promiscuity is his development of Darwin's biological argument. Darwin had pointed out that the extreme jealousy of males among the higher mammals made promiscuity

[1] *Op. cit.*, pp. 175–176.
[2] *The History of Human Marriage* appeared originally in 1889. In 1921 a 5th ed., rewritten in 3 vols., was published.

exceedingly unlikely. The typical original family probably took
the form of a group comprising one male with one or more
females whom he jealously guarded against all other males. On
this basis, and pointing to the fact that marriage between single
pairs and the individual family play a conspicuous part in some
of the most primitive existing societies, Westermarck takes a
firm stand as the champion of pair-marriage as the original
form of the family.

Briffault and Other Recent Advocates of Matriarchal Theories.
In *The Mothers*, Briffault engages in a detailed attack on Westermarck's position.[1] Drawing a clear distinction between the
products of biological and social heredity he holds that "the
social characters of the human mind are, one and all, traceable
to the operation of instincts that are related to the functions
of the female and not to those of the male." [2]   The mind of
woman must have exercised a profound influence on the earliest
stages of social development.   Briffault accordingly thinks it
necessary to postulate, as the prototype of society, maternal
groups which were the extension of the natural groups composed
in each case of a mother and her offspring.   Daughters would
remain in the group in which they were born, but mate with
men from other groups. Sons would leave the group. Women
were thus the founders of the home, the originators of the arts;
in the enduring maternal group were forged the bonds knitting
its members together in ties of kinship.   The maternal clan, by
fostering social sentiments, provided the conditions for all
social and mental development.   The maternal clan is thus
supposed to antedate the family, and to have been the essential
unit of social organization.

In spite of his insistence on the feminine sentiments, Briffault
seems strangely to underestimate the importance of individual
motherhood, believing that cultural influences can override
the individual attitude of a mother to her own child. He cites
the prevalence of adoption and interchange of children in support of his contention that mother-love operates irrespective
of real relationship, and may thus be directed by each mother
of a group to all the children of the group. Individual marriage
and the family are, according to Briffault, of far later origin,
being the outgrowth of economic influences. The mother, needing economic and social protection for herself and her children

[1] See E. A. Westermarck, " 'The Mothers,' A Rejoinder to Dr. Briffault," *Three
Essays on Sex and Marriage* (1934), pp. 163–330.
[2] *Op. cit.*, Vol. I, p. v.

was able in time to convert the casual and wholly sexual interest of the male into a more lasting attachment. The husband and father secured in return the individual economic services of the woman. Individual economic association tended to lead to individual sex association, and in this way the individual family came into being. In common with other recent advocates of matriarchal theories, Briffault over-emphasizes the economic aspects of marriage. He points out that sexual and economic aspects have been combined in the European marriage tradition, with the sexual regarded as primary. "The institution, its origin and development, have hence been almost exclusively viewed and discussed by social historians in terms of the operation of the sexual instincts, and of the sentiments connected with those instincts." But to this valid criticism he adds the following comment: "The origin of individual marriage being essentially economic, these psychological factors are the products of the association rather than the causes and conditions that have given rise to it." [1] Keller also over-emphasizes the economic, though not to quite such a degree as Briffault. While careful to distinguish between fact and inference, and, unlike Briffault, holding that "the family is the unit cluster of societal organization," he is still influenced by the theory of evolutionary stages and contends that the mother-family preceded the father-family, insisting that there still survive traces of the former in the latter, while the reverse is not the case. [2]

The Family versus the Clan as the Basis of Social Organization. And so, what Malinowski calls "the great anthropological rift" still remains open and a matter of acrimonious dispute. Broadly speaking, one school affirms an original communism in sex, economics, and kinship, while the other defends individual marriage and kinship, and the importance of the family. For the former, the original unit of social organization was the clan or some group larger than the family; for the latter, it was the family itself. Both sides are considered by Malinowski to be in error; each overlooks one essential aspect of human kinship and over-emphasizes the other. Neither family nor clan can be ignored; they exist, not as exclusive of one another, but as mutually complementary. What, then, is their relationship to

---

[1] *Op. cit.*, Vol. II, p. 2.

[2] *The Science of Society* (4 vols., 1927), Vol. III, p. 1486. Keller is responsible for the final form of these volumes, for the compilation of which he used the masses of materials gathered by Sumner before his death in 1910.

one another? In approaching the problem from this new angle one may hope to break the deadlock and substitute for the clash of rival hypotheses some measure of empirical understanding of the actual functions of the family.[1]

A functional analysis of culture, according to Malinowski, "aims at the explanation of anthropological facts at all levels of development by their function, by the part which they play within the integral system of culture, and by the manner in which they are related to one another within the system, and by the way in which this system is related to the physical surroundings. . . . The functional view of culture lays down the principle that in every type of civilization, every custom, material object, idea, and belief fulfils some vital function, has some task to accomplish, represents an indispensable part within a working whole."[2] Social anthropology from such a viewpoint becomes a branch of social psychology. With the resources of modern psychology at its command it attempts a genetic study of the way in which innate biological tendencies are transformed by means of specific social environment into the cultural forces of habit, disposition, and sentiment.

As an approach to the puzzles of kinship, this method of studying the life histories of individuals has hitherto been neglected. Only as they are viewed as correlated component parts of an organic whole, can we "see in all the facts of sexuality, marriage, family, and clanship one integral institution: the Procreative Institution of mankind."[3]

PARENTHOOD AS THE BASIS OF SOCIAL STRUCTURE

The Family as Core of the Procreative Institution. Central to the life of society is "the institution which controls the mating of the sexes, the procreation of offspring and the education of the young, and fulfils the integral function of racial and cultural continuity."[4] "The core of this institution is the human family; that is, parenthood culturally defined and marriage as a

---

[1] The foregoing outline of the divergences in anthropological opinion is included not only as an aid in understanding the actual facts, but also as a guide to the literature. Only through realization of the hypothetical basis of so many books on the family, is the student shielded from uncritical acceptance of the theories of the first author he or she may happen to read.

[2] *Encyclopaedia Britannica* (14th ed., 1929), Vol. 20, p. 864, *s.v.* "Social Anthropology." By permission.

[3] Malinowski, *Parenthood—The Basis of Social Structure*, in Calverton and Schmalhausen, *op. cit.*, p. 131.

[4] Malinowski, *Encyclopaedia Britannica*, Vol. 20, p. 865, *s.v.* "Social Anthropology."

social contract." [1] Within marriage, "economics are, like sex, a means to an end, which is the rearing, education and dual parental influence over the offspring." [2] At the same time, "Every human culture is built upon its own system of kinship, that is, upon a special type of personal bonds primarily derived from procreation and family life." [3] In primitive societies there are always relations between groups, though not necessarily clans, in addition to relationships between individuals. In its study of the relationships between the members of the family, functional anthropology finds the clue to an understanding of wider social relationships. The formation of the sentiments and ties of kinship may be traced from their origin in the earliest experiences of childhood.

Individual Maternity as a Cultural and Social Fact. The intimate relationship between mother and child is an obvious biological fact. But motherhood is never, in any culture, allowed to remain a mere biological fact. Almost universally there is reënforcement by cultural influences of the original individuality of the biological tie, and a social imposition upon the mother of individual responsibilities. The relation of mother to child is clearly dictated by natural inclination; yet conception, pregnancy, childbirth, and suckling are all socially regulated through ritual, religious and moral conceptions, and legal obligations and privileges. Of particular importance is the sharp distinction drawn between sexual freedom and freedom in becoming a mother. A legitimate socially approved conception must be based on an individual legal contract of marriage between one man and one woman. [4] A prospective mother must observe ceremonial rites and keep taboos, all of which have as their motive the welfare of the unborn child. "The tie of kinship between mother and child is defined by tradition long before birth, and defined as an individual bond." [5] At the crisis of birth customs and ceremonies further reaffirm the important functions of individual motherhood. In each culture, moreover, motherhood is remolded in a fashion specific to that culture and in correlation to the whole structure of the community.

[1] Malinowski, *Parenthood—The Basis of Social Structure*, in Calverton and Schmalhausen, *op. cit.*, p. 162.

[2] Malinowski, *Encyclopaedia Britannica*, Vol. 14, p. 943, *s.v.* "Marriage."

[3] Malinowski, *ibid.*, Vol. 13, p. 404, *s.v.* "Kinship."

[4] This by no means implies *monogamy*. Plural marriage, *polygamy*, is also based on legal contracts between one man and one woman, the difference being that the contract may be repeated once, or more often, between the same man and another woman (*polygyny*); or between the same woman and another man (*polyandry*).

[5] Malinowski, *Parenthood—The Basis of Social Structure*, in Calverton and Schmalhausen, *op. cit.*, p. 135.

Cultural Paternity and Sexual Freedom. What of the father? The male is biologically necessary for impregnation alone. "And yet in all human societies the father is regarded by tradition as indispensable. . . . Among the conditions which define conception as a sociologically legitimate fact there is one of fundamental importance. The most important moral and legal rule concerning the physiological side of kinship is that no child should be brought into the world without a man—and one man at that—assuming the rôle of sociological father, that is, guardian and protector, the male link between the child and the rest of the community."[1] This, Malinowski says, is a generalization of such universal applicability, that, in spite of endless variation in detail, it may be regarded as a fundamental sociological law. As such, he calls it the "principle of legitimacy."[2]

Further to clarify this principle Malinowski emphasizes the fact that, although the two aspects of procreation, sex and parenthood, are linked both biologically and culturally, yet the cultural link differs radically from the natural link. "Sex and parenthood are obviously linked biologically. Sexual intercourse leads at times to conception. Conception always means pregnancy, and pregnancy at times means childbirth. We see that in the chain there are at least two possibilities of a hiatus; sexual intercourse by no means always leads to conception, and pregnancy can be interrupted by abortion and thus not lead to childbirth. The moral, customary, and legal rules of most human communities step in, taking advantage of the two weak links in the chain, and in a most remarkable manner dissociate the two sides of procreation, that is, sex and parenthood. Broadly speaking, it may be said that freedom of sexual intercourse, though not universally, is yet generally prevalent in human societies. Freedom of conception, outside marriage, is, however, never allowed, or, at least in extremely few communities and under very exceptional circumstances."[3]

Where pre-nuptial intercourse is regarded with disapproval, children are legitimate, that is, vested with full social status, only when produced within the socially approved contract of

---

[1] *Ibid.*, p. 137.

[2] The cultural determination of individual paternity is the rule even in communities where the fact of biological fatherhood is unknown. In the Trobriand Islands, Malinowski found that conception is attributed to the agency of "spirits," and children are considered of the "same flesh" only with the mother. *The Father in Primitive Psychology* (1927).

[3] *Parenthood—The Basis of Social Structure*, in Calverton and Schmalhausen, *op. cit.*, p. 138.

marriage. There are many tribes, however, where pre-nuptial intercourse is customary, but where, nevertheless, marriage is regarded as essential if children are to have full tribal position. In some tribes extra-marital pregnancy is not penalized, although the girl and her lover must marry. Often, indeed, pregnancy is a prerequisite to the full conclusion of marriage. In other tribes, unmarried mothers and their children suffer definite penalties. Resort may be had to abortion, or else illegitimate children are killed at birth. No satisfactory explanation has, as yet, been given for the scarcity of illegitimate children where pre-nuptial intercourse is customary.

Parenthood and Regulated Sexuality. Facts such as these lead to yet another important generalization. "Marriage cannot be defined as a licensing of sexual intercourse, but rather as the licensing of parenthood . . . [as] a contract legitimating offspring. . . . Since marriage is the institution through which the inchoate, at times even disruptive, drives of sex are transformed and organized into the principal system of social forces, it is clear that sexuality must be discussed, defined, and classified in relation to marriage."[1]

The Christian monogamous ideal wholly subordinates sex to marriage. This is also the case, as applied only to women, in a number of non-Christian communities. The virginity of the bride is a prerequisite to marriage, sometimes even being enforced by a surgical operation. Wives are jealously guarded, and adultery on their part severely punished. But such conditions are rare among savage races. For correct perspective, one must consider the numerous communities in which there are socially recognized and regulated forms of non-conjugal intercourse. Sexual license among savages does not mean lack of regulation. But, within the prescribed limits of lawful intercourse, there occur certain forms of chartered freedom.

By far the most prevalent form is the liberty of intercourse given to unmarried youths and girls. From his study of this custom in Melanesia, Malinowski concluded that in savage society, pre-nuptial intercourse is an institutional method of arranging marriage by trial and error, serving two functions: in the first place it is a safety vent, drawing off the merely sexual motives from affection; and, secondly, it provides an empirical basis for a more mature choice of a mate. A greater selectiveness is possible, leading to "the conclusion of marriages based on an affinity of character combined with sexual compatibility."[2]

[1] *Ibid.*, p. 140.   [2] *Ibid.*, p. 142.

There are also, among many tribes, recognized relaxations of the marriage bond itself. These practices, which have been regarded by so many anthropologists as survivals of group-marriage, appear in an altogether different light when considered in relation to marriage. Such temporary cohabitation never implies community of children. It functions as an approved way of satisfying the desire for sexual novelty. Occasionally, where it leads to divorce and remarriage, it is also a form of trial and error making for better sexual adjustment.

At the primitive level regulated extra-marital intercourse, far from being destructive or subversive, is "one of those cultural arrangements which allow of a greater stability of marriage and the family, of easier adjustment within it, and of a more suitable choice of partner."[1] "To satisfy the fundamental function of sex, we have the institution which makes full sex, that is, parenthood, exclusive and individual. To satisfy the correlated selective components of sex, we have the dependent institutions of regulated license."[2]

Parenthood in Its Direct Growth and One-Sided Distortion. As a child grows, he comes into contact with the members of his own immediate family, and also with those of related households. His most important relation is likely to be the mother's sister. The mother, the absolutely indispensable parent, may fall ill or die. The mother's sister then serves as a substitute mother; in matrilocal communities she is on the spot, but even in patrilocal communities she is likely to be a frequent visitor and available if needed. There being no form of social insurance against death or misadventure in primitive communities, there is "an extraordinary development of what might be termed the substitution by kinship and a definite system of vicarious duties and responsibilities devolving on the nearest of kin."[3] This is evident in the way children are taught to regard the mother's sister as a substitute mother and to call her by the same name as their own mother. The father's brother for similar reasons is called father and his wife mother, and the children of the mother's sister and the father's brother are called brothers and sisters. These new individual relationships are formed by direct extension of family ties. The *bilaterally* defined system of kindred, the product of the grouping of other households around the original household is what has been called the *Grosse Familie*.

But a second process, that of unilateral extension of kinship ties, accompanies the process of bilateral extension. In the

[1] *Ibid.*, p. 140.   [2] *Ibid.*, p. 143.   [3] *Ibid.*, p. 150.

earlier stages of nurture father and mother usually coöperate. Education, however, means a transmission of skilled procedures and, sooner or later, a handing over of the prerogatives of social status. At this stage the first break occurs in the simple, direct growth of family relationships. In *matrilineal* societies the father must now step back and leave the further education of the child to the mother's brother. In *patrilineal* societies the relationship to maternal relatives comes to be considered for many purposes irrelevant. The unilateral extension of kinship ties furnishes an orderly and simple solution of the problem of transmission of possessions and social privileges. So important to social cohesion is the elimination of ambiguity with regard to descent and inheritance, that in no human society are they left undetermined.

Parenthood as the Controlling Force of the Social Process. With the formation of the new kinship ties, the early relationships of the child to father and mother are changed, more or less profoundly. But they still persist, and, even when with marriage the whole kinship outlook is still further modified, parental ties on each side of the newly created household are not wholly broken. Accordingly, "right through life there is . . . the process of growth and constant reaffirmation of the simple bilateral family pattern. . . . Side by side with this, there is a breaking-up connected with a unilateral over-emphasis of the legal side of the maternal or the paternal bond."[1] The *clan* is the outcome of the latter process. While neither the equivalent of, nor a substitute for, the family, it is by no means a merely legal institution. It is pervaded by ideas of kinship, traces descent from a common ancestor, and stands in an intimate relationship to the family. "Both the family and clanship begin at home. When a child is born it becomes *ipso facto* a member of its mother's or father's clan and subsequent clan relations are derived from this fact."[2]

Sex and the Building of Kinship. A further clue to the relationship between family and clan is to be found in an important aspect of the unilateral extension of family bonds: the development of rules of exogamy out of rules of incest, eliminating sex from within the clan and the household respectively.[3] The prohibition of any sexual interest between members of the same household, other than husband and wife, is universal in human

---

[1] *Ibid.*, p. 153.   [2] *Ibid.*, p. 151.

[3] There have been numerous attempts at explaining the origin of incest taboos and rules of exogamy. These are summarized and criticized by Briffault, who then proceeds to suggest a most ingenious theory of his own. *The Mothers*, Vol. I, Chapter VI.

societies, quite independently of father- or mother-right, of patrilocal or matrilocal residence, and of varying forms of marriage. There are variations, the chief emphasis sometimes being laid on the taboo between brother and sister, elsewhere between mother and son. Very seldom in savage societies is incest between a father and daughter regarded with equal horror. Malinowski explains the universality of incest taboos by the fact that inclinations to incest are utterly incompatible with the cultural function of the family. Appearing, as they would, at that stage in the life of the household when the family is the indispensable educational medium, "the fundamental pattern of all social bonds, the normal relation of the child to the mother and father, would be destroyed."[1] The disruptive forces of sex thus meet with their first restriction within the life of the household. The function of incest taboos is their elimination from the practical coöperation of everyday life.

Rules of exogamy have a similar function within the clan, being the full unilateral extension of incest taboos, and prohibiting marriage between members of the same clan. Cousins in the households of father's brother and mother's sister, the substitute parents, are addressed in early life as brothers and sisters. But a distinction would soon be made, depending on the one-sided extension of kindred bonds. One of these households would become legally kindred, and definite taboos would hold between those legally brothers and sisters. Under mother-right the household would be that of the mother's sister. Gradually more and more households related on the mother's side would be included in this type of relationship. A similar extension on the father's side would take place under father-right. Family terms of relationship come to be extended to all clansmen and clanswomen; they may own property together; they associate in hunting, in war, and in religious ceremonial. Above all between the men and women of the same clan the relationship is one of coöperation undisturbed by sex.[2]

The Functional Theory of Kinship. The extension of kinship bonds beyond the individual family thus fulfills several important functions: it meets the need for substitute parents; it establishes order in matters of inheritance; and it eliminates sex from the household and the clan. The life of primitive tribes has, in

---

[1] *Sex and Repression in Savage Society* (1927), p. 252; and see pp. 243–252 for a full discussion.

[2] This does not mean that lapses from the laws of exogamy are unknown. See Malinowski, *Crime and Custom in Savage Society* (1926).

general, two main phases, the private phase of its everyday concerns and its public ceremonial phase. The greater part of life is everywhere spent in economic concerns on a small scale. This phase of existence is dominated by the household. Sometimes economic needs are satisfied by communal hunting or from communal stores. The clan here dominates, as it does, preëminently, on all ceremonial occasions and in the making of war and peace. It is on such legal and ceremonial occasions that "classificatory" kinship terms are applied to "solid blocks of kindred." But while a number of different people may accordingly be addressed as "father," "mother," "sister," or "brother," "in actual use kinship terms have always a distinct and concrete meaning and there is never any doubt in the mind of the speaker or hearer as to who is designated in each case."[1] Emotional tone, circumlocutions such as adjectives and suffixes, and, finally, the context of the situation make possible discrimination of meaning. "Thus, in reality, each so-called classificatory term is a class label for a number of distinct words, every one of which has its own specific individual meaning."[1]

While in Melanesia, Malinowski was able to observe the first steps in the process of extension of both kinship ties and kinship terms. Only with difficulty is the child at first induced to extend the term "mother" to the mother's sister; there is never complete assimilation of meaning any more than there is an identical relationship between the child and his mother and maternal aunt respectively. In the same way the term "father" comes to be extended to the father's brother, and the terms "brothers" and "sisters" to those first cousins with whom, under a unilateral system, kinship establishes unity of descent. There are, however, among the parents' kin certain individuals to whom no direct extension of already existing kinship attitudes is possible: the grandparents, the father's sister and the mother's brother and the children of the two last named. To these children anthropologists give the name "cross-cousins" to distinguish them from what they call "parallel cousins," the children of the mother's sister and father's brother. All these relatives occupy special positions and are almost always designated by special terms.

Classificatory nomenclature, Malinowski points out, always refers to the tribe or a large part of it, never to one clan only. It is thus "the tribe as a correlated system of clans which corresponds to the widest circle of kinship extensions and so to the

[1] Malinowski, *Encyclopaedia Britannica*, Vol. 13, p. 405, *s.v.* "Kinship."

family on the classificatory level of kinship."[1] The clan may thus be defined functionally "as the institution which standardizes one-sidedly the extended aspect of parenthood. The clan, however, unlike the family, is always part of a larger system, never a self-contained unit. The full functional reality of clanship is only achieved by the integration of the clans as correlated units in a larger tribal whole." Kinship may be defined "as, in the first place, the personal bonds based on procreation socially interpreted, and, in the second place, as the complex system of wider bonds derived from the primary ones by the two-fold process of direct extension and of unilateral reinterpretation."[2]

"Where empirical facts yield a sufficient explanation," says Malinowski, "hypotheses are superfluous—they are a disease of method."[3] The chief error in most fanciful speculations has been the neglect of domesticity and of the influences of everyday life in early childhood, combined, very frequently, with over-emphasis on sex. "Sex, far from being the principal clue to kinship, plays only a subordinate part in its formation. . . . It is the elimination of sex and not indulgence in it which, through the rules of incest and exogamy, really influences kinship and clanship."[3]

"Parenthood is invariably the starting point of wider social relationships."[4] "Through the building of strong emotional attitudes on biological foundations, it endures, it leads to the establishment of a life-long social relationship of mutual obligations and services. This, however, since human beings never live in single families but in groups of them, entails the building of new ties in virtue of the parental ones and directly on the pattern of them."[5] "The study of kinship, far from demonstrating the small importance of the family, proves the tenacity of its bonds and their persistence through life as a standard for all wider social relations. The age-long experience of mankind . . . teaches us that the institutions of marriage and family have never been absent in human history, that they form the indispensable foundation for the structure of human society, and that, however they might become modified in the future, they will never be destroyed nor their influence seriously impaired."[6]

---

[1] *Parenthood—The Basis of Social Structure,* in Calverton and Schmalhausen, *op. cit.,* p. 165.

[2] *Ibid.,* p. 165.   [3] *Encyclopaedia Britannica,* Vol. 13, p. 409, *s.v.* "Kinship."

[4] *Parenthood—The Basis of Social Structure,* in Calverton and Schmalhausen, *op. cit.,* p. 163.

[5] *Ibid.,* p. 162.   [6] *Encyclopaedia Britannica,* Vol. 13, p. 409.

THE FAMILY AND SOCIAL ORGANIZATION IN PREHISTORIC
SOCIAL GROUPS

The Family and the Group. From empirical studies of savage societies to-day certain inferences with regard to prehistoric groups may be made with a fair degree of assurance. Further light is thrown on the relation of the family to the group in prehistoric times by the study of anthropoid apes. Westermarck's argument for pair-marriage as the original form was partially based on an account of the family among gorillas. Briffault, scorning Westermarck's reliance on one "unreliable" report, accumulated a mass of evidence to show that gorillas invariably live together in groups of from ten to twenty or thirty individuals. The progenitors of human beings must have lived in groups larger than the individual family, Briffault argues, for only through such wider associations could language have originated. A recent study proves conclusively, however, that some, at least, of the gorilla hordes are composed of individual families.[1]

In his *Social Life in the Animal World*, Alverdes gives an account of Reichonow's study of the habits of gorillas in Africa.[2] Each gorilla horde occupies a well-defined and limited area, the size of which is dependent on the number of animals in the horde. The only solitary gorillas, very old males, have their own smaller domains, which they obstinately defend against intrusion. Gorillas feed exclusively on fresh shoots, and must accordingly be constantly on the move. In every direction throughout their domain, they wander as a horde, never spending two successive nights in the same place. But every night they build themselves nests, used for that one night only. It was from a study of the arrangement of nests that Reichonow was able to draw conclusions as to the family life of gorillas.

There are variations in nest-building habits in different parts of Africa. In the northern forests the nests of all but females with very young offspring are built on the ground. These mother-apes build nests in the trees about one and a half meters up. The arrangement of the nests in the north is particularly significant. They are arranged in ordered groups, each group

[1] For further evidence of the existence of individual families among gorillas, chimpanzees, orang-outans, and gibbons, see E. A. Westermarck, "On Primitive Marriage, A Rejoinder to Mr. V. F. Calverton," *American Journal of Sociology*, Vol. XLI (March, 1936), pp. 565–589.

[2] E. Reichonow, *Biologische Beobachtungen an Gorilla und Schimpansee* (1920). For a summary of this study see F. Alverdes, *Social Life in the Animal World* (1927).

being separated from the next by a space of fifteen to eighteen meters. In each group there are two large nests for the parent apes and one or two smaller nests for the half-grown offspring, who from the age of three or four occupy their own sleeping places. When younger, they spend the night with the mother in a specially soft nest placed high. The horde is thus shown to consist of a number of pairs of apes with their offspring. There are never more than five families in the horde.

A few other species of apes are known to live in pairs within a horde. Among the members of one South American species, the female, who sometimes bears as many as three young at one birth, is able at times to induce her mate to carry their offspring. More usual are the large ape hordes consisting of numerous polygynous families. Even here, however, the males protect their families while jealously guarding their marital rights. Constant quarreling is the rule in every ape horde.[1]

The family, consisting of a male and one or more females with their offspring, appears to be the fundamental social unit among many anthropoid apes.[1] There is every reason to infer that the monandrous individual family was also the constant and essential unit in the earliest human groups. Among the most primitive peoples living to-day, groups of related families range over a limited area, rarely making a permanent settle-ment. The general rule appears to be toleration, each group respecting the territory of others. There is no reason to believe that all the many and varied primitive peoples now at the lowest levels have lost a culture they once enjoyed. It is far more likely that the majority, at least, represent a type of community which has persisted for untold ages with relatively little cultural ad-vance. As such, they afford insight into the organization of the earliest human societies.

Masculine and Feminine Rôles, as Determined by Parenthood. Men and women have always been obliged to coöperate with one another, their rôles being determined, not primarily by differences in physical strength, but by their respective shares in reproduction. Intercourse entails no burdensome physical consequences for man. The pregnant woman, on the other hand, is under a severe handicap. For even primitive women childbirth involves temporary disability. In the earliest human

[1] See S. Zuckermann, *The Social Life of Monkeys and Apes* (1932), for significant comparisons between the social arrangements of the anthropoids and of man. He suggests that, when men began to go far afield hunting, they could no longer guard a number of wives. The change to a meat diet would thus, he believes, tend to limit polygyny.

societies the increasingly heavy infant would have to be carried about for a year or more and fed from the breast for an even longer period. Another child would in all probability be conceived as soon as, or even before, the first was weaned. From girlhood on, women must ceaselessly have carried children within or upon their bodies, feeding, tending and protecting them, as best they could, from omnipresent dangers. Menaced by wild beasts and engaged in a constant search for food, mothers and children would have found survival even more difficult had it not been for the coöperation of men in supplying food and protection.

Among human beings, moreover, the need for the father is far greater than among anthropoid apes. Not only is human infancy of longer duration, but the young must remain in contact with the older generation, even when physically independent, in order that they may be educated, that they may acquire the culture of their group.

There is no reason to believe, however, that human paternity can be naturally established as is maternity. The mother's native endowment secures the well-being of her baby. His need for nourishment is met by her milk, his need for warmth and protection by her longing to clasp and fondle him. There are no such innate ties binding a father to his offspring. It is probable, however, that in early human groups men would tend to protect those with whom they were closely associated. Making use of such tendencies custom must have fashioned the socially indispensable function of paternity. Coöperation between men and women would, moreover, bring with it advantages for men, as well as for women and children. Let us picture a human family in the days when fire had been discovered, but was hard or impossible to rekindle if once extinguished. A man with one or two women and their children would be a natural unit within the larger group. He would be more efficient as a hunter, if he could divest himself of such tasks as tending the precious fire and carrying burdens of extra weapons and food; if, when the chase was over, others cut up and carried home the meat and prepared it for food. Women, on the other hand, could tend their children in greater safety, if gathered with their possessions round the *hearth:* the center from earliest times, of domestic life. So would begin the fundamental dichotomy between the masculine and feminine rôles in life; the women because of their vital function as mothers, accepting the more passive rôle, their lives absorbed in the petty details and relatively unskilled drudgery of everyday existence; the men, as providers and protectors, finding an active and interesting existence as skilled hunters and warriors. The ownership and use of weapons early became prerogatives of men, a fact which must have reënforced the dominance of men over women.

Social Cohesion and Tendencies Strengthening the Father-Family. So essential to society is an ordered pattern of family relationships that the family was, in all probability, the first group to take traditional form. Social cohesion is assured by a well-defined system of kinship bonds, within the family, between families, between the family and the clan, and between clans within the tribe. There is usually restriction on marriage outside the tribe, solidarity being ensured by endogamy.[1] But the principle of exogamy is of far greater importance for social organization. By its means there is, on the one hand, cohesion between intermarrying groups, usually clans, within the tribe; while, on the other hand, within the clan, coöperation is facilitated through the elimination of the distracting influences of sex. Exogamy, according to MacIver, is "the source of the primary articulation of society beyond the family, and the greatest agency towards the maintenance of the tribal structure."[2]

There is no evidence in favor of there having been any fixed sequence of maternal and paternal descent. In general, where matrilineal descent prevails this is due, Lowie says, to special conditions.[3] It appears probable that where such conditions were either not present or passed into abeyance father-right prevailed. In the mother-family authority was divided within the household. The father-family on the other hand was a more compact social unit. In the patrilineal and patrilocal family, authority over the children and responsibility for both their early nurture and later education in tribal affairs was concentrated in the father supported by his kinsmen. A society in which the male heads of families, with their sons, brothers, and nephews, could coöperate in industry, hunting, and, above all, in war possessed potentialities for more effective organization than a society which separated sons from their fathers and divided authority between a man and his wife's male relatives. Ties within family and clan reënforce one another with the concentration of authority in the male heads of families, the elders

[1] Where too narrowly applied, as within a social class, endogamy may tend, on the contrary, to isolation and stagnation.
[2] *The Modern State* (1926), p. 28.   [3] *Primitive Society*, Chapter VII.

of the clan. As a concomitant of political and military organization came the full development of the *patriarchal* family which, when history begins, is found, with some variations in form, but with well-defined general characteristics, as an established integral part of ancient civilization.

THE PATRIARCHAL FAMILY AND THE ANCIENT CIVILIZATIONS

General Characteristics of the Patriarchal Family.   In the earliest stages of civilization the family and kinship were still the basis of the social structure. "Ancient Law," Maine points out "is concerned not with Individuals, but with Families, not with single human beings but with groups. . . . The life of each citizen is . . . but a continuation of the existence of his forefathers, and it will be prolonged in the existence of his descendants."[1] Society had for its units not individuals but groups of kindred, united by the reality or the fiction of blood relationship. Through the custom of adoption, family ties were extended to include strangers, who thenceforth shared rights and obligations with the members of the group of kindred and even assumed descent from their common ancestor.

The fundamental importance of ancestor worship in the patriarchal family is evident. The kinship group included all departed members of the family, its cohesion being reënforced by the bonds uniting the living with the spirits of the dead. In the patriarchal family, departed ancestors in the male line were the chief objects of worship. In conducting the religious rites the patriarch, or living male head of the family, was also the high priest. Religious and political authority were thus combined. As warrior, as the protector of life and property, and as living representative of the family ancestors, the authority of the patriarch was supreme. He was the owner of land, of flocks and herds, of weapons and tools, and was accordingly considered as the provider of food and raw materials. Women and children and all subordinate members of the household were dependent upon him and subject to his rule.

The varied aspects of life in the patriarchal family in the ancient civilizations are considered in succeeding chapters. The present chapter concludes with examples of the relation of the patriarchal family to social organization in India and China, and among the Hebrews, Greeks, and Romans.[2]

[1] Sir Henry Maine, *Ancient Law* (5th ed., 1874), p. 258.

[2] Egypt and Babylon are omitted at this point. Certain exceptions from typical patriarchal practices are to be noted in these two countries.

The Patriarchal Family, and Social Organization in India and China. Indian institutions are for the most part of immense antiquity. The Hindu village community, in particular, is regarded by authorities as a well-nigh indestructible institution. The great households of which it is composed are believed to be surviving representatives of the patriarchal Aryan households of ancient India. Each joint family is a coöperative corporation generally having its oldest male member at its head. All contribute their labor and earnings to the common stock. Cousins are called brothers and sisters, and with certain exceptions there is no intermarriage between cousins. In the course of several generations such joint families become unwieldy; they then divide, whole villages being peopled by members of the same clan. Every member of the household, even the servants, participate in the worship of the household gods.

In China the whole social structure has been dominated by the patriarchal family system. Nowhere else has greater emphasis been laid on ancestor worship. According to Confucius, man is first of all a member of a family, and then of the state which should model itself on the family. Filial piety is foremost among the virtues. Systems of local government have been provided through the association of families in villages. The extended father-family has, accordingly, been, through countless generations, the real and effective unit of society.

The Patriarchal Family and Social Organization among the Hebrews. The Old Testament presents a vivid picture of the patriarchal family, first among the Hebrew tribes as pastoral nomads, and later as agriculturalists settled in village communities. The tribes broke up into smaller groups, the families or houses consisting of several households. The heads of these households constituted the village council of "elders" or "fathers." By the time of King David (c. 1055–1015 B.C.) the villages were expanded into cities.

There are traces of an earlier system of mother-right in the Old Testament, but the Law was framed from the point of view of a patriarchate.[1] Ancestor worship had been relinquished by the time the Hebrew tribes became welded into one nation, bound together as the people chosen of Jehovah. Although no longer deriving his priestly duties as a representative of his ancestors, the patriarch still served as priest in the numerous religious observances connected with family life. His authority

[1] For example, Abraham and Sara were half-brother and sister, but could marry because, although having the same father, they had different mothers.

was, indeed, in no way diminished by this fact, being inherent rather than derivative, and patterned on the government of the all-powerful Jehovah.

The Patriarchal Family and Social Organization among the Greeks. The Greek father, on the contrary, derived his power as representative of the family and as priest of the domestic worship of ancestors. Interestingly enough, the word "father" in Hebrew, Greek, and Latin signifies not so much the paternal relationship as authority, dignity, and power. In the time of Solon (c. 600 B.C.), the Athenians were divided into four tribes, each tribe being subdivided into three *phratries* or religious brotherhoods and these in turn into about thirty *gentes*, kindred or family groups tracing descent to a common ancestor. Unlike the early Hebrews among whom such groups held land in common, the Greeks very early established the institution of private property. The *gens*, however, had power to prevent the alienation of land from the kinship group. With the development of democracy in Athens, the older form of social organization disintegrated after a period of transition in which "the aristocracy of the kin-organized . . . fought a losing battle for privilege against the commonalty, the peasant-farmers, and the 'work-people.' "[1]

The Patriarchal Family and Social Organization in Rome.[2] Rome, the city stronghold of the Latins, was built on "a strategic ford near seven defensible hills."[3] Through one desperate struggle after another Rome gained the control of Italy, achieving for the first time "a political unit based upon metropolitan citizenship."[3] The civic structure of Rome in its early period was based upon the *curiae*, which were divisions of tribes. Each *curia* comprised a group of *gentes*. The *curiae* had religious and administrative functions. They formed the privileged order, the *patricians*, and provided the council of elders and the senate. To these were gradually added, as an inferior class, the unorganized and landless plebeians, men who had sought refuge or employment in the city.

The city-state in time absorbed and subordinated the family government out of which it had arisen. "Men began to have immediate connection with the state no longer touching it only

[1] Robert MacIver, *The Modern State*, p. 79.

[2] The word "family" is derived from the Roman *familia*, which signified the members of the closely knit patriarchal household, including the slaves, over all of whom the paterfamilias held the *patria potestas*. In its original use it denoted the household slaves alone.

[3] *Ibid.*, p. 92.

through their family chief.   Citizenship began to dissociate itself from kinship."[1] At the same time, Rome, yielding to the claims of the plebeians for civil and political rights, moved towards civic democracy and became a republic. The privilege of Roman citizenship had been used in the consolidation of Italy. With the spread of empire it was extended even further, but in this process the association of citizenship with self-government was destroyed. While Rome failed "to devise a political basis for an empire of the civilized world," yet it was she "that liberated the universality of law . . . and that first embodied in one comprehensive and unified code the distinctive order of the State."[2] "The contrast between the first great monument of Roman Law, the Twelve Tables, and the last, the system contained in the Institutes, Digest, Code and 'Novels' of Justinian . . . is very striking. The old jurisdiction of the *pater familias* has shrunk to insignificance before the universal jurisdiction of the State. The conception of personality as the basis of legal right and obligation has been disentangled from the claims of kinship."[3]

SUGGESTED READING

Briffault, R., *The Mothers*, 3 vols., 1927, Vol. I, Chs. I–VII; Vol. II, Chs. XIII–XIV.

Goodsell, W., *A History of Marriage and the Family*, rev. ed., 1934, Chs. I–IV.

Groves, E. R., and Brooks, L. M., *Readings in the Family*, 1934, Ch. I.

Howard, G. E., *A History of Matrimonial Institutions*, 3 vols., 1904, Vol. I, Chs. I–III.

Lowie, R., *Primitive Society*, 1920, Chs. I–VII.

MacIver, R., *Society*, rev. ed., 1937, Ch. XI.

Malinowski, B., *Encyclopaedia Britannica*, 14th ed., 1929, Vol. XIII, *s.v.* "Kinship"; Vol. XIV, *s.v.* "Marriage"; Vol. XX, *s.v.* "Social Anthropology."

———, "Parenthood—The Basis of Social Structure," *The New Generation* (eds. Calverton, V. F., and Schmalhausen, S. D.), 1930, pp. 113–168.

Sumner, W. G., and Keller, A. G., *The Science of Society*, 4 vols., 1927, Vol. III, Part V.

Westermarck, E. A., *The History of Human Marriage*, 3 vols., 5th ed., 1921.

---

[1] Woodrow Wilson, *The State* (rev. ed., 1898), p. 138.
[2] MacIver, *op. cit.*, pp. 114, 105.   [3] *Ibid.*, p. 107.

CHAPTER IV

THE FAMILY AND RELIGION

PRIMITIVE RELIGIOUS CONCEPTIONS IN THEIR RELATION
TO SEX AND THE FAMILY

The Supernatural in Savage Experience. Human progress has
been due to daring and adventure; to the fact that human
beings invent the means of making possible pursuits for which
they are not naturally equipped. They fashion weapons with
which to subdue ferocious animals; they build boats to carry
them on the water. But hard-won experience and technical
ability are often insufficient to secure success, not alone in more
spectacular and dangerous pursuits, but even in the daily round
of practical activities. It is then, when "in spite of knowledge
and effort, the results turn unaccountably against him . . . ,
when forces completely beyond his control baffle him," that the
savage has "resort to supernatural means of filling the lacunae
in his practical power."[1] Natural means are wanting by which
abundant supplies of game and favorable weather may be
assured, or accident, disaster, disease, and death may be averted.
Supernatural means are sought for influencing the mysterious
unseen powers which control human destiny.

Chance and the unforeseen often prove the decisive factors
in human affairs. In moments of suspense and uncertainty
emotions are aroused: hope, picturing vividly the longed-for
object of desire, struggles with the fear of frustration. At such
moments a magical ritual can give confidence and courage; for
belief in magic affirms man's power to cope with a situation by
means of rite or spell. Faith in success supplants fear of failure,
and the actual uncertainty and insecurity of the future are
mercifully veiled in illusion. The efficacy of ritual and the truth
of religious belief are further substantiated by means of myth.
Such sacred stories function, according to Malinowski, as warrants for the magical and religious cult of the social group,
explaining and sanctioning its traditions and customs.

Among prehistoric peoples, all that was in any way extraordinary or mysterious would perforce have been considered supernatural and treated with religious awe. Ghosts of the dead

---

[1] Malinowski, *Encyclopaedia Britannica*, Vol. 20, p. 867, *s.v.* "Social Anthropology."

and other spirits and intangible influences formed an ever-present imaginary environment. When such unseen powers were considered as beneficent, beliefs gave solace; but, even where dangerous, they might be propitiated or rendered impotent through exorcism and magic. Where there is no knowledge of actual causal continuities, superstition can flourish unchecked. Any association, actual or merely symbolic, any casual sequence in time, may be taken as evidence of causal connection. A natural calamity would be explained, whenever possible, in terms of the omission of some ritual or the breach of some taboo. In ways such as these, has the vast and complicated network of religious beliefs and rituals been built up, entwining in its often intangible, but none the less tenacious, grasp the destinies of men. It was inevitable that religion should have exercised a determining influence on social life, most of all in matters of crucial import to the group, including sex, marriage, and the family. Only to-day are we beginning to free ourselves from superstitions with regard to sex, which are directly derived from the beliefs of our prehistoric ancestors.

The General Character and Function of Taboos. In the hope of averting the wrath, malice, or envy of unseen powers certain restrictions come to be imposed on conduct. The savage's ignorance of what evil consequences to expect, the very indefiniteness of his dread, only increases his superstitious fear of neglecting any means of propitiation and exorcism. As Lowie says, "the Extraordinary is potentially ambivalent. . . . It may be credited with either a mysterious power to confer benefits or a weird tendency to destroy."[1] Tabooed objects are conceived of as "unclean" and "holy" at the same time, and are regarded, either with extreme aversion and horror as impure, a source of contamination and pollution, or else with extreme reverence as sacred. While the two sentiments are often not clearly differentiated,—the sacred, for instance, being highly dangerous to the sacrilegious and impious,—the predominant emphasis in primitive thought is upon avoidance of the unclean. Such is their terror of breaches of taboo, that savages have been known to die of fright when these have occurred.[2]

Taboos came to be extended from objects to actions, till finally they comprised a series of restrictions preventing all behavior believed to be harmful to any social interest. As a

[1] *Primitive Religion* (1924), p. 283.
[2] Some insight into the character of taboos may be gained from the horror still experienced at the very thought of incest.

negative method of control they have had an important disciplinary and selective function, and have served as powerful factors in the building of traditions and customs. By proscribing the *indecent* and improper they defined codes and established norms.[1] Breach of taboo constitutes a *sin*.[2] The sinner is regarded as not only himself in danger, but also as a source of danger to others, a plague center, as it were, one who is contagious and must be secluded. Fear of danger thus converts a private sin into a public crime; banishment or death are considered not too drastic methods of eradicating the source of evil.

Universality of Taboos on Women. Among the most strictly observed taboos are those having reference to women and their reproductive functions. Their mysterious powers cause them to be regarded as dangerous at all times, but especially so before and after parturition and during menstruation.[3] Immature girls and old women are sometimes exempt from these taboos, which are, on the other hand, apt to be more severe at puberty. At the first menses a girl is often rigorously secluded, sometimes even treated as a corpse, so unclean is she; sewn in a hammock, fumigated and starved, with death as an occasional result. Among the majority of tribes, the menstruous woman is subject to an endless variety of restrictions. She must live in seclusion, shun daylight, abstain from certain foods, from cooking for others, from picking fruit, and from other ordinary pursuits; her very presence and still more her touch are a source of contamination. Similar restrictions are placed on the mother in childbirth. Often she must be confined in a separate shelter constructed for this purpose; among some tribes she is driven outside into the forest, even in winter, to bear her child alone. She may have been considered impure during the greater part of her pregnancy; and among some peoples restrictions are placed upon her for the whole period of lactation.

Women's reproductive functions must very early have been regarded as closely associated with supernatural life-giving agencies.[4] In some mysterious manner new life was formed in

---

[1] The term "decent" is derived from *quid decet*, meaning that which is *customary* or becoming.

[2] In both Hebrew and Greek the words for "sin" mean "to miss." Those who violate custom fail to do the correct thing, they *miss* the mark.

[3] See Havelock Ellis, *Studies in the Psychology of Sex* (7 vols., 1898–1928), Vol. I, Appendix A.

[4] Cowry shells, which figure so widely as amulets, are symbols of the life-giving power of women, from the association of their shape either with the lower part of the feminine body or with the female genitalia.

their wombs, supposedly from the menstrual blood. Early religious cults and myths bear witness to the sacred but dangerous character of women. Moon cults, in particular, associated the phases of the moon with women's sexual periodicity, and frequently held the moon to be the actual cause of impregnation and the source of all fertility.[1] No wonder that women were credited with magical powers, and that some among them were, in ancient days, regarded with reverence and awe as priestesses and prophetesses; or that others were regarded with fear and hatred as witches.

In most primitive cultures to-day, as well as in the higher religions, women are debarred from participation in religious ceremonies. Although early considered as givers of life and promoters of fertility, their dangerous qualities seem to have received greater emphasis. Woman's witchcraft was early believed to have been the original cause of death. Many myths imply that man gave up immortality because of his subjection to woman. Death was not regarded as inevitable, and it was believed that if man could change his skin, as did the serpent, he might live forever. The same weird associations of ideas, connecting women with serpents, the moon, and other sacred objects, are found again and again all over the world, and are present in refined and symbolized form in the dogmas of the higher religions. The superstitions of our savage ancestors branded woman as the source of all evil; a primeval curse, the results of which endure to this day.

Modesty and Purity. Avoidance of a breach of taboo is a dominant motive in conduct among people at lower levels of culture. Fear of black magic, of the power of a curse, a spell, or the evil eye leads inevitably to attempts at concealment and disguise; fear of the envy of unseen beings leads to abstention from actions which might excite such envy. Abstention is considered particularly valuable, as insurance against inauspicious influences, when affairs of special moment are afoot.[2] In the same way, disguise is most prominent in the protection of the most highly valued objects and functions.

It seems very probable that, far from being due to shame at

[1] See M. Esther Harding, *Woman's Mysteries* (1935), and Robert Briffault, *The Mothers*, Vol. II, Chapters XIX–XXII; Vol. III, Chapters XXIII–XXV.

[2] Abstention from work is very frequent at inauspicious seasons; during an epidemic or an eclipse or any period considered unlucky. The "Sabbath" was derived originally from the custom of abstaining from work during certain phases of the moon, the waning moon being symbolic of death: a fact of interest when we recall the part played by observance of the Sabbath among the Jews and Puritans.

sex functions, as many have believed, modesty was originally due to a desire for protection of the sex organs from magical influences.[1] Protection by amulets and charms probably preceded actual concealment. Ornaments serve not only to ward off evil influences but usually have positive virtues as well. For example, certain Indians believe that the porcupine gives birth to its young with great ease. Their young women accordingly wear belts made of porcupine quills to ensure easy childbirth. Certain forms of clothing were originally worn on account of their magical properties. At a later date, the proprietary claims of men over women, and notions of the impurity of sex functions, readily coalesced with and reënforced more primitive reasons for concealing sex organs and regulating clothing. Ludicrous illustrations of this fact are to be found in the experiences of missionaries, who have endeavored to arouse a becoming sense of modesty among unclad natives. Father Gilii was so successful in his exhortations to the Orinoco women, that they could not be induced to remove any part of their clothing before going to bed. "This," exclaimed the pious Father, "is a matter of great consolation."[2]

One of the several reasons for the values which have been set upon purity and chastity is to be found in the notion of ritual purity, the belief that the envy of maleficent powers may be warded off by abstention from enjoyment, by self-abasement and voluntary suffering. Abstinence from sexual intercourse has been frequently practised before some important enterprise, such as a hunting expedition or warlike raid, a religious ceremonial or an agricultural event such as the sowing of crops. Continence was enforced on certain occasions and for certain periods by strict taboos.[3]

Religious Rites in Connection with Sex and the Family. Birth, puberty, and marriage are all celebrated with appropriate rites, varying in different savage societies, but with the same general intent: individual and group welfare and the avoidance of danger. At birth, means are taken to guard the child from evil

---

[1] As one corroborating example, Briffault points to the fact that, whereas in Europe a nursing mother may expose her breasts, which at all other times must be modestly concealed, among many savages the nursing mother alone must conceal her breasts, for fear of magical influences which might impair their function.

[2] Quoted by Briffault, *The Mothers,* Vol. III, p. 306.

[3] Crawley in *The Mystic Rose* (rev. ed., 1927) suggests that the temporary lassitude induced by sexual intercourse is regarded as a contamination of the man with feminine weakness, a result specially to be feared when engaged in some undertaking where his full strength and vigor are needed. Crawley considers this to be a probable source for taboos enforcing continence.

influences. The peculiar custom of the *couvade*, where the father simulates the weakness of the mother and is believed to expose himself to dangers imminent at such a crisis, is probably designed to avert harm from mother and child.

Puberty rites indicate the attainment of adult social status. Sexual intercourse is sometimes made part of these rites and there may be artificial defloration of girls. Particular dangers are supposed to attend defloration. Accordingly, where it has not taken place at puberty, it may form a rite preliminary to marriage. Since the bridegroom is then considered to be in danger, the strange custom may prevail of intercourse on the part of the bride with some other man or men, often strangers or those of a group into which she may not marry. Very frequently marriage may not be consummated for a certain period after the ceremony, in the effort to avert dangers by abstinence. A wedded pair may be considered dangerous to others, but as exercising, at the same time, a mysterious beneficent influence.

Marriage rites center on promotion of the interests of the new social entity, the formation of which is sanctioned in the wedding ceremony. Even where little ceremony attends a marriage, there is always the essential element of publicity, the acknowledgment by the group of a new alignment of family ties. The rupture of old bonds and the formation of new may be symbolized in the rites. There may also be symbolic anticipation of the later occupations and privileges of the wedded pair. The licensing of parenthood is ceremonially expressed in innumerable ways. All stages of the generative process are supposed to be facilitated by appropriate rites. Phallic symbols may be employed, grain may be sprinkled to promote fertility, and knots may be untied to procure easy delivery.

In lower cultures there are few examples of divorce rites. There are, however, widespread observances connected with persistence of matrimonial bonds after death, bonds usually more tenacious for widows than widowers. Both, however, are frequently required to observe a long series of taboos, before remarriage may take place. The chief function of all funeral ceremonies, in primitive cultures, appears to be an endeavor to avert the envy of the ghost of the departed. The survivors conceal themselves in black garments or cover themselves with dust and ashes, they fast and are chaste. At the same time they strive to alleviate the lot of the dead, by burying his belongings with him and supplying him with food.

THE PATRIARCHAL FAMILY IN ITS RELIGIOUS ASPECTS

General Characteristics. Rites such as those we have been discussing must have been characteristic of prehistoric social groups. For, in the ancient civilizations and still through the greater part of the civilized world to-day, we find religious rites and ceremonies which are their direct derivatives. In most parts of the East every phase of family life is attended by innumerable ritual observances.

Ancestor worship, as already noted, was of supreme importance in the ancient civilizations. While fear of ghosts, even those of ancestors, seems to have been universal, ancestors would readily have been considered as beneficent influences. Trust would be felt in ancestral spirits united to the living by bonds of consanguinity. To ensure their favor, there would, however, be need for ceremonial observance and sacrifice on the part of their descendants. Thus was constituted a tenacious religious bond, binding together successive generations of the family.

Family ties thus provided a pattern for religious cult and dogma. Sons were considered necessary to carry on the cult of ancestors. Daughters, on the other hand, were almost always obliged to relinquish the gods of their fathers and worship those of their husbands. Women, indispensable as the mothers of sons, still bore in the ancient civilization the taint of uncleanness derived from primitive taboos. Even in Greece, the impurity of women at certain periods was shunned as equal to that of a corpse.

Despite this fact, women among the Aryan peoples seem to have had some share in religious rites around the sacred hearth-fire. In the midst of both Greek and Roman houses was the hearth, the fire on which was carefully tended by the wife and mother. In Greece, women had little share in the worship of hearth gods and ancestors. The Roman mother, on the other hand, served as a priestess with her husband and her children, girls as well as boys serving as acolytes.

THE INFLUENCE OF RELIGION ON THE FAMILY AND ON ATTITUDES TOWARDS SEX AMONG THE HEBREWS

Orthodox Family Life. Our concern must be with religious influences on European and American family life. We must turn, accordingly, to the religious development of the Hebrews. Strongly established among Jewish ideals were those of the endurance of the family and the increase of the race. Jehovah had ordered his chosen people to "be fruitful and multiply and replenish the earth."[1] The promise had been given to Abraham that his "seed" should possess the land. Celibacy was regarded as akin to murder and was not tolerated for any man over twenty, not even for the priests. Family life, the devotion of fathers and mothers to their children, the reverence of children for parents are stressed throughout the Old Testament. It even includes numerous stories of women and children, such, for instance, as that of Hannah and Samuel.[2]

Women had little part in public worship, but the greater part of Jewish religious ceremonial was connected with home life. The Sabbath and Passover were observed primarily in the home, and every phase of family life was governed by ritual in such a way as to make the wife and mother a prominent participant in religious observances. Further to enhance the prestige of the Jewish woman and the value of children, came the prophetic promise of the birth of a Messiah.

The Chosen People and Ritual Purity. Punctilious observance of traditional ceremonies made possible the remarkable persistence of orthodox family life, through conquest, captivity, and dispersion among hostile peoples. The vitality and endurance of the religion of the Jews was probably due in large part to their intense nationalism, their belief in themselves as the people chosen of Jehovah, a deity who would surely, despite temporary failures, ultimately triumph over all other gods. The Hebrews appear to have been originally a confederation of Semitic tribes, united in the worship of Yahweh, a jealous and vindictive tutelary deity, but one who kept the covenant made with his chosen people. Their insistence, in spite of national humiliation, on the claims of Jehovah to be the one true god led in time to the triumph of monotheism and the amazing transformation of Jehovah into the loving Father of the Hebrew prophets and of Christianity.

Meanwhile it was essential that the chosen people should be distinguished from all other peoples by their righteousness, their obedience to the Law of God.[3] The Ten Commandments

---

[1] *Genesis*, I, 28.

[2] In his *Dawn of Conscience* (1933), Breasted has conclusively demonstrated the fact that in morals, religion, and social thinking the Hebrews built on Egyptian foundations. We may conjecture then that the wholesome family life of the Egyptians had its influence on Hebrew family life. Egyptian family life is discussed in Chapters VI and VII.

[3] See *Leviticus* XX, 26. "And ye shall be holy unto me: for I the Lord am holy and have severed you from other people that ye should be mine."

were directly imposed by God: "And it shall be our righteousness, if we observe to do all these commandments before the
Lord our God, as he hath commanded us."[1] Such an idea of
righteousness was very similar to that prevailing in primitive
communities. The same supernatural origin and authority were
assigned to rules of conduct, rooted in the requirements of
social life, and also to ritual rules and prohibitions derived directly from the taboos of superstitious savages. Indeed, the
ritual rule was often regarded as of greater importance than the
social rule. For example, "Every one that defileth" the Sabbath "and doeth any work therein . . . shall surely be put
to death."[2] All forms of transgression are sacrilegious and the
concern of the whole community, on whom divine wrath may be
visited for the sin of any of its members.[3] Jewish adherence
to moral principles was far stricter than that of neighboring
peoples, but this was because observance of religious rules
constituted the whole of their morality. In Briffault's words,
"Moral excellence was synonymous in the Jewish conception
with accurate observance of the prescriptions whereby the
state of ritual purity, and therefore magic power over evil,
might be attained."[4] Every orthodox Jew must be ritually
undefiled.

Sex and Defilement. Among the Jews, as among all patriarchal
peoples, certain sex restrictions were imposed to protect the
property interests of men in their wives or their betrothed.[5]
But numerous other restrictions represent an attempt to free
the community from evils believed due to certain forms of sex
expression. Many of these are very similar to sex taboos among
savages. Incest in various forms was, of course, accursed, and
in some cases punished by death.[6] Of peculiar significance, however, are restrictions imposed in condemnation of the sexual
practices associated with the cults of foreign deities. Heresy
was of all offences the most heinous; it was the duty of a family
to slay its recusant member, to cast the first stone or to thrust

[1] *Deuteronomy*, VI, 25.

[2] *Exodus*, XXXI, 14; and see *Leviticus*, VII, 20, 25; XVII, 3, 4; and *Deuteronomy*,
XII, 23 *et seq.*

[3] See *Joshua*, VI, 18, and VII, 1, 11 *et seq.;* also *Leviticus*, XIX, 7, 8; XX, 4, 5.

[4] *The Mothers*, Vol. III, p. 361.

[5] See *Leviticus*, XX, 10: "The adulterer and the adulteress shall surely be put to
death"; and see *Deuteronomy*, XXII, 22–29, where it is decreed that a *betrothed*
damsel and her seducer shall be stoned to death, unless she was forced and could obtain
no help, in which case only the man was to die. If the damsel were unbetrothed, there
is no question of drastic penalty.

[6] *Leviticus*, XX, 11, 12, 17–21; *Deuteronomy*, XXVII, 20–23.

through with the sword.[1] The excessive sinfulness of certain
sexual aberrations and the infliction on them of the death penalty
was undoubtedly due to the abhorrencé felt for foreign cults
which allowed such practices.[2] Religious prostitution, so frequently practised in connection with the cults of antiquity,
was banned for the same reason.[3] Mixed marriages were bitterly
condemned, although they appear to have taken place, as did
extra-marital intercourse with foreign women, although strictly
forbidden.[4]

Sex expression in any of these forms was considered a defilement. But defilement was also incurred in the normal exercise
of sex functions. Women, the daughters of Eve, were the source
of all evil.[5] The sex functions of women were regarded with
peculiar horror. At childbirth a woman became unclean, her
uncleanness enduring for *twice* as long a period if she bore a
girl. Only through burnt and *sin* offerings could she be made
clean.[6] During menstruation anything she touched was defiled,
while anyone who touched her, or her bed, must bathe and
remain unclean "until the even." On the eighth day she might
become clean by means of burnt and *sin* offering.[7] Sexual intercourse during this period was strictly forbidden: one text states
"both of them shall be cut off from among their people," and
another that "the man shall be unclean seven days."[8] At any
time, however, intercourse rendered both man and woman unclean "till the even," the notion of sex functions as defiling being
thus extended from women to men.[9] Throughout, stress is laid
on sexual undefilement as a major element in ceremonial
cleanness.[10] Continence was practiced by way of propitiation
before certain events of particular importance.[11]

[1] *Deuteronomy*, XIII, 6–10; and *Zechariah*, XIII, 3.
[2] *Exodus*, XXII, 9; *Leviticus*, XVIII, 22, 23; XX, 13–16; *Deuteronomy*, XXVII, 21.
[3] *I Samuel*, II, 22.
[4] *Deuteronomy*, VII, 1–4; *Nehemiah*, XIII, 23–27; *Deuteronomy*, XXIII, 17; and
Hosea, IV, 12.
[5] There are two accounts of the creation of woman. In the first chapter of *Genesis*,
both man and woman are created on the sixth day in the image of God. In the second
chapter there is found a more primitive legend, very similar to those of other peoples.
Man is created before the other animals and woman is formed from his rib, almost,
it seems, as an afterthought. In one version of this legend it is the devil who fashions
woman from a bone of man. See Sir J. G. Frazer, *Folk Lore in the Old Testament*
(1918).
[6] *Leviticus*, XII, *passim*.
[7] *Ibid.*, XV, 19–30.
[8] *Ibid.*, XX, 18, and XV, 24.
[9] *Ibid.*, XV, 18; and see *Deuteronomy*, XXIII, 10, 11, 16, 17.
[10] *Leviticus*, XV, 31.
[11] *Exodus*, XIX, 15; *I Samuel*, XXI, 4, 5.

The Essenes and Other Reformers. Despite these restrictions, sexual license was prevalent in the centuries preceding the Christian era. Reformers were of several types: those with the largest following were the Pharisees, who were particularly scrupulous on questions of ritual purity and non-contamination. In the *Testament of the Twelve Patriarchs*, written about 100 B.C., is found, for the first time in Jewish tradition, a condemnation of non-heretical fornication. Women are spoken of as evil plotters against men, being "overcome by the spirit of fornication more than are men." The Sadducees, who tended to adopt Greek ideas, interpreted the law in a more liberal spirit. Most important, in view of the similarity of their doctrines and practices to those of the early Christians, were certain mystical sects who followed sterner and more rigorous codes, in seclusion from the evils of contemporary life. In Judaea, the Essenes were the most prominent of these sects. Escaping the immorality of the cities they wandered from place to place or else lived in communistic brotherhoods. Marriage was held in aversion, although many Essenes married, believing themselves enjoined to procreation, even at the cost of pollution. But all sensual desires were sinful; virtue consisted in continence and mastery over passions. *Asceticism*, or the practising of spiritual exercises with a view to preserving personal purity, became the outstanding aspect of morality.

Christ and the Pharisees. The Hebrew prophets have been omitted from the foregoing account. In them, the spirit rather than the letter of the Jewish religion is made manifest. Obedience to a divinely given law meant for them submission to the divine will, expressed in the inward purposes and social conduct of men, rather than in exact conformity to law. "Shall I come before him with burnt offerings . . . ?" said Micah. "He hath shewed thee, oh man, what is good, and what doth the Lord require of thee, but to do justly, and to love mercy, and to walk humbly with thy God?"[1] The prophets came with warnings of destruction at the hands of an angry God, but they promised salvation to the repentant sinner, for God "delighteth in mercy" and "will have compassion on us."[2] "Let him return unto the Lord," said Isaiah "and he will have mercy upon him . . . for he will abundantly pardon."[3]

By the time of Christ the ritualistic conception of life, no longer held in check by the prophets, had led to an almost exclusive stress on the letter of the law. Steeped in the poetic

[1] *Micah*, VI, 6–8.   [2] *Micah*, VII, 18, 19.   [3] *Isaiah*, LV, 7.

vision of the prophets, Christ denounced the hypocrisy of Pharisees and Scribes, insisting that no mere ceremonial uncleanness could defile, but only evil thoughts and actions proceeding from within.[1] Through a living faith in God as Father and an all-embracing love of humanity, the formalism of the letter of the law was transmuted by Christ into the joy of service and the freedom of spiritual growth.

Christ's Sayings on Marriage, Women, and Children. Apparently Christ never entered of his own accord into a full discussion of marriage. Yet his answers to the Pharisees' questions are recorded in several well-known passages.[2] It is, of course, uncertain whether Christ actually spoke the words attributed to him in the Gospels. There are discrepancies; and several interpretations are possible. Bitter and endless has been the controversy among those who, literally accepting every word, have endeavored to decide whether Christ advocated the indissolubility of marriage, or whether for certain reasons the marriage bond might be severed.[3] Far more important than the letter of such sayings is the spirit underlying them. Consistently throughout is service of God and man placed first. There are, indeed, passages advocating the abandonment of family relationships for the sake of such service.[4] And the same context must be given to the passage referring to those "who have made themselves eunuchs for the kingdom of heaven's sake."[5] There is no indication of an advocacy of celibacy or chastity as states of greater purity. Christ attended the wedding at Cana, and his attitude to women would indicate that he held an ideal of marriage in which the bonds were spiritual and women were the companions of men. Mary's interest in the things of the spirit was commended as of higher value than Martha's preoccupation in the traditional household services of women. Even sinful women were not shunned, nor would Christ condemn the woman taken in adultery; but simply said, "Go and sin no more."[6]

Finally, Christ's attitude towards children enhances the value given to childhood by the Jews and is central in his

[1] *Mark*, VII, 1–23.

[2] *Matthew*, XIX, 1–12; *Mark*, X, 2–10; *Luke*, XVI, 18, and compare *Matthew*, V, 31, 32.

[3] See Ralph de Pomerai, *Marriage* (1930), Chapter XI. The word "fornication," the interpretation of which is crucial in this discussion, is derived from the Greek translation of an unknown Aramaic word.

[4] *Matthew*, XIX, 29; *Luke*, XIV, 26.

[5] *Matthew*, XIX, 12.

[6] *John*, VIII, 3–11.

gospel. "And he took a little child and set him in the midst of them: and when he had taken him in his arms, he said unto them, whosoever shall receive one of such children in my name, receiveth me; and whosoever shall receive me, receiveth not me, but him that sent me."[1] "Suffer little children to come unto me and forbid them not: for of such is the Kingdom of Heaven."[2]

THE INFLUENCE OF THE CHRISTIAN CHURCH ON MARRIAGE AND THE FAMILY IN THE ROMAN EMPIRE

St. Paul and the Earlier Christians. The influence of Christianity on the family is only in a slight degree the influence of Christ himself, and almost wholly the influence of St. Paul and the Church Fathers in the first four centuries of the Christian era. Very early the followers of Christ seem to have concentrated their hopes on a Kingdom of God which had no relation to the social life of their day. The decadent and disillusioned world around was regarded as a scene of temporary probation for those filled with the certain hope of a glorious future. This explains their lack of interest in social problems and their all but exclusive attention to individual conduct. Within the Christian communities, it is true, the spirit of brotherhood prevailed; but an increasing emphasis was laid on holiness, purity, freedom from sin as a breach of moral law.[3]

It was under these abnormal conditions that the Christian Church formulated its ethics of marriage and family life. How could a wholesome view have been held when, as St. Paul said, "the time is short," and it were better to remain unmarried in order to "attend upon the Lord without distraction"?[4] Or, when the birth of children into this wicked world was regarded by many as a misfortune for them and for their parents?

St. Paul was himself unmarried, and had evidently been much influenced by the dualistic Eastern doctrine of the evil nature of matter and the consequent war between spirit and flesh.[5]

---

[1] *Mark*, IX, 36, 37; and see 42 in which the striking warning is given of the gravity of any offence against "one of these little ones." See too *Matthew*, XVIII, 2–6; *Luke*, IX, 46–48; and XVII, 1, 2.

[2] *Luke*, XVIII, 15–17, and XIX, 13–15; *Mark*, X, 13–16.

[3] The Essenes held much the same views as did the Therapeutae in Egypt and a growing number of sects throughout the Roman Empire. It is not to be wondered at that the attitude of the early Christians was profoundly modified by such widespread tendencies.

[4] *I Corinthians*, VII, 29–35.

[5] *Galatians*, V, 17, 19; *Romans*, VII, 14–25; *I Corinthians*, VI, 13, 18; *Colossians*, III, 5; *I Thessalonians*, IV, 3.

Sex would obviously be regarded as the most unruly of the lusts of the flesh, and therefore evil: an idea which among many of the earlier ascetic sects coalesced with notions of ritual purity and undefilement. While St. Paul censured some of the more extreme Christian ascetics, he yet held "it is good for a man not to touch a woman."[1]

St. Paul's utterances on sex and marriage, fundamental in the formation of Christian ethics, are the outcome of an ambiguity of attitude, the consequences of which have been far-reaching and deplorable. As a disciple of Christ he could not altogether condemn marriage. Indeed, he held marriage to be symbolic of the union between Christ and his church, which "is a great mystery."[2] But, on the other hand, he declared "it is better to marry than to burn," of which it has been said that few texts have done more harm.[3] His whole attitude is one of conviction as to the superior merits of celibacy. Marriage is, however, not a sin and may be necessary to avoid fornication.

St. Paul's attitude to women bears little resemblance to the attitude of his master, although he called certain women his fellow-laborers. Women participated at first in all the activities of the Christians; but very soon the older attitudes reasserted themselves, reënforced by a constantly growing distrust of women as lust-inspiring creatures. As has been well said, "in attempting to desexualize the idea of man, ascetic Christianity succeeded only in over-sexualizing the idea of woman."[4] The woman, said St. Paul, was created for the man, "the head of the woman is the man."[5] "Let the woman learn in silence with all subjection. But I suffer not a woman to teach, nor to usurp authority over the man, but to be in silence,"[6] for "it is a shame for women to speak in the church."[7] Women's heads must never be uncovered when they prayed, and they must "adorn themselves in modest apparel, with shamefacedness and sobriety."[8] Even the charitable work of the churches was

---

[1] *I Corinthians*, VII, 1; and see VI, 18, 19, where fornication is spoken of as a sin against the body as the temple of the Holy Ghost. Its *social* consequences are left unconsidered. See too *I Timothy*, IV, 3, where St. Paul refers to those who forbid marriage and the eating of meat. One reason for the distinction made between meat and fish was the fact that fish propagate without sexual intercourse!

[2] *Ephesians*, V, 32. Jerome translated the Greek word for "mystery" by the Latin word *sacramentum;* to this fact is due, in part at least, the later doctrine of marriage as a sacrament.

[3] *I Corinthians*, VII, 9; and see the whole chapter.

[4] Geoffrey May, *Social Control of Sex Expression* (1931), p. 54 and see Chapter III.

[5] *I Corinthians*, XI, 1–15.   [7] *I Corinthians*, XIV, 34, 35.

[6] *I Timothy*, II, 11, 12.   [8] *I Corinthians*, XI, 1–15; *I Timothy*, II, 9.

entrusted to none but widows over sixty. Younger women were advised to "marry, bear children, guide the house."[1] Because of the sin of Eve, women needed discipline: "notwithstanding she shall be saved in childbearing, if they continue in faith and charity and holiness with sobriety."[2]

The Increasing Hold of Asceticism. As time passed, the fathers of the Church became more and more convinced of the sinfulness of sex. Clement of Alexandria conceded marriage to be "a sacred image," yet declared that it "brings shame" to a woman "even to reflect of what nature she is." A woman, he said, should never go abroad, save to church or to visit the sick, and must always be closely veiled. Tertullian is less moderate: "You are the devil's gateway," he said in his letter, *On Female Dress*. "You destroyed . . . God's image, man. . . . Natural grace must be obliterated by concealment and negligence, as being dangerous to the beholder's eye."[3] Virginity is a superior state, according to Tertullian and most of the later fathers. Wives were but of a second degree of modesty, having "fallen into wedlock."[4] Widows occupied an intermediate position between virgins and wives, and their charitable ministrations were before long superseded by those of unmarried deaconesses.

The spread of Christianity among the cities of the Roman Empire only served to intensify the Christian hatred of sex. The utmost emphasis was placed on its repression by the Christians in their revulsion from the prevalent sexual license. As time went on, many, both men and women, repaired to the solitude of the deserts. They were joined by others who fled persecution or who deplored the growing worldliness of the Christian Church. The spread of the monastic movement was so rapid that Lecky characterizes it as due to an "epidemic" of asceticism.[5] Many lived as hermits, unwashed and filthy,

---

[1] *I Timothy*, V, 9–14.   [2] *I Timothy*, II, 14.

[3] *De Cultu Feminarum*, i, 1, and ii, 2: quoted by James Donaldson, *Woman; Her Position and Influence in Ancient Greece and Rome and among the Early Christians* (1907), pp. 182, 184. The subject of dress received the attention of several church fathers. St. Cyprian, writing in the third century, deplores the weakness of Christian young women for necklaces, earrings, paint, rouge, and beautifully colored garments. "God neither made the sheep scarlet nor purple," he exclaimed. "Be such as God the creator made you. . . ." (Quoted by Dorothy Stuart, *The Girl through the Ages* [1933], pp. 70–71.) St. Jerome, writing in 403 to Laeta on the upbringing of her daughter Paula, forbids all personal adornment including the "reddening her hair" to "make it suggest the fires of Gehenna." (Quoted by E. P. Cubberley, *Readings in the History of Education* [1920], p. 61.)

[4] Donaldson, *op. cit.*, p. 179.

[5] W. E. H. Lecky, *History of European Morals* (2 vols., 4th ed. rev., 1880), Vol. II, pp. 107 *et seq.*

in an all too actual "odor of sanctity," covered with sores and inflicting horrible tortures on themselves. Others lived in monasteries. Morbidly obsessed by sex, the men among these "saints" were confirmed in their aversion to women as the curse of mankind. The sexual aspect of holiness had become supreme. Anthony had fled to the desert in 305, and, before the end of the fourth century, there were numerous monasteries, monasticism having been introduced in Greece by Basil, and in Rome by Athanasius and Jerome.

What of marriage? Tertullian, while not forbidding it, told his own wife it was "a voluptuous disgrace," consisting "of that which is the essence of fornication." Ambrose said that married people ought to blush at the state in which they were living. To change the state of virginity in which human beings are born is to deface the work of the Creator. Some questions must have arisen as to the reason for organs of generation. Gregory of Nyssa declared that Adam and Eve were sexless; if they had not sinned the human race would have been propagated in some wholly innocent manner. John of Damascus argued that Adam and Eve could not have possessed sex organs before the fall, because not until then were they ashamed when they saw themselves naked.

Under such circumstances, the theological conception of marriage was far removed from the wholesome view of mature Roman law: "a partnership in the whole of life, a sharing of rights sacred and secular."[1] The Church did not interfere with Roman marriage customs, other than those which were clearly opposed to Christian views. Very early, however, Christian couples were urged to secure the blessing of a priest, although for many centuries this was not essential to the validity of marriage. The Church was chiefly interested in devising restrictions and enforcing prohibitions. Adultery was, of course, regarded as the most heinous of crimes, so evil that, for the first three centuries, the single standard was not only upheld but actually enforced. Guilty husbands, as well as guilty wives, were excluded from the sacraments. There was some hesitation as to the justification of divorce for adultery, especially on the part of the wife. All agreed it was criminal for any other cause. While all second marriages were looked on with disfavor, that of a divorced person in the lifetime of his or her former partner was bitterly denounced.

[1] *Nuptiae sunt conjunctio maris et feminae et consortium omnis vitae, divini et humani juris communicatio.* C. E. Howard, *History of Matrimonial Institutions* (3 vols., 1904), Vol. I, p. 329.

St. Augustine. It was St. Augustine, influential above all other Church Fathers on later European thought, who paved the way for the final doctrine of the indissolubility of marriage.[1] Adultery, though a ground for separation, did not dissolve the nuptial bond. By the time of St. Augustine, the transformation of Christianity into an ecclesiastical institution, based on belief in dogma, was complete.[2] Love and charity were only nominally the foremost Christian virtues. Chastity and abstinence had taken their place.[3] Lecky cites instances of "the intense hardness of heart and ingratitude manifested by the saints towards those who were bound to them by the closest of earthly ties. . . ."[4] Natural affection had to be sacrificed where it interfered with individual salvation. Continence within marriage led to such difficulties that the Church was obliged to intervene. Bishops and priests had early been advised not to marry, although it was not until 402 that the celibacy of the clergy became obligatory.

In the Papal Encyclical of 1931, St. Augustine is quoted as a final authority on the doctrine of Christian marriage. In much that he wrote, after his conversion, horror and disgust are manifest in his attitude towards sex. He was filled with remorse at the sins of his youth: his relations with two mistresses, by one of whom he had a son. He saw no justification for marriage "save for the sake of children." Marriage is pardonable, however, if entered into in order to avoid worse evils. With the doctrine of original sin, of which St. Augustine, though not the originator, was the most influential exponent, sex becomes the agency for the transmission of evil. The deliberate sin of Adam, Augustine believed, was the cause of original sin and death. Both sin and death became the heritage of the human race, all of whom were justly damned. A few, however, would be saved by the grace of God.

---

[1] Promulgated by the Council of Carthage in 407. St. Augustine lived 354–430.

[2] The last great persecution under Diocletian occurred in 303; and in 313, under the Christian emperor, Constantine, Christianity became part of the official state religion. In 392 Theodorus forbade all pagan worship.

[3] The full appreciation of these virtues was, according to Athanasius, one of the supreme revelations and blessings brought to the world by Christianity. Briffault points out that the Greek word for chastity was "agneia," a term denoting rites of mourning and of warding off evil: a significant indication of the derivation of the Christian insistence on chastity from primitive sex taboos. *Sin and Sex* (1931), pp. 56–59.

[4] *Op. cit.*, Vol. II, pp. 125–136, 320–324.

THE MEDIAEVAL PERIOD

The Roman Church and the Barbarians. The Christian Church had become the Church of Rome. In less than five centuries the members of a once despised Jewish sect had gained control of the empire of the Caesars. Only, however, at a great cost. The joyful hope of imminent salvation had faded. The fiery zeal and unflinching courage of the martyrs—many of them women—was a thing of the past. A growing worldliness had overtaken the Church, whose bishops became statesmen. Converting the Roman genius for government to its service, the Church made full use of one of its less admirable aspects, the regulation of daily life by legislation. Armed with a metaphysical creed, prescribed forms of worship, and the prohibitions of an ascetic morality, the Church proceeded to convert the barbarians. Lecky ascribes an "admirable missionary power" to the doctrine of exclusive salvation, backed up by the threat of pestilence and disaster in this life and hell-fire in the world to come.

Moral conditions among the barbarians could not fail to accentuate still further the ascetic tendencies of the Church. Monks and prelates of the sixth, seventh, and eighth centuries deplore what Alcuin called "the flood of fornication, adultery, and incest," not among the laity alone, but among secular clergy, monks, and nuns. In an endeavor to remedy this evil the Church made use of the discipline of penance; absolution was made conditional not only on repentance but on acts of self-abasement. In the seventh century Theodore of Tarsus, the seventh Archbishop of Canterbury, prepared a *penitential;* and others, notably those of Egbert and Bede, were compiled in the next three centuries. Confession of sins was made necessary to salvation; and the Church gained unprecedented control over the private lives of its members. The emphasis throughout was on the uncleanness of sex. All the old Jewish restrictions were repeated and even extended. Hell was said to contain a lake of mingled lead, pitch, and resin for the future reception of those who had intercourse on fast or feast days. All manifestations of sex were subject to minute regulation, the stress being laid wholly on the taint of sin with no consideration of the social consequences of sex expression.

Increasing Control of the Church over Marriage and Divorce. Sexual conduct, being considered primarily as a matter of "spiritual" significance, was subject to ecclesiastical jurisdiction.[1] Naturally the Church endeavored to gain control over marriage and divorce. Between the fourth and tenth centuries the custom became established for the newly wedded pair to attend the "bride-mass." This marks the beginning of a marriage liturgy. Nothing, however, was added to the validity of the marriage contract. Between the tenth and twelfth centuries, marriages came to be directed by priests and took place at the church door immediately preceding the bride-mass.

It now became possible for the Church to condemn all but canonical marriages as illegal. On the other hand, all marriages, legal or illegal, contracted *in words of the present tense* were held by canon law to be equally *valid*.[2] The ambiguity of the orthodox attitude towards marriage is evident; marriage is both a sacrament and a remedy for concupiscence, so must not be made too difficult, or greater evils might result.

It was not until 1164, however, that the seven sacraments were clearly recognized by the Church. Marriage was included among them; and the Church, while reaffirming the indissolubility of marriage, claimed exclusive jurisdiction in all matrimonial cases. Canon law was responsible for many abuses in its distinction between *legality* and *validity*, and its acceptance of clandestine marriages *per verba de praesenti* as valid and indissoluble but not legal.[3] The jurisdiction of ecclesiastical courts was frequently arbitrary; and the situation was further complicated by the doctrine of impediments to marriage.

In theory, marriage had been regarded as indissoluble since the Council of Carthage. In practice, divorce and even remarriage seem to have been commonly allowed until the ninth century. Canon law, formulated three centuries later, did in actual fact grant two forms of divorce. Marriage was declared null and void (*divortium a vinculo matrimonii*) when certain impediments existed: 1. a previous verbal contract *per verba de praesenti;* 2. consanguinity within the seventh degree; 3. spiritual affinity, arising from common participation in some

[1] Occasionally where sexual conduct constituted a breach of the peace, or where there was infringement of property rights, it might also be dealt with by temporal powers.

[2] The distinction between a contract in words of the present tense and one in words of the future tense is derived from the Teutonic custom whereby a contract of betrothal preceded the surrender of the bride, which completed the marriage.

[3] Not until the Council of Trent (1545–1563) did the Catholic Church free itself from the evils of irregular marriage. In England, on the other hand, no definite step was taken to remedy the situation until the middle of the eighteenth century.

sacrament, for example as godparents at a baptism.[1] Secondly, canon law allowed separation (*divortium a mensa et thoro*) on grounds of adultery, heresy, and cruelty. The results of such legislation, as administered by ecclesiastical courts, was disastrous. As Howard says, "The annulling of marriages . . . became a flourishing business. . . . For a sufficient consideration a canonical flaw could be found in almost any marriage."[2]

Another source of abundant revenue came from the commutation of penances into money payments. So frequent were sex offenses and the consequent impositions of public penance, that every parish church was provided with sheets to be worn by penitents, on the occasion of "the usual penance." The Knight of La Tour Landry gives an account of one such penance. After warning his daughters that "the synne of lechery stinketh afore God and his aungeles" and that a maiden who lost her chastity would "abide in the brennyng fere an hundred yere," he recounts the earthly results of "doing suche filthe": "they that dede the dede were ioyned to penaunce, to go naked afore the procession thre Sondayes, beting himself and recording his synne to fore the pepille."[3]

Chivalry and Romance. The Church had little success in its direct efforts at the suppression of sexual license. But the *indirect* influence of ascetic ideals, through their embodiment in literature, was to determine the whole future course of European sentiment. The period during which asceticism achieved its codification in canon law was also that of the Crusades, of the development of chivalry, of the *trouvères* of Northern France and the troubadours of Provence. The knights of feudal Europe considered themselves "noble" in contrast to the servile remnants of conquered peoples. They were warriors on horseback, or *chevaliers*. So long as they were valiant, of "gentle" birth, and preserved their "honor," which at first meant merely warlike fame, they were "chivalrous," according to the earlier *chansons de geste*. Treachery, cruelty, arson, pillage, wholesale massacre, and mutilation of prisoners were not inconsistent with such an ideal. Nor was the brutal treatment of women. Luchaire remarks that it became almost a

[1] So complicated was the doctrine of forbidden degrees that it was codified under thirteen heads. The Lateran Council of 1214 relaxed the prohibition on consanguinity to include only the fourth degree.

[2] *History of Matrimonial Institutions* (University of Chicago Press, 3 vols., 1904), Vol. II, p. 57.

[3] Quoted by May, *op. cit.*, pp. 105, 117. This famous book of moral stories and precepts for the benefit of his daughters was written by the knight in 1370.

habit for knights to strike their ladies on the nose with their fists.[1]

In such an age the romances of chivalry attained popularity and, by a retrospective idealization of an even cruder and more barbarous age, exercised increasing influence on current customs and ideals. Romantic literature, originally derived from pagan tradition, transformed the warlike and amatory adventures of heathen heroes into the chivalrous deeds of Christian knights. At the same time the eroticism of the early legends was transmuted into an idealization of romantic love, of chivalry towards women, and of chastity. From a later standpoint, the actual conduct of the knights in some of these romances does not appear particularly chivalrous. In one early French poem a knight meets an unprotected lady in a forest. When she rejects his advances, he knocks her down and ravishes her. The lady, however, forgives him, for she has recognized in him a "courteous and well behaved, a good, generous, and honorable knight." As a matter of fact, romantic love was then believed only possible outside of marriage. The lady, whether maiden or wedded wife, repaid with her favors the knight who served her. In the book of Andreas the Chaplain, *De Amore*, it is stated that "love can deny nothing to love; that marriage cannot be pleaded by a lady as an excuse for refusing love." And again "conjugal affection and the true love between lovers have nothing in common. . . . We say definitely and considerately that love cannot exist between married people."[2] Despite a veneer of ascetic morality, love-making seems to have been a major preoccupation in mediaeval castles, where life was dull except in times of war. There was little privacy and extreme freedom of social intercourse between the sexes.[3]

The ideal of courtly love which became an integral part of the romances of chivalry was due in large part to the lyrical poetry of the troubadours of Provence. An esoteric code of love developed, an idealization of extra-marital relationships, as the privilege of those of gentle birth and in complete dissociation from the mere licentiousness of the vulgar. It was only in its later development that romantic love became platonic. In

[1] *Social France at the Time of Philip Augustus* (English translation, 1912), p. 355.

[2] Quoted by Briffault, *The Mothers*, Vol. III, p. 428.

[3] Young men and maidens visited each other's bedrooms as a matter of course, in spite of the fact that it was the custom to go to bed naked. Illustrated manuscripts prove that nightclothes were not worn before the sixteenth century, if we except the elaborately beribboned headdresses which adorn some of the ladies.

order that the love song might survive, it, too, was finally obliged to conform to the ascetic morality of the Church and sing the praises of chastity. And yet, "as the freedom of pagan barbarism became gradually abolished, the idealization by which it had been sought to justify and excuse it was transferred to legitimate relations, and came to be regarded as leading to, and as the foundation of monogamic marriage."[1]

PROTESTANTS AND PURITANS

The Moral Revolt of the Puritans. The moral revolt of Protestantism was but one aspect of the social and political revolt of an increasingly powerful burgher class against the arrogant aristocracy. The whole way of life of the aristocrats was at variance with that of the merchants; a complete negation of their own solid qualities and economic virtues: the diligence and industry, caution and thrift to which their class owed its rise to power. How better could they assuage their wounded self-esteem than by a bitter denunciation of the "ungodly" ways of the aristocrats, their "vanities," or love of amusement, and their "whoredoms," or sexual laxity. This is most evident among the Puritans, despite the sincerity of their belief in their own superior righteousness, their moral zeal, and portentous earnestness.

The reformers turned for authority to the word of God as found in the Bible. The spirit of Christianity revealed in the New Testament held little real significance for them. In the Old Testament, with its fierce separatism and its denunciation of the impious ways of the ungodly, they found a religion which fitted their every need. With the Puritans, as with the Pharisees of old, superior self-righteousness found expression in moral restrictions and a rigid regulation of conduct, particularly the conduct of others. Not only were they plentifully provided with Old Testament models, but they extended their taboos to all forms of behavior not fitting to a sober and godly Puritan.[2] The Jewish Sabbath, discarded by the Christians in favor of Sunday as a day of rejoicing, was reëstablished in even more solemn and gloomy form.

---

[1] Briffault, *op. cit.*, Vol. II, p. 506.

[2] For example, the long hair and beards of the Cavaliers were fiercely denounced as the "beastlinesse of ruffians." In 1644 the Puritan Parliament condemned the Maypole because of its association with sex excitement. There were differences of opinion, however, with regard to music. Some believed it "Satan's snare," but others upheld music, even though they would not allow organs or trained choirs in their places of worship.

The Puritan attitude towards sex was also Jewish, though modified by Christian asceticism. Agreeing with the Catholics as to the sinfulness of sex, except as the means for procreation, the Puritans did all in their power to enforce its repression. On coming into power in England, they passed an act, in 1650, "for the suppression of the abominable and crying sins of incest, adultery, and fornication, wherewith this land is so much defiled, and Almighty God highly displeased."[1] Adultery was made a felony punishable by death, and fornication was punishable by three months imprisonment. In spite of Cromwell's proclamation commanding execution of this law against "acts of uncleanness," it was found impossible of enforcement even in a Puritan commonwealth.[2]

Protestant Conceptions of Marriage and Divorce. In his revolt from the evils of ecclesiastical jurisdiction, Luther repudiated the doctrine of the sacramental character of marriage, and declared it to be a "temporal worldly thing," of no concern to the Church. But, as a protest against the low ideals of professed ascetics and the evils of sacerdotal celibacy, Luther laid stress on the holiness of marriage, a most "spiritual" state, "ordained and founded" by God, and proclaimed the right of priests to marry. As a monk himself, he set an example by marrying a nun and, with her, rearing six children.

Despite disagreement among Protestant leaders, more liberal ideas of divorce followed the renunciation of the sacramental view of marriage. Luther and Calvin agreed on absolute divorce for adultery, both of them feeling that death was an appropriate penalty. The tendency, in general, was to cling to the letter of Scriptural authority and to broaden its interpretation, rather than to admit new grounds for divorce. Some reformers were even more liberal. Milton, for example, in his *Doctrine and Discipline of Divorce* asks, "What thing ever was made for man alone and less for God, than marriage?" He denounced the intolerance of those reformers who but substituted new tyrannies for old.

In the reëstablishment of religious despotism Calvin was the most influential of the great reformers. His *Institutes of the Christian Religion*, published in 1536, provided the first clear and logical presentation of Protestant Christianity. The two functions of marriage, according to Calvin, are procreation and

---

[1] See May, *op. cit.*, pp. 192 *et seq.*

[2] In Scotland there was similar legislation, "ducking in the foulest pool in the parish" being prescribed as one remedy for sexual license.

the provision of a safe and legitimate remedy for incontinence, which is an unpardonable sin. Since man's nature was corrupted, marriage had become a medicine, and we need not wonder to find "a bitter taste mixed with its sweetness." "Marriage is a veil by which the fault of immoderate desire is covered over, so that it no longer appears in the sight of God."[1] Certain aspects of Puritan family life are better understood in the light of such a view and of the complacency with which Calvin comments on the Scriptural account of a massacre of children. "We may rest assured that God would never have suffered any infants to be slain, except those who were already damned and predestined to eternal death."[2]

The Puritan Control of the Family in New England. The "Puritan mind," still so influential in American life, had its source in the Puritan rule of the New England colonies. Calvinism was later reënforced by the settlement in America of Huguenot, Presbyterian, and Dutch colonists, while Lutheranism came in with Swedes and Germans, and the Anglican Church was in control of the Southern colonies. The population of the American colonies was thus overwhelmingly Protestant, and puritanism was fundamental in the making of America. In Howard's words, "the zeal with which the Pioneers of Plymouth and Massachusetts proscribed the ceremonies and usages of the Roman and Anglican churches," the fanatic fervor wherewith they sought to restrain vice by legislation has "much to do with the character and the civil institutions of the United States."[3] The unparalleled freedom afforded by their colonization of a virgin wilderness meant to the Puritans the opportunity to impose the tyranny of a rigid theocracy. The similarity of their position to that of the ancient Hebrews in the midst of the heathen but reënforced their belief in themselves as a "chosen people," carried by God "into the wilderness upon the design of a glorious reformation."[4]

Paradoxically enough, in view of their domination by religious dogma, the Puritans, through their insistence on marriage as a civil contract, did much to facilitate the separation of church

---

[1] *Opera*, XLIX, 406, quoted by Georgia E. Harkness, *John Calvin* (1931), p. 133.

[2] *Opera*, XXIV, 363, quoted *op. cit.*, p. 109.

[3] *Op. cit.*, Vol. II, p. 125.

[4] These are the words of Cotton Mather. The same author speaks of a "divine slaughter" of the Indians; and it was generally believed that the "Prodigious Pestilence" which had caused the death of many Indians shortly before the arrival of the Pilgrim Fathers, had been sent by God to prepare New England for his people. In Mather's words, "the woods were almost clear of these pernicious creatures to make room for a better Growth."

and state. Suspicious of ecclesiastical control and finding a
precedent in Jewish law, they declared both the celebration
and dissolution of marriage to be civil functions. In Connecticut,
in particular, the policy adopted was so liberal as to anticipate
"in all the more essential respects . . . the present policy of
civilized nations by nearly two hundred years."[1]

The early colonial codes were modeled on Mosaic law. At
least three persons, two men and one woman, were put to
death for adultery in Massachusetts Bay Colony.[2] But it was
difficult to enforce the death penalty, so other penalties were
devised. It must, of course, be remembered that the Puritans
were embued with the ancient idea of sin, as endangering not
only the sinner's soul, but the community; and that misfortune
of any kind was regarded as a punishment for sin. When Cotton
Mather's child burnt himself, his pious father exclaimed, "Alas
for my sin, the just God throws my child into the fire."

The Puritans were desirous of following to the letter the
commandments of God delivered on Mount Sinai. But since
these did not always afford appropriate solutions to colonial
problems, they were led to adopt the procedures of public
penance with which they had been familiar in England. Public
ignominy and confession of sin were the characteristics of punishments for such crimes as drunkenness, wanton, unclean, and
lascivious behavior, incontinence, disturbing of public worship,
and blasphemous words. Rhode Island, more humane than
the other colonies, prescribed that an adulterer is "to be
publickly set on the Gallows in the Day Time with a Rope
about his or her Neck, for the Space of One Hour; and on his
or her Return from the Gallows to the Gaol shall be publickly
whipped on his or her naked Back, not exceeding Thirty
Stripes."[3] Scarlet letters were frequently imposed in the New
England colonies. The earliest typical instance was that of a
woman, who in Plymouth, in 1639, was sentenced to be
"whipt at a cart tayle" through the streets, and to "weare
a badge upon her left sleeve." If found without the badge, she
was to be "burned on the face with a hott iron."[4]

[1] Howard, *op. cit.*, Vol. II, p. 353.

[2] See May, *op. cit.*, p. 240, for an account of the trial and death of poor Mary La-
tham, aged eighteen. She died exhorting all young maids to be obedient to their
parents.

[3] Quoted by Howard, *op. cit.*, Vol. II, p. 173, from the Acts and Laws of Rhode
Island.

[4] *Op. cit.*, p. 171. Scarlet letters were worn for other offenses besides adultery.
For example a man who married his deceased wife's sister was sentenced for incest to
wear an I.

Punishment for fornication was far less severe, and a further distinction was introduced when betrothed couples guilty of incontinence were punished comparatively lightly. Howard considers that this put a premium on sexual intimacy in the period between espousals and nuptials; particularly in view of the prevalence of "bundling."[1] Numberless such cases of "uncleanness" are on record. The following is typical: "A. F. for having a child born six weeks before the ordinary time of women after marriage, fined for uncleanness and whipt, and his wife set in the stocks."[2] If parents of children born less than seven months after marriage did not make public confession, their children were refused the rite of baptism, and so consigned to eternal damnation.

Although even the Puritans were unable to suppress sexual immorality by legal means, the laws of many of the states still provide punishments for fornication and adultery. In New York where no statutory provision existed for the punishment of adultery, the National Christian League for the Promotion of Purity succeeded in having such a law enacted in 1907.

THE EFFECTS OF CHRISTIANITY ON THE FAMILY

There are those to-day who denounce the influence of Christianity on the family as wholly harmful. While such a sweeping generalization is unjustifiable, the material presented in this chapter effectually disposes of the contradictory generalization, that the effects of Christianity on the family have been wholly beneficial.

Christianity has not, Chesterton said, "been tried and found wanting; it has been found too difficult and never tried." This famous aphorism, despite its ambiguity, reveals an essential truth. Countless men and women in the nineteen centuries since the death of Christ have faithfully sought to follow him. To the extent in which they were inspired by his vision, they *have* tried Christianity and have *not* found it wanting. But the history of the organized institutions of Christianity is a wholly different matter. Most, if not all, embody principles at variance with the spirit of Christ. By these, Christianity has, therefore,

---

[1] The practice in which lovers "shared the same couch, with the mutual understanding that innocent endearments should not be exceeded," quoted, *op. cit.*, p. 182, from Stiles, *Bundling in Its Origin, Progress, and Decline* (1871). One motive for this strange custom is indicated in the following verse by Israel Perkins: "Since in a bed, a man and maid may bundle and be chaste, It does no good to burn out wood, it is a needless waste"!

[2] Quoted by Howard, *op. cit.*, p. 186.

never really been tried. Supremely ironical has been the long story of distortions and perversions, whereby the living spirit of the gospel of Jesus has been killed by the letter: stifled by the imposition of orthodox belief and an external code of morals. All too soon did the majority of Christians turn from service to concentration on purity from sin and the salvation of their souls. And with the spread of Christianity came all the subtle and insidious temptations which accompany the acquisition of power. Christ had said, "Judge not, that ye be not judged"; but, by the fourth century, the Christian Church was already showing signs of that intolerance which was to culminate in the fiendish cruelties of the Inquisition and the equally barbarous persecution of Catholics by Protestants.

The benefits which are usually credited to Christianity, higher ideals of marriage and the improved status of women and children, have been due indirectly, if at all, to the influence of official Christianity. To its direct credit are due such social values as the cohesion and efficiency which accompany discipline and unswerving faith. And the Church has also had direct influence for good, in so far as it has sustained those individuals through whom the spirit of Christianity has remained active to this day.

A stage in social development has been reached where the vision of human brotherhood is more possible of achievement than ever before. All the more important, therefore, that attention should be directed to positive values and away from negative endeavors to suppress sin. This chapter has been one-sided in emphasis, its chief purpose being the promotion of insight through knowledge of the facts. Release from irrelevant dogmas and restrictions should facilitate the solution of family problems from a constructive ethical standpoint, which owes much of its inspiration to the original teachings of Jesus.

SUGGESTED READING

Briffault, R., *The Mothers*, 3 vols., 1927, Vol. II, Chs. XVII–XXII; Vol. III, Chs. XXIII–XXIX.

Donaldson, J., *Woman: Her Position and Influence in Ancient Greece and Rome and among the Early Christians*, 1907, Book III.

Goodsell, W., *A History of Marriage and the Family*, rev. ed., 1934, Ch. V.

Howard, G. E., *A History of Matrimonial Institutions*, 3 vols., 1904, Vol. I, Chs. VII–X; Vol. II.

Lecky, W. E. H., *History of European Morals*, 2 vols., 4th ed. rev., 1880, Vol. II, Ch. IV.

Lowie, R., *Primitive Religion*, 1924.

May, G., *Social Control of Sex Expression*, 1931.

Sumner, W. G., and Keller, A. G., *The Science of Society*, 4 vols., 1927, Vol. II.

Westermarck, E. A., *The History of Human Marriage*, 3 vols., 5th ed., 1921, Vol. I, Chs. XI, XII.

CHAPTER V

THE FAMILY AND ECONOMICS

ECONOMIC CONDITIONS AS DETERMINING INFLUENCES ON FAMILY ORGANIZATION

Chapter I provided us with a general introduction to the economic aspects of family life in the past. The pattern of a culture, we saw, is directly derived from the prevailing type of maintenance activities. Efficient industrial activity, even in the early stages of social evolution, must have required association in coöperative groups and a certain degree of specialization. Sex differences have formed a natural basis for division of labor; and, in all ages, sex specialization in industry has exercised a determining influence on family organization. As such, it forms one of the two main topics of this chapter. The other topic is concerned with the influences on the family exercised by usages and beliefs with regard to property. Questions of inheritance, of marriage as a form of economic contract, of the status of women and children when regarded as the property of the husband and father, have been of profound significance for family life.

THE PRIMITIVE FAMILY IN ITS ECONOMIC ASPECTS

Division of Labor between the Sexes. Fundamental patterns of sex specialization must gradually have emerged among hunting peoples. Women and children stayed at "home," the trysting place near the fire, and would gather such food as might be found in the immediate vicinity. The men, free of all burdens but their weapons, would range far afield in the pursuit of game. Hunting and fighting became the preëminently "manly" pursuits; and a life of strenuous activity developed strength and skill, discipline and organization. Save for the fashioning of weapons, "home," for the men, was primarily the place of rest. For women it was the scene of never-ending work. This is as true of savage peoples to-day, as it must have been in prehistoric groups.[1] The economic activities of primitive woman are undertaken as an accompani-

[1] And it is also true of peasant women and of most women of the lower classes, even in the most highly civilized countries.

ment to her primary business of motherhood. She must give birth to, nourish, care for, and carry her offspring, with as little interruption as possible in her industrial work.

Women were naturally the tenders of the fire, constantly gathering the fuel necessary for its replenishment. They were the burden-bearers, as they moved from one hunting ground to another. It was essential for the safety of all that men should be free and alert to repel attack or to engage in the chase. A plentiful supply of fresh water must, at all times, have been the chief requisite of a camp site. Women were the water-carriers. Skins, carefully removed from carcasses with stone knives, hollowed gourds, containers of bark and wood, woven baskets, and, later, clay vessels would provide them with means for transporting and storing water. Baskets would also be used to carry seeds or nuts, and babies could be transported in woven cradles, or in skin hoods as they still are among the Eskimos. The more primitive forms of shelter were also the work of women, rushes or branches being woven together, or skins stretched on poles to form a tent.

Skins, already in use for transportation, storage, and shelter, must also have provided the materials for the earliest forms of clothing, whether for ornament or protection. Women were probably in charge of all the industrial processes connected with skins, from the separation of the hide from the flesh, to the manufacture of vessels, tents, clothing, and shoes. Bone scrapers form a large part of all paleolithic tools. With these the women scraped off the flesh, and the hair as well, where leather articles rather than furs were desired. The skins must then have been dried and dressed in various ways: chewed, or soaked, or rubbed with marrow or brains to make them supple. With bone awls and, later, with needles, garments were fashioned, held together by strips of skin, by sinews, or vegetable fibers.

While men supplied the game, women prepared and cooked the flesh. They cut it up with stone knives and cracked the marrow bones with stone malls. Meat, when not eaten raw, must have been roasted on sticks, or baked in the ashes or dried in the smoke or sun. But, in time, women devised ovens of stones and discovered the possibilities of boiling by means of hot stones dropped into clay-lined pits, or, later, in vessels of steatite, which could withstand the heat of the flames, unbroken.

Most important of all, perhaps, was women's supplementation

of the food supply by means of vegetable products. Flint sickles and stone mortars have recently been found in Palestine, indicating that, as long as 20,000 years ago, grains were reaped and their seeds ground for food.[1] At first, nuts, fruits, roots, and seeds were gathered wherever they were found, but the time came when they were deliberately planted, and the industrial life of women centered largely around the staple vegetable products; their cultivation with digging stick and stone hoe, their storage and preparation for food. Weaving and basketry must have developed largely because of the need for food-containers. Clay daubed on gourds and baskets to render them water- and air-tight gave rise in time to pottery, again of primary importance for the storage of food and water. The arts of basketry and pottery in their earlier stages must have been almost entirely in the hands of women.

Besides engaging in all these varied pursuits, women must themselves have made all the necessary appliances. The grain, for instance, had to be ground before it could be used for gruel or griddle-cakes. Pestles and mortars and various kinds of hand-mills had to be invented and fashioned from stone or hardwood. Not only were women the first bakers, but the first brewers as well. Drinks were made from vegetable juices, and their discovery of the medicinal properties of herbs made women the first practitioners of the healing art.

In the practice of the industrial arts, moreover, fine art had its place. Basic needs and the essentials of maintenance are not the sole controllers of primitive industry. Pride in workmanship, joy in artistry, in the perfected form, and the decoration of the finished product became dominating motives.[2]

One must not assume, of course, that the division of labor between the sexes has always and everywhere followed the same lines. Undoubtedly, however, among hunting peoples, hunting has been and still is the chief occupation of the men. As an Australian native told Howitt: "A man hunts, spears fish and sits about." There are exceptions: a woman may occasionally hunt or even fight, and fishing is at times an exclusively feminine occupation, as with the Fuegians where the women are sole owners of the canoes. The general char-

[1] See *New York Times*, April 22, 1933, for a report of the finds of the American School of Prehistoric Research in Palestine and the Near East.

[2] An interesting example of primitive artistic development is afforded by the fact that patterns on clay appear to have been derived from the braidings on basketry, so that the ornamentation as well as the form of primitive pottery preserves traces of its origin.

acteristics of the division of labor among primitive peoples to-day are summarized by Malinowski as follows: "the husband is the protector and defender of the family, and he also performs all the work which requires greater strength, courage, and decision, such as hunting game, fishing, heavy building of houses and craft, and clearing the timber. . . . The wife normally looks after the preparation of the food, she almost invariably provides the fuel and the water, is the actual attendant at the hearth or fireplace, manufactures, tends, and owns the cooking vessels, and she is also the main carrier of burdens."[1]

Outside these immediate household tasks, the division of labor between husband and wife is very much a matter of convention. There are marked differences in the allotment of masculine and feminine pursuits in different cultures. Sewing and weaving, for instance, are often the work of men, while hide preparation is more likely to devolve upon women. It is of interest to note that, whatever be the prevailing division of labor, there is a tendency for men to regard their work as superior to that of women, to safeguard it with taboos and to consider it degrading for a man to engage in a woman's work![2]

There is no doubt, as Mary Beard so forcibly points out, that woman's share in the building of society has been neglected by historians. In all ages and in all lands the majority of women have worked hard, often from childhood, to what we should now consider an early death. The daily monotonous round of the necessary tasks has been, and still to a considerable extent is, theirs. Exceptional conditions have occasionally given rise to classes of women exempt wholly or in part from useful work. But there can have been no idle women among our prehistoric ancestors. For full appreciation of the invaluable productive services of women in early times, we need subscribe to no exaggerated theory of woman as the inventor and originator of all the industries and arts. Over-emphasis on women's contributions to culture is very natural as an offset to previous neglect. Briffault, for example, suggests that flint-knapping may possibly have been a feminine invention, in which case, not only the first tools, women's stone knives and scrapers, but also the first weapons, axes and lance-heads, were due to women's ingenuity. Keller, on the other hand, contends that the arts of peace were contributions from the arts of war. Men

---

[1] *Encyclopaedia Britannica*, Vol. 14, p. 943, *s.v.* "Marriage."
[2] Even where, in case of need, the sexes help each other, a man is ashamed of doing a woman's work if a stranger is present!

were the inventors of weapons. Tools were once weapons or modified from weapons. He does not, of course, deny that some of the arts may have originated with women. Whatever may have been the actual facts, there need, at least, be no dispute as to the importance of the economic functions of primitive women.

The Influence of Economic Changes on Division of Labor between the Sexes. A detailed theory of the relation between family organization and typical forms of maintenance was developed by the German writer Grosse in *Die Formen der Familie und die Formen der Wirtschaft* (1896). He maintained that, "under every form of culture, the form of family organization prevails which is best suited to economic needs and conditions," and thus that "in its essential features, the character of each particular form of the family may be explained by the form of economy in which it is rooted."[1] Grosse's theory may be criticized for over-emphasizing economic influences. Many of its details may be rejected. But it is valuable in its insistence on the close connection between the family and current industrial conditions.

Modern anthropologists are cautious; they hesitate to accept theories and generalizations without the fullest empirical evidence. It has long been held, for instance, that with the development of herding the status of women was lowered. Lowie shows that the case for a necessary causal connection here is not so strong as at first appears. "It is the preëxisting culture," he finds, "that largely determines how a new economic factor shall affect woman's status."[2] Bearing this caution in mind, it still seems worth while to point out some of the probable results of early economic development.

Women must have had their full share in the domestication of animals. Mason suggests that they alone were responsible for the domestication of the cat, its purpose being to guard their granaries from the depredations of rodents. But, even though they must have tended the young wolf pups, kids, lambs, and calves, brought back by the hunters, these were probably the exclusive property of men. The raising of flocks and herds was the derivative of hunting; and men became the herdsmen and the owners of a new and highly productive form of property.[3]

[1] Quoted by Howard, *op. cit.*, Vol. I, p. 63.　　　[2] *Primitive Society*, p. 200.

[3] Masculine prerogatives with regard to cattle are jealously guarded by taboos, even now, among some primitive peoples. In many parts of Africa women may not touch cattle; all activities connected with cattle-tending, even milking and the care of hides, being the work of men. The Todas go so far as to forbid their women to cook food of which milk is an ingredient. See Lowie, *op. cit.*, p. 75.

Horticulture, or hoe-tillage, probably remained in the hands of women, agriculture only becoming a masculine pursuit when the ox owned by man, or the slave captured in war, was harnessed to the plough. Men had more leisure when a reliable food supply liberated them from hunting. They turned to the development of the occupations hitherto carried on by women.[1] The potter's wheel, for instance, must have been a masculine invention, for while hand-made earthenware is the work of women, wheel-turned pottery is produced by men. The advance from crude stone to metal tools and weapons was made by men, who everywhere have been the workers in metal. The plough was undoubtedly invented by men.

With the domestication of wool-bearing animals, activities connected with the use of wool, preëminently spinning, but also dyeing, weaving, and fashioning the wool into garments, would have been added to the regular work of women. In spite of these services, where men have been, as in this case, the owners and producers of raw materials, women have been considered as economically dependent. Economic power, when derived from ownership of property, rather than from power of production, is largely in the control of men.

Keller's general conclusion is that "proficiency in the application and organization of force enabled man to coerce woman to whatever activities repelled him most. . . . Nothing stands out more clearly than that man did what he wanted to much more consistently than did the woman."[2] We must not assume, however, that primitive women were unwilling victims of an inequitable division of labor. Even at higher levels of culture, with the increasing dominance of men, the majority of women have seen nothing inappropriate in the customary allotment of tasks.

The Influence of Property on Marriage and the Family. Individual marriage in primitive groups is a publicly recognized association, having as its purpose the procreation of children and the "founding of a self-sufficient economic aggregate."[3] Economic considerations are involved in the choice of a partner. A woman is prized for her industrial and horticultural skill. Sometimes a marriage is not formally celebrated until she has demonstrated her capacity as a housewife. A man, on the

---

[1] A high degree of skill had, of necessity, been developed by men in the invention and perfecting of weapons. A faulty weapon meant disaster or death.

[2] W. G. Sumner and A. G. Keller, *op. cit.*, Vol. I, p. 139.

[3] Lowie, *op. cit.*, p. 64.

other hand, must give proof of his functional fitness as protector and food-provider: his prowess as a warrior and his skill as a hunter must be put to the test. The tests of courage and endurance, which so often form part of initiation rites and are sometimes made preliminaries to marriage, give proof of a man's qualifications as a husband.

Sometimes a man acquires a wife by contributing his services to her family. He may be obliged to remain permanently with his wife's family, or else he may serve a stated but limited period before marriage, or even after marriage. "Marriage by service" has been made much of, in theories of the development of the family, as one of the chief "modes of concluding marriage," the others being "marriage by capture" and "marriage by purchase." Malinowski considers such a classification unjustified, based as it is on an exaggeration of the influence of some one aspect.[1] Least of all can "capture," "service," and "purchase" be considered as stages in the evolution of marriage. The "capture" of a wife must always have been a rare exception. In most ages women have been captured in war, but they have become slaves, concubines, or prostitutes rather than legal wives. While Briffault believes that "marriage by service" constituted the earliest form of marriage contract, and that the "bride-price" first came into use as a commutation of service, Malinowski considers service to be but "a detail in the economics of certain marriages."

Another error, according to Malinowski, is "the tearing out of some one economic trait, and giving it a special name and thus an artificial entity."[1] This has been done notably with regard to "marriage by purchase," a term which falsely implies that the initial gifts at marriage, particularly those given by the husband, are in the nature of a commercial transaction. The presents given at marriage should be considered as a *link* binding together two groups, rather than two individuals. Sometimes there is an exchange of brides between two groups, but most frequent is the gift of property in exchange for a bride. The gift may be very small, or else it may be large enough to warrant the current anthropological term of "bride-price"; provided it be understood that among primitive peoples, at least, no ordinary "purchase" is implied. The exchange of property for a bride takes many different forms. Cattle, for example, are the most frequent form of bride-price in all herding communities. They may be provided by the bridegroom

[1] *Encyclopaedia Britannica*, Vol. 14, p. 943, *s.v.* "Marriage."

himself, or by the father or other relatives. Sometimes these cattle must be distributed among the bride's relatives according to fixed tribal custom. There are many cases, too, in which the bride's family must present the bridegroom with a return gift. Sometimes this gift is the husband's property only as long as the marriage lasts. In other cases the return gift takes the form of a *dowry*, which, though benefiting the bridegroom, is given to the bride.

Marriage may be easily dissolved among many primitive peoples. Considerations of property, however, tend to stabilize the relationship and act as a deterrent to divorce. Where a bride-price has been given the woman's liberty of divorce tends to be restricted. Even so, if the husband repudiates his wife without just cause, he often loses his right to reclaim the bride-price, and may even suffer further penalties. If the wife, in such a case, brought a dowry with her, this is very usually returnable. If she unjustly leaves her husband, or is justly repudiated for certain recognized causes, she may lose all she brought with her and compel her kindred to return the bride-price.[1]   In general, there is apt to be discrimination against the party at fault: the man or woman who arbitrarily dissolves marriage, or whose conduct is the cause of separation, is usually put at a disadvantage in property settlements.

We have seen in Chapter III that questions of descent and inheritance have been influential on family organization. One of the special conditions which has probably been a chief cause for the matrilineal counting of descent is the ownership of gardens by women. The ownership of live-stock seems, on the other hand, to have strengthened patrilineal ties. The advantages of filial inheritance would have become more obvious when, with the increase of the herds, wealth began to accumulate.

Changes Brought About by the Development of Agriculture and the Beginnings of Civilization. In some cultures the development of agriculture probably superseded the horticulture of women without any marked intervening development of herding or the pastoral life. Such a course of events would have had favorable results for women. Among some agricultural peoples, for example, the common land still descends through maternal ancestors only. On the other hand, as Briffault points out, the most pronounced types of patriarchal society have arisen where agriculture has developed among owners of flocks and

---

[1] Economic inefficiency is usually included among just grounds for divorce; bad temper, sterility, and adultery are others.

herds. With accumulation of wealth, class inequalities began
to appear. Women were more likely to be regarded as valuable
property, capable of a wide range of labor, and adding children
to the other possessions of the husband. While monogyny was
perforce the rule for the poor man, the man of wealth had the
means to "purchase" numerous wives; increasing not only
his wealth but his power and social importance. It is under
conditions such as these that the bride-price takes on more
of the character of a genuine purchase. Particularly where
there is slavery, it may tend to become identified with the
payment made for a slave. With the introduction of slavery,
moreover, there would be less demand for economic production
on the part of wives of wealthy men. As in some Eastern
civilizations, large numbers of women would cease to be workers
and become the property of wealthy men, rigorously secluded
in harems and valued for their sex alone.

With the development of agriculture, land becomes, in time,
the chief form of private property. Earlier it was held in
common, and there are to this day instances of land being held
in common by villages, as in India, or by joint-households
as in parts of Eastern Europe. But where land is the property
of an individual man, the problem of its inheritance gives to
woman a new function as the producer of legal heirs. Where
there are several wives, the chief wife is usually the mother
of the heir. In Europe, monogamy became the prevailing form
of marriage.[1] Where women were heiresses to lands they were
desired as a means for acquiring property. In any case it was
their chief function to be the mothers of heirs.

Where women are regarded as the property of the husband,
and particularly where emphasis is placed on the legitimacy
of the heir, a new importance is attached to any infringement
of a husband's exclusive marital rights. Adultery becomes a
peculiarly heinous form of theft. Girls may be betrothed very
young. There is added insistence on the chastity of unmarried
girls; for brides must be virgins.

ECONOMIC ASPECTS OF THE PATRIARCHAL FAMILY AMONG THE
HEBREWS, GREEKS, AND ROMANS

The Hebrew Family: Property and Inheritance. The Old
Testament affords abundant illustration of the economic changes

---

[1] According to Briffault, this was due to the fact that in Europe, as distinct from
many parts of the East, no pastoral life on a large scale preceded the development
of agricultural settlements.

alluded to in the last section. In the days of the patriarchs, individual ownership was restricted to cattle and movable possessions. With the development of agriculture, came settlement in village communities, in which pastures and cultivated lands were at first held in common and portioned out for the use of households. Individual ownership of land was well established by the time when King Ahab coveted the vineyard which Naboth had inherited from his fathers.[1]

The ties of kinship were strong among the Hebrews. Tracing descent back through the generations, each head of a family looked forward to the perpetuation of his name in the future and the transmission of his property to his descendants. The usual custom, at first, appears to have been the division of possessions among all the sons, the first-born son receiving a double portion. It was later decreed that, failing sons, a daughter might inherit; failing daughters, the next of kin was the heir.[2] The next of kin was held responsible in many ways; he must care for the widow and orphans of a deceased relative and manage the property of those not yet of age. In the well-known story of Ruth, Boaz will not marry Ruth, nor buy her father-in-law's land, until the right of purchase is relinquished by the kinsman "nearer" than he. When this has been arranged, Boaz announces that he has bought the land and that "Ruth . . . have I purchased to be my wife, to raise up the name of the dead upon his inheritance."[3]

The custom of *levirate*, to be found among a number of primitive peoples, persisted among the Jews until the Middle Ages. If a man died childless, his brother was expected to marry his widow, and "the first-born which she beareth shall succeed in the name of his brother which is dead, that his name be not put out of Israel."[4] Such an obligation might, however, be avoided by the surviving brother.

The Hebrew family was polygynous and included both wives and concubines. When a wife gave her handmaiden as concubine to her husband, she often claimed the offspring as her own. In the days of the patriarchs, wives were acquired in exchange for gifts, as in the case of those given by Abraham's servant for Rebekah as the wife of Isaac; or else by service, as in the case of Jacob, who served fourteen years before Rachel

---

[1] "And Naboth said to Ahab, The Lord forbid it me, that I should give the inheritance of my fathers unto thee." But Jezebel, it will be remembered, had Naboth falsely accused of blasphemy and stoned to death. *I Kings*, XXI.

[2] *Numbers*, XXVII, 6–11.   [3] *Ruth*, IV.   [4] *Deuteronomy*, XXV, 6.

was finally given to him. If a man seduced an unbetrothed damsel, it was ruled that he "shall give unto the damsel's father fifty shekels of silver, and she shall be his wife."[1] If a bride were found not to be a virgin, she was stoned to death.

The Hebrew husband possessed unlimited rights of divorce. The wife, on the other hand, was not protected in any way or given any rights of divorce until shortly before the Christian era. The law of the marriage deed, promulgated about this time, required every husband to convey to his bride a certain sum from his estate, to provide for her, in case of his death or of her divorce without due cause.

The Hebrew Family: Industry. While the Hebrew wife had few rights, her duties as housewife and mother were very numerous. The household appears to have been largely self-sustaining even as late as the time of Solomon. A great variety of productive industries were carried on under the housewife's direction; where there were slaves, she worked with them and directed their work and that of her daughters. All members of the household, including slaves, must be fed and clothed and tended when ill. The famous passage in Chapter XXXI of *Proverbs* gives a picture of some of the manifold activities of the virtuous housewife: "She seeketh wool and flax and worketh willingly with her hands. . . . She bringeth her food from afar. She riseth also while it is yet night, and giveth meat to her household and a portion to her maidens. She considereth a field, and buyeth it: with the fruit of her hands she planteth a vineyard. . . . She layeth her hands to the spindle, and her hands hold the distaff. . . . She is not afraid of the snow for her household; for all her household are clothed in scarlet. She maketh herself coverings of tapestry; her clothing is silk and purple. . . . She maketh fine linen and selleth it; and delivereth girdles unto the merchant." After which, it seems superfluous to add that "she . . . eateth not the bread of idleness." Nor is it to be wondered at that "Her children arise up and call her blessed; her husband also, and he praiseth her." As a modern writer has observed, this seems somewhat condescending on his part; all we learn of him being that "he is known in the gates, where he sitteth among the elders of the land."[2]

The Greek Family: Property and Inheritance. The family estates of the Athenian Greeks were passed on to the oldest

[1] *Deuteronomy*, XXII, 29.
[2] Abraham Myerson, *The Nervous Housewife* (1920), p. 7.

son. If the head of the family died having no sons, his daughter could be forced by her kinsmen to marry her father's nearest male relative, in order that he might become the head of the family. In Sparta, on the other hand, women might inherit land and personal property directly. Aristotle speaks in his *Politics* of the "number of heiresses" among the Spartans and the "large dowries which are customary."[1]

The Athenian wife's chief function was the provision of a legitimate heir who would inherit the estates and, as head of the family, officiate as priest in the worship of ancestors. Marriage was monogynous and, being purely juridic, was often regarded by men simply as a duty, unavoidable except where it might be evaded through adoption of an heir. The Athenian did not desire many children; daughters, indeed, were a liability, since they must be provided with dowries if they were to be legally married. Child exposure, particularly of girls, was common. The oldest son alone could inherit the family estates, while movable property was inherited equally among the sons.

In the Homeric age no dowry had been needed by a woman: on the contrary, a bride-price in the form of "gifts" was presented to a maiden's father by her suitor. She was regarded as "one who yields to her parents many oxen" as presents from her suitor. But by the time of Solon it was already customary in Athens to set aside a dowry in money and personal effects for each daughter. As Euripides has Medea say, "We must pay our store of gold, hoarded for that one day, to buy us some man's love." When the father was dead, the oldest brother must provide a dowry for his sister and make arrangements for her marriage. This dowry did not, however, become the property of the husband, and he usually gave securities for its return under certain conditions. He might administer it during his married life, and, if his wife predeceased him, he controlled it until his death or remarriage. In these events the dowry passed to the children or, if there were none, reverted to the wife's guardian, the father or male head of her family.

It was easy for a man to divorce his wife. Indeed, if she were known to be an adulteress, the law commanded annulment of the marriage. It was also considered justifiable for a man to divorce a childless wife. The fact that the dowry of the repudiated wife had to be returned to her family doubtless

[1] 1270,a.

served as a restriction on divorce.[1] A wife might lawfully leave her husband, taking her property with her, but, except in cases of mutual consent, she must make a written statement to the *archon* in which she gave evidence of her husband's neglect of, or cruelty to, his family. "The whole intention of Greek law," says Whibley, "seems to have been to preserve property in families, principally with a view to prevent the extinction of families and the disuse of family *sacra*."[1]

The Greek Family: Industry. According to Demosthenes, the wife had two functions, both primarily economic. Men took wives, not only that they might "beget legitimate children," but also that they might have "faithful housekeepers." Even in the Homeric age the chief preoccupations of the mistress of the household seem to have been weaving and spinning, as was the case indeed in all early civilizations. The carvings and wall-paintings of ancient cities everywhere give graphic evidence of the close connection of women with all forms of the textile industry, and particularly with spinning and weaving.

By the fifth century B.C. in Athens, the household had for the most part ceased to be economically self-sufficient. Many crafts and trades had developed, and these, including some of the processes connected with the making of clothing, were carried on professionally outside the home. In the households of the poorer citizens the wife was doubtless hard-worked, although even the less well-to-do usually owned a slave or two. Nor was the wife exempt from work in the wealthier households with their numerous slaves. She must instruct these slaves, apportion and oversee all their tasks, see that they were provided with food and clothing, and care for them in illness. A vivid picture of what this involved is given by Xenophon in his *Economics:* a dialogue between Socrates and the young husband Ischomachus, who obligingly gives full details of the instructions he has given his meek little fifteen-year-old bride with regard to the management of his household.[2] All she was expected to know, "when she came," was "how to take wool and make a garment, . . . and how to apportion the tasks of spinning among the maidservants." Now, however,

[1] See L. Whibley, *A Companion to Greek Studies* (1931), pp. 613–614. It is uncertain whether the dowry was returned where the wife was divorced for just cause. For a full discussion see F. Baudry, *Dictionnaire des Antiquités Grecques et Romaines* (5 vols. in 10, 1877–1919), Vol. II, *s.v.* "*Divortium*" and "*Dos.*"

[2] Extracts from the *Economics* are given by Paul Monroe, *Source Book of the History of Education for the Greek and Roman Period* (1928), pp. 37–50. Quoted by permission of The Macmillan Company, publishers.

as a wife she must not only direct the work of the entire household, but is "guardian of the laws established in the home." She is in charge of all household stores and must keep strict account of all provisions. Clothes, shoes, bed-coverings, vases, implements and utensils, for spinning, preparing corn, kneading bread, cooking, for the table and for the bath, must each be kept in good condition in its appropriate place. Ischomachus complacently remarks that "the gods . . . have plainly adapted the nature of the woman for works and duties within doors, and that of the man for works and duties without doors."

The Roman Family: Property and Inheritance. An insistent emphasis was placed on patriarchal authority in earlier Roman law. But, despite the power conferred on the paterfamilias, actually the Roman matron held a more independent and dignified position than was usually accorded to a wife among patriarchal peoples. An interesting explanation of this paradox is suggested by Briffault. He believes there to have been a rapid change in current usage, patrician marriage being deliberately instituted as a means of transmitting property from father to son. It is significant that, in the absence of a legal heir, property still reverted under the Law of the Twelve Tables to the *gens.* The propertied patricians did not even recognize the marriage arrangements of the propertyless plebeians. Nor could *matrimonium justum* take place between a patrician and a plebeian prior to 445 B.C. In the case of *matrimonium justum* alone, could the husband acquire the rights of *patria potestas* and *manus.* In other marriages the child was considered as having no father and would take the name and condition of his mother. The very term *matrimonium* seems to be derived from this latter form of marriage. These facts give evidence, Briffault holds, of a sudden transition from a very different state of affairs.

Patrician marriage rites in early times were those of *confarreatio,* and included the sharing of a cake of *far* and the transference of the bride from the *potestas* of her father *in manum viri.* Her *dos,* or dowry, agreed upon at the time of betrothal, now belonged to her husband.

Coemptio was a more archaic form of marriage, probably significant of the transition from bride-price to dowry through an exchange of gifts. The Roman jurists interpreted it as "mutual purchase," and it appears to have been the usual form of marriage between plebeians when they first acquired the right of legal marriage. The right of *manus* became attached, in time, to *coemptio*, as it did even to *usus*, a form of marriage where a woman, who had willingly lived with a man for a year and had never absented herself for three consecutive nights, thereby became his wife.

All these earlier forms of marriage were superseded in the period following the Punic wars, by the custom of "free marriage" without *manus*. The husband still had the right to administer his wife's dowry, but it was no longer his property. Wealth had been flowing into Rome; and Roman fathers became reluctant to part with large dowries to the daughter's husband. The wife now remained a member of her father's family and under his power. But a father's or guardian's control became in many cases only nominal, and many wives were in actual control of their dowries or even became possessed of independent means.

Marriage now rested on consent, and was a union which might not only be freely entered but also freely left. Where divorce had been difficult and comparatively rare in earlier days, it now became extremely frequent, at least among the wealthy and influential. In an effort at restriction, pecuniary penalties were placed on the guilty party. In case of a wife's infidelity, a husband might retain one-sixth of her dowry, while, where he was guilty, he was obliged to restore the whole amount of the dowry to his divorced wife.

The Roman Family: Industry. In the Roman home of the earlier period the *atrium* or central room was the headquarters of the wife. Here she sat, spinning and weaving and directing her household. Most Romans were farmers, cultivating their lands themselves, with, perhaps, a few slaves to help them. Raw materials were supplied by the husband, to be prepared for use by his wife and her household assistants. A few industries had developed even in the earlier period: the crafts of the dyer, coppersmith, and goldsmith, and, curiously enough, of the fuller. The family clothing was sent to the fuller to be cleansed together with the woven cloth freshly come from the loom.

Even in the days of the later Republic and Empire, the majority of Roman matrons were, probably, still engaged in much the same manner as of old. The inscription on a tombstone of the year 8 B.C. contains these words: "You were assiduous at your spinning," and on another of a later period it is written "She . . . kept her house and spun." But among the very wealthy all was changed. The country villas or city households were often all-inclusive industrial units, dependent on the labor of multitudes of slaves whose work was directed by slave-overseers. The mistress of such a household was no longer its manager and director, far less did she engage in any productive work herself. For the first time in history, economic conditions made possible a class of purely *parasitic* women: idle, pleasure-loving ladies who were mere consumers of the goods produced by others.

ECONOMIC ASPECTS OF THE FAMILY IN THE MIDDLE AGES AND DURING THE RENAISSANCE

The Marriage Contract in the Old English and Teutonic Codes. In his *Germania* Tacitus wrote of the customs of the Teuton barbarians. "The wife," he says, "does not offer a *dos* to the husband, but the husband offers one to the wife . . . , oxen, a bridled horse, a shield with sword and spear. For these gifts the wife is obtained, and she, in turn, brings something of arms to her husband."[1] Tacitus was probably mistaken on one point, for the gifts must have been given to the bride's guardian, not to the bride herself. With this correction, however, here is an account of the custom of "wife purchase," long prevalent among all Teutonic peoples. *Bewedding*, or betrothal, took the form of a contract where the bridegroom made payment of the *weotuma* or *witthum*, the bride-price. *Gifta*, or nuptials, consisted in the transference of the bride to the husband by her father or guardian. Authorities differ as to how far a woman was regarded as property. The bride-price, according to some, must be looked upon rather as the cost of protectorship. On the other hand, a law of Alfred speaks of the *weotuma* as "the worth of her maidhood," and another law provides that, if a betrothed woman were unfaithful, a penalty had to be paid to the betrothal sureties.

Before the tenth century various changes had occurred. The full payment of the bride-price at the *bewedding* had given place to the *handgeld*, or *arrha*, a small sum given as guarantee of later payment. In time this came to be given to the bride herself and, much later, took the form of a betrothal ring. The actual purchase money itself was gradually transformed into provision for the wife from the husband's property in case he died before her. From the tenth century on, the *bewedding* was no more than a contract, or *wed*, to pay the bride-price to the wife in case of the husband's death. Another custom

[1] Quoted by Howard, *op. cit.*, Vol. I, p. 262.

had arisen of the morning gift to the bride on the day after marriage. This too was provided for in the marriage contract, and in time was merged with the bride-price as a provision for the wife in case of her husband's death.

The Marriage Contract in the Feudal Period and during the Renaissance. Limitations of space make it impossible to follow the further modifications and developments of the marriage contract. Married women and widows had been possessed of considerable property rights before the establishment of the feudal system. These rights were now curtailed and the general position of women was lowered. The Anglo-Norman lawyer Glanvill, living in the twelfth century, states in his *Tractate* that the wife was granted, as *dower*, the life-use of one-third of her husband's real estate at the time of marriage, and one-third of his personal property. The oldest son was almost invariably the heir, the inheritor of the landed estates of the family. Some provision was made for daughters, however, for the Roman custom of a dowry at marriage was revived during the feudal period. The "lady" was indeed frequently married wholly for the sake of her dowry, or if a widow, for her dower. She, as well as the serf, "went with the land."

In the later Middle Ages and during the Renaissance, a girl was very generally considered eligible in proportion to the size of her dowry. The drawing up of a marriage contract took on the character of a business bargain, and marriage itself was looked upon as a business partnership. Indeed, through the seventeenth and eighteenth centuries, and in many parts of Europe even to this day, marriage is considered primarily as a contract whereby social and economic benefits may be secured.

Changes in the Economic Basis of the Family. The economic basis of the patriarchal family in Europe is evident from such facts. Its traditional pattern is to a large extent derived from the ownership of land. Wealth in the form of land does not admit of division, if the power and prestige of the land-owners is to be maintained. Only the oldest son and very few daughters could be provided for. Superfluous sons became priests or adventurers, or, in later times, joined the professional or commercial classes. Unmarried daughters had the convent as sole alternative to life-long dependence on father or brother. The wife and her children thus had their fates determined very largely by the dependence of the aristocracy on the ownership of land.

Even among the landless classes, family standards were derived from the dominant class. It was largely on this account that the traditional pattern of the patriarchal family survived, long after its foundations in land-ownership had been undermined. For, with the rise of the middle class to wealth, economic security was derived from commerce and industry and no longer solely from the land. No longer was there any need for a strict limitation on the division of property, nor for primogeniture, in any families except those still wholly dependent on landed estates. Of even greater importance was the fact that the successful professional man or merchant must be enterprising and independent. His status was determined by capacity rather than by a share in the family inheritance. The dominance of the father over his family and his authority over their careers thus ceased to rest on a foundation of economic necessity.

Paradoxically enough, the patriarchal family pattern received further reënforcement from the Protestant Reformation, despite the inception of the latter as a middle-class movement. Biblical tradition sanctioned the full exercise of patriarchal authority. It was a long time, accordingly, before the changed economic basis of the family made itself felt, a fact which will be apparent in succeeding chapters, particularly those dealing with the treatment of children.

Industry in the English Home. Records show the English housewife to have been ceaselessly occupied. Even the "lady" in Anglo-Saxon times must have spent much time in household tasks and in directing the work of others. While the term "lord" comes from the Anglo-Saxon *hlaf-ord*, meaning loaf-owner or guardian, "lady" is derived from *hlaf-dig*, or loaf-kneader.

Throughout the Middle Ages the chief occupation of all women of rank seems to have been needlework and embroidery. But, even if the lady was to a certain extent relieved of industrial tasks, this was by no means true of the great majority of women. Theodore, in his *Penitentials*, forbids Anglo-Saxon women to occupy themselves on Sunday with shearing sheep, carding wool, beating flax, washing garments, weaving, spinning, and sewing. The textile industry was evidently altogether in the hands of women. All activities connected with the preparation of food and drink were home industries. Candles had succeeded rushlights, and must be made at home.

Women and the Gilds.   Industrial changes came about more rapidly in towns.   With greater density of population there is greater demand for goods and a tendency for each individual to spend his time at the work for which he is best fitted.   Production on a large scale is only possible with division of labor, a principle essential to the development of industry.   While most of the people of mediaeval England lived in scattered country villages, London had a population of some 25,000 in the thirteenth century, and there were numerous smaller towns with populations of 4,000 or less.   Already a number of industries had been established; some of them, such as public baking and brewing, catered to the needs of the townspeople; others, in particular the making of woolen cloth, were undertaken with a view to sale at fairs and markets.

Such industries, although specialized, were still carried on in the household; a master workman, possessing a few tools and a small supply of raw materials, directed the work of apprentices and journeymen.   For the protection of their rights and privileges such master workmen were collected together into craft gilds, organizations which controlled conditions of work, fixed prices, maintained high standards of quality and workmanship, and looked after the interests of their members. As early as 1130 there were gilds of weavers in London, Lincoln, and Oxford.

Many industries which had formerly been in the hands of women thus became skilled trades for men.   Women, however, continued to share in the work even under these changed conditions, the wife and daughter of the master being employed in the industrial activities going on in the household.   In some cases they carried on the business after the death of the gildsman. As a general rule, however, women were not admitted to independent membership in the craft gilds.   There were exceptions, particularly on the Continent.

English Industry in the Later Middle Ages and during the Renaissance.   Many industries still remained in the hands of women; silk-weaving, for instance, knitting, candle-making, and, most important of all, the carding and cleaning of wool and the spinning of it into yarn.   Efforts were made by the gilds to prevent women, other than the wives and daughters of members, from sharing in men's occupations.   Nevertheless, although women occupied an inferior position in all branches of trade and industry, a great part of the work of the community was done by women, as is shown by the number of surnames ending in the feminine suffix "ster," such as Webster, Brewster, and Baxter.   The survival of the term "spinster," not as a surname, but as denoting an unmarried woman, is significant. "So universal was spinning," says Salzman, "that 'spinster' became the general legal description of any woman who had no particular rank or trade and was independent—that is to say, unmarried, for in the eyes of the law a married woman had practically no existence apart from her husband. . . . The distaff was the inseparable companion of the medieval dame; it could be carried under the arm, or thrust into the waist-belt, and formed on occasion a useful weapon of offense, particularly for the taming of husbands, as medieval artists delight to show; it became the recognized symbol of Woman."[1]

While the lady of the castle spent much of her time in spinning, embroidery, and making tapestry, she also knew how to cook. Even if seldom engaging in the heavier forms of cookery, she would make sweetmeats, conserves, and wines. She supervised the household at all times, and was its sole ruler when her husband was away at the wars. She was skilled as nurse and even as doctor, and engaged in the manufacture of soothing ointments and medicines.

Society was for long divided into three groups: the churchman, the knightly landowner, and the workers who produced the food and goods required by all classes.   This last group was, by the close of the Middle Ages, subdivided into three: the trading and industrial class living in the rapidly growing towns, the yeomen or free farmers, and, lastly, the serfs, bound to the soil and owing services to their masters.   Even in the prosperous middle classes the housewife was incessantly busy. In addition to household management, she might help her husband at his trade, and, if the wife of a farmer, "would look after the herb garden, help with such work as haymaking, go into market with butter, cheese, eggs, poultry and so forth, make malt, and brew ale, and, presumably do most of the cooking."[2] If this were insufficient, "her distaff should be always at hand for a pastime, it stops an idle gap."[3]

The life of the poorest classes was miserable indeed. Some were crowded together in the most squalid parts of the towns, often short of food and other necessaries. The majority eked

---

[1] *English Life in the Middle Ages* (Oxford University Press, 1926), pp. 258–259.
[2] *Ibid.*, pp. 256–257.
[3] *Ibid.*, p. 86. A quotation from a sixteenth century *Book of Husbandry* by Sir Anthony Fitzherbert.

out a meager subsistence farming their share of the village lands. Men, women, and children, clad in rags, living in mud and plaster cottages, possessing only the absolute necessities, toiled from dawn till dark. Some of the produce might have to be given to the lord of the manor or else the men had to work part of their time on the lord's land. Arduous toil, hunger, cold, and privation, the bearing and tending of numerous children were the inescapable lot of poor women. As the writer of *Piers Plowman* says, "pity 'tis to narrate . . . the woe of the women, that dwell in the cottages." The condition of the laboring class was, however, somewhat improved following the Black Death. This catastrophe, by wiping out, in 1349, from one-third to one-half of England's population, caused a great demand for labor, and both men and women were able to command higher wages and to achieve a greater measure of independence.[1]

THE LESSENING SPHERE OF HOME INDUSTRY

Productive Labor of the Housewife in England and the American Colonies in the Seventeenth and Eighteenth Centuries. One outstanding fact emerges from even the briefest account of women's work through the ages. Sustaining and making possible the exploits of men, which alone are commonly regarded as making history, women have, through their productive services, provided the fundamentals of everyday living. The "lady," who has at her command the labor of others, has to a certain degree been exempt from the hardest toil, but she has seldom been idle. The majority of women have always been abundantly occupied in caring for the needs of their households, and the character of their work has remained comparatively unchanged as the centuries passed by.

In the seventeenth century, English housewives were still the active producers of a great variety of goods. In *The English Housewife*, Gervase Markham places foremost among her "vertues," "the preservation and care of the family touching their health and soundness of body." To this end she must maintain an herb garden from which to brew the requisite medicinal draughts. Next comes cooking. If a woman cannot cook, "she can then but perform half her vow, for she may obey, but she cannot cherish, serve and keep with that true duty which is ever expected." Endless culinary details follow, and

---

[1] See G. T. Warner, *Landmarks in English Industrial History* (3rd ed., 1903), Chapter VI.

attention is given to the "Ordering of Banquets," both "great Feasts" and "humble ones." Even the humble feast must include "no less than two and thirty dishes." Next comes the clothing of the household, including all processes in the preparation of raw wool and flax before it is "delivered into the hands of the weaver." The woven cloth, when returned, must be made into garments. The housewife must also be proficient in dairy work and in making wine and brewing ale.[1]

With this as her background, the prodigious industry of the American housewife of colonial days is more readily understood. Bakers and bakeshops became established fairly early in New England. But, except for the baking of bread, all other industries connected with the preparation of food remained part of the housewife's labors. Candles were home-made, and home manufacture of clothing and house-linen was the rule, although cloth was imported from England and weaving early became a professional craft.

The Southern plantation homes were very nearly self-sufficient. Except for imports from England, all necessaries were produced and prepared for consumption by the labor of numerous slaves. The mistress of such a plantation must oversee and direct the work of all its members, caring for their needs in health and tending them in illness.

The Transition from Domestic Industry to the Factory System. The handicraft system, associated with the gilds and carried on in towns, long represented the only form of organized industry. It was gradually replaced by the domestic system, a term which indicated the centering of activities in the cottages of rural England. This change was in part due to the fact that the manufacture of woolens had become, next to agriculture, the most important and widespread industry.[2] By the eighteenth century the woolen business was centered in Yorkshire, in the Southwest, and in East Anglia. DeFoe in his *Tour through the Whole Island of Great Britain* (1724) gave a vivid picture of domestic industry. He tells of the numerous small clothiers who "buy the wool of the Dealer, and, in their own homes, assisted by their wives and children, and from two or three, to six or seven Journeymen, . . . dye it . . . and through all

---

[1] Quoted by Willystine Goodsell, *A History of Marriage and the Family* (rev. ed., 1934), pp. 341–343.

[2] Owing to the Black Death and the consequent scarcity of labor, much hitherto cultivated land had been turned to pasture in the fourteenth century, and henceforth used for sheep-raising.

the different stages work it up into undressed Cloth."[1]   In such a household he saw "The Women and Children carding or spinning; all employed from the youngest to the oldest; scarce anything above four Years old but its Hands were sufficient for its own Support."[2]

Everywhere this system was connected with a partial dependence on agriculture. Each clothier owned or rented a little land, kept a horse, two or three cows and perhaps a few sheep, while the small plot was cultivated by his wife for garden produce. In some parts of England, particularly in the South-west, the growth of capitalism manifested itself in larger scale production and increased division of labor.   The majority of the workers remained in their homes but worked for wages, being directed in their work by capitalist clothiers who rented out wheels and looms, provided raw materials, and marketed the finished goods. Already in some cases skilled craftsmen lived on the premises of their employers, while in others journeymen gathered in workshops.   Such conditions represent an intermediate stage between the domestic system and the factory system.

Women in their homes were still the spinners. Wool spinners were found all over the country, but there were fewer flax and cotton spinners. Much of the linen produced in the eighteenth century was still made in private families, while cotton was of minor importance until the end of the century.   At that time, owing to the importation of fine Indian muslins, chintzes, and calicoes, cotton goods became extremely popular, and the cotton trade increased rapidly. The manufacture of cotton goods was carried on as a domestic industry. The cotton was picked clean by the weaver's younger children, was carded and spun by his wife and daughters, and woven by himself and his sons.

It took several spinners to supply one loom, so that a weaver might provide work, not only for his wife and daughters, but for several neighboring "spinsters" as well. Before long, however, hand work with the spinning wheel and loom could not keep pace with the increasing demand for textiles in England and abroad; and the situation was made more difficult by Kay's invention, in 1733, of the flying shuttle, a device which

---

[1] Quoted by Ivy Pinchbeck, *Women Workers and the Industrial Revolution* (1930), p. 119.

[2] Quoted by Goodsell, *The Family as a Social and Educational Institution* (1915), p. 414.

enabled a weaver to accomplish almost twice as much work as formerly. When this came into general use, about 1760, the demand for spinners became even greater. It was met by the invention of machines and the inauguration of a new industrial era.

THE INDUSTRIAL REVOLUTION AS A DETERMINING INFLUENCE ON THE FAMILY

Mechanical Inventions and the Factory System. In 1767 Hargreaves, a weaver and carpenter, invented the spinning-jenny which multiplied the number of spindles worked by turning one wheel. By 1784 a model was produced with eighty spindles, making possible an enormous increase in the production of thread. In 1768 Arkwright invented a frame, or roller-machine, for spinning, which was driven by water-power and produced a better quality of thread. Finally, in 1779 Crampton combined features of both the jenny and the frame in his mule, which, driven first by hand, later by water-power, produced a cotton thread fine enough for the manufacture of muslins.

The smaller jennies and even mules were used in the cottages, but the frames driven by water-power and the larger jennies and mules necessitated the setting up of the earliest factories. Finally, before the end of the century, the progress and expansion of the cotton industry was given renewed stimulus from the use of steam-power. From the time when Watt managed to use steam to produce rotary movements, there followed a series of inventions revolutionizing one industry after another. In the cotton industry the first power-loom was patented by Cartwright in 1785. The tremendous demand for raw cotton was before long supplied largely from the United States where, in 1793, Eli Whitney invented the saw-gin, a device making possible the expeditious cleaning of short-stapled cotton.

The use of power machinery meant a rapid increase in the number of factories, and industrial centers arose in the districts where domestic textile industries had hitherto been carried on.[1] Meanwhile, with the use of steam-power coal became of major importance. The iron industry was revolutionized, iron mills were set up near the coal fields, and the "black country" came into being.

In England alone did the Industrial Revolution precede the development of railways. The sea was nowhere far distant, and

---

[1] The cotton industry was the first in which the transition to the factory system took place, but similar changes took place before long in the wool industry.

canals and roads gave easy access to ports. In America industrial expansion became rapid only in the second half of the nineteenth century. Here too, however, the textile industry was the earliest to develop. In spite of the fact that England carefully guarded the secrets of the new machinery, successful experiments were made in America, leading, in 1789, to Slater's establishment in Rhode Island of a cotton mill fully equipped with spinning machines. The power loom was not introduced till 1814, after which date both spinning and weaving were carried on largely in factories.

The Industrial Revolution as the Basis of Modern Economy. Scientific discovery and the use of machinery have transformed civilization. A society which has passed through an industrial revolution is characterized, by Hammond, as one which "makes great use of machinery, conducts its operations in industry and commerce on a large scale, and supplies the needs of its simplest members by an elaborate series of world-wide exchanges." Industrial Revolution means "the change that transforms a people with peasant occupations and local markets into an industrial society with world-wide connections."[1]

The results of such a change depend, of course, on the conditions which precede and accompany it. In England, the Industrial Revolution combined with the later phases of the Agrarian Revolution, and caused the final destruction of the old peasant type of life in which agriculture and village crafts were combined. Ownership of land came to be concentrated in the hands of a diminishing number of proprietors, a movement accompanied by enclosure of the common lands which had for centuries been a chief support of small farmers and cottagers. For a time, a precarious subsistence was still possible by means of home industry combined with agriculture. With the loss of home industry the rural population was faced with the choice of becoming agricultural wage-laborers or of following industry to the new manufacturing towns.

English Workers in Factories and Cities. The concentration of labor in factories and mills gave rise to great manufacturing cities, whose growth was subject to no control during the earlier stages of the Industrial Revolution. In the already existing cities conditions had been bad enough: the streets were dirty and ill-paved, with wide gutters filled with refuse; the poor lived in indescribable squalor. Such evils were multiplied

[1] J. L. Hammond, *Encyclopaedia Britannica*, Vol. 12, pp. 303–304, *s.v.* "The Industrial Revolution."

and intensified by the concentration of population in industrial centers. The problem of housing the workers became acute, leading to the crowding together of cheap, ugly, and insanitary dwellings in the neighborhood of the factories.

But we must not idealize home conditions in the rural districts from which so many of the factory workers were drawn. Extreme poverty and continuous hard work were the usual portion of every member of a cottager's family. Six or eight persons would work, eat, and sleep in a cottage of two or three small, low-ceilinged rooms.

After the first period of adjustment, factory conditions compared favorably with conditions in the domestic industries. The workers clung, however, to a system which held the family together and gave a measure of independence. Once in the factory, the worker was wholly dependent on the capitalist for wages and working conditions. From these new industrial relationships pressing problems soon arose. Undoubtedly the conditions were very bad indeed in some of the early factories. Low wages and long hours of work were the rule; worst of all was the exploitation of children. Here again, as Ivy Pinchbeck points out, it is often not realized that exactly the same conditions prevailed in the domestic industries where children went to work at an even earlier age.

The labor of the children of the poor was, indeed, taken as a matter of course until attention was called to the hardships of children employed in the factories. Owing to the efforts of public-spirited men, chief among whom was Lord Ashley, later the Earl of Shaftesbury, a series of Factory Acts were passed. In 1833 the hours of labor for children were limited and in 1850 the working day for women and children was restricted to the hours between 6 A.M. and 6 P.M. in summer, and an hour later in each case in winter, with no Saturday work after 2 P.M.

Once the hours and conditions of factory workers became regulated by the State, the new system was to advance along lines rendering it far superior to the domestic system from the standpoint of the workers. "For the majority of workers," says Ivy Pinchbeck, "the factory meant higher wages, better food and clothing and an improved standard of living. . . . This was especially so in the case of women."[1]

With regard to women, Ivy Pinchbeck's conclusions are authoritative. She shows that the evils accredited to the factory

---

[1] *Women Workers and the Industrial Revolution* (F. S. Crofts and Co., 1930), p. 311. By permission.

system by contemporary critics must be viewed "in the light of previous standards and those prevailing among the working classes generally at this period."[1] The great change brought about by the Industrial Revolution was "that a far greater number of women than ever before were compelled to follow their work out of the home and become wage-earners in the outside world."[2] As one industry after another was taken from the home, "the family-wage disappeared, and agrarian and industrial changes combined to deprive women of their earning capacity in the home. In the misery and stress of the transition, these changes at first appeared to affect many women adversely. The family income was seriously depleted by the loss of their earnings, and for a time, until men's wages were readjusted to meet the change, lack of employment for married women had serious consequences. . . . When a little later working women were reabsorbed into industrial work outside the home, they were regarded by many contemporaries as victims of the new industrial regime."[3]

Contemporary critics exaggerated the extent of married women's work in factories. At first, they do not seem to have been extensively employed, although there was an increase in their numbers after the introduction of steam-power and with the limitation of children's labor. Successive Parliamentary commissions revealed the conditions under which women worked, not in factories alone, but in mines and metal trades, in the remaining domestic industries, and as dressmakers and milliners. Extremists were anxious to withdraw women, not only from heavy and unsuitable labor, but from all forms of industry. Fortunately the moderate party triumphed, and by securing women a recognized but more protected position in industry, began the process of the emancipation of the working woman. The married woman became, it is true, financially dependent on her husband; for her earnings rarely balanced the loss to her family where she was withdrawn from family duties. The assumption was thus reached that "a man's wages should be paid on a family basis" and the way prepared "for the more modern conception that, in the rearing of children and in homemaking, the married woman makes an adequate economic contribution."[4]

---

[1] *Ibid.*, p. 309.
[2] *Ibid.*, p. 1. In view of women's age-long association with textiles, it is of particular interest that the textile industries should have been the first to develop.
[3] *Ibid.*, p. 4.   [4] *Ibid.*, p. 313.

The Industrial Revolution has "on the whole proved beneficial to women. It has resulted in greater leisure for women in the home and has relieved them from the drudgery and monotony that characterized most of the hand labour previously performed in connection with industrial work under the domestic system. For the woman worker outside the home it has resulted in better conditions, a greater variety of openings and an improved status."[1]

The influence of industrialism upon the American family is discussed in detail in later chapters. At this point it must suffice to say that, while there were striking differences between England and America in the early stages of the factory system, with the influx of foreign labor after 1850 and the rapid growth of industrial centers, the same pressing problems which had arisen in the Old World were reproduced once again in the New.

SUGGESTED READING

Briffault, R., *The Mothers*, 3 vols., 1927, Vol. I, Ch. IX; Vol. II, Chs. XV, XVI.

Goodsell, W., *A History of Marriage and the Family*, Chs. I–IV, VI–X.

Howard, G. E., *A History of Matrimonial Institutions*, 3 vols., 1904, Vol. I, Ch. VI.

Lowie, R., *Primitive Society*, 1920, Chs. VIII, IX.

Mason, O. T., *Woman's Share in Primitive Culture*, 1910.

Monroe, P., *Source Book of the History of Education for the Greek and Roman Period*, 1901, pp. 37–50.

Pinchbeck, I., *Women Workers and the Industrial Revolution*, 1930.

Salzman, L. F., *English Life in the Middle Ages*, 1926.

Sumner, W. G., and Keller, A. G., *The Science of Society*, 4 vols., 1927, Vol. I, Part II; Vol. III, Chs. XLI–LIII.

Tickner, F. W., *Women in English Economic History*, 1923.

Westermarck, E. A., *The History of Human Marriage*, 3 vols., 5th ed., 1921, Vol. II, Ch. XXIII.

[1] *Ibid.*, p. 4.

CHAPTER VI

THE FAMILY AND SEX

THE BIOLOGICAL BASIS OF THE FAMILY

The Evolution of Sex. In *Creative Evolution*, Bergson likens the vital impulse to a mighty whirlwind, sweeping irresistibly onwards, while in its wake the transient eddies of dust sink down and die. Less poetically, but in equally forceful metaphor, Havelock Ellis speaks of Nature as "obsessed with one idea—the reproduction of the species."[1] The distinguishing characteristic of living substance is the capacity for self-renewal. In its interaction with environing conditions each response of the organism entails partial destruction of its substance; ceaselessly it restores itself and rebuilds its structure.

Even under the most favorable conditions there is a limit to the self-renewal of an individual organism. The simplest living forms then reproduce themselves by subdivision. The first step towards the development of sex is found where reproduction occurs, not by fragmentation, but by conjugation. Through the fusion of two cells rejuvenation takes place, the resulting individual being endowed with revived powers of self-renewal. As Briffault puts it, "the most favorable effects will naturally result when an organism which has acquired varied activities and adaptations in its struggle against unfavorable conditions conjugates with one which has retained a greater power of nutrition."[2] That is, where cells of a male and of a female type coöperate in reproduction.

Through the lower ranges of life there are innumerable variations in methods of reproduction.[3] Where sexual reproduction is more fully developed, impregnation of the female is necessary. She bears ova within her, large food-storing cells, which are penetrated by the minute and actively moving spermatozoa, the product of the reproductive cells of the male

[1] *Man and Woman* (rev. ed., 1929), p. 234.
[2] *The Mothers*, Vol. I, p. 88.
[3] For example, Darwin describes a female cirripede which "in the two valves of her shell, had two little pockets, in each of which she kept a little husband." *Life and Letters* (edited by Francis Darwin, 2 vols., 1911), Vol. I, p. 345. In some species the female devours the male in the act of fertilization.

organism.[1]   The physiological differences between male and
female become more and more manifest in the higher organisms,
until, with the mammals, the female is profoundly modified
through her specialization for reproduction.   From the time
of sexual maturity, there is periodic renewal of ova, until
with impregnation comes gestation, birth, lactation and care
of offspring.

The evolution of motherhood has meant increasing dependence of the offspring on the mother and longer association of
mother and young.   In the higher mammals the period of
gestation is prolonged, the development of the individuals
proceeds more slowly and the young are born more immature.
As Briffault says, "In exact proportion as the immaturity of
the offspring is prolonged the mammalian animal is superior in
intelligence, in power of learning from experience, and of adapting itself by modifications in its behavior."[2]   In the implications
of this fact lies the paramount significance of the prolongation
of human infancy, clearly enunciated for the first time by
John Fiske in his *Excursions of an Evolutionist* (1883).   As
Briffault puts it, "the very springs of action and behavior
are transformed by the new relations that are established by
the protracted tutelage of mother-care.   That prolonged individual education is not only the supreme factor of mental
development, but, owing to the nature of the means by which
it is effected, the sentiment of maternal affection, it constitutes
a new psychological development by which the individual mind
is linked up with others to form a new organism, the group
bound by social ties.   It is, in fact, through that process that
the social products of evolution have become super-imposed
upon the biologically inherited animal mind, and that mind
has become human."[3]

Satisfaction of sexual impulse does not necessarily imply
mating.   Sexual reproduction is ensured primarily by means
of an overwhelming urge leading the male to seek for and
impregnate one or more females.   Yet, even among animals,

---

[1] Even the highest organisms give evidence of nature's prodigality: the lavish
production of countless thousands of male and female cells in order that a few individuals may survive. A single ejaculation of human semen contains on an average
more than 200,000,000 spermatozoa.

[2] *Op. cit.*, p. 104.

[3] *Ibid.*, p. 116. The origin of social sentiments is undoubtedly to be found in the
prolonged association between mother and child. To accept this fact does not, however, necessitate our drawing the further conclusion, as does Briffault, that the
maternal group, and not the family, is the original unit of social organization: see
p. 54.

there are instances of paternal care of offspring and many more of true mating, in the sense of a more or less enduring association between parents and their coöperation in rearing the young. Among the higher anthropoids and among human beings the young are dependent for several years; before the older offspring reach maturity, others are born, and a whole complex of habitual activities tends to intertwine with the nurture of the young, endowing the mating relationship with greater stability and endurance.

The Cultural Determination of Sexual Behavior. In the human family group is found "the link between biological cohesion and social cohesion."[1] The relationships in the animal family are the outcome of inherited behavior patterns. Human beings, on the other hand, are governed in their behavior not so much by innate tendencies as by acquired attitudes and habits. In the intimate associations of the family group tendencies become organized into socially acceptable behavior patterns. In this way, it has come about that the same human impulses express themselves through an amazing diversity of social customs and institutional forms. This holds true, moreover, for the sexual impulse, although "because its paths of motor outlet or discharge are comparatively few and fairly well-defined" it is often thought of as a separate "psychic force."[2] As a matter of fact sexual behavior has a complex pattern, whose actual content varies with its social context, and is largely the result of cultural determination.

The family has, as we saw, always provided for the more stable satisfactions of sex needs. But, although the biological impulses basic to family life are relatively unalterable, social conditions have produced wide divergencies of emotional attitude and customary behavior. Within each culture sexual behavior is part of an integrated whole of thought and action. Something of this has been already evident. We have seen how cultural influences, in particular those due to religious belief and economic usages, have influenced the pattern of family life. We must now consider more directly the cultural determination of sexual behavior and of the interrelationship between the sexes. Emphasis falls on the position of women for two reasons. In the first place, women are so highly special-

[1] Malinowski, *Sex and Repression in Savage Society*, p. 239.

[2] Dewey, *Human Nature and Conduct*, p. 150. For example, some psychoanalysts treat sex in a way which, according to Dewey, "flagrantly exhibits both the consequences of artificial simplification and the transformation of social results into psychic causes." *Ibid.*, p. 153.

ized for reproductive purposes, for marriage and family life, that the socially acceptable fulfillment of these functions has always remained what has been called the "dominant chord" of woman's destiny. Her life, whether married or unmarried, has been "oriented from wedlock and has taken its values from that status."[1] Secondly, this fact, and the further fact of her relative passivity and dependence on man, has rendered her even more susceptible than man to cultural conditioning.

Very early, women must have been generally ranked as the inferior sex. Fighting and hunting were spectacular; in times of crisis men gained prominence: the successful hunter was the savior in time of famine; the brave warrior was the heroic defender of his people. It is in the fully developed military state, where man as warrior is supreme, that women's status is almost invariably at its lowest.[2] Her status cannot be taken as an index of cultural advancement. She has been at a greater disadvantage, relative to men, in many civilized societies, than at more primitive levels of culture. The same despotic spirit is shown by man as war-leader in the state and as patriarch in the family: the weaker, in each case, being protected by, but subject to the stronger. Woman as life-giver has been least regarded, save as the mother of warriors, where man has been primarily concerned with dealing death. So strong, however, is the hold of custom and tradition that she has apparently been glad to produce numerous sons, destined to destroy others and be themselves destroyed.

Sex Differences. It can no longer be taken for granted that the relationships of men and women have been determined primarily by innate differences, either physical or mental, or by their actual reciprocal functions as mates and parents. It is only recently, indeed, that it has become evident that very little is known with regard to any but anatomical and physiological differences between the sexes. In 1869, John Stuart Mill wrote as follows: "in regard to that most difficult question, what are the natural differences between the two sexes . . . , while almost everybody dogmatizes upon it, almost all neglect and make light of the only means by which any partial insight can be obtained into it. This is an analytic study of the most important department of psychology, the laws of the influence of circumstances on character. For, however great and however

[1] W. G. Sumner and A. G. Keller, *The Science of Society*, Vol. III, p. 1735.
[2] Herbert Spencer assembled a mass of evidence in support of his contention that the status of women varied inversely with the degree of militarism in a social group.

ineradicable the moral and intellectual difference between men and women might be, the evidence of their being natural differences could only be negative. Those only could be inferred to be natural which could not possibly be artificial—the residuum, after deducting every character of either sex which can admit of being explained from education or external circumstances. The profoundest knowledge of the laws of the formation of character is indispensable to entitle anyone to affirm even that there is any difference, much more what the difference is."[1]

Despite the wide range of opportunity accorded to women, despite the development of scientific psychology, we are still to-day far from reaching any solution of the problem so clearly stated by Mill. The differential treatment accorded boys and girls from earliest infancy at present puts insuperable obstacles in the way of the necessary experimentation. It is, indeed, to a great extent still true that "what is now called the nature of women is an eminently artificial thing, the result of forced repression in some directions, unnatural stimulation in others. . . . No other class of dependents have had their character so entirely distorted from its natural proportions."[2]

Great advances have been made in exact knowledge of the fundamental biological differences between the sexes.[3] Sex is determined at the moment of conception. All ripe ova are alike in containing what has been designated as an X-chromosome. But the spermatozoa are of two kinds, bearers respectively of X- and Y-chromosomes. The resultant embryo is a female where the ovum has been fertilized by an X-bearing sperm. A female has two X-chromosomes in every body cell, a male only one, of maternal origin. The influence of sex thus pervades the whole organism. At an early embryonic stage, however, the reproductive organs are neither male nor female. Later, due probably to the chemical balance of endocrine

---

[1] *The Subjection of Women*, Sec. 20. For a recent edition see Everyman's Library No. 825 (E. P. Dutton and Co., Inc., New York, 1929), pp. 239–240.

[2] John Stuart Mill, *op. cit.*, p. 238.

[3] It was not until 1672 that Swammerdam discovered that the contact of spermatic fluid with the ovum was necessary to generation. The actual male germ cells were discovered by Spallanzani only in 1785. The fusion of male and female cells was demonstrated adequately for the first time in 1879. Hippocrates, it is true, divined the existence of male and female germ cells; but the view prevailing until a few hundred years ago was that of Aristotle, that the male contributed an "impulse to movement," the child being formed from the menstrual blood retained during pregnancy. Such a view accorded with the patriarchal conception, expressed by Sophocles, when he spoke of woman as a "ploughed field" in which man sows his "seed."

secretions, specialization comes about both in the genitalia and in other anatomical, physiological, and biochemical characteristics. In the female there is further specialization for the prenatal care of the foetus, for its delivery at birth, and for lactation. In spite of these facts, few individuals can be considered, even physically, to be 100% male or female, all being blends due to the endocrine balance, even though predominantly masculine or feminine.

Psychological experimentation aimed at the discovery of sex differences in mental traits has been in progress some forty years. It was soon discovered that individual differences *within* each sex enormously outweigh any differences *between* the sexes. Intelligence tests and psychometric methods have demonstrated the mental equality of the sexes in the major aspects of intellect and in various special fields such as musical, artistic, mathematical, and even mechanical ability. There is still, however, a general acceptance of a dichotomy between masculine and feminine personality types, of characteristic differences in sentiments, interests, attitudes, and modes of behavior which are supposed to be derivatives of differences in instinctive and emotional equipment. Recent researches in anthropology have, on the other hand, furnished abundant evidence for the plasticity of temperament and personality, and for the patterning of sex differences through cultural influences. Margaret Mead's *Sex and Temperament* (1935) is an outstanding contribution; a description of a first-hand study of three primitive tribes in New Guinea, and of the way in which accepted norms of masculine and feminine conduct are inculcated from earliest childhood.[1] These norms, moreover, are in marked contrast, not only with each other, but with those current in Western society.[2] Even so, we have as yet no final answer to the problem of the respective influence of nature and nurture as determiners of sex temperament.

The same conclusion is reached as the result of a recent

[1] Psychoanalysts, such as Paul Bousfield, *Sex and Civilization* (1928), have stressed the influences of early childhood in creating artificial distinctions between the sexes. Only when boys and girls have the same freedom, the same education, and the same opportunities will there be any possibility of discovering to what extent the actual biological differences between the sexes express themselves in divergencies of temperament.

[2] In one case, that of the Arapesh, both males and females exhibit much the same temperamental pattern, one which we should consider typically feminine. The Mundugumor, a tribe of head-hunting cannibals, also have a single norm, this time typically masculine. Among the Tchambuli, the males approximate what we should call feminine in temperament, and the females the masculine! Ruth Benedict's *Patterns of Culture* (1934) also presents a study of three primitive cultures, to illustrate the wide diversity of cultural patterns and their profound influence on temperament.

experimental investigation in this field, by Terman and Miles. Tests of masculinity and femininity were devised, based on experimentally established differences between male and female groups. One dominant principle of sex difference emerges: "the males included in the standardization groups evinced a distinctive interest in exploit and adventure, in outdoor and physically strenuous occupations, in machinery and tools, in science, physical phenomena, and inventions; and, from rather occasional evidence, in business and commerce. On the other hand, the females of our groups have evinced a distinctive interest in domestic affairs and in aesthetic objects and occupations; they have distinctively preferred more sedentary and indoor occupations, and occupations more directly ministrative, particularly to the young, the helpless, the distressed. Supporting and supplementing these are the more subjective differences—those in emotional disposition and direction. The males directly or indirectly manifest the greater self-assertion and aggressiveness; they express more hardihood and fearlessness, and more roughness of manners, language, and sentiments. The females express themselves as more compassionate and sympathetic, more timid, more fastidious and more aesthetically sensitive, more emotional in general (or at least more expressive of the four emotions considered), severer moralists, yet admit in themselves more weaknesses in emotional control and (less noticeably) in physique."[1] In other words, the traditional dichotomy between masculine and feminine temperaments is evident. Nevertheless, the experimental evidence is inconclusive as to the innateness of even such distinctive tendencies as maternal tenderness and masculine aggressiveness, however probable it may seem that physiological sex differences have their temperamental counterpart.

One conclusion may, however, be drawn. There is no basis in our present knowledge for dogmatic statements as to differences between men and women, and as to their consequent place in society. As Havelock Ellis says, "it is safer to trust to the conservatism of Nature than to the conservatism of man. We are not at liberty to introduce any artificial sexual barriers into social concerns. The respective fitness of men and women for any kind of work or any kind of privilege can only be ascertained by actual open experiment."[2]

[1] *Sex and Personality* (McGraw-Hill Book Company Inc., 1936), pp. 447–448.
[2] *Man and Woman* (Houghton Mifflin Company, rev. ed., 1929), p. 480. By permission.

SEX RELATIONSHIPS AND THE POSITION OF WOMEN IN PRIMITIVE
SOCIETY

A few points remain to be noted in connection with the social
regulation of sexual behavior in primitive societies.[1] First with
regard to the choice of a mate. The qualities considered typically
"manly" are valued in a husband, these being, very frequently,
prowess in hunting and battle. In women the qualities valued
most frequently are industry and fertility. But compatibility
of character, social considerations, and physical appeal also
determine choice. Youth is usually valued in a wife, and
beauty also, if we remember that the term is strictly relative
and that for many savages beauty is synonymous with plump-
ness. As an extreme instance, Briffault cites the unfortunate
Tuareg girls of good family who, systematically fattened with
rich foods, massaged, and rolled on the sands, in spite of their
tearful entreaties that "they may remain ugly," are, "by this
regimen and complete idleness," forced "towards the age of
eighteen" to become "monstrously beautiful," unable henceforth to rise "without the support of several slaves."[2]

Abnormalities such as this belong, however, to a relatively
high level of cultural development. In most uncivilized societies
women lead active lives and have well-developed muscles. The
relative ease of childbirth among savage women is attributed
to these facts, and also to the fact that infants tend to be
smaller at birth than among civilized women. Nevertheless, the
courage and endurance of primitive women in childbirth must not
be underestimated. There are many reports of their fortitude
in difficult cases. They have little or no assistance, a fact
freeing them from danger of infection, but, in cases of malforma-
tion, or where the position of the foetus makes normal birth
impossible, they have no recourse but to die unaided, after a
labor protracted sometimes for several days. Among the ancient
Mexicans, women who died in giving birth were honored
equally with warriors who fell in battle, or with those whose
hearts had been torn out on the stone altars as a sacrifice to
their bloodthirsty gods.

The actual position of women in any primitive society is the
resultant of many factors. The exigencies of savage life must

[1] Sexual behavior in a large number of savage societies has been studied in detail
by anthropologists. In addition to references already given we may note here Malinowski, *The Sexual Life of Savages in North-Western Melanesia*, 2 vols. (1929); also
J. D. Unwin, *Sex and Culture* (1934).

[2] *The Mothers*, Vol. II, p. 162.

not be forgotten, as is done where, judging from a civilized standpoint, the conclusion is reached that primitive women are oppressed drudges, because of the onerous work they perform. Among the majority of peoples this is not the case: the division of labor is equitable, and maltreatment of women is rare. What is more, regardless of any theories as to their inferiority or impurity, they exercise a considerable degree of influence upon masculine decisions. They have, as a rule, fewer prerogatives than men, and less freedom. Even where matrilineal descent and women's property rights give them a certain social position, they are not necessarily accorded any exceptional rights. Among the Australians, Lowie points out, women's lot is no more dignified in matrilineal tribes than it is in patrilineal. A woman may profit where, with matrilocal residence, she stays with her own people, but her status may still be one of complete subservience.

The correlation of women's status with their economic services has been emphasized by many writers. The intricacy of this problem has already been touched upon. It may have been due to historical accident that women have been excluded from participation in economic development following such advances as the cultivation of cereals, the domestication of animals, and the invention of the plough. Through dissemination, the empirical association of their inferior status with certain types of economy would be preserved and propagated. And it must further be remembered that peoples in contact with each other may adopt only part of a diffused complex. Economic factors, Lowie concludes, have undoubted potency, but "of a strictly limited kind, liable to be offset and even negatived by other determinants."[1]

Where polygyny prevails among savages things seem to go smoothly on the whole. The first wife very frequently asks for other wives to share the work. The women may differ among themselves, but they may also unite against the husband. Where established in individual households, as is usual in Africa, there is less disruption of the typical pattern of sexual relationships than where, as among North American tribes, several wives live together in the same household. Polygyny is not, at this level of society, any sign of a woman's inferiority, nor is it felt to be degrading. The first wife is quite commonly accorded a position of authority; and further distinctions of status may be introduced among the women of a household,

[1] *Primitive Society*, p. 201.

or, indeed, of a community, where they gauge their respective positions in terms of the bride-price: very frequently the number of cows for which they were "purchased." Among the Kaffirs a woman for whom no cows are paid is no better than an outcast. Briffault reports the case of a Christian Kaffir who taunted his wife as follows: "You are no better than a cat. I paid nothing for you!" Here, of course, we are no longer at the simplest levels of social organization. With the development of wealth, ideas derived from the ownership of property have increasing influence on the position of women.

SEX RELATIONSHIPS AND THE POSITION OF WOMEN IN THE ANCIENT CIVILIZATIONS

The Legendary Heroines of Antiquity. There is a striking contrast between the position almost universally accorded to women in heroic legend and their actual status at the beginning of the historic period. Most modern anthropologists have, as we saw, discarded the theory of a matriarchal stage when women held civil and religious rights of which they were later deprived. Nevertheless, feminine prerogatives must, in many cases, have reached a high degree of development. There were many instances of women as queens, and, in the great agricultural civilizations, the worship of fertility and the exaltation of the life-giving feminine principle led to the cult of goddesses and the dedication of innumerable priestesses to serve their shrines.

In prehistoric times women's powers as life-givers were emphasized. The earliest extant drawings of women, made by Stone Age artists, seem designed to promote fertility by magic. Woman is shown as "a faceless lump of fecundity"; often without arms or legs and with grossly exaggerated breasts, thighs, and sexual characteristics.[1] At a far later stage came the organized cults of the great goddesses Cybele, Ishtar, Astarte or Ashtoreth, and Isis. Under many names the feminine principle of life was worshiped, often with sexual rites and sometimes with human sacrifices. Priestesses were still found in the service of goddesses in the classical periods in Greece and Rome, despite the fact that masculine dominance of social institutions had long been an accomplished fact.

[1] Gerald Heard, *The Source of Civilization* (1935), p. 132. Recent discovery of a woman's skeleton in the Cave of Oxen in Palestine indicates that this Stone Age woman "was not much to look at"; barrel-chested, big-jointed, with unusually wide hips, a narrow forehead, a low flat skull, and small brain. Sir Arthur Keith in the *New York Times*, March 18, 1937.

Women in Babylon, Egypt, and Minoan Crete. The code of
Hammurabi, who reigned in the twenty-first century B.C.,
accorded women certain property rights and a more independent
legal position than was typical in most ancient civilizations.
Among a people whose chief interest was commerce and its
regulation by law, women conducted business, in certain cases
disposing of property and carrying on processes of law.   In
marriage, a woman could protect herself against the possibility
of her husband taking a second wife by pecuniary penalties
in the contract. The dowry given her by her father was to
be returned to her in case of divorce, or on the death of her
husband. All this, however, only in the case of the blameless
wife, for, if she proved "uneconomical" or a "goer about . . . ,
one shall throw her in the waters." Her marriage was arranged
by her male relations, so that patriarchal power, though in
some ways curtailed, was still in evidence.

Greek travelers in Egypt were amazed at the freedom of
Egyptian women. Herodotus exclaimed: "They have established laws and customs opposite for the most part to those
of the rest of the world. With them the women go to the market
and traffic, the men stay at home and weave!"[1] Late in the
history of Egypt women are known to have taken part in
commercial life; they could make contracts, and little restraint
was put upon their social intercourse with men. In the marriage
contracts drawn up after the eighth century B.C. it was usual
for a wife's property to remain at her disposal, while she retained
the right of leaving her husband and of keeping her property
together with the bride-gift.

Perhaps this is not so surprising when it is realized that, two
thousand years before this time, family life had reached a
high stage of development in Egypt. The tomb reliefs at
Memphis, dating back to between 3000 B.C. and 2500 B.C.,
form, as Breasted says, "the first graphic revelation of family
life which has survived to us from the ancient world," and
picture "delightfully amiable family relations."[2] The wife
walks or sits by her husband's side; "she shares with him all
his life and work, and is his hourly companion. Their children
are ever with them."[2] In the tomb inscriptions dating from
the twenty-seventh century B.C. the following words occur
repeatedly: "I was one beloved of his father, praised of his

[1] Quoted by C. G. Hartley, *The Truth about Women* (1913), p. 81.
[2] *The Dawn of Conscience* (Charles Scribner's Sons, 1933), p. 120. By permission.

mother, whom his brothers and sisters loved."[1] In the maxims of Ptah Hotep at about this time, the husband is advised: "Love thy wife in the house as is fitting. . . . Make her heart glad as long as thou livest."[2] And again, after thirteen centuries, the art of the fourteenth century B.C. reveals Iknaton's "charmingly natural and unrestrained relations with his family."[3] One statuette "not only shows the king seated with his little daughter on his knee, but depicts the Pharaoh in the very act of kissing the little girl."[3]

Judging from the art of Minoan Crete, dating from about this same period, women there too mixed freely in the life of the day. Interestingly enough, the elaborate clothing of the women is often constricted at the waist with the effect of accentuating the allurement of feminine characteristics.[4] By the seventh century B.C. the Cretan family was definitely patriarchal, as is shown by the laws inscribed on the walls of the temple at Gortyna; but women were still accorded legal rights far superior to those possessed by them in the classical Grecian period.

The Domestication of Women in the Patriarchal Family. In all the ancient civilizations men finally attained supreme control in politics and religion. Excluded from participation in public affairs, and relegated to the secluded life of the household dominated by its patriarchal head, woman became *domesticated*. Müller-Lyer summarizes her situation as follows: "In order to be more easily dominated, she had to be inexperienced and ignorant, chaste, obedient, submissive and timid, her life had to merge entirely with man's life; in a word she had to possess the so-called 'feminine' characteristics if she would please him." But "Since all who are menial degenerate, woman took on still other (secondary) characteristics which embittered man's dominion. As he had the power, she became sly, scheming, lying; since all larger activities were denied her, she became petty, querulous, garrulous and tearful; since she was not an equal associate for man, a deep mental abyss separated those bound together in perpetual monogamy."[5] The term *monandry* would appear to fit the actual situation better than *monogamy*. In the patriarchal family in ancient times very rarely was monogamy

---

[1] *Ibid.*, p. 117. [2] *Ibid.*, p. 133. [3] *Ibid.*, p. 295.
[4] Probably the first known instance of this deforming custom which has recurred so often, despite the criticism of physicians as early as Hippocrates and Galen, who pointed out its deleterious effects on the maternal function.
[5] *The Evolution of Modern Marriage* (Alfred A. Knopf, Inc., 1930), p. 73. By permission.

more than nominal, even where it was the only legal form of marriage; it was almost always supplemented by concubinage and prostitution. Most Eastern civilizations were legally polygynous.

Characteristic of this patriarchal pattern is the view that the husband possesses "marital rights," and that it is the wife's duty to submit.[1] All virtuous women, moreover, must conform to exactly the same pattern of behavior, a fact explicitly stated in first-century Rome in a panegyric on Murdia: Women's gravestones must be alike, "because their virtues admit of no heterogeneity and it is enough that all have shown themselves worthy of the same good report."[2] The virtues cited are "modesty, rectitude, chastity, obedience, household work, carefulness, and loyalty." Very obviously the patriarchal pattern of the family is wholly man-made.

Women in India. Patriarchal power was fully developed in India. Women were in perpetual tutelage: "Day and night women must be kept in dependence by the males of their families," decrees a law of Manu.[3] "In childhood, a female must be subject to her father, in youth to her husband, when her lord is dead, to her sons."[4] Woman is "a cause of dishonor," she "is to be shunned." When created, women were allotted "a love of their bed, of their seat, of ornament, impure desire, wrath, dishonesty, malice, and bad conduct."[5] Women must serve their husbands when living and be faithful to them when dead.[6] A husband, on the other hand, can take other wives and supersede his first wife for various failings: in the eighth year if she is barren, in the tenth if her children are all dead, in the eleventh if she has borne only daughters; "but she who is quarrelsome without delay."[7] The husband owned his wife and her children; he could even force her to bear a child by another man, for "men who have no marital property in women, but sow their seed in the soil of others, benefit the

---

[1] In contrast to this attitude, still widely prevalent, Malinowski reports that in the matrilineal society of the Trobriand Islands, the husband believes himself "indebted to his wife for sexual services, that he has to deserve them and pay for them." His chief way of doing this is "by performing services for her children and showing affection to them." *Sex and Repression in Savage Society,* p. 30.

[2] Quoted by L. Hobhouse, *Morals in Evolution* (rev. ed., 1915), p. 212.

[3] *Manu,* IX, 2, quoted by Hobhouse, *op. cit.,* p. 190.

[4] *Manu,* V, 147, 148, quoted by *ibid.,* p. 192.

[5] *Manu,* IX, 17, quoted by *ibid.,* p. 190.

[6] There are still several hundred cases of *suttee* every year in India despite the most vigilant precautions of the government. The term is derived from the Sanskrit *sati,* meaning a faithful wife, and denotes the burning alive of a widow on her husband's funeral pyre. For an account of a recent case see *New York Times,* Oct. 10, 1936.

[7] *Manu,* IX, 80–82, quoted by *ibid.,* p. 191.

owner of the woman."[1]   Unauthorized adultery on her part would, on the other hand, be barbarously punished.[2]

Occasionally a wholly different attitude towards women is embodied in the laws of Manu; for example: "The father [is] a hundred times more honorable than the teacher, but the mother a thousand times more than the father."[3]   In actual practice, the mother has been reverenced; and the influence of Indian women within the household is often very great, the dominance of mothers over their sons being regarded, by a recent writer, as leading to continued subservience to custom and a theoretical regard for women, in compensation for which the actual woman tends to be degraded.[4]   In the long history of Indian marriage, a combination of causes have produced a joint-family in which mother-dominance, the immolation of widows, purdah, and child marriage have been outstanding features.   Even sympathetic interpreters of Indian life are obliged to admit that the horrible picture presented by Mayo in *Mother India* depicts actual conditions, yet they insist that the perspective is false, facts being torn from their context in Indian family life.   Hauswirth points out, moreover, that it ignores the changes which are revolutionizing modern India.

The Position of Women in China and Japan.   The position of women in China was profoundly affected by the influence of Indian asceticism.   The widow and divorced woman were no longer permitted to remarry.   Paradoxically enough, this led to a sentiment against divorce, despite the fact that the classics laid down seven conditions for divorcing a wife, among them jealousy, failure to bear sons, and talking too much. But there were also three conditions under which she could not be divorced, one of which was if she had no home to return to.   Adultery became the only justifiable cause for divorce; and husbands could not otherwise rid themselves of wives, who, in consequence, often became the despots in the family.[5] Despite the actual power of the older women, the lives of

---

[1] *Manu*, IX, 51, quoted by *ibid.*, p. 193.

[2] If she be of high rank, it is decreed, "the king shall have her devoured by dogs in a very frequented public place" and "the king shall condemn her accomplice to be burnt on a bed of red hot iron." VIII, 371, quoted by de Pomerai, *Marriage*, p. 143.

[3] *Manu*, II, 145, quoted by Hobhouse, *op. cit.*, p. 190.

[4] Frieda Hauswirth, *Purdah: The Status of Indian Women* (1932). Of Swiss extraction, the author, Mrs. Das, married a Hindu. Purdah denotes the rigid seclusion of high-caste women in special quarters in the household.

[5] Hu Shih, *The Chinese Renaissance* (1934), pp. 102–110.

women have been completely controlled by the old family system. Only to-day indeed is this system being undermined.[1] Great families still endure in much the same form as they have for a thousand years or more.[2] Betrothals between mere children are legally binding, the subsequent marriage being a contract between families involving considerations of ancestors, descendants, and property. The sons remain at home to perpetuate their own family, while daughters go forth to "complete" a family other than their own.

Every daughter is entitled to maintenance in her home until a marriage has been arranged for her. She has a right to demand marriage. A man marries a first wife with much ceremony; but he may also introduce into the household as many lesser wives as he can support. These wives and also concubines have a recognized status, and their sons share the family inheritance. It is only when her husband is father to a child that his relationships with other women concern his wife; she must then accept the child as a member of the household. Adultery is a wholly feminine vice for only in the wife is it a breach of family-building. The punishment is decreed to be death by strangulation, which must be deferred if the wife is pregnant.

The subjection of women to men has been even more rigorous in Japan, and even to-day girls are taught to bow and crawl before men and to use a special language of self-abnegation. Obedience, submissive sweetness, unselfishness, sacrifice, and endurance are required of women. While marriage is legally monogamous, in reality there are often many concubines in the house; the young women in waiting being divided into the "Honorable Pure" and the "Honorable Impure" who "were honorably touched by the lord."[3]

Despite these facts, in both China and Japan there have not been wanting women famous in literature. One leading Chinese poetess of the ninth century, Yü Hsuan-chi, repudiated submission as the aim of feminine education, actually sued her husband for divorce when he discarded her, and traveled about the country with a fellow poet. Unfortunately, she was

[1] The younger generation are now taking advantage of the new "Law of Family Relations and Succession" of December, 1930. The earliest move towards the recognition of the economic, social, and legal equality of women was made by the First National Congress of the Kuomintang party in 1924. Details of the law are given by Hallett Abend in the New York Times, July 26, 1931.

[2] An illuminating picture of such a family is given by Nora Waln in The House of Exile (1933).

[3] See Baroness Shidzue Ishimoto, Facing Two Ways (1935); a fascinating account of her life and of the newly awakened feminist movement in Japan.

unjustly accused of murder and executed before she was thirty.[1]
The Tale of Genji is now famous everywhere. In it Lady Mura-
saki analyses the emotions of the accomplished ladies and
gentlemen of the Japanese court in the eleventh century,
ceaselessly engaged, as they were, in romantic amours.

In both China and Japan the inevitable corollary of the
segregated and often ignorant and uninteresting wife has
been the development of a numerous class of courtesans. In
both countries girls are still obtained in very early childhood
and are given long and careful training. In the highest ranks
are those distinguished for beauty, charms, and talents. They
sing, dance, play musical instruments, and provide educated men
with feminine companionship.

SEX RELATIONSHIPS AND THE POSITION OF WOMEN IN GREECE AND ROME[2]

The Pattern of Sex Relationships in Sparta. The warlike
Spartans had but one social ideal: military prowess, to which
end the breeding and training of warriors was the necessary
means. Women were the mothers of warriors and, as such,
must be themselves hardy and brave. Accordingly they underwent a course of rigorous physical training. Stripped of all
clothing, they engaged in public exhibitions of gymnastics and
wrestling. At eighteen they married, their husbands visiting
them only at night. All men and boys over seven lived in
military barracks undergoing training of drastic severity. While
it was understood that they must marry for breeding purposes,
there was deliberate encouragement of homosexual attachments;
the boys vying with each other for the favor and approbation
of the young men who were their immediate superiors. Each
such man in his turn endeavored to make the youth "whom he
had taken into his affections . . . as accomplished as possible."[3]

Marriage was nominally monogamous, but the married women
frequently had lovers; any children born of such unions belonged
to the husband. The softer sentiments of motherhood were

---

[1] See the first English translation of her poems by Genevieve Wimsatt, *Selling
Wilted Peonies* (1937).

[2] Sex relationships and the position of women among the Hebrews have been
sufficiently discussed in Chapters IV and V, and are therefore omitted here.

[3] Such attachments, moreover, were not confined to boys and men alone. Plutarch
speaks of the love of the "adopters of favorites" as "so honorable and in so much
esteem, that the virgins too had their lovers amongst the most virtuous matrons."
Life of Lycurgus, quoted by Cubberley, *Readings in the History of Education* (1920),
p. 4.

not allowed to interfere with social purposes. The state decreed
the death of all infants not physically perfect; and a mother's
highest joy was supposed to be found in the sacrifice of her
sons in battle. Daementa, whose eight sons were buried in
one tomb, shed no tears, but shouted, "Victory! Sparta, I
bore them but to die for thee!" Another poem tells of a mother
whose son fled to her from battle, whereupon she "struck him
dead."

The Pattern of Sex Relationships in Athens. The situation was
one of much greater complexity in Athens. While the Athenians
maintained on the whole a naturalistic attitude towards sex,
yet all forms of emotion were regarded as to some extent
interfering with the well-ordered life. Plato speaks of a man
being "thrown off his balance by sickness or love or it may be
by intoxication or some other misfortune."[1] In the *Symposium*
a contrast is drawn unfavorable to those whose love leads to
the begetting of children: far superior are poets and artists
whose souls give birth to beauty.[2]

The pattern of sexual relationships had developed in Athens
in response to social exigencies. Athens being a commercial
city did not exclude strangers; but at the same time required
the perpetuation of the Athenian patriarchal families by means
of pure-bred heirs. Their production was the sole purpose of
legal marriage, which could take place only when both bride
and groom belonged to the families of citizens. Marriages
were arranged into which entered no element of individual
choice. Chaste and docile girls of fifteen, ignorant of all save
a few feminine accomplishments and the rites of religion, were
handed over by their families to husbands more than twice
their age.

After dedicating her dolls and other toys, together with her
maiden girdle, to Artemis or some local goddess, the high-born
bride was given to her husband in an elaborate ceremony, at
the conclusion of which she ate a quince, the symbol of fruitful-
ness, as she was led to the bridal chamber. The middle-aged
husbands, to many of whom a wife was, in Menander's words,
"a necessary evil," probably did not always treat their brides
with the condescending kindness shown by Ischomachus. "She
came to my house," he told Socrates, "when she was not
fifteen years old and had spent the preceding part of her life
under the strictest restraint, in order that she might see as
little, hear as little, and ask as few questions as possible." No

[1] *Republic*, 346.   [2] *Symposium*, 208, 209.

wonder the poor little wife tells him, "Everything rests with you; my duty, my mother told me, was to conduct myself discreetly."[1] Emotionally the wife was supposed to remain a dutiful child, carefully secluded in special apartments where she lived with her daughters, sons under seven, and women slaves. She was also expected, as we have seen, to be the housekeeper, but not to satisfy her husband as a sexual mate, or as a companion.

As Müller-Lyer points out, the traits, which were later to characterize full heterosexual love, made their appearance in Athens, not only in separation from one another, but as caricatures. Loyalty, permanence, and exclusiveness of affection belonged almost entirely to homosexual relationships; while physical passion, if left unsatisfied, found an outlet in relationships with courtesans, concubines, and prostitutes. Among these were the *hetairai*, who as mistresses gave in addition the cultivated feminine companionship, so seldom found by the men in their own households. Nowhere else has such a pattern of sexual relationships been so openly accepted as a social norm, however frequent it may have been in practice. The three distinct types of heterosexual relationships are summarized in Demosthenes' well-known words, "Mistresses we keep for pleasure, concubines for daily attendance upon the person, wives to bear us legitimate heirs and be our faithful housekeepers."[2]

Prostitution was an established institution in Greece by the time of Solon. *Dicteria*, or houses of prostitution, were a state monopoly, and their inmates were forbidden to enter the superior part of the town, or take part in religious services, and were compelled to wear a distinctive dress. They were the only women with whom young men might freely associate; in that typical form of sexual relationship where the woman is socially helpless and regarded as degraded, and the man is free from any responsibility for his sexual mate or for their possible offspring.

In later times the regulation of prostitution was not nearly so rigorous. Forbidden to wear purple or scarlet, prostitutes wore flowered robes and either dyed their hair or wore blond wigs. The presence of the *hetairai* probably contributed to the growth of a more tolerant attitude. These well-educated,

---

[1] From Xenophon's *Economics*, Chapter VII, quoted by Monroe, *Source Book of the History of Education in the Greek and Roman Period*, pp. 37–50.
[2] *Orations*, Bohn Classical Library (1889), Vol. V, p. 272.

beautiful, highly gifted women were usually foreigners and thus excluded from legal marriage with Athenian men. They accordingly became the "companions" of the leading men of Athens. In some cases they and their children entered into more normal family relationships with men. Many of them were noted philosophical disputants, Diotima being acknowledged by Socrates as his teacher, while others were members of the schools of Plato, Aristotle, and Epicurus. Their influence very probably accounted in part for the more liberal views of some of the greatest Greeks.

Aristotle's comments on women are an outstanding example of the still prevalent fallacy of attributing to nature, and so justifying, existing arrangements which are the outcome of social conditions. He complacently accepts the *effects* of women's complete exclusion from education and of their subservience to older husbands, as proving the *natural* superiority of the male, "who is by nature fitter to command than the female. . . . For the slave has no deliberative faculty at all; the woman has, but it is without authority; . . . the temperance of a man and woman, or the courage and justice of a man and of a woman, are not, as Socrates maintained, the same; the courage of the man is in commanding, of a woman in obeying; . . . as the poet says, 'silence is a woman's glory.' "[1] On the other hand, Aristotle states that "between husband and wife friendship seems to exist by nature . . ."; they "live together not only for the sake of reproduction but also for the various purposes of life."[2] He believed it disgraceful for either husband or wife "to be found in any way unfaithful."[3] As a physician he deplored too early marriage, not only because of the likelihood of weak offspring, but because, "in childbirth younger women suffer more, and more of them die."[4]

Aristophanes in some of his plays bore witness to the growing restlessness of Athenian women, although he attacked Aspasia and satirized such feminists as Plato and Euripides. But he was also critical of the cloistered and conservative women who "dip their wool in hot water according to the ancient plan, all of them without exception, and never make the slightest innovation. They sit and cook as of old. They wear out their husbands as of old. They buy sweets as of old."[5] Euripides alone sought to understand women, presenting them in his tragedies as beings having personality, intelligence, and emotions.

[1] *Politics*, 1260a.   [2] *Ethics*, 1162a.   [3] *Politics*, 1136b.   [4] *Ibid.*, 1335a.
[5] Quoted by Mary Beard, *On Understanding Women* (1931), p. 167.

In the *Medea* he actually exposed the injustice of an Athenian man to a barbarian woman and gave eloquent expression to her wrongs.

> "Of all things upon earth that bleed and grow
> A herb most bruised is woman. . . .
>
> Home never taught her that—how best to guide
> Towards peace this thing that sleepeth at her side.
>
> And then, forsooth, 'tis they that face the call
> Of war, while we sit sheltered, hid from all
> Peril. False mocking. Sooner would I stand
> Three times to face their battles, shield in hand,
> Than bear one child."[1]

No more than mention can be made here of Plato's famous suggestion for a community of women and children. His advocacy of the state control of marriage and of a system of eugenic breeding had no influence on the actual life of his day. We may note, however, that he held "the difference between the sexes to consist simply in the parts they respectively bear in the propagation of the species." He therefore contended that, "so far as her nature is concerned, the woman is admissible to all pursuits as well as the man; though in all of them the woman is weaker than the man."[2] Most remarkable of all is the rebuke put into the mouth of Socrates, when Glaucon assumes that the rulers of the republic will be men: "Say leading women too, Glaucon. For do not suppose that my remarks were intended to apply at all more to men than to women, so long as we can find women whose talents are equal to the situation."[3]

The Roman Matron. In early times in Rome the *patria potestas* was held throughout the lifetime of the paterfamilias over all members of his family, even over adult males, who might hold state offices and be married. The wife and her children were legally very nearly in the position of slaves owned by the paterfamilias. The law spoke of her *imbecillitas* (weakness) and transferred her at marriage from the *potestas* of her father to the *manus* of her husband. Yet despite all these facts the position of the Roman matron was one of dignity. As Bryce says: "One can hardly imagine a more absolute subjection to one person of another person who was nevertheless

---

[1] *Medea*, trans. by Gilbert Murray (1915), pp. 15, 16.
[2] *Republic*, 454, 455.   [3] *Ibid.*, 540.

not only free but respected and influential, as we know that the wife in old Rome was."[1] Roman marriage in those days seems to have been a normal institution successfully fulfilling its essential functions. It was far more generally monogamous in actual fact than Greek marriage had ever been, and combined sexual mating and economic coöperation with a partnership of husband and wife in the maintenance of the family honor, in domestic religious observances, and, above all, in the nurture and education of children.

The honorable position of the Roman wife and her relation to her husband were expressed in the ancient marriage formula: *Ubi tu Caius, ego Caia:* where thou art lord, I am lady. Cornelius Nepos, in criticizing the customary treatment of Grecian wives, exclaimed: "What Roman would be ashamed to bring his wife to dinner, or who amongst us does not regard the mother as occupying the first place in the house and in our regard."[2]

The Law of the Twelve Tables allowed a husband to repudiate his wife by means of the following formula: "*Tuas res tibi habebo.*" Later too, Cato the Censor, a defender of ancient institutions, upheld the right of a husband to kill with impunity a wife found in adultery. She, on the other hand, "has no right to so much as lay a finger upon" a husband who committed adultery. The husband, he believed, was judge of the wife and should punish her for her faults, among which the drinking of wine was numbered as serious. Nevertheless, in the earlier period, divorce was a matter of complicated negotiations between the families of husband and wife, and was probably of very rare occurrence.

The Emancipation of Roman Women. While the austere ideals of early Rome undoubtedly survived in many households, the Punic wars had far-reaching results in undermining the stability of the family, and in fostering individualism and the pursuit of pleasure among women as well as men. The Punic wars lasted from 264 to 249 and from 219 to 202 B.C. During all those years, a large proportion of the citizens of Rome had been obliged to leave their households in the charge of their wives. Changes in marriage customs came about, as we saw in the last chapter. By the end of the second century marriage was no longer regarded as a social and religious obligation; many evaded marriage altogether; others who married remained childless. In 131 B.C. the censor Metellus Macedonicus proposed

---

[1] *Studies in History and Jurisprudence* (1901), Vol. II, p. 790.
[2] *Praefatio*, 6, 7, quoted by Briffault, *The Mothers*, Vol. II, p. 349.

that all citizens should be compelled to marry, at the same time declaring, "if we could get along without wives we should all dispense with the nuisance."[1]

Under the circumstances it was natural enough that the Roman men should blame women for the decay of ancient customs and ideals, and that they should seek to restrain the growing wealth and independence of women by legislation. In 215 B.C. the *Lex Oppia* sought to restrict extravagance in dress and adornment, and in 169 B.C. the *Lex Voconia* forbade women to be made heirs to fortunes above a certain sum. Evasion of the latter law was easy by means of trusts or by non-registration of the amount of a fortune. The *Lex Oppia*, on the other hand, was finally repealed in 195 B.C. largely through the concerted efforts of its women opponents. Livy records the speeches of Cato, who opposed repeal, and of Lucius Valerius, who answered Cato. "Our ancestors," said Cato, "thought it not proper that women should direct any, even private business, without a director. We, it seems, suffer them to interfere in the management of state affairs. Will you give the reins to their intractable nature and their uncontrolled passions? This is the smallest of the injunctions laid upon them by usage or the laws, all of which women bear with impatience; they long for liberty, or rather for license. . . . Remember all the laws by which our fathers have bound down the liberty of women, by which they have bent them to the power of men. As soon as they are our equals, they become our superiors." In answer to which Lucius Valerius, pointing to the public services of women in the past, asked: "Why should men grudge them their ornaments and their dress? Women cannot hold public offices, or priesthoods, or gain triumphs; they have no public occupations. What then can they do but devote their time to adornment and dress?"[2]

Fortunately not all Roman women were as destitute of worthwhile occupations as Valerius' words imply. There were many Roman women of exceptional character and talent. Cornelia, the mother, not only of the two famous Gracchi, but of ten other children, was a woman of great social influence and intellectual prominence. Agrippina, the wife of Germanicus, the mother of nine children, assisted her husband in his campaigns and finally, after retaliating against her husband's

---

[1] Livy, *Epistle* 59, quoted by E. J. Putnam, *The Lady* (1910), p. 48.
[2] Quoted by Putnam, *op. cit.*, p. 47; Briffault, *op. cit.*, Vol. I, p. 428; and J. Langdon-Davies, *A Short History of Women* (1927), pp. 178–179.

murderers, starved herself to death. The mothers, wives, sisters, and daughters of the early Caesars were many of them women of outstanding character. Only later do we find among the imperial women those "monsters of iniquity" who did so much to cast discredit on the independent Roman woman of the Empire. Among the Stoics, too, there were many noble women. The Stoics held particularly high ideals of marriage, stressing equality and community of feeling between husband and wife. Towards the end of the first century G. Musonius Rufus advocated the same education for men and women because "they have the same reason" and "their virtues are the same." Moreover, "perhaps all human tasks are open to all and common to men and women." A woman student of philosophy, which "is the pursuit of a noble character," would be bound "to love her children more than life; . . . she should be able to suckle the infants to whom she gave birth, and minister to her husband with her own hands, and fulfil without reluctance tasks which some consider as work only fit for slaves."[1]

It must be admitted, however, that the dark pictures painted by satirists and Christian ascetics, although exaggerated, were not without justification. The evils of easy and frequent divorce, of celibacy and childlessness increased, despite all legislative endeavors, such as the *Lex Julia et Papia Poppæa*, rewarding parents and penalizing celibacy, which was passed by Augustus in 9 A.D., and laws imposing pecuniary penalties on the guilty party in a divorce. Abortion and child exposure were very prevalent, children were neglected, and there were many women who abused the new freedom that was theirs; some, brilliant but unscrupulous, sought power in politics; others, lazy and luxury-loving, turned liberty into license. All forms of sexual license became common. Prostitution had been comparatively rare in the period before the Punic wars. Alone among the ancients, the Romans considered it shameful for a married man of standing to frequent the company of prostitutes. Restrictive measures were now introduced, but in vain. There was registration of prostitutes, who were licensed and taxed and obliged to wear special clothing and a yellow wig, or else to dye their hair. The very word "fornication" is derived from the arched areaways, or *fornices*, running along the sides of public buildings or larger private houses in Rome; a fact recalling Catullus' lament for the mistress he had been forced to discard, Lesbia, who "now in alleys sells herself for the obscene pleasure of the young Roman gentry."

[1] Quoted by Monroe, *op. cit.*, pp. 401 *et seq.*

SEX RELATIONSHIPS AND THE POSITION OF WOMEN IN WESTERN
EUROPE UP TO THE EIGHTEENTH CENTURY

Christianity and the Patriarchal Family in Europe. A contrast
is often drawn between Roman decadence and the virility of
the Teutonic barbarians. The Romans were even forced to
unwilling admiration of the barbarian women, their loyalty
to family and tribe, their warlike spirit and dauntless courage.
Florus tells how, in defeat, the Cimbrian women first strangled
their children and then hung themselves with the sashes which
bound their hair. And Tacitus wrote that the barbarians
"believe that there is in all women some spark of prophecy,
and they do not despise their advice nor neglect their words."[1]
Yet the husband held all but complete control in the family;
for, although the wife retained her membership in her own
great family, she had been given into her husband's power.
In some tribes masculine dominance was symbolized by the
husband treading on his bride's foot.[2] He might further enforce
his authority by blows, and divorce his wife for various causes,
although in cases of extreme cruelty or injustice the wife's
kin might interfere to protect her.

These were the people who came more and more fully under
the influence of the Roman Church and its ascetic standards.
Distrustful of women, the Church discarded the liberal doctrines
of the Roman jurisconsults and adopted the various forms of
guardianship of women current among the barbarians. However,
Maine points out that, in the code of the Middle Ages, "the
principle of Roman jurisprudence is so far triumphant that
unmarried females are generally . . . relieved of the bondage
of the family; but the archaic principle of the barbarians has
fixed the position of married women, and the husband has
drawn to himself in his marital character the powers that once
belonged to the wife's male kindred."[3]

At first, it is true, the Church attempted to enforce a single
standard of morality on husband and wife. St. Augustine had
approved the Stoic maxim: "It would be unjust that a husband
should exact a fidelity he does not himself keep."[4] But this
view had little effect on actual practice. The Church was soon
forced to compromise, prostitution being defended as an outlet
for lust and a safeguard to respectable society. The ascetic

[1] Quoted by Briffault, *op. cit.*, Vol. I, p. 414.
[2] Hence the association of shoes with marriage.
[3] *Ancient Law*, p. 157.
[4] Quoted by Lecky, *History of European Morals*, Vol. II, p. 313.

hatred of sex and bitterness against women were evident in the decision of the Council of Auxerre (578) that women, because of their impurity, might no longer receive the sacrament with naked hands, and in the debate at the Council of Macon (585) as to whether women possessed souls!

Losing all that had been gained in Rome, women once more became the dependents of men in an unsettled and brutal era. From such conditions emerged the pattern of the European patriarchal family, a pattern which, though modified in some of its features, endured for many centuries and is only now beginning to break up. It is adapted to a society for which war is a constant feature, and where the strong who forcibly seize and hold the land become the ruling class of land-owners. The weaker, whether the laboring classes, serfs, or slaves in the state, or the women and children in the family, attained protection only at the cost of dependence, subservience, and exploitation.

Marriage, for the owners of land, was primarily a mode of determining inheritance and, as such, was a matter of arrangement between families, with very rarely any choice on the part of bride or even groom. Freedom of sexual choice on the part of men found an outlet in temporary and irresponsible relationships with unprotected girls of the lower class. The wife, forced into marriage without affection, was doubtless in some cases unfaithful.[1] But the exaggerated possessive jealousy of the husband and the masculine assertion of the inconstancy of women were caused quite as much by the unsatisfying character of the relationship between husband and wife.

The Position of Women in the Middle Ages. With the full development of the feudal system land was held in exchange for military service. Where a knight was killed in battle, his lady was usually given in marriage by his overlord with as little delay as possible, in order that she might have a stout defender of her deceased husband's property. The picture drawn of this situation by Luchaire is truly amazing, depicting as it does the incessant violent disputes over the acquisition of heiresses to lands.[2]

There remained one notable way of escape for women: the religious life, which offered to all freedom from the dominance

---

[1] As we saw in Chapter IV, romantic love was at first entirely extra-marital, a revolt not only against asceticism but against the artificial and cramping bonds of the patriarchal family pattern.

[2] *Social France at the Time of Philip Augustus,* Chapter XI.

of men, and to some the opportunity for power and influence. Many men escaped the stormy life of the period by seeking refuge in monasteries; those who cared for learned pursuits or those younger sons who did not wish to become soldiers of fortune. Both sons and daughters were frequently dedicated by their parents to monasteries or convents. For the undowried daughter, in particular, the convent was the sole recourse, also for daughters brave enough to oppose their fathers' arrangements for their marriages. Finally, many daughters of the nobility were sent temporarily to convents to receive such education as was then given.

The convent, however, was no mere refuge; it offered an outlet for feminine energy and ambition. Eckenstein says of the nun, "provided she agreed to forego the claims of family and sex, an honorable independence was secured to her, and she was brought into contact with the highest aims of the age. . . . Many women devoted themselves to managing settlements which, in the standard they attained, vied in excellence with the settlements managed by men."[1] Women were thus given a chance for a professional career in which some of them, usually of noble birth, held positions of great power as abbesses. As administrators, scholars, and educators, abbesses entered fully into the life of larger affairs. Hilda of Whitby was one notable example, another was Hildegard of Germany.

Eckenstein relates how the nun Hrotswith, famous for her Latin dramas, while holding Terence in admiration was yet forced "to blush by the wicked passion of illicit love . . . and the tempting talk of the amorous."[2] Doubtless large numbers of these "Brides of Christ" piously kept their vows, mindful that "the precious liquor of virginity" was borne in a "frail vessel more brittle than glass," which "is broken by an unchaste thought" and "once broken can never be mended."[3] Evidently the erotic images of religious symbolism were not considered "unchaste thoughts." Nevertheless, the ascetic repression of sex was responsible for widespread evils. The gross superstitions of the age must be remembered; the fact, for instance, that both Christians and those who secretly still practised the rites of older fertility religions believed in the existence of devils.

While the influence of these older faiths on Christianity is shown most clearly in the firm establishment by the thirteenth century of the worship of the Virgin Mary, there is no doubt,

---

[1] *Woman under Monasticism* (1896), p. 478.   [2] *Ibid.*, p. 169.
[3] Langdon-Davies, *op. cit.*, p. 274. Paraphrased from an ancient treatise.

on the other.hand, that witchcraft involved highly licentious practices. Langdon-Davies believes that many women became witches in the Middle Ages because it offered yet another means of escape, despite the grave danger they ran of persecution and death. Pope Innocent VIII actually issued a solemn Bull in 1484 that provided the faithful with a formula protecting them from enforced sexual intercourse with demons, either male *incubi* or female *succubi*. As a modern writer remarks, "the male demons were far more numerous and enterprising than the female demons."[1] Many nuns confessed a devil had visited them, and some actually believed it!

An equally sinister and more sordid indication of the temper of the times was the justification by both church and state of prostitution as a necessary evil. In those days of bitter poverty and oppression of the working classes, Europe was overrun with vagabonds, criminals, and abandoned women. Prostitutes gathered at first in loosely organized companies of "itinerant wives and maidens," but before long public houses of prostitution were once more established, licensed, and regulated, proving profitable investments, not only for city and university, but even for sacerdotal funds.[2] As an example of prevailing regulations, certain German *Frauenhäuser* in the fourteenth century were forbidden to admit married men, the clergy, and Jews, and were ordered closed on Sundays and Saints days! Regulations increased in severity in the fifteenth and sixteenth centuries, partly owing to the moral fervor of the Reformation, but even more to the realization of the connection between promiscuity and the spread of venereal disease. Eventually the clergy and other reformers demanded that there be no recognition of prostitution at all. But all efforts at its total suppression failed, as they do to this day.

The patterns of sex relationships for all classes of society were largely derived from the aristocratic patriarchal family. Among the poor, and in the middle classes, which began to come to power in the later Middle Ages, the father and husband was master and his wife and children were supposed to be meek and obedient. In England, at least, the common people seem to have held a low view of women. In church they heard

[1] Howard W. Haggard, *Devils, Drugs, and Doctors* (1929), p. 287.

[2] In England in the fourteenth century sacerdotal.funds were sometimes invested in brothels whose inmates were refused the rites of the Church during their lifetime and Christian burial at death. The revenues of church authorities were augmented (in Catholic countries) by means of taxes paid by clergy for the privilege of keeping concubines.

praise of celibacy and disparagement of women, while popular literature was full of stories of women's fickleness, deceit, extravagance, and, above all, their total inability to keep a secret or to keep silence. Salzman tells of a thirteenth century preacher who thus addressed "Ye women": "Ye never let your mouths rest from unprofitable babble."

The Influence of the Renaissance. With the gradual amelioration of manners the actual position of women was in many ways improved by the fifteenth and sixteenth centuries. From the Paston Letters, written between 1422 and 1509, we get a vivid picture of everyday life through several generations of a prosperous family living in a Norfolk village. While the men became judges, lawyers, soldiers, and sailors, the women transacted the business of house and estate and, on occasion, played a leading part in village affairs. The discipline and education of the children was largely in their hands, as were arrangements for the marriages of daughters.

The influence of the Renaissance on women was most evident in increased opportunities for education and in added freedom of social intercourse for married women of the upper classes. Gifted women played a notable part in the intellectual and social life of sixteenth-century Italy and France. In *The Book of the Courtier*, Castiglione has one of his characters say, "A little girl ought to learn Latin; it completes her charm." While mental liberation may have been effected, or at least symbolized, by Latin, it was offset by physical imprisonment in the tightest of corsets. A chief reliance of the ladies of this period in their pursuit of charm seems to have been cultivation of the extremes of extravagance and artificiality in dress: dyed hair, costly perfume (to make up for lack of bathing), and, above all, the fashionable tapering waist, secured by means of a billowing farthingale below and a tight constriction of the upper part of the body. "Their ribs were made to overlap each other," said the famous French surgeon Paré. The one thing which remained consistent in ladies' fashions for hundreds of years was the long trailing skirt: a significant fact, considering the filth of the steeets and that through a great part of this period the floors of houses were none too clean.

In England, also, young ladies of the upper class were given remarkable educational opportunities. The classical scholarship of Lady Jane Grey, Mary Queen of Scots, and Elizabeth are familiar. A fascinating account of the education and life of a less known lady is given in the Conway Letters, containing the correspondence of Anne, Countess of Conway, with ℓ notable group of contemporary scholars. She was the pupil of Henry More, the Cambridge Platonist, and was influential in a group which included Boyle, Newton, Hobbes, Leibniz, van Helmont, and Harvey.

Little or no progress was made, however, in freeing women from legal disabilities. Marriage was still largely arranged by parents. Clandestine marriages were, however, very frequent until the passage of the Hardwicke Act in 1753 secured the public regulation of marriage by the State. While there is evidence of affection between many a husband and wife in the fifteenth and sixteenth centuries, yet the attitude of the wife was still supposed to be one of complete subservience. A French writer describes what was expected of her as follows: "To pay honour, reverence and respect to her husband, as to her master and sovereign lord . . . , obedience in all things just and lawful, adapting herself and bending to the habits and disposition of her husband, like the useful mirror which faithfully reflects the face, having no private purpose, love or thought."[1] The husband might enforce obedience by blows; and the law would not intervene except in case of severe bodily injuries. While adultery on the part of husbands was lightly regarded, wives were expected to be strictly chaste and, in Italian court circles, were sometimes put to death for infidelity. It was in Italy, moreover, that jealous husbands compelled their wives to wear padlocked "girdles of chastity" of which the husbands kept the keys.

Married women in England appear to have had more freedom than those on the Continent, although even there the intellectual impulse imparted by the Renaissance soon ceased to have much influence. The Elizabethan period was followed by a decline in women's status. The Puritan emphasized anew the fitness of women's subjection. John Knox, attacking, it is true, the Catholic Marys of England and Scotland, yet dared to issue in the reign of Elizabeth his *First Blast of the Trumpet against the Monstrous Regiment of Women.* Typical of Puritan standards are Milton's lines in *Paradise Lost:* "He for God only, she for God in him." Eve speaking to Adam says:[2]

---

[1] Quoted by Goodsell, *A History of Marriage and the Family*, pp. 278–279. Such a view of a wife's functions is by no means entirely a thing of the past. As Virginia Woolf says, "Women have served all these centuries as looking-glasses possessing the magic and delicious power of reflecting the figure of man at twice its natural size." *A Room of One's Own* (1929), p. 60.

[2] Book IV, lines 299, and 635 to 637. Hillaire Belloc has pointed out that the humiliation suffered by Milton, because of the temporary although prolonged desertion of his first wife, accounted for passages such as these and for the violence of his views.

"My author and disposer, what thou bidds't
Unargued I obey; so God ordains:
God is Thy law, thou mine."

With the Restoration and its reaction against Puritan standards
the women of the upper classes did not escape the prevailing
decline of manners and morals.

The Care of Women in Childbirth. Before concluding this
chapter with a few comments on the American colonial family,
one further topic calls for consideration. Dr. Haggard believes
that "the position of woman is gauged best by the care given
her at the birth of her child."[1] While this statement may need
qualification, it remains true that an understanding of women's
status at any period is incomplete unless something is known
of the social attitude towards childbirth. Not until the sixteenth
century were women as well cared for in Europe as they had
been in antiquity. The ancient Egyptians are known to have
been skillful in providing effective assistance at birth. The
Hebrews seem to have confined their interest to the hygiene
of pregnancy and labor. In Athens the art of midwifery was
subject to legal regulation. With the great Hippocrates, moreover, medicine for the first time was dissociated from religion
and became a science based on observation. In Rome there
was a partial revival of Greek medicine, the last period for
many centuries in which the treatment of illness was free from
the control of superstition. It was in the second century A.D.
that Soranus of Ephesus wrote his work on midwifery and the
diseases of women. He practised obstetrics, a branch of medicine
from which, shortly after, physicians were to be wholly excluded
for fourteen centuries. Soranus reintroduced podalic version,
a practice known to the Egyptians, whereby an unborn child
might be turned into a position making birth less difficult and
dangerous. Not till the sixteenth century was podalic version
revived by Paré. The intervening centuries were the "ages
of faith": of superstition, asceticism, filth, and disease. From an
early age women bore children incessantly, and yet the population was barely maintained, kept down as it was by war,
famine, and pestilence. Infant mortality was very high, and
the lives of countless mothers were sacrificed to ignorance, infection due to lack of cleanliness, and brutal treatment.

Neglect would have been preferable to the actual treatment
often received by mothers in childbirth. The Church taught
that the pains of labor were justly suffered by women as a

[1] *Op. cit.*, p. 3.

penalty for Eve's temptation of Adam and responsibility for the fall of man.[1] The matter of chief importance to the Church was the baptism of the child. Accordingly, in cases where birth was believed to be impossible the mother was further tortured by the use of the intra-uterine baptismal syringe which was supposed to ensure the salvation of the unborn infant's soul.[2] The Church never allowed abortion under any circumstances, but advocated a Caesarian operation to be performed on the living woman where a child could be saved at the expense of the mother.[3] There were, of course, no anesthetics, their use being unknown before the nineteenth century. In actual practice it was more frequent for the unborn infant to be killed and removed piecemeal. Such operations were considered the only justification for masculine assistance at childbirth, and were in the hands of barbers or of men accustomed to the gelding of animals. In 1580 a law was passed forbidding shepherds and herdsmen from attending obstetrical cases! Physicians strictly avoided obstetrics; and no wonder. As late as 1522 Dr. Wertt of Hamburg was burnt at the stake for having attended a case, dressed as a woman. There are records too of midwives who were burnt as witches for showing undue skill in their attempts at easing labor.

Not until 1513 was any book written for the direction of midwives. Its author, Eucharius Roslin, had probably never seen a child born, but his manual is the first indication of a new concern for mother and child. *The Garden of Roses for Pregnant Women: For Midwives* was translated into Latin, French, Dutch, and English, its English translation being *The Byrthe of Mankynde*. Not long after, Paré came to Paris, to rise from a position of barber's assistant and surgical dresser in the Hôtel Dieu to be the foremost surgeon of his day.[4]

---

[1] *Genesis*, III, 16.

[2] In 1280 at the Council of Cologne it was decreed that, if a mother died in labor, her mouth was to be gagged open! This was supposed to prevent the infant's suffocation, while being removed as quickly as possible, for baptism, even if it too could not ultimately survive.

[3] Contrary to the popular story, a Caesarian operation was never performed on living women at the time of Julius Caesar. Haggard says the phrase is probably derived from the fact that in the *Lex Regia* of Numa Pompilius it was decreed that the infant should be removed from every woman who died far advanced in pregnancy, even if the child could not survive. Mother and child might then be buried separately. The *Lex Regia* was later called *Lex Cesare*.

[4] Unutterable conditions prevailed within the Hôtel Dieu and in other hospitals in the sixteenth century. Three to six patients suffering from a variety of contagious diseases would be placed in the same five-foot bed. The dead were not removed for hours.

Better training was given to midwives at the Hôtel Dieu and, not long after, physicians once more began to practice obstetrics. The fashion was set for this change when Louis XIV called in a physician to attend his mistress. It was not until the nineteenth century, however, that great advance was made in the care of childbirth.

Apart from the inevitable risks of childbirth, another grave danger menaced the lives of innocent mothers and children. With grim irony Holbein's woodcut, Death and the Newly Married Lady, calls attention to the prevalence of venereal diseases. More than any other diseases they have been regarded as punishment for sin,—even though this punishment falls most heavily in a vicarious form on women and children. The effective treatment of venereal diseases has thus been obstructed, and their continued prevalence constitutes one of the most crucial problems of public health to-day.

SEX RELATIONSHIPS AND THE POSITION OF WOMEN IN THE AMERICAN COLONIES

With the settlement of America, the European patriarchal family was transplanted and took root in a land free from many of the restrictive conditions of the Old World. Although men took the leadership in subduing hostile forces, women worked side by side with their husbands, sharing all the hardships and dangers of pioneer life. So strong, however, was the patriarchal tradition of the intellectual, social, and legal inferiority of women, that in spite of the services of the hardy pioneer wives, there was little actual change in their subservient position.[1] There were, of course, variations in the form assumed by the patriarchal family in various parts of America, but in each case the European pattern was reproduced as nearly as possible under the new conditions. In the Southern plantations, with their dependence on slave labor, there was actual retrogression to an archaic form of family.

One aspect of the new conditions was of paramount importance to family relationships. The economic limitations of the Old World were escaped in the New. There was unlimited free land for those resourceful and courageous enough to take and hold it. In this enterprise a wife and a numerous family were a desirable asset and a premium was put upon early

[1] "A hyacinth follows not the sun more willingly than she her husband's pleasure," is the approving description of one colonial wife. Quoted by Goodsell, *Problems of the Family* (1936), p. 87.

marriage. So strong, moreover, was the belief in the salutary effect of family life, that "incurridgement" to wedlock was offered by some communities in the shape of home-lots, while many others taxed what colonial Hartford called "the selfish luxury of solitary living." An unmarried woman of twenty-six was regarded as a "superannuated maid," for whom, however, it was still important to preserve "the two great virtues essential to the Virgin-State, . . . Modesty and Obedience." Such "antient maids" were looked on, in Boston and probably elsewhere, as "such a curse as nothing can exceed it, . . . a Dismal Spectacle."[1]

Numerous children were ardently desired, and they were fully believed to be "a heritage of the Lord." Calvin's views on marriage have already been alluded to, and Luther had said, "If a woman becomes weary or at last dead from bearing, that matters not; let her only die from bearing, she is there to do it."[2] Literal acceptance of such attitudes probably accounts for the seeming heartlessness and the self-righteous complacency of colonial husbands confronted by the "slaughter of womanhood in incessant childbearing." Calhoun does not hesitate to say, however, that "colonial wives, dependent on men for the opportunity to live, . . . were the instruments of male gratification" and "the vicarious sacrifice to the peopling of a continent."[3] One writer speaking of his deceased wife, whom he had married at fifteen, says: "She always went through the difficulties of childbearing with a remarkable steadfastness, faith, patience and decency. . . . Indeed she would sometimes say to me that bearing and burying children was hard work and that she had done a great deal of it for one of her age (she had six children, whereof she buried four and died in the twenty-fourth year of her age), yet would say that it was the work she was made for, and what God in His providence had called her to, and she would freely do it all for Him."[4] Cotton Mather has left us a "catalog" of "fruitful vines by the side of the house," among whom he mentions one mother who "had twenty-two children, whereof she buried fourteen sons and

---

[1] Quoted by Goodsell, *A History of Marriage and the Family*, pp. 368–370.

[2] Quoted by Schreiner, *Woman and Labor* (1911), p. 56. Luther, of course, believed that God had ordained woman's subservience to man: "she must bend before him as before a master, whom she shall fear; and to whom she shall be subject and obedient."

[3] Reprinted by permission of the publishers, The Arthur H. Clark Company, from Calhoun's *The Social History of the American Family*, Vol. I, pp. 80, 105.

[4] *Ibid.*, p. 90.

six daughters."[1]   An appalling number of children died in infancy. One Plymouth gravestone reads, "Here lies———— with twenty small children." Even less attention was paid to obstetrics than in Europe. Not till the middle of the eighteenth century is there any record of a male physician practising obstetrics, and even then "modest" women preferred the assistance of a midwife and of women friends. There was one woman physician, Margaret Jones, in Massachusetts Bay Colony, but she was executed for witchcraft.

In many an old New England graveyard there are to be seen groups of graves. The largest headstone in each is that of the father, who passed away in the *"fulness* of his days." There are the graves of two or more wives and of numbers of little children. Beatrice Hale says: "When one counts the many, many tiny headstones with footstones so pathetically near, when one remembers the mother's anguish at these children's birth, and her greater anguish at their death, one can appreciate the full flavour of the good old times."[2]

SUGGESTED READING

Briffault, R., *The Mothers*, 3 vols., 1927, Vol. I, Chs. VIII, X–XII; Vol. II, Ch. XVI.

Calhoun, A. W., *A Social History of the American Family*, 3 vols., 1917– 1919, Vol. I, Chs. III–V, VII, XVI.

Donaldson, J., *Woman: Her Position and Influence in Ancient Greece and Rome and among the Early Christians*, 1907.

Ellis, H., *Man and Woman*, rev. ed., 1929.

Geddes, P., and Thomson, J. A., *The Evolution of Sex*, 1899.

Goodsell, W., *A History of Marriage and the Family*, rev. ed., 1934, Chs. I–IV, VI–IX.

——, *Problems of the Family*, rev. ed., 1936, Chs. I–V.

Groves, E. R., and Brooks, L. M., *Readings in the Family*, 1934, Chs. II–V.

Guttmacher, A. F., *Life in the Making*, 1933.

Haggard, H. W., *Devils, Drugs, and Doctors*, 1929, Chs. I–IV, X, XI.

Hobhouse, L. T., *Morals in Evolution*, rev. ed., 1915, Chs. IV, V.

Howard, G. E., *A History of Matrimonial Institutions*, 3 vols., 1904, Vol. I, Chs. IV, V.

Jennings, H. S., *The Biological Basis of Human Nature*, 1930.

Langdon-Davies, J., *A Short History of Women*, 1927.

Lecky, W. E. H., *History of European Morals*, 2 vols., 4th ed. rev., 1880, Vol. II, Ch. V.

Malinowski, B., *Sex and Repression in Savage Society*, 1927.

[1] *Ibid.*, p. 88.   [2] *What Women Want* (1914), p. 39. Out of print.

Malinowski, B., *The Sexual Life of Savages in North-Western Melanesia*, 2 vols., 1929.

Mead, M., *Sex and Temperament*, 1935.

Parshley, H. M., *The Science of Human Reproduction*, 1933.

Putnam, E., *The Lady*, 1910.

Richmond, W., *An Introduction to Sex Education*, 1934.

Stern, B. J., ed., *The Family Past and Present*, 1938, Chs. I–IV, VI.

Sumner, W. G., and Keller, A. G., *The Science of Society*, 4 vols., 1927, Vol. III, Chs. XLI–LIII.

Terman, L. M., and Miles, C. C., *Sex and Personality*, 1936.

Unwin, J. D., *Sex and Culture*, 1934.

Westermarck, E. A., *The History of Human Marriage*, 3 vols., 5th ed., 1921.

CHAPTER VII

THE FAMILY AND EDUCATION

THE FAMILY AS THE FUNDAMENTAL EDUCATIONAL INSTITUTION

Education and Social Continuity. The central function of the institution of the family is to be found in the nurture of childhood. Its diverse forms have one and all subserved the same purpose; its several functions have, in the last analysis, been means to the same end: the rearing and education of the young. In the two concluding chapters of this historical section, we directly consider the child and the way in which the family has fulfilled through the ages its function of education.

The immature members of a social group are closely associated with certain of its mature members, and, to an increasing extent as the years go by, they participate in group activities. Not only is education implicit in these relationships between the young and their elders, but it is the sole means whereby the social group is enabled to perpetuate its existence. The traditions of the group, their knowledge, skill, and customs are in the possession of the adult members, all of whom must in time die. To ensure social continuity, the renewal of the characteristic cultural life of the group, "there is the necessity that these immature members be not merely physically preserved in adequate numbers, but that they be initiated into the interests, purposes, information, skill and practices of the mature members."[1] "Speaking generally," Dewey says, "education signifies the sum total of processes by means of which a community or social group, whether small or large, transmits its acquired power and aims with a view to securing its own continued existence and growth."[2] "Society exists through a process of transmission" which "occurs by means of communication of habits of doing, thinking and feeling from the older to the younger."[1] The plastic and flexible impulses of the young are molded by these cultural patterns, and the mind of the individual is largely a product of contemporary culture. The springs of human conduct, the origin and continuance of customs, beliefs, and institutions are found by social psychology

[1] John Dewey, *Democracy and Education* (1916), p. 3.
[2] *Cyclopedia of Education* (5 vols., 1910–1913), Vol. I, p. 398, *s.v.* "Education."

164

to be dependent on education. "In directing the activities of the young, society determines its own future in determining that of the young."[1]

The Family as the Focal Agency in the Transmission of Culture. The experiences of the earliest years of life are decisive in the educational process and determine all future development. The social environment of infancy and early childhood, the family, is thus the fundamental educational institution and the basic formative influence in society. It brings to a focus, as it were, the socially acceptable behavior patterns, and, by constantly impressing these on the awakening experience of the young, transforms inborn tendencies into the cultural forces of habit, disposition, and sentiment. The efficacy of family education is assured, because of the peculiarly close bonds uniting the child to his parents. He is wholly dependent, over a protracted period, upon beings whose authority is for him unquestioned. In the very process of learning his *mother*-tongue, the fundamental patterns of mental development are acquired, each word being fraught with the intellectual and emotional meaning given to it by those who surround him. The family thus occupies a strategic and focal position in the transmission of culture.

In simpler societies the family is not only the fundamental educational institution, but is also the chief educative agency. In more complex societies, particularly in societies where culture is transmitted by means of written symbols, the gap between the interests and activities of the immature and the mature becomes so great that the social heritage can be efficiently transmitted only by means of deliberately instituted agencies and specially designated persons. Formal education comes into being; schools, studies, and teachers are its instruments. The education within the family becomes related to and in some degree conditioned by formal education.

Everywhere and in all ages, the final determinant of the treatment of children has been the valuation set by society on childhood. Social attitudes are, in each instance, related to the whole cultural complex, and are the result of many factors; although here again the influences of religious belief and economic conditions and usages have been marked. Social attitudes determine to a large extent how many children will be born, whether, when born, they will be permitted to survive, their treatment, and the education given to them. Such influ-

[1] Dewey, *Democracy and Education*, p. 49.

ences take effect first of all through the family. It is the mother who must make away with an unborn, unwanted child; she or the father must kill or expose it at birth; or, if it is to be reared, must nurture it in the formative years of early childhood. Nevertheless, fortunately for children and for the formation of social sentiments, it has been comparatively seldom that the natural tenderness of parents for their young children— of the mother at least, if not always the father—has not tempered for a few years the influence of social attitudes, however harsh and unfeeling these may be.

THE FAMILY AS THE CHIEF EDUCATIONAL AGENCY IN PRIMITIVE SOCIETY

Infanticide. Among many uncivilized peoples, the parents not only have the right of destroying a new-born infant, but are obliged to do so under certain circumstances. Custom frequently decrees the number of children who shall be permitted to survive. Sometimes, as in Madagascar, infants born on certain days or in certain months are destroyed. Among many peoples the child of an unmarried mother is killed; as are deformed or diseased babies and those about whom there appears something uncanny or unusual. In some parts of Africa a child born with teeth is regarded as unlucky; and very prevalent indeed is the destruction of one or both of a pair of twins. Multiple births are very frequently held to portend bad luck, although occasionally they are treated as good omens. Sometimes the difficulties in the way of rearing more than one child may be the decisive factor leading to the destruction of one twin. In the same way practical and superstitious motives combine when the child of a mother who dies in childbirth is buried alive in her grave. Not only is the infant bereft of a nurse, but the mother's ghost is believed to be restless till reunited with her child.

The hardships of savage life and above all scarcity of food are undoubtedly the chief reasons for infanticide. Where food is very scarce, fewer children can be successfully reared. If an infant is born while an older child is still at the breast, the new-born must be sacrificed. Where there is not enough food to go around, the least wanted are killed, for, as Mead reports of certain tribes in New Guinea, it is a question of "strangulation or starvation." In this case, since girls leave at eight to marry outside the tribe, the natives prefer to rear boys. Hence the practice of strangling new-born girls. Such sex discrimination is of frequent occurrence. Among many peoples, the political or economic value of girls being less than that of boys, female infanticide is the only or more frequent form.

Among so-called more highly civilized peoples, unwanted children are usually abandoned or exposed. Among savage races exposure is not so frequent as actual destruction; strangulation, drowning, a blow, and burial alive are the most frequent methods.[1] Foeticide is extensively practiced, many of the same motives responsible for infanticide being operative in causing attempts at abortion. Fear of disgrace is one prominent motive; as in the case of the pregnancy of unmarried mothers, where this meets with social disapproval.

The Treatment of Surviving Children. Infanticide takes place almost invariably only at birth. If a baby is allowed to live, it usually becomes at once the object of its parents' solicitude and affection. Should this seem paradoxical, it must be remembered that infanticide does not necessarily imply cruelty. Many cases are reported of mothers putting their babies to death to save them from inevitable hardship. Many do so in the belief that the spirits of dead infants will be reborn in more prosperous times. Savage mothers are wont to love their children with intense devotion and will sacrifice their lives in their children's defense. Both parents often show the greatest indulgence to their young children. Among the Hopi Indians, even to-day, young children who die are often buried under the floors of houses, so that their spirits may remain near their mothers. If buried away from the house, a string may be placed with one end in the grave and another near the mother's place in the house, so that the tiny ghost may find its way back to receive comfort.[2]

The infant mortality rate among savage peoples is usually very high; scarcity or unsuitability of food, unwholesome conditions, and disease cause the death of great numbers of babies and children. While the survivors are almost always treated with tenderness in their earliest years, when a little older they may be looked upon as valuable economic assets in the form of additional workers, and may meet with harsher treatment.

[1] Among the Eskimos when food is scarce new-born infants may be put naked in the snow with their mouths stuffed with snow so that no cry may be heard. In Australia the unwanted baby's mouth is filled with sand.

[2] Recent excavations in the thirteenth-century pueblo ruins in Kinishba, near Fort Apache in Arizona, constantly uncovered the skeletons of babies and young children under the floors. *Los Angeles Times*, Sept. 18, 1933.

Some peoples welcome all children. Even the illegitimate child is accepted and soon acquires full social status through adoption by relatives or by the husband of the mother.[1] Among most peoples, however, the illegitimate child, if allowed to survive, is severely handicapped. The harsh attitude towards illegitimate children is shown in extreme form where they are kept alive to be used for sacrifices, to ensure the good-will or assuage the wrath of some deity.

Educational Methods. Prior to puberty, the young are initiated into the life of the social group, and acquire its practices and beliefs, through direct participation in home activities. The little children accompany their mothers as they bring in wood or water, gather nuts, or till the ground. They watch them cook and weave. Later the boys help their fathers make weapons, traps, and nets, and may even go on hunting and fishing expeditions. The girls, on the other hand, share their mothers' work. In addition to such direct apprenticeship in adult tasks, there is the indirect sharing in group life through dramatic play in which children reproduce the activities of their elders. In these ways savage children gradually become proficient in the arts of daily life and at the same time do each thing in the prescribed and customary manner. In learning the ways of acting current in the group, they absorb, at the same time, its ways of feeling and thinking.

Among most savage peoples, however, moral and theoretical education is not entrusted to the family alone. Before the youth is admitted to adult status, the customs and beliefs of his people, with their traditional interpretation, must be indelibly impressed upon him. By means of fasting and ordeals, impressive and awe-inspiring ceremonials, he becomes a full initiate. Initiation rites very commonly take place at puberty, and it is usual for instruction to be given the youth by the elders of the group or by certain leaders such as the medicine men. On account of the prevalent exclusion of women from full participation in the political and religious activities of the group, such ceremonies as may take place in the case of girls are more likely to be limited to their initiation at sexual maturity and preparation for marriage.

The Years of Infancy and Early Childhood. Only very recently

---

[1] Westermarck reports that the Wanyamwesi of Eastern Africa sometimes leave their property to illegitimate rather than legitimate children, on the ground that the former require more assistance than do those of assured social status. *The Origin and Development of the Moral Ideas* (2 vols., 1906–1908), Vol. II, p. 46.

has there been any attempt to study the psychology of primitive children. In *Sex and Repression in Savage Society*, Malinowski gives a detailed account of family relationships in the Trobriand Islands, and of the ways in which character is molded by cultural conditions. Mead's *Coming of Age in Samoa* (1928) and *Growing Up in New Guinea* (1930) give accounts of field studies of children and adolescents in which for the first time the central interest of the investigator has been the social psychology of youth. In all her field studies, whatever the problem she is investigating, Mead seeks its solution through an endeavor to trace the influence of the social environment on individual behavior.[1]

The amazing diversity of cultural patterns and the innumerable differences in detail in the education of primitive children are at once apparent from such objective studies. Even so general an account as that given in the last section is found to admit of exceptions. A few illustrations from the cultures studied by Malinowski and Mead should, however, serve to give a more concrete idea of primitive educational methods.

In the Trobriand Islands the family is patrilocal though matrilineal. The father is the benevolent friend and companion of his children, in spite of the fact that his actual blood-kinship with them is unrecognized.[2] He is not even the sole provider, for the proceeds of his work must go largely to his sisters' families. The mother's brother, on the other hand, contributes to the support of the family and "represents the principle of discipline, authority and executive power within the family."[3]

Mothers are deeply devoted to their babies, nursing them from two to three years. Weaning occurs without shock when the child can run about. During this period the father shares the mother's tasks and is the children's chief nurse. Great indulgence is shown by both parents, and there is scarcely any discipline or moral education. The father is the playmate of early childhood and never a domestic tyrant. There is no

[1] See Margaret Mead, "The Primitive Child," *Handbook of Child Psychology* (2nd ed. rev., 1933), pp. 909–926. In *Sex and Temperament*, a report on the cultural determination of sex differences, she tells how she was able among the Mundugumor to study the differences between twins reared by different women. One of a pair of twins is frequently adopted, on being discarded by its mother, and the foster mother usually shows greater affection than the real mother.

[2] He is called the *tama*, that is "the man married to the mother." The reason given by the Trobriand Islanders for their disapproval of unmarried motherhood is that there would then be "no man to take it [the child] in his arms." Malinowski, *The Sexual Life of Savages*, Vol. I, p. 195.

[3] Malinowski, *Sex and Repression in Savage Society*, p. 11.

inculcation of shame over natural functions, nor reprobation
of infantile sexual play, when it manifests itself at about five
or six.

Mead's account of the early years on the island of Tau in
Samoa differs in details, but also presents a picture of indulged
babyhood. She describes the ceremonies attending birth, there
being no privacy for the Samoan mother. Twenty or thirty
people throng around her, and she must show no sign of pain.
When weaned after two or three years, the baby is handed
over to the care of a little girl of six or seven, who carries it
astride on her hip or the small of her back. It is she who is
responsible for the education of her little charge: the inculcation
of a series of simple avoidances, "enforced by occasional
cuffings and a good deal of exasperated shouting and ineffectual
conversation."[1] The children must be house-broken, must stay
out of the sun, must not tangle the weavers' threads or scatter
the drying cocoanut, and "must keep their scant loin cloths
at least nominally fastened to their persons."[1] Parents do not
exert themselves to discipline younger children, if an older one
can be made responsible and punished for any breach on the
part of her charges. Just as a child is getting unbearably
willful, a younger one is saddled upon it, each child being disciplined and socialized through such a responsibility. The boys
are not exempt from this task, although relieved of it at eight
or nine, much younger than the girls.

Very different is the picture of child life in New Guinea,
where shame, inculcated early in life, is used as a most effective
disciplinary measure. Habits of personal prudery, of responsibility for property, and of physical proficiency are instilled
by the time a child is three.[2]

Later Childhood and Adolescence. In addition to baby-tending,
Samoan girls engage in simple household tasks and are at
the beck and call of their elders. They have no opportunity,
as have the boys, of engaging in organized activities and
learning the more complex practical techniques. This must be
done in adolescence, when, released from baby-tending, they
work on the plantations, go fishing, and learn to weave. The
girl's chief preoccupation at this period is, however, clandestine
sex adventures; marriage with its adult responsibilities being

---

[1] *Coming of Age in Samoa*, pp. 23–24.

[2] Among the cannibal Mundugumor the lot of children is even harder. Infants
are born into a hostile world and must early accustom themselves to lack of affection, prohibitions, and punishments. Only the hardiest survive. Mead, *Sex and
Temperament*, Chapter XI.

postponed as long as possible. There are no special puberty rites for the boys, but they must become proficient in many ways and at about seventeen become members of a society called the "strength of the village."

One particularly interesting aspect of Samoan education is the absence of any desire to protect children from shock, or to keep them in ignorance of the biological facts of life and death. Sexual intercourse, miscarriages, birth, and death hold no mystery to young children. About half the children interviewed by Mead had even witnessed a post-mortem Caesarian, when the partially developed foetus is cut from its dead mother's body in an open grave, for fear that it may become an avenging ghost. Apparently such an experience had no sinister effects. There being strict avoidance of one another by boys and girls after the age of nine or ten, there is no sexual play at this time, although masturbation is almost universal, again seemingly with no bad effects.

In the Trobriand Islands, on the other hand, "playing at marriage" is considered a normal amusement of children between six and seven and adolescence. Groups of girls and boys play freely together, except for the fact of the strict separation of brothers and sisters from the day a little girl dons her grass petticoat for the first time. Here too there is no sharp turning point at puberty. As he passes to manhood, the boy takes a more active part in economic pursuits and tribal concerns. Adolescent boys and girls spend their nights together in special houses, where, provided there is rigid observance of the brother and sister taboo, there is no restraint upon their sexual activities.

Childhood in Samoa, or in the Trobriand Islands, thus presents a picture in marked contrast to that of childhood in the patriarchal family. In other primitive groups, however, paternal authority and sexual repression may be much more fully developed. In the Amphlett Islands, for example, another matrilineal society only thirty miles south of the Trobriand Islands, the treatment accorded children more closely resembles the discipline typical of the patriarchal family.[1]

THE PATRIARCHAL FAMILY AND EDUCATION IN THE ANCIENT CIVILIZATIONS

The Influence of the Patriarchal Family Pattern on Childhood. In the fully developed patriarchal family, supreme authority is vested in the father, and his power meets with little or no

---

[1] Malinowski, *Argonauts of the Western Pacific* (1922), Chapter XI.

social restraint. In earlier days and at simpler social levels the larger kinship group curtails paternal power, and again in later times the state does likewise as in increasing measure to-day. In the intervening stage, however, children are viewed as the inheritors and transmitters of family tradition, prestige, and power, and as the support of their parents in old age. Daughters are frequently regarded as liabilities rather than assets. They leave their families, and their dowries deplete family coffers. Nor is there room for the weak or deformed. Together with unwanted daughters, they are often rejected at birth by the patriarch and doomed to exposure or death. Interpretations of legitimacy vary, as we have seen, in different societies, but in general the patriarch only assumes responsibility for children born to him by his legal wives.

The awe-inspiring authority of the father is impressed on children in their years of helplessness, the years of greatest suggestibility. Even when his physical superiority over his sons wanes, he remains their superior in wisdom. Over his daughters he continues to maintain his physical and mental dominance. At an earlier stage, paternal superiority is often reënforced by a superstitious regard for the father's curse or blessing. As the children grow older, they are still economically dependent, and expected to remain obedient and passively to accept the arrangement of their lives, both in their marriages and occupations. Unrestrained in any way, the patriarch is all too likely to become a domineering despot, even a brutal tyrant. The extravagant filial piety, so often insisted upon, but disguises the hostile relationships thus engendered between children, particularly sons, and their fathers. Parricide is considered the most frightful of crimes. Even in the best of circumstances, the typical sentiment towards the all-powerful father, while it may include reverence, is not unmixed with fear and dislike.

Towards the mother, on the other hand, the children in the typical patriarchal family respond with enduring affection. In Japan it is believed that spirits of dead mothers still guard their children; while the Koran says, "Paradise lies at the feet of the mother."

Childhood in Babylon and Egypt. In Babylon, and still more in Egypt, family life differed, as we have seen, from the typical patriarchal pattern. While in Babylon most cruel punishments were decreed for "the son of a devotee" who repudiates his father and mother, who hates them, or who strikes his father, there is, on the other hand, evidence that girls were more highly regarded than was usual in patriarchal society.[1] Since women might engage in business, be scribes or priestesses, girls were given an education almost equal to that of their brothers. There are records showing that girls, as well as boys, were adopted on occasion. Some little girls of noble birth must have been very highly regarded, judging from the skeleton of the seven-year-old girl found by Woolley in 1930. Not only was she decked with a golden headdress, earrings, and necklaces, but miniature cups and bowls of silver and gold were buried beside her. All authorities agree in believing Egyptian childhood to have been unusually happy. Children of both sexes were welcomed, and Donaldson states that "no civil disadvantage attached to illegitimate children, and the Egyptian papyri of Roman times recognize no social distinction between the legitimate and the illegitimate."[2] Among the names given to little boys were "Beautiful Morning," "Young Wild Lion," "Pretty Kitten," and "I have wanted you," while little girls might be called "Beautiful" or "Sweet." Numbers of delightful toys have survived, showing that Egyptian children played with wooden and clay models of animals: a wooden horse on wheels, lions, crocodiles, a hippopotamus with movable snapping jaws, and a cat with inlaid crystal eyes and movable jaw studded with metal teeth. Egyptian children also kept pet monkeys and gazelles, porcupines and young crocodiles, and sometimes grasshoppers in cages of plaited rushes. Even the upper-class children wore few clothes; in early childhood the boys usually wore only a girdle and a necklace, from which swung a golden charm or tightly rolled talisman of papyrus. The very little girls wore nothing but a necklace. Both boys and girls had their heads shaved save for the tightly plaited "lock of youth" dangling over one ear. Upper-class children were taught table manners and allowed to be present at banquets, although they touched no food till their elders had finished.

Plato comments with approval on the arithmetical games played by Egyptian children.[3] Actual work in arithmetic, however, as well as education in general, seems to have been confined almost wholly to boys. Women might be priestesses, but after 1600 B.C. no woman could become a scribe. The

---

[1] E. C. Parsons, *The Family* (1906), p. 78. A son committing these offences was to have his tongue cut out, or his eyes plucked out, or his fingers cut off.

[2] *Op. cit.*, p. 196.   [3] *Laws*, 819.

average boy at twelve had learnt to read and write and do
some simple figuring.   Only those destined to be scribes or
priests continued their education.   According to the schoolmasters of the "House of Books," "a boy's eyes are in his
back," and a liberal use of the cane was required to impress
the need for learning on their pupils.   Nevertheless the Egyptian
family, in which children were treated with tenderness by
both parents and where the mother was highly honored, was
far removed indeed from the typical patriarchal family.[1]

Childhood among the Hebrews.   Despite the warm welcome
given children among the Hebrews, the provisions of the Mosaic
law with regard to both sons and daughters are framed with
the harshness characteristic of the typical patriarchal family.[2]
Typical too is the power of the father.   He arranged his children's marriages, as when Abraham chose Isaac's wife.[3]   He
might sell his daughter as servant or concubine, although he
might not prostitute her.[4]   He might condemn an incontinent
daughter-in-law to be burnt.[5]   He that "curseth" or "smiteth"
his father or mother "shall surely be put to death."[6]   "The
stubborn and rebellious son, which will not obey the voice
of his father, or the voice of his mother, and when they have
chastened him, will not hearken unto them shall be stoned to
death."[7]   The extreme importance placed on filial duty is
shown by its position in the Ten Commandments, immediately
succeeding the duties to God.

The position of the Jewish mother was one of responsibility
for and authority over her children.   She took an active share
in their education; although boys, at five, came more directly
under the care of the father, who instructed them in Mosaic
law and oversaw their training in a trade.   Not till about the
time of Christ were schools established apart from the education
given at home.   Discipline was probably stern, in keeping with
Solomon's maxims: "Spare the rod and spoil the child," and

[1] The famous passage from the Boulak Papyrus inculcating honor for a mother is
quoted by Hobhouse, *Morals in Evolution*, pp. 186–187.   "Thou shalt never forget
thy mother, or what she has done for thee, that she bore thee, and nurtured thee in
all ways. . . . For she carried thee long beneath her heart as a heavy burden. . . .
Three long years she carried thee on her shoulder and gave thee her breast to thy
mouth.   She nurtured thee, nor knew offence for thy uncleanness.   And when thou
didst enter school, and wast instructed in the writings, daily she stood by the master
with bread and beer from the house."

[2] For example, "a bastard shall not enter into the congregation of the Lord:
even to his tenth generation." *Deuteronomy*, XXIII, 2.

[3] *Genesis*, XXIV, 4.   [4] *Exodus*, XXI, 7 *et seq.;* and *Leviticus*, XIX, 29.
[5] *Genesis*, XXXVIII, 24.   [6] *Exodus*, XXI, 15, 17.   [7] *Deuteronomy*, XXI, 18.

"The rod and reproof bring wisdom."[1] Nevertheless the education in the Jewish family has been of great social value and has been largely responsible for the continuity of Jewish traditions from biblical times to the present day.

Childhood in China. In China we have an outstanding example of the great family where the oldest living male possesses supreme authority as representative of the ancestors. Filial piety is the fundamental duty and, according to Confucius, "In filial piety there is nothing greater than the reverential awe of one's father."[2] Each member of the family has his or her place in a hierarchical order. Not even grown-up sons can act in matrimonial matters independently of the wishes of the family Elder. All, even illegitimate children, have their portion in the family inheritance. Such conditions have prevailed, of course, only among the well-to-do. For untold centuries, China has been densely populated, and it has been the custom among the poor to kill unwanted girl babies at birth and to sell boys and girls into slavery.[3]

The disparagement of girls is justified in one treatise as follows: "That you have not been born a male is owing to your amount of wickedness in a previous state of existence having been very deep and weighty." Discussing the correct training of girls, it decrees: "Their feet must be bound; they must stay at home and must not be allowed to run here and there and play";[4] thus complacently dismissing in a sentence the long-drawn-out torture and misery of countless tiny girls, while the bones of their feet were being slowly crushed together into the deformities euphemistically styled "golden lilies." Girls were to be taught to be docile and obedient, to spin, weave, and do women's work, to attend to sacrifices, to garments, liquors, and sauces. As soon as old enough to speak a girl must learn to respond submissively and low, but a boy always boldly and clearly.[5]

---

[1] *Proverbs*, XVII, 10, XIII, 24, and XXIX, 15.

[2] *Hsiao King*, 9, quoted Westermarck, *op. cit.*, Vol. I, p. 608.

[3] Probably children who are sold are, in some cases, better off than if they had remained to starve in the mud-houses of their parents. Public opinion in consequence still supports this custom as against the laws enacted in 1932 for its suppression. Laws have also been enacted designed to do away with female infanticide. The destruction or abandonment of girl babies in the Eastern civilizations has, however, by no means been limited to the poor. It became a frequent custom in India among the Rajputs, because of the expenses connected with the wedding ceremonies of daughters.

[4] Quoted M. B. Messer, *The Family in the Making* (1928), p. 71.

[5] *Li Ki*, X, 11, 32, 36, Max Müller, *Sacred Books of the East* (50 vols. 1879–1910), Vol. XXXVII, pp. 477–479.

In Japan, too, girls have been trained completely to submerge their own individualities in those of a husband and his family. Even the younger boys used to be discriminated against under the old family system. According to Baroness Ishimoto, in the ruling class, all babies after the heir were coldly received, if at all, for they would consume the limited family income. Younger children were even called "cold rice," for, while the heir would get the freshly cooked rice, they were fed on what was left over.[1]

THE FAMILY AND EDUCATION IN GREECE

Education in Sparta. Education in both Athens and Sparta had as its deliberate aim the development of citizens. In Sparta emphasis fell on military prowess, while in Athens the Homeric ideal of the harmonious development of mind and body remained dominant. Plutarch's life of *Lycurgus* gives an account of Spartan education. In it he tells how the most ancient men examined each child and, "if it was weakly or deformed, they ordered it to be thrown into the place called Apothetœ, which is a deep cavern near the mountain Taygetus; concluding that its life could be no advantage either to itself or to the public."[2] For every boy was destined to be a warrior and every girl the mother of warriors. Even girls, therefore, received the training necessary to the formation of "strong and vigorous bodies."

Contrary to the custom of so many peoples Spartan babies were not swaddled. "Great care and art were also exerted by the nurses; for as they never swathed the infants, their limbs had a freer turn and their countenances a more liberal air; besides they used them to any sort of meat, to have no terrors in the dark, not to be afraid of being alone, and to leave all ill-humour or unmanly crying."[2]

The boys had to leave their mothers at seven and thenceforth lived in barracks with other boys. Here they were hardened by being made to endure cold, hunger, pain, and all manner of hardships with unflinching fortitude. They were taught to steal and if caught were severely flogged for want of dexterity. Aristotle, while praising the Spartans for their great interest

---

[1] Despite such facts attention has often been called to the sympathetic attitude of the Japanese towards children; note, for example, the following epitaph of a little boy:
    "Ah, little hunter of the dragon-fly;
        To what far realms art hunting gone?"
[2] Quoted by Monroe, *Source Book of the History of Education in the Greek and Roman Period*, p. 15. New-born infants were washed with wine in the belief that "sickly and epileptic children sink and die under the experiment, while healthy become more vigorous and hardy."

in education, yet said, "they brutalize their children by laborious exercises which, they think, will make them courageous."[1] Of the boy under twelve, Plutarch said, "his whole education was an exercise in obedience." From twelve on his physical and military training continued till thirty, when he must marry to breed a new generation of warriors.

Education in Athens. In Athens, for the first time, "some expression of individuality is thought compatible with, even desirable for, social stability and welfare."[2] The education of the period preceding the close of the Persian Wars (479 B.C.) was highly successful in preparing for citizenship at the same time as it secured personal development. The state only granted citizenship to men whose education had continued till twenty.[3] On the other hand, responsibility for education was placed on parents. Only reading, writing, music, and gymnastics were obligatory and many boys did not pursue their studies beyond thirteen or fifteen.[4] But, where education was thus neglected, the laws of Solon freed the son from all obligation for the support of his parent in old age.[5] The state supervised all schools but directly established only the gymnasia for boys from sixteen to eighteen.

The training of boys up till the age of seven and of girls till their marriage was in the hands of the family. At birth the midwife carried the child to the father on whom *alone* rested the responsibility of deciding for or against exposure. Girls must have been thus abandoned, on some hillside or the steps of a temple, far more often than were boys.[6] At the birth of

[1] *Politics*, 1337a and 1338b.

[2] From Monroe, *Textbook in the History of Education* (1905), p. 52. By permission of The Macmillan Company, publishers. And see Monroe, *Source Book*, p. 80, for the account of Athenian educational aims Thucydides put into the mouth of Pericles.

[3] By the time of Aristotle the last period of education was lengthened from two to three years, making twenty-one the age for full citizenship.

[4] The term *music*, in Greek education, included the study of literature and the chanting of poems to the accompaniment of a seven-stringed lyre.

[5] In this connection Ischomachus' words to his wife on the subject of children are significant. "If . . . the gods should ever grant children to be born to us, we shall then consult together . . . how we may bring them up as well as possible; for it will be a common advantage to both of us to find them of the utmost advantage as supporters and maintainers of our old age." Xenophon, *Economics*, quoted by Monroe, *op. cit.*, pp. 39–40.

[6] There is a letter extant to this day in which a Greek writes to his wife, saying, "If it is a male, let it live; if a female, expose it." No wonder women often underwent abortions; in performing which Athenian midwives were proficient. Both Plato and Aristotle calmly sanction abortion and exposure under specified circumstances. Aristotle insists, however, that abortion should not be lawful after sense and life have begun. *Politics*, 1335b; and *Republic*, 461.

a boy an olive wreath was hung on the house-door symbolizing the honors which might be his. A knot of woolen thread, symbolizing her future industry, announced the birth of a girl. The new-born infant, after being bathed in warm water and oil and swaddled in soft woolen bands, had a cluster of little charms hung round his neck and was laid in a wicker cradle. On the fifth day, he was put under the protection of the household gods by being carried round the hearth. On the tenth day, the child was formally recognized and named by the father.

Among the wealthier families babies were almost wholly in charge of nurses, and were very commonly not even suckled by their mothers; slaves or Spartan women being employed as wet-nurses. Discipline was strict and great care was taken in their training according to approved standards.[1] Boys and girls played together in charge of their mother and nurses until the seventh year. They kept pets; dogs, tortoises, and ducks; and sometimes ran holding cockchafers tied to strings. All sorts of clay and lead models were used as playthings. Aristotle's remarks on the rattle as "a toy suited to the infant mind" testify to the high spirits of the little Greeks.[2] In the enclosed courtyards of their homes the boys played ball, blind-man's buff, and tug-of-war, and balanced themselves on inflated wine-skins made slippery with grease. The girls had dolls, and little clay dishes, and played with balls and knuckle bones. The courtyard meant more to them than to their brothers, for, except on the rare occasions when they went abroad in some religious procession, it was their sole escape from the house. They had swings and see-saws on which, according to vase paintings, they amused themselves when no longer little children; and they joined in singing and dancing. No education was considered necessary save instruction in spinning, weaving, embroidery, and sometimes cooking.

The boy, on the other hand, from the time he was seven went forth daily at an early hour to school, accompanied always by a trusted slave, his pedagogue. Only at sixteen were boys freed from supervision of pedagogues and, though still under

---

[1] In the *Protagoras*, 325, Plato comments on the interest shown by all members of the household "in the improvement of the child." "And if he obeys well and good; if not, he is straightened by threats and blows like a piece of warped wood." A brief account of the stages of the Athenian educational system follows.

[2] "Children should have something to do, and the rattle of Archytas which people give to their children, in order to amuse them, and prevent them from breaking anything in the house, was a capital invention, for a young thing cannot be quiet." *Politics*, 1304b.

the guardianship of the father, brought more fully under the supervision of the state. In the public gymnasia they engaged in physical contests and enjoyed free association with their elders, that they might "learn the laws and live after the pattern they furnish."[1] At eighteen the youths passed from the control of their fathers, who presented them as candidates for citizenship. If accepted, a youth solemnly took the Ephebic Oath and was enrolled for two years of severe military training, the successful completion of which entitled him to full citizenship.[2]

The Educational Theories of Plato and Aristotle. As Athens lost its conservative isolation and became more of a cosmopolitan state, the older education was gradually replaced by newer forms looking more to individual achievement than to preparation for citizenship. Far greater emphasis came to be laid on grammar and rhetoric, for skill in discussion was highly prized, opening the way, as it did, to a political career. With the breaking up of the older ideals came a gradual decay in political power till finally, in 146 B.C., Athens became part of the Roman Empire. Though losing her position as a free political entity, her art, science, literature, and philosophy were spread throughout the world. Greek educational ideas and in particular the theories of Plato and Aristotle were destined, in this way, to exercise a determining influence on the educational institutions and ideals of the West.

A brief consideration of these theories is, therefore, apposite at this point, not so much because of their relation to the education of their own period, whether in family or school, but because in the writings of Plato, and, in a lesser degree, in those of Aristotle, we find the earliest expression of certain educational insights of enduring value. Of Plato, Dewey says: "No one could better express than did he the fact that a society is stably organized when each individual is doing that for which he has aptitude by nature in such a way as to be useful to others (or to contribute to the whole to which he belongs); and that it is the business of education to discover these aptitudes and progressively to train them for social use."[3] In developing this point of view Plato "laid down the fundamental principle of a philosophy of education."[4]

[1] Plato, *Protagoras*, 325.

[2] The Ephebic Oath is quoted by Cubberley, *The History of Education* (1920), p. 35. Its most significant sentence is perhaps the following: "I will transmit my fatherland, not only not less, but greater and better, than it was transmitted to me."

[3] *Democracy and Education*, p. 102.   [4] *Ibid.*, p. 361.

Plato and Aristotle both agreed that education must prepare the citizen for the good life, and that education is a life process in which the service of the state is the chief aim, and the control of life by reason man's highest end.[1] Aristotle's remarks on the general problems of education, in his *Ethics*, include a penetrating discussion of the significance of the formation of good habits in childhood and youth. The details of a proposed system of education are given in his *Politics*, only a fragment of which remains. The legislator, Aristotle holds, should be guided by eugenic considerations in his regulation of marriages. His medical experience leads him to advocate exercise for pregnant women, but he adds that "their minds, unlike their bodies, they ought to keep quiet, for the offspring derive their natures from their mothers as the plants do from the Earth."[2] His suggestions owe much to the customary education of Athens; but his admiration for the Spartan view, that education is of paramount concern to the state, led him to say that "education should be one and the same for all; . . . it should be public and not private."[3] However, in contradistinction to Plato, and as against Spartan custom, Aristotle insists on the importance of the family in the nurture of children.[4] Moreover, this public liberal education, advocated by Aristotle, was only for those capable of living the free life of reason. Slaves, artisans, and women were, on the other hand, fitted by *nature* to furnish the means of subsistence in order that the few may lead "the life of leisurely concern with things intrinsically worth while."[5] In thus reflecting in theory the social customs of his day, Aristotle was influential in perpetuating a dualism between liberal education, culture, and knowledge, on the one side, and practical training, utility, and action, on the other, which endures, in modified form, to this day.

Plato held just as strongly as did Aristotle that the only practical activities in which the highest type of human being

---

[1] In the *Republic* Plato lays down the stages of the educational process, which is to select those best fitted to be rulers. For them, fifty years of education, both theoretical and practical, are required.

[2] *Politics*, 1335*b*.   [3] *Ibid.*, 1337*a*.

[4] Plato, in Book V of the *Republic*, suggested that the family with its private interests and individual relationships should be superseded by a larger group, in which all interests were to be shared, and all those of the same generation were to consider those of the next as their children. Matings arranged by the rulers for eugenic reasons were to produce children who were never to know their own parents, but were to be at once put in charge of the educational officers of the state.

[5] Dewey, *op. cit.*, p. 296. The Greek word from which "school" is derived meant leisure.

might worthily engage were war and statecraft. But, according to Plato, the educational process itself was to select and train those capable of the life of reason. All would have an equal chance; the children of laborers, and women as well as men, might prove themselves to have sufficient wisdom to be safely entrusted with power. If once the ideal Republic were to come into being, Plato believed, it should then be preserved unchanged. In the Laws, where he sketched a conservative state which is an approximation to the ideal, he insisted that even children's games should always remain the same; for "the plays of childhood have a great deal to do with the permanence or want of permanence in legislation; . . . to change from anything except the bad, is the most dangerous of all things."[1] Plato very clearly recognized the influence on subsequent health of mind and body of the earliest and most impressionable years of childhood; and, hence, the fundamental importance of these earliest stages of education.[2]

THE FAMILY AND EDUCATION IN ROME

The Early Period of Home Education. For many years in ancient Rome the family was the sole educational institution. Elementary schools furnishing the rudiments of reading, writing, and calculation began to appear in the fifth century B.C., but probably did not become common before the third.[3] Before that time the home gave a most effective education in the virtues and abilities which gave Rome her military and political preëminence. Its purpose was to produce citizens, soldiers, and heads of households, who should be guided in their duties by certain stern and practical moral ideals, the essence of which was unswerving devotion to the service of the state.[4] Beginning with the inculcation of habits of industry and self-control, the boy later learnt through actual participation in the daily life of his father as farmer, soldier, and citizen. His father, the

[1] *Laws*, 797. Curiously enough, Plato suggests here that children should be trained to use both hands, the difference between right- and left-handedness being due, he believed, to habit.

[2] *Republic*, 377, 378; *Laws*, Book VII.

[3] They were known as *ludi*, from *ludus*, meaning a diversion, a play, or sport; indicating that they were concerned with non-essentials, the serious education of Roman youth being of a moral and practical character.

[4] The Roman virtues were: Piety (including obedience to and filial regard for parental control), Modesty, Manliness or Firmness (*constantia*), Courage, Prudence, Honesty, and Earnestness (*gravitas*). Polybius, a Greek who spent much time in Rome in the second century B.C., considered the outstanding characteristic of Romans to be strength and determination of character.

outstanding Romans of the day, and those of old who had left illustrious names, all provided him with impressive examples of the virtues of which his life was to be an embodiment. After 450 B.C., when the Law of the Twelve Tables was formulated, full understanding of its meaning became part of the education of every boy.

The fourth of the Tables dealt with the rights of a Father. Included among these was provision for the immediate destruction of monstrous or deformed children. The father had the right, during the whole life of his sons and daughters, to scourge, imprison, keep at rustic labor in chains, sell, or slay. A father's duties consisted primarily in his responsibility for the education of his children. An illegitimate child had claims on his mother, but none on his father; and no child born more than ten months after the death of his reputed father was to be considered legitimate. While apparently legally permissible, neither exposure nor infanticide was common in Rome until far later.[1]

The family ceremony of *lustratio* took place nine days after the birth of a boy, eight after that of a girl. The baby was lifted from the floor by his father and given the name to be later entered in the public registers. The *bulla*, an amulet of gold or gilded bronze, was hung about the baby's neck, and numerous small trinkets, the *crepundia*, were presented by relatives. Plautus described one set as including a tiny gold sword inscribed with the father's name, a tiny gold axe inscribed with the mother's name, a little silver sickle, two clasped hands, and a miniature pig.

The children spent their time with their parents. According to Tacitus, in the old days, the infant "was reared and cherished in the bosom of its mother, whose highest praise it was to take care of the household affairs and attend to her children." An "elderly female relation of approved conduct" might help in the nurture and discipline of the children.[2] From earliest years children were trained to be frugal, industrious, and obedient. Family life centered in the *atrium*, in which were placed the waxen masks of ancestors, and the shrines of the *Lares*, the guardians of the fields, and of the *Penates*, who watched

---

[1] Lecky refers to an old Roman law which restricted parental rights by requiring a father to bring up all his male children and his oldest female child; and further forbidding the destruction of any well-formed child till the end of the third year, by which time she would be supposed to have a secure hold on her parents' affection. *History of European Morals*, Vol. II, pp. 26, 27.

[2] In his *Dialogue concerning Oratory*, passages from which are quoted by Monroe, *op. cit.*, p. 362.

over the house. All free-born boys and girls wore the purple-bordered *toga praetexta* as acolytes in the service of these deities and of Vesta, the goddess of the hearth. The mother, while she spun and wove, would tell the children stories of their ancestors and of other heroes "in the brave days of old." Her daughters, sharing in her pursuits, would, by the time of their marriage at fourteen or fifteen, have become proficient in their future duties as housewives and mothers.[1] After six or seven, the little boy became his father's constant companion, on the farm or in the Forum.[2] From the father too, before the introduction of *ludi*, he learnt to read, write, and count.[3]

Such was the education of the patrician. For a plebeian it must have been much more limited in scope and probably included preparation for the pursuit of a trade. At sixteen or seventeen the patrician boy solemnly relinquished his *bulla* and the toys of his childhood. As a symbol of his manhood, he donned the *toga virilis*. Domestic and public ceremonies solemnized his accession to the dignities and responsibilities of citizenship.

The Introduction of Greek Schools and Changes in Family Education. Greek educational influences began to make themselves felt in the third century B.C. At first efforts were made to stem the tide of hellenization. But by 92 B.C. the Censors could do no more than express their disapproval of the new schools of rhetoric as "novelties, contrary to the customs and instructions of our ancestors." Before long an almost wholly literary education, conducted largely outside the home, replaced the old practical education in the home. The orator became the ideal of the well-educated man, a conception first fully exemplified and formulated by Cicero, who in 55 B.C. published his work *On Oratory*. Tacitus and Quintilian, who also wrote on oratory, concur with him in defining the perfect orator as a

[1] From Livy's story of Virginia it would appear that girls too attended the *ludi* even at the time of their earliest appearance. She was on her way to school when abducted by order of Appius Claudius.

[2] Monroe points out that "when the Romans came to develop the conception and process of education, they gave to it the term indicative of this process, and *cultura*, culture, came to signify in the intellectual and spiritual life what agriculture, the cultivation of the fields, meant for them in their practical life." *History of Education*, p. 182.

[3] Arithmetic was difficult for Romans because of their system of notation. Yet it became a subject of fundamental importance, at first for household accounts, and later in the pursuit of world-wide commercial interests. Much time came to be given to finger-reckoning (hence the word *digit*) and to calculation by means of an *abacus* or counting board. Horace spoke of a bag of pebbles (*calculi*) for use on the *abacus*, as a necessary part of every school-boy's equipment. Hence the term *calculation*.

good man who, endowed with consummate ability in speaking and with every excellence of mind, makes practical use of his talents.

Discipline was very harsh in the elementary schools, and there was much flogging either with a bundle of rods (*ferula*), "the schoolmaster's sceptre," as Martial called it, or with a thonged scourge. In another of his epigrams Martial apostrophized an "abominable schoolmaster, object abhorred alike by boys and girls. Before the crested cocks have broken silence, you begin to roar out your savage scoldings and blows."[1] The *magister* in an elementary school might be a slave, or a "starveling Greek." In Horace's case he was an ex-trumpeter of the army, Orbilius, upon whom Horace conferred the epithet *plagogus*.

In the homes of many of the wealthy, the earlier simplicity of Roman family life gave way to luxury. Cruel and brutal public spectacles were the fashion. The comparatively few children born to pleasure-seeking parents were subjected from infancy to the most deleterious influences. Tacitus, Quintilian, Plutarch, and Juvenal, all bitterly criticized the unworthy parents of their times. The least worthy slave, even "one that is a drunkard or a glutton, and unfit for any other business," is put in charge of a child.[2] The parents themselves set "the first examples of luxury and licentiousness."[3] "The unfortunate children learn these vices before they know they are vices."[4] They "acquire a confirmed habit of impudence and a total disregard of that reverence they owe both to themselves and others."[5] Juvenal appealed to parents: "The greatest reverence is due the child. If you are contemplating a disgraceful act, despise not your children's tender years, but let your infant son act as a check on your purpose of sinning."[6]

In combating adverse educational influences, Juvenal was thus led to enunciate the fundamental principle of all education, reverence for the child. Plutarch, too, made a plea for the family as the center of education. Mothers, he said, should nurse their own children. Since "childhood is a tender thing and easily wrought into any shape," the utmost care should be taken in the choice of pedagogue and of playfellows, and "it

[1] Epigram 68. Book IX, quoted by Monroe, *Source Book*, p. 399.
[2] Plutarch, *The Training of Children*, quoted by Monroe, *op. cit.*, p. 309.
[3] Tacitus, *Dialogue concerning Oratory*, quoted by Monroe, *op. cit.*, p. 363.
[4] Quintilian, *Institutes of Oratory*, quoted by Monroe, *op. cit.*, p. 461.
[5] Tacitus, *ibid.*, quoted by Monroe, *op. cit.*, p. 363.
[6] *Satire*, XIV, quoted by Monroe, *op. cit.*, pp. 419–420.

is my advice to parents that they make the breeding up of
their children to learning the chiefest of their cares."[1] "Praise
and reproof" should be the incentives to study; "on no account
. . . whipping or any other contumelious punishment."[2] "I
would not have fathers of an over-rigid and harsh temper,
but so mild as to forgive some slips of youth, remembering
that they themselves were once young. . . . The chiefest thing
that fathers are to look to is this, that they themselves become
effectual examples to their children."[3]

It must not be imagined that such ideals were without actual
embodiment in the later Republic and Empire. The first
chapter of the *Meditations* of Marcus Aurelius, the Stoic
Emperor, proves that even in the highest circles the old ideals
of family life and education were still potent. Horace, living
two centuries before, left a memorable tribute to the early
training given him by his farmer-father and to his watchful
supervision of the future poet's education at school.[4] From
Horace too, information can be obtained of some of the children's
amusements; these were to build houses, to yoke mice to a
small cart, to play odd-and-even, and to ride on a hobby-horse.
Games were also played with tops, marbles, balls, and very
commonly with nuts. Many Roman toys still survive: chariots
with wheels, models of gladiators and wild beasts for boys;
dolls and tiny bronze and ivory animals for girls.

Horace and other poets testify to the fact that the Roman
paterfamilias was not always stern.[5] He sometimes gave pet
names to his little ones and brought home treats when he
went to a banquet. Particularly interesting are certain epitaphs
as giving evidence of tenderness and affection for little girls.
"Little sweet Erotion, as Martial called her, was buried at
six, between two older people. In their company he hoped
'her little slender shade' will not be so frightened."[6] In another
he spoke of "Antulla, too soon torn from her parents; here

[1] *The Training of Children*, quoted by Monroe, *op. cit.*, pp. 308, 312.
[2] *Ibid.*, p. 317.
[3] *Ibid.*, p. 324.
[4] *Satires*, Book I, 6, quoted by Monroe, *op. cit.*, p. 397.
[5] There was a marked tendency under the Emperors to restrict the rights formerly
held by the paterfamilias over his children.
[6] D. M. Stuart, *The Girl through the Ages* (1933), p. 67. One is forcibly reminded
of its modern counterpart, the poem by Walter de la Mare, An Epitaph.

> "Here lies, but seven years old, our little maid
> Once of the darkness, oh, so sore afraid.
> Light of the World—remember that small fear
> And when nor moon nor stars do shine—draw near!"

(in this tomb) will each of them be united with her."[1]   There
were Roman children not only in Rome and Italy, but sometimes
in the distant parts of Rome's far-flung empire.   A small sar-
cophagus unearthed at York bears an inscription in imperfect
Latin: "To the sacred shades of Simplicia Florentine, a most
innocent being, who lived for ten months, Felicius Simplex,
of the victorious Sixth Legion, her father, erected this."[2]

THE INFLUENCE OF CHRISTIANITY

The Condemnation of Abortion, Infanticide, and Child Exposure.
Nowhere has the contrast been more tragic between the teaching
of Jesus and the beliefs and practices of his professed followers,
than in Christian attitudes towards childhood.   It is true that,
on occasion, Jesus emphasized man's relationship to God as
of greater importance than the closest earthly tie, thus affording
some basis for an exaggerated concern over individual salvation
even at the expense of family claims.   But the importance of
family claims was not minimized; rather was it exalted, by
one who believed the relation of God to humanity was that
of a loving and tender father to his children.   Jesus' attitude
towards children is consistent and unmistakable.   He affirmed
the supreme value of the unspoiled nature of the child and
demanded such nurture as would make for growth and fulfillment.   In Christian doctrine these teachings were narrowed
into an insistence on the supreme value of the immortal soul
of every human being.   Hence the life of the individual became
sacred, even that of the new-born or unborn babe.

It is not to be denied that such a point of view was in itself
of value, and was destined to have immediate and beneficial
results for child life.   Prior to this time, rarely, if ever, was
the child held to have a right to life, for his or her own sake.
In the days of the Empire, abortion had become very frequent;
and increasing numbers of new-born children were abandoned.
Neither of these practices met with much censure in the pagan
world.   Infanticide, however, had been severely condemned,
and laws had been passed, endeavoring, though vainly, to
restrain it.   The Christian attitude was unequivocal from the
first.   Abortion and infanticide were regarded alike as murder.
The Stoics had held that the soul was inhaled with the infant's
first breath.   Tertullian, on the other hand, insisted that the
foetus had a soul and that it is equally sinful "to take away

[1] *Ibid.*, p. 66.   [2] *Ibid.*, p. 67.

a life when formed, or drive it away when forming."[1] Exposure of the new-born, which, if the infant survived, was the prelude to a life of slavery or prostitution, was also condemned by the Church, and severe penances were imposed on guilty parents. Besides imposing ecclesiastical penalties, the Church made every effort to secure legislation against these evils. The various measures devised for the protection of exposed children met with little success. But infanticide was made a capital offence by the Christian Emperor, Valentinian, in 374 A.D.[2]

The Doctrines of Original Sin and Infant Damnation. In all its efforts to eradicate abortion and infanticide the Church was moved not so much by the fate of the murdered babies, as by the fact that they died in sin, unbaptized: "Every soul, even the soul of the infant," said St. Augustine writing to Jerome, "requires to be delivered from the binding guilt of sin." A special anathema was pronounced against those who interpreted "in my Father's house are many mansions" to mean that in the Kingdom of Heaven there will be a place in which infants may live in happiness, who have gone forth from this life without baptism. In this way the Church extinguished what must have been a last spark of hope for many a bereft mother. There was some difference of opinion, however, as to whether the foetus was liable to damnation. One point of view was expressed by St. Fulgentius in the sixth century: "not only men who are come to the use of reason, but infants, whether they die in their mother's womb, or after they are born, without baptism, . . . are punished with everlasting punishment in eternal fire, because, although they have no actual sin of their own, yet they carry along with them the condemnation of original sin from their first conception and birth."[3] Others were not so harsh; and, according to the finally accepted doctrine, Catholics believe that infants dying unbaptized, and thus in original sin, must suffer privation of the sight of God. The Protestants, however, later revived the doctrine of infant damnation.

[1] *Apologeticus*, 9, quoted by Westermarck, *op. cit.*, Vol. I, p. 416. St. Augustine made the distinction between the formed and unformed embryo. The embryo *informatus* was held to be without a soul, and only a fine need be imposed for its abortion. An embryo *formatus* had a soul, and its abortion was murder, punishable by death. This view influenced the formation of later laws. At one time it was held that a male embryo became animate in forty days, a female only after eighty days!

[2] This does not, of course, mean that it was wholly suppressed. Indeed both infanticide and child exposure were common in the Middle Ages up to the eleventh century: often, it is true, as the result of desperation in times of famine or war.

[3] *De Fide*, 27, quoted by Westermarck, *op. cit.*, I, 416–417.

The same influences which conspired against normal family life explain the almost hostile attitude towards childhood among the early Christians. The time was believed to be short in which the faithful might cleanse their souls from sin. Human nature was intrinsically evil and asceticism alone offered escape. Clement of Alexandria interpreted the infant's first wail as follows: "Why, Oh mother, didst thou bring me forth to this life. . . . Why hast thou brought me into this troubled world?"[1] Tertullian spoke of "the bitter, bitter pleasure of children, . . . burdens which are to us most of all unsuitable as being perilous to faith. . . . No wise man would ever willingly have desired sons."[1] Jerome described motherhood as follows: the tumefaction of the uterus, the care of yelling infants, and fond feelings which death at last cuts short. The earlier Christian writings altogether neglect the subject of education. Later on fathers were admonished to teach their children not only the Scriptures, but also such trades as were suitable in the world. They must not be afraid of severity. Children should be made subject from infancy, being brought under "with cutting stripes." In 403 Jerome wrote to Laeta outlining the education he considered desirable for her daughter Paula.[2] She was to "take as her model some aged virgin of approved faith, character and chastity, apt to instruct her by word and by example." Advocating that she be brought up in a monastery, he concluded, "let her be ignorant of the world; . . . while in the flesh, let her be without the flesh, and let her suppose that all human beings are like herself."

Family life was sometimes, as we saw, disrupted by ascetics who won admiration for their sanctity, even when it meant neglecting or leaving their children. Even when not destroyed, family life must have been profoundly modified by ascetic attitudes.[3]

Where the procreation of legitimate offspring was regarded as a concession to the weakness of the flesh, illegitimate births were naturally regarded with the strongest disapprobation. Sex expression outside marriage was utterly sinful, with the result that the illegitimate child was wont to fare even worse than it would otherwise have done, wherever Christian influences made themselves felt. During the Middle Ages the illegitimate child was regarded as an outlaw and deprived of all rights of

---

[1] Quoted by Donaldson, *op. cit.*, pp. 180–181.
[2] Quoted by Cubberley, *Readings in the History of Education*, pp. 59–63.
[3] See Lecky, *History of European Morals*, Vol. II, pp. 125–136.

inheritance. On the whole, however, the treatment of illegitimate children and their mothers has been less harsh under Catholicism than under Protestant influences.

The Church Control of Education. For many centuries, the lives of all children, in all ranks of society, were largely determined by attitudes formulated under the abnormal conditions within which the early churches developed. The harshness of such attitudes must of course have been tempered in many cases through the natural feelings of parents. For a long time, moreover, the Church was in complete control of all organized efforts at education. The only use for learning in the early Middle Ages was in the service of the Church. It was obliged to educate its priests in order that its government and worship might be maintained; and the monastic orders educated those who expected to take vows. Schools were accordingly attached to cathedrals in cities, or to monasteries and convents. By the tenth century schools of the latter type were divided into inner schools for those preparing to take vows and outer schools for others who might wish to attend. Meager as was the instruction in the inner schools, it was probably even more rudimentary in the outer. Corporal punishment was a prominent feature. Interestingly enough, it was in convents that more extensive education in outer schools was first developed. Reading and writing, music, the copying and illuminating of Latin manuscripts were engaged in, much as in the monasteries, but in addition there was instruction in weaving, spinning, and needlework.

By the time that Alfred the Great effected a temporary peace in 878 after the Danish invasions, churches and monasteries had been burnt and plundered, and so many books had been destroyed and learning was in such decay, that he at once set himself to attempt its revival. He established a palace school for the education of noble children, and translated books from Latin into Anglo-Saxon, to encourage the reading of the English language on the part of all free-born youths. Before this, in 782, Charlemagne had called Alcuin from the cathedral school of York to assist him to organize a palace school and to institute reforms designed to improve the education of the clergy.[1] New types of schools began to develop as society

---

[1] An example of the catechetical instruction prepared by Alcuin for Charlemagne's sixteen-year-old son survives in a list of questions with their appropriate answers: For example, "What is man? The slave of death, a transient traveller, a host in his dwelling. . . . What is the body? The domicile of the Soul." Quoted by Cubberley, *op. cit.*, p. 88.

became more settled; all, however, under Church control. Finally gild schools were established by gild members for the education of their children. While taught by clergy, they were freer than any other type from ecclesiastical control. In time the gild schools and some of the parish schools became, in many communities, burgher schools, largely supported and controlled by the secular authorities.

But in all the centuries from the fall of Rome to the opening of the thirteenth century, school instruction was wholly dominated by the Church. Under the weight of its absolute authority education, in the sense of stimulation of inquiry and investigation ceased to exist. Instruction was designed primarily to fit for the service of the Church and the life of the world to come. It was imparted only to the few, the future members of clerical orders and a number of the nobly born. The mass of peasant-workers remained wholly uneducated.

SUGGESTED READING

Cubberley, E. P., *The History of Education*, 1920, Chs. I–V.

——, *Readings in the History of Education*, 1920, Chs. I–V.

Goodsell, W., *A History of Marriage and the Family*, rev. ed., 1934, Chs. I–V.

Malinowski, B., *Sex and Repression in Savage Society*, 1927.

Mead, M., *Coming of Age in Samoa*, 1928.

——, *Growing up in New Guinea*, 1930.

Monroe, P., *A Text Book in the History of Education*, 1905, Chs. I–IV.

——, *Source Book of the History of Education for the Greek and Roman Period*, 1901.

Parsons, E. C., *The Family*, 1906, Lectures II–V.

Stoddard, L., *The Story of Youth*, 1928.

Stuart, D., *The Boy through the Ages*, 1926.

——, *The Girl through the Ages*, 1933.

Westermarck, E. A., *The Origin and Development of the Moral Ideas*, 2 vols., 2nd ed., 1912, Vol. I, Chs. XVII, XXV.

CHAPTER VIII

THE FAMILY AND EDUCATION (*Continued*)

THE FAMILY AND EDUCATION IN WESTERN EUROPE UP TO THE EIGHTEENTH CENTURY

Aspects of Child Life in the Middle Ages. Only gradually did barbarian customs yield to the influence of the Church. The Teutonic father had the power to reject a child and so doom it to exposure, provided the child had not tasted food.[1] Save for limitations set by the kin on the father's power to kill or sell his children, his authority over them, in childhood, was absolute. But the Teuton boy was freed from paternal authority as soon as he was able to bear arms, even though only twelve or fifteen years old. Partial freedom was gained among the Anglo-Saxons, by both sons and daughters, at the age of twelve.

Harsh as the conditions were in pre-Christian days, children were probably better off then than in the centuries of disorder which were to follow.[2] Above all, for the children of the conquered peoples, who were to become the poor working classes, life was insecure and full of misery. War, waged with barbaric cruelty, frequent famine, and the unchecked ravages of pestilence took their heaviest toll among infants and little children. Luchaire draws a terrible picture of the intolerable hardships suffered by the poor in the twelfth and thirteenth centuries in France. Superstition, he says, became the characteristic trait of the Middle Ages, nourished by the prevailing atmosphere of misfortune and fright. Thus was made possible the Children's Crusade of 1212, as a result of which thousands of children never saw their homes again; many were sold into slavery and many more perished.

The death-rate among children was very high, even in noble families where they were well-fed and protected. For example,

---

[1] If the child's lips had been touched by milk or honey, he became a member of both his father's and mother's kin and was entitled to their protection. Exposed children were frequently adopted, an eventuality possibly foreseen among the Norsemen, where the herdsman, whose task it was to abandon the new-born babe in the forest, would leave with it a piece of salt pork to suck!

[2] The barbarians were trained to endurance from birth. Aristotle relates that, in his day, the new-born infants were plunged into cold streams to harden them. *Politics*, 1336a.

seven of the children of Edward I of England died at an early age. The drastic remedies prescribed for children when ill may, in many cases, have hastened death. Baths were infrequent events. It was generally considered excessive that Edward's children should receive four a year, and some of the clergy advocated bathing only on the advice of a physician. Through many centuries, a baby was invariably swaddled at birth. In order to shape the head and straighten the limbs, head and body were swathed in tight bandages which were usually not removed more than once a day.[1] On their release from swaddling clothes children were clad in stiff and often splendid garments, almost exactly like those worn by their elders, and were allowed to eat the rich and highly spiced food common at that time. Such well-born children as survived became, in many cases, what Luchaire calls "only the figures on a chess-board"; marriages being arranged between mere boys and girls, as part of the policy of the holders of landed estates.

Children of all classes were treated with the utmost severity both at home and at school. Flogging was considered a necessary accompaniment of learning, as one "sory ladde" found, who sadly complained that "the byrchen twigges ben so sharpe." A twelfth-century writer said, "When the child is most loved of the father, it seemeth he loveth him not, for he beateth and grieveth him oft lest he draw to evil manners and faults." Yet children "lead their lives without thought and care, and dread no perils more than beating with the rod."[2] There are, indeed, many tales of pranks and escapades on the part of mediaeval boys, and many pictures and accounts of the merry games they played, such as whipping tops, ninepins, battledore and shuttlecock, and "hoodman's blind."[3] The girls too had their share of fun and mischief, and we find churchmen complaining of their frivolity and urging a stricter maternal discipline.

The Influence of Chivalry on Education. The development of chivalry not only modified attitudes towards women and towards

[1] One cannot help speculating on the psychological result of such treatment, which, indeed, is still customary in some parts of the world. Since restraint very early arouses aggressive patterns of response, it seems possible that such repression may not only have facilitated "breaking the will" of young children, but have led to a more sinister warping of character.

[2] Salzman, *English Life in the Middle Ages*, p. 135.

[3] In his rhymed Testament, the fourteenth-century writer, John Lydgate, tells how, as a youth, he was "lik a young colt that ran withoute brydel," and how, though afraid of the rod, he played truant, preferring to steal apples and grapes above saying matins, and counting cherry stones above "gon to chirche." F. J. Furnivall (editor) *The Babees Book* (1868), pp. xliii—xliv.

sex, but provided a definite system of training in the pursuits of secular life in the feudal period; a form of education which, beginning at the end of the ninth century, endured through the Crusades and had passed out of existence by the sixteenth century. However superficial their action, knightly ideals were influential in effecting an amelioration of manners. The very word "courtesy" refers to the code of manners prevailing in the court or household of the lord and lady. Lesser knights sent sons and daughters to the households of their feudal superiors or of eminent churchmen to be educated. The children of the greater nobles were sent to the King's court. From seven to fourteen, the boy, as a page, performed many humble tasks, waiting on table, serving the ladies, putting his lord's bed-chamber to rights, and, last thing at night, he must remember "to dryve out dogge or catte, or els geve hem a clout." Not only did he learn to serve and obey, but was trained by the ladies in etiquette, religion, music, chess and other games, and by the men in wrestling, riding, swimming, and the use of weapons. In the later centuries of chivalry he might learn to read and write and was sometimes taught Latin. At fourteen he became a squire and personal bodyguard of the lord, caring for his horse and weapons and attending him in battle. Only when his prowess had been thoroughly tested might he achieve knighthood. Girls were attached as bower maidens to the lady, and, besides sharing in the instruction given to the pages, learnt to embroider and to make tapestry. They must also have learnt how to ride, for falconry was a favorite pursuit; and, on occasion, they hunted the stag.

The gradual refinement of manners among the nobility was influential in setting standards for the increasingly powerful and prosperous burgher class. Small books of etiquette became common.[1] The greatest stress was laid on table manners; although in one German manual many aspects of polite conduct are considered, and boys are told not to start trouble, when sleeping with a brother, by pulling off the bed-clothes. The advice given in the English manuals indicates that manners there left even more to be desired than on the Continent. The following are some of the less startling instructions for correct deportment at table: Do not "claw . . . youre hed

---

[1] A remarkable collection of those popular in fifteenth-century England was made by Furnivall and published by the Early English Text Society, in one volume, in 1868, under the title of *The Babees Book*. Included among the contents are *The Lytylle Childrenes Lytel Boke*, *Stans Puer ad Mensam*, and *Lerne or be Lewde*.

ne bak . . . a fleigh as thaughe ye sought"; "suppe not lowde of thy Pottage . . . as a Pigge eating draffe"; nor "spytte you over the table boorde"; "pick not thy teeth with thy knyfe, nor with thy fyngers ende, but take a stick or some cleane thyng, then doe you not offende."[1]

Included in Furnivall's collection, are the verses, "How the Good Wife taught her daughters," of particular interest since they concern girls and give a picture of middle-class manners. No offer of marriage was to be despised; and daughters were admonished to speak meekly to their husbands, to begin collecting goods for their girls' marriages from the day of their birth, and not to curse their children when they misbehaved, but to "bete" with a "smert rodde." They are further advised not to be too often drunk or "it falle thee to schame." The Paston letters give further evidence of the harsh treatment of daughters. Because Elizabeth Paston, at the age of twenty, refused to marry a wealthy but deformed man of fifty, a letter tells how "She hath since Easter . . . been beaten once in the week or twice; and sometimes twice on a day, and her head broke in two or three places."[2] In a letter written by Agnes Paston, the mother who thus chastised Elizabeth, she prays a London Schoolmaster that he "will truly belash" her fifteen-year-old son, if he "hath not done well, nor will not amend."

The Revival of Learning. Not until the middle of the fifteenth century did the revival of learning spread beyond Italy, when scholars, who had gone from other countries to Italy, brought back with them an enthusiasm for the new humanism. A new type of education developed for middle- and upper-class youth, one designed to fit them not only for the service of the Church, but for leadership in the state and in commerce.[3] Guarino, describing the new learning in 1459, spoke of *Humanitas*, as embracing "the pursuits, the activities, proper to mankind."[4] All too soon, however, the study of classical literature became not so much a means to this end as an end in itself, and the narrow form of humanistic education came into being which was to dominate secondary schools for over three centuries.

[1] Quoted by Furnivall, *op. cit.*, pp. 134, 76–78.

[2] *Ibid.*, p. vii.

[3] As Sir Thomas Elyot puts it in *The Boke named the Governour* (1531), "a trained governing class must henceforth take the place of the privileged caste and the clerk education under the mediaeval disciplines." Quoted by Cubberley, *History of Education*, p. 275. This was the first work on education written in English.

[4] Quoted by Monroe, *History of Education*, p. 370.

In Germany and England, moreover, humanistic education was influenced from the first by being associated with religious reform. No northern school provided for all-round development as did the court school at Mantua, where from 1423 to 1446, Vittorino da Feltre gave the ideal of liberal education its first modern embodiment. In the Pleasant House, in meadows beside a river, boys and girls led an active self-governing life, in which physical training through sports, and the cultivation of aesthetic appreciation supplemented studies based on natural interests and activities. Typical of German classical schools, on the other hand, was Sturm's *gymnasium*, where physical training was omitted and the curriculum consisted of ten years of drill in idiomatic Latin and Greek. Marked liberal tendencies were nevertheless evident among the leaders of the educational reform in the North. Wimpfeling based all his work on the principle that "the better education of the young is the foundation of all true reform, ecclesiastical, national, and domestic."[1] Erasmus' book, *On the First Liberal Education of Children* (1529), recommended personal care and direction of the child's studies and stressed the importance of play and exercise. He emphasized the function of the mother and advocated the free dissemination of knowledge to women as well as men.[2] Roger Ascham, in his treatise, *The Scholemaster* (1571), denounced the inordinate use of corporal punishment, saying, "boys are bet from learning by lewde scholemasters." He complained that parents took more care in the selection of a "cunnynge man for their horse than a cunnynge man for their children." As a result they possess "a tame and well-ordered horse, but wilde and importunate Children."[3]

Aspects of Child Life and Education during the Renaissance and Reformation. The Reformation in England resulted in the abolition of the old system of religious charity and almsgiving. As a result the problem of poor-relief became acute. The sixteenth century saw the development of relief legislation culminating in the Poor Law of 1601, in which the care of the poor was recognized as an obligation of the state. All poor

[1] Quoted by *ibid.*, p. 363.

[2] Although girls did not attend secondary schools, the new learning gave an impetus to their education at the hands of private tutors and governesses. The first Renaissance treatise on the education of girls was written for Mary, later called Bloody, by her Spanish tutor Vives, in 1523. While recommending the study of Latin and Greek, he advocated a simple and severe regimen and would have girls learn to handle wool and flax and not despise the work of the kitchen.

[3] Quoted by Furnivall, *op. cit.*, p. viii.

children were apprenticed to learn a useful trade, and the funds for these purposes were to be provided by the taxation of persons with property. Here, Cubberley says, "we have the germ, among English-speaking peoples, of the idea of the general taxation of all persons by the State to provide schools for the children of the State."[1] In England, however, no system of elementary schools was developed till the latter half of the nineteenth century.

On the Continent, as early as 1350, there had come into existence in commercial centers a large number of elementary vernacular schools, where reading, writing, business arithmetic, and accounting were taught to girls, as well as boys, and often to older people besides. Such schools were for the common folk, but did not spread beyond the cities, until, with the printing of the Bible in the common tongue and the insistence of the Protestant reformers on study of the Scriptures, an entirely new emphasis was put on reading. In Catholic countries a revival of educational zeal, to offset the Protestant movement, resulted in the elementary and religious instruction of the poor in parish schools, or by the members of teaching orders.

The rate of infant mortality was still very high, as, indeed, it continued to be till recent times.[2] Toleration of filthy and insanitary conditions seems to have been even more marked in England than on the Continent. Erasmus ascribed the frequency of plague and sweating sickness in England, "partly to the filthiness of the streets, and to the sluttishness within doors. The floors . . . are commonly of clay, strewn with rushes, under which lies unmolested an ancient collection of . . . fragments, bones, spittle, excrements . . . , and everything that is nasty."[3] Personal cleanliness seems to have been almost wholly neglected, and "creepers" were found even in the costly apparel of the rich.[4]

Children were treated with the utmost severity at home, as well as in school. They had to kneel to receive a parental

---

[1] *History of Education*, p. 326.

[2] For example, John Colet, the founder, in 1510, of St. Paul's School, was the oldest of twenty children, and the only one of them to survive childhood.

[3] Quoted by Furnivall, *op. cit.*, p. lvi.

[4] Bathing seems to have been as rare as ever, although there may have been a slight improvement in the seventeenth century, judging from Mouffet's *Theater of Insects*, a treatise which included information on varieties of "lice and worms," sent by God to humble man when he affects to know too much. "The daintiest dames," it is said, hate "these filthy creatures." The condition of the poor, however, was appalling. A "bonde man" is described as "in a tawny tabard, Al so torn and baudy, And ful of lys creeping." Furnivall, *op. cit.*, lxiv.

blessing, might not sit unbidden in their parents' presence, and addressed them in formal and respectful terms. In his *Scholemaster*, Ascham quotes Lady Jane Grey's account of her " sharpe and severe Parentes." "I am so sharplie taunted, so cruellie threatened . . . with pinches, nippes, and bobbes, and other waies which I will not name for the honor I beare them, . . . that I thinke myself in hell."[1] The prevalent severity was undoubtedly considered as the dutiful fulfillment of parental responsibility. The Catholic and Protestant Churches alike warned parents of the supreme importance of the moral and religious upbringing of their children.

Despite the harsh assertion of parental authority, children of this period were in many ways treated as old beyond their years. They were dressed, from an early age, exactly as were their elders, and both boys and girls were uncomfortably cramped in heavy, stiffened, and padded garments. Child marriages and betrothals were astonishingly prevalent in the sixteenth century. Girls, in particular, were often betrothed by their parents while still in the cradle. Records of child marriages and divorces in the diocese of Chester, between 1561 and 1566, were collected by Furnivall, who found instances where both bride and groom were carried in arms before the priest. Such marriages seem very frequently to have been mere money-bargains contracted among the less well-to-do. One father "to get somme money . . . to the discharge of his debtes" married his son to another's daughter. No wonder some of these children who were bold enough to seek divorce pled, "at the time of their marriage they knewe not what they did"!

The Treatment of Children and Their Education in England in the Seventeenth and Eighteenth Centuries. Children in the sixteenth and seventeenth centuries seem in some cases to have been singularly unchildlike and remarkably precocious. Many portraits of royal children have been preserved, and there are fuller records of their upbringing than is the case with those of less exalted status. James I of England could, at eight, translate the Bible from Latin into English and French. His son "Baby Charles," later the ill-fated Charles I, was, on the other hand, refreshingly natural and childlike. Extant letters

---

[1] Quoted by *ibid.*, p. vii. There were, of course, exceptions. Sir Thomas More, for instance, was on terms of loving comradeship with his daughters; and his friend, Sir Thomas Elyot, keenly interested in the education of his nephews and full of solicitude for children, advocated gentle methods of discipline.

to his brother show him to have been a most affectionate and generous little boy. In the nurseries of the well-to-do, children learnt their letters from blocks; the abacus and horn book were in use, and primers began to appear in the seventeenth century. Boys, as usual, were more fortunate than their sisters. Their tasks done, they might engage in outdoor sports. Little girls were often forced to stay indoors. Among the fashionable they were tightly laced and must shun the sunlight in order to preserve a waxen pallor. In the seventeenth and eighteenth centuries their inevitable employment was the "exemplar," or sampler. In this way, they became fine needlewomen, and were believed to acquire habits of industry and to be inspired by the pious and edifying sentiments with which their efforts were adorned.[1]

In Puritan households, in particular, children were not only brought up in an atmosphere of gloomy severity, but were haunted by terrors of the devil and hell-fire. In the preface of one of the earliest children's books, its author, Janeway, warns parents that their children "are not too little to die, . . . not too little to go to hell." The children themselves are told that they are "by Nature, Children of Wrath, brands of Hell," and that "Hell is a terrible place that's worse far than whipping," whereas, if they attained Heaven, "they shall never be beat any more, never be sick or in pain any more."[2] Children were exhorted to gain conviction of sin, through reading the Bible with groans, tears, and sobs; and "searching" books about the early deaths of "godly" infants were recommended for lighter reading. One boy, who died at eight, was reported to have wept for fear of hell; in his secret diary he had noted, as misdeeds, that he had "whetted his knife on the Lord's day," and that, finding his "Heart dead," he had omitted prayer.

The eighteenth century was, in many respects, a brutal age. Laws were harsh, there being, as late as 1800, more than two hundred crimes punishable by death; and all punishments

[1] The brevity and uncertainty of life are frequently dwelt upon, even the perils of the hereafter. The following verse appears on a late eighteenth-century sampler:

"The Lord delights in them that speak
The words of truth, but every liar
Must have his portion in the lake
That burns with brimstone and with fire."

Another verse embroidered by a poor mite of six runs:

"This I have done, I thank my God,
Without correction of the rod."

[2] F. J. Harvey Darton, *Children's Books in England* (1932), pp. 54, 55, and 59.

were public spectacles.[1] There was much drunkenness and many cruel sports; bull- and bear-baiting and cock-fighting were particularly popular. There were even prize-fights arranged between women. Sanitation and drainage were unknown; the streets were filthy and unlighted and dangerous at night. To offset ugly realities, the era was one of artificiality and superficial elegance. Many charges were brought by the more serious against parents. DeFoe wrote: "It becomes a little unfashionable for the mothers to give themselves any trouble with their children . . . but to order their dress and make them fine and to make a show of them upon occasion."[2] Girls were often sent to "select" boarding schools to be turned into "accomplished" young ladies. The repression of the natural activities of childhood was well symbolized by the adult clothing and wigs, or powdered hair, worn by little boys and girls of the upper classes, until the middle of the century.

The infant death-rate remained almost as high as in the Middle Ages. Hygienic principles were unknown and the old prejudice against bathing was still strong. Harsh discipline was the rule; and, even of the delicate, there must be no coddling. Only one of Queen Anne's seventeen children survived infancy to live to eleven; and he was thrashed for obstinacy, when the real trouble was water-on-the-brain. John Wesley attributed all his qualities to the rigorous training given him by his "devoted" mother. Early indulgence was held by her to be cruelty. At one year old, each successive baby in Epworth Rectory had to learn to bear the rod without tears.

Books meant for children were written, at this time, wholly for instruction and never for amusement. *Pilgrim's Progress* (1678), *Robinson Crusoe* (1719), and *Gulliver's Travels* (1726) were written for adults, not children, despite their enduring popularity among young people. Locke says, in his *Thoughts on Education* (1693), that *Aesop's Fables* and *Reynard the Fox* were the only story books he knew fit for children. Very shortly after this time the first great collections of fairy tales were issued in France and later reached England. The earliest collection of nursery rhymes was brought out in 1744. Meanwhile Isaac Watt's *Divine and Moral Songs for Children* (1715) were typical of what was considered suitable.

[1] Men of fashion used to arrange parties to witness the whipping of women. Not till 1790 was the public burning of women abolished; they were, it is true, usually strangled first.

[2] *The Compleat English Gentleman* (ed. 1730), p. 71.

While upper-class children were left to the care of nurses and servants and led a restricted, often joyless life, the lot of the children of the poor—the majority of all children—was unbelievably wretched. It has been estimated that a sixth of the population of England, in the eighteenth century, were all but destitute: half-starved, clad in rags, and living in filthy hovels. Children under such conditions were early brutalized by hard labor, beating, and even by strong drink and vicious habits.

CHILDREN IN THE AMERICAN COLONIES

The Transplantation of Educational Patterns. Despite their freedom from religious oppression and from economic limitations, the early settlements in America reproduced, at first with little change, the characteristic institutions and social and religious attitudes of their European prototypes. In the absence of a nobility, the land-owners, the prosperous middle-class merchants, and professional men constituted the highest level of society. The patriarchal family with its typical subservience of women and children was transplanted all but unmodified, as were the attitudes determining educational institutions and opportunities.

English attitudes towards education were most evident in Virginia, where the owners of large plantations engaged tutors for their children or sent them to private schools in the colony and mother country. Class distinctions were sharply drawn, because of the introduction of large numbers of indentured white servants, and later of negro slaves. The only attempts at public education were made in the spirit of English Poor Law legislation. Orphans and the children of the poor were to be apprenticed and trained to trades. Not until 1705 were masters of apprentices required to have them taught to read and write.

In the other colonies religious purposes were paramount in education. The majority of schools were of the parochial type. In New England, however, despite its domination by Calvinism, the first steps were taken which were to lead to the state school systems of to-day, entirely separated from religious influence. Massachusetts best represented the Puritan attitude towards education. For the perpetuation of their faith all must learn to read the Bible and to take an intelligent part in family and public worship. Above all, there was need for an educated ministry. Children were instructed at home by their parents, or in the case of poor apprentices, by their masters. Congregations organized themselves into towns and established grammar schools, in which Latin was the chief subject of study. Harvard College, founded in 1636, provided the instruction considered necessary for ministers.

In accordance with English precedent the educational system was, at first, voluntary. But the zealous Puritans soon found that their purposes would not be accomplished in this way. "Accordingly," says Cubberley "the Church appealed to its servant, the State, . . . to assist it in compelling parents and masters to observe their religious obligations."[1] The Law of 1642 directed the "chosen men" of each town to supervise the home education of children, and to ascertain if they were being taught "to read and understand the principles of religion and the capital laws of the country."[2] Even though supervised, education was thus left in the home. But a five-year trial of this plan showed the necessity for a further step. In 1647, it was ordered that every town of fifty householders must appoint and pay for a teacher of reading and writing, and every town of one hundred householders must provide a grammar school to fit youths for the university. "Not only was a school-system ordered established," says Cubberley, "but, for the first time among English-speaking peoples, there was an assertion of the right of the State to require communities to establish and maintain schools. . . . This law became the cornerstone of our American state school systems."[3]

Child Life in Puritan New England. Contemporary accounts of colonial New England provide illuminating glimpses of the lives of children. Although the picture is not wholly typical of children in other colonies, it vividly portrays, even if in extreme form, their domination by religious influences and by adult authority. Life in the colonial South for the children of the well-to-do was undoubtedly less rigorous, more easy-going and genial than in New England; but much the same attitude towards children prevailed even there, as it did in the other colonies and in the European countries from which their settlers had come.

The moral earnestness of the Puritans pervaded every detail of their daily lives. The very names given to children must have early impressed upon them the solemnity of life. Many were selected with meticulous care from the Bible; others emphasized traits thought particularly desirable: "Submit," "Endurance," "Silence," "Wait still" or, in one instance of

[1] *History of Education*, p. 364.   [2] Quoted in *ibid.*, p. 365.   [3] *Ibid.*, p. 366.

three brothers, "Return," "Believe," and "Tremble"! In the early days, the pioneers had to contend with very real dangers and hardships.[1] When savage men and beasts no longer menaced, there still remained the ever-present threat of incomprehensible disease and sudden death. Disease and disaster of every kind were regarded as punishments for sin, and to anxiety over actual danger was added the overshadowing terror of hell and damnation. According to Cotton Mather, "Sickness is in Fact the whip of God for the sins of Man." When a distracted mother appealed to him on behalf of her ailing baby, he comforted her as follows: "Think! Oh! the grievous Effects of Sin! This wretched Infant has not arrived unto years of sense enough to sin after the similitude of the Transgression committed by Adam. Nevertheless the transgression of Adam . . . has involved this Infant in the guilt of it. And the poison of the old serpent which infected Adam . . . has corrupted all mankind, and is a seed unto such disease as this Infant is now laboring under. Lord, what are we, and what are our children, but a Generation of Vipers?" Somewhat inconsistently, however, he recommends a stiff dose of tincture of "sowbugs": "take . . . half a pound, put 'em alive into a quart or two of wine."[2]

There was no lack of devotion on the part of Puritan parents. But all in authority, ministers, teachers, and parents took for granted the corrupt nature of the child, which could only be subjugated through stern repression and harsh correction. As John Robinson, pastor of the Pilgrims while in Holland, put it: "Surely there is in all children (tho not alike) a stubberness and stoutnes of minde, arising from naturall pride, which must in the first place be broken and beaten down, that so the foundation of their education being layd in humilitie and tractableness, other virtues may in their turn be built thereon."[3] In general, there was acceptance of the belief that the rebel against parental authority was a "monster," the disobedient son being indeed worthy of death.[4] Implicit prompt obedience, profound respect for parents and teachers, and meek acceptance of the minute ordering of their daily lives were expected from all children.

[1] "Concerning of ye earlie days I can remember but little save Hardship. . . . After ye Red Skins, ye grate Terror of our lives . . . was ye Wolves." A description of boyhood experiences in the Connecticut Valley quoted by Stoddard, *The Story of Youth*, pp. 256–257.

[2] Quoted by Haggard, *Devils, Drugs, and Doctors*, p. 189.

[3] A. M. Earle, *Child Life in Colonial Days* (1899), p. 192.

[4] The early colonial codes, following *Deuteronomy*, actually decreed that the unruly child should be put to death. There exists no record, however, of such sentence being carried into effect.

In case parents were unable to enforce such discipline, it was ordered in 1654, in Massachusetts, that "Magistrates have authority to whip divers children and servants who behave themselves disrespectfully, disobediently and disorderly towards their parents, masters and governors."[1]

The use of the rod was universal, discipline being, however, not usually so harsh in homes as in schools. Birch trees were plentiful in America, as Mrs. Earle points out, but birching was not enough for many of the schoolmasters of that period. The more cruel and brutal among them preferred such instruments of torture as the "taws," a hickory club with leather thongs. Some fathers—Judge Sewall and Cotton Mather among them—seem, on the other hand, to have used the rod but sparingly. Cotton Mather condemned "the *Slavish* way of *Education*, carried on with raving and kicking and scourging (in *Schools* as well as in *Families*)." He would never "give a Child a *Blow;* except in case of Obstinancy or some gross Enormity."[2] Judge Sewall's diary refers twice to the punishment of his children. Ten-year-old Sam is "corrected . . . for breach of the 9th Commandment, saying he had been at writing-school when he had not." And little four-year-old Joseph "threw a knob of Brass and hit his sister Betty on the forehead so as to make it bleed and swell; upon which, and for playing at Prayer-time and eating when Return Thanks, I whip'd him pretty smartly. When I first went in . . . he sought to shadow and hide himself from me behind the head of the Cradle: which gave me the sorrowful remembrance of Adam's carriage."[3]

Locke's *Thoughts on Education* served as a handbook for many colonial parents. His idea of inuring the body to hardship was thoroughly congenial to the Puritan mind. Colonial homes were often dismally cold and damp, and babies and little children wore linen undergarments. Nevertheless,

---

[1] Quoted by Goodsell, *History of Marriage and the Family*, p. 417. A regular censorship of family life was thus instituted. There was enforcement of strict discipline and religious instruction in the home, and of seemly behavior in the meeting-house, or elsewhere abroad in the community.

[2] Quoted by Lothrop Stoddard, *op. cit.*, p. 267. It was Cotton Mather who gave the following warning to children in *A Family Well-Ordered*. "If by undutifulness to your Parents, you incur the Curse of God, it won't be long before you go down into Obscure Darkness, even into Utter Darkness: God has reserved for you the Blackness of Darkness forever." This is preferable, certainly, to the "Unquenchable Flames of Hell" in which the souls of children were pictured by some preachers as "melting in the midst of the blazing heat of God's endless, dreadful wrath." Sandford Fleming, *Children and Puritanism* (1933), p. 103.

[3] Diary (1674–1729), edited by Mark van Doren (1927), entries for Sept. 15, 1688, and Nov. 6, 1692.

three-year-old Josiah Quincy was further "hardened" by being taken from his bed, winter and summer, to be dipped three times in water fresh from the pump. Whatever the weather, the new-born infant must be carried to the icy meeting-house to be baptized at the earliest possible moment. Little Henry Sewall, baptized in December when four days old, became "extream sick," and in spite of prayers, died at thirteen days old, apparently from pneumonia. On Christmas Eve, Judge Sewall records, "We follow little Henry to his Grave."[1] Two years later Stephen survived his baptism on a stormy winter day, but six months later teething proved fatal. "The Body of my dear Son Stephen is carried to the Tomb."[2]

Henry and Stephen were but two among fifteen brothers and sisters, of whom eight died in infancy. One was still-born, and the others died, two of them at five weeks, one at sixteen months, and two at two years old. More than any other of these bereavements Judge Sewall deplores the loss of the still-born son, which occurred during his absence from home. He was "grievously Stung," and exclaims: "The Lord pardon all my Sin and Wandering and Neglect, and sanctify to me this singular affliction."[3] His concern arose from the belief that the procreation of children was not enough, the all-important duty being "to offer children to God in Baptisme." On the occasion of Judith's birth, he is grateful for having "had my health and opportunity" to offer nine. He does not mention the fact that four were already dead. A few weeks later he writes: "My little Judith languishes and moans, ready to die. I rise, read some psalms and pray with my dear Daughter; . . . in the evening the child died and I hope sleeps in Jesus."[4]

Of Mrs. Sewall's feelings at the death of her children there is almost no mention. When she was told that her nineteen-year-old daughter Mary had died after the birth of her first child, the diary records, "a dolefull Cry was lifted up." With what becomes almost monotonous regularity the Judge records briefly, "My wife brought to Bed" of a Son, or Daughter. Once Mrs. Sewall had been at a funeral and "was so ill she

[1] *Ibid.*, Dec. 4, 13, 22, 24, 1685.
[2] *Ibid.*, Feb. 6, 1686/7, and July 27.
[3] *Ibid.*, May 18, 1696. The fear of infant damnation, was, of course, the cause for very early baptism, as well as for religious conversion at a tender age. Jonathan Edwards, it is true, depicted parents in heaven, "with holy joy upon their countenances," contemplating the torment of their little ones. But one doubts whether any mother can have been reassured by such a prospect.
[4] *Ibid.*, Sept. 21, 1690.

could hardly get home"; another time the family are called to prayer for "my wife was in great and more than ordinary extremity"; at still another, he comments on my "wive's hard Time." On the birth of the fourteenth child he writes: "My Wife is very ill and something delirious. . . . What through my wive's many Illnesses, more than ordinary, . . . her thoughtfulness between whiles whether she were with child or no; her Fears what the issue would be, and the misgiving of our Unbelieving hearts God has been wonderfully merciful to us in her comfortable delivery. . . . It may be my dear wife may now leave off bearing."[1]

Most New England homes were thus shadowed in actual fact by recurrent illness and death. An added gloomy solemnity was given to everyday life by a belief in the portentous religious significance of all events, sometimes of the most trivial incidents. When, afraid "she should dye," Susan Sewall sought her parents in the dead of night, the Judge writes: "I was the more startled because I had spilt a whole Vinyard Can of water just before we went to Bed; and made the reflection that our Lives would shortly be spilt."[2] Even feeding the chickens reminds him of his need for spiritual food. When Mary fell into the cellar and cut her head, her father says, "The Lord sanctify to me this bloody Accident."[3] When "the body of Jane Sewall" is "laid in the Tomb," he writes, "Lord teach us to profit."[4]

What of the effect on the surviving children of such an atmosphere? The tendency to precocity already manifest in Europe was accentuated.[5] The sooner the sinful and unregenerate natures of children were subdued and their stubborn wills broken, the sooner might their anxious parents hope for their conversion. The most popular and widely read of all children's books in New England bore the following title: *A Token for Children, being an Exact Account of the Conversion, Holy and Exemplary Lives and Joyful Deaths of Several Young Children, by James Janeway. To which is added a Token for the Children of New England or Some Examples of Children in Whom the Fear of God was remarkably Budding before they died, in several parts of New England. Preserved and Published for the Encourage-*

---

[1] *Ibid.*, Jan. 6, 1701/2.   [3] *Ibid.*, July 26, 1695.
[2] *Ibid.*, Oct. 25, 1711.   [4] *Ibid.*, Sept. 15, 1693.

[5] Here too the children were dressed in imitation of their elders from the day their baby clothes were discarded. Mrs. Earle gives many contemporary pictures of solemn and amazingly mature looking little children, the boys till six or seven being dressed as adult *women;* then, when "coats" were left behind, they changed to the dress of adult manhood.

ment of Piety in other Children.[1] Among other similar instances, it is recorded that Elizabeth Butcher, "when two and a half years old as she lay in the Cradle, would ask herself the Question, 'What is my Corrupt Nature?' And would answer herself, 'I am empty of Grace, bent unto Sin, and only to Sin, and that Continually.'"

Other books bore titles such as *The Afflicted Parents, or the Undutiful Child Punished; The Prodigal Daughter, or the Disobedient Lady Reclaimed.* One of the most popular of all books was not written for children, but was very often committed to memory by them. This was written by Wigglesworth in 1662 and was called *The Day of Doom.* After a lurid description of the eternal tortures of the damned in the flames of Hell, it records God's answer to a plea for salvation from "reprobate infants";

> "In bliss, you may not hope to dwell,
> But unto you, I shall allow
> The easiest room in Hell."[2]

Even at school there was no escape from such preoccupations, for there, as at home, the famous New England primer was in universal use. There were many successive editions with slight alterations, such for example, as the later inclusion of John Cotton's catechism: *Spiritual Milk for Babes drawn out of the Breasts of Both Testaments for Their Soul's Nourishment.* All editions included the chief features, such as the rhymed, illustrated alphabet beginning, "In Adam's fall, we sinned all"; the Lord's Prayer, the Apostle's Creed, the Shorter Catechism, and the picture of John Rogers being burned at the stake, apparently very cheerfully, with his wife and nine children as amazingly unconcerned spectators! Among the twelve five-syllabled words included in the tables, *five* were as follows: *abomination, edification, humiliation, mortification,* and *purification.*

In Judge Sewall's diary there is evidence of the effect on children of such teaching, and of constant Bible reading, prayers, and sermons, and of the frequent participation at funerals.[3] After Stephen's funeral the Judge writes: "Sam

---

[1] The first part of this book was written by the Janeway to whom reference has already been made. It was extremely popular in England. The second part was written by Cotton Mather, and, in Mrs. Earle's words, "out-Janeways Janeway."

[2] Quoted by Earle, *op. cit.,* p. 253.

[3] Funerals were social events where the whole community gathered together. Before the funeral of his daughter Sarah, on Christmas Day, 1696, Judge Sewall visits the family tomb to determine where Sarah's coffin shall be placed. "I was entertain'd with a view of and converse with . . . the family coffins [including those of] my Six Children. . . . Twas an awful yet pleasing treat; Having said, 'The Lord knows who shall be brought hether next,' I went away."

and his sisters cryed much coming home and at home and could not be quieted. It seems they looked into Tomb and Sam said he saw a great Coffin, his Grandfather's."[1] Sam was then nine. When he was nearly twelve, his father records: "Richard Doumer, a flourishing youth of 9 years old, dies of the Small Pocks. I tell Sam of it and of what need he had to prepare for death." At the moment, Sam "seem'd not much to mind, eating an Aple." But when Sam was saying the Lord's Prayer that evening, "he burst out into a bitter cry and said he was afraid he should die. I pray'd with him and read Scriptures comforting against death."[2] One hopes Sam's nervous apprehensions were allayed, particularly when not long afterwards he was "put . . . to Bed, having the Small Pocks come out upon him."

Betty seems to have been the most sensitive of the Sewall children. When she was eight, the Judge records, "It falls to my Daughter Elizabeth's share to read the 24 of Isaiah which she doeth with many Tears, not being well."[3] Six years later, the Judge came home one day to be told by his wife, "Betty had surprised them." After being dejected all day, a "little after dinner she burst into an amazing cry." Questioned by her mother, it appeared she had been brooding, for days, on texts from sermons she had recently heard or read: "Ye shall seek me and shall die in your sins, ran in her mind and terrified her greatly. . . . Why hath Satan filled your heart, which increased her Fear. Her Mother asked whether she pray'd. She answer'd; Yes, but feared her prayers were not heard because her Sins not pardon'd." On all of which the Judge comments: "The Lord bring Light and Comfort out of this dark and dreadful Cloud, and Grant that Christ's being formed in my dear child, may be the issue of these painful pangs."[4] But later entries show that Betty "was afraid she should go to Hell" and that she was "not Elected."[5] And four months later, she "can hardly read her chapter for weeping; tells me she is afraid she is gone back, does not taste that sweetness in reading the Word which once she did."[6] Two years later she is overcome with nervousness at the prospect of suitors. After much hesitation she married at eighteen, bore children, one of whom was still-born, and after years of failing health died at thirty-four.

[1] *Ibid.*, July 27, 1687.
[2] *Ibid.*, Jan. 12, 1689/90.
[3] *Ibid.*, Jan. 10, 1689/90.

[4] *Ibid.*, Jan. 13, 1695/6.
[5] *Ibid.*, Feb. 22, 1695/6.
[6] *Ibid.*, May 3, 1696.

Even when not morbidly preoccupied with their souls, Puritan children were apt to be nervously anxious over their moral well-being. In the "Monitor" of Mary Osgood Sumner, a diary with a black-list on one page and a white-list opposite, a record is found of such wrongdoings as: "I left my Staise on the Bed," "Part of this day I did not improve my time very well." The white-list is far more extensive, filled with occasions on which she was "midlin Diligent" or sought, as she did at all hours, to "improve her time."[1] The stress on constant industry and occupation was one of the aspects of Puritan teaching which was destined to have far-reaching social consequences, making possible as it did the approval of child labor. Isaac Watt's famous line, "Satan finds some mischief still, for idle hands to do," expressed the Puritan hatred for idleness as a form of original sin.

Undoubtedly the participation of little children in daily work was necessary under the conditions of pioneer life. Even in later days there was always plenty of work for children on farms, pulling weeds, sowing seeds, feeding the stock, and working with flax and wool. Tending cattle was not considered a sufficiently industrious pursuit, so that a Massachusetts law of 1624 bade the selectman see that the small herdsmen and herdswomen "be set to some employment withal, as spinning upon the rock [hand-distaff], knitting, weaving tape, etc." For little girls, when their tasks within and without permitted, there was the inevitable sampler. The worst aspects of the situation were of course to be found among orphans and the children of the poor, who were apprenticed and began their industrial training at a very early age.

While children's play was not forbidden, it was not encouraged. Cotton Mather wrote, "I must think of some exquisite and obliging Wayes to abate Sammy's inordinate Love of Play." A little later he exclaimed, "What shall be done, for the raising of Sammy's Mind above the debasing Meannesses of Play?" Poor Sammy evidently could not withstand his father's zeal, for a year later he "is united with a Society of sober and pious lads who meet for Exercises of Religion."[2]

But even in Puritan New England youthful exuberance was hard to quell. Boys seem very frequently to have behaved in a boisterous manner in the solemn atmosphere of the meeting-house. Here they were all crowded together in the boys' "pue," in the least comfortable part of the building, and relieved their

---

[1] Earle, *op. cit.*, pp. 166, 169.   [2] Quoted by Stoddard, *op. cit.*, p. 267.

tedium, according to the note-book of a Connecticut justice by "pulling hair, smiling, larfing and intiseing others to the same evil," and other forms of "Rude and Idel behavior in time of public worship." Elsewhere it is recorded that, when the girls went forth to gather "daisies and butter flowers," the boys kicked them "to make them pipe"!

As in England, it was not till the eighteenth century that there were any story books for children other than those of a pious type.   The children seem, however, to have had a fair number of toys and to have played numerous games in spite of all restrictions.

CHANGING ATTITUDES TOWARDS CHILDHOOD

The Shift in Emphasis from Conformity with Social Patterns to the Personality of the Child.   The modern enlightened attitude towards children is in complete contrast to the attitudes which have just been described.   Education, throughout the ages, has been, in Dewey's words, "the art of taking advantage of the helplessness of the young," of treating their plasticity as though it were "putty to be molded according to current designs."[1] The emphasis has fallen on preëxisting social patterns to which the young must perforce conform.   However diverse have been the ways in which the goal of education has been envisaged, it has ever been a predetermined goal; and the educational curriculum, true to its Latin derivation, has been the course which must be traversed to reach the goal.   In Dewey's essay, *The Child and the Curriculum*, there occurs a passage which, perhaps better than any other, summarizes the contrasting emphasis of the modern viewpoint: "The child is the starting point, the center and the end.   His development, his growth is the ideal. It alone furnishes the standard.   To the growth of the child all studies are subservient; they are instruments valued as they serve the needs of growth.   Personality, character is more than subject matter.   Not knowledge or information, but self-realization is the goal."[2]

Freedom for the child, and education by means of an environment which will ensure the realization of his potentialities for wholesome physical and mental growth, of his full development as an individual: this is the ideal of twentieth-century educational leaders.   From such a point of view, the history of childhood through the ages presents a poignant picture.   "The genera-

[1] *Human Nature and Conduct*, p. 64.
[2] *Op. cit.* (University of Chicago Press, 1902), p. 13.

tions running to waste like rapids," Wells once exclaimed. Generation after generation, the lives of children have been bound in the fetters of current social custom, of economic institutions, and of religious dogmas; and their mental growth has been, too often, stunted or distorted. Economic injustice still warps the lives of the majority of children; but the situation is no longer accepted as irremediable. Many children have not, even to-day, escaped from the repressions of Puritan morality or from traditional religious fears. But such influences are recognized by enlightened thought for what they are, fetters from which childhood must be freed. It is significant, indeed, that a new day for childhood only began to dawn, as the darkness of the doctrine of original sin was dispelled. Modern educational theory takes its rise in a complete repudiation of the view that the child's nature is evil, and that education must repress natural tendencies, and regenerate the child, by molding him into conformity with traditional ways of thinking and feeling and doing. In the opening sentence of Rousseau's *Émile* (1762)— "Everything is good as it comes from the hand of the author of nature"—we have, accordingly, the proclamation of a new era.

GREAT EDUCATIONAL REFORMERS OF THE EIGHTEENTH AND NINETEENTH CENTURIES

Locke and Comenius as Forerunners.[1] Rousseau, influential as he was in shaping modern social and educational attitudes, owed much to certain of his predecessors, in particular to John Locke. Locke, it is true, stresses the necessity of discipline for mind and body, saying in his *Thoughts* (§ 33): "And the great Principle and Foundation of all Virtue and Worth is plac'd in this: —That a man is able to *deny himself* his own desires, cross his own Inclinations, and purely follow what Reason directs as best, tho' the Appetite lean the other way." His experience as a tutor, and his habit of dispassionate observation gained through the study of medicine, led him to give expression to the highest ideals of his day for the education of gentlemen. But there is a new note in this book, which, first among books on education, deals primarily with the child. Despite the emphasis on discipline and the control of natural tendencies, Locke as a doctor

---

[1] Although these men belong to the seventeenth century, they must be referred to in any account, however brief, of the development of educational theory and practice in succeeding centuries. Comenius lived from 1592 to 1671, and Locke from 1632 to 1704.

recognized the great importance of physical activities and of sound health. He also believed that early education should take advantage of the child's natural curiosity, and should be a training in sense perception rather than in memory, and that it should be pleasurable.

One other predecessor of Rousseau must be mentioned, who, though he exercised comparatively little influence on the actual development of the modern attitude, was nevertheless one of its first and greatest exponents. Johann Amos Comenius was a bishop of the Moravian Church and suffered life-long persecution. His wife and children were murdered, his books and manuscripts burnt. As a result, his writings were for the most part unknown until nearly two centuries after his death. Although he believed this life to be but a preparation for eternity, yet natural tendencies should not be eradicated, for "nature" means man's original condition before the Fall. All alike, rich and poor, boys and girls, have been born in order to become "rational creatures," and so should be sent to school. With this end in view, Comenius outlined a system of education for the first twenty-five years of life. Education, he held, must begin at birth, and for the first six years the mother is the teacher. In *The School of the Mother's Knee* (1628) he anticipated many of the ideas of the kindergarten. In the same way, with no psychology to guide him, other than that derived from his own insight and experience as a schoolmaster, Comenius developed practicable school methods, embodying many features commonplace to-day, but at that time wholly new. Discipline was to be gentle, learning was to proceed from observing and doing, and emphasis was shifted from words to things. His *Orbis Sensualium Pictus* (1658), a reader in which a picture was followed by its explanation in Latin and translation, was the first illustrated book ever made for children.

Rousseau.[1] The liberal thought of the eighteenth century owed much to Locke, who had pointed the way to the substitution of individual experience and reason for tradition and authority in the conduct of human affairs. It was not, however, till after the middle of the century that criticism was directed against the injustice of the social order. In this movement the leader was Rousseau, the "first voice," according to Morley, ever to appeal for justice for the common people. Human powers, he believed, were hampered and distorted by corrupt social and political institutions, by artificial man-imposed restrictions. A

[1] 1712 to 1778.

return to *nature* meant for Rousseau the substitution of a kingdom of humanity for the existing inequitable social order.

As a first step Rousseau advocated a new education in accord with nature. And yet, as contemporary critics were not slow to point out, many of his educational ideas were not original. *Émile* was even described as a "patchwork of plagiarisms." Nevertheless, not only did Rousseau's style and method of presentation give *Émile* great influence, but its originality lies in the fact that it enunciates certain fundamental principles in a wholly new form.

Nature being the work of God, Rousseau held that the natural tendencies of the child are good. Faulty education is responsible for the notion of natural depravity. According to McAllister, Rousseau not only "proclaims his faith in the child's nature. . . . He shows how the supposed defects of the child's nature enclose the germs of later development and is at pains to teach us how the helplessness of childhood is a positive factor in forming the man of strength and independent judgment."[1] Rousseau's "insistence that education be based upon the native capacities of those to be taught and upon the need for studying children, in order to discover what their native powers are, sounded," in Dewey's words, "the key-note of all modern efforts for educational progress."[2]

Certain specific aims become apparent when attention is centered on the child. Health is necessary to natural growth, and, since Rousseau would "let children be children," he stressed spontaneous activities and play. Again, the study of children reveals the fact of individual differences, and in the letter on education in the fifth part of *La Nouvelle Heloïse* (1760), Rousseau dwells on the fact that "every child at birth possesses an individual temperament."

Natural development, Rousseau insists, must determine the educational process. Valuable as this principle proved, much of the paradox and inconsistency of Rousseau's own work arises from his faulty interpretation of natural development, as an independent and spontaneous process with which educational processes must be brought into harmony.

Pestalozzi and Froebel.[3] Rousseau's contention that education is an unfolding of natural capacities led to the realization that individual development can be hindered or helped by educa-

---

[1] *The Growth of Freedom in Education* (1931), p. 231.
[2] John Dewey and Evelyn Dewey, *Schools of To-morrow* (1915), pp. 1–2.
[3] Pestalozzi lived from 1746 to 1827; Froebel from 1782 to 1852.

tional methods. The need was apparent for more accurate psychological knowledge. Pestalozzi and Froebel were foremost among those who, influenced by Rousseau, attempted to base education on a study of the early years of childhood. For the first time the center of educational interest was shifted from the higher stages of education to the elementary stage. Two important corollaries followed: in the first place, since all can profit by the earlier stages of education, interest in universal education was stimulated; secondly, the need for knowledge of the child's interests and activities led to that sympathy for childhood which is characteristic of the modern attitude.

Pestalozzi himself was fully aware that his efforts were tentative, that he was an experimenter and learner, even more than he was a teacher. Most of his educational ventures failed, yet throughout he held to his original purposes: the regeneration of all, even the poorest, members of society through education, and the introduction into the school-room of the sympathetic relationships of the home. To these purposes was later added a third: to "psychologize" education through the discovery of a new method, by which concrete educational procedures might be based on and related to the actual growth of the child. Comparing the child to a plant, Pestalozzi held that education must protect from adverse influences and foster the "natural, symmetrical, and harmonious development" of the child, of "head, hand, and heart." The child learns through his own activities, and the teacher must seek to provide such educative experience as is fit for each stage of development. Since "the first hour of its teaching is the hour of its birth," Pestalozzi held that the mother is the natural teacher of the child.[1] "Yes! I would say the mother is . . . qualified by her Creator himself, to become the principal agent in the development of her child; . . . what power can be more influential, more stimulating than maternal love? . . . What I would demand of her is only a thinking love. . . . Let me repeat that we cannot expect any real improvement in education . . . unless we begin by educating mothers."[2]

While Pestalozzi was more successful in developing educational principles than in putting them into practice, "his very failure was a witness to a faith that refused to abandon an

[1] *How Gertrude Teaches Her Children* (1801), quoted by Ilse Forest, *Preschool Education* (1927), p. 148.
[2] *Letters on Early Education* (1818), quoted by *ibid.*, pp. 150–151.

ideal, and his tenacity and conviction [inspired] real belief in the humanizing influence of education in the elementary school."[1] In several of his ventures he failed from the financial standpoint alone. In some of his schools not only did he support and educate numbers of orphans, but his method of combining education with industrial activities was influential in the later development of education for dependent, delinquent, and defective children.

Among those who taught under Pestalozzi in his school at Yverdun was Froebel, the founder of the kindergarten, and the man from whom more than any other "have sprung the chief streams of present educational thought."[2] In the first paragraph of his *Education of Man* (1826), Froebel states his mystical conviction that "all things live and have their being in and through the Divine Unity. . . . The divine effluence that lives in each thing is the essence of that thing."[3] The child's nature is thus not only good, but *divine*, a conception investing the activities of childhood with a new and profound significance. Education becomes the *unfolding* of the divine essence of man. Fortunately Froebel did not fully carry into practice his notion of the unfolding of ready-made tendencies. His sympathetic understanding of childhood brought him success as an educator despite the limitations of his philosophy.

In its general spirit, indeed, Froebel's educational philosophy is constructive. His larger educational aim is expressed as follows: "But I will protect childhood, that it may not, as in earlier generations, be pinioned, as in a strait-jacket, in garments of custom and ancient prescription that have become too narrow for the new time. I shall show the way and shape the means, that every human soul may grow of itself out of its own individuality."[4] Education must nurture and cultivate, and provide the environment for the realization of the child's potentialities through *self-activity*. *Play* being the characteristic spontaneous activity of early childhood, it became for Froebel the basis of early education. When in 1837, inspired in part by Comenius, Froebel founded the first *kindergarten*, he created a miniature society in which play, games, songs, handwork, and occupations involving self-activity provided children with educative and ethically desirable experience. Since social

[1] McAllister, *op. cit.*, p. 280.
[2] Monroe, *History of Education*, p. 646.
[3] Quoted by *ibid.*, p. 648.
[4] Bertha von Marenholtz-Bülow, *Reminiscences of Friedrich Froebel* (Eng. trans. 1887), p. 53, quoted by Forest, *op. cit.*, p. 160.

relationships are essential to self-realization, helpfulness and coöperation characterized this school, which was designed to supplement the primary educational institution of the family.

In the family, the earliest development of the child through self-activity must be fostered. Like Pestalozzi, Froebel stressed the need for the education of mothers. All women should be trained in all types of child care. "Women, whatever their stage of culture, ought to take their rightful position with regard to the development and education of the human race; and this position ought to be universally acknowledged whether with regard to the individual child, the family, or the entire nation."[1] "We must cultivate women, who are the educators of the human race, else the new generation cannot accomplish its task."[2]

ASPECTS OF CHILD LIFE IN THE NINETEENTH CENTURY

Children in England. Among the majority of nineteenth-century parents in England the leaven of these new attitudes was to work but slowly. By the end of the century, however, all but the most conservative were influenced by views which at the beginning of the century had even been attacked as *unchristian.* An English review of Pestalozzi's *Letters on Early Education* deplored its having been "put into . . . any language into which the word of God has been translated, for it belies it utterly. . . . We have no such children to educate, and therefore the book is useless to us." The reviewer contrasts Pestalozzi with a "Christian author" whose words she quotes with approval: "No sooner do children begin to act at all, but we discover how universally sin has pervaded all the sources of intelligence; . . . the evil passions grow and flourish, and the good are educated with difficulty." "The Christian mother," concludes the reviewer, "will compare these opposing principles with the testimony of Scripture and her own heart, and will have no difficulty in deciding in which author to study the principles of education."[3]

It must be admitted, of course, that religious societies had been responsible for most of the efforts hitherto made to give free instruction to the very poor. In England the *Society for*

---

[1] *Letters on the Kindergarten* (Eng. trans. 1896), p. 257, quoted by Forest, *op. cit.,* p. 162.

[2] *Reminiscences of Friedrich Froebel,* p. 4, quoted by *ibid.,* p. 162.

[3] Quoted by Monroe, *op. cit.,* pp. 589–590.

Promoting Christian Knowledge founded and supported a number of Charity Schools. Children were clothed, instructed in the Catechism, in spelling, reading, writing, and the rudiments of arithmetic. Later some form of labor was added, partly in order to "effectually obviate an objection against the Charity Schools, that they tend to take poor children off from those servile offices . . . for which the wise Governor of the world has by His Providence designed them."[1] It was complacently assumed that it would never do "to puff the children up and set them above their rank and order; or to make them disdain any of the lowest kind of work or service, such as they are born to, and wherein they may be most useful."[2] Such an attitude formed the basis for frequent protests against the education of the poor, for fear it would "unsettle" them.[3]

Terrible conditions prevailed among the children of the poor in the first half of the nineteenth century. Cruel exploitation of children was not new, but it attracted little attention before the concentration of child labor in the early factories. Such a pursuit as pin-heading could "be done by a child as soon as it acquires the use of its arms and legs." In 1833, a Factory Commissioner declared that one such establishment "reminded him more of an infant school than anything else."[4] Most unfortunate of all, perhaps, were the numerous small "climbing-boys," or chimney-sweeps. Boys as young as four or five were stolen or bought from parents, and forced by kicks and blows, by pins stuck in their bare soles, or by burning straw beneath them, to climb the narrow, crooked, pitch-dark chimneys, common in old houses. The majority were stunted and became lame or deformed, after suffering some six months of torture from raw and bleeding knees and elbows, before these became permanently calloused. There were a number of fatal accidents, the boys being suffocated with soot, or else burnt when sent

[1] Quoted (from a sermon preached in 1733) by E. H. Reisner, *The Evolution of the Common School* (1930), p. 103.

[2] Quoted (from a sermon preached in 1717) by Forest, *op. cit.*, p. 38. In the *Charity School Spelling Book* written by Mrs. Trimmer, highly regarded as an authority on children, is included a prayer for "strength and cheerfulness . . . to labor and do my duty in that state of life which Thy Wisdom has seen fit to allot me." Mrs. Trimmer believed that "the lower sort of children" might be so far civilized by education "as not to be disgusting."

[3] Furnivall tells of a nineteenth-century squire who would not allow arithmetic taught in the village school, for fear the boys would get to know too much about wages. *The Babees Book*, p. xlvii.

[4] Ivy Pinchbeck, *Women Workers and the Industrial Revolution*, p. 273.

up to extinguish a fire. At night they slept in cellars on their soot-bags.[1]

In the coal mines children of five to eight were everywhere employed opening and shutting doors, from twelve to eighteen hours at a time, sitting alone in the damp and the inky blackness. Even younger children were taken down the shafts to keep the rats from the miners' food. There were instances of children becoming mentally deranged from sheer terror of the dark and the swarming rats.

A regular juvenile slave-trade existed for a time where paupers, waifs and strays, and children obtained from poverty-stricken and grasping parents were dispatched by the wagon-load to the cotton mills. Some of them were not over five and looked "like little wild things out of cages." Worn out by the long hours of work, weak from undernourishment and disease, the required amount of work was yet wrung from them by the blows of a heavy leather strap, held in the middle so that two cuts were given with every blow. Nor were the children, inappropriately named "free," those who lived with their parents, much better off. Parents were often refused poor-relief unless their children worked. Crying mothers were seen dragging their crying, shivering children through the snow to the dreaded mill, before it was yet light.

Robert Owen, instrumental in the establishment of infant schools for the poor, did not wait for the slow processes of law and changing public opinion to better prevailing conditions among the children of the poor.[2] Himself the owner of cotton mills in New Lanark, Scotland, he was eager to help his workers. A follower of Rousseau, he believed that "it is through the education or the influence of circumstances, or of the conditions in which he is placed, that man becomes good or bad, inferior

[1] The Hammonds estimate that there were in England in 1817 about four hundred master chimney-sweeps and some thousand climbing-boys. Very occasionally girls were employed, but they were usually the children of the master sweeps. *The Town Labourer, 1760–1832* (1917), pp. 176–192. In one pamphlet on the subject, addressed to the mistresses of families, the writer deplores the apathy of "ladies," which must, he thinks, be due to "false delicacy," leading them to shun a "subject so filthy, vulgar and uninteresting." One argument against legislation was that of Mr. Ommaney, who asserted that "The boys generally employed in this profession were not the children of poor persons, but the children of rich men, begotten in an improper manner."

[2] Even as late as 1883 there was much opposition to the establishment of the Society for the Prevention of Cruelty to Children. One newspaper ridiculed "the benevolent old women of both sexes who are desirous of forming a Society for the Purpose of Washing the Faces of Dirty Children." It was protested that to save children from cruelty was to interfere with the rights of parents.

or superior."[1] He forbade the work of children under ten, and provided schools for the workers' children as soon as they could walk. Each child was told that "he must endeavor to make his companions happy." Unfortunately Owen's educational practices had little effect on the later infant schools.[2] Nevertheless, his idea appealed to liberals like Lord Brougham, James Mill, and Jeremy Bentham, and societies were founded for the support of infant education.[3] Not until 1870 was a system of national elementary schools established in England.

Although exempt from the miseries of the poor, the children of the upper and middle classes often led a life of repression, sometimes of harsh treatment or neglect. The Earl of Shaftesbury, the humanitarian leader, was in his childhood lonely and neglected, ill-treated by servants, and terrified of his parents. While a kindlier spirit began to permeate family life in the nineteenth century, "those impressive potentates, 'Papa' and 'Mamma,' continued for a long time to stand high above the level upon which their children lived, high upon pedestals from which they seldom came down. And when they did descend, it was more often to chastize the erring than to reward the deserving child."[4] "Papa," in particular, was apt to be pompous and awe-inspiring.

Children in America. The emancipation of the child progressed more rapidly in America. In the New World with its great resources and wide range of opportunity men looked to the future and worked for the generations to come. Children acquired a new value. Wherever frontier conditions prevailed, not only were children very useful, but they had early need for independence, fearlessness, and competence. Relationships between children and their parents were, of necessity, modified;

[1] Journal (1852), Vol. IV, p. 202, quoted by Forest, *op. cit.*, p. 54.

[2] This was probably due, in part, to the distrust felt for Owen's hostility to religion and his radical political views. In his *Life of Robert Owen, Written by Himself* (1857), he writes that "religions have been, and are to this day, the strongest causes of repulsive feelings between individuals and nations; and while any of these deranging systems of human intellects shall be forced into the young mind by the insane contending sects over the world, the spirit of universal charity and love must remain unknown among all nations and all peoples." P. 142, quoted by Forest, *op. cit.*, p. 58. As an example of the slight impression made by Owen on later infant schools, the case may be cited of one school where tiny tots were solemnly instructed in "all the sins recorded in Scripture, beginning with that of Jezebel."

[3] Lord Brougham, speaking in advocacy of infant schools in the House of Lords, May 21, 1835, said, "I am going to expose myself to ridicule when I state that I consider the establishment of infant schools in large towns, where crime is rife, . . . would be the most simple and efficacious preventative of crime." Quoted by Forest, *op. cit.*, p. 49.

[4] D. Stuart, *The Boy through the Ages* (1926), p. 259.

and travelers from the Old World commented on the indulgence of American parents and the wilfulness of their children, who, as one writer complained, "are seldom taught that profound reverence for, and strict obedience to their parents, which are at once the basis of domestic comfort and of the welfare of the children themselves."[1] Doubtless there were spoilt, precocious, and wayward children, but, on the other hand, some travelers testified that, what they at first took for disrespect and impudence, they later found to be intelligence and independence. One English writer in 1881 speaks of the intelligent and affectionate obedience of American children.

There were, of course, many American critics of the newer attitudes. One writer, in 1840, deplored "the laxness of family government" and "the opinion that punishments are rarely, if ever, necessary." The root of the trouble, he believed, lay "in setting aside the teachings of Scripture in regard to natural depravity." Further, since the father of the family was responsible to God alone, no power on earth had the right to interfere between him and his family, save in extreme cases of neglect and abuse.[2] In many families, however, particularly early in the century, the old severity still prevailed. And, in many cases, children were still terrified into submission by belief in the devil, a hell of fire and brimstone, and the "wrath of a just God."[3] Belief in original sin was inculcated even in infant schools; one manual of 1830 contained these lines: "Yes! I was even born in sin, and all my heart is bad within." Discipline in the schools retained much of its old-time harshness until the middle of the century. An average public school in Boston, in 1845, numbered four hundred pupils and gave sixty-five whippings a day, or one every six minutes.

By this time the development of a graded series of secular schools controlled and supported by the state was well under way. The characteristic American system of education, for children of the poor and the privileged alike, exercised an enormous influence in concentrating attention on childhood. American elementary education was reorganized after 1860

[1] Reprinted by permission of the publishers, The Arthur H. Clark Company, from Calhoun's *Social History of the American Family*, Vol. II, p. 65.

[2] *Op. cit.*, pp. 63, 68.

[3] Henry James, Sr., who was born in 1811, used to recall "bedewing my pillow with tears" and "beseeching God to grant me forgiveness." He was brought up to fear the "vengeance of an angry God," and was long unhappy, "encompassed with the terrors of hell and dread of estrangement from God." C. Hartley Grattan, *The Three Jameses* (1932).

through the introduction of Pestalozzi's ideas, and the first public school kindergarten was opened in 1873. The earliest important scientific study of children was made in 1879, based on the physical measurements of 1,000 Boston school children; and movements for the protection of children began about the same time.

CHILDREN'S BOOKS AS ILLUSTRATIVE OF CHANGING ATTITUDES TOWARDS CHILDHOOD

In his fascinating study, *Children's Books in England*, Darton points out that, before the middle of the eighteenth century, children's books did not stand out as a definite branch of literature, however subordinate. To-day they stand second only in number to works of fiction. The modern movement may be said to have begun when John Newberry published books deliberately designed, not only to *instruct*, but to *amuse* children. From that time on, according to Darton, "children's books were always the scene of a battle between instruction and amusement, between restraint and freedom, between hesitant morality, and spontaneous happiness."[1] The Puritan distrust of pleasure and spirit of solemn didacticism influenced the majority of children's books till well beyond the middle of the nineteenth century. Many were devastatingly pious; almost all, in Rosenbach's words, were "dripping with solemn virtue."[2] Goodness was shown to be uniformly profitable, while mischief and carelessness, not to speak of worse sins, brought inevitable catastrophe. In the illustrations, the bad boys look miserable, the good, smugly prosperous; tomboy girls are a source of endless embarrassment, while the prim are a joy to all. Exemplary children, perfect models of decorum, are made to indulge in the most absurdly priggish and well-informed conversation. One schoolmaster, writing as late as 1840, advises his young reader that "his looks should be complacent and composed, modest yet confident, affable and condescending." He further reminds him that "the circumstance of your being sent to school places you above numbers of vulgar and indigent children who are suffered to wander about the streets."[3]

Condescension appears to have been a prevailing characteristic on the part of the writers themselves. Those so desirous

---

[1] *Op. cit.*, pp. v–vi.

[2] "Gleaming Pageant of Children's Tales," *The New York Times Magazine*, Sept. 10, 1933.

[3] Quoted by Stoddard, *op. cit.*, pp. 315, 316.

of "improving" the minds of the young felt themselves superior to their little readers. Mrs. Barbauld praised Watts, "For the condescension of his Muse, which was very able to take a loftier flight," adding, "But it may well be doubted, whether poetry *ought* to be lowered to the capacities of children."[1] She herself, according to her brother, had been "censored for employing talents of so superior a kind in the composition of books for children"; yet, as he was kind enough to assure her, such a task is "by no means an ignoble employment." What Darton calls the "full-blown moral tale," was preceded by a period in which Rousseau exercised a great influence on the writers of children's books. Not only was there a tremendous crop of books in imitation of Robinson Crusoe (the only book Émile was allowed to read); but excellent stories, such as those of Maria Edgeworth, fill the reader with "the oppressive certainty that a calamity with a vivid moral will befall the injudicious child."[2] Some of Rousseau's followers censured fairytales for not being useful, but many of the more orthodox moralists, such as Mrs. Trimmer, considered them definitely evil. The most intense moralist of them all was Mrs. Sherwood, who, in *The Fairchild Family*, still adhered to the doctrine that "all children are by nature evil, and while they have none but the Evil principle to guide them, pious and prudent parents must check their naughty passions in any way that they have in their power, and force them into decent and proper behavior."[3] The Quaker moralists were far more gentle, but even they wrote tales such as: *Idle Ann, or the Dunce Reclaimed*, and *Industry and Idleness, a Pleasing and Instructive Tale for Good Little Girls*.

With the Taylors' *Original Songs for Infant Minds* (1804), the moral tale turns into humorous verse. A host of other books of verse for children followed this successful volume, which included such verses as "Twinkle, Twinkle Little Star."

[1] Quoted by Darton, *op. cit.*, p. 156.   [2] *Ibid.*, p. 142.
[3] The first part of *The Fairchild Family* appeared in 1818, the fourth in 1847. In it occurs a passage where Mr. Fairchild uses appalling means to "force" his children to desist from quarreling and to "love each other with perfect and heavenly love." Not content with "whipping their hands till they smarted again," he solemnly and mysteriously conducts them to see "something very shocking." This turns out to be "the corpse of a man hung in chains; it had not yet fallen to pieces, although it had hung there some years; . . . but the face of the corpse was so shocking that the children could not look on it. . . . The wind blew strong and shook the body upon the gibbet, rattling the chains by which it hung." The children beg, "Oh! let us go." "Not yet," says the inexorable Mr. Fairchild, and proceeds to tell "the history of that wretched man, . . . a murderer, one who first hated, and afterwards killed his brother." The children thereupon ask if they may "kneel down and pray for new hearts." Quoted by Darton, *ibid.*, pp. 175–177.

In some of these was to be found the "dawn of levity," verses which were simply good fun with no trace of "archness" or "be-good-ness." In 1846, Edward Lear's *Book of Nonsense* takes "the whole insane liberty of being absurd," whereas, in the English translation (1848) of Hoffman's *Struwelpeter*, "The Taylorian Awful Warning was carried to the point where Awe topples over into helpless laughter."[1]

Apart from such instances, however, it was not till 1865, with *Alice in Wonderland*, that "children's literature was emancipated from the thralldom of the older generation." Darton calls *Alice*, "the spiritual volcano of children's books, . . . the first unapologetic . . . appearance in print . . . of liberty of thought in children's books. . . . It was to be enjoyed . . . with neither forethought nor remorse. . . . The turning-point had at last been reached in the long struggle of joy against solemnity."[2]

SUGGESTED READING

Calhoun, A. W., *A Social History of the American Family*, 3 vols., 1917–1919, Vol. I, Chs. VI, XVII; Vol. II, Ch. III; Vol. III, Ch. VII.

Cubberley, E. P., *The History of Education*, 1920, Chs. VI, VII, XV.

——, *Readings in the History of Education*, 1920, Chs. VI, VII, XV.

Darton, F. J. H., *Children's Books in England*, 1932.

Earle, A. M., *Child Life in Colonial Days*, 1899.

Forest, I., *Preschool Education*, 1927.

Furnivall, F. J., ed., *The Babees Book*, 1868.

Goodsell, W., *A History of Marriage and the Family*, rev. ed., 1934, Chs. VI–IX.

Monroe, P., *A Text Book in the History of Education*, 1905, Chs. V–XIV.

Reisner, E. H., *The Evolution of the Common School*, 1930.

Salzman, L. F., *English Life in the Middle Ages*, 1926.

Sewall, S., *Diary* (ed. Van Doren, M.), 1927.

Stoddard, L., *The Story of Youth*, 1928.

Stuart, D., *The Boy through the Ages*, 1926.

——, *The Girl through the Ages*, 1933.

[1] *Ibid.*, pp. 249–250.

[2] *Ibid.*, pp. 267, 268. The leading English children's books have always formed the nucleus of children's libraries in America, and here too there has been the same transition from the religious attitude, through the didactic to the sympathetic attitude prevailing to-day. Since the middle of the century there have been numerous American authors producing excellent books for children. The mass of inferior and pious literature distributed through Sunday School libraries was superseded by worthwhile juvenile literature distributed by the children's departments in public libraries.

THE MODERN FAMILY

CHAPTER IX

EDUCATION IN THE CENTURY OF THE CHILD

THE CHILD AND SOCIETY

Education as the Supreme Human Interest. Writing in the opening years of the present century, Ellen Key foresaw "the time . . . in which the child will be looked upon as holy"; when the central duty and responsibility of society will be for the generations to come, that they may be well-born and well-educated. Thirty years have gone by, and we still have grounds for believing that the twentieth century may prove worthy to be called *The Century of the Child*. Ellen Key based her hope on the fact that a new factor had entered the situation: with scientific knowledge as to the nature and needs of the child, we are at last supplied with means to realize our educational ideals. She was thus in agreement with the greatest educational leader of to-day, John Dewey.

The fundamentals of Dewey's educational philosophy are world-wide in their application. But, fortunately for the purposes of this book, his views are the outgrowth of American conditions, and his practical proposals are primarily for the reorganization of American education. He sees in education the supreme human interest; for the hope of the future lies ever in the younger generation. In the past, however, except where chance has effected alteration, the younger generation has been modeled after the old. "Docility is looked upon," Dewey says, "not as ability to learn whatever the world has to teach, but as subjection to those instructions of others which reflect *their* current habits. To be truly docile is to be eager to learn all the lessons of active, inquiring, expanding experience. . . . When we think of the docility of the young we think first of the stocks of information adults wish to impose and the ways of acting they want to reproduce."[1] "That the most precious part of plasticity consists in ability to form habits of independent judgment and of inventive initiation has been ignored. . . . The weight of adult custom has been thrown . . . against those [tendencies] which make for variation and

[1] *Human Nature and Conduct*, p. 64.

independence.''[1] ''But with the dawn of the idea of progressive betterment and an interest in new uses of impulses, there has grown up some consciousness of the extent to which a future new society of changed purposes and desires may be created by a deliberate humane treatment of the impulses of youth. This is the meaning of education; for a truly humane education consists in an intelligent direction of native activities in the light of the possibilities and necessities of the social situation.''[2]

Dewey is the leader of contemporary educational reform because he combines social idealism with a perception of the full significance of scientific method. While there is increasing recognition of the value of childhood and of the responsibility of society to its immature members, few fully appreciate the lesson taught by scientific method: that ideals are realized only when dependable means are developed for the attainment of specific aims. Social institutions must be judged by their consequences for human well-being, and deliberate attempts must be made to remedy specific evils. Of central importance are the educational institutions: the family and the school. For, as Dewey says: ''the chief means of continuous, graded, economical improvement and social rectification lies in utilizing the opportunities of educating the young to modify prevailing types of thought and desire.''[3]

The Haphazard Expansion of American Education. Schools are responsive to social change, and an enormous expansion of educational facilities has taken place in America.[4] It is in education more than anywhere else that Americans have sought to realize what James Truslow Adams has called the ''American Dream''; and the result is the achievement, for the first time anywhere, of the physical and administrative basis for universal education. The American people, Hart says, are animated by ''a profound, almost a pathetic faith in education, though we are not sure what education is.''[5] Such uncertainty is of recent origin. The public school system developed in the confident belief that education was the key to individual success and should be equally available to all, a belief fostered under

---

[1] *Ibid.*, pp. 97–98. [2] *Ibid.*, p. 96. [3] *Ibid.*, p. 127.

[4] In 1850 there were less than *twenty-five* public high schools in America, as against 6,085 private and denominational academies. In 1930 there were 20,000. Over 50% of all boys and girls of high school age, some 4,750,000, attend these schools. Judd has estimated that approximately a quarter of the population of the United States are directly engaged in educational activities, while something like $2,250,000,000 is spent annually on education.

[5] *A Social Interpretation of Education* (1929), p. 236.

frontier conditions. It was the business of the school to equip
with the tools of learning. Schools were supplements to the vital
educational influences of home and community life. Traditions,
skills, disciplines, and development of character were all acquired
by the young through their participation in everyday activities.

Now, however, all is changed. There is continued expansion,
it is true, but, as Dewey says: "at the present time education
has no great directive aim. It grows, but it grows from specific
pressure exerted here and there, not because of any large or
inspiring social policy. It expands by piecemeal additions, not
by the movement of a vital force within."[1] Take, for example,
the transference to the city of the typical elementary school, developed under frontier and agricultural conditions. In the city
the child is deprived of all opportunities for education through
participation in the activities of home and community; and
even of facilities for safe outdoor play. Earlier changes in
the schools were largely administrative, to meet the problem
of dealing with larger numbers, and only recently has there
been effort to supply the deficiencies in the lives of city children
and to make the schools places where, in Kilpatrick's words,
"actual living goes on." Public schools have accordingly, as
Hart points out, never been made truly democratic, except in
a geographic sense. There are public schools "everywhere, but not
for all children according to their needs."[2] The realization and
even the fair trial of the democratic ideal is prevented, moreover,
so long as culture is still identified as the possession of an upper,
leisure class, while the education of workers is conceived as
utilitarian, its sole purpose being to enable them to earn a living.

The dualism between culture and utility, inherited from non-
democratic societies, has, paradoxically enough, been reënforced
by the American tradition of "rugged individualism," developed
in an era when there seemed unbounded opportunity for individuals to make their way, particularly if equipped with an education.
But in the present era of corporate interdependence, there are no
longer great opportunities for individual advancement, except for
a favored few. As has been well said, individualism to-day is the
prerogative of these alone, while the ruggedness is reserved for
the masses. Education can no longer retain its individualistic
aims unrevised if it is to keep abreast of social realities.

[1] From an address on the radio given Oct. 25, 1931; reported in the *New York
Times*, Nov. 1, 1931.
[2] *Op. cit.*, pp. 182–183. Fuller realization of this fact has led to the current movement for Federal school grants. See *New York Times*, Feb. 24, 1938.

CENTRAL AIMS OF EDUCATION

The Development of Individual Capacity, of Social Insight, and Critical Intelligence. The educational confusion of the present "is due ultimately to aimlessness. Only new aims," says Dewey, "can inspire educational effort for clarity and unity. They alone reduce confusion; if they do not terminate conflict they will at least render it intelligent and profitable."[1] It goes without saying that these aims cannot be fixed, preconceived ends, imposed from without, and used in a rigid control of educational processes. They must, on the contrary, arise within experience as the outgrowth of existing social conditions and the needs of individuals. They must be principles for guidance, and lead to the suggestion of specific procedures to be tested by the results they achieve.

The fundamental purpose of education, as envisaged by Dewey and his disciples, has many important aspects. Of these, three outstanding aspects may be emphasized as representing central aims of education. As aspects, they are not mutually exclusive but rather reënforce each other, in the measure in which they integrate, one with another, to form the democratic ideal. In the first place, education must aim at securing the *full growth of every individual.* Dewey says: "What the best and wisest parent wants for his own child, that must the community want for all its children."[2] This means that "the right of every person to realization of his potential capacities," must be "effectively recognized," and all must be provided with opportunity "to develop rich and diversified experience."[3] As Bode puts it: "To be truly democratic, education must treat the individual himself as an end, and set itself the task of preparing him for that intellectual and emotional sharing in the life and affairs of men which embodies the spirit of the Golden Rule."[4] To encompass this end, according to Dewey: "School facilities must be secured of such amplitude and efficiency as will in fact and not simply in name discount the effects of economic inequalities, and secure to all the wards of the nation equality of equipment for their future careers."[5] A democratic society must, moreover, "have a type of education which gives individuals a personal interest

---

[1] *The Way out of Educational Confusion* (1931), pp. 40–41.

[2] *The School and Society* (1st ed., 1900; rev. ed., 1930), p. 3.

[3] Dewey and Childs in *The Educational Frontier* (D. Appleton-Century Company, 1933), p. 317.

[4] *Fundamentals of Education* (1921), p. 62. [5] *Democracy and Education*, p. 114.

in social relationships and control, and the habits of mind which secure social changes without introducing disorder."[1]

In this last quotation, two other central aims of education become apparent. As social relationships become more complex, there is pressing need for individuals in whom enrichment of experience means, at the same time, development of *social insight*. A central aim of education must be the initiation of children into responsible membership in society. Each should be prepared for work through which he may find individual happiness and contribute to the service of others. Education must aim at the production of vocational ability which is not antagonistic to, but synonymous with, personal culture, and serves as a point of departure for informed social insight and a sense of social responsibility.

A third aim must be the development of *critical intelligence*. To establish a "moving stability," a "dynamic equilibrium" between thought and social change, "we must," in Kilpatrick's words, "free our children to think for themselves."[2] The development of science has disclosed the methods by which intelligence can operate most effectively. It should, accordingly, become a central aim of education to foster scientific attitudes of thought, observation, and inquiry. The future of our civilization depends, says Dewey, "upon the widening spread and deepening hold of the scientific habit of mind; and . . . the problem of problems in our education is, therefore, to discover how to mature and make effective this scientific habit."[3]

Education must facilitate the realization of the fact that, as Bode says: "the whole adventure of the human race on this planet *is* an adventure, an experiment, and that our institutions, our beliefs, our practices must all be held subject to revision as we go along."[4] "Those who hold the remaking of institutions and traditions is as much the office of conscious education as is the transmission of values attained in the past, will not see their ideal realized even in a fragmentary way until the formation of an experimental attitude of mind becomes the unified and unifying goal of education in its intellectual phase."[5]

The development of critical intelligence implies that each individual must learn to think for himself. Students must learn not *what* to think, but *how* to think. While education

[1] *Ibid.*, p. 115.
[2] *Education for a Changing Civilization* (1926), p. 60.
[3] *Character and Events*, Vol. II, p. 774.
[4] *Op. cit.*, p. 32.
[5] Dewey and Childs in *The Educational Frontier*, p. 62.

must foster the social spirit, the power to share in common activities and to act socially, it must retain, and indeed intensify, individualism in thought. The following motto for education is proposed by Dewey: "Learn to act with and for others, while you learn to think and to judge for yourself."[1] Dewey's hope for the future of education rests on the fact that, in education, meet three of the most powerful motives of human activity: affection for children, as shown particularly in the desire of parents that their children may have the fullest opportunities; the concern of thoughtful people for social welfare, for the reform and future progress of society; and, finally, the intellectual and scientific motive. "If the good will, the loyalty, the political faith and hope of the American people can be united with the affection which parents have for their children, and the union can be directed by the spirit of free scientific inquiry, there is no ground for fear of failure."[2]

The Development of Reliable Methods for the Realization of These Aims. Bertrand Russell has said: "There is only one road to progress in education as in other human affairs, and this is science wielded by love. Without science, love is powerless; without love, science is destructive."[3] Improvement in educational methods has come about through the efforts of those who not only loved children, but who made full use of all available scientific data. The development of objective methods of child study was first made possible by Séguin's work with the feeble-minded; a most significant fact. These subnormal children could not be regarded as morally responsible, and were accordingly observed in a scientific manner apart from considerations of praise or blame. The great influence of the medical mind on child psychology and the development of educational methods is not always realized. Many notable contributions to psychology have been made by doctors, and their work has helped to bring about a realization that the medical insistence on prevention rather than cure has nowhere a more important application than in education.[4] Long ago Horace Mann said, "Where anything is growing, one former

---

[1] Radio address, reported in the *New York Times*, Nov. 1, 1931.

[2] *Ibid.*

[3] *Education and the Good Life* (1926), p. 234.

[4] A few well-known names may be mentioned: Itard, Pereira, and Séguin, pioneers in the study and treatment of deaf-mutes and mentally defective children, and Montessori, whose educational methods were first developed for use among the subnormal; William James and Stanley Hall in this country; Havelock Ellis, pioneer in the psychology of sex; Binet and Simon, pioneers in the development of mental tests; and Freud, Jung, and Adler, leaders in the development of psychoanalysis.

is worth a thousand re-formers." The profound truth of this statement is attested to by all psychologists, who, however far they differ in methods of approach or in their interpretation of data, yet are unanimous in their emphasis on the fundamental influence of the nurture and education of the early years of childhood.

Enthusiasm for scientific method has led to certain exaggerations, it is true; to a mechanical over-simplification of the processes of human behavior, as with certain behaviorists; or to the premature application to education of insufficiently verified theories and procedures, as in the enormous development of mental testing, and the use of statistical methods. The whole movement for the development of accurate measurements in education is, of course, of fundamental value. Where mistakes have been made, they have been due to a departure from the scientific spirit of experimental inquiry, of holding results as tentative and in need of constant revision. Instead of this, results have been taken as final and as the basis for dubious educational practices.[1] It is true, nevertheless, that the development of mental testing in recent years has greatly increased the accuracy of estimates which may be made of ability and achievement. The results of tests have also been shown to have diagnostic value for child guidance. Great advances have been made in accurate knowledge of the growth and development of children. As the first enthusiasm for immediate results gives way to the development of more reliable experimental techniques, further advances may be confidently expected.

Added emphasis has been placed on the extreme significance of the early years of childhood by the development of abnormal psychology with its practical applications in clinical psychology, psychoanalysis, and mental hygiene. It has been conclusively shown that pathological conditions are largely due to the development of emotional maladjustments in early childhood. Attitudes injurious to individual happiness, and preventing adequate social adjustment, have been found in greater or less degree, in the majority of so-called normal individuals.

The development of psychiatry has been profoundly influenced by the different schools of psychoanalysis. In his diagnosis of neurotic patients, Freud found himself forced to the conclusion that, in the forgotten experiences of early childhood, lay the clue to an understanding of character and behavior in later life. Techniques were discovered whereby the "unconscious"

[1] See Dewey, *The Sources of a Science of Education* (1929).

might be explored and the memories of childhood to some extent recovered, and in many cases distressing symptoms have been alleviated where their original cause has thus been uncovered. For Freud, the "unconscious" is primarily the realm of ego-centric and asocial primitive impulse, and, above all, of "infantile sexuality"; and he presents the now familiar and exaggerated picture of the stormy conflict supposed to be waged in the soul of the young child, with his possessive love of his mother, and his "ambivalent" attitude of jealousy and admiration for his father. In Adler's interpretation, the "unconscious" is related, as is the whole of life, to the individual's struggle against inferiority. The child naturally finds himself in a position of inferiority toward his parents and older brothers and sisters; and wise treatment may be necessary to free him from a sense of inferiority and a compensatory impulse to dominate. Jung agrees with Freud and Adler that the personalities of the parents and family relationships are the most important formative influences in the child's life: he does not deny the importance of sexual impulses or of the longing for self-expression and power. He believes, however, that the "unconscious" is the result not only of repressed personal experiences, but of a "collective unconscious," memory traces, as it were, of the experiences of the race.

Some of the psychoanalysts have been guilty of dogmatic and exaggerated claims and of fantastic distortions of fact. In particular there has been neglect, on the part of Freud and some of his followers, of the cultural determination of sexual behavior. Malinowski has shown conclusively that the "Oedipus Complex," which Freud calls the "nuclear complex of the neuroses," far from being the effect of fixed native impulses, is the product of the typical patriarchal family. In the matrilineal society of the Trobriand Islands, a study of customs, myths, and dreams reveals the fact that the characteristic repressions are those engendered by this radically different pattern of family relationships. Malinowski concludes that, whether in Europe or in the Trobriand Islands, "the complex is *not* a cause but a by-product, not a creative principle but a maladjustment."[1]

Psychoanalysis has, nevertheless, rendered a variety of valuable services. Its insistence on the profound importance of unconscious forces in determining not only conduct, but desire, belief, and judgment, has revolutionized the theories and prac-

[1] *Sex and Repression in Savage Society*, p. 279 and *passim*.

tices of psychiatry. The emphases placed on individual development, on the supreme influence of family relationships, and on the fundamental importance of the experiences of early childhood are all to the good. Even the most critical must admit, as does Adolf Meyer, that there is "some truth in much of this." He accordingly advises students "to search for the facts along this line, where real facts suggest such a procedure."[1]

Psychoanalysis has finally to its credit the great stimulus it afforded to the development of the mental hygiene movement, a widespread effort to prevent and cure maladjustments of personality. An increasing number of Habit Clinics, or Child Guidance Clinics are working with young children in their formative years in an endeavor to correct defects and build the foundations of wholesome character. This movement is of very recent origin, particularly in its emphasis on the preschool child. As Gesell puts it: "The study of child development has become at once a branch of human biology and of social science. . . . Child development is a focal area for psycho-biological and medical knowledge converging upon the central problem of early human growth."[2] "It seems certain that the preventive methods of pediatrics contain a germ capable of endless development in the supervision and control of early human growth."[3]

UNSATISFACTORY FUNCTIONING OF THE HOME AS AN EDUCATIVE INFLUENCE

The Crucial Significance of Early Childhood. With the discovery that human nature can no longer be regarded as fixed and unalterable, that modification of intellectual and emotional dispositions may be brought about by specific changes in the social environment, education becomes an instrument for the progressive and reciprocal amelioration of human nature and of social institutions.

The perception of this fact, reënforced by the convergence of many lines of scientific investigation, focuses attention on the crucial significance of early childhood; and on the imperative need to supply the child from birth with conditions favorable for his full, free growth as an individual, and as a responsible and intelligent member of society. The original tendencies of the child will require redirection and reorganization, but

[1] "Normal and Abnormal Repression," *Bulletin* No. 13 of the Progressive Education Association (1922).

[2] From *The Guidance of Mental Growth in Infant and Child* (1930), p. 11. By permission of The Macmillan Company, publishers.

[3] *Ibid.*, p. 317.

never mere repression. There is much, indeed, in the native and unspoiled attitudes of early childhood which should be preserved as infinitely precious. Burnham points to the fact that the child already possesses that integration of personality, the achievement of which is the goal of mental hygiene.[1] He is socially responsive, trustful, free from self-consciousness, from inhibitions and repressions, delights in activity and in the performance of his chosen tasks, and is capable of concentrated attention. Dewey points out that in his "ardent curiosity, fertile imagination and love of experimental inquiry," the attitude of the child is "very near to the attitude of the scientific mind."[2] All too soon this first response of little children to the world loses its early freshness, and becomes blurred and covered up by the impress of the adult world. Everyone possesses originality, everyone is a unique center of experience, but individual potentialities can only be realized by the provision of conditions which ensure wholesome growth.

Home and school gain new significance. As the institutions most influential in guiding the mental growth of children, their opportunities and responsibilities are more clearly revealed than ever before. This is particularly true of the home, for family relationships are now recognized as the fundamental formative influence in the life of the child. Authorities are for the most part in agreement that the individual family is not only the natural agency for the nurture of children, but that it alone can provide the most favorable conditions for their growth. The infant needs individual attention and a fostering love, not only in order that his physical needs may be met, but that he may have that sense of security, which is the essential foundation and support of independent growth.

Influences Adverse to Successful Nurture. There need be no surprise at the unsatisfactory functioning of the modern family as an educative influence. The child may best learn the rudiments of social living and grow to emotional maturity within the close relationships of family life, *provided* these relationships are wholesome and harmonious. But the extreme susceptibility of the little child to the influences of his social environment exposes him to almost inevitable maladjustment, whenever these relationships are in any way unwholesome or discordant. Authorities are agreed in stressing what Gesell calls, "the axiomatic importance of the normal parent-child relationship," and "the superlative importance of preserving from day to

[1] *The Normal Mind* (1924), p. 681.   [2] *How We Think* (rev. ed., 1933), p. v.

day, and from month to month, the most vital thing of all—
a wholesome consistent parent-child relationship; . . . there is
but one fundamental problem—namely, the normalizing of the
relationship between parent and child."[1]

The number of obviously *bad* parents is relatively few: those
who do not love their children, are cruel to them, or neglect
or desert them; even those who are too selfish and shallow
to be capable of more than a possessive love. The vast majority
of parents love their children; their own children at least are
precious to them, even if they fail to extend their sympathy
to the children of others. And yet it is these well-meaning
parents who to-day are becoming more and more bewildered,
and conscious, if not of their failures, yet of the difficulties
of nurture. A wide variety of social and economic conditions
have, it is true, an adverse influence on family relationships.
These are discussed in later chapters; and may, for the moment,
be disregarded, while we consider the influence of parental attitudes on the behavior of children.

In matters of health there is increasing reliance on expert
guidance. But this is very far from being the case, as yet, in
matters of character or behavior. The Lynds, in their study
of Middletown in 1924, found that mothers who safeguarded
the health of their children in an empirical, matter-of-fact way
frequently adhered blindly to traditional prejudices and procedures when it came to problems of personality and behavior.
Many parents were bewildered, but "the traditional view that
the dependence of the child carries with it the right and duty of
the parents to enforce 'discipline' and 'obedience' still prevails."[2]

Good children have been traditionally conceived as those
who give as little trouble as possible to their elders, who do
what they are told and conform to the standards of the people
about them. Parents who to-day cling to such conceptions
betray not only ignorance, but a lack of understanding of the
needs of a changing civilization; and are entirely unfitted to
interpret the world to their children. Quite apart from emotional
maladjustments caused by repressive methods, the child who

---

[1] *Op. cit.*, p. 15.

[2] *Middletown* (Harcourt, Brace and Company, 1929), p. 142. At club meetings,
such as the Mother's Council, there was little discussion of specific situations, but
a manifest tendency to sentimental generalization. For example: "Children are not
a problem but a joy. We can trust them and God will lead them"; "There are three
notable words in the English language, mother, home and heaven. . . . There is
nothing like being a good home-maker to be able to raise up a child in the way he
should go." *Ibid.*, pp. 177, 178.

has been taught unquestioning obedience and acceptance of the standards of narrow-minded parents is ill prepared to cope with the complexities of modern life with its conflicting standards.

One of the most frequent causes for failures in home nurture is the unwise use of parental authority. In general the behavior problems of children fall into two groups.[1] The child may have been spoilt and indulged and given inadequate incentives to independence; or else the environment has been too harsh, and social requirements are beyond his capacity. In the first case, dependence is unduly prolonged, emotional patterns and attitudes endure long after they should have been outgrown.[2] Moreover, the spoilt child will inevitably, sooner or later, encounter the other class of problems; for he will find his environment too difficult. When the latter is the case, the child tends either to escape his difficulties by withdrawal, or else to become aggressive. If life is too difficult for a little child, typical symptoms make their appearance which, if unalleviated, often lead to permanent maladjustments.

Typical of the evasion of social requirements by withdrawal are such traits as shyness, dreaminess, dependence on adults and on fixed routines, solitary and unsocial attitudes, suspicion, fear of criticism, inefficiency, and inability to bear responsibility. In extreme form such traits may lead to a variety of neuroses, to alcoholism or drug addiction, or to suicide. Typical of more assertive methods of escape are temper tantrums, aggressiveness, disobedience and defiance of authority, antagonistic and contentious attitudes, a desire for domination. Delinquency and crime may be a final result.

The child's emotional development is thus largely determined by the atmosphere of the home: by the interrelationships between family members. The relationship between the parents is of first importance, and what has been called the "friction home" is perhaps the most frequent and potent source of maladjustments in the children. The breaking up of a home by death, desertion, or divorce almost always has deleterious effects, but discord between parents who continue to live together is even more harmful.

Inconsistent discipline is a chief source of danger, particularly

---

[1] To state the matter thus is to run the risks of over-simplification. For present purposes, this seems justifiable, however, particularly in view of the more detailed discussion of the nurture of children, given in Chapters XXIII and XXIV.

[2] Fixations at an immature stage of emotional life are sometimes due, not to over-indulgence, but to *deprivation* of emotional experience at its appropriate stage, as in the case of an unwanted and unloved baby.

where there is open disagreement between the parents, each thereby undermining the influence of the other. Integrated personality is impossible, where opposing dispositions are being fostered by, for example, harshness on the part of a father, and weak indulgence on the part of a mother. Where parents make favorites among their children bitter antagonisms and jealousies are a frequent result. Extreme instances of discord between brothers and sisters are found where a parent, discontented with his or her relationship with the other parent, seeks compensation in possessive love for a child. A child who is the object of such love rarely achieves independence, or that emancipation from parental control, which should be the goal of all home education.[1]

Another form of discrimination occurs when parents seek to use their children as a means for satisfying their own ambitions. A disappointed parent may hope that a child will accomplish what he or she has failed to achieve. A successful parent may favor the child who seems most likely to follow in his or her footsteps.[2] Children whose abilities and interests are at variance with those of their parents are discouraged and made to feel inferior, and so, in the long run, often fail to accomplish what they might otherwise have done. An exaggerated interest in school marks, and a rating of children in terms of these symbols of achievement in school, have been shown to be most harmful practices.

Abuse of authority is a frequent cause for a child's failure to achieve an independent well-balanced personality. The frequency with which parents, particularly fathers, still dominate their children is due to several causes. In the first place, it is wholly in accord with patriarchal traditions, and disciplinary ideas are often accompanied by complacent notions of the peculiar obligation of children to their parents. In the second place, disciplinarians justify themselves as good "managers," by pointing to the correct conduct which may be secured through terrorization, ignoring its less obvious, but always harmful and more lasting, emotional consequences.[3] And

[1] Possessive love for a child of the opposite sex is most frequent, and to this situation have been traced many failures to reach heterosexual maturity.

[2] The phrase "a chip off the old block" summarizes the traditional attitude, with its neglect of individuality, and its endeavor to force the lives of children into prearranged patterns.

[3] Van Waters has called attention to the frequent use of the word *management* in this connection; a term which was originally applied to the handling of a horse. Her well-known indictment of parenthood, "Nineteen Ways of Being a Bad Parent," should be studied by all parents and by everyone interested in the nurture of children. *Parents on Probation* (1927), pp. 61–99.

finally, a certain degree of self-assertion is natural. An individual who finds himself repressed and feels inferior in most of life's relationships frequently satisfies his thwarted impulses by dominating the weaker members of his family. The most frequent cause of domineering conduct on the part of a parent, again particularly a father, becomes clear. He was, himself, domineered over in childhood, and even though he then did not openly rebel, he has carried, into adulthood, "a habit of reacting to every interference with anger." Controlling himself in his relations with superiors, he lets himself go with dependents, particularly with children, on whom he "may vent his anger in the sacred name of discipline."[1] Arbitrary demands for explicit obedience, impatient repression, intolerant criticism, sarcasm or even cruelty may all be rationalized as justifiable severity by the self-righteous parent.[2]

"Bad" parents are almost always found to be in their turn the children of "bad" parents. As Glueck puts it, emotionally maladjusted parents can rarely escape doing "violence to child nature, by using the child-parent relationship as a battlefield for their own unresolved problems."[3] The warped personalities of parents contaminate the home atmosphere and create fresh distortions in their children. A vicious circle, or rather a chain, often of many links, thus comes into being, in which the psychological sins of the parents are indeed visited upon the children to the third and fourth generation, or even beyond.

It must be remembered, as Glueck points out, that "the forces which make for family conflict, for maladjustments and disruption, have their roots in the same natural dispositions of man and woman which make possible a healthy and happy adjustment to family life."[4] Thoughtful parents will not be slow to realize their unique responsibilities and to utilize the resources which are now being made available for their guidance. Self-criticism is stimulated by the knowledge that the manners, morals, and emotional and mental habits of their children are being fashioned through daily living, in which they, as

[1] Mary B. Sayles, *The Problem Child at Home* (1928), p. 60.

[2] It is now becoming the practice to pay special attention to the early family history of the parents of a maladjusted child. When possible, the search is pushed even further back. In one family a violent and cruel father of a delinquent boy was found to be reproducing the exact methods of discipline, including incessant beatings, by means of which his own childhood had been made miserable by his father, a cruel schoolmaster.

[3] D. C. Fisher and S. E. Gruenberg (editors), *Our Children* (1932), p. 176.

[4] *Ibid.*, p. 169.

parents, furnish concrete models and should be sympathetic companions, guides, and interpreters.

The parent-child relationship is, moreover, a changing, progressive relationship. "Weaning and security," Van Waters says, "must grow on the same stem."[1] Support should be gradually withdrawn and the child encouraged to choose his own path. It is no exaggeration to say that "the business of parenthood is the greatest in life." Its aim should ever be "that the child should grow up a better parent for the next generation."[2]

UNSATISFACTORY FUNCTIONING OF THE SCHOOL AS AN EDUCATIVE INFLUENCE

The Need for a Scientific Treatment of Behavior Problems in Schools. There is to-day a growing appreciation of the fact that problems of mental development cannot be treated in isolation from considerations of health and character. Society is assuming fuller responsibility for the health of school children, but only very recently has there been any realization of the need for a scientific treatment of behavior problems. Not only are multitudes of children poured into the schools from failing homes, but there are many factors, in the average school situation itself, which tend to produce further maladjustments. Strained relationships arise with teachers and others in authority, and the whole competitive system, in which an education, suited only for the few, makes failures out of the many, tends to produce feelings of inferiority, and to hinder wholesome development through the stimulation of individual interests. Wickman, in his study of *Children's Behavior and Teacher's Attitudes*, found the average teacher ignorant of the principles of mental hygiene, and wont to deal directly with the *symptoms* of behavior disorders, with no consideration whatever of their underlying causes. The teacher's first concern is to preserve an orderly routine, by means of obedience to classroom rules and subservience to the requirements of the curriculum. In most schools independent activity on the part of children, tendencies to sociability and free inquiry are sternly repressed. An artificial situation is created in which, the more normal the child, the harder it is for him or her to be "good." Transgressions against authority and aggressive conduct constitute the most serious problems from the teacher's point of view. Withdrawing and

[1] *Parents on Probation* (1927), p. 50.
[2] H. Crichton-Miller, *The New Psychology and the Parent* (1922), p. 12.

recessive behavior traits, suspected by mental hygienists as symptomatic of serious disorder, are disregarded by teachers, because they do not disturb the order of the classroom. It is obviously important that teachers should be familiar with the principles of mental hygiene. If they are able to detect early symptoms of maladjustment, they may then coöperate with a visiting-teacher, able, through special training as a psychiatric social-case-worker, to make a study of the child both in home and school.[1] Were all schools adequately staffed to deal with behavior problems in this way, much might be done for the prevention of serious maladjustment and delin-quency.

Failure of Schools to Realize the Central Aims of Education. Not only does the average school foster rather than prevent defects of personality, but, on its ethical side, as Dewey says, "the tragical weakness of the present school is that it endeavors to prepare future members of a social order in a medium in which the conditions of the social spirit are eminently wanting."[2] Traditional school procedures give little opportunity for the cultivation of social responsiveness. So far as social habits are learned in school, this is largely by means of so-called extra-curricular activities. As is so well illustrated in *Middletown*, there is a marked tendency to reproduce in these activities the social and political customs of the community, along with uncritical acceptance of its standards.[3]

The typical school tends to inculcate a sterile conformity with things as they are. Intellectually there is not only failure to provide conditions under which habits of independent think-ing are acquired, but the doses of ready-made information administered in the form of school subjects are selected in such a way as to enforce adherence to currently accepted opinions. A majority of the social science classes in the last two years at Middletown High School were indoctrinated with the prejudices of "100% Americanism." Far from fostering habits of informed criticism, such education reënforces other social pressures, and prevents the development of social insight and independent thought.

[1] For a detailed account of such work in a large elementary school, see E. Irwin and L. Marks, *Fitting the School to the Child* (1924).

[2] *The School and Society*, p. 12.

[3] In *Middletown in Transition* (1937), a study of the same city ten years later, the Lynds report conflict between contradictory trends, with the community pres-sure-forces, business, and the patriotic groups mobilizing against elements favoring change. Chapter VI.

This situation is not to be wondered at. The final authority in public education lies largely in the hands of those who are themselves the products of miseducation, and whose standards, moreover, are those of business efficiency. The American public school system, designed originally to furnish universal education and equal opportunities for all, has met its problems by applying factory methods of mass production to the training of the masses. For only *training*, and not education in the full sense, can result. Business methods of organization have put the control of schools in the hands of executives trained to combine business with educational administration. Authority and responsibility become centralized, and the work of schools is carried on by means of successive clean-cut divisions of labor. As Thayer says: "our machinery of administration runs counter to the professed purposes of public education. . . . The motive lying back of the prevailing conception . . . is . . . business efficiency, [while] the dominant aim of public education is to prepare . . . for intelligent participation in democratic living." Such a marked divergence has fostered "a progressive insulation of the school from forces without the school."[1]

The effect on teachers is particularly unfortunate. Personality and teaching qualifications tend to be subordinated in proportion as the emphasis is laid on the smooth working of a machine in which they are little more than the necessary cogs. To compensate for their exclusion from participation in the guidance of the work of the school, they are wont to be frequently and publicly thanked for their coöperation, in other words for meekly doing what they are told to do.[2] The efficiency of teachers is measured largely by their success in the distribution of ready-made information and in the imposition of standard patterns of thought and behavior. The work of a teacher thus tends to be reduced to the job of a factory hand, a fact symbolized in some schools by the spectacle of a long line of teachers, secretaries, janitors, scrub-women, and other employees of the school system punching a time clock, as they arrive or leave. The regimented world of school presents other features of a factory. Thousands are herded in gigantic buildings, seated in rows in immovable desks, occupied in set tasks for certain fixed periods marked by the ringing of

[1] *The Educational Frontier*, p. 220.

[2] Sometimes teachers are rated on a series of traits by administrative authorities. A *minus* rating on coöperation is frequently given to those of greatest ability as scholars and teachers, because they have shown themselves critical of prevailing abuses.

bells. Promotion from grade to grade is dependent on the *completion* of subjects and the acquisition of required numbers of *units*.

The schools cannot, of course, wholly escape the impact of social change; but, as the Lynds point out, too often "creakings in the system are met not by changes in its foundations, but by adding fresh stories to its superstructure; . . . strains or maladjustments in education are being met by further elaboration and standardization."[1] Uncritical acceptance of so-called scientific results and lack of insight into fundamental educational values are responsible for what Dewey characterizes as "the uncontrolled succession of one-sided, temporarily dominating interests and slogans that have affected educational theory and practice."[2] Failure is inevitable in all such *external* efforts at reorganizing a system of schools which has grown up, as Dewey puts it, by "piecemeal additions."[3] Each unit of the American school system developed in isolation from the others and with its own purposes to serve. No wonder that integration of the formal agencies of education with one another and with the community is lacking, in the absence of any concept which shall unify the process of education from within.

Contemporary educational arrangements contravene the principle of education as growth and enrichment of experience. Little opportunity exists for the all-round development of the majority, and few are prepared for social responsibility or intelligent participation in social reconstruction. Commenting on H. G. Wells' remark that we are engaged in a race between education and catastrophe, Dewey sees the race, in America, to be between a possible education which will face the future, and "a *miseducation* which will bear no vital relation to the needs and conditions of the modern world."[4] No complete escape is, of course, possible from the circle within which education must move. It is a matter rather "of accelerating momentum in the right direction, and of increasing the effective energy of the factors that make for removing obstacles."[5] Of recent

---

[1] *Middletown*, p. 210.

[2] *The Sources of a Science of Education*, p. 51.

[3] See *The School and Society*, for a brief but graphic account of this development.

[4] Radio address, reported in the *New York Times*, Nov. 1, 1931. Sir Norman Angell attacks the failures of education as a chief cause not only of social disorder, but of war. "Education has failed to develop in the millions, that pass through its mills, the particular skill and aptitude for discerning the social meaning of the facts that stare us in the face." *From Chaos to Control* (1933), p. 192.

[5] John Dewey, *Philosophy and Civilization* (1931), p. 316.

years this process has been facilitated by the influence of so-called *progressive* education.[1]

PROGRESSIVE EDUCATION

Dewey's Statement of Progressive Principles: The Utilization and Guidance of Present Interest. In the growing complexity of the modern world, there is increasing need for a special environment—the school—which is deliberately instituted and regulated with reference to educational purposes. The school should provide a simplified environment, one in which certain features are selected and arranged in a progressive order to facilitate the transmission of cultural resources. Unworthy features of existing society may be eliminated, only the more desirable being reproduced and so reënforced by the school. And the school should finally endeavor to provide a wide, inclusive, and well-balanced environment.

The general aims of education are promoted, if the work of the school contributes to experience, which, in Dewey's words, is "marked by executive competency in the management of resources and obstacles encountered (efficiency); by sociability, or interest in the direct companionship of others; by aesthetic taste or capacity to appreciate artistic excellence in at least some of its classic forms; by trained intellectual method, or interest in some mode of scientific achievement; and by sensitiveness to the rights and claims of others—conscientiousness."[2] The business of the school is, accordingly, to use present impulses, interests, and capacities in such a way that desirable dispositions and habits may develop. The healthy child is already "intensely active, and the question of education is the question of taking hold of his activities, of giving them direction."[3] The child's impulses and interests may, for this purpose, be grouped under four heads. First there is a social impulse, and interest in communication and conversation; secondly there is a constructive tendency, the interest in manipulating and making things; thirdly the child is led from manipulation to exploration, in which his tendencies towards inquiry and investigation find outlet. Finally, growing out of his interest in communication and construction, there are the expressive, artistic tendencies. The free and active expression

[1] At this point, progressive education is discussed in relation only to the school. Its further significance for family life is made apparent in Chapters XXIII and XXIV, where it is found that adequate home nurture embodies progressive principles and procedures.

[2] *Democracy and Education*, pp. 285–286.   [3] Dewey, *The School and Society*, p. 37.

of impulses has long been recognized as essential to healthy physical growth. Only recently has there been realization of the fact that desirable mental and moral growth is best secured through utilizing the spontaneous activities of childhood for educational purposes.

Dewey's Statement of Progressive Principles: Learning by Doing. Play and active work must be assigned a place in the curriculum for social and intellectual reasons. Learning is most effective when it is an outgrowth of activities which cause reflection; and coöperative association in such activities fosters desirable social dispositions. Play passes gradually into work where there is greater attention to the specific results to be achieved by an activity. Both are most efficiently utilized by the school where there "is the consistent use of simple occupations which appeal to the powers of youth and which typify general modes of social activity."[1] Methods of education are most effective, Dewey points out, where "they give the pupil something to do, not something to learn; and the doing is of such a nature as to demand thinking, or the intentional noting of connections; learning naturally results."[2] "Processes of instruction are unified in the degree in which they center in the production of good habits of thinking."[3] An educative experience must therefore embody the essentials of reflection. "They are first that the pupil have a genuine situation of experience . . . , a continuous activity in which he is interested for its own sake; secondly, that a genuine problem develop within this situation as a stimulus to thought; third, that he possess the information and make the observations necessary to deal with it; fourth, that suggested solutions occur to him which he shall be responsible for developing in an orderly way; fifth, that he have opportunity and occasion to test his ideas in application, to make their meaning clear and to discover for himself their validity."[3]

Dewey's Statement of Progressive Principles: The School as a Typical Community. Effective moral education is only possible where school conditions make possible a permeating social spirit. Schools must reproduce typical social life, for social living can only be learnt through actual experience. Education through constructive activities affords "a genuinely social medium—one where there is give and take in the building up of a common experience. . . . In place of a school set apart from life as a place for learning lessons, we have a miniature

[1] *Democracy and Education*, p. 241.   [2] *Ibid.*, p. 181.   [3] *Ibid.*, p. 192.

social group in which study and growth are incidents of present shared experience."[1]

In a progressive school the teacher shares in the activities of the pupils. His or her function is no longer that of direct, external, or coercive control; but simply that of providing stimulation and guidance. In this way the child identifies himself with work which arouses his interest. Attention and persistence are necessary to success. Discipline is the result. Moreover, in social situations, where all, teacher and pupils alike, participate in common efforts and purposes, there is that "common understanding of the means and ends of action [which] is the essence of social control."[2]

Dewey's Statement of Progressive Principles: The Use of Subject Matter. The teacher must be thoroughly familiar with the subject matter of school studies. Good teaching does not mean efficiency in securing appropriation of organized subject matter by the pupil, but rather the use of subject matter in interpreting and finding the pupil's interests. Learning will then mean that the child's experience gains in significance, he understands better what he is doing, he can more fully foresee consequences, and he acquires an added power of direction and control. The occupation upon which a child is engaged provides a center for the assimilation of information which adds significance to present activities.

The most obvious method by which experience may be enriched and given context and perspective is by placing it in its setting of space and time connections, by relating it with nature and with the activities and experiences of other human beings. For purposes of information and interpretation, geography and history are the fundamental school subjects. They are best treated as interdependent aspects of a common topic, the associated life of man in his enduring home, the Earth. Where children are engaged in an occupation which reproduces some typical art or industry, by means of which human beings have adapted natural forces to social uses, a vital center is found for a realization of the natural and human connections of their activity.[3] Social progress is seen to depend upon human intelligence as manifested in inventions and discoveries, and history becomes a means for cultivating a socialized intelligence. Occupations, moreover, furnish opportunity for insight into experimental method and for fostering a scientific habit

---

[1] *Ibid.*, p. 416.   [2] *Ibid.*, p. 47.
[3] Examples of such occupations are given on pp. 248–249.

of mind.[1] What of the famous 3 R's, so long considered almost the sole essentials of the elementary curriculum? The most effective motive to their mastery is found when these formal subjects are introduced as methods for coping with difficulties which arise in the course of constructive or expressive activities. Techniques thus exhibit themselves in their proper function, as the tools or instruments for the communication and control of experience.

Dewey's Statement of Progressive Principles: The Furtherance of the Democratic Ideal. A society is democratic, Dewey says, in so far as it "makes provision for participation in its good of all its members on equal terms and . . . secures flexible readjustment of its institutions through interaction of the different forms of associated life."[2] Education through shared activities furthers the qualities most necessary for the realization of the democratic ideal. Opportunity is provided for the discovery and development of individual capacity, and at the same time a social return is demanded of each member of the group. The function of intelligence in the direction of useful activity is revealed, and the age-old dualism between theory and practice, between culture and utility is destroyed. If all schools were reconstructed in accordance with progressive principles as envisaged by Dewey, the time would be hastened when the traditional distinctions between leisure and labor, between liberal and vocational education will be abolished. A truly democratic society would then be possible, "a society where all share in useful service and all enjoy a worthy leisure."[3]

The Development of Experimental Schools. Progressive schools are experiments in devising educative environments. Resembling one another in spirit to the extent in which they are animated by genuinely progressive principles, there is great diversity among them in their specific objectives and methods of procedure. These new schools, however, only fully deserve the name of progressive if they look upon their work as of a laboratory type; if their activities, while centered in the individual children committed to their charge, are yet conducted with such careful noting of conditions and consequences that they are able to contribute the results of their experiences to the sum of educational knowledge. The criteria for evaluating the results of school work in the experiences of pupils are the

---

[1] Only for advanced students should science be the study of technical organized subject matter, of the *abstract results* of tested thought.

[2] *Op. cit.*, p. 115.   [3] *Ibid.*, p. 300.

qualities of character enumerated by Dewey. Kilpatrick summarizes these criteria very simply. The question, he says, is
always, how are the children *growing?* "Are they *more thoughtful*
about what they do and say? . . . Do they work *more persistently?* Are they *more considerate* of others? Good character,
good habits of thinking and good habits of working—these will,
in time, take care of all else."[1]

Bertrand Russell has said that "reverence for human personality is the beginning of wisdom, in every social question, but
above all in education."[2] The new schools have at least entered
the path leading to wisdom, for, one and all, they make the
child the central figure, and endeavor, while conserving initiative and elasticity of mind, to provide conditions favorable to
intellectual growth and the integration of personality.[3] In a
changing civilization individuals must be prepared to meet the
new and unexpected, and individual variations should be conserved as precious assets, and possible means for social growth.
Washburne sums the matter up as follows: "Each single child
must be developed just as fully as possible as an individual—not
at the expense of his fellows, but with them, and in order that
he may contribute his own particular gifts to the common weal."[4]

Colonel Francis W. Parker, according to Dewey, was the
father of the progressive educational movement. This title,
however, is often bestowed on Dewey himself, who in 1896
started the first little laboratory school, later merged in the
School of Education of the University of Chicago, of which
he became director, in 1902, on the death of Colonel Parker.
School and Society gives a brief account of this experiment.
At first there was difficulty in finding desks and chairs for the
new school; "finally one dealer, more intelligent than the rest,
made this remark: 'I am afraid we have not what you want.
You want something at which the children may work; these are
all for listening.' "[5] Other experiments were soon under way,

---

[1] Fisher and Gruenberg (editors), *Our Children*, p. 189.
[2] *Sceptical Essays* (1928), p. 205.
[3] Burnham says: "the minimum essentials of education and mental health alike
are a task, a plan, and freedom. . . . The function of the teacher is to provide opportunity for a suitable task and the conditions that make success for the individual
possible." *The Normal Mind*, p. 228. Hart points to the significant distinction between the concept of an *instructor*, a word derived from building with inorganic
materials, and the concept of a teacher as a *cultivator*, one who provides favorable
conditions for growth. *A Social Interpretation of Education*, p. 199.
[4] C. Washburne and M. M. Stearns, *Better Schools* (1928), p. 15.
[5] *School and Society*, p. 34. For a detailed account of this laboratory school, see
K. C. Mayhew and A. C. Edwards, *The Dewey School* (1936).

but it was not until the second decade of this century that the new schools became numerous.[1] Experimentation was carried on at first very largely outside the public school system. And yet, so strong has been the influence of Dewey and other educational leaders, such, for example, as Kilpatrick, on public school teachers, that what Stanwood Cobb calls the *new leaven* has permeated the schools of the country.[2] At the same time a similar movement has been taking place in Europe.[3]

Programs of Work in Progressive Schools. The atmosphere of a progressive school is natural and informal. The old-time schoolroom with its regimentation, restraint, and "noisy silence" has vanished. Small groups of children are busily at work, eagerly discussing their problems with one another and moving freely about. They have pets and gardens, they work in kitchens, shops, and laboratories; build, cook, sew, weave, paint, model, dance, sing, write poetry, and stage dramas. At other times they go on excursions or are absorbed in books. Certain plans are made in advance, but the program is flexible enough to respond to children's needs in connection with the occupation on which they are engaged.

The term *project*, though sometimes abused, is much in use to indicate the typical educative unit, or integrative center of interest, which forms the basis for work in progressive schools. To be worthy of the name, a project must not be trivial or too easy, nor must it be too difficult. It must come within the capacity of the learner, and yet be of sufficient scope to raise new questions, initiate new undertakings, create a desire for knowledge, and so lead the learner out into ever-widening fields of experience. Such projects as the following are representative of work in progressive elementary schools: a food study, fruits and vegetables; a study of milk, or of wool; the raising and

---

[1] Many new-type private schools have been initiated at the instigation of intelligent parents, dissatisfied with the opportunities offered to their children by the existing school system.

[2] In *Schools of To-Morrow*, the Deweys include, among the accounts of experiments, those carried on in the public schools of Winnetka and Gary. In *Better Schools*, Washburne, superintendent of schools at Winnetka, gives an account of progressive education in American public schools. An experiment in a public school is described by Irwin and Marks, *op. cit.*

[3] Washburne and Stearns give a brief account of some of the newer schools in Europe in *New Schools in the Old World* (1936), while *The Activity School* (1928) by Adolphe Ferrière is a translation of the standard French work on progressive education in Europe. The New Education Fellowship has headquarters in a number of cities and publishes a tri-language international magazine, the *New Era*. In this country *Progressive Education* is published by the Progressive Education Association, founded in 1919.

care of chickens or rabbits; how man has made records; a study of cave men; a study of Egyptian life; the story of the growth of the city (in which the school is located). Any one of these projects is "rich in group and individual activity; in opportunity for developing responsibility, initiative, coöperation and scientific attitude; in the need of information and skill; and in social meaning."[1] In any one period the children may be engaged in manual activities, in getting and using facts, and in practice in reading, writing, and arithmetic; the motive for this practice being the need felt for the efficient use of these tools. References must be looked up and books read; notes must be taken, records kept of experiments, and letters of inquiry written. Even very young children find it useful to keep accounts, or learn the use of measurements in connection with activities such as building chicken-coops, laying out gardens, buying feed, or selling produce.

The emphasis placed by the new school on creative self-expression has achieved its greatest successes in the field of the arts. It has been conclusively shown that every child is to some extent a creative artist, and that, in an atmosphere conducive to self-expression, he may develop talent in one or more directions, and be led to an enhanced appreciation of the qualities of experience and to the formation of standards of cultivated taste.

Difficulties and Weaknesses of the New Education. The very success of progressive schools in furthering artistic self-expression is associated with a one-sided emphasis which mars the outlook and limits the achievements of many schools. Dewey believes this to be due to the origin of progressive schools in a reaction against traditional education. Colonel Parker frequently stated that teachers had been teaching *subjects*, instead of *children*. This antithesis has not only been preserved, but over-emphasized in many *child-centered* schools, with the result that they "suffer from exactly the same fallacy as the adult-imposition method of the traditional school—only in an inverted form. That is, they are still obsessed by the personal factor; they conceive of no alternative to adult dictation save child dictation. What is wanted is to get away from every mode of personal dictation and merely personal control. When the emphasis falls upon having experiences that are educationally worth while, the center of gravity shifts from the personal factors, and is

[1] J. S. Tippett and others, *Curriculum Making in an Elementary School* (1927); quoted by H. Rugg and A. Shumaker, *The Child-Centered School* (1928), p. 72.

found within the developing experience, in which pupils and teachers alike participate."[1]

The new schools are wholly right in centering attention upon the child. Their great danger lies in treating the child's present impulses as *finalities* rather than potentialities for growth. This results in some schools—as in some families—in a "fear of adult imposition" amounting to "a veritable phobia," and may lead to indulging pupils in "unrestrained freedom of action and speech, of manners and lack of manners." "Ultimately it is the absence of intellectual control through significant subject matter which stimulates the deplorable egotism, cockiness, impertinence, and disregard for the rights of others apparently considered by some persons to be the inevitable accompaniment, if not the essence, of freedom."[1]

Rugg and Shumaker analyze some of the outstanding defects in the curricula of child-centered schools. One and all may be traced to revolt from specific features of traditional methods, a revolt which has been one-sided, due to false conceptions of individual development and freedom. The indispensable functions of the teacher in contributing to the coöperative development of well-integrated curricula have often been overlooked, if not expressly repudiated. Rebelling against the formal organization of subject matter in a graded series of steps, enthusiasts have adopted the extreme position that no advance plan is needed. As Childs points out, there has been frequent misinterpretation of Dewey's statement that education is growth, with no end beyond itself, and a consequent neglect of the need for constant and careful planning of an environment adequate to provide for continued growth in our complex modern world. This is not surprising. Progressive schools have been started in many instances by those whose thoughts are centered in the child, sometimes to the exclusion of vital or intelligent interest in the moving forces of the social world in which these children will some day have to play their part. Such schools tend to be lop-sided in their curricula; they utilize the resources of their immediate locality, and reflect the special interests of their organizers. In some schools well-integrated programs may be developed for each year, but seldom is the program of work for all the years of school efficiently integrated. There is need for coöperative planning if a curriculum is to serve successive stages of growth and conduce to

[1] Dewey, "How Much Freedom in New Schools?" *The New Republic*, Vol. LXIII (July, 1930), p. 205.

certain desirable outcomes in the developing experience of the pupil.

The newer methods are frequently criticized because they fail to secure sufficient mastery of fundamental techniques. While there is much truth in this contention, the remedy is not a return to the traditional drill. The necessary repetition may be introduced when the need is felt for mastery of numerical and verbal techniques. Children can, moreover, be brought to take a keen interest in this work for its own sake; and in many progressive schools the pupils in the long run acquire as thorough a mastery of spelling, reading, writing, and arithmetic as has ever been attained by drill in complete isolation from other activities.

A more fundamental criticism is to be found in the fact that the rebellion against knowledge for the sake of knowledge has led to an over-emphasis on activity for its own sake, and a consequent neglect to provide for practice in reflective thinking, and for the ordered, well-balanced interpretation of personal experience, which is essential to a critical evaluation of modern life. The greatest weakness in so-called progressive schools to-day, according to Dewey, is the lack of development in pupils of "understanding and capacity that are relevant to contemporary social life." Work should be undertaken to lead the mind back of present happenings "to the understanding of basic causes." "The relation of science to industrial society" must be brought out, and "its potentialities for a planned control of future developments." "Only schools which take the lead in bringing about this kind of education can claim to be progressive in any socially significant sense."[1] Over-emphasis on the present experience of the child has combined with lack of social purpose and insight, in isolating the progressive school from the actual life of the community, and so frustrating the development of that social responsibility which is a central aim of the new education.

Hitherto progressive programs have been most successful in elementary schools. It is far harder to relate the work of the secondary school to the life outside its walls. Another reason for the difficulty in developing progressive secondary school curricula has been the dominance of college entrance requirements over secondary education. Of first importance therefore is a crucial experiment now being made on the basis of which much should be discovered as to the actual possibilities and

[1] *Ibid.*, p. 206.

results of progressive methods in secondary schools. A commission under the auspices of the Progressive Education Association has developed a plan whereby, for five years beginning in 1936, 280 of the leading colleges of the country are waiving their regular entrance requirements to permit the attendance of graduates of thirty schools which have undertaken to experiment with progressive methods. Admission to college from these schools is upon recommendation of the principal, supplemented by a record of the student's activities and interests and achievements, and other evidence of the quantity and quality of his work. Some of these schools are private, some public, but all have concrete programs for significant reconstruction of their curricula and teaching methods along progressive lines. The experiments vary in detail, but show homogeneity of purpose and general pattern. Provision has been made for a systematic following of records in order to obtain a significant evaluation of results. Widespread adoption of progressive ideas and methods would probably result if the experiment proved successful. In any case it should bring about significant gains in educational theory and practice, and should further the development of experimental attitudes in education.[1]

Achievements of the New Education. As Rugg and Shumaker point out: "In spite of the errors and gropings and mistakes of an imperfect methodology one fact stands supreme: The new education has re-oriented educational thinking about its true center—the child."[2] It has conclusively proved that all future educational experimentation must be rooted in the concept of growth. Perhaps the best summary of the achievements of progressive education is given by Stanwood Cobb in *The New Leaven*. He describes the work of progressive schools under ten principles.

(1) *Health comes first.* The environment of progressive schools is in every way conducive to health. There is freedom from strain of any kind, from overwork or fear of failure or enforced silence and inactivity. Instead, there is joyous absorption in

---

[1] A preliminary report indicates that the 900 boys and girls, who entered the colleges in September, 1936, have secured as good grades as their more traditionally trained classmates. Of these students, 332 were concentrated in 18 colleges, and with these, appraisal experts worked all the year, checking success in academic studies, college life, and attainment of personal objectives. A several-volume report is planned for 1941. The experiment has influenced the development of similar plans in California, Michigan, and Ohio. *New York Times*, Aug. 1, 1937.

[2] *Op. cit.*, p. 325.

active occupations allowing for and, indeed, requiring freedom of movement.   Progressive schools are, as far as possible, open-air schools, making much of outdoor activities, and arranging buildings and rooms in such a way as to secure a maximum of air and sunshine.

(2) *Constructive activities as a starting point.* Some form of handwork may be found to enlist the interest of every child, and varieties of capacity are discovered in this way. A valuable beginning is being made in progressive schools, looking towards a new integration of vocation and culture. Some will early be led along the lines of their future vocation; others find means for the worthwhile utilization of leisure. But all *learn by doing*. The future manual worker and the future scholar alike are released from narrowness of outlook, and are led to an appreciation of the relation of intelligence to action and the worth and necessity of both intellectual and manual labor.

(3) *Freedom from restraint and from external compulsions* makes possible, under wise leadership, the substitution of *internal* for *external* compulsions. Children in progressive schools have actual experience of free self-expression combined with self-restraint for the benefit of group purposes. The condemnation of other members of a group is usually sufficient discipline for those absorbed in group activities. In extreme cases, Cobb has found a short period of suspension beneficial. Coöperative methods of self-government are usual in progressive schools; and the children *develop in ability to direct their own affairs intelligently*.

(4) *Adapting education to meet the individual needs of students.* Each individual is thus given opportunity for development along lines for which he has particular aptitude. Even for the slow or inferior student some line of activity can be found in which success is possible, while the benefits to be derived from the fullest development of the gifted are self-evident.

(5) *Coöperative group work definitely fosters social-mindedness and the ability to live and work in harmony with others.* Competition is replaced by a desire to contribute to group achievement. Proficient pupils are encouraged to help the slow. Enterprises of value to the community are encouraged and included in the school program.

(6) *The release of ability in one or more of the arts.* In this, as we have seen, progressive schools have had remarkable success.

(7) *Control of the tools of learning, and learning how to learn and to think.* The best progressive schools definitely encourage such achievements as opposed to the mere assimilation of information.

(8) *Happiness and zest for work.* All other achievements of progressive schools may be summed up in the happiness which children experience, when they have the opportunity to cultivate their interests and abilities, and progress brings a glow of success.

(9) *The tyranny of marks and examinations is abolished.* External motives in the shape of rewards and punishments are done away with, and the temptation to cheat is reduced to a minimum. Tests and records of achievement are not wholly eliminated, but they are not used in such a way as to produce strain and anxiety and the familiar evils of competitive marking—the self-consciousness and conceit of the brilliant child, the bitter sense of failure and inferiority on the part of the slow-minded. Children are encouraged to surpass their own previous records and achievements.

(10) Progressive schools finally provide opportunity for *highly gifted teachers* to serve as guides to childhood. Unhampered by the demands of a system, they are encouraged to make their full personal contribution to education. The success of progressive schools depends on securing "a new type of teacher, a teacher possessed of personality and culture and capable of awakening and developing the creative powers of childhood."[1]

Progressive education is not a system but a spontaneous movement, expressive of the new attitude towards childhood. The new spirit in education must devise new and ever better methods, but beginnings have been made which are full of hope for the future. The right path has been found to the fuller and freer development of more truly *human* beings.

SUGGESTED READING

Bain, W. E., *Parents Look at Modern Education*, 1935.
Basset, C., *The School and Mental Health*, 1931.
Bode, B. H., *Conflicting Psychologies of Learning*, 1929.
——, *Fundamentals of Education*, 1921.
——, *Modern Educational Theories*, 1927.
Burnham, W., *The Normal Mind*, 1925.
Children's Bureau, *Publication 135*, "Habit Clinics for Children of Preschool Age," 1924.

[1] Cobb, *The New Leaven* (1928), p. 24. Cobb emphasizes the success achieved by *mothers* who are teaching in progressive schools.

Children's Bureau, *Publication 225*, "Guiding the Adolescent," 1933.

Cobb, S., *The New Leaven*, 1928.

——, *New Horizons for the Child*, 1934.

Dewey, J., *Democracy and Education*, 1916.

——, *The School and Society*, rev. ed., 1930.

Dewey, J. and E., *Schools of To-morrow*, 1915.

Fisher, D. C., and Gruenberg, S. M., eds., *Our Children*, 1932.

Groves, E. R., and Brooks, L. M., *Readings in the Family*, 1934, Ch. XXIII.

Hart, J. K., *A Social Interpretation of Education*, 1929.

Irwin, E., and Marks, L., *Fitting the School to the Child*, 1924.

Judd, C. H., "Education," *Recent Social Trends*, 2 vols., 1933, Vol. I, Ch. VII.

Kilpatrick, W. H., *Education for a Changing Civilization*, 1926.

Lynd, R. S. and H. M., *Middletown*, 1929, Chs. XI, XIII–XVI.

——, *Middletown in Transition*, 1937, Ch. VI.

Morgan, J. J. B., *The Psychology of the Unadjusted School Child*, 1931.

Rivlin, H. N., *Education for Adjustment*, 1936.

Rugg, H., and Shumaker, A., *The Child-centered School*, 1928.

Sayles, M. B., *The Problem Child at School*, 1926.

——, *The Problem Child at Home*, 1928.

Sherman, M., *Mental Hygiene and Education*, 1934.

Stevenson, G. S., and Smith, G., *Child Guidance Clinics*, 1934.

Van Waters, M., *Parents on Probation*, 1927.

Washburne, C., and Stearns, M. M., *Better Schools*, 1928.

Watson, M. E., *Children and Their Parents*, 1932.

Wickman, E. K., *Children's Behavior and Teachers' Attitudes*, 1928.

CHAPTER X

THE RECIPROCAL FUNCTIONS OF HOME AND SCHOOL

THE SCHOOL AS SUPPLEMENT TO THE HOME

Ideally the school should supplement the home in such a way that the growth of the child is fostered through the medium of an integrated environment. The ideal home possesses all the essentials of an educative environment. Sharing so far as he is able in the daily life, experiences, and occupations of a small and sympathetic group, the child finds protection, stimulation, and guidance. Sheltered and secure within the family, he receives at the same time an introduction to the larger life around him, and an interpretation of the world of thought and action which becomes an integral part of his developing experience. Here in the ideal home is the best opportunity for securing individual development, for fostering independence of thought and socialized disposition: the fundamental habit of subordinating individual activities to the general interest.

The ideal school, according to Dewey, should grow gradually out of home life; it should embody those elements which make for growth in the preschool years, but should do this systematically and in an organized and enlarged fashion. The child needs contact with more children and more grown people. He needs to participate in a wider range of occupations and activities than is usually possible at home. The child's education is not the *primary* aim of many home activities. The school is needed to supplement the home by providing a selected, enlarged, and organized environment whose sole and all-controlling aim is educational.[1]

If even an ideal home would need supplementing by the

[1] In a delightful speech, Dewey envisaged the schools of Utopia as assembly places where children and older people gather in groups of not more than two hundred. These schools are like homes, but with more open spaces and with books everywhere as well as in the library, and with large gardens, workshops, museums, and scientific laboratories. The adult leaders combine special knowledge of children with special abilities and are all engaged in carrying on work of their own with the children as apprentices. They are married and have children of their own. *New York Times*, April 23, 1933. See the anonymous *Mother's Letters to a Schoolmaster* (1923) for concrete suggestions for a Children's Community Center, based on an experiment in education planned and carried out by a mother and her little son.

school, much more do the vast majority of the homes of to-day which for one reason or another are failing to provide even a moderately good educational environment. In the case of most children, the school is called upon, not only to supplement the home, but, in from five to seven hours daily, to counteract the harmful influences of all the remaining hours and of the preceding preschool years as well. So far the chief progress along these lines has been achieved in promoting health. Beginnings are now being made in mental hygiene. On the whole, however, most public schools are not very successful as supplements to the home, and even less so as influences counteracting the illiberal and antisocial tendencies which are so often the result of miseducation in homes. Where progressive tendencies make themselves felt, there is likely to be deliberate effort to supplement the home, and a greater measure of success in providing a wholesome and integrated environment for the child.

THE NURSERY SCHOOL

The Nursery School Movement. In the recent development of nursery schools, we have, perhaps, the most successful example of ways in which the school may provide extension and supplementation of present resources, and may also be used to correct the defects of home environment. It was for the second of these purposes that the nursery school originated in England; as an effort to save little children from the blighting effects of poverty. Increased facilities for medical inspection led to the discovery that, by the time of school admission at five, from 35% to 40% of those who had been born healthy bore marks of preventable physical defects. Meanwhile the pioneer work of the McMillan sisters in a Southeast London slum was demonstrating the striking changes in the health, happiness, and development of children, brought about by wholesome diet and open-air nursery school facilities. The Education Act of 1918 gave official sanction to the establishment of nursery schools by local education authorities. A governmental report, in 1923, found that the few existing nursery schools had fully demonstrated their value, but regretfully acknowledged that their cost offered a serious bar to their extension. Indeed, by 1930 there were still only twenty-seven nursery schools in England and Wales, and of these only twelve had been established by local education authorities.[1]

---

[1] Gesell, *The Guidance of Mental Growth in Infant and Child*, p. 104. Since then, however, others have been established, in some cases at very slight cost, through

Not until 1933, with the establishment of nursery schools by the Federal Emergency Relief Administration, in coöperation with the United States Office of Education, were nursery schools in the United States developed to any extent as self-protective social measures.[1] The earlier American nursery schools were the outcome of a scientific interest in early childhood and of experimental efforts in the field of mental hygiene. Several agencies have been responsible for their establishment, of which the chief were: (1) university departments of psychology and education, and individuals and groups interested in research; (2) parents who have realized the need for supplementing home facilities by organized pre-kindergarten education; (3) individuals and associations interested in improving the educational status of day nurseries.[2] The American nursery school movement was antedated by the establishment of research center pre-kindergarten groups.[3] But, while some nursery schools have been organized for laboratory purposes and many others as demonstration and training centers, the great majority now have, as their primary, if not sole, object, the education of children and their parents.[4]

As early as 1916, a group of mothers connected with the University of Chicago formed a coöperative nursery school group, to secure expert direction of their children and to widen their own experience. Provided trained leadership is secured, a coöperative plan has many advantages. Most nursery schools, other than the emergency schools, are private enterprises supported by tuition fees or philanthropy. Very few are supported by public school systems. The cost of a well-conducted nursery school is beyond what can be secured for public elementary education. The nursery school group must

using the services of the unemployed. Margaret Wintringham, "Giving Children a Chance" in *The Christian Science Monitor*, weekly magazine section, July 24, 1935. The percentage of physical defect in children who have attended a nursery school from two to five is reduced to 7%.

[1] Already, by April, 1935, there were approximately 1,900 emergency nursery schools unevenly distributed in forty-seven states and in Puerto Rico. In these, 55,000 needy children between two and four were being given nourishing food, medical supervision, and healthful, happy conditions for rest and play. Grace Langdon, "Salvaging the Children," *New York Times*, April 28, 1935.

[2] Day nurseries are briefly discussed in Chapter XII. They were originally established for the sole purpose of providing shelter and physical care for the babies of working mothers.

[3] In 1920, Gesell began the study of a group of two-year-olds at the Yale Psycho-Clinic, and in 1921 The Iowa Child Welfare Research Station opened a preschool laboratory. The latter is now operated as an experimental nursery school. The Merrill-Palmer Nursery School, organized in 1921, is a research and training center.

[4] In 1930 there were some 500.

be small, and one director is needed for each ten children. If teachers in training and high school students were used as assistants, the expense might be reduced, and a further possibility is the partial financing from secondary school funds of nursery schools as laboratories for work in child psychology.[1]

The emergency nursery schools are, of course, a different matter, having been financed as part of the Federal Relief program. They are being staffed by needy unemployed teachers to whom special training is given free. Quite apart from the question of costs, some experts, such as Gesell, have feared that premature standardization might result from the inclusion of nursery schools in the public school system. Privately supported enterprises, particularly those operating as research centers, are best able to secure experimental conditions in which more efficient methods and techniques may be devised for the conduct of nursery schools and the training of directors. As the years pass, however, there is a growing belief that nursery schools should be incorporated in the public schools, to form with the kindergarten a preschool unit.

Values of Nursery School Education. The social importance and influence of nursery schools has been out of all proportion to their number. Education at the preschool level is being given a scientific basis and progressive principles are being recognized as valid and put into practice. It is hoped that the nursery school may not only "furnish a more solid support to the educational ladder," to quote Gesell, but that its influence may extend up through kindergarten and primary school until "the education of the child will become a continuous scientific procedure based upon child psychology, with all the scientific resources of our great universities available for guidance and teacher training."[2]

Nursery school education endeavors to secure an integrated environment for children. There is full realization of the central importance of the parent-child relationship, and deliberate

---

[1] A nursery school was conducted for a time as part of the Los Angeles City School system, at a cost of $250, per capita, for a ten-month year. The highest sum which is allowed for elementary education is $80. Dr. Elizabeth Woods, Director of Psychology and Research, believes that, if nursery schools were regularly established, before very long much money might be saved which is now required for psychological and mental hygiene work in the schools. The depression caused the discontinuation of the Los Angeles nursery school, in keeping with the country-wide retrogressive policy of the elimination of "fads and frills"; in most cases, the most valuable and progressive features of public education.

[2] Cobb, *The New Leaven*, p. 265; and see Gesell, "The Nursery School Movement," *School and Society*, Vol. V (1924), pp. 642–652.

attempts are made to supplement home facilities and to help
parents to understand and guide their children. The nursery
school makes use of the child's regular daily activities, with
only such modifications as are imposed by association with
others and by provision of more and better equipment than is
usually possible in a home. The aim throughout is to secure
close coöperation between home and school in providing for
the child's physical well-being and his normal adjustment to
his surroundings, and in encouraging independence and consideration for others.

Where there are defects in home conditions, the benefit of
nursery school education is obvious, even though the best
results cannot be secured where home coöperation is lacking.
But even in a good home, where the child is assured of the
best of care, there are indisputable advantages in a nursery
school; which make it probable that, for almost all children
over two, attendance at a nursery school for the half-day,
at least, would prove definitely beneficial. Few mothers to-day
are experts in child guidance, and in their handling of children
they have not the ability born of special knowledge and wide
experience. Even if they should be experts, rarely can the
modern home, particularly in the city, provide the child with
adequate facilities for play. But, even when these are present,
one essential is almost always lacking: sufficient companionship
with other children of the same age. In the nursery school,
children learn to share the life of a social group. Courtesy,
good manners, and a variety of social and individual habits,
which are sometimes difficult to acquire in the small family
circle, become a matter of course as part of a pleasant group
routine.[1] Even in the best of homes, moreover, it is frequently
difficult to secure gradual detachment of the child from too
great dependence on the mother. The brief daily separation
of mother and child is beneficial to both. Emotional tensions
are lessened, and the child learns self-reliance. In all of these
ways the nursery school lays the foundations of mental health.
In its facilitation of personality adjustment may be found
its unifying aim and its central significance.

The distinctive services of the nursery school in parent
education are considered later in this chapter. The re-education
of parents is effected by various means designed to secure
coöperation between home and school. Another valuable service

---

[1] A restless child will settle quietly to a nap where all the others do likewise, or
the formerly "faddy" child will quietly eat what is set before him.

performed by nursery schools is the use made of them to vitalize pre-parental education in child care. Teachers and those who are not yet parents are led to take an interest in problems which would otherwise not come within their experience. For the nursery school, as Gesell says, is designed, not to reduce, but to sharpen the responsibilities of parents. "Far from being an insidious encroachment upon the power and prestige of the home, the best principles of the nursery school may permeate the practice of family life and impart perfecting impulses to the parent-child relationship of the coming generation."[1]

INTERRELATIONSHIPS OF HOME WITH SCHOOL IN THE EARLIER YEARS

The Kindergarten. At one time the kindergarten was in much the same position as the nursery school to-day. In 1873, when the first public school kindergarten was established, there were forty-two private kindergartens. The earlier kindergartens were strictly Froebelian, but, towards the end of the century, the progressive kindergarten developed under the leadership of Anna Bryan and Patty Smith Hill, assisted by Dewey and those responsible for the child-study movement. The progressive kindergarten makes use of modern scientific findings and is interested in the all-round development of the child.

Although kindergartens are a recognized part of the public school system, comparatively few children are enrolled.[2] The present organization of schools gives the kindergarten a strategic position, according to Gesell. At the growing edge of the school system, the kindergarten should be deliberately used as an experiment station to discover methods for "the readjustment and extension of present educational and hygienic control of early child development in relation to home and parent."[3] The new interest in the preschool child "signifies a social movement comparable to the democratization of elementary education." It is now realized that opportunity for school instruction is not enough: "We must equalize the earlier developmental opportunities of earlier childhood. This can only be done by replacing the historic concept of education with the

[1] *The Guidance of Mental Growth in Infant and Child,* p. 113.
[2] In 1930, only about 695,490 out of the 16,000,000 children under six, in the United States at that time, were enrolled in public school kindergartens. An immediate need is for the extension of kindergarten facilities to far greater numbers of four- and five-year-old children.
[3] Gesell, *op. cit.,* p. 119.

modern biological concepts of development, initiating a policy of developmental supervision with the birth of the infant, and projecting that supervision medically and educationally throughout the whole period of preschool childhood. Such a system of developmental safeguards is part of the fundamental right of the infant of this century."[1] And this implies "the shifting of educational approach to the whole family," an attitude already operative in nursery school procedure and which the kindergarten is in a better position to adopt than any other part of the school system.[2]

Close relationships already exist between home and school wherever progressive methods have influenced the work of kindergartens and primary grades. Parents' conferences are the rule; and home visits were initiated at the kindergarten level; so that the public school kindergartner was actually the first visiting teacher. If organized on a more flexible basis, the kindergarten might extend its work in parental education and guidance and make fuller use of its opportunities for preventive work in health and mental hygiene. Finally, it affords a laboratory for use by older students in pre-parental education.

The Elementary School. In many elementary schools to-day, the traditional curriculum is being superseded by programs of activities and the encouragement of methods of *inquiring*, as well as *acquiring*. In preparation for the 1930 White House Conference the sub-committee on pre-parental education conducted a nation-wide survey of experiments in education for home and family life. While existing programs were found inadequate, the number and variety of the attempts being made were highly significant.

The elementary grades beyond the first two or three years constitute the most difficult period from the standpoint of family education. School life at this stage is not so closely integrated with home life as in the case of the little child. And there is not yet, as with adolescents, a growing awareness of the possibility of founding a new home. Efforts are frequently made, however, to relate subject matter to the individual's life in the family; arithmetic, for example, may be vitalized by its use in the formation of family budgets. Social science courses are designed to give perspective on the relation between home and society. Activities in connection with food, clothing, and shelter furnish appropriate starting points. This being the case, it is not surprising that home economics courses

[1] *Ibid.*, p. 124.　　　　　　　　　　[2] *Ibid.*, p. 121.

should lead in programs of education for family life. Difficulty is reported, however, in elevating work in home economics above the acquisition of housekeeping skills, so as to develop appreciation and understanding of home, and a desire to participate in its activities. Of particular interest is the growing realization that *boys* as well as girls are in need of education for home and family life. One such course given to eighth-grade boys in Denver endeavors to help adjustment within the family group, and to give boys understanding of the relation of food and clothing to health, and of their share in the financial problems of the home.

INTERRELATIONSHIPS OF HOME WITH SCHOOL IN THE LATER YEARS

The Junior High School. Of recent years a new administrative unit, the junior high school, has become the accepted method of caring for the last two years of the older elementary school and the first, sometimes the second, year of high school. While growth is continuous, broad stages may be recognized which call for appropriate educational procedures. At this transition period between elementary and secondary education, the well-educated child should have sufficient direct acquaintance with the world around him and sufficient mastery of the tools of thought, inquiry, and activity to be able to specialize upon selected studies and arts for technical or intellectual purposes. "The ideal junior high school," according to Van Denburg, "is . . . a finding and sorting school where pupils may, through actual experience, be led to make a more rational selection of their senior high school work, or their occupation in the world of industry, than would be otherwise possible."[1]

Broad integrated courses in several fields are being included during this period. For example, a ninth-grade course, in a Washington school, complements the elementary work in housekeeping with a course in homemaking; it supplements work being done in the social and natural sciences, which deal, respectively, with the home and society and the biological conception of family life. In New York, in coöperation with the Vocation Service for Juniors, life-career and occupation courses have been developed for the seventh grade, preparing the way for the vocational counselling of individuals. The reduction of school failures is a definite objective of those in charge of the New York schools, in the belief that the public schools are responsible for organizing work on the basis of individual capacity. No

[1] *The Junior High School Idea* (1922), p. 16.

longer should the dull child be repudiated as non-educational material. Indeed, Irwin and Marks advocate that "every child should continue his education in all-day schools until the age of eighteen, no matter what his I. Q. is."[1]

The High School. Secondary education can no longer be conceived as the prerogative of a selected minority with predominantly intellectual interests; but must be planned with a view to helping each and every individual adjust himself or herself to life in the complex modern world. At present the waste of opportunity is great, even in the case of potential scholars: they are left unprepared to face the problems of the real world; and docile mastery of facts and techniques needed for college entrance too often replaces the development of independent thought. The non-academic-minded student is thus sacrificed to a system which does not provide adequate education even for those for whom it was originally planned.

As early as 1918, the National Education Association recommended educational reorganization in the interests of the democratic ideal, and with the following definite objectives: health, command of the fundamental processes, worthy home membership, vocation, citizenship, worthy use of leisure, and ethical character. But no fundamental changes followed: a failure attributed by Thayer to the reactionary tendencies following the war. These, combined with faulty scientific pedagogy, resulted instead in "a sterile emphasis on things as they are."[2] According to Dewey, the root of the present confusion lies in the fact that prevailing schemes for vocational education take their point of departure in the present industrial situation, and maintain the traditional distinctions between a narrow technical education, as vocational, and an education "which has to do chiefly with preparation for the pursuit of conspicuous idleness, for teaching, and for literary callings and for leadership," as "non-vocational and even as peculiarly cultural."[3]

Realization of the relation between individual capacity and social needs brings perception of the fact that, in addition to vocations as specialized occupations, everyone has a variety of vocations in which he or she should be intelligently effective, as a citizen, for instance, or as a family member. Moreover, in Dewey's words, ": the dominant vocation of all human beings

---

[1] *Fitting the School to the Child,* p. 254.
[2] Fisher and Gruenberg (editors), *Our Children,* p. 232.
[3] *Democracy and Education,* p. 365.

at all times is living—intellectual and moral growth."[1] "It will not be easy," Dewey warns, "to develop secondary education so that practical and semi-vocational courses will absorb within themselves the liberal training and the social and scientific outlook which is needed. . . . It is not easy to find teachers having this point of view, while the problem of selecting and arranging subject matter and activities which will accomplish the end desired requires patient, thorough inquiry and careful testing."[2]

Starting with the major interests and abilities of students, high schools must endeavor to develop their vocational and cultural possibilities. Certain central questions should form the core of the course of study, questions having to do with "plans and methods for furthering the life of the community."[3] Such central problems organize subject matter in a vital manner, acting, as Dewey says, "like a magnet to draw facts from different fields together. . . . The outcome is a continually growing intellectual integration."[4]

The Depression and the Development of Services to Youth. The exigencies of the depression years forced attention to the vocational and educational needs of young people over sixteen. In 1934, between six and seven million of those between sixteen and twenty-five had no work to do and no means for further education. Of the nine or ten million employed, many were in routine occupations, blind alleys affording no entrance to anything better and offering no educational advantages. The Civilian Conservation Corps camps were already providing work and a realistic education for thousands of unemployed young men; and the Federal Emergency Relief Administration made possible the continuation of high school and college education by means of work-scholarships for some 100,000 boys and girls by the end of 1934.

On June 26, 1935, the National Youth Administration was created, a federal youth service looking towards a solution of the vocational and educational problems of youth. Through state and local agencies endeavors are made to find employment for young people, to assist with the continuation of education and with vocational training, and to foster the development of apprenticeship systems through coöperation between employers

[1] *Op. cit.,* p. 362.
[2] *The Way Out of Educational Confusion,* p. 28.
[3] Dewey, *The Educational Frontier,* p. 67.
[4] *The Way Out of Educational Confusion,* pp. 33–34.

and the public schools. The whole problem is, of course, too vast to admit of rapid solution, and millions of young people have found their plight unalleviated. Impatient with what it feels is the slow progress made under the Youth Administration, the American Youth Congress has been active in urging the passage of a National Youth Act to provide wages and living expenses for 5,000,000 unemployed young people.[1]

Meanwhile a five-year program of investigation is being undertaken by the American Youth Commission, financed by the General Education Board.[2] Research began in October, 1935, and already certain discoveries have been made. Employment is the greatest need of youth, and there has been a trend since 1919 to exclude those under twenty-one from employment. Since three-fourths of all young people are out of school by eighteen there is a widening gap between the completion of school and the beginning of work. The second great need universally expressed by youth is: "How can I prepare for a happy home life?" In the third place, the need for guidance is keenly felt. There is a sense of bewilderment amid the complexities of modern life and the conflicting standards between which the young are compelled to choose.

Education for Home and Family Life. The secondary schools have not been unaware of the growing demand for education for home and family life, or of their strategic position in supplementing the home in the adolescent years.[3] Education at this period should help in the readjustment of relationships within the parental home and lead towards the development of wholesome family relationships in the future homes, of which to-day's youth will be the founders. All this is part of the necessary process of emancipation from the home and of adjustment to the world outside its protective atmosphere. Questions of adjustment to their own generation, particularly of the opposite sex, and to the older generation and the community at large, are all of vital interest to boys and girls in the last two years of high school. They need help in their present

[1] The American Youth Congress first met in August, 1934, and claimed a million and a half members by March, 1936, when a Senate committee held hearings on the National Youth Act.

[2] A Rockefeller benevolent corporation.

[3] Some years ago a questionnaire was answered by 5,000 seniors in the Los Angeles schools. Of these, 93% were emphatic on the need for courses on parenthood. In one mixed class on family relationships in a Los Angeles high school questions are handed in, for the most part anonymously, in which the same topics recur over and over again: methods of courtship, contraception, pre-marital sexual intercourse, venereal diseases, prostitution.

problems; and use may be made of these to give them an insight into social relationships, in particular those involved in family life.

The public schools must become responsible for education for family life if its advantages are to be shared by all. Only so, moreover, can this vital matter be guarded from exploitation by faddists, pseudo-scientists, and sensationalists. The White House report admitted that but meager beginnings had been made by 1930. Certain factors were already apparent, however, as contributing to the success of experiments in this field. First of all comes the importance of individual teachers, and of their ability to arouse vital interest. The report suggests that a good teacher with actual experience as a wife and mother would be particularly well fitted. It is being found, too, that men who are themselves fathers are frequently very successful, particularly in classes conducted for boys.[1] Educational partnership between home and school was found of the greatest value. The attitude of administrators was, on the contrary, discouraging: though there was much talk of better children and better homes, the mechanics of the school system took precedence over actual efforts to achieve success along these lines.

The trend towards the education of boys, as well as girls, for family life is of the utmost importance, as indicating a genuine effort to meet changing conditions.[2] Home economics departments have led the way, and, while the greater part of their work is still planned for girls, an increasing number of courses are being given for boys alone or for mixed groups. Boys show themselves fully as interested as girls in child care provided they have opportunities for contact with children in nursery schools, kindergartens, or child-centers.

[1] In the Rochester high schools elective courses in home and family life for boys are entirely in the hands of men. To the discussion of practical problems is added instruction in the care of children. This has immediate practical value, for, according to Rochester statistics, one of the chief means by which boys earn money outside of school is by caring for small children. A number of other courses for boys are given in the home economics departments, dealing with food, clothing, etiquette, and household management. New York Times, March 1, 1936.

[2] Experts in the field of family life, such as Andrews, Groves, and Lindquist, comment on difficulties frequent to-day, where wives are in touch with recent scientific facts regarding health, mental hygiene, and child care, while husbands, in default of education in these matters, cling to traditional notions. Ruth Lindquist says: "As a condition, therefore, for the promotion of healthful and satisfying family life, the training of boys and of men is not less important than that of girls and women. To center attention upon one sex is educating but half the parents, and this policy may actually lead to less rather than more harmonious relationships." The Family in the Present Social Order (University of North Carolina Press, 1931), p. 159.

Home economics departments still teach the techniques and skills of good housekeeping, but there is a definite tendency towards expansion to include education in the wider aspects of family relationships. In many cases a point of departure is found in group discussions of the personal problems of young people in their own homes. Sometimes definite home projects are undertaken, under the joint supervision of teacher and mother, designed to be helpful in the home as well as of educative value.[1] Many schools now have practice houses, which serve as social centers where the boys and girls may carry on housekeeping and homemaking activities, and learn high standards of order, cleanliness, and taste. In some schools there is co-operation, between parents of nursery school children, the school doctor and nurse, and several school departments, in the maintenance of a nursery school. Work in home economics departments may readily be related with work in other school departments, and there are several schools where there is a definitely planned integration of all resources around the practical problems of home life. Social science departments have also, in a number of instances, introduced comprehensive courses on the family.

Some of the courses in family relationships, and others in hygiene or biology, endeavor to provide adequate sex instruction: not mere biological information, but understanding of the physiological, psychological, and ethical problems of adjustment between the sexes. The White House report concluded, however, that less had been done to offer adequate instruction in this field than in any other; far too frequently courses purporting to give sex education fail to face fundamental problems. Yet the school has a definite responsibility in this matter, particularly at the present time. The majority of the older generation of parents are incapable of dealing wisely with sex education, on account of either ignorance or miseducation. The school, moreover, can deal with such questions in a more objective and impersonal manner than can the home, particularly where school laboratory facilities are available and the instructors are scientific specialists.

The White House report found that no school had as yet integrated the whole of its curriculum around the objective of participation in family life. The North Shore Country Day School of Winnetka presents the *majority* of courses so as to show their application to family life. The school is limited to

---

[1] "Helping my little brother to become more self-reliant" was one project which turned out most successfully for all concerned.

three hundred and fifty pupils and organized like a large family with opportunities for all ages and both sexes to work and play together. Parental and pre-parental education proceed simultaneously by means of a well-devised plan of coöperation between parents and the life of the school. Adolescent boys and girls have opportunity for natural social contacts with one another and for developing responsibility for those younger than themselves. The parents not only keep in touch socially and mentally with their children, but are themselves provided with opportunities for a social life centered on educational interests. Such a school indicates the possibilities open not only to private but to public schools, were their resources more fully organized as community centers.

Brief mention of two controversial questions is apposite at this point. The White House report takes co-education for granted, it being almost universal in this country. In private preparatory schools and abroad, the reverse is the case. Criticism of co-education is frequently combined with attacks on the education of boys by women. Boys over eight are said to be in need of competent and authoritative masculine guidance, to meet not only their physical but psychological needs.[1] At present there are no means for deciding with any scientific precision how far this contention is true. In large part it is undoubtedly due to prejudice and adherence to tradition. From the experience of progressive schools, and from the standpoint of education for family life, it would appear probable that the more nearly schools provided opportunity for natural association between boys and girls, and for both with men and women teachers, the more beneficial would be the result. Boys undoubtedly need plenty of opportunity for association solely with boys, and girls with girls. And boys should also be to a considerable extent under masculine guidance. But such ends are even now successfully secured without complete segregation.[2]

[1] Count Keyserling is scathing in his comments on the infantilism of American men due to the "ascendancy" of women in the social and educational system; and the public school system of the United States was held up as a horrid example by the 1934 conference of the National Association of Schoolmasters in London. Critics of the "feminization" of the public schools are not wanting in America either. It is of interest to note, particularly in view of the tendency towards equal salaries for men and women, that the proportion of men teachers in the high schools rose between 1920 and 1930. The proportions in 1930 were 35.2% men to 64.8% women.

[2] The problem is harder to solve in a boarding school than in a day school, and yet Bedales at Petersfield, England, has operated successfully as a co-educational boarding school for some forty or more years. See Washburne and Stearns, *New Schools in the Old World*.

The flexible curriculum of a progressive school can be more easily adjusted to the differing needs of the sexes, as to both subject matter and adjustment to differing rates of mental growth, if such are finally proved to exist.

A Suggestion for an Integrated Program. For both boys and girls the broader aims of education are the same. Education must orient the student to the life of which he is a part. Modern problems become most vital when they are given the perspective of history and are seen as phases of a process in which human beings are gradually discovering the methods of progress and the forces favoring coöperation. Life becomes a great adventure with the destiny of humanity in its own keeping. As a guiding thread through the complexities of life, each new generation may face its task inspired by "the conception of the human race as a whole, fighting against chaos without and darkness within, the little tiny lamp of reason growing gradually into a great light by which the night is dispelled."[1] Each boy and girl needs thorough preparation if they are to have their full share in this adventure. Special interests and capacities must be developed in such a way as to secure wholesome all-round living and skilled competence along certain lines.

By way of a concrete suggestion for an experimental program, would it not be possible to integrate the work of the last three high school years with reference to the interrelated foci of *home* and *work?*[2] Activities of present significance, which at the same time prepare for future living, would be used under such a plan to discover capacity and to develop social and scientific insight. Individual guidance would be essential to success. Highly competent counsellors or tutors would be needed, with expert knowledge of mental hygiene and of the relationship of different subjects and disciplines to vocations and professions.[3] Every student must be closely supervised in the selection of a course of study to meet his or her special needs. For, while the central core would be the same for all, it serves as a main trunk from which branch the varied special interests.

[1] Bertrand Russell, *Education and the Good Life*, p. 267.

[2] Of the many experimental programs now being developed, none, so far as the writer is aware, takes exactly this form.

[3] Of particular importance at present is the guidance of girls, in an era when an integrated outlook on life is far harder of achievement for a woman than for a man. Boys for the most part are more far-sighted in their attitude to their vocation or profession. While the plan here suggested would increase homemaking ability, it would also give girls a greater appreciation of the value of a vocation. The education of women is more fully discussed in Chapter XVI.

The detailed development of such a course would be a matter for experts in curriculum construction. Possibly it would be simpler to present the core course in the form of two parallel courses each emphasizing one aspect of the development of civilization. (1) The *maintenance* of civilization or *vocational history*, dwelling on occupations, industries, and professions. (2) The *transmission* of civilization, or *educational history*, dwelling on the physical and social heritage of humanity, and the family as the chief agency for its transmission. There would, of course, be close interrelationships between the two courses. Both would be taught in such a way as to make clear the influence of economic and social forces, and the contributions of science to human welfare. Geography, political and intellectual history, and literature would be introduced throughout, while practice in written and oral English would be given by reports and group discussions. Foreign languages might be introduced at appropriate points. Both, finally, would contribute to an objective of the highest importance at the present time: better understanding of each other and a consequent facilitation of coöperation between men and women.

(1) In the course centered on maintenance activities, the basic necessities of food, clothing, and shelter would form initial nuclei for scientific investigation and practical work in the mechanical, homemaking, and fine arts. In connection with the study of *food*, biology, chemistry, hygiene, dietetics, and cooking may be introduced; with that of *clothing*, botany, chemistry, weaving, dyeing, sewing; with that of *shelter*, botany, leather work, carpentry, physics, chemistry, and architecture. Many points of contact are found for the fine arts. In the study of occupations the significance of the economic aspects of family life becomes clear. The emergence of specialized pursuits, industries, and professions may be traced, with stress on the inventions making progress possible. A study of the development of medicine is of particular value as illustrating the long struggle of science with superstition and the contributions of science to well-being. First aid and the fundamentals of nursing may be introduced in this connection.

(2) In the course centered on transmission of the physical and social heritage, emphasis falls on the *child* and on biology and psychology. A study of the evolution of sex serves as introduction to the family as the fundamental educational institution. There must be study of heredity and of hygiene, while psychology and mental hygiene may be introduced in

connection with the social patterning of the minds of the younger generation. The history of education may be used as a vital introduction to intellectual history. The laboratory study of children would, of course, have an important place. With adequate knowledge of the physiological and psychological foundations of the family and realization of its values, the way is prepared for a realistic study of the modern family and of the full implications of coöperation in family life.

INTERRELATIONSHIPS OF HOME WITH COLLEGE AND UNIVERSITY

Experiments in Reorganization. The educational confusion of the present is nowhere more apparent than in the college. Higher education is in increasing demand, but the attitude and outlook of many applicants is very different from that of the comparatively few who came to college a few generations ago.[1] At the worst, colleges have acquired the characteristics of the factory type of education.[2] Even so, the number of failures in the freshman year is often phenomenal. Attention has accordingly turned to college entrance requirements, and certain colleges which are in a position to do so are devising new and more rigorous methods of selection. Experimentation is also in process looking to the reform of methods of instruction and of curricula. The "honors" or "tutorial" system has tended to introduce methods of independent study, while the widespread development of orientation courses has indicated a felt need for integrated surveys, as affording general culture and as a basis for later specialization.

Since 1917 there has been a rapid development of junior colleges. Many progressive educators are in favor of the so-called 6–4–4 plan, in which the last two years of high school are combined with the first two years of college as a terminal *college* unit, succeeding the *secondary* and preparatory unit of the four year junior high school, which in turn succeeds the six years of *elementary* education. The plan opens possibilities for the extension of popular education to the eighteenth or twentieth

---

[1] Writing in the twenties, Bode pointed out that student activities meant almost everything *but study.* Many leading college educators now testify to an increase in intellectual seriousness among college students, due, it is supposed, to the depression and to the menacing aspects of economic and international unrest.

[2] Frequent examinations secure credit for the reproduction of memorized material in a number of unrelated subjects, and graduation results from the amassing of a sufficient number of units. The following case may be cited: a valuable member of a junior college football team found himself a hopeless failure in philosophy. He was overjoyed to discover that he might still secure a junior certificate if he substituted R.O.T.C. for philosophy!

year. Colleges as at present organized would tend to disappear, and only those with scholarly or professional interests would enter the universities. There is one very great danger in this plan, that such reorganization may mean, as it has already done in many cases, the extension of the high school into the college.[1] It *should* mean, on the contrary, the extension of the college into the high school, and the development of a real collegiate institution comparable to the French lycée.

The extension of public education to the twentieth year would afford valuable opportunities for correlating education with the interests of young adults.[2] College work could be vitalized by being organized with reference to individual interests. Those whose interests were primarily intellectual would, as always, be in the minority, but they too would have their needs met by the college years, being given wide perspectives, as well as being prepared for future specialization at the university.

Education for Home and Family Life. If reorganization along such lines becomes general, education for family life will undoubtedly center in the college unit where all young people can take advantage of such education. With the present system the need is perhaps greatest in the secondary schools; but it is almost equally great in the colleges, partly because of the inadequacy of secondary education and partly because the colleges can best develop leadership along these lines. As matters stand at present, not very much is being done to prepare individual students for the fundamental issues of life. The large number of maladjusted individuals who break down in college, or soon after, testifies to the great need for constructive work in mental hygiene. Already by 1930, however, mental hygiene services, though not yet extensive, were developing rapidly in leading colleges and universities.

The White House Conference sub-committee on *Pre-parental Education in Colleges*, made a survey of 269 accredited institutions of higher learning in this country. Out of 157 direct replies received to questions, fifty-eight stated that they pursued

[1] Where public junior colleges are controlled by high school administrators, not only is there sacrifice of the possibilities inherent in the new unit, but there is a frequent lowering of standards as the junior college is dragged into the machinery of the public school mill.

[2] The remarkably high cultural level of the people of Denmark and their ability and desire to enter into all forms of coöperative enterprise are, at least in part, attributable to their unique system of People's High Schools, attended by from a quarter to a third of the whole rural population, usually between the ages of eighteen and twenty-five. See "The Danish People's High School," *Bulletin* No. 45 (1915) of the U.S. Bureau of Education.

a conscious policy directed towards personality adjustment and fitting the student for marriage, parenthood, and family life. Courses in the family were offered by only a third of these institutions: by two men's colleges, eleven women's colleges, and thirty-nine co-educational institutions. Six of the women's colleges and ten co-educational institutions reported the use of nursery schools in this type of education. All replies indicated an increasing interest on the part of both men and women in the problems of family life.[1] A more recent survey of about 250 of the best known undergraduate colleges has been made under the auspices of the American Social Hygiene Association.[2] A definite tendency towards the development of courses concerning marriage and the family is apparent. Few of these are general courses open to all seniors and juniors without prerequisites, although there is a significant trend towards interdepartmental courses in which several instructors coöperate. In the majority of leading colleges a course on the family is offered, usually with prerequisites, in the department of sociology. Many colleges emphasize topics related to the family, in their appropriate setting, as aspects of diverse courses.

On the basis of her survey of the offerings in home economics departments in nine Mid-Western institutions, Lindquist summarizes the relation between educational trends and the practical problems of modern family life as follows: "the training of the past has been primarily in the techniques of homemaking, with emphasis upon good standards in the routine processes carried on in the home. . . . At the present time, a transition from processes to persons, particularly the young child, is occurring; and . . . in the future one may anticipate more emphasis upon philosophy, perspective, personnel of the family, factors promoting successful marriage and family life, the use of leisure, and the rôle of home managers as citizens and community builders." She believes, moreover, that "the college training of the future will not be limited to special groups nor will it be provided so largely within a single department. If courses can be made valuable for men and women who are majoring

[1] One course of particular interest is offered for *men* at North Dakota Agricultural College by Dean Alta Bates of the School of Home Economics, and deals with the problems of family life when men bear their full share of responsibility. She is convinced of the value of such courses offered by women who are able to interpret the point of view of modern women to men. In a detailed study of divorce she finds opportunity for a frank discussion of the physiological and psychological aspects of women's lives.

[2] M. A. Bigelow and Helen Judy-Bond, "Courses on Marriage and the Family in Undergraduate Colleges," *Journal of Social Hygiene*, Vol. XXII (1936), pp. 25–32.

in other fields, and if the prerequisites for such courses are few, the time is not far distant when one need no longer choose between education for marriage and parenthood and that for earning."[1]

The White House report commented on the enthusiastic response of students to orientation courses in the family, provided they were *well-given*. Much depends on the conduct of such courses. As Lindquist points out, there is a real danger inherent in courses in the field of human relations, when "given by persons lacking a background of experience or without a realization of the many points at which their statements are likely to be applied—sometimes misapplied, to be sure —in dealing with other individuals."[2] In no other field is faulty information or misinterpretation so likely to have serious results.

Further progress in education for marriage and family life evidently depends upon improvement in the quality of teachers in this field. Possessing a well-balanced personality, they should have had a wide experience of life and be well equipped as scholars. They should be themselves persuaded of the enduring values of family life, and should be capable of comradeship with young people and a sympathetic understanding of their problems and their point of view. The White House sub-committee found a few institutions for teacher-training experimenting in the preparation of teachers in this field, but such work was, on the whole, in its earliest stages. Valuable work is being done in many states in the further education of teachers already in service.

SEX EDUCATION

The Need for Organized Effort in a Period of Transition. Were pre-parental education adequate, there would be little need for the type of parent education, so necessary to-day, as a remedial and emergency measure. It is essential to meet the needs of children by supplying so far as possible the deficiencies in their parents' education. Not only does the physical and mental health of children so largely depend on the home environment, but one fundamental aspect of education for parenthood, sex education, is almost entirely in the hands of parents.

[1] *The Family in the Present Social Order*, pp. 135–136.
[2] *Op. cit.*, p. 96. For example, it was found by the survey of the American Social Hygiene Association that many instructors, most of whom had had no satisfactory family life, were impressing on students their view that the family was doomed to rapid disorganization and perhaps ultimate extinction. M. A. Bigelow and Helen Judy-Bond, *op. cit.*, p. 26.

The present interest in sex education tends to be exaggerated, as is probably inevitable in view of the recent and rapid transition from a policy of silence, on the part of parents, and ignorance and supposed innocence, on the part of children.[1] To-day we oscillate between the extremes of modern sex obsession and traditional prudishness. The concentration of attention on sex education is justifiable, moreover, since "the surest way to dethrone sex as a supreme interest is to restore it to simple naturalism."[2]

Sex education should in the future be taken as a matter of course, constituting as it does, when adequately defined, an indispensable foundation for wholesome living, and for successful marriage and parenthood. A broader view of sex education is a very recent development, being to some extent a result of organized effort begun in the first decade of the century to combat the ravages of venereal diseases. It is now realized that the control of these is the task of medicine, and the so-called *social hygiene* movement has become a movement for sex education in the widest sense, meaning the preparation of young people to meet all the problems of life which have their center in sex. In 1918, the Federal Government, alarmed at the prevalence of venereal diseases in the army camps, engaged in a movement for sex education in coöperation with state departments of health. Numerous pamphlets are available for use by parents and teachers and by boys and girls, and studies have been made of the status of sex education in the schools.

The situation with regard to sex instruction in the schools is, as we saw, far from satisfactory, and the same is true of the majority of homes: an even more important matter. In 1915, Exner reported the results of a study of 948 college men, which revealed the following facts: that a large majority of boys got their first permanent impressions about sex from improper sources before the age of twelve, and that the ideas then received had bad effects, leading in many cases to some

---

[1] There were, it is true, certain eighteenth-century educational pioneers who advocated frank sex instruction: Basedow in his *Elementarwerk* (1774) and Salzman in his *Elements of Morality*, translated into English by Mary Wollstonecraft in 1790, and illustrated by Blake. These remarkable anticipations of the modern attitude may be contrasted with a conversation, held at the same period, between Hannah More and one of the dissolute sons of George III, on the subject of keeping from the young all knowledge which might "taint the mind with evil." "No boys were ever bred up in greater ignorance of evil; at fourteen years old, we retained all our natural innocence," explained the Duke!—Mrs. C. S. Peel, *The Stream of Time* (1931), p. 37.

[2] David Seabury, *Growing into Life* (1928), p. 172; and see Chapter XII.

form of sexual practice between twelve and fifteen. Instruction from parents or teachers, though often crude or meager, appeared to have been helpful, but such instruction had generally been given from four to six years too late.[1] In 1924, Isabel Davenport published a significant study, based on the anonymous questions of 160 high school graduates, in training to become teachers. These questions reveal, not only the densest ignorance, but the prevalence of unwholesome and superstitious attitudes, the prevailing tone being one of morbid curiosity with regard to matters which had evidently been shrouded for these girls in a veil of shame and secrecy. The outstanding impression made was "the almost entire lack of constructive idealism displayed in regard to just those sentiments and institutions upon which human happiness most vitally depends—and the fairly incredible lack of penetration of the viewpoint of modern science into the thought of girls relative to their own bodily functions as women."[2]   In Middletown, in 1925, there appears to have been a definite trend in the direction of more teaching of sex hygiene in the home, although actual sex instruction by parents was very far from universal. Of 600 high school boys and girls, 32% of the boys and 68% of the girls named their parents as their chief source of information. These percentages are in significant agreement with the findings of the extensive study conducted in 1930 by a sub-committee of the White House Conference.[3] Among white public school boys, 33% received their first information from their parents, as against 76% of the girls of the same group. Of the college men, 21% had received first information from parents, as against 56% of the college women. This difference between boys and girls was found to be related to the fact that boys confide less in their parents than do girls. Sex education in the home was found to be a function of the degree of intimacy between parents and children.[4] The college students had in the majority of cases received their first information between nine and

[1] M. J. Exner, *Problems and Principles of Sex Education* (1915).

[2] *Salvaging American Girlhood* (1924), pp. 175–176. Much the same impression is gained from P. Blanchard and C. Manasses, *New Girls for Old* (1930). Less than a quarter of these girls had gained their information of sex from their mothers; the majority picked it up in a haphazard fashion between thirteen and sixteen.

[3] *The Adolescent in the Family* (1934), pp. 192–211. A most revealing report, including as it does a number of excerpts from the actual comments made in reply to a questionnaire. Many are very critical of their parents, but, where parents have been successful, their children are warmly appreciative.

[4] In *Middletown in Transition*, the Lynds report that in 1935 the gap between parents and children had grown even wider than it was in 1925.

fourteen, while 7% of the boys and 17% of the girls were actually kept in ignorance until they were over fifteen! Altogether parents were found to be failing badly in giving their children accurate information about sex, and in gaining their children's confidence to an extent making possible the seeking of advice from parents and friendly discussion between parents and children. Little children turn naturally to their parents with their questions, but so far as these in any way concern sex the majority of parents are both reluctant and ill-equipped to answer.[1]

Pre-adolescent Sex Education. Substantial agreement has been reached as to what constitutes adequate sex education. In the first place, it should not be treated as a special branch of instruction. In answering their children's questions, parents must not only give accurate information, but they must do so in an objective manner, casually and calmly; without hesitation or the slightest sign of embarrassment or shame. On no account must sex be treated as a solemn mystery to be spoken of with a hushed voice and in a special manner. In answer to early questions, sex should be treated as a biological and not a moral matter.

Where the parent's own attitude is natural and wholesome this is simple. From the child's point of view, the earliest questions on matters supposedly appertaining to sex are not sexually motivated, but are simply part of his general curiosity. The normal child from two years on is "an animated question mark," and will inevitably inquire into everything he observes.[2] If these questions are simply and truthfully answered, curiosity is satisfied, for the time being. If, on the other hand, he is rebuffed and told his question is "not nice," or if he is met by shamefaced evasion or lies, several unfortunate results follow.

---

[1] Average middle-aged parents are themselves the product of what Havelock Ellis has called "the policy of silent obscurantism." Elementary text books of anatomy and physiology at the end of last century described the human body as though the organs and functions of reproduction had no existence. That the attitudes of parents have been slow to change was very evident in 1929, when Mary Ware Dennett was convicted by a jury of married men of sending *obscene* literature through the mails. The pamphlet found obscene, *The Sex Side of Life*, was originally written by Mrs. Dennett for her own sons and was upheld by leading doctors, psychologists, and educators as a valuable contribution to sex education.

[2] For example, the entirely natural interest taken by children in the differences between boys and girls are no sign of "depravity," as too many parents still seem to believe. Children are humiliated and bewildered when some wholly accidental happening is interpreted as due to preoccupation with sex, as where a little boy was called "horrid" for inadvertently going into a room where a woman guest was undressing.

Not only does his whole attitude to sex become unwholesome, but attention becomes morbidly concentrated on forbidden knowledge. Even if fictions, such as the familiar stork or doctor's bag, momentarily satisfy, they never do so for long. The child will no longer question parents who have shown themselves capable of deceit and evasion, and will turn for information to others, usually other children, from whom he is apt to acquire all sorts of erroneous notions. Some of these may give rise to fears, for which, in the absence of confidence between himself and his parents, there is no antidote. Loss of confidence in parents is perhaps the most disastrous result; for a child's greatest safeguard is his assurance that he can rely on his parents to give a sympathetic and honest answer to every question. In this way alone can parents fully utilize their unique opportunity to lay the foundations of wholesome emotional and mental development. Lively interests, wholesome attitudes, and a scientific spirit are thus encouraged from the first.

The almost universal first question, "Where do babies come from?" or "Where did I come from?" is not a real sex question, although whenever it is asked, usually in the third year, the time is ripe to begin sex education. A foundation should already have been laid by giving information as to the names and care of the different parts of the child's body; something which can be done naturally and incidentally as the child is being bathed. Otherwise the child's interest is the guide and should not be forced. It is better not to go beyond what the child wants to know at the moment. As a matter of fact, when the first questions of a little child are answered, his attention will almost always be turned to something else. In order effectively to relate new knowledge to present interest and capacity, questions should be answered briefly, simply, and *often*. There is danger at the present time that well-meaning but over-anxious parents will proceed to tell far too much, and, in so doing, create the very impression of uneasy solemnity which should be avoided.

Although the earliest stages of sex education consist in giving information, interpretation is implicit from the first, even before there is conscious effort on the part of parents. Their attitude toward the facts is absorbed by the child, both in their manner of discussing them, and in the daily experiences of family life.[1]

[1] For example, a small boy of six, whose every question had been answered by a scientifically trained mother, on discovering the mechanism of sexual intercourse, remarked rather dubiously: "But it doesn't seem very polite": a good illustration too of the difficulties encountered by parents in ridding their manner of attitudes acquired in childhood.

The child of happily married parents has the best chance to acquire thoroughly wholesome attitudes towards sex. Children can most readily be encouraged to think of sex constructively when it is seen first of all as a *family* matter, and when the earliest questions are answered by *both* father and mother. The responsibility for the earliest stages of sex education rests squarely on parents, and cannot with equal hope of success be delegated to any agency outside the home.

There is also substantial agreement as to the content of pre-adolescent sex education. Correct names for external genitalia can be taught, just as they are for ears or nose, as the baby discovers and explores the different parts of his body. Not only should no impression of wickedness be attached to sex organs, but, while sanitary measures are adopted as a matter of course, it is important that disgust should not become attached to excretory functions. When little children are accustomed to see both parents and their brothers and sisters naked, their observation of the differences between the sexes affords a natural opportunity for acquiring the correct terms for the external genitalia of the opposite sex. Very tiny children readily understand that little girls will be mothers some day, and little boys, fathers, and in consequence differ from each other.

Children should become gradually acquainted with the facts of reproduction in response to their questions. The coming of a new baby, or the observation of animals may facilitate matters. It is particularly important to avoid sentimentality and to make clear that both parents have their share in reproduction.[1] If only the mother's relation to the baby is explained wrong conclusions are often drawn as to the father.[2] In connection with this information the correct names of internal genitalia are readily learned. The linking up of knowledge

---

[1] The charge of undue sentimentality may even be leveled against some of the government pamphlets. *The Wonderful Story of Life* is issued in two editions: *A Mother Talks with Her Daughter Regarding Life and Its Reproduction*, and *A Father Talks with His Little Son*, etc. The suggestion is given, moreover, that a boy should be instructed between six and ten, and a girl between seven and ten. This is too late to begin and there seems no good reason for these distinctions. Karl de Schweinitz, *Growing Up* (1928) is an excellent book for children to read to themselves; even if already familiar with the facts, they are interested in the diagrams.

[2] It is generally considered injurious to a child to have any opportunity to observe specifically sexual behavior on the part of parents or other adults. This has been known to produce shock and to lead to mistaken impressions. As we saw on p. 171, under simpler and uncivilized conditions a calm and matter-of-course attitude was the result of Samoan children's early observation of sexual intercourse and childbirth.

of reproduction with keeping pets, and with elementary biology, either in home or school, is helpful in giving the child an impersonal and scientific viewpoint. The boy or girl whose sex education has included these measures will for several years need merely additional information and interpretation along the same lines.

It is most important, however, that physiological changes be fully and clearly explained *before* their culmination in sexual maturity. It is of greater importance that girls be prepared for the sex manifestations of adolescence: that their attitude towards menstruation should be calm and responsible, and concerned only with the establishment of a hygienic regimen conducive to normal functioning.[1] But a boy should also be forewarned, or he may find a first experience of seminal emission alarming. It is advisable too that boys should understand something of the changes taking place in girls. Reasonable caution against masturbation or over-stimulation of the sex organs may be given either boy or girl, if required; but entirely without any threat of punishment or disaster as has so often been the case in the past, sometimes with definite pathological results. At all times emphasis should fall on the constructive aspects of sex and on positive social adjustment, rather than upon the all too prevalent sexual disorders of our times. Information on venereal diseases, though necessary, should not be overstressed, and is best introduced, at first, in connection with the study of bacteriology and communicable diseases, rather than in specific association with sex.

Sex Education in Adolescence. The distinction must again be made between remedial measures necessary because of the neglect of sex education in the pre-adolescent period, and normal sex education during adolescence. A great part of what must be undertaken nowadays falls in the former class.[2] When pre-

[1] Mothers have been most neglectful. Particularly where girls have been brought up to consider sex as shameful, the shock, horror, and disgust inspired by the unexpected onset of menstruation have often had disastrous emotional consequences. Neglect of adequate hygiene and morbid attitudes of mind have been responsible for much invalidism among women. Fortunately a great change for the better has recently been taking place. In an English study, 70% of the girls were found free from menstrual difficulties; after a single educative talk this number was raised to 93%.

[2] A document of the greatest interest as revealing the results of parental silence is to be found in *A Young Girl's Diary* (1921), edited by Freud. This is a private record of the experiences, thoughts, and emotions of an upper-class Austrian girl between the ages of eleven and fourteen and a half, and of her consuming curiosity with regard to sex. Such information as she and her equally ignorant friends are able to glean is largely derived from servants. Her fearful but intense preoccupation

adolescent sex education has been adequate, the girl or boy is already provided with the best safeguard for this difficult period; indeed, some of its chief difficulties will be lessened where the parents have equipped their child with knowledge and a sense of responsibility and an open-minded outlook on the conflicting standards of contemporary life. While they must be prepared to give added information and interpretation, to help and advise, on the whole, their attitude must be one of *trust*. There are obvious risks. But they can be minimized only through the development of voluntary self-control. The central task of education at this period is to help young people to work out their own standards for the guidance of sexual behavior, on the basis of genuine preference and enlightened aspiration.

Adolescence in civilized societies is a difficult period even under the most auspicious circumstances. However socially necessary may be the interval elapsing between the achievement of sexual maturity and actual sex expression, it is from the biological standpoint abnormal. Certain tensions and strains are inevitable. In spite of this fact, there is now general agreement that sexual experience, even in later adolescence, is not necessary to health. This is the time, moreover, when young people naturally love adventure and reach out eagerly for all that may widen and deepen their experience. As an aspect of the adolescent's endeavor to become independent there is very likely to be some withdrawal of confidence from even the most understanding parents. In matters of sex, it often appears easier to speak impersonally with those outside the immediate family circle. All these circumstances combine in complicating the problems of individual and social adjustment in adolescence.[1]

Some added knowledge of fact is necessary during this period. Young people, as they grow older, desire far more detailed knowledge of the physiology and psychology of sex, and information on such matters as the use of contraceptives. An increasing number of books now furnish such information. Not all, however, are scientifically accurate, and still fewer adequately discuss sexual problems in their wider social setting. Young people need a

---

affords illuminating first hand evidence of the realities of so-called "girlish innocence." Already, in 1891, in Germany, Wedekind in *Spring's Awakening* had given dramatic form to the reverse side of youthful innocence and the tragedies which result from the thwarting of natural curiosity. This play had great influence in stimulating interest in sex education. Yet even to-day, according to Judge Lindsey, nine-tenths of girls who "go wrong" do so because of the inattention of parents who imagine their children to be ignorant and innocent.

[1] The problems of adolescence are more fully discussed in Chapter XXIV.

realization of sex as an integral part of life and closely related with the best that life has to offer them. The high school or junior college has, at this point, its chief opportunity to prepare young people for marriage and family life. Both home and school should provide, during these years, as many varied and constructive outlets as possible. Boys and girls must have ample opportunity for active participation in physical, intellectual, and artistic interests. Most important of all is the encouragement of wholesome comradeship in work and play, and the development of genuine companionship between boys and girls. Sex education in adolescence must be very broadly conceived if it is to fulfill its two-fold function of helping young people to live happy and healthy lives, while they gain the experience and knowledge necessary to equip them for successful marriage and responsible parenthood.

PARENT EDUCATION

The Parent Education Movement. The emphasis which has recently come to be placed on the education of those who are already parents is a corollary of the modern realization of the crucial significance of the preschool years. Medicine, psychology, and mental hygiene unite in their insistence on the preschool period as "the most fundamental, the most formative, the most precarious portion of the whole life cycle."[1] The scientific attitude of prevention through control of causes points, accordingly, to the imperative need for a new art of parenthood, based no longer on tradition and routine, but upon science. Emphasis on physical welfare came first. With the publication in 1894 of Dr. Holt's *The Care and Feeding of Children*, an increasing number of mothers were led to seek expert medical guidance rather than rely on the traditional lore of their mothers and grandmothers.[2] Before long, researches in psychology and mental hygiene proved that mental health was fully as much dependent on early nurture as was physical well-being. The supreme social importance of the home as the environment of early childhood made evident the need for the preparation of parents for their responsibilities.

The rapid spread of the movement bears witness to the fact that parents in increasing numbers are realizing their need for

[1] Gesell, "The Preschool Child and the Present Day Parent," *Intelligent Parenthood*, Proceedings of the Mid-West Conference on Parent Education (1926), p. 259.

[2] The fifteenth revised and enlarged edition of Holt's manual was published in July, 1934.

enlightenment. There is still much indifference, even hostility. Many parents still believe themselves naturally endowed with the wisdom necessary for child nurture, while even more believe obedience to be all important, and disobedience a sign of natural depravity. It is particularly important, moreover, that fathers should share more fully in the benefits of the movement.[1] Already, however, despite its initiation as an emergency measure, parent education is passing beyond the stage of being a movement and is becoming an established branch of education.

It is only within the last twenty years that widespread efforts have been made to collect and disseminate organized material in this field, although the movement had its earliest beginnings fifty years ago, when in 1888 *three* mothers formed a group which became the nucleus for the present Child Study Association of America.[2] Gradually other groups gathered until in 1908 a central organization, known as the Federation for Child Study, came into being. In 1923 this organization was incorporated under its present name, The Child Study Association of America.

Early in the nineties, the Association of Collegiate Alumnae, now the American Association of University Women, began a systematic study of children. Not, however, until 1922 was a definite parent education program developed. In 1925, the American Home Economics Association, founded in 1908 to promote homemaking, undertook systematic work in child care and parent education. In the same way, the study of homemaking included in the program of the Federal Board of Vocational Education soon led to the formation throughout the country of classes in parent education. Parent education is also one of the projects of the Coöperative Extension Service in Agriculture and Home Economics of the United States Department of Agriculture, while the United States Public Health Service and the Children's Bureau have consistently carried on programs of education in child health. Finally parent education is becoming incorporated as an integral part of state, county, and city systems of public instruction, and is included on university programs. The National Council of Parent Education was organized informally in 1925 and definitely launched in 1928 to serve as a coördinating and counseling agency in the field of parent education.

[1] See note 2, p. 267.
[2] Herbert Spencer, in 1860, had advocated the need for special knowledge on the part of parents and teachers in preparation for the rearing and education of children.

Programs, Objectives, and Methods. Most of these agencies employ both individual and group methods of parent education. In study and discussion groups, behavior problems are very naturally the chief interest. The White House survey found that other problems frequently discussed were those of child care and feeding, mental and physical development, family relationships, and sex education. Adolescent problems were not found to be dealt with as frequently as might be expected, and relatively little emphasis was placed on specialized subject matter dealing with handicapped, retarded, or superior children, and vocational guidance or educational techniques. Most of the work clearly centers on the practical problems of parents; which accounts for the emphasis on problems within the home, on behavior crises, discipline, and parent-child relationships.

Far too many of the parents who are thus seeking aid still want rules which may be automatically followed, devices to be applied in a specific situation; instead of a grasp of principles, as a prelude to further learning, and the only safe guide in the intricate and complex problems of parenthood. There is, of course, need for factual knowledge derived from a study of nutrition, hygiene, sanitation, growth, behavior, sex, mental and emotional development, social relationships, and education. In addition certain skills and techniques may be acquired, very generally helpful in child nurture. But all this is not enough. The wise use of principles of child guidance is largely a matter of insight and attitude. It is essential that parents should be led to adopt scientific habits of thought. This demands in the first place a calm objective attitude only too hard to acquire when dealing with their own children. It may, however, be facilitated by the study of other children. Secondly, it is essential to look for underlying causes, and to seek the meaning of a child's behavior in terms suggested by an analytical study of the whole situation. Self-criticism is of particular importance, and will follow realization of the determining influence exercised by parents on their children. From an objective *socio-psychiatric* standpoint the child's behavior is no longer the subject of praise or blame.

Respect for the child's personality undermines older concepts of discipline. Not that discipline becomes unnecessary or devoid of meaning. Far from it. As Mrs. Gruenberg says, "Obedience having ceased to be a cardinal virtue, parents must find effective substitutes." "To-day we must realize that children need to be trained not for obedience, but through obedience. Obedience is a useful instrument of control whereby those responsible for guiding the child's development lead him to formulate and eventually to obey his own rules of life."[1] Parental authority, exercised in the endeavor to make children conform to fixed patterns of conduct, must be superseded by parental responsibility for the provision of an environment in which growing powers may be liberated and self-direction be gradually achieved. This is no easy problem; but its solution in each individual case may be facilitated if parents hold fast to the conviction that the purpose of discipline is the attainment of responsible freedom.

The actual content of group work is to a considerable extent determined by the group leader or by the study outlines or publications of various organizations.[2] In addition to educating parents, either singly or in groups, the national programs have concentrated on the preparation of material and on the stimulation of interests and activities. State programs, on the other hand, are more concerned with the training of the professional and lay leaders upon whom so much of the success of study groups depends.[3] The universities, with their facilities for research and teaching, supply many leaders. For example, the Child Development Institute of Teachers College, Columbia University, has been experimenting since 1923 in the preparation of professional leaders in parent education.

Emphasis is beginning to be laid on the relationships between parents and leaders. Successful methods of parental education involve not so much instruction as thinking and feeling together, with free expression of emotions and ideas. It is also being discovered that practice in the handling of children under supervision is invaluable. Gesell has found concrete demonstration of the way problems are met and solved to be of the greatest

[1] "Parent Education and Child Welfare," in *Parent Education* (D. Appleton-Century Company, 1932), p. 17; and "New Parents for Old," in *The New Generation*, p. 521.

[2] The National Council of Parent Education publishes the magazine *Parent Education*, while the magazine *Child Welfare* is brought out by the National Congress of Parents and Teachers. *Child Study* is the monthly publication of the Child Study Association of America. *The Parents' Magazine* has been published since 1926, with the technical advice and coöperation of Teachers College, Columbia University, The Child Study Association, the Universities of Minnesota and Iowa, and Yale University. In addition to these magazines, whose primary purpose is parent education, a number of others include materials of special interest to parents: *Progressive Education*, *Mental Hygiene*, *Journal of Social Hygiene*, *Journal of Home Economics*, and *Child Development*. Women's magazines enlist the services of authorities in their departments of child care, and six of them now have a circulation of over two million.

[3] In California in 1935 there were eighty parents leading study groups.

aid in parent guidance, even though, as at the Yale Psycho-Clinic, the parent remains removed from the situation in the observation alcove. The experience of those who have experimented with coöperative nursery schools is significant. In such nursery schools mothers, and sometimes fathers, participate in the school activities. Very successful results have followed in several schools, both for the children and for their parents, although parent education had not been an original objective. The Northampton Coöperative Nursery School was organized in 1925 by the Smith College Institute for the Coördination of Women's Interests. Both fathers and mothers participated in all phases of the venture, from the formulation of detailed plans for the school to assistance in its regular activities. On the basis of her experience as director Mrs. Howes concludes: "a nursery school which is not coöperative in . . . the sense that the work of the parents is . . . known to be needed . . . misses its greatest opportunity. . . . We have learned from our successful experiment that the most effective instrument of parental education is participation by the parents in their children's education under direction."[1]

Teachers College at Columbia embarked on a new program of parent education, in the summer of 1937, based on the progressive concept of "learning by doing." Parents live with their children in a summer camp, they observe classroom procedure, help to determine school policies, and even teach. Thus by actual practice they learn how to live with their children and to coöperate with the school in their education.[2] The full potentialities of coöperation between home and school in the provision of an integrated educative environment are thus beginning to be appreciated. Since 1897 this has been, it is true, one of the chief objectives of the National Congress of Parents and Teachers which, by 1930, included more than 20,000 parent-teacher associations, fathers' clubs, mothers' clubs, preschool associations, and study circles, with a membership of 1,500,000. Adequate and widespread parent education should do much to make the work of this organization more effective.

Parent Education as a Focus for Adult Education. In the future it is to be hoped that much of the work now being done will be unnecessary, because adequate pre-parental education will have become universal. There will still, however, be enduring need for parent education as part of a general program of

[1] *Parent Education*, p. 281.   [2] *New York Times*, July 18, 1937.

adult education. Parents will wish to keep abreast of the developing body of scientific materials which can aid them in the nurture and education of their children; there will always be need too for the discussion of parents' problems under the guidance of experts, and for the participation of parents in the work of the school.[1]

Parent education occupies a focal position in the current adult education movement. Indeed, as Lindeman points out: "parent education . . . becomes a point of departure for a thorough inventory of the qualities of adult experience in this modern world. . . . The primary motivations of parent education emerge from actual problems, real situations. . . . The parent in meeting a specific situation may acquire knowledge which will become useful in other situations; he or she may be a center of educational infection for a group, a neighborhood, a community; and he or she may acquire the method of learning which may thenceforth become operative in all phases of life and living. Thus, the motive to become an effective parent may be seen to expand so as to interfuse all experience, to become the stimulus for widening circles of motivation, making of life itself an adventure in learning."[2]

In proportion as parents come to realize the influence of social conditions on the welfare of all children, they may assume leadership in making contemporary society a more fitting environment for childhood. There are already signs indicating that parent education is emerging as a social movement. If this is indeed the case, says Lindeman, "parents may become . . . the new ferment for making our society more flexible and more progressive."[3] Parent education will then appear as a major force determining the destiny of future generations.

Moreover, if parenthood becomes, as Lindeman hopes, "an adventurous intellectual pursuit without sacrifice of its emotional qualities," there should follow a new and fuller realization of education as an essential function of enduring family life.[4] Interest in education may become an integrating force in the community, uniting homes with schools and other agencies, in the service of youth. Since to serve youth effectively, adults must continue their own education, the result should be the enrichment of adult experience and a social life based on common

[1] A thorough study of family life, such as was earlier suggested as the core of an integrated curriculum, would adapt itself very readily to the purposes of parent education through participation in school activities.

[2] "Sociological Backgrounds of Family Life," in *Parent Education*, pp. 11–12.

[3] *Our Children*, p. 290.   [4] *Parent Education*, p. 8.

interes'ts and shared pursuits. As Miriam Van Waters says,
"the movement of parental education is the most hopeful sign
in American life to-day."[1]

SUGGESTED READING

Bain, W. E., *Parents Look at Modern Education*, 1935.

Bigelow, M., *Sex Education*, rev. ed., 1936.

Blatz, W. E., Millichamp, D., and Fletcher, M., *Nursery Education,
Theory and Practice*, 1935.

Bossard, J. H. S., and Weaver, W. W., eds. *The Prospect for Youth,*
in *The Annals of the American Academy of Political and Social
Science*, Vol. CXCIV, Nov., 1937.

California State Department of Education, *Bulletin*, "Objectives and
Suggested Procedures for Parent Education in California," 1934.

Fisher, D. C., and Gruenberg, B. M., eds., *Our Children*, 1932.

Forest, I., *Preschool Education*, 1927.

Gesell, A., *The Guidance of Mental Growth in Infant and Child*, 1930.

Groves, E. R. and G. H., *Sex in Childhood*, 1933.

Gruenberg, B. C., *Parents and Sex Education*, 1932.

Hanna, P. R., *Youth Serves the Community*, 1936.

Johnson, H., *Children in the Nursery School*, 1929.

Lindquist, R., *The Family in the Present Social Order*, 1931.

Maclean, M. S., "A College of 1934," *Journal of Higher Education*,
Vol. V, May and June, 1934, pp. 240–246, 314–322.

National Youth Administration, *Youth, a World Problem*, 1937.

Office of Education, *Bulletin 9*, 1932, "Nursery Schools, Their Development and Current Practices in the United States."

——, *Bulletin 3*, 1935, "Parent Education Opportunities."

——, *Bulletin 18*, 1936: I, "How Communities Can Help"; II, "Lei-
sure for Living"; III, "Education for Those Out of School"; IV,
"Vocational Guidance for Those Out of School"; V, "Finding
Jobs"; VI, "Community Surveys."

Public Health Service, Division of Venereal Diseases, *Bulletin 75*,
"High Schools and Sex Education," 1922.

——, *Bulletin 86*, "Sex Education," 1927.

Strain, F. B., *New Patterns of Sex Teaching*, 1934.

White House Conference, *Education for Home and Family Life*, 1932.

——, *Home and School Coöperation*, 1932.

——, *Nursery Education*, 1931.

——, *Parent Education*, 1932.

——, *Social Hygiene in Schools*, 1932.

——, *The Adolescent in the Family*, 1934.

[1] *Parents on Probation* (1927), p. 279.

CHAPTER XI

THE ASSUMPTION OF PUBLIC RESPONSIBILITY FOR CHILD WELFARE

RECENT TRENDS IN SOCIAL WELFARE WORK

Private Social Welfare Agencies. Modern educational ideals envisage the extension of opportunities for full development to every child alike, irrespective of social status. Actually we have very far to go before the children of America are assured of equality of opportunity. Educational reform cannot of itself rectify present injustice. Characteristic of our day, as Dewey points out, is "the recognition that mere schooling is not enough": if social disintegration and disorder are to be averted, there must be "the unremitting devotion of society to serve the needs of the young who are component members of future adult society."[1]

Only recently has society concerned itself with the needs of children. In 1853 the Children's Aid Society was founded with the primary object of caring for orphans and deserted children. Not until the seventies, were any steps taken to protect children from cruelty or exploitation at the hands of incompetent or greedy parents. Humane societies of that period were organized for the protection of animals. An appeal made against the brutal mistreatment of a little girl to the New York Society for Prevention of Cruelty to Animals resulted in 1875 in the formation of the Society for the Prevention of Cruelty to Children, incorporated under the first statute of its kind anywhere in the world. In general, social reconstruction in the United States lagged behind similar movements in England and on the Continent.[2] Nevertheless, although postponed till the nineties, the growth of public concern for social welfare gives cause for hope that the "American dream," of a richer and fuller life for all, may in time be realized, through the

---

[1] *New York Times*, April 10, 1932.

[2] Jane Addams points to several factors which contributed to this result: the rapidity of industrial expansion, the attitude towards the immigrants who composed the bulk of the working classes, and the fact that the moral energy of America had been concentrated on abolition and on finding remedies for commercial and political corruption. "The Process of Social Transformation," in *A Century of Progress* (ed. Charles Beard, 1932), pp. 235–237.

potent means of securing opportunity for development to every child.

A significant change of attitude in social work has taken place with the growing concern for child welfare, and consequently for the welfare of families as providing the natural environment of childhood. In contrast to the frequent obtuseness to the personal feelings of recipients of charity or relief at the close of last century, there has been increasing emphasis on consideration for personality; and case work, with its methods of individualized treatment, has become the recognized technique for social work. Case workers were first employed by family and child welfare agencies, and it is upon the basis of their experience that the preservation and development of family life is now regarded as a major objective of social work. In the first decade of the century, the breaking-up of families was frequently resorted to when the environment appeared unfavorable for children. Extensive experience with children has now brought realization of their essential need for family relationships.

A significant and steadily growing trend in social work has been the emphasis on preventive and constructive measures rather than on temporary alleviation. Already by 1910, Jane Addams was urging a positive policy, which would make the raising of life to its highest levels the objective of social work.[1] Here too, concern for children has had decisive influence; their development is so obviously handicapped by adverse conditions, and they are so obviously responsive to constructive influences. Higher standards of relief have been the result of the new attitude.[2] In 1907 Mary Richmond protested against the still too prevalent practice of giving just enough "to tide the recipient over the next week's misery." Relief is now considered a *tool* of good case work, but not a sure remedy for maladjustment.

Another conspicuous trend has been the employment of the

[1] Lilian Wald expresses the same aim as follows: "The goal of a social program based on personal interests is to help individuals to the highest level of which each is capable. . . . Intelligence, disinterestedness and respect for people will show how best they can be served. . . . I hold to my faith that the first essential of sound human relations is respect. No one who has that sense of respect will patronize, or insult, or feel alien to human beings." *Windows on Henry Street* (Little, Brown and Company, 1934), pp. 8, 10.

[2] Sydnor H. Walker says: "The fact that promotion of child welfare transcends all other social welfare interests, and that optimism in regard to his future supplies the basis for most preventive and constructive activities, must be emphasized for real understanding of the motivation of private social work." "Privately Supported Social Work," *Recent Social Trends* (McGraw-Hill Book Company, 1933), Vol. II, p. 1172.

psychiatric approach in social work, an approach which reënforces the emphasis on prevention and individual treatment and the early emotional experiences of childhood. Finally, and of utmost significance for future developments in social work, is the trend towards the absorption of welfare activities as a part of public administration. This had been in process for at least fifteen years before the depression. "The private agency has experimented with methods of meeting new situations, demonstrated the effectiveness of certain methods, and stimulated social legislation to make possible the transfer of social services to public funds."[1]

A new social philosophy is thus making itself felt; a philosophy inspired by the spirit of those pioneers whose voluntary efforts made possible the development of private social work. Among these, none have had a larger share, both in saving the unfortunate and in interpreting their needs to the more fortunate, than the workers in social settlements. Hull House and the Henry Street Settlement are leading examples, founded respectively by Jane Addams and Lilian Wald.[2]

Despite the expansion of the public welfare program there was a marked increase in private social welfare activities before the depression, and a trend towards their coördination and systematization through a centralization of authority in nationally organized associations.[3] Another interesting development is that of independent organizations chartered for the financing of certain stated forms of philanthropy. Twenty of the three hundred and fifty such foundations, existing in 1930, controlled the greater part of the fifty million expended that year. Of this, $19,000,000 went to medical research and public health, not quite $2,000,000 directly to social welfare, and a little over $1,000,000 to child welfare.

The work of these foundations in financing experiments and

[1] Walker, *ibid.*, p. 1222.

[2] Hull House was founded in 1889 and the Henry Street Settlement in 1895, although Miss Wald began her work as a district nurse in the neighborhood in 1893. The whole public-health nursing movement originated in her concrete demonstration of the value of such organized service. Miss Addams tells how the Hull House workers were at once impressed by the numerous instances in which "the promise of youth was frustrated by premature labor and by malnutrition in childhood. . . . It was perhaps inevitable that a child labor law should have been our first venture into the field of state legislation." *Op. cit.*, p. 241.

[3] The first Charity Organization Society in the United States was founded in 1877 in Buffalo. By 1930 there were 378 national agencies, 117 of which had local branches. Of the organizations participating in the National Conference of Social Work, 73 were organized prior to 1900, 53 between 1901 and 1911, 108 between 1911 and 1921, and 144 between 1921 and 1930.

demonstrations, such as those of the Commonwealth Fund
with child guidance clinics and visiting-teacher services, makes
clear one reason for the important place maintained by private
social work as a necessary supplement to public social work.[1]
Private agencies are the community's "path-finding and experimental arm in dealing with social problems."[2] Private social
work is more flexible, freer from legal restrictions, and is able
to use its funds to meet needs not yet recognized as part of
public responsibility. More time and attention can be bestowed
on individuals, and in this way valuable experience and training
are furnished for those who are to become leaders in public
social work. Even prior to the depression, relief-giving was
becoming more and more of a public function, but the advice
and care given to individuals in their own homes remained
very largely the work of private welfare agencies.

The development of social welfare work has been most
uneven, the standards of fifty years ago being sometimes found
in areas not far removed from the centers of greatest progress.
Modern trends have been largely the outcome of urban development. All the worst features of industrialism are manifest in
the congested areas of the cities. In the cities alone, moreover,
is it possible to accumulate the large funds necessary for effective
work. In some parts of the country, little or no aid was derived
from public funds before the depression, while in others many
activities of social value have long been undertaken as a matter
of course.

Public Welfare Activities. "Public welfare," says Odum, "is
the social welfare function of government. . . . It is social
work financed by federal, state, county or city governments
and controlled and directed by them. That is, public welfare
is an extension or development of the techniques and methods
of private social work into the field of government. . . . Within
a few decades the changes in the field of public welfare . . .
have been so numerous and so radical as to transform the
whole field and method and give it a new place among social
forces now remaking the nation. . . . The significance of techni-

[1] Miss Wald says: "It is impossible to wait upon government appropriations for
all the emergencies that clamor at the door. . . . One of the great lessons of the
depression is that the government must take more responsibility for social welfare,
although we have a long road to travel before public relief alone is sufficient or even
desirable. Satisfactory human relations are built upon expressions of compassion,
of understanding, of willingness to help, and upon the recognition of the fact that we
are all interrelated as human beings." *Op. cit.*, p. 128.

[2] Joanna Colcord, director of the charity organization department of the Russell
Sage Foundation, *New York Times*, Nov. 11, 1934.

cal public welfare in American life . . . is not only indicated by the quantitative changes . . . , but by the aspiration of America to devise and operate technical functions of government which will assist in the equalization of opportunity and facilitate adaptation to economic and social change. The demand is not merely for a philosophy but for something so real and vital that it will serve the actual maladjusted individual, family and community, in practice as well as theory."[1]

This development has been in part motivated by an increasing realization that the individual cannot be held responsible for misfortunes arising from natural handicaps or from maladjustments in the economic system. Public aid, following the lead of private social work, is endeavoring to provide protection for individuals and for families. Rapid development began in 1917, when the National Conference of Charities and Corrections became the National Conference of Social Work, and the characteristic terminology of public welfare became current. Approved methods of social work are being incorporated in each of the four major fields of public welfare work: relief; penology; provision for the mentally handicapped; and child welfare; the underlying philosophy of the whole movement being a change in attitude, "away from the old condescending charity . . . to the newer ideals of democratic service."[2]

The Depression. Despite these developments, the nation was unprepared to meet the emergencies of a depression of unprecedented magnitude, which deprived increasing numbers of their means of livelihood. It is true that, between 1921 and 1927, in only two years did the number of unemployed fall below 1,750,000. But by 1927 the number employed in manufacturing industries was 12% lower than in 1923, and by 1928 the situation was already very serious. In 1929 the storm broke. According to estimates of the American Federation of Labor, an average of 4,000,000 were unemployed in 1930, of 7,500,000 in 1931, of 11,500,000 in 1932, of 12,000,000 in 1933 with a peak of 13,000,000 in the spring of that year. By 1934 the situation was beginning to improve, though with 10,000,000 still out of work.[3]

The result was a rapid and enormous increase in the number of persons dependent upon social agencies for support. A study of relief expenditures in 81 cities for the years 1929–1931,

[1] "Public Welfare Activities" in *Recent Social Trends*, pp. 1227, 1226, 1224, 1271. It is to be noted that the derivation of the connotation of *public* welfare, from the sources of expenditure, is in contrast to that applying in the field of *public* health, which means health of the public, whether supported by public or private funds.

[2] *Ibid.*, p. 1224. [3] *New York Times*, Jan. 5, and Feb. 17, 1935.

made by the Russell Sage Foundation, indicated a 300% increase. In general, relief expenditures increased annually in geometric progression until the peak in the spring of 1933. In July, 1933, 15,500,000 persons were receiving unemployment relief out of public funds, more than the whole population of the United States a hundred years ago.[1] Adding other recipients of public and private care to these figures, about *one-sixth* of the whole population were being maintained wholly or in part, in 1933, by public or private agencies.

The seriousness of the situation was not fully apparent till 1932. At first there had been reliance on existing public and private relief agencies. But the emergency did not pass, local funds became exhausted, relief was inadequate, and suffering was pronounced. In turning to outside aid, the first recourse was to state funds. New York was the first state to undertake extensive assistance to local communities, $20,000,000 being appropriated by the New York State Temporary Emergency Relief Administration Act in September, 1931. Other states very soon followed the example of New York, and there was a gradual assumption of state leadership in the relief program. But by the summer of 1932 all emergency funds, both state and local, were becoming exhausted. Recourse was finally had to federal aid. In July, 1932, the Wagner Relief Bill set up a federal fund of $300,000,000 to be disbursed by the Reconstruction Finance Corporation. The primary purpose was business relief, and there was no federal leadership in the formulation of a program of relief. Accordingly, in May, 1933, the Federal Emergency Relief Administration began to function, after the passage of the Federal Emergency Relief Act, appropriating $500,000,000 to be spent through the states in coöperation with the federal government. The new policy is one of public relief to be extended through public agencies, and making a three-fold partnership—federal, state, and local— under federal leadership. Since the Works Progress Administration began to function in 1935, there has been a liquidation of the FERA, as work relief replaced home relief. State and local agencies now have full responsibility for direct relief.

Prior to the depression, efforts to coördinate and consolidate the welfare activities of the federal government met with little success. Owing to historical accident or political expediency the offices and bureaus in charge of public welfare are to be found in several of the departments of the government. The

[1] Federal Emergency Relief Administration, *Monthly Report*, for Sept., 1933.

Department of the Interior includes the Office of Education and touches health services in several ways. But the Public Health Service itself functions under the Treasury Department. The Children's Bureau, founded in 1912, and the Women's Bureau, founded in 1920, are included in the Department of Labor. The reorganization of departments and outlying bureaus was recommended to Congress in 1937; judging by the action of a House committee, reorganization will include the establishment of a new federal department of public welfare.

THE 1909 WHITE HOUSE CONFERENCE AND THE CREATION OF THE
CHILDREN'S BUREAU

The White House Conference on Dependent Children. Recent years have seen what Frank calls "a change in the major strategy of child welfare." Attention has been transferred "from exclusive concern with the diagnosis and treatment of the individual child in isolation to a consideration of indirect methods of furthering the welfare of children in general, especially as methods of preventing the ills, defects and handicaps that are so expensive and difficult to remedy."[1] The new emphasis on individualized home care led to added concern for the problems of dependent children. Accordingly, on Christmas day, 1908, President Roosevelt invited 200 child welfare workers from all parts of the United States to assemble in Washington for two days in January, 1909, for a consideration of measures to be taken for the care of dependent children. A report containing fifteen specific recommendations was unanimously adopted and transmitted to Congress and to the Governors of states. The dominant note of this conference was the elemental importance and value of the family as a basic institution for child care.[2]

Among specific suggestions were the following: that greater provision be made for the assistance of needy children in their own homes; that greater use be made of family care for children who must be removed from their own homes; that child-caring

---

[1] "Childhood and Youth," *Recent Social Trends*, Vol. II, p. 752.

[2] "Home life," it was declared, "is the highest and finest product of civilization. It is the great moulding force of mind and character. Children should not be deprived of it except for urgent and compelling reasons. Children of parents of worthy character, suffering from temporary misfortune, and children of reasonably efficient and deserving mothers who are without the support of the normal breadwinner, should as a rule be kept with their own parents, such aid being given as may be necessary to maintain suitable homes for the rearing of children." Quoted by E. O. Lundberg, "Public Aid to Mothers with Dependent Children," *Children's Bureau Publication*, No. 162 (1928), p. 1.

agencies be responsibly organized and be inspected by the state; that dependent children receive better medical care, that prevention of child dependency is better than cure; that the causes of child dependency be ascertained and, if possible, controlled; and that a Federal Children's Bureau should be established.

The Children's Bureau. The creation of a Children's Bureau had been discussed for several years before the 1909 Conference. The experiences of social workers provided daily evidence of the great need for an organized and centralized source of information on all matters pertaining to child welfare. The government in its program for the conservation of natural resources had overlooked its obligation "toward the greatest wealth of the nation: the children."[1] There was no responsible governmental agency to which appeal might be made for guidance in the conservation and protection of children. Accordingly, the National Child Labor Committee, of which Miss Wald was a leading member, became sponsor for the propaganda necessary to the creation of a Children's Bureau. In 1912 a law creating the Bureau was passed. Under its terms the new unit of the Department of Labor shall "investigate and report . . . upon all matters pertaining to the welfare of children and child life among all classes of people, and shall especially investigate the questions of infant mortality, the birth rate, orphanage, juvenile courts, desertion, dangerous occupations, accidents and diseases of children, employment legislation affecting children in the several States and Territories." Julia Lathrop was appointed first chief of the Bureau, and, with an appropriation of $25,640, made a beginning in this vast field of social research, which at once established the scientific character of the Bureau's work, and demonstrated its practical value, in establishing relationships with child-caring agencies and groups throughout the country concerned with child welfare problems, and in making its conclusions available to individual parents. In her first annual report, Miss Lathrop declared: it is "the final purpose of the Bureau to serve all children, to

[1] These are Miss Wald's words. As a matter of fact the idea of a Federal Children's Bureau had emanated from the Henry Street Settlement. Lilian Wald and Florence Kelley "had made the first outline of the matters to be investigated by such a bureau, an outline which corresponded closely to the act creating the Bureau as finally passed." From Addams, *Twenty Years at Hull House* (1910), p. 22. By permission of The Macmillan Company, publishers. Miss Kelley and the first two chiefs of the Children's Bureau, Julia Lathrop (1912–1921) and Grace Abbott (1921–1934), had all been associated with Hull House.

try to work out the standards of care and protection which shall give to every child his fair chance in the world." Although similar bureaus were soon thereafter established in other countries, the United States Children's Bureau was the first public agency directed to consider as a whole the problems of childhood.

Infant mortality was selected as the subject of the initial inquiry to be conducted by the Bureau. It was soon discovered that few states had satisfactory laws with regard to birth registration. A campaign for birth registration followed, the first of many important pieces of work which have been undertaken in coöperation with the national women's organizations throughout the country, as well as with professional organizations in the field of child care. In Grace Abbott's words the first task of the Children's Bureau thus became the enumeration of "fuzzy heads and tiny coffins." At the same time the popular bulletins on prenatal care, infant care, and child care were published, the first of a long series, none of which have exceeded in popularity the first three.[1] In addition to the maternity and infancy division, responsible for the study of infant mortality, the Bureau, as originally organized, had a child hygiene division; an industrial division, concerned with the problem of child workers; and a division of social service, whose field of research included children in need of special care: the dependent or neglected, the delinquent, and the physically and mentally handicapped.[2] A statistical division is in charge of investigations which are primarily statistical, and an editorial division edits the Bureau publications and prepares materials for exhibits and for newspapers and magazines.

In 1918, when faced by the additional problems of child welfare occasioned by the World War, the Children's Bureau was asked to coöperate with the women's committee of the Council of National Defense to sponsor a national program of

[1] Until the time of their publication, the most popular government bulletin had been "Care of the Horse." The demand for these three bulletins has increased year by year until they have exceeded all records as best sellers. By 1930, they had reached a circulation of 10,000,000. By September 29, 1934, "Infant Care" alone had reached a circulation of 8,000,000. It was compiled in 1914 by a group of leading baby specialists and was revised in 1929.

[2] Reorganization of these divisions has since taken place. Before the passage of the Social Security Act in 1935, the divisions other than editorial and statistical were: child and maternal health; social science; delinquency; industrial; social statistics. To enable the Children's Bureau to administer the maternal and child welfare provisions of the Act, further reorganization took place: crippled children, child welfare services, public health nursing, and research in child development were added; and social statistics dropped.

child welfare. "Children's Year" was proclaimed in April, and an educational campaign ensued, in which all but two states participated. Altogether 17,000 committees including 11,000,000 women were formed in 16,500 communities. Weighing and measuring tests were conducted for children of preschool age, both for their immediate value and to furnish a basis for a follow-up program. As a fitting close to Children's Year, a second White House Conference was organized by the Children's Bureau at the request of President Wilson, and financed by his war emergency fund; its aim being to formulate "certain irreducible minimum standards for the health, education and work of the American child."

MOTHERS' AID

The Development of Mothers' Aid. Before turning to the work of the 1919 White House Conference, brief consideration must be given to the development of mothers' aid, a movement which may be traced to the 1909 Conference, and whose rapid progress has been assisted by the work of the Children's Bureau. A revolution has been wrought by the policy of never removing a child from his own home, nor from the custody of his parents, because of poverty, or illegitimacy, alone. Money formerly available to care for children in institutions is more and more being used to keep homes intact. The Missouri legislature, in 1911, was the first to make legal provision for the payment of public funds to mothers of dependent children.[1] Illinois in the same year enacted the first *state-wide* mothers' aid law. Beginning in 1913, with Colorado's Mothers' Compensation Act, eighteen states had by the end of that year enacted similar legislation. For a time there was much opposition. Revisions and numerous amendments were found necessary as the earlier laws were put in operation. By 1932, however, only two states had failed to enact such statutes.[2]

The earlier laws had tended to restrict public aid to *widows*, thus denying relief to mothers whose husbands were incapacitated or had deserted. By 1931 only two states limited the grant to widows. Aid is being administered, not so much in the guise of a "pension," which the phrasing of laws often implies, as in accordance with methods of social case work. There was

[1] The law applied at first only to the county in which Kansas City was located.
[2] Care of dependent children in their own families has been found less expensive than their maintenance in institutions, so that economic motives have reënforced humanitarian in securing this significant development.

steady growth in the number of families aided and in the amounts expended up to 1930.[1] In that year, in the thirty-three states where data were available, over $30,000,000 was spent in aiding an average of 220,000 children and their mothers, almost as many children being helped in this way as in institutions and foster homes combined.[2]

State Laws Relating to Public Aid for Children in Their Own Homes. An analysis of the laws in operation by 1931 revealed variations from state to state.[3] With regard to the persons to whom aid may be given, the prevailing methods are to permit aid to any mother with dependent children, or else to limit aid to certain types of cases including those where the father is dead or deserting, divorced, physically or mentally incapacitated, or imprisoned. In twenty states the laws are very liberal. Seven states permit aid to be granted to expectant mothers, and three states authorize aid to unmarried mothers. Aid is sometimes allowed to relatives or guardians having custody of a dependent child. In five states fathers are eligible for aid. Eligibility requirements as to residence and citizenship vary in the different states. Most laws include further conditions as to economic need and the mother's ability to give the child proper care. The age period during which children are regarded as dependents tends to conform with the compulsory school attendance and child labor laws. In the majority of states the age is sixteen, but there are four in which aid is authorized only for children under fourteen.

Great diversity is also found in the amounts granted. Experience has shown that it is desirable to avoid strict limitation of grants, in order to permit of assistance adjusted to individual need. But the majority of laws provide for a maximum amount per month for each child. In eleven states and in the District of Columbia, however, legal provision is made for aid sufficient

[1] For examples of typical rural and city conditions, figures may be cited for Wisconsin and New York City. In 1913 Wisconsin spent $9,632 in aiding 187 families. In 1928, 6,274 families were assisted at a cost of $1,533,900. In New York City in 1916, the first year when aid was given, $165,000 was spent, while in 1929 the sum was $6,479,000. Grace Abbott, "Safeguarding the Child in America," *Current History*, Vol. XXXIII (1931), p. 824.

[2] So great has been the need for relief for the unemployed and their children during the depression, that the needs of other children have been to some extent overshadowed. In November, 1934, it was estimated that 300,000 children were being cared for through mothers' aid, while approximately 400,000 were being cared for through 1,900 public and private agencies or institutions. J. P. Murphy, "Children in the New Deal," *Annals of the American Academy of Political and Social Science*, Vol. CLXXVI (Nov., 1934), p. 125.

[3] "Mothers' Aid, 1931," *Children's Bureau Publication*, No. 220 (1933).

to enable mothers to bring up their children properly in their own homes. Various agencies are responsible for the administration of these laws. A few states have established new agencies. In the others, juvenile courts, or county or city boards serve as local administrative agencies in coöperation with the state.

In 1922 a Conference on Mothers' Pensions was held under the joint auspices of the Family Division of the National Conference of Social Work and of the Children's Bureau. Adequate state supervision was urged, and recommendations made to the effect that aid should be sufficient to meet deficiencies in family budgets, which should be made out in each case with the guidance of a standard budget schedule. The *principle* of home-care for dependent children is now generally accepted. The problem, even by 1928, was not so much the need for new legislation, as "to obtain adequate appropriations and to raise standards of administration so that the laws may mean adequate care for the children they are intended to benefit."[1] Those in charge of this work have an unequalled opportunity for family case work, in helping mothers in the care of their children and in supervising their education or employment. Sometimes such opportunities have been neglected, in other cases excellent work is being done.[2] But wherever financial aid is given regularly, in a friendly spirit, it is found to bring security and stability, and to enable large numbers of families to function efficiently and on a par with self-supporting families in their community. Mothers' aid laws are much more than relief measures; stress being laid on the responsibility of mothers for their children. It has been definitely shown that the provision of mothers' aid does not encourage dependency, but, on the contrary, has developed self-confidence, initiative, and, generally, a desire for economic independence on the part of mothers receiving assistance. Federal aid to dependent children was included in the Social Security Act of 1935. Although the grants are regrettably small, this acceptance of national responsibility for needy and dependent children is of the utmost significance.[3]

[1] Lundberg, *op. cit.*, p. 24.

[2] The importance of an adequate personnel has not been sufficiently realized. The possibilities of intensive case work diminish as the number of families per worker rises above 50 or 60. In some agencies workers were found to be in charge of from 90 to 250 families, in addition to making new investigations.

[3] The Act authorized $24,750,000 for the current fiscal year and such amounts as shall be needed in future years, to assist the states in providing aid to dependent children. Grants are to be made on the basis of one-third by the federal government, and two-thirds by the states, with the federal allowance limited to $6 a month for a

THE 1919 WHITE HOUSE CONFERENCE AND THE MATERNITY AND INFANCY ACT

The Widened Scope of the 1919 Conference. The Conference which met in May, 1919, was limited in size, but included guests from the countries allied with the United States during the war. Eight regional conferences followed at which attendance was large and representative. The discussion was no longer limited to the problems of dependent children, but included the following topics: child labor and education; public protection of the health of mothers and children; children in need of special care. Under the last heading were included, in addition to the topics dealt with in 1909: mental hygiene, juvenile courts, children born out of wedlock, rural social work, and scientific literature on child care. It reaffirmed in all essentials the conclusions of the first Conference, emphasizing the need of every child for a normal home life, and declaring that no child should be removed from his own home unless it were impossible to reconstruct family conditions so as to make the home safe for the child.

A tentative draft of minimum standards of child welfare was drawn up at the Washington Conference, which, after its discussion and modification by the regional conferences, was published by the Children's Bureau. It exercised a marked influence on the development of legislative and administrative practice in the states.

An Act for the Promotion of the Welfare and Hygiene of Maternity and Infancy. In her 1917 report on the Bureau's investigation of infant mortality, Miss Lathrop called attention "to the method of coöperation between the national and local government adopted by Great Britain in the so-called grants-in-aid for maternity and infant welfare work, and suggested that the United States should use the well-established principle of federal aid as a basis of national and state coöperation in reducing the unnecessarily high death-rate among mothers and babies."[1] The Sheppard-Towner Act which became law on November 23, 1921, was in all essentials the plan submitted

single child, and $4 a month for any other child in the same household. It is feared that standards may be lowered, by the specification of a maximum which was *surpassed* in the laws of 17 states prior to the Act, while no maximum was set in a number of others.

[1] Abbott, "Ten Years' Work for Children," *Children's Bureau Publication* (1923), pp. 3–4. Miss Abbott, who had been secretary of the 1919 Conference, succeeded Miss Lathrop in 1921, and was herself succeeded in 1934 by Katherine Lenroot, a member of the staff of the Bureau since 1914 and its assistant chief since 1922.

by Miss Lathrop in 1917. An annual appropriation of $1,240,000 was authorized for a five-year period; of this sum, not more than $50,000 might be spent for investigation and administration by the Children's Bureau; and the balance was to be divided among the states accepting the act as follows: $5,000 to be granted outright to each state and $5,000 more if matched; the balance to be allotted to the states on the basis of population and granted if matched by equal state appropriations. Plans of work were to originate with and be carried out by the states. A federal board might approve or disapprove, but *must* approve these plans "if reasonably appropriate and adequate" to carry out the purposes of the act.[1]

By June, 1923, forty of the states had accepted the provisions of the act, and by 1927, five other states had done so, leaving only Massachusetts, Illinois, and Connecticut, unwilling to accept federal aid, with its accompaniment of federal supervision in the administration of state welfare work for mothers and their babies.[2] In January, 1927, the provisions of the act were extended for two more years beyond the original five-year period. But in spite of all efforts for its continuance, even in a modified form, federal aid to the states came definitely to an end on June 30, 1929.[3] Not until the passage of the Social Security Act in August, 1935, was it again forthcoming; an appropriation of $3,800,000 a year being authorized for grants-in-aid to assist in promoting the health of mothers and children, "especially in rural areas and in areas suffering severe economic distress."

Results of the Act and of the Work of the Children's Bureau before 1930. However widely they differed in their plans, all the states have sought, first of all, to educate the public with regard to the saving of life and improvement of health which may be brought about through better care of mothers and babies. The aim has been to stimulate such interest that the work once begun would be continued by the local community. Mothers have been helped in their homes or at health-centers,

[1] This board was composed of the Chief of the Children's Bureau, the Surgeon General of the U. S. Public Health Service, and the U. S. Commissioner of Education.

[2] A noticeable growth of similar activities took place in these states.

[3] The reasons given by the gentlemen who opposed such efforts are illuminating. According to Senator King: "This bill is obnoxious to our theory of government. It is backed by Miss Grace Abbott . . . and a number of communistic ladies, by women who may be charming, but who have no idea of the functions of the state and are willing to have superimposed on the states a federal bureaucracy." *New York Times,* Jan. 10, 1931. One representative even broke into impassioned verse about the "struck eagle" shot by a "poisoned arrow" of federal control.

and there has been instruction of groups of adolescent girls, teachers, midwives, nurses, and physicians.[1] A total of 2,978 permanent prenatal or child health centers were established. During the last six years of the act, public health nurses made 3,131,996 visits to homes, and during the last four, 4,000,000 infants and preschool children, and 700,000 expectant mothers were reached by some form of maternity and infancy work.

Apart from its direct effects on health, the act has had certain permanent results. The birth registration area has been extended until, by 1933, it included the entire United States.[2] Also, a number of state child hygiene bureaus and divisions have been created.[3] Finally there has been a great increase in state appropriations for maternal and infant welfare work.[4] These developments have been due very largely, of course, to the work of the Children's Bureau. Most encouraging changes have come about in the years since its creation. In 1912, there were 300,000 baby deaths annually: 124 out of every 1,000 born died in the first year of life. By 1930 this rate had been lowered to 64, and only about 150,000 died annually, in spite of a large increase in population. The reduction of child labor; the development of juvenile and family courts and of psychiatric and child guidance clinics; and a great extension of home care for dependent children have been notable features of this period.

THE 1930 WHITE HOUSE CONFERENCE ON CHILD HEALTH AND PROTECTION

Scope and Purposes. In July, 1929, twenty years after the first White House Conference, President Hoover sent out a call for a third Conference: "To study the present status of the health and well-being of the children of the United States and

---

[1] A total of 183,252 health conferences were held in the seven-year period; during the last five years, 22,030,489 pieces of literature were distributed, and, in the last four years, 176,733 sets of *prenatal letters* were sent. The average expectant mother was best helped, it was found, not by a booklet on prenatal care, but by the receipt of a friendly letter of advice and information at the beginning of each month during pregnancy. Recipients of these letters might ask questions which would be answered.

[2] Only 10 states registered births in 1915. In 1922 the number was 30 and the District of Columbia. By 1930, 16 more states were added.

[3] When the Children's Bureau was founded in 1912, there was only one such bureau; 12 more were established prior to 1919, 16 more in Children's Year, 9 more in anticipation of the Maternity and Infancy Act and 10 more after its passage.

[4] In 1930, a year after federal aid was no longer forthcoming, 19 states and Hawaii reported the appropriation of amounts equaling or exceeding the combined state and federal funds under the act. Florida continued the full program by a special tax levy. Twelve states increased their appropriations although these fell short of the combined amount. In the other states work had to be curtailed through lack of funds.

its possessions; to report what is being done; to recommend what ought to be done and how to do it." Miss Abbott was a member of the planning committee and secretary of the executive committee, while the directors of the divisions of the Children's Bureau and other staff members served on committees in all four major divisions of the Conference. These divisions, with their committees, were organized as follows:

Section I. Medical Service: Committee A, Growth and Development; Committee B, Prenatal Maternal Care; Committee C, Medical Care for Children.

Section II. Public Health Service and Administration: Committee A, Public Health Organization; Committee B, Communicable Disease Control; Committee C, Milk Production and Control.

Section III. Education and Training: Committee A, The Family and Parent Education; Committee B, The Infant and Preschool Child; Committee C, The School Child; Committee D, Vocational Guidance and Child Labor; Committee E, Recreation and Physical Education; Committee F, Special Classes; Committee G, Youth outside of Home and School.

Section IV. The Handicapped (Prevention; Maintenance; Protection): Committee A, State and Local Organizations for the Handicapped; Committee B, The Physically and Mentally Handicapped; Committee C-1, The Socially Handicapped (Dependency and Neglect); Committee C-2, The Socially Handicapped (Delinquency).

The enlarged scope of this Conference is at once apparent. Concern for the dependent and handicapped is in no way diminished, but interest in the problems of children has broadened to include *all* the children of the nation, while reaffirming the emphasis of the two earlier conferences on the needs of the *whole* child.[1] Sixteen months were devoted to preparatory study and research on the part of 1,200 experts, working in nearly 150 sub-committees, and the main Conference was finally held in November, 1930, with the Medical Section Conference following it in February, 1931.

[1] Significantly enough, the one major dispute concerned the recommendation, by the Committee on Public Health Organization, that the child health and maternity and infancy work of the Bureau be transferred to the Public Health Service. Miss Abbott, in a dissenting opinion, said: "To remove the health work from the Children's Bureau would not merely remove one section of the Bureau's activities, but would destroy it as a children's bureau." *Public Health Organization* (1932), pp. 336–337. The storm of protest was countrywide, and Secretary of Labor Davis, in pleading that the Bureau be kept intact, suggested "assembling in the Children's Bureau the scattered welfare activities which bureaus charged with other major responsibilities are now attempting to perform." *New York Times*, Nov. 20, 1930.

Never before had such a wealth of coördinated material been brought together in an endeavor to diagnose conditions affecting children and to define goals for their welfare and protection. The Conference met, according to Secretary Wilbur, "in the hope that we could bring up the general level of child care to the point reached by the outposts of science and weighed social experience. . . . Parental responsibility is moving outward to include community responsibility. Every child is now *our* child."[1] The great need is the development of means for putting all the facts and findings, brought together at the Conference, to work for the good of all children.

More than Ten Million Handicapped Children. Out of the more than 45,000,000 young people under eighteen in the United States in 1930, 35,000,000 were reported as reasonably normal; of these 1,500,000 were reported as specially gifted. Some 16,000,000 of the nation's children were still under six. Grouped under the general term of handicapped were some 10,000,000 young people.[2]

3,000,000 with impaired hearing; of whom 18,000 were deaf.
    64,400 visually handicapped; of whom 14,400 were blind.
1,000,000 with defective speech.
    300,000 crippled children.
    382,000 tuberculous children, and 850,000 suspected cases.
1,000,000 children with weak or damaged hearts; of whom 375,000 had serious organic heart disease.
2,500,000 children with well-marked behavior difficulties, including the more serious mental and nervous disorders.
6,500,000 children were mentally deficient, including 850,000 definitely feeble-minded and 5,650,000 intellectually subnormal.
    150,000 epileptic children.

In addition, it was revealed that over 18,600 children were killed by accidents in a year; that between 20,000 and 25,000 under eighteen, and 3,000 under sixteen, in *sixteen* states, were injured in industry; that at least 1,100 in *thirteen* states were killed or permanently injured in industry; and that 14,000 lost their fathers in industrial accidents. There were 200,000 appearing each year before the courts as delinquents, and 1,200,000 inmates in child-caring institutions. More than 6,000,000 were reported as improperly nourished. Finally, it

[1] *White House Conference, 1930* (D. Appleton-Century Company, 1931), pp. 15, 16.
[2] *White House Conference, 1930*, pp. 292–293. It must be remembered that these figures were collected at the beginning of the depression. Since then the numbers in many of these groups, particularly of the malnourished, have increased.

was discovered that more than 80% of the children included in these groups were not receiving adequate care. Standards are rising, it is true, and increasing numbers are thereby listed as handicapped. But these figures bring overwhelming realization of the gap that exists between the newer knowledge of child nurture and its application in daily practice.

The Children's Charter. Further realization of how much remains to be done is derived from the *Children's Charter*, whose nineteen points embody the aims towards which the Conference hoped to lead public thought and action:[1]

I. For every child spiritual and moral training to help him to stand firm under the pressure of life

II. For every child understanding and the guarding of his personality as his most precious right

III. For every child a home and that love and security which a home provides; and for that child who must receive foster care, the nearest substitute for his own home

IV. For every child full preparation for his birth, his mother receiving prenatal, natal, and postnatal care; and the establishment of such protective measures as will make child-bearing safer

V. For every child health protection from birth through adolescence, including: periodical health examinations and, where needed, care of specialists and hospital treatment; regular dental examinations and care of the teeth; protective and preventive measures against communicable diseases; the insuring of pure food, pure milk, and pure water

VI. For every child from birth through adolescence, promotion of health, including health instruction and a health program, wholesome physical and mental recreation, with teachers and leaders adequately trained

VII. For every child a dwelling place safe, sanitary, and wholesome, with reasonable provisions for privacy; free from conditions which tend to thwart his development; and a home environment harmonious and enriching

VIII. For every child a school which is safe from hazards, sanitary, properly equipped, lighted, and ventilated. For younger children nursery schools and kindergartens to supplement home care

[1] *White House Conference, 1930,* pp. 46–48.

IX. For every child a community which recognizes and plans for his needs, protects him against physical dangers, moral hazards, and disease; provides him with safe and wholesome places for play and recreation; and makes provision for his cultural and social needs

X. For every child an education which, through the discovery and development of individual abilities, prepares him for life; and through training and vocational guidance prepares him for a living which will yield him the maximum of satisfaction

XI. For every child such teaching and training as will prepare him for successful parenthood, home-making, and the rights of citizenship; and, for the parents, supplementary training to fit them to deal wisely with the problems of parenthood

XII. For every child education for safety and protection against accidents to which modern conditions subject him—those to which he is directly exposed and those which, through loss or maiming of his parents, affect him indirectly

XIII. For every child who is blind, deaf, crippled, or otherwise physically handicapped, such measures as will early discover and diagnose his handicap, provide care and treatment, and so train him that he may become an asset to society rather than a liability. Expenses of these services should be borne publicly where they cannot be privately met

XIV. For every child who is in conflict with society the right to be dealt with intelligently as society's charge, not society's outcast; with the home, the school, the church, the court, and the institution when needed shaped to return him whenever possible to the normal stream of life

XV. For every child the right to grow up in a family with an adequate standard of living and the security of a stable income as the surest safeguard against social handicaps

XVI. For every child protection against labor that stunts growth, either physical or mental, that limits education, that deprives children of the right of comradeship, of play, and of joy

XVII. For every rural child as satisfactory schooling and health services as for the city child, and an extension to rural families of social, recreational, and cultural facilities

XVIII. To supplement the home and the school in the training of youth, and to return to them those interests of which modern life tends to cheat children, every stimulation and encouragement should be given to the extension and development of the voluntary youth organizations

XIX. To make everywhere available these minimum protections of the health and welfare of children, there should be a district, county, or community organization for health, education, and welfare, with full-time officials, coördinating with a state-wide program which will be responsive to a nation-wide service of general information, statistics, and scientific research. This should include:

(a) Trained, full-time public health officials, with public health nurses, sanitary inspection, and laboratory workers
(b) Available hospital beds
(c) Full-time public welfare service for the relief, aid, and guidance of children in special need due to poverty, misfortune or behavior difficulties, and for the protection of children from abuse, neglect, exploitation, or moral hazard.

For every child these rights regardless of race, or color, or situation, wherever he may live under the protection of the American flag.

SAFEGUARDING THE HEALTH OF THE CHILD

Growth and Development. Significant of recent trends is the recognition of the right of the child to "health protection, from birth through adolescence," and the further recognition that only through adequate knowledge of the mental and physical growth and development of children can such protection be secured. In a four-volume report, the Committee on Growth and Development sought to appraise the rapidly increasing body of knowledge descriptive of growth and development from conception to maturity, to point out obstacles to normal growth and development, to indicate gaps in present knowledge, and to suggest promising lines of approach to fuller knowledge.

The two terms *growth* and *development* were used advisedly. Physical growth was taken to mean increase in size; and physical development, increase in complexity. No such clear distinction can be made in regard to mental growth and development, and in practice the terms are used interchangeably. Emphasis falls on each child as a unique individual, and too much stress must not be laid on the average or standard. Many individuals who differ from the average are normal; the most important meaning that attaches to this term being absence of ill-health or incapacity. Attention is thus focussed on the practical problem of determining whether each individual realizes his own inborn potentialities. For the appraisal of individual growth statistical norms are necessary, but they are misused if too absolute a status is ascribed to them. Intelligence tests, for example, are peculiarly apt to be misleading unless interpreted in terms of the child's total individuality and previous development.

Each individual grows and develops physically in accordance with a unique inherent design, and mentally in accordance with his own genetic pattern of behavior. But nurture must coöperate with nature: detrimental conditions must be eliminated, and a favorable environment provided, if optimum growth and development are to be secured. The aim must thus be to "secure for each child the best environment for *that* child. . . . Study each child as a lock, unique in its mechanism; and then devise the special key that will fit the lock; so will the door of opportunity be thrown open, as widely as constitution permits, for each child to develop under individual training his individual innate capacities."[1]

Far fuller knowledge is needed. Meanwhile practical problems must be dealt with on the basis of present *best* knowledge. But, at the same time, intensive studies should be undertaken of a relatively small number of individuals over a long period. Through a sufficient number of such *longitudinal* studies valuable data should be secured, data hitherto unrevealed through group methods which give information of general trends alone. There are two periods of peculiar importance which are as yet far less completely understood than any others in the developmental process; the neonatal and adolescent periods; the early weeks of life and the transition to maturity. There is pressing need of longitudinal studies which will give special consideration to these periods of most rapid change and critical adjustment.

The important bearing of mental and emotional factors on physical health must not be overlooked. Physicians should seek to understand the causes of behavior, and become able to assist parents "to develop a sound point of view in regard to the general management of their children."[2] To this end, "they must be as well acquainted with the healthy child as with the sick child. Their standard of comparison must be one of

[1] *Growth and Development of the Child*, Part I (D. Appleton-Century Company, 1932), p. 43.
[2] *White House Conference, 1930*, p. 65.

positive health, and not merely one of relative freedom from disease, and they must learn the importance of asking themselves the question not only, 'Is the child well?' but also, 'Is the child happy?' for the truly healthy child is also a happy child."[1]

Infant Mortality. As a result of the intensive study of the causes of infant mortality made by the Children's Bureau, not only have countless babies been saved, but there has been a great increase in accurate knowledge of the factors and conditions detrimental to infant health.[2] Social and economic conditions were found to have a decisive effect on infant mortality. In Baltimore, in the homes of the well-to-do, one baby died out of every twenty-seven born; but in the homes of the poor, one in seven. Low wages, unemployment, insanitary housing, the employment of mothers away from home were all shown to be prevalent where the infant death-rate was high. It was already established, moreover, even before the studies by the Children's Bureau, that the excessively high rate of infant mortality in certain industrial cities was not due, as had been thought, to the widespread employment of mothers, but to ignorance of proper feeding, proper care, and the simplest requirements of hygiene. To this one cause all others are secondary, a fact substantiated by all later studies. Mothers employed away from home are obliged to resort to artificial feeding sooner than otherwise, and the baby is earlier deprived of their care, which, though lamentably inadequate, is better than neglect.

The breast feeding of all babies was urged by several committees of the Conference; although it is possible, in case of necessity, to provide substitutes, these are satisfactory only under medical supervision and with the strictest regard to freedom from contamination; requirements met with difficulty in rural districts or among the lower socio-economic groups in cities.[3] In spite of all difficulties, however, the dissemination of information, as to the importance of breast feeding and the proper

---

[1] *Growth and Development of the Child*, Part I, p. 11.

[2] Studies were made in eight cities, by means of which detailed information was secured regarding 22,967 live births and 813 still births, occurring in selected years between 1911 and 1920. Careful histories were compiled of the growth and feeding of babies from birth till death, and a study made of all conditions connected with each infant's chances of life. Further studies followed, surveying the care available to mothers and babies in typical rural communities.

[3] In discussing the work of the public health nurse, Miss Wald testifies to "the intelligent reaction of the tenement house mother," and adds, "In the last analysis babies of the poor are kept alive through the intelligence of mothers"; poverty and ignorance being "the twin roots" of the "social disease of infant mortality." *The House on Henry Street* (1915), pp. 54, 55.

preparation of artificial substitutes, has resulted in a radical decline in the number of deaths from gastrointestinal diseases, formerly second only to *natal* and *neonatal* causes of infant mortality.[1] Respiratory diseases were the third chief cause, with social and economic factors largely responsible for the prevalence of contagion. There has been little success hitherto in reducing the number of deaths from this cause, now second in importance. An actual increase occurred, even before the lowering of standards of living produced by the depression. There has been only a slight decline in the leading group of causes responsible for death in early infancy, natal and neonatal causes; and the chief hope of a further reduction of infant mortality now lies in the better care of mothers.[2]

The decline in infant deaths, hitherto, has been almost entirely due to the more hygienic treatment of babies from one month to one year old. There has been almost no decrease in neonatal deaths, approximately 75,000 annually, nor in the number of still births, from 86,000 to 100,000 annually, or at least four for every 100 live births.[3] The chief cause in both these cases is *prematurity*, this being followed by *intracranial injury* or *hemorrhage* due to factors connected with the process of birth. Hitherto, moreover, insufficient attention has been given to the expert care of infants in the first few weeks of life.

The Hygiene of Maternity in Its Relation to Infant Welfare. The same measures which would prevent the deaths of innumerable new-born babies would also save the lives or promote the health of their mothers. Accordingly, as a first and fundamental method of protection for childhood, the Children's Charter stresses the prenatal, natal, and postnatal care of mothers. The close relationship between maternal and infant welfare, hitherto taken more or less for granted, has become invested with crucial importance. The foetus is, of course, absolutely dependent on the mother for life and the conditions of normal growth. Anything affecting the mother detrimentally

---

[1] In the eight cities studied by the Children's Bureau, the rate of mortality from natal and neonatal causes was 36.1, while gastrointestinal diseases were a close second with a rate of 32.4. During the seven years work under the Maternity and Infancy Act the death-rate from gastrointestinal diseases for the country at large was reduced from 14.8 to 7.9.

[2] Comparison of the infant death rate in the United States with that of New Zealand makes it obvious that the irreducible minimum has not been reached. Here the 1930 rate was 64 per 1,000 live births, while in New Zealand it was 34, 47% lower. Since 1930 it decreased until the rate of 57.6 was reached in 1932; but then began once more to *increase*, being 58.1 in 1933 and 60.1 in 1934.

[3] Over 2,200,000 babies are born annually.

may have a serious effect on the child. Where mothers are in poor physical condition, many more babies are prematurely born or die in infancy. Complications during labor often lead to the disability or death of mother, or child, or of both. After birth the dependence of the infant on his mother, though no longer absolute, is very real. A healthy mother who can nurse her infant and devote herself to his nurture is the surest guarantee for his well-being. Moreover, in considering maternal mortality, the disastrous effects of a mother's death must be taken into account, where other children besides the new-born baby are left motherless.

Despite growing realization of the tragedies involved in the deaths of mothers, there has been no material decrease in maternal mortality in the United States, which has one of the highest maternal death-rates among civilized nations.[1] Moreover, out of the 15,000 mothers who die annually, 10,000 do so from preventable or controllable causes. "When about 40% of maternal deaths are due to infections, approximately 25% to toxemias, and 8 to 10% to hemorrhages, which, if not absolutely preventable are at least controllable, it would seem possible to do something to diminish the number of deaths." Some good has evidently resulted from the greater emphasis laid in recent years on prenatal care, but "only conservative and intelligent rational obstetrics at the time of delivery, followed by postnatal observation for a period of two months after birth, will ever raise our maternity care to proper standards." However, "if our present day obstetric knowledge could be universally and skilfully applied, several thousands of maternal lives, and tens of thousands of fetal and infant lives could be saved annually and much suffering and injury avoided."[2]

Although social workers had for years been only too well acquainted with the tragedies attending childbirth in city slums, it was not till 1909 that a beginning was made in organized prenatal work. In 1917, with the publication of a Children's Bureau pamphlet, the first attempt was made by the federal government to bring the risks of childbearing to public attention. In 1918, the Maternity Center Association was founded in

---

[1] In 1928 the rate was 69 for 10,000 live births. About 7 mothers die in childbirth, as compared with the best rate abroad of 3, for every 1,000 live births. Childbirth in the United States is the second chief cause of death for women between 15 and 45. The very high mortality rate among the colored population is a contributing factor, and lower rates in the states where systematic efforts have been under way for some time are offset by high rates in states where this work has been neglected.

[2] *White House Conference, 1930*, pp. 78–80.

New York, and soon afterwards a great impetus was given by the Sheppard-Towner Act to the education of both physicians and the laity. The work done under this act saved many lives; but there are still parts of the country where no maternal help is available. In many Western counties there were found to be no hospitals or nurses, and a doctor could only be reached by traveling thirty to sixty miles.[1] In the Southern states, numbers of mothers were wholly dependent for such help as they received on untrained, superstitious, and often dirty midwives. Prenatal conferences are now conducted in many parts of the country, and nurses are sent to care for mothers; many in the cities, and others in the remote country districts, some going long distances over the mountains on horseback. During six years of work under the Maternity and Infancy Act, 3,000,000 such home visits were made. Another important phase of remedial work has been the instruction and registration of midwives. It was found that some 45,000 midwives attended about 15% of all deliveries.[2] Some of these women, including many foreign-born, were intelligent and well trained; but many others, including superstitious Negro women who had been "ketchin' babies" by the most primitive methods for years, were found totally unfit. Some of these Negro midwives resigned voluntarily, saying, "there's too much law in this here work nowadays." On the other hand, many were enrolled among the 55,000 who attended classes for midwives as part of the maternity and infancy program.

It was pointed out, at the White House Conference, that European countries, in which well-trained midwives were largely employed, had a maternal mortality rate comparing very favorably with this country. It is now realized that midwives are needed here, especially in rural localities, because of racial and economic conditions. With more adequate provision for their training and supervision they should be able to give a satisfac-

[1] Of Idaho mothers who had died in childbirth, nearly half had received no medical attention or had had a doctor only when dying. In 12 states nearly one-half of the mothers who died received no prenatal care at all. Such lack of attention is still very common. A more recent study, covering the deaths of 7,537 women in childbirth, in 15 states, showed that 9% had either no medical attention or none until they were dying. Less than 1% had adequate prenatal care. *New York Times*, May 13, 1933.

[2] Some 80% of these are in the Southern states. And among foreign populations in the cities, tradition and economic necessity cause a large proportion of mothers to receive help from midwives. Miss Wald was chairman of an investigation, in 1905, which disclosed that 40% of babies in New York City were brought into the world by midwives; 98% among the Italians. Ample evidence was found of neglect, ignorance, and criminality. Five years later the first school of midwives in America was established at Bellevue Hospital. *The House on Henry Street*, pp. 58 *et seq.*

tory type of care in normal cases. A recent study of maternal deaths between 1930 and 1932 made by the New York Medical Association found only 2.2% of the preventable deaths chargeable to midwives. Nearly 66% of all the deaths studied were held to have been needless: more than one-third were the fault of the patient, in that she failed to take advantage of available facilities. Most startling, however, was the charge that physicians were directly responsible for 61.1% of all preventable deaths.[1] There was no decline in the number of deaths due to puerperal septicemia, which has been known for the last seventy years to be preventable by the use of aseptic methods. There has, moreover, been an actual increase in the numbers of mothers dying from operative procedures or careless methods. Maternal mortality was twice as high among operative deliveries, which were shown to be far too prevalent, being necessary in only about 5% of all cases.

Adequate obstetric education was accordingly stressed as an urgent need, as it had been by the White House Conference Committee on Prenatal and Maternal Care. Physicians, nurses, midwives, social workers, and the laity in general, are urged to assume "the only sane and reasonable position" towards childbirth: to consider it "not as an event so natural and devoid of danger as to be regarded with indifference, nor yet so abnormal as to place it in the category of a surgical specialty. Rather should it be regarded as a process of such intrinsic importance as to call for increasing vigilance, for masterly inactivity matched with timely though controlled interference."[2] In the last analysis it is the education of the average citizen which is of fundamental importance; prospective mothers must as early as possible secure expert supervision, and husbands must insist that their wives receive the full advantage of the latest contributions of science to maternity.[3] When the laity faces reality, fully realizes how many maternal deaths are preventable, and "demands that this terrible, needless loss of life of the most necessary group of our citizens cease, then there will be a marked improvement in the maternal welfare situation."[4]

[1] New York Times, Nov. 20, 1933.

[2] Obstetric Education (D. Appleton-Century Company, 1932), p. 50.

[3] Many methods are now being tried of educating expectant mothers and the public at large. While the stress has been laid hitherto on prenatal care, it is now being emphasized that good delivery care is also essential and postnatal care of extreme importance. The Maryland Bureau of Child Hygiene distributes, to all who apply for marriage licenses, a pamphlet calling attention to the responsibility of both parents for insuring the health of mother and baby.

[4] Obstetric Education, p. 249.

Accidents and Diseases Chiefly Responsible for Children's Deaths. In the first year of life, *whooping cough* follows *natal* and *neonatal causes*, *respiratory* and *gastrointestinal diseases* as a chief cause of death. From the age of one onwards *accidents* are included among the chief causes of death for children.[1] In the age group, one to four, *respiratory* and *gastrointestinal diseases* and *accidents* are the three chief causes, followed by *diphtheria*, *whooping cough*, and *tuberculosis*. From five to fourteen, *accidents* are the *chief* cause of death. In the age group, five to nine, *diphtheria* comes second, followed by *respiratory* and *heart diseases;* for ten to fourteen, *tuberculosis* and *heart disease* follow in the order named. From fifteen to nineteen, *tuberculosis* leads all other causes of death, followed however by *accidents*, and then, in turn, by *heart disease*. The first five years of life are by far the most hazardous; whereas, from five to nineteen, there have, since the beginning of the century, been notable decreases in mortality from diseases where preventive medicine, public health, and sanitary measures have been operative.[2] In diseases of a constitutional character and in deaths from accident the trend is *upward*.

From five to nine, the death rate for accidents in 1928 was *45.2* for each 100,000. In the ten to fourteen group it was *36.1*. Accidents caused more than three times as many deaths as any single disease between the ages of five and fourteen. Although, from fifteen to nineteen, accidents rank second to tuberculosis, the rate here is even higher, *57.4*, there having been a great increase in accidents in this group in recent years. For children under five, *burns* are by far the most common cause of accidental death, followed by *automobiles, suffocation, poisoning, drowning, falls*.[3] From five to nineteen, *automobiles*

---

[1] *Growth and Development of the Child*, Vol. I, p. 362. The tables given in this volume are for 1927. Figures given in *Safety Education in Schools* (1932) are for 1928; and in *Communicable Disease Control* (1931) cover deaths of children from 1926 to 1928. For further study of the leading causes of child mortality and of changes in the rates, see the successive volumes of *Mortality Statistics*, compiled annually by the Bureau of the Census.

[2] It must be noted, however, that the high death-rate from diphtheria between five and ten is totally unnecessary, since diphtheria is now absolutely preventable through immunization. There is, however, very marked and continuing improvement in certain cities and states. Outside of New York City there were in the state, in 1924, 5,883 cases, and in 1934 only 442, a reduction in ten years of 92%. Binghamton and Niagara Falls each with 50,000 population reported no cases in 1934, an event which has never occurred before. Yet only 40 to 43% of the children of the state were immunized, as all should be in the first year of life. *New York Times*, Jan. 20, 1936.

[3] According to figures made public by the U. S. Public Health Service in September 23, 1936, burns cause one-third more deaths among children of preschool age

lead all other causes, followed for the five to nine group, by *burns, drowning, falls, firearms;* for the ten to fourteen group, by *drowning, firearms, falls;* for the fifteen to nineteen group, by *drowning* and *firearms.* It must also be remembered that this appalling loss of child life is only part of the toll levied by accidents. For every death, many more suffer injuries, some of which result in permanent maiming.[1]

The Prevention of Accidents. That this tragic state of affairs is in large part preventable seems proved by the success which has attended the intensive efforts, of the last twelve or more years, to provide safety education in the schools. This movement is part of a larger protective and educative safety program. More city playgrounds have been provided and organized camping has given valuable training; police and fire departments have assisted, as have the American Red Cross, automobile clubs, and the National Safety Council, directly or through its local affiliations. A great part of the Boy and Girl Scout programs is concerned with safety. The combined effect of these efforts was shown, by 1928, when the number of accidental child deaths was not greater than in 1922; whereas there had been a 32% increase among adults. Motor vehicle deaths were chiefly responsible, having caused an increase of 106.9% in adult deaths, while the increase in child deaths from this cause was 22.9%. Most significant of all was an actual decrease, between 1927 and 1929, in deaths from automobiles among *school* children of five to fourteen. Among preschool children there was a 10% increase in the same period.

A survey of 1,862 school systems, conducted by a White House sub-committee, showed that some form of safety education was included in the curricula of 86% of elementary schools and 56% of secondary schools.[2] Schools appear to be increasingly alive to the right of the child to "education for safety and

than automobile accidents. Burns are still the leading cause of accidental death for children under five. Figures showed a steady decline since 1925, but in 1930, 1,876 children under 6 were burned to death in accidents. Children of 2 were the most frequent victims except in the Southeast, where there were more deaths from this cause than elsewhere and where the age of greatest frequency was 3. Deaths of this type were lowest in the Western area. *New York Times,* Sept. 23, 1936.

[1] In a study of accidents to school children from September, 1929, to January, 1930, it was found that out of 246,700 children from kindergarten to high school in various parts of the country, *26* were killed and *2,880* received major non-fatal injuries. *Safety Education in Schools* (1932), p. 10.

[2] In the majority, safety is taught in connection with other subjects; in some there are separate courses; and, in many, safety education forms part of the extra-curricular activities. Junior Safety Patrols or Safety Councils were found in some third of the school systems.

protection against accidents to which modern conditions subject him." The weight of responsibility accordingly falls more and more on parents. Not only are they in charge of the earlier habit-forming years, but the pressing need for safety education in the home is evident from the excessive loss of life in the preschool years. Besides the 2,800 under five who, in 1928, died of burning or scalding, 75% of all those who die of suffocation are under five, and of these 97% are infants of less than a year. The automobile death-rate is particularly high between three and nine, and highest of all between four and eight, years which account for as many deaths as all the remaining years of childhood put together.[1]

Gesell believes that the importance of safety education in the home has been obscured by the romantic notion that children should be spared from fear. Genuine safety education calls for elements of courage and fortitude as well as of caution. Bold and intelligent alertness is necessary for adjustment to the hazards of modern civilization. Basic attitudes of wholesome caution are utterly essential for young children. In teaching these attitudes, reliance must not be placed on warnings or descriptions of disaster. While certain physical safeguards are, of course, necessary, at a very early age a child should begin to acquire actual habit patterns through their exercise in concrete situations. "Two years of unremitting training in caution between the ages of two and four are indispensable to any plan of safety education."[2] Those parents who are the intimate companions of their children can most effectively and directly impart the necessary instruction and guidance.

Agencies Safeguarding Health. Many individuals and agencies must combine their efforts if the health of children is to be adequately safeguarded. Parents are responsible for the first and fundamental line of defense: the well-born, well-nourished, and carefully-nurtured child is already protected against disease and its worst effects. Constructive health programs in schools should coöperate with good homes, and should endeavor to remedy the defects of adverse home conditions. The organization of public health agencies is also essential to secure sanitary conditions, pure food, milk, and water supplies, and effective control of communicable diseases.

The progress of preventive medicine in the twentieth century

---

[1] Fatal automobile accidents are three times as common for boys as for girls; the difference between the sexes is not so marked before ten as later.

[2] *Guidance of Mental Growth in Infant and Child*, p. 189.

has been phenomenal.[1] Already some of the chief scourges of childhood have so yielded to control that it is possible to foresee their complete elimination if the accepted preventive measures were universally applied. In the early years of the nineteenth century one-fifth of all children died of smallpox before they were ten, and one-third of all the deaths of children were due to smallpox. If every baby were vaccinated, the disease could be completely eliminated, as could diphtheria through immunization, the reduction between 1900 and 1930 being from 43.3 to 4.9 per 100,000. Less than 50 years ago about 75% of all children had rickets. It is still far too prevalent, despite the fact that exposure to sunshine and the addition of cod liver oil to diet secure the growth of strong bones.[2] The importance of the teeth as an index of health, growth, and usually of nutrition, is being increasingly realized; but 95% of all children in 1930 were found to have dental defects which could probably have been prevented through better nutrition.[3] The death toll from communicable diseases is diminishing; but these diseases, of which half the cases still occur in children, cause about 15% of all deaths. To the deaths and economic and social losses due to these diseases, must be added the far greater toll of disabilities; the crippled children, 50% to 75% of whom owe their condition to infantile paralysis or tuberculosis; the blind; and those with damaged hearts and kidneys. Much has been accomplished, but far more remains to be done. Knowledge is available which could prevent a great part of this waste of life and health and happiness; but the knowledge is not being fully utilized.[4]

[1] It must be remembered that Pasteur undertook his epoch-making study of contagious diseases in animals as late as 1875.

[2] The Child Hygiene Division of the Children's Bureau has recently been engaged in two intensive studies of rickets: one in New Haven and the other in Puerto Rico. Negro children and those of South European stock are unusually susceptible to rickets. Its crippling effects are particularly disastrous for girls, since they include pelvic deformities, making childbirth difficult or impossible without resort to operative procedure.

[3] These conditions prevailed before the depression. The disastrous results of malnutrition on mothers and children during the last seven or eight years are noticeable in the increase of dental ailments. In Los Angeles, 90% of children who are free clinic patients have serious dental troubles, as against 5% of children who are attended by dentists in private practice. There are thousands of children under 10 who will probably be toothless by 35. *Los Angeles Times*, March 14, 1937.

[4] In *A City Set on a Hill* (1934), Dr. Winslow, of the Yale School of Medicine, gives an account of an experiment in public health conducted for 10 years in Syracuse, N. Y., with the financial assistance of the Milbank Memorial Fund. It has conclusively proved that effective public health work pays dividends: not only has there been a striking lowering of the death-rate in several groups of diseases, but the annual

The White House Conference Committee on the School Child reported a definite trend towards a comprehensive preventive and diagnostic service within the public schools of the country. Physicians, dentists, oculists, psychologists, nurses, visiting-teachers, nutritionists, supervisors of health instruction, health counselors, and teachers of physical education, all have their part in this program. Medical service was given in *some* schools in *every* state, while forty states in 1930 had laws providing for medical inspection of school children, of which twenty-seven made this service mandatory. This development is all the more encouraging because of its recency. The first law was passed in Connecticut in 1899, and the first law making medical inspection mandatory was that passed in 1906 in Massachusetts.[1]

The Need for Constant Supervision of All Children. As a final essential in the safeguarding of health, all children should be under the constant supervision of pediatricians, or of doctors with at least some special training in pediatrics, whose primary concern is the preservation of health and the promotion of normal growth and development. A survey by a White House sub-committee of the work being done by hospitals, convalescent homes, child-health centers, and nutrition experts found evidence of the growth of preventive pediatrics, but also revealed the need for more adequate training in pediatrics for doctors and nurses. A survey of pediatric education further revealed its inadequacy. Special stress was laid, as a result of another study, on the need for scientific investigation of the relation of body mechanics or "posture" to health and well-being. Insufficient intelligent attention is being paid to this matter by parents and by the majority of physicians.[2]

The report on *Psychology and Psychiatry in Pediatrics* is of special interest. It is strongly urged that pediatricians make it their business to "acquire psychiatric intelligence and become

economic saving is shown to be about four times the health budget of $500,000. In *Middletown*, Chapter XXV, the Lynds give an illuminating account of the obstacles to progress in the application of preventive medicine and the promotion of public health. Little improvement was noticed ten years later according to *Middletown in Transition*, Chapter XI.

[1] New York was the first city in the world to employ school nurses, after Miss Wald had demonstrated, through the work of public health nurses, that children could be given treatment and in most cases kept in the classroom, instead of being simply kept out of school as previously. The first school nurse was employed in 1902 and by 1914 there were 374 in New York City.

[2] In this connection see the books of F. M. Alexander, *Man's Supreme Inheritance* (rev. ed., 1918), and *Constructive Conscious Control of the Individual* (1923), to which fuller reference is made in Chapter XXV.

sensitive to the educational implications of the situations which arise in their practice."[1] This does not mean that they should master all the technical resources of psychology and psychiatry, but that they should add to their supervision of the child's physical well-being an active and sympathetic concern for the growth of personality. Psychiatrists and child guidance clinics must continue to care for the more extreme cases of maladjustment; and they have besides a major function to fulfil, in devising methods whereby "appropriate instruction can be available to all parents whose children are failing to meet life adequately and happily. In a measure such instruction can be profitably given directly to parents and teachers. But in larger measure, the interpretation and utilization of the advances in psychiatry and psychology by parents demand the intervention of a skilled and resourceful adviser."[2] It is indeed impossible to give adequate medical service without a consideration of intellectual and emotional factors. Invaluable service may be rendered by the physician who is in charge of a child from birth to puberty.

All experts are agreed on the importance of periodic medical and dental examinations, and also on the need for universal vaccination and immunization, to safeguard against smallpox and diphtheria respectively. An illuminating report on *Health Protection of the Preschool Child* gives the results of a national survey of preventive medical and dental service for children under six. The study covered 146,000 children in 156 cities, and 37,000 in the country or in towns of under 2,500 inhabitants. It was found that 51% of preschool children in cities and 37% in rural areas had had health examinations.[3] Most of these, however, had been given prior to the first birthday. The attitude of parents to periodic examination becomes less favorable as the child grows older, until at school age very few are willing to have such an examination made.

Only about 13% of the preschool children studied had had dental advice. About 21% of city children had been vaccinated and 7% of rural children. While vaccination is recommended by one year old, in most cases it is postponed till school age. In the urban areas 21% of the children were immunized and, in the rural, about 18%.[4] There is abundant evidence of the

---

[1] *Op. cit.* (D. Appleton-Century Company, 1932), p. 43.   [2] *Ibid.*, p. 29.

[3] This means they were taken to a physician, not because they were ill, but for health supervision. The cities differed widely from 82% in Berkeley, California, to 11% in Roanoke, Virginia.

[4] A parallel study reported in *The Young Child in the Home* (1936), surveyed the health protection of children from birth until twelve. In many particulars the studies

lack of appreciation of the value of preventive measures by parents and the public at large. Countless children are growing up handicapped by defects which could have been prevented or corrected if discovered early. All authorities agree on the enormous gains in national health and vigor which would result from the better care of childhood.

SUGGESTED READING

Addams, J., *Twenty Years at Hull House*, 1910.

——, *The Second Twenty Years at Hull House*, 1930.

Children's Bureau, *The Children's Bureau Yesterday, Today and Tomorrow*, 1937.

——, *Causes and Prevention of Neonatal Mortality*, 1929.

——, *Publication 9*, "Infant Mortality, The Results of a Field Study in Johnstown, Pa.," 1925.

——, *Publication 20*, "Infant Mortality, The Results of a Field Study in Manchester, N. H.," 1917.

——, *Publication 68*, "Infant Mortality, The Results of a Field Study in New Bedford, Mass.," 1920.

——, *Publication 105*, "Infant Mortality and Preventive Work in New Zealand," 1922.

——, *Publication 119*, "Infant Mortality, The Results of a Field Study in Baltimore, Md.," 1923.

——, *Publication 142*, "Causal Factors in Infant Mortality," 1925.

——, *Publication 233*, "Infant Mortality in Memphis," 1936.

——, *Publication 223*, "Maternal Mortality in Fifteen States," 1934.

——, *Publication 57*, "Maternity Benefit Systems in Certain Foreign Countries," 1919.

——, *Publication 95*, "Text of the Act of Nov. 23, 1921, for the Promotion of the Welfare and Hygiene of Maternity and Infancy," 1922.

——, from *Publication 203*, "Seven Years of the Maternity and Infancy Act," 1931.

——, *Publication 82*, "The Administration of the Aid-to-Mothers Law in Illinois," 1921.

——, *Publication 109*, "Proceedings of the Conference on Mothers' Pensions," 1922.

——, *Publication 162*, "Public Aid to Mothers with Dependent Children," 1928.

——, *Publication 184*, "The Administration of Mothers' Aid in Ten Localities," 1928.

corroborate one another. There are certain differences, however, the figures for dental advice being higher in this study of 3,000 families. Over one-half of the urban children had had their teeth examined by the time of school entrance, as against a slightly smaller percentage of rural children. More children too were found to be immunized and vaccinated. *Op. cit.*, pp. 155–177.

Children's Bureau, from *Publication 209*, "Family Welfare, Summary of Expenditures for Relief, General Family Welfare and Relief, Mother's Aid, Veterans' Aid," 1932.

——, *Publication 220*, "Mothers' Aid, 1931," 1933.

——, *Legal Chart 3*, rev., "A Tabular Summary of State Laws Relating to Public Aid to Children in Their Own Homes, in Effect Jan. 1, 1934," 1934.

——, *Publication 205*, "Posture and Physical Fitness," 1931.

Galdston, I., *Maternal Deaths: The Ways to Prevention*, 1937.

Glover, K., and Dewey, E., *Children of the New Day*, 1934.

Goodsell, W., *Problems of the Family*, rev. ed., 1936, Ch. X.

Groves, E. R., and Brooks, L. M., *Readings in the Family*, 1934, Ch. XXII.

Guttmacher, A. F., *Into This Universe*, 1936.

Odum, H. W., "Public Welfare Activities," *Recent Social Trends*, 2 vols., 1933, Vol. II, Ch. XXIV.

Public Health Reprints, 1763, 1767, 1772, *Studies on Fatal Accidents of Childhood*, 1936.

Wald, L., *The House on Henry Street*, 1915.

——, *Windows on Henry Street*, 1934.

Walker, S. H., "Privately Supported Welfare Work," *Recent Social Trends*, 2 vols., 1933, Vol. II, Ch. XXIII.

White House Conference, *Communicable Disease Control*, 1931.

——, *Growth and Development of the Child, Part I, General Considerations*, 1932.

——, *Growth and Development of the Child, Part IV, Appraisement of the Child*, 1932.

——, *Health Protection of the Preschool Child*, 1931.

——, *Psychology and Psychiatry in Pediatrics*, 1932.

——, *Safety Education in Schools*, 1932.

——, *The School Health Program*, 1932.

——, *The Young Child in the Home*, 1936.

——, *The White House Conference, 1930*, 1931.

CHAPTER XII

CHILDREN IN NEED OF SPECIAL CARE AND PROTECTION

CHILD LABORERS

Child Labor Legislation Prior to 1930. Healthy development can be promoted only if children are protected "against labor that stunts growth either physical or mental, that limits education, that deprives . . . of the right of comradeship, of play and of joy." And yet, in 1930, a hundred years since the beginning of the struggle to protect children from exploitation, more than 2,000,000 young people under eighteen were at work in the United States, and 180,000 under sixteen had left school in that year to go to work. At about the time Robert Owen was denouncing the labor of young children in factories, Hamilton, in this country, was advocating the employment of women, and of children of eight to ten, "who would otherwise be idle," in order that the new industries might not deplete the supply of laboring men needed for agriculture. The machinery from England was specially built to accommodate little children, and only too soon the same tragedies were being enacted here as in the factories in England. In this country, moreover, apart from a few laws which generally went unenforced, the movement for the abolition of child labor did not get under way till after 1890.[1] In 1870 the percentage of all children *ten* to *fifteen*, gainfully employed, was 13.2%, while in 1890 it had risen to 18.1%. Despite twenty years of progress in state legislation, it was still 18.4% in 1910; but by 1920 it had fallen to 8.5% and by 1930 to 4.7%.[2]

As a result of the investigations of Florence Kelley of Hull House, the first factory law of Illinois was passed. The National

[1] A committee of the Massachusetts legislature, in 1866, stated that factory representatives made systematic canvasses in an effort to draw children from schools into the mills. One witness said, "They'll take them at any age they can get them, if they are old enough to stand." In 1874, it was estimated in Massachusetts that at least 25,000 children from five to fifteen received no education at all on this account. Calhoun, *Social History of the American Family*, Vol. III, pp. 136–138.

[2] *Recent Social Trends*, Vol. I, p. 327. The 1920 percentage is misleading, since the census, being taken in January, omitted many children engaged in agriculture, included in the 1910 census taken in April. In 1910, 1,990,225 children from 10 to 15 were engaged in "gainful occupations."

Child Labor Committee, organized in 1904, largely through her efforts, has had great influence in securing improved state legislation. Its advocacy of the movement for federal legislation, begun in 1906, was influential in securing the passage of the first federal child labor law of 1916, a law prohibiting the shipment in interstate or foreign commerce of goods produced by child labor in violation of specified age and hour standards. Unfortunately, this measure and its successor, a child labor tax law, passed in 1919, were both held to be unconstitutional.[1] After the second decision in 1922, some twenty-eight proposals for a child labor amendment were introduced in the Senate and House. Finally, in June, 1924, the following amendment to the Constitution was submitted for ratification by the states:

SECTION I. The Congress shall have power to limit, regulate, and prohibit the labor of persons under 18 years of age.
SECTION II. The power of the several states is unimpaired by this article except that the operation of the state laws shall be suspended to the extent necessary to give effect to legislation enacted by Congress.

Arkansas proceeded to ratify the amendment at once, and was followed by California, Arizona, and Wisconsin, in 1925, and by Montana in 1927. A number of states promptly rejected the amendment. All who are concerned with the well-being of children are agreed as to the deplorable effects of child labor: the social and industrial loss due to impaired health for the individual, and physical deterioration for the race; the loss of education and training, and consequent industrial inefficiency; the increase in juvenile delinquency. Several factors reënforced one another, however, in rendering the electorate of many states reluctant to ensure the effective control of child labor through federal legislation. Poverty is a chief cause of child labor; even where the child's earnings are not indispensable they are desired in order to raise the level of family subsistence. Some parents exploit their children; many more do not realize the values of an education of which they themselves were

[1] The passage of these laws had an important effect in raising state standards between 1917 and 1922. The age level in the federal statutes was 14 for children employed in mills and factories, 16 for children in mines and quarries. The hours of work for children, 14 to 16, were eight a day and forty-eight a week. There was retrogression when the federal laws were declared unconstitutional: a longer working day returned, and more children were employed under 16; also there was an appreciable increase in the violation of state laws.

deprived, and are ignorant of the dangers and disadvantages of child labor. The attitude of children is a contributory cause; many gladly leave a school where they have been failures, in the hope of earning money and independence.

Ignorance of the conditions and results of child labor has been largely responsible for public apathy. Active opposition is due, however, not so much to ignorance as to selfish industrial interests. Employers profit when a supply of cheap labor is available. Every effort to raise standards is met first of all by some of the ancient arguments which have opposed every advance in social legislation, particularly where federal control is involved. These will shortly be considered in some detail in their connection with the child labor amendment. It is also urged that children's earnings are necessary to their families; a contention in which there is too much truth; but the remedy is worse than the disease. Adult standards are lowered, and, as a matter of future policy, poverty is an insufficient reason for the continuation of the vicious circle of poverty, child labor, and impaired physical and mental development.[1] Others insist that fourteen is not too young for work, that work is better than idleness and provides an education in itself, which may be supplemented by continuation schools. Several insidious fallacies are involved in such statements. More adequate school education, rather than idleness, should be the alternative to work. Moreover, child labor rarely possesses educational value, proving in most cases a blind alley of unending monotonous drudgery, which precludes access to more skilled and higher paid forms of work.

The Textile Codes of 1933 and the Recent Movement for Ratification of the Child Labor Amendment. In 1931 Colorado became the sixth state to ratify the amendment. In 1933, however, *fourteen* more states ratified the amendment, a result very largely attributable to the agreements made under the National Recovery Act. In signing the first of these, the cotton textile code, President Roosevelt pointed to its significance in prohibiting the employment of children under sixteen. Employers could now do by agreement what none of them could do separately and yet survive competition. In 1930 there were 20,625 children under sixteen employed in textiles, about half of their

---

[1] Commenting on "the well-fed gentlemen" who wait in the lobbies of Congress and urge legislators to "think of the poor homes which need the money these children will bring," Grace Abbott says, "If you continue to use the labor of children as the treatment of the social disease of poverty, you will have both poverty and child labor to the end of time." *World Tomorrow*, Vol. XIV (Sept., 1931), p. 295.

number being in cotton mills alone, more than in any other manufacturing industry. The minimum age and other raised standards, established by the cotton code, were followed in the codes of many other industries.[1] Renewed impetus was afforded to the movement for ratification in an effort to ensure the permanence of these raised standards on a national basis. Four more states ratified in 1935, but in May the industrial codes were rendered invalid by the Supreme Court in the Schechter decision; an event leading at once to nation-wide increase in child labor.

Accordingly, when by the beginning of 1937 only twenty-four states had ratified the amendment, a determined effort was made by its supporters. President Roosevelt sent letters to the Governors of nineteen states urging them to make the proposal a major item in regular 1937 legislation. By the end of March four more states had ratified, but seven had defeated the amendment, including New York where it was passed by the Senate but defeated by the Assembly.[2] The Chief of the Children's Bureau urges the continuance of the fight for the present amendment, but suggestions are also being made for substitute amendments and for federal laws restricting child labor.[3] Senator Borah suggested a new amendment setting the age limit at *fourteen* instead of eighteen, while Senator Vandenberg offered an amendment, with the unanimous endorsement of the Senate Judiciary Committee, fixing the age limit at sixteen, omitting the word "regulate," and introducing the words "for hire." These measures are thought by their supporters to eliminate some of the chief objections to the original amendment, and also to obviate difficulties which might arise, even if it were ratified in a year or so, because of the length of time elapsed since its proposal.[4]

Arguments for and against the Child Labor Amendment.

[1] The Children's Bureau placed the reduction of child labor in industries affected by the NRA at 90%, 18% of which was attributed to the depression, and 72% directly to the NRA. *New York Times*, March 22, 1936.

[2] Others, besides New York, defeating the amendment this year were North Carolina, South Dakota, Texas, Connecticut, Massachusetts, and Nebraska. In addition to these, the following states have either rejected the amendment or have not considered it: Alabama, Delaware, Florida, Georgia, Louisiana, Maryland, Mississippi, Missouri, Rhode Island, South Carolina, Tennessee, Vermont, Virginia.

[3] As an example of the latter, the Fair Labor Standards Bill, which passed the Senate in July, 1937, endeavors to prevent child labor by forbidding interstate shipments of products so produced, and by making such products subject to the anti-child-labor laws of states into which they are shipped. *New York Times*, Aug. 1, 1937. The bill failed to come to a vote in the House.

[4] *New York Times*, March 25, March 27, and June 22, 1937.

Among the opponents of the amendment are those whose views are, as Dewey says of President Butler's, "sincere, honest, straightforward" even when "completely wrong."[1] Many are concerned because they believe the amendment to constitute an invasion of state's rights, promoting centralization and growth of bureaucracy.[2] But the amendment gives Congress no rights that states do not possess. It does not take away from the states the right to regulate or prohibit child labor, but merely establishes what will be in effect a minimum standard of protection for all American children. "This is no question of state's rights versus national rights, but of coöperation to secure children's rights."[3] Closely allied to this argument is the further contention of opponents of the amendment, that the states are fully capable of dealing adequately with the situation, and indeed are already doing so. In answer to this it is pointed out that the problem is national. Manufacturing and industry operate on a national rather than state basis, and must be regulated on the same basis. Employers in states with high standards are handicapped in competition with those where standards are low. In many cases, "fly-by-night" industries migrate to a nearby state to avoid more rigid laws, and child laborers are frequently brought across state lines for the same purpose. Such conditions can only be eliminated when equal protection is given in every state.

In the second place, state regulation has in most cases proved wholly inadequate. Only nineteen states had laws in effect in 1927 which measured up in all respects to the conservative standards of the federal laws of 1916 and 1919, even as regards work in factories; and of these only thirteen measured up to federal standards in every particular. Federal legislation has been found to encourage good state legislation, and the effect of the invalidation of federal measures is actual retrogression. In the seven months after the NRA codes went out of operation, more children went to work in factories and stores than in the whole year of 1934. Moreover, only three states, New York, Pennsylvania, and Connecticut, raised their child labor requirements to the level of the standards of the invalidated codes.

---

[1] *New York Times*, April 21, 1934.

[2] For many, undoubtedly, this argument is the result of sincere conviction; nevertheless it has been well characterized as a "smoke screen," transferring opposition from the basis of selfish interest to that of old political philosophy, and so giving it a standing it could not otherwise have attained.

[3] "The Children's Amendment," *Publication* of the League of Women Voters (1927), p. 13.

As a result child labor conditions were found to be as bad as before the introduction of the codes.[1]

Finally, much alarm is expressed, by Catholics and other conservative citizens, for fear Congress will abuse the powers conferred by this amendment.   They suggest that federal legislation might mean the regulation of the private lives of all young people under eighteen.   Boys and girls, they say, might even be forbidden to help their parents in the household or on the farm.   A National Committee has been formed for the Protection of Child, Family, School, and Church, which devotes itself to opposing the amendment and to pointing out that progress is being made in state legislation and that conditions are not really very bad.

As the National Child Labor Committee and other upholders of the amendment point out, such an interpretation is utterly indefensible.   Secretary Wallace characterized as utter nonsense the contention that children might not be allowed to help with farm and household chores.   The amendment, moreover, is not a *prohibitory* but an *enabling* amendment, conferring power on Congress which in no way surpasses that already possessed by the states.[2]   This power is given over the labor of children for hire, and over nothing else: inspection could only be authorized where work for hire was being carried on. The "invasion of the home" and the "subversion of family government" are very old arguments.   In view of their frequent use by the opponents of the amendment, it is ludicrous to find Secretary Perkins' advocacy cited as proving that women in politics are sentimental rather than thoughtful.[3]

The Children's Bureau and White House Conference Studies of Child Labor.   The actual facts as to the employment of children and as to the failure of the majority of states to regulate or control child labor are not nearly well enough known.   The Industrial Division of the Children's Bureau and the National Child Labor Committee have for years carried on intensive studies of all aspects of the child labor problem.   The results of their investigations and all other available material were

[1] *New York Times*, Nov. 30, 1935, Feb. 2 and Nov. 23, 1936. It is true that the child labor line had started downward by 1930 and fell along with the general fall in industrial employment until 1933. But in the first half of 1929 there had been a particularly sharp upward trend. *New York Times*, Dec. 15, 1930, and Oct. 9, 1932.

[2] This is an important point since the Child Labor Amendment has been compared to the Eighteenth Amendment. No prohibition or regulation of the employment of children is found in the amendment itself.

[3] Julia Johnsen (editor), *Selected Articles on Child Labor* (1925), p. 365, and *New York Times*, Feb. 17, 1934.

brought together for the first time to provide a basis for the report and recommendations of a White House Conference sub-committee. The report deals with the employment of children in non-agricultural occupations and in agriculture, with hazardous occupations and industrial accidents, and with the laws affecting the employment of minors.[1]

Hundreds of thousands of children under 16 are toiling in factories, shops, canneries, and laundries, as errand and messenger boys, and in almost every type of monotonous, mechanical, and unskilled work. The places where they work are often poorly lighted and ventilated, and altogether insanitary. The hours are long and unregulated. The moral hazard, moreover, is great for children engaged in street occupations, such as selling newspapers late at night, peddling, or junk-collecting. Too often these occupations are not only blind alleys, but easy paths to delinquency and crime.

The White House report is emphatic in its recommendation of an age minimum of sixteen for full-time work, and an even higher age minimum for hazardous occupations.[2] Children from fourteen to sixteen should be allowed to work in a restricted list of occupations, only outside school hours for a limited time, and in vacations. All children should be required to attend school full-time until sixteen, or until eighteen unless legally employed, or in cases where the high school course is completed earlier.[3] Only the physically sound should work, and periodic

[1] The figures of the 1930 census were not available when the White House Conference report was issued. In 1920, 2,773,506 or 17% of the population from 10 to 18 were gainfully employed, and in 1930, 2,142,973 or 11.3%. In 1920, 1,060,858 were 10 to 15; 61% of these, including 87% under 14, were engaged in agriculture. Children *under* 10 were not reported, although large numbers were engaged in agriculture, street work, and industrial home work. In 1930, 667,118 children were 10 to 15. The decrease is to some extent attributable to the depression. In Georgia and South Carolina, the two states permitting the longest hours of work for children under 16 (from sunrise to sunset in Georgia), there was an actual increase in their numbers between 1920 and 1930.

[2] While a greater proportion of those *under* 16 work in agriculture, by far the larger proportion of boys and girls of 16 and 17 are employed in non-agricultural work, the great majority in manufacturing and mechanical pursuits. At 16 many of the prohibitions relating to dangerous machinery, which serve to protect those under 16, are removed.

[3] Vocational guidance was stressed by a separate sub-committee as of even greater importance to the child laborer than to others. Many children might be kept in schools if their interest was enlisted in their work. In some cities not only are schools endeavoring to meet the actual needs of children, in their curricula and through counselling, but committees have been formed to provide scholarships to keep children in school. Educational opportunities including those for vocational guidance are usually least adequate in rural communities.

health examinations should be compulsory for all under eighteen. No one under eighteen should work more than an eight-hour day for six days a week; and no night work should be allowed except for boys over sixteen until ten o'clock. Minimum wage standards must be established and employment certificates made obligatory.

The problem created by the wide prevalence of industrial home work is peculiarly difficult, since complete prohibition seems impossible. When the home is converted into a work shop, family life suffers, and children of all ages work long hours before and after school. Almost a fourth of these child workers are under ten, many under six; and almost all under fourteen. Girls do this work rather more commonly than boys, but both are engaged in a wide variety of such tasks as stringing beads, carding buttons or snaps, stringing tags, or pulling out basting threads; monotonous tasks, particularly trying for children since they require the constant exercise of the finer eye muscles and are often carried on by artificial light. Home work is paid by the piece at a pitifully low rate.

The problem of the *agricultural* child laborer is almost as serious a problem and far harder to solve than that of the child engaged in industrial pursuits. Compliance with the school attendance laws should be insisted on for all farm children, and further control should be exercised over children who are *hired*, and work under a family wage or contract system. These children, many of whom are as young as six, work long hours at monotonous and frequently over-heavy work; often in unnatural and cramped positions; sometimes in the blazing sun in cotton or tobacco fields, sometimes damp and chilled through at the end of the beet and cranberry seasons. The problems of their supervision and school attendance are difficult, particularly when they are migratory workers, moving from place to place, as crops mature and fruits ripen. The housing of these workers is often appalling; their camps are crowded and insanitary, and breeding grounds for contagious diseases. Here too the White House report recommends that children under sixteen should not be employed in agriculture while school is in session. Working permits should be required in all cases. Children under fourteen should not be hired out, except that those over twelve may be employed in light tasks a few hours daily outside school hours. No child under sixteen should work more than nine hours a day, nor more than eight hours at school work and agriculture combined.

The majority of states do not compile regular statistics of industrial accidents to minors.[1] In addition to those killed or permanently disabled or injured less seriously, many thousands more are harmed by dust and vapors, by excessive heat and cold and over-fatigue. In many cases these children of the poor are malnourished or suffer from latent infection. Most of them have low resistance to infection, and because of their youth are peculiarly susceptible to industrial poisons. Because of their immaturity, heavy and cramping work results in curvature of the spine and other malformations. Finally, being awkward and playful, heedless and easily distracted, young people are far more liable to accidents from machinery than are their elders. The highest proportion of all injuries befall boys of sixteen and seventeen; the Children's Bureau cites cases of fingers chopped off and of mangled arms, of legs burnt in molten metal, of eyesight destroyed by steel splinters, and arms twisted off at the shoulder.

Recent reports indicate that work permits are once again being issued in large numbers to children under sixteen.[2] In its annual report for 1936 the National Child Labor Committee presented the results of surveys of the lumber industry in the South, the beet sugar industry in the Middle West, and the making of candlewick bedspreads in homes. Appalling conditions of exploitation and misery were revealed in all three.[3]

THE PHYSICALLY AND MENTALLY HANDICAPPED

Special Education of the Handicapped as Sound Public Policy. The modern attitude towards childhood makes doubly poignant the appeal of the multitudes of children who suffer from physical or mental handicaps. Their needs in general are those of all children; but they also require a far greater measure of special attention if their potentialities are to be realized, and their lives made even moderately successful and happy. A special *Bill of Rights for the Handicapped Child* was framed by the White House Committee for the Physically and Mentally Handicapped.[4] He has a right:

[1] Such figures as are available were given on p. 306.

[2] In ten states and ninety-eight cities in other states which reported to the Children's Bureau, 8,400 children of fourteen and fifteen obtained regular work certificates in the first five months of 1936, as against 3,350 during the same period of 1935. *New York Times*, Nov. 23, 1936.

[3] *New York Times*, Nov. 23, 1936.

[4] *White House Conference, 1930*, pp. 291–292.

(1) To as vigorous a body as human skill can give him

(2) To an education so adapted to his handicap that he can become economically independent and have the chance for the fullest life of which he is capable

(3) To be brought up and educated by those who understand the nature of the burden he has to bear and who consider it a privilege to help him to bear it

(4) To grow up in a world which does not set him apart, which looks at him not with scorn or pity or ridicule—but which welcomes him, exactly as it welcomes every child, which offers him identical privileges and identical responsibilities

(5) To a life on which his handicap casts no shadow, but is full day by day with things which make it worth while, with comradeship, love, work, play, laughter, and tears—a life in which these things bring continually increasing growth, richness, release of energies, joy in achievement

Here, indeed, is a program whose realization, even in part, demands the best efforts of all concerned, of parents and of agencies both private and public. Most important of all perhaps is the education of public opinion. Experts are now agreed that thousands of handicaps are preventable, thousands more susceptible of cure, and that special education will permit the majority of those who cannot be cured to take a useful place in normal society. To afford handicapped children the necessary treatment is then not in any sense charity, but *sound public policy*. The initial cost is considerable, but in the long run it is a mere fraction of the cost entailed by the support at public expense of neglected and handicapped dependents and delinquents, who, had they been afforded the opportunity, might have been self-supporting citizens. Until recently such efforts as were made were charitable endeavors to protect the handicapped from physical neglect, and their educational needs were almost entirely overlooked. To-day, permanent care in institutions is recommended for none but hopelessly insane adults and the lower grades of the feeble-minded.

The vast majority of handicaps are due to accident, disease, poverty, and ignorance. The earliest possible diagnosis is essential. Remedial treatment, even when it cannot cure, may provide the appropriate training by which the effects of the handicap may be as far as possible overcome, abilities and interests may be explored, and such special education provided as will make the most of existing possibilities. Vocational guidance is even more difficult to provide than with normal children, and placement in appropriate employments presents peculiar problems.[1] Handicapped children are much in need also of appropriate recreation, of play which will foster self-confidence and aid in overcoming the neurotic tendencies so frequently resulting from a sense of inferiority. For certain purposes they must be segregated, but they should also have plenty of opportunity of mingling with normal children and becoming adjusted to ordinary social life. Everywhere and always, their disability should be minimized, and emphasis placed on constructive possibilities.[2]

Constructive Treatment for the Physically Handicapped. Largely because of the cost of adequate treatment few handicapped children as yet receive it. Special education is in the main confined to the cities, and, in general, the more serious the handicap, the more and better is the care available. Extreme cases are, however, far less common than less severe and neglected cases. Whenever possible children should not be separated from their family and normal social environment. Local agencies, public and private, should be coördinated under state supervision.

The first state hospital for the special care of the *crippled* was opened in 1897; and the earliest public school classes, in 1899 in Chicago. Of recent years public interest in crippled children has been stimulated by the infantile paralysis epidemics. Yet by 1930, of the 100,000 cripples in need of special education, only 10,110 were enrolled in public schools and 1,480 more in state and private schools.[3]

In 1832, the first effort was made on behalf of the *blind*, when a private residential school was opened. In 1837, Ohio provided the first state-supported school. Not until 1900 were the first public school classes for the blind opened in Chicago. By 1930 some 6,000 of the 14,400 blind children were receiving education in state or private schools or in public school braille classes in eighteen cities. Of the 50,000 children with defective eyesight only 5,000 were receiving attention in 348 special

[1] The additional needs of the handicapped for vocational education are recognized by the Smith-Fess Act of 1920, whereby federal aid may be secured by states coöperating in this work. Some school systems employ special vocational advisers or teacher-coördinators who study the employment possibilities of the handicapped and coördinate instruction with the commercial and industrial pursuits of the local community.

[2] For example, special classes should be named wherever possible in terms of their constructive *function*, and *not* in terms of the handicap they seek to alleviate.

[3] The Social Security Act authorized the appropriation of $2,850,000 a year for assistance to the states in providing surgical, corrective, and other services and facilities for crippled children.

sight-saving classes.[1] The first such classes were established in 1913, one of them in Cleveland where pioneer work is now being done in the development of a visiting-teacher service for the preschool blind. The normal development of blind babies is impossible unless they are given attention at a very early age.

An even worse handicap is *deafness*, either congenital or acquired in infancy, since mental development is dependent upon the acquisition of means of communication with other human beings.[2] By 1929 there were over 18,000 pupils in schools for the deaf, but there is reason to believe that there are many more cases of children, not totally deaf, who are unrecognized and given no treatment. Many *hard of hearing* are being discovered by recent tests among those previously considered mentally subnormal. There are approximately 3,000,000 of these, all of whom need medical attention and should attend lip-reading classes. By 1929 sixty school systems had established such classes. Many of the deaf also require special attention for speech correction, as is also the case with a surprisingly large number of children. Of these, however, 85% have defects which might be removed by standard methods of speech correction.

Very little is as yet being done to provide special treatment in schools for large numbers of children with lowered vitality: those in danger of becoming tuberculous; the sufferers from heart disorders; the anemic; the malnourished, either essentially or secondarily on account of some infection.[3] A beginning is being made to provide home instruction for cardiopathic cases and for epileptics and encephalitis cases for whom school attendance is usually inadvisable. Open air classes for the tuberculous were first provided in 1908 in Boston; and there are now certain others throughout the country. For all these groups of children the danger of over-fatigue and discouragement is very great, and special adjustments should be made, adapted to their physical condition.

[1] Altogether 3,000,000 children in the United States have been found to be handicapped in their school work by defective eyesight; far-sightedness being most common, then astigmatism, and near-sightedness third. A study was made recently under the auspices of the National Education Association, the American Medical Association and the National Society for the Prevention of Blindness. *New York Times*, March 6, 1935.

[2] The most sadly handicapped and the most utterly neglected of all groups are the *blind deaf*, 608 of whom are known to exist in the United States, including 100 children. In dealing with cases of multiple handicap, the greater disability must determine placement and treatment, at least in its earlier phases.

[3] Of all children 60% were found to be malnourished in some counties of Alabama because of hookworm; and in some Texas counties because of malaria.

The Mentally Retarded. Many children are backward in school because of impaired eyesight or hearing, because of nose and throat affections, or infected teeth. Appropriate treatment often brings marked improvement. There remain, however, those who are *mentally* retarded in various degrees.[1] In Europe special classes for the backward were provided as early as 1867 in Germany, but in this country the first such class was established in Providence in 1896. There are state programs and institutions for the mentally handicapped in almost every state, but much of the care is custodial rather than educational. The great need is the training and supervision of those on the higher levels of subnormality, in order that they may become socially adequate, law-abiding, and self-supporting in the simplest occupations.[2]

In concluding its survey of the handicapped the White House Committee laid emphasis on the meager facilities existing for the care of children with *behavior problems*, the sufferers from nervous disorders, the emotionally unstable, and the maladjusted. Increasing stress is being laid on the need for mental hygiene, which should, as we have seen, become everywhere an integral part of educational procedure. Through the safeguarding of mental health in childhood much might be done to offset the present alarming prevalence of mental disease; and many might become socially adjusted who would otherwise be led into delinquency and crime.[3]

THE SOCIALLY HANDICAPPED: DEPENDENT AND NEGLECTED CHILDREN

Dependency as a Major Social Problem. Dependency, neglect, illegitimacy, and delinquency are *social* handicaps having their roots in some of the most complex social and economic problems of the day. It is not surprising, therefore, that their prevention

[1] Mental defect may be hereditary, it may be caused by injury at birth, by syphilitic infection, or by serious illness in early infancy or childhood. In a large number of cases it can be diagnosed very early by periodic examinations which reveal consistent developmental retardation.

[2] The White House Committee further recommended selective sterilization, to eliminate the possibility of reproduction on the part of those mentally deficient persons whose social adequacy is precarious.

[3] Patients in the state hospitals for the insane increased 110% from 1904 to 1929 and the feeble-minded and epileptics in state institutions increased 45% from 1922 to 1929. This may, however, mean that many more are put into institutions, not only that there has been an increase in numbers. In the same way the fact that 60% of the hospital beds of the United States are occupied annually by mental patients is partly accounted for by the longer hospitalization required. Nevertheless the situation is serious enough, with some 125,000 new cases annually.

and alleviation present even greater difficulties than is the case with physical handicaps.[1] Several orphan asylums were founded in the eighteenth century; but the majority of children deprived through death, misfortune, or neglect of the security of home and the fostering care of parents were placed in mixed almshouses, sometimes even in gaols, along with destitute, defective, and criminal adults; or else they were indentured, placed out to work with some person who agreed to be responsible for them. Not until 1875 did the revolt against keeping children in mixed almshouses become nation-wide; and by this time, also, the movement begun in 1853, for placing children in free foster homes without indenture, was well under way.

In 1923 the Bureau of the Census estimated that the number of dependent and neglected children cared for *away* from home was 12,000 in public institutions, 120,000 in private institutions, 31,000 in foster homes under public care, 38,000 in foster homes under private auspices. Despite the marked trend to secure for children, wherever possible, adequate care with their own families, the Committee on Dependency and Neglect voiced profound regret and disappointment at the tremendous numbers of children who still "suffer, unrelieved, in their own homes, or are separated from their homes because of poverty."[2] Little is being done to prevent many of the causes which deprive children of parental care. Invalidism, accidents, premature death, irregular employment and unemployment, and insufficient wages, on the part of parents, still leave thousands of children homeless, or deprived of the essentials of adequate care.

Individualized treatment, now universally recognized as essential to the well-being of children, may best be secured by the care of children in their own homes or in carefully selected foster homes. Wherever possible, aid to dependent children should secure unbroken care within their own homes, yet, despite the assistance rendered by mothers' aid, there are still many mothers obliged to leave their children unsupervised in their working hours. Day nurseries are an evident necessity in such cases. Their spread in this country was the result of endeavors to prevent such neglect, and also to offset the excessive institutionalization of children of destitute parents which

---

[1] The large majority of the physically handicapped are also socially handicapped. Neglect and adverse social conditions are the direct or indirect causes in many cases of disease and accident.

[2] *White House Conference, 1930*, p. 319.

had been increasing to an alarming extent towards the end of last century. Between 1905 and 1915 the number of day nurseries nearly doubled; since then the spread of the mothers' aid movement has doubtless prevented their more rapid expansion. There were about 700 day nurseries in the United States in 1936.[1]

In some cases, despite all endeavors at amelioration of family conditions, it is necessary for the child's welfare to remove him temporarily, or even permanently, from his own home. This may be the case with motherless children; or with children whose mothers, or both of whose parents, are ill or incapacitated; in the case of irremediably bad home conditions; and even in the case of problem children. As the authors of *Reconstructing Behavior in Youth* say, "for the majority of children who have become difficult to manage, family life in carefully selected homes . . . will prove to be of far greater value than institutional life."[2] Much more obviously is this the case with the thousands of little orphans, and illegitimate, abandoned, or neglected children who simply need the security and affection of normal home life.

Substitutes for the Care of Children in Their Own Homes. "About 1,500 institutions and 350 child-placing agencies cared for approximately 250,000 dependent children during the year 1928, one-third of the children being in foster families. They expended a total of $60,000,000."[3] Not only has there been a great increase in the number of children placed in foster families rather than institutions, but there is growing uniformity in methods of dealing with those deprived of home care. There

---

[1] Day nurseries of the type now in operation are modeled on the French crêche, the first of which was opened in Paris in 1844. The movement spread rapidly in Europe; and the first day nursery in the United States was opened in 1854, by the Nursery and Child's Hospital in New York City. Working mothers who had been in the hospital could leave their babies with the nurses during the day. The importance of day nurseries was not so fully recognized here as abroad; and only a small proportion of those for whom they are intended have had the benefit of their services. Owing to the efforts of public-spirited individuals and to organizations, such as the National Federation of Day Nurseries, founded in 1898, standards have been much improved and the scope of their work has broadened.

[2] W. Healy, A. F. Bronner, E. H. Baylor, J. P. Murphy, *op. cit.* (1929), p. 4. Although the authors believe that "foster home care . . . should be utilized to a far greater extent before institutional treatment is considered for any normal young person . . . , even when a behavior problem is involved," they concede that for those children who refuse to recognize authority in a family or community "a well-directed and constructive institutional policy can accomplish much." Indeed, "group care is the only hope" in the occasional cases where a child is "entirely controlled by his impulses and proves unmanageable even in a good environment." Pp. 4, 221.

[3] *White House Conference, 1930*, p. 328.

should, in the first place, be an institutional receiving station for the intensive treatment of children before placement in families: foster boarding homes may then be selected for temporary or more lengthy periods of care, or else children may be placed in free foster homes either for adoption or for a long period without adoption. More and more the emphasis is being placed on thorough investigation before acceptance of a child for care, in order to preserve or reconstruct the child's home where it is possible to do so; or, where this is impossible, to insure that a careful study be made of each child with a view to understanding his situation and needs. Competent social case-work is required, in order that the foster home may provide the environment suited to the individual child.

Standards for the selection of foster families must be "based on the same principles found necessary for the best functioning of natural families."[1] Of particular importance is the motive leading a family to assume care of a foster child: it is essential that all the family members be capable and willing to give the child everything necessary for normal development.[2] The temperamental and emotional qualities of the members of the family are also of first importance and must in each case be considered in connection with the temperament of the child proposed for foster care. Such considerations reach their maximum importance where adoption is under consideration. Impetuous adoption is always to be discouraged, and every possible safeguard should surround so decisive a step.[3] Recent legislation, recognizing the complexity of the problems involved, stresses the welfare of the child as a primary consideration, but also seeks to safeguard the rights of all concerned.

While undoubted progress has been made towards the realization of "a new and inclusive ideal of suiting the action to the real needs of the individual child," much yet remains to be done.[4] First of all, there should be complete elimination of methods recognized as without justification to-day. There are still children in county almshouses; and in many states it is

[1] According to the National Children's Home Welfare Association. M. C. Elmer, *Family Adjustment and Social Change* (1932), p. 215; and see pp. 209–220.

[2] See Mary B. Sayles, *Substitute Parents* (1936), pp. 16–28 and *passim*.

[3] Gesell holds that the risks of adoption would be much reduced by the use of adequate diagnostic methods: "a carefully considered clinical judgment of mental status, taking into account as many factors as possible, will make the work of child placement more discriminating and prevent gross error." *Guidance of Mental Growth*, p. 197. For a recent and thorough study of adoption see Eleanor G. Gallagher, *The Adopted Child* (1936).

[4] H. W. Thurston, *The Dependent Child* (1930), p. 259.

legal for them to remain there until two years of age.[1] **Nor** is indenture entirely a thing of the past. In 1923 six states still allowed children to be "bound out," and a Children's Bureau survey disclosed shocking conditions among indentured children in Wisconsin: many were overworked, kept from school, neglected, spitefully and cruelly treated.[2]

A survey made by the Child Welfare League of America in 1924–1925 disclosed abuses in many child-caring institutions: insanitary conditions and absence of health supervision, undernourishment and lack of recreation. Too frequently unauthorized individuals and groups receive needy children for profit, and oppose supervision by public agencies. Every state should assume responsibility for the effective supervision of all public and private agencies caring for dependent children. There is improvement now, however, in many of the institutions for children; numbers of them have rebuilt in cottage groups or have altered their buildings to provide for the care of children in small groups.

The work being done with dependent children needs improvement and extension. Each community should provide, "not only for such a variety of resources as will best meet every variety of child need, but also for such a balanced and flexible supply of each variety of care as will meet the need of the child as soon as the need is discovered."[3]

THE SOCIALLY HANDICAPPED: CHILDREN BORN OUT OF WEDLOCK

Significance of Illegitimacy. The child born out of wedlock suffers from a handicap which more than any other is of purely social origin, his birth having occurred without the sanction of the law. Not until every so-called *natural* child is also considered *legitimate*, will newer attitudes towards childhood have finally triumphed over ancient prejudice and custom. In 1915 Norway abolished the status of illegitimacy. North Dakota, following Norway, decreed in 1917 that "all children are declared to be legitimate children of their natural parents." Arizona followed suit in 1921. While there is an undoubted trend towards emphasis on the welfare of the child born out

[1] In 1922 there were 4,715 children in almshouses.

[2] "Children Indentured by Wisconsin State Public School," *Children's Bureau Publication*, No. 150 (1925). One foster father told the investigator that he would "never take on another child unless I can get one young enough, so that I can break 'em in to work."

[3] Thurston, *op. cit.*, p. 260. Under the Social Security Act an appropriation of $1,500,000 was authorized to aid state welfare agencies in caring for homeless and neglected children.

of wedlock, he is as yet afforded very inadequate legal protection, and almost nothing has been done to remove the stigma of illegitimacy. Justice will not be done until public opinion accords him an unimpaired social status, and until he receives special care and consideration as a wholly innocent victim of *illegitimate parenthood*.

In Christian countries the lot of unmarried mothers and their "bastard" children has been miserable indeed. In English law bastards were held to be *nullius filii*, the sons of nobody, with no legal ancestors and no claims to support.[1] With the sanction of a nominal Christianity, intent on suppressing and punishing sin, hundreds of thousands of innocent children have been repudiated by society, scorned, and neglected. As for their unfortunate mothers, so heavy has been their burden of suffering, ostracism, and punishment, that many have been driven to kill or abandon their new-born babies, practices by no means unknown to-day.[2] Until very recently the father has almost entirely escaped either censure or responsibility, apart from minor contributions for support.[3] Not until 1924 was there substantial alteration in English laws dealing with illegitimacy; at that time provision was made for legitimization through subsequent marriage of the parents. In France, Article 340 of the Napoleonic Code decreed, "*la recherche de la paternité est interdite*," and not until 1912 was this law amended. American legislation has been only slightly more progressive. Nor indeed can legal advance be secured and made effective, save through a thoroughgoing change of attitude. *Irresponsible* parenthood is not to be condoned, and all efforts must be bent on its prevention, but the stigma of illegitimacy should be removed from childhood. Parents must be held *equally* responsible and helped to do their best for the welfare of their child. The plight of the unmarried mother, often herself a mere child, is hard enough without any added cruelty on the part of society. Those who still consider her as irretrievably "ruined," "fallen," and, even when "rescued" and "reformed," still without the pale, are substituting outworn taboos for a constructive morality.

---

[1] The maxim of law being, according to Blackstone, "*qui ex damnato coitu nascuntur, inter liberos non computantur.*"

[2] As late as 1744, in England, a woman who wandered, begged, and gave birth to a child in a parish where she did not belong, was to spend six months in the house of correction, after being publicly whipped, stripped to the waist, till she became bloody.

[3] Birth certificates commonly in use in the United States carefully designate that, where the child is illegitimate, facts about the father need not be entered.

Prevalence and Causes of Illegitimacy. The problem of illegitimacy, rooted as it is in a complex of biological, economic,
and social forces, is one of the most serious from the standpoint
of child welfare. The number of illegitimate births in the
United States registration area in 1933 was 77,167; which
means that forty out of every 1,000 babies born were illegitimate.
Of these 34,890 or 45.2% occurred among the *white* population.[1]
Investigators are in substantial agreement as to the causes
of illegitimacy. Kammerer, as a result of his study of 500
unmarried mothers, found *bad home conditions* to be the outstanding factor; others are lack of home protection, as in the
case of girl immigrants; vicious neighborhood influences; conditions of employment, particularly in domestic service in hotels
and restaurants; evil companions; educational disadvantages;
demoralizing recreation; sexual suggestibility; and mental abnor-
mality.[2] All studies find that many of these girls come from
poverty-stricken, overcrowded homes, with male lodgers frequently added to the family circle. The character of the parents
is the most potent factor in the deterioration of home conditions.
There is frequent insistence that girls contribute all their wages
to family support, leaving nothing for recreation and dress.
Many parents are unable to guide or control their daughters
owing to ignorance or indifference; others are cruel, drunken,
or immoral. Many families have been broken by death or
desertion. A large proportion of the girls are mentally abnormal,
some are epileptics, many more subnormal or feeble-minded or
psychopathically inferior. Such girls often have several illegitimate children.[3]

Many of these unfortunate girls are very young. As Ruth
Reed points out, the treatment accorded them can no longer
be smugly considered as a punishment for irregular sex relations.
The sophisticated and mature may repeatedly offend and yet
escape, while the young, ignorant, and inexperienced are left
to suffer the full consequences of what may have been a single

---

[1] *Birth, Stillbirth and Infant Mortality Statistics,* U. S. Bureau of the Census (1936).
The remaining 42,277 illegitimate births occurred among Negroes, who comprise less
than 10% of the population.

[2] P. G. Kammerer, *The Unmarried Mother, A Study of Five Hundred Cases* (1918).
Among unmarried mothers there are also a number of young women of good character
and social position who have been deceived by false promises. Another group are the
definitely delinquent girls, for whom maternity is only an incidental evidence of
repeated immorality.

[3] It is not only the girls of inferior mentality who give birth to more than one illegitimate child. The same conditions responsible in the first case are very often aggravated after the child's birth.

mistake.[1] Out of 1,562 cases in New York City, in 1930, 77 or 4.9% were under sixteen, one was only eleven, and one girl of fourteen gave birth to her *second* illegitimate child.   Under twenty years of age were 42.2%, and under twenty-five 81.6% .[2] Where information is available about the fathers, they are found to be somewhat older than the mothers, comparatively few being under twenty.

The Treatment of Illegitimate Children and Their Mothers. Illegitimacy is an important contributory factor in the already grave problems of infant mortality, dependency, and delinquency. European statistics have shown that mortality among illegitimate babies is uniformly higher than among others. Such statistics as are available here show the disparity to be even greater. Approximately three times as many illegitimate babies die in early infancy as do babies born in wedlock. The number of stillborn illegitimate babies is also very great. Of those who survive many disappear, being handed over to unscrupulous persons who profit from the mother's longing for concealment. Many are cared for in institutions. The lack of normal home life, of security, of social status, tend to develop in these children a morbid outlook, leading sometimes to delinquency, and almost always to maladjustment.[3] To this tragic toll of death and misery must be added the heavy drain on public resources. Most states require the father to contribute to the support of his illegitimate child, but in many cases this provision cannot be enforced, and in others the support is entirely inadequate.

An important part of the whole problem of child dependency is thus concerned with the care of illegitimate children. Numbers of the children offered for adoption are illegitimate and this solution of the problem is very frequently for the best interests of the child.[4] On the other hand there has been a growth of sentiment, recently, in favor of keeping mother and child to-

[1] *The Modern Family* (1929), Chapter XV.

[2] Ruth Reed, *The Illegitimate Family in New York City* (1934), p. 115. Figures in other studies are in close agreement. In 1923 about half the illegitimate births in the registration area were to girls under twenty, four-fifths to girls under twenty-five. Jane Addams tells of two forlorn and prematurely aged children arriving at Hull House straight from the Maternity Ward of Cook County Hospital, each with a baby in her arms, and afraid to go home for fear of "being licked."

[3] For concrete examples see "Children of Illegitimate Birth and Measures for Their Protection," *Children's Bureau Publication*, No. 166 (1926).

[4] See Gallagher, *op. cit.*, pp. 134–217, for arguments in favor of adoption as soon after birth as possible, and consequently opposing legal requirements obliging mothers to keep their children for a certain number of months.

gether at least during early infancy. At present there are too few agencies giving effective help and guidance to unmarried mothers. Few of the hospitals in whose maternity wards so many of these children are born have adequate social service departments. Many private maternity homes, managed on a purely commercial basis and avoiding publicity, are definite social menaces. They have little interest in either mother or child, and the babies are, in traditional fashion, regarded as outcasts to be disposed of as soon as possible.

In some cases the parents of illegitimate children subsequently marry and provide a home for their child. *Forced* marriages are, however, most inadvisable and, being almost foredoomed to failure, offer no real solution.[1] Where unmarried mothers have been accorded friendly care and helped to reconstruct their lives, they have often made successful marriages, and in numbers of cases illegitimate children find a happy home with their mother and stepfather. Others support themselves and their babies, although under these circumstances the child must often be placed in a boarding home.[2] There is great need, as Mangold points out, for "mothers' and babies' homes," where mothers can live and their babies be cared for while they are at work. Another need is for the further extension of mothers' aid to unmarried as well as married mothers.

Laws Relative to Illegitimacy. Perhaps the most urgent need is for humane, comprehensive, and constructive legislation, giving protection to illegitimate children, and at the same time ensuring the fulfilment of obligations on the part of both parents. American laws, in general, recognize paternity chiefly for the purpose of obtaining support. Actions must usually be brought by the mother, although she is frequently assisted by some agency. But comparatively few actions are brought and fewer still are pressed. Where payments are secured, they are most inadequate. Apart from the two states where all children are declared legitimate, a child may often be legitimated by action of his father, most usually by marriage with the mother. The most adequate provision is that secured by the Minnesota laws where the legislative code is reënforced by effective administrative procedures. Large powers of guardianship are conferred

[1] Mary E. Richmond and Fred S. Hall, *Marriage and the State* (1929), pp. 155–162.
[2] So intense is popular prejudice that many social workers have found it necessary to help in deceiving all but those most nearly concerned as to an unmarried mother's true status. Otherwise her social and economic readjustment may be too severely handicapped. "Children of Illegitimate Birth Whose Mothers Have Kept Their Custody," *Children's Bureau Publication*, No. 190 (1928), pp. 11–14.

on the State Board of Control, a department concerned with problems of delinquency and dependency. Minnesota is the first state to assume centralized public responsibility for the protection of illegitimate children.[1] Recent legislation in other states has also been clearly designed for the welfare of the child. There is no suggestion, however, in any state, of the revolutionary reforms introduced by the Castberg law in Norway.[2] According to Mangold: "The Norwegian law goes to the heart of the problem, for if a law can enforce for the illegitimate a standing that makes illegitimacy a grievous burden to men, then a powerful deterrent force will have been set in motion. The Norwegian law adapted to American needs, but without substantial modification, should be adopted in every American state. . . . There is good reason for the contention that the status of illegitimacy should be entirely abolished and each child become the legal child of his natural parents."[3]

THE SOCIALLY HANDICAPPED: JUVENILE DELINQUENTS

The New Approach to Problems of Juvenile Delinquency. No longer must children who come into conflict with society be considered as criminals and their delinquencies treated as crimes for which appropriate punishment should be inflicted. The endeavor must be to *understand* the delinquent child, and, viewing his antisocial acts as symptoms of deeper disorders, to reach a diagnosis on the basis of which treatment may be prescribed. The first juvenile *houses of refuge* were established a century ago to care for children who would otherwise have been committed to prison; court procedure, however, remained

---

[1] The primary purpose of the Minnesota law is declared to be: "To safeguard the interests of illegitimate children and secure for them the nearest possible approximation to the care, support and education that they would be entitled to receive if born in lawful marriage, which purpose is hereby acknowledged and declared to be the duty of the State." S. P. Breckenridge, *The Family and the State* (1934), p. 478. North Dakota now has an administrative board similar to that of Minnesota.

[2] "Norwegian Laws concerning Illegitimate Children," *Children's Bureau Publication*, No. 31 (1918). According to this law "a child whose parents have not married one another shall have the same legal status, except as elsewhere provided in this law, in the relation to the father as to the mother." The burden of establishing paternity and fixing the obligation of maintenance is placed on the state, although the mother is required to report the facts to the local authorities. Paternity established as a biological fact carries with it all the obligations of legal paternity; when only fair presumption is established, the alleged father is obliged to support mother and child. In Soviet Russia distinctions between legitimate and illegitimate children have been swept away; and in 1934, in Germany, legal measures were taken greatly to improve the status of the illegitimate child. *New York Times*, Nov. 4, 1934.

[3] From *Problems of Child Welfare* (rev. ed., 1924), p. 509. By permission of The Macmillan Company, publishers.

all but unmodified until the juvenile court movement developed the idea of safeguarding and salvaging the child. The first juvenile court in this country was established in 1899 in Cook County, Illinois. In 1909, this Court became the scene of the first psychopathic clinic for the systematic study of delinquent children.[1] Under the leadership of the pioneer psychiatrist, Dr. William Healy, real progress began to be made in the discovery of the underlying causes of delinquency.

Despite the validity of the new approach and excellence of procedure in some juvenile courts, the total results have been disappointing. Apparently there has been no lessening of delinquency; if anything it is on the increase.[2] The money costs are enormous. The human costs in sorrow and suffering, in the tragedy of wasted lives and blighted hopes cannot be measured. Most ominous is the fact, that adult crime has its roots in juvenile delinquency.[3]

Many factors contribute to the prevalence of delinquency. Only a few communities and comparatively small numbers of children as yet have the benefit of the best present knowledge. The treatment of delinquent children still very frequently violates humane principles and is deficient in dispassionate consideration of the reasons for their lack of social conformity. There is also need for fuller understanding of the causes of delinquency and of methods for its treatment. One outstanding lack has been the failure sufficiently to take into account the social relationships which have woven themselves into the texture of personality. Maladjustment and delinquency result almost inevitably when the child's needs, being afforded no

[1] By 1932 there were 600 psychiatric and child guidance clinics.

[2] There is also a very high percentage of *recidivism*. For example, 88.2% of 923 cases were found delinquent in the five years following official treatment. S. Glueck and E. T. Glueck, *One Thousand Juvenile Delinquents* (1934), Chapter IX. Four-fifths of the delinquents who pass through juvenile courts are boys, the most common offenses being against property. Girls are most frequently brought into court for sex offenses. For this reason girls are rather more likely than are boys to be committed to institutions, and so the proportion of males in institutions is not quite so large as among children appearing before the courts. In 1923, 19,656 boys and 7,582 girls were in institutions for delinquents. "Children under Institutional Care," *Bureau of the Census Publication* (1923), Part III.

[3] In the Gluecks' studies of 500 adult male and 500 adult female offenders, from two-thirds to three-quarters of them were found to have been delinquent in childhood. In the 1934 survey of the New York City slums undertaken by Langdon Post, it was discovered that one particular slum area of Manhattan bordering the Harlem River had the highest felony conviction rate, 1.66 per 1,000, and also the highest proportion of juveniles judged delinquent, 18.39 per 1,000. The arrest rate for this section was 72.31 per 1,000, also the highest for any area. *New York Times*, Aug. 5, 1934.

wholesome means of satisfaction, clash with the needs of those around him and with social needs embodied in institutions. Because of lack of understanding of stresses and strains, so easily developed in the complex network of human relationships, much of "our present mode of handling these problems" of social maladjustment "is but the endless monotonous task of sweeping up the debris of life."[1] It is not so much the problem child that must be studied as "the problem of the child."[1]

Were every child assured of an environment securing for him full opportunity for normal growth and development, particularly for emotional development and social adjustment, delinquency might be prevented. Even under the best conditions, adjustments between the individual and the group are delicate matters. Small wonder, then, that under present social and economic conditions delinquency is so prevalent. Even so, much more might be accomplished, if when a child *first* got into trouble, he were given the full benefit of scientific diagnosis and treatment.

Treatment of the Delinquent Child. All the elements of a delinquent child's physical and social environment should be investigated in an effort to discover and eradicate factors provocative of maladjustment. First, however, a physical and mental picture of the individual is essential, not only of weaknesses and defects, but of assets and potentialities for a fuller life. For it is largely through cultivation of assets that better courses of conduct may be encouraged. Research has led to complete abandonment of the idea that delinquency and crime are the result of inborn physical constitution. Nor are most delinquents physically inferior or mentally deficient. In not a few cases the native equipment of the offender is markedly superior. Nevertheless, mental or physical defects or peculiarities have an important bearing on the incidence of misconduct.

In the first place certain abnormalities affect the individual's powers of inhibition and unfit him for the stresses of social living. Diseases affecting the brain often lead to great instability of behavior. Intellectual handicaps are not found to be as important as was once thought. The relationship between subnormality, feeble-mindedness, and delinquency, although actual, has been overemphasized. The mentally alert delinquent is far more likely to escape detection and institutional treatment; so that the number of mentally defective delinquents in courts

---

[1] *The Delinquent Child* (1932), p. 20. The Report of the White House Conference Committee on Delinquency.

and institutions is disproportionately high. The mental defective is suggestible and less likely to withstand temptation, but with special care and education he is unlikely to become delinquent. A large number of delinquents have abnormal personalities; the psychopathic or constitutionally inferior or those possessed of markedly peculiar characteristics and behavior tendencies. Few of this latter group respond to any treatment so far devised. There is also another way in which handicaps or deformities may lead to delinquent conduct; not directly, but *indirectly*, through setting the child apart from others, causing him to feel inferior and thwarting him in the fulfilment of his natural ambitions. It is therefore of the greatest importance, not only to detect defects, but to discover the child's attitude towards his handicap.

To help any delinquent child, it is essential to discover why a particular delinquent act seemed natural to him. The clue is to be found in habitual behavior tendencies, in interests and ambitions, and above all in his emotional and ideational life. He is frequently found to be very unhappy, his desires are unsatisfied, he feels himself inferior, not trusted, not wanted, frustrated, and unable to succeed.[1] Where there is no legitimate outlet for his natural longing for achievement and adventure he may readily resort to antisocial conduct; particularly is this the case where, through association with undesirable companions, from sensational reading or films, and crime news, he is thrilled by the idea of achieving notoriety and eluding the police. As Florence Mateer has said, "if the child cannot be famous, he will be infamous." Only through an attitude of sympathetic understanding can the investigator hope to discern the actual thoughts and emotions preceding a delinquent act. The most hopeful plan for the prevention of further delinquency is the provision of wholesome recreation and of opportunities for successful achievement in worth-while occupations suited to individual interest and capacity.

Environmental Factors in Delinquency. Adverse home conditions are an important factor in delinquency. The majority of delinquents come from homes blighted by poverty and economic stress. Deprivation of physical necessities, of food,

---

[1] A study of 105 children who have appeared in the courts, comparing them with non-delinquent brothers and sisters, included eight sets of twins ranging from six to seventeen. Every one of the delinquent twins proved to have deeply felt emotional discomfort, whereas the non-delinquent twin in each case proved to be free of inner stresses. William Healy and Augusta F. Bronner, *New Light on Delinquency and Its Treatment* (1936).

clothing, and a decent and uncrowded dwelling place leads to ill-health and unsatisfied desire. The worry and insecurity of life under such conditions leave an indelible impress on the maturing character of the child, particularly since these conditions are also productive of bitterness and discord among the older members of the family. The home broken by death or desertion or divorce and the home where discord prevails have been conclusively shown to be among the chief causative factors of delinquency.[1] A sense of security is impossible in homes marred by incessant quarreling, or by alcoholism, immorality, and criminalism; in homes where parental severity alternates with parental neglect, due sometimes to indifference, and sometimes to the enforced absence of the mother at work.[2] Healy and Bronner found that among 2,000 young repeated offenders in Chicago and Boston, only 7.6% were living under reasonably good home conditions.[3]

The majority of delinquents are school children, and for most of them truancy is the first overt break with social authority. Retardation and failure in school are shown in some studies to accompany delinquency more frequently than any other condition.[4] Persistent failures, constant reprimands, and ridi-

[1] Clifford Shaw and H. D. McKay, "Broken Homes and Delinquency," *Social Forces*, Vol. X (1932), pp. 514–523. Evidence is here presented to show that it is not the actual break, such as occurs in the death or desertion of a parent, which is a factor in delinquency, but the subtler influences of family interaction under such circumstances. Blanche Weill, in *The Behavior of Young Children in the Same Family* (1928), enumerates the factors which tend to be interwoven in an undesirable family situation. The four chief classes, which include many subdivisions, are poor personal relations, physical and mental disabilities, social and moral maladjustments, and economic pressures. For a recent discussion of the interplay of social and psychological factors in delinquency see F. Alexander and W. Healy, *Roots of Crime* (1935), Chapter X.

[2] Many accounts of such homes are found in the recent case studies. In none perhaps is the impression more vivid, because presented in the course of the delinquent's own story, than in *The Natural History of a Delinquent Career* (1931), by Clifford Shaw and M. E. Moore. The mother in this tragic account was forced by circumstances, an alcoholic and deserting husband and extreme poverty, to leave her son unprotected while she worked.

[3] *Delinquents and Criminals, Their Making and Unmaking* (1926), p. 129.

[4] In "A Warden Looks at Education," *New York Times Magazine*, Jan. 31, 1932, Warden Lawes stresses this fact. The great importance of vocational guidance is attested to by the fact that less than 5% of those admitted to Sing Sing had any such opportunity. The visiting-teacher is invaluable, but in 1931 there were only seventeen in New York City, or an average of one to about 12,000 retarded or maladjusted children. There is no telling how much human wreckage and financial waste might be prevented through adequate treatment of young delinquents when first apprehended. One prisoner in Sing Sing had been arrested 80 times since he was 13. Fines to the amount of $347 were collected from him, whereas for many years he will cost the state $400 annually. In view of Lawes' indictment of the schools, present developments in New York City are encouraging; in particular the

cule create an unbearable situation for the child. But when the child is thus driven to leave school and goes to work the situation is no better. According to the White House report: "one of the pervasive elements of our present problem of delinquency is this difficulty that the young person has in finding real satisfaction in his actual earning life."[1] According to Maude Miner Hadden of the Girls' Service League, most of the 16,000 runaway girls who come to her every year do so because their life in their home, at school, or at work is dull, sordid, or confining. "Can't I get a job at something I wouldn't hate?" they ask.[2] Emotional compensation is very naturally sought in a feverish pursuit of pleasure and adventure in the few free hours of the day.

Clifford Shaw has emphasized the fact that delinquency is a symptom of the disintegration of social controls, those formative influences inherent in social tradition and in orderly community life which make for socially acceptable ways of acting. In the past the church has been a potent influence. To-day, while the functions of family and school remain clear, there is no general agreement as to the function of the church. Undoubtedly the need for security in its deepest and most inclusive sense can be satisfied only through a harmonious relationship to the whole of life. Yet more than two-fifths of the population of the United States, thirteen years of age and over, are not members of any church, and millions more have but nominal religious affiliations. Such a situation places an added responsibility upon the home.[3]

When home, school, and church fail to exercise a stabilizing effect, the pervasive influences of the community become all-powerful. Particularly where the intimate life of the family group fails him, the child will go outside the home in search of recognition, companionship, and adventure. Children in the best of homes cannot be wholly protected from influences beyond the control of parents, the hurry, confusion, and noise of crowded city life, the conflict of standards, the vulgarity and bad taste and more sinister influences of popular commercial

extension in principle of the Peyser plan for delinquency prevention which has been in successful operation for many years in Public School 181 in Brooklyn, of which Dr. Peyser was principal before his death in 1936. The personality of each child is studied and teachers coöperate with parents and other community agencies in providing a wholesome integrated environment.

[1] *The Delinquent Child*, p. 44.

[2] "The Runaway Girl of To-day: a Problem and Its Solution," *New York Times*, Nov. 19, 1933.

[3] See Chapter XXIV.

amusements; the thrill of the crime news and the meretricious glamour imparted to the doings and misdoings of publicized individuals, the rich, the notorious, and the popular entertainers of the day. All these factors combine to create an atmosphere wholly subversive, an atmosphere of money-seeking and of restlessness, if not lawlessness, permeated by "the vicious belief that somehow more can be gotten out of life than one puts in it."[1] Obviously the child, when unprotected by home and school, is entirely at the mercy of such factors.

Delinquency Areas. This explains in part the influence of slum areas as breeders of delinquency and crime. Slums, as the products of larger social and economic forces, are characterized by a combination of deleterious conditions: "bad housing, low income levels, the weakened grip of regulatory institutions such as the family, objectionable groupings, and unwholesome and inadequate recreational outlets."[2] The slum child is "surrounded by attitudes of apathy and indifference toward individual modes of behavior; lowered cultural levels, a preoccupation with the bare necessities of existence and an almost complete lack of understanding of and concern with the necessity for social conformity."[2] Frequently malnourished and physically handicapped, surrounded by squalor, bitterness, discord, how can the slum child be expected to make desirable social adjustments?

Young people everywhere band together in spontaneous social groups. Where there are wholesome outlets and opportunities for play and recreation, and where community traditions are those of orderly social life, these groups seldom become delinquent. In slum areas they frequently develop into antisocial, even dangerous, *gangs*. These are in large part the result of unsupervised contacts of street life, and compensate their members for repression and adversity by giving them a sense of companionship and social recognition. Robbery and all forms of violence and law-breaking are natural developments where the most interesting play for children consists in petty thievery and the excitement of flight and escape. Few delinquents commit offenses alone; and those social agencies which

[1] *The Delinquent Child,* p. 351.
[2] F. M. Thrasher, "City Slums Are Shown as Breeders of Crime," *New York Times,* Aug. 5, 1934. Studies in a number of large cities corroborate the fact first emphasized by Clifford Shaw in his Chicago study of *Delinquency Areas* (1929): that different community backgrounds were productive of different rates of truancy, delinquency, and crime, by far the highest rates being found in the so-called *slums*. Cf. note 3, p. 346.

are most successful in diverting lawless youths to more wholesome pursuits have worked with whole groups and have not made the mistake of undermining the loyalty of members to their group.

No analysis of the influence of demoralizing neighborhoods on youth can compare with the vivid testimony afforded by Clifford Shaw in his case-histories of boys as told by themselves.[1] The sordid and insecure home life, the early initiation by companions into the thrills of shoplifting, the later gang associations and matter-of-course familiarity with corruption, vice, and crime, all illustrate conclusively the smothering of the "divine fire of youth." The "spirit of youth" with its freshness and eager longing for life and happiness, of which Jane Addams wrote nearly thirty years ago, has still to-day small chance to escape the blighting influence of the city streets.[2]

Remedial Agencies: Juvenile Courts. The police are the first representatives of law and order for the child, and possess an unparalleled opportunity for influencing the behavior of individuals and groups *before* critical delinquent situations arise. But if the work of the police is to be constructive, rather than merely restrictive, it is imperative that they deal with children in a manner wholly different from that used with adult offenders. They must be the friends and protectors of the young, rather than their enemies. Individual police officers in many communities have become alert to the needs of youth; and there are juvenile bureaus attached to police departments in a few communities. Particularly valuable are coördinating councils, which secure the coöperation of the police with the school and other community agencies. Policewomen have been specially successful in work with young people. But on the whole there is far too much violence, far too many arrests and detentions of children in police stations and gaols. It should often be unnecessary to do more than secure name and address and return the delinquent to the custody of his parents.

Juvenile courts were established in order that children might be removed from the jurisdiction of criminal courts to special tribunals of their own, the purpose of which would no longer be the meting out of appropriate punishment, but the discovery and removal of the underlying causes of delinquency. In general the juvenile court is "charged with providing for children the care, discipline, education and training which

[1] *Op. cit.*, and *The Jack-Roller, a Delinquent Boy's Own Story* (1930).
[2] *The Spirit of Youth and the City Streets* (1909).

should have been given them by their parents."[1]   The best courts use the methods of social case-work: medical, psychological, and psychiatric examinations determine the child's assets and handicaps, while probation officers make a study of the child in relation to his environment.   Court procedure is informal and private: only the child, his parents, and those immediately concerned in the case are present.   The judge then prescribes treatment.   In most cases the child should not be separated from his home, but placed on probation under the supervision of a probation officer.   The success of juvenile-court procedure depends primarily upon personnel.   Probation officers should be specially selected for their qualifications as social case-workers.   The work of such men as Judge Cabot, in Boston, and Judge Hoyt, in New York, offers conclusive proof of what may be accomplished by judges well qualified for the supervision of a juvenile court.[2]

In spite of the principles involved in the establishment of juvenile courts, their jurisdiction over children charged with violation of the law is by no means complete in all states.   In a number of states those charged with certain serious offences come before the criminal courts regardless of age.   Defects in juvenile court laws and in the courts themselves are due largely to the fact that traditional attitudes towards juvenile delinquency are still widely prevalent.   The legalistic concept of the court as a disciplinary agency precludes acceptance of the fundamentals of social case-work.   As a result, few juvenile courts approximate the standards formulated in 1923 by the Children's Bureau and the National Probation Association.

Remedial Agencies: Institutional Treatment.   When it is not possible to allow the child to remain in his own home, pending the hearing and disposition of his case, further problems arise. Hardly anywhere is detention of children in the care of the

---

[1] *The Delinquent Child*, p. 274.

[2] There has been a tendency for juvenile courts to become agencies for dealing with children's problems in all cases where the child is in need of protection from the state; for example in cases of adoption, of controverted custody, of dependency, or neglect. A further step in unification has been taken in domestic-relations courts. The first of these was established in Buffalo in 1910. By 1933, 16 states and Hawaii had authorized domestic-relations courts in 146 jurisdictions. In New Jersey and Virginia they were found in every county. They differ somewhat in the scope of their jurisdiction. Some are fully developed family courts with juvenile and broad adult jurisdiction in children's cases, and in cases of divorce, desertion, or non-support, and contribution to delinquency or dependency. In New York City on Oct. 1, 1933, the Court of Domestic Relations was amalgamated with the Children's Court to form such a family court.

juvenile court carried on with fully satisfactory results. Well-equipped and well-conducted detention homes and carefully selected boarding homes are valuable as affording temporary treatment and observation.

Commitment to correctional institutions is still far too often ordered by the court without sufficient understanding of the needs of the child. If the child cannot be placed on probation in his own home, good foster-home care should in most cases be preferred to institutional care. This is all the more advisable because of the uneven quality of institutions. Some are still unbelievably bad, reformatories in the old sense of correctional institutions, gaols in reality, where no attempt is made to understand the children's needs or to facilitate social rehabilitation. Worst of all, first offenders are frequently in daily contact with hardened criminals.[1] Warden Lawes is emphatic in his conviction that the professional criminal is the product of institutionalism; no boys under sixteen except the mentally deficient should be confined in institutions.[2] Even with progressive management it is hard to offset the contamination of evil communications where delinquents are herded together, without opportunity for normal social contacts, and with the sense of inferiority due to an institutional record. "You're never the same if you go there," said one youthful offender.[3]

Nevertheless, some institutions are becoming genuine diagnostic laboratories, designed to ascertain and correct the causes of social failure and to prepare their inmates for normal community life. An outstanding experiment of this kind is that undertaken by New York State in coöperation with the Columbia Medical Center at the Warwick School. It is designed as a medical and psychiatric research laboratory, while affording the best possible chance of rehabilitation for the boys who are sent there. In common with other good reform schools it in no way resembles a gaol, its features being those of a well-

---

[1] One reformatory, investigated by Dr. Peyser in 1932, made no attempt at classification or segregation of the 700 inmates whose ages ranged from 16 to 29. The sole object of the institution was incarceration, the daily routine being a "deadly monotonous grind." There was no vocational training, no recreation. After a day of hard labor the inmates, most of them adolescent boys, were locked in their cells to remain there from 4 P.M. to 6:30 A.M. *New York Times*, Sept. 27, 1932.

[2] *Op. cit.*, and *Twenty Thousand Years in Sing Sing* (1933), pp. 356 *et seq.*

[3] The Children's Bureau has recently conducted a study of five state institutions for delinquent boys, and made case studies of 751 boys who had undergone treatment. The majority of these failed in making satisfactory adjustment to community life. *Children's Bureau Publications* No. 228 (1935) and No. 230 (1936).

conducted school making ample provision for health, education, vocational training, and recreation.[1]

At the time of the first White House Conference it was hoped the juvenile court would solve the problems of delinquency. But there has been no such assuaging of these problems as was expected. An essential step has been taken, however, in the adoption of the dispassionate socio-psychiatric attitude which does not find fault or accuse or lay the blame, but sees in the delinquent act the natural result of some deeper trouble. Research and experiment should in time bring fuller understanding of the causes of delinquency and improved methods of treatment. But with these must come, as well, increasing realization of the fact that there can be *no enduring solution* of the problems of delinquency, without amelioration of social and economic conditions. "We have gone along for years now," Thrasher says, "sending one crop of criminals to the electric chair . . . and watering a new crop in the slums." Many a slum boy compensating for his sense of social inferiority by attitudes of bravado, early becomes a delinquent, until, "in the end, we have the pathetic picture of the anemic youth . . . turning up with a smoking gun in his hand, and finally sitting in the electric chair with bitterness in his heart and bleak wonder in his mind."[2]

In the meantime, it is of the greatest importance that educational rather than penal methods of treatment be extended to include all young people throughout childhood and adolescence. This would mean that those from seventeen to twenty-one should be viewed by the court as wards to be trained, protected, and guided. Already, in seventeen states, the age limit for juvenile courts is eighteen and in four states it is twenty-one.[3]

[1] "The State Calls in Science to Aid Its Delinquent Boys," *New York Times*, Aug. 7, 1932.

[2] *New York Times*, Aug. 5, 1934. In "Gangsters: Why? A Resounding Question," *New York Times*, March 17, 1935, Thrasher points out that the spectacular method of attacking the crime problem is to deal with the finished criminal. Getting rid of "public enemies" is, however, but a temporary means of suppressing symptoms which will very shortly reappear. Crime prevention should center on efforts to provide wholesome influences for children who are the victims of vicious environment. Those who believe that society is *just* to its young offenders should read the story of Two-Gun Crowley in Lawes' *Twenty Thousand Years in Sing Sing*. This youthful murderer of a policeman was the illegitimate son of a policeman. Not till some time after he was lodged in the death-house, was Warden Lawes able to penetrate beneath his mask of defiance and discover his unusual artistic talents. A new life began for Crowley, to be cut short in the electric chair.

[3] It must be remembered that the largest single age group in the prisons of the country is *19*, although all ages from *18* to *26* are represented in almost equal numbers. The prison population has been increasing steadily until by January, 1936,

Van Waters deplores the tendency to speak of "a protective court attitude as sentimentality, pity or leniency"; rather should it be understood "that we are seeking to modify childish behavior by means of psychological and ethical knowledge."[1]

All community agencies must coöperate in conserving childhood. Unwholesome local conditions should be eliminated wherever possible, facilities for wholesome recreation established, and agencies provided for the treatment of problem behavior in home and school, culminating in an intelligent juvenile court service with qualified probation officers. Coöperation of federal, state, and local agencies is necessary. The state should provide expert leadership for local organizations and specialized services which are beyond the scope of the local community. Through research and education the federal government may afford a basis for nation-wide development.

SUGGESTED READING

Abbott, G., "The Juvenile Courts," *Survey*, Vol. LXXII, May, 1936, pp. 131–133.

Bentley, J. E., *Problem Children*, 1936.

Breckenridge, S. P., *Family Welfare Work*, 1924, Section VI.

——, *The Family and the State*, 1934, Sections VI–VIII.

Burt, C., *The Backward Child*, 1937.

Children's Bureau, *Publication 152*, "Industrial Accidents to Employed Minors in Wisconsin, Massachusetts and New Jersey," 1926.

——, *Publication 187*, "Children in Agriculture," 1928.

——, *Publication 188*, "Child Workers on the City Streets," 1928.

——, *Publication 197*, "Child Labor, Facts and Figures," 1930.

——, *Publication 198*, "Children in Fruit and Vegetable Canneries," 1931.

——, *Publication 227*, "Children Engaged in Newspaper and Magazine Selling and Delivery," 1935.

——, *Publication 210*, "Employment of Mentally Deficient Boys and Girls," 1932.

——, *Publication 62*, "Minimum Standards of Child Welfare," 1919.

——, *Publication 136*, "Foster-Home Care for Dependent Children," rev., 1929.

there were 235,500 persons confined for various offences, more than double the number in 1910. Sanford Bates, "Penal and Reformatory Institutions for Adults," *Social Work Year Book 1937*, issued by the Russell Sage Foundation.

[1] "When a Child Runs Afoul of the Law," *New York Times*, May 15, 1932. In commenting on the Children's Charter, XIV, she says: "When we refuse to consider any child society's outcast, we refuse to send any child to death, to prison, or to show hate, fear or antagonism to any child offender . . . . We will regard every offending child as our challenge and moral responsibility."

Children's Bureau, *Publication 150*, "Children Indentured by the Wisconsin State Public School," 1925.

——, *Publication 171*, "The Work of Child-Placing Agencies," 1927.

——, from *Publication 209*, "Care of Children in Day Nurseries," 1932.

——, from *Publication 209*, "Care of Dependent and Neglected Children," 1932.

——, *Publication 216*, "The A B C of Foster-Family Care for Children," 1933.

——, *Publication 31*, "Norwegian Laws concerning Illegitimate Children," 1918.

——, *Publication 42*, "Illegitimacy Laws of the United States, Analysis and Index," 1919.

——, *Publication 66*, "Illegitimacy as a Child-Welfare Problem," Part I, 1920.

——, *Publication 75*, "Illegitimacy as a Child-Welfare Problem," Part II, 1921.

——, *Publication 128*, "Illegitimacy as a Child-Welfare Problem," Part III, 1924.

——, *Publication 166*, "Children of Illegitimate Birth and Measures for Their Protection," 1926.

——, *Publication 190*, "Children of Illegitimate Birth Whose Mothers Have Kept Their Custody," 1928.

——, from *Publication 209*, "Protective Case Work for Young People and Maternity Homes," 1932.

——, *Chart Series, 16*, "Analysis and Tabular Summary of State Laws Relating to Illegitimacy in the United States, in effect Jan. 1, 1928, and Text of Selected Laws," 1929.

——, *Publication 193*, "The Child, the Family and the Court," 1929.

——, *Publication 215*, "Facts about Juvenile Delinquency, Its Prevention and Treatment," 1933.

——, *Publication 226*, "Juvenile Court Statistics, 1932," 1933.

——, *Publication 228*, "Institutional Treatment of Delinquent Boys, Part I, Treatment Programs of Five State Institutions," 1935.

——, *Publication 230*, "Institutional Treatment of Delinquent Boys, Part II, A Study of 751 Boys," 1936.

Donahue, A. M., "Children Born Out of Wedlock," *The Annals of the American Academy of Political and Social Science*, Vol. CLI, Sept., 1930, pp. 162–172.

Gallagher, E. G., *The Adopted Child*, 1936.

Glover, K., and Dewey, E., *Children of the New Day*, 1934.

Glueck, S., and E. T., *One Thousand Juvenile Delinquents*, 1934.

Goldberg, J. A., and R. W., *Girls on City Streets*, 1935.

Goodsell, W., *Problems of the Family*, rev. ed., 1936, Ch. XVI.

Groves, E. R., and Brooks, L. M., *Readings in the Family*, 1934, Ch. XVII.

Healy, W., and Bronner, A. F., *Delinquents and Criminals, Their Making and Unmaking*, 1926.

——, *New Light on Delinquency and Its Treatment*, 1936.

Healy, W., Bronner, A. F., Baylor, E. H., Murphy, J. P., *Reconstructing Behavior in Youth*, 1929.

Inskeep, A. D., *Teaching Dull and Retarded Children*, 1926.

Johnsen, J., ed., *Selected Articles on Child Labor*, 1925.

Kammerer, P. G., *The Unmarried Mother, A Study of Five Hundred Cases*, 1918.

Lumpkin, K. Du P., and Douglas, D. W., *Child Workers in America*, 1937.

Mateer, F., *The Unstable Child*, 1924.

Mangold, G., *Problems of Child Welfare*, rev. ed., 1924.

National Child Labor Committee, *Publication 368*, "Handbook: the Federal Child Labor Amendment," 1937.

——, *Publication 369*, "Child Labor Facts," 1937.

Office of Education, *Bulletin 11*, 1936, "A Guide to Curriculum Adjustment for Mentally Retarded Children."

——, *Bulletin 13*, 1936, "The Deaf and Hard of Hearing in the Occupational World."

Pendleton, O., "New Aims in Adoption," *The Annals of the American Academy of Political and Social Science*, Vol. CLI, Sept., 1930, pp. 154–161.

Reed, R., *The Illegitimate Family in New York City*, 1934.

Sayles, M. B., *Substitute Parents*, 1936.

Shaw, C., *Delinquency Areas*, 1929.

——, *The Jack-Roller, A Delinquent Boy's Own Story*, 1930.

——, and Moore, M. E., *The Natural History of a Delinquent Career*, 1931.

Thrasher, F. M., *The Gang*, 1927.

Thurston, H. W., *The Dependent Child*, 1930.

Van Waters, M., *Youth in Conflict*, 1925.

Vernier, C. G., *"American Family Laws"* (5 vols., 1931–1938), Vol. IV.

White House Conference, *Child Labor*, 1932.

——, *The Delinquent Child*, 1932.

——, *Dependent and Neglected Children*, 1933.

——, *The Handicapped Child*, 1933.

——, *Organization for the Care of Handicapped Children*, 1932.

——, *Special Education: The Handicapped and the Gifted*, 1931.

——, *A Survey of Day Nurseries*, 1931.

——, *Vocational Guidance*, 1932.

CHAPTER XIII

RECIPROCAL RELATIONS BETWEEN CHILD WEL-FARE AND SOCIAL WELFARE

POVERTY AND CHILD WELFARE

Poverty and Industrialism. In the case histories of children in need of special care or protection, the same sinister factors occur repeatedly. First and foremost stands poverty. Poverty is at least as old as civilization; wealth has been for the few, and the many have lived in want. To-day, despite an unprecedented increase in resources and a general rise in scales of living, there are even greater inequalities in the distribution of wealth. In 1929, of the twenty-two million non-farm families, *one-third* enjoyed nearly *half* the food, *three-fifth* of the clothes, *two-thirds* of the housing, and *three-quarters* of all the other good things of life.[1] In 1927, less than 10% of the income receivers secured 25% of the national income and 1% secured 12%. Of the workers, more than 90% were exempt from a federal income tax because their incomes averaged $1,500 or less.[2] The average earnings of an unskilled laborer were insufficient to maintain a wife and *one* dependent child, far less two or more children.[3]

Until 1929 actual money wages have shown a consistent trend upward and, in the post-war years, real earnings also showed increases.[4] Yet, owing to a concomitant rise in the cost of living, wages, even in the most prosperous times, were not proportionately high. While the cost of living is the chief

[1] Mordecai Ezekiel, *$2,500 a Year* (1936).

[2] Stuart Chase, *Poor Old Competition* (pamphlet published by the League for Industrial Democracy, 1932). Among these, of course, are all the poorer elements of the rural population, who still *produce* rather than buy most of their living. But many of them are in an even worse situation than the urban poor. According to the 1930 Census, 1,000,000 farmers had less than $400 income, including the value of all produce, whether sold or used for family living.

[3] *A Study* of *the Income and Standards of Living of Unskilled Laborers in Chicago* (1927) was made by Leila Houghteling. Of 467 families with at least one dependent child, 70% were unable to maintain, on the father's earnings alone, a scale of living recommended by the United Charities for dependent families. In 45% of the families the total income including the money derived from lodgers and the work of mothers was insufficient to maintain this level.

[4] *Real* income signifies the commodities and services which can be procured with *money* income, and the satisfaction of needs through their use.

factor in determining adequacy of income, other factors are the size of the family, skill in household management, and the wisdom of the wife in buying the family living. Leaving the last two factors out of consideration, estimates can be made at any particular time of the average income necessary to maintain families of specific size at a minimum level of health and decency.[1] Serious discrepancies are always found between the average income of the majority of workers and estimated budgets of *necessary* yearly expenditures.[2]

The Pervasive Influence of Poverty. Insufficiency of the father's income to support the family is the primary cause for the labor of married women and of children at the lower economic levels.[3] Poverty is so closely associated with many of the conditions which undermine the integrity of family life that it is often difficult to distinguish cause from effect. The poor are caught in a vicious circle, where, from poverty, ensue results which once more bring poverty in their wake. Illness, either chronic or acute, follows unemployment as a leading cause of poverty, and here the reciprocal connection is very close. Food insufficiencies and bad housing lead to malnutrition and susceptibility to disease. Ignorance, owing to deprivation in youth, aggravates the situation. Illness, mental disturbances, and accidents are all more prevalent in poverty-stricken homes. Many homes are broken by the premature death of father or mother. In others they are broken when the unbearable strain leads to desertion on the part of the husband. Escape is frequently sought through recourse to drink or drugs. Poverty makes utterly impossible the provision of a dwelling place adequate as an environment for childhood and youth. No wonder the young seek escape from their squalid tenement homes, from the misery of their overworked mothers, and the bitterness or brutality of unemployed or intemperate fathers, and fall an easy prey to the more vicious among the purveyors of commercialized amusements. In many poor families, of course, family life is rendered as adequate as it can be, under

[1] One of the first to attempt scientific budget study was the Frenchman, Le Play. This was in 1855; but not until the present century were similar studies undertaken in this country.

[2] It must be remembered, in speaking of *average* incomes, that, while those *above* the average might be sufficient for family support, all those below would be even less adequate than the average.

[3] In 1930, families with only one gainful worker constituted 62.1% of all families, those with two paid workers comprised 21.1%, those with three 7.2%, those with four or more 3.6%. "Population Bulletin: Families," *Publication* of the U. S. Bureau of the Census (1930).

the circumstances, owing to the courage of parents. All social workers bear testimony to the devotion of poor mothers to their children and to the kindness of the poor to one another. The fact remains, however, that poverty lies at the root of most of the conditions deleterious to the welfare of children.

UNEMPLOYMENT AND CHILD WELFARE

Unemployment as a Permanent Hazard. Many wage earners, even when steadily employed, are unable to earn enough for family support. Many more live close to the margin of want. Their tragic insecurity becomes all the more evident if one considers the hazards of illness, accident, and unemployment. Besides the millions who fall ill, over two million workers are killed or injured each year in accidents. Many workers are not protected at all by the compensation laws, and, in the case of those who are, the benefits are frequently inadequate. But the gravest menace of all is unemployment, which, even in so-called prosperous times, has become a permanent feature of industry.

Irregular employment is involved in the seasonal character of many trades. But, in the non-seasonal forms of industry, complete "shut-downs," or else "lay-offs" of numbers of employees, are a common feature. Many factors contribute to this situation. Supply may not be adjusted to changing demands, the number of workers in a particular occupation may be excessive, or else, owing to new inventions and more efficient technical processes, fewer workers are needed and so-called "technological employment" results. In addition to these factors, others more complex and obscure result in business cycles with recurring periods of depression.

The Effects of Unemployment on Children. At the National Conference for the 1935 Needs of Children, it was stated by Miss Lenroot that, during 1934, the numbers under the age of sixteen who were dependent on unemployment relief had risen to 7,400,000, and that these constituted more than two-fifths of the whole relief population and *one-sixth* of the total child population of the United States.[1] In 1933 almost a quarter of a million infants began life in families on relief. Besides all these children dependent on more or less inadequate relief, there have been multitudes of children whose parents barely succeeded in doing without public assistance; and finally there have been thousands of vagrant young people, wandering

[1] *New York Times*, Jan. 5, 1935, and Feb. 17, 1935.

about the country as a result of the break-up of their homes. It is probably impossible to paint too dark a picture of what the depression has meant in the lives of the unemployed and of their children, or of its menace to future welfare.[1]

At all times, indeed, whether widespread or not, unemployment is disastrous to family welfare. When a father loses his job, the mother must seek work, as must the older children, who are taken from school. The savings of years are swept away, credit becomes exhausted, and dangerous attempts are made to save on food and other necessities. Cherished possessions, even necessary household goods, are sold. Sometimes lodgers are taken into already restricted quarters, or else the family moves to a cheaper and even less adequate dwelling. Finally, overwhelmed with debt, the family is driven to the humiliation of seeking charitable aid. Even more disastrous than deprivation of material needs is the effect on family morale. Those who are in touch with the daily lives of the unemployed stress the *psychological* aspects of the situation. Miss Wald speaks of "the creeping daily change," the uneasiness and "thickening fog of anxiety and fear" which permeated the neighborhood of Henry Street in the early days of the depression. When uncertainty is succeeded by the dreaded reality, a "black pall" envelops the unemployed worker and his family, a pall which may overspread the rest of their lives.[2] After desperately trying to make ends meet, many families are broken up; in others, which still cling together, the children live in a cloud of fear, insecurity, and hopeless despondency. The greatest tragedy of unemployment is the devastation of family life. No wonder there is a marked increase in illnesses and that recovery is delayed.[3] Even the alarming spread of

[1] While the tendency towards public relief is all to the good, it must be remembered that funds have been insufficient for adequate relief. The situation in 1937 was in many cases particularly bad, because, since the substitution of work relief for direct relief by the federal government, state and local facilities have in many cases found themselves in such difficulties, that essential items have had to be eliminated from relief allowances, and harsh policies have governed the acceptance of applications. Social workers are advocating a renewal of federal grants to states for direct relief, to supplement the federal works program. *New York Times*, Feb. 18, 1937.

[2] This last analogy is used by the Lynds, in describing the effects of unemployment on working-class families in Middletown.

[3] A study made under the auspices of the Milbank Fund revealed 48% more sickness in the families of the unemployed than in families having full-time workers. An analysis made in 1934, under the auspices of the Citizen's Family Welfare Committee in New York, disclosed the fact that in 51% of the families under the care of welfare agencies there was physical illness, and in 16% there was mental illness. *New York Times*, Nov. 11, 1934.

malnutrition among children during the depression is not caused by lack of nourishing food alone, but by the more imponderable aspects of the vicious circle in which unemployment has involved millions of children.[1]

Altogether during the worst of the depression the situation was such that the child-welfare gains of many years were at stake. No wonder Judge Thaxter of the Baltimore Children's Court was led to assert that "the Children's Charter is not worth a snap of the fingers and will never have meaning until jobs are made sacred for parents who want work and will work."[2] As one result of the depression, however, American communities will never again be so wholly unprepared to deal with the social problems involved by unemployment. Hitherto the lessons of depressions have been forgotten as soon as prosperity returned, despite the warnings and explicit recommendations of the more far-sighted. Now, at last, it has been realized that private effort alone cannot cope with large scale unemployment, and that it has become a public responsibility not only to give relief in emergencies, but to provide protection against the hazards of unemployment by means of social insurance.[3]

FAMILY DISORGANIZATION AND CHILD WELFARE

Homes Broken by Death or Desertion. A definite connection between unemployment and the break-up of the home was shown by the increase of 134%, between 1928 and 1931, in the number of men arraigned for deserting wife and children.[4] The phrase *family disorganization* is now used by sociologists to indicate the process undermining the unity and stability of the family, which leads in many cases to *family disintegration.* Family disorganization may be due to death or to discord, and homes may be broken by death or by the extreme results of discord: divorce (including separation and annulment) and

---

[1] Data gathered by the Children's Bureau indicated that in the spring of 1933 about *one-fifth* of all preschool and school children were below par in health. The great proportion suffered from malnutrition; many were anemic or suffered from rickets. At the time of greatest need the funds of health agencies and child-welfare agencies were curtailed.

[2] *New York Times,* Apr. 2, 1931.

[3] The Social Security Act provides a federal-state system of unemployment compensation, based upon a payroll-excise tax upon employers. The widest discretion in setting up laws suited to their own requirements is allowed to the states, and credit up to 90% is allowed to employers on account of taxes paid into strictly state unemployment funds. Federal subsidies of $4,000,000 in 1936, and $49,000,000 annually thereafter, are granted to assist the states in administering their laws.

[4] *New York Times,* Oct. 16, 1932. The *arraignment* statistics represent only a fraction of the actual number of abandonments.

desertion. The actual number of broken homes has shown no appreciable increase since the beginning of the century, because the rapidly increasing divorce rate has been offset by the marked decline in the death-rate.   There are no adequate data on desertion, but it is believed to be on the increase.[1]

The proportion of broken homes for families not yet completed, which means that the wife is forty-four or younger and the husband forty-nine or younger, is about *one* in *seven* or *eight*. They occur about twice as often in cities as in rural districts.[2] About *one* in *six* families with children are still deprived of one parent by death, a proportion which would be much higher in the families of the workers.[3] The loss of a parent is a critical experience in family life, and may have most deleterious effects on a young child's development. The total situation is much more difficult where the mother dies. If, despite a father's death, a mother and children can be kept together, the atmosphere of the home is more nearly normal than when motherless children are left with relatives, or a paid housekeeper. Fresh difficulties may develop if the father remarries. In many cases homes are permanently disintegrated by the death of a mother.

Divorce is discussed in Chapter XVIII. It is the more appropriate to limit ourselves at this point to desertion, since it is so largely confined to the lower economic classes among whom divorce is comparatively rare.[4] Desertion has frequently, though inaccurately, been called "the poor man's divorce." The deserter

[1] W. F. Ogburn, "The Family and Its Functions," *Recent Social Trends*, pp. 688–696. A response to a questionnaire sent in 1928 by the National Desertion Bureau revealed desertion to be a vexing problem in 134 out 145 communities. The probable rate of desertion is 100 per 100,000 urban population; which means about 50,000 annually. A. Cahen, *Statistical Analysis of American Divorce* (1932), pp. 16–17.

[2] The stability of the rural family, its adherence to tradition and resistance to change were noted in several researches carried on by committees of the White House Conference. But it was found that city children were better adjusted than rural children. Large families are the rule, with separation and divorce almost nonexistent. Much time is spent in household tasks with little educational value. The superficial unity of the family, the long hours of leisure time and of work spent together do *not* result in identification of interests. There is more reserve between members of the rural family than in urban families. Children tend to be critical of their parents and do not confide in them. Altogether "the physical proximity of the members of the rural family apparently does not necessarily lead to psychological unity." *The Adolescent in the Family*, p. 29 and see pp. 8–29.

[3] In 9,471 families receiving mothers' aid, over 71% of the fathers had died before 45. *White House Conference, 1930*, p. 334. In 1926 the leading causes of death for men, between 20 and 55, were violence, tuberculosis, pneumonia, and heart disease; for women between 15 and 45, they were tuberculosis, childbirth, and heart disease.

[4] *Desertion* is to be distinguished not only from divorce, but also from *separation* and *non-support*. Separation is a legal arrangement whereby wife and husband live apart. A man who does not provide for his family is guilty of non-support. *Desertion*

does not usually intend to cut himself off finally from his family; indeed, many desert their homes more than once. Desertion is an escape from strain and responsibility, a form of vacation, or moral holiday. Statistics of causes of desertion are misleading, according to Colcord; "there is no one cause or group of causes"; for desertion "is itself only a symptom of some more deeply seated trouble in the family structure."[1] Statistics indicate one significant fact: the presence of children does not act as a deterrent from desertion. Indeed, as is shown by the frequency of what is known as "pregnancy desertion," the birth of a child may be the determining factor in causing desertion.

Alcoholism and Desertion. Alcoholism bears a close relation to desertion. A great majority of so-called "justifiable" deserters have alcoholic wives. Alcoholism in men is so closely related to desertion, that Colcord believes it should frequently be listed as a direct cause; as it is of non-support and many other antisocial acts.[2] Intemperance is itself the result of personality maladjustment or of nervous instability, and provides an escape from feelings of inferiority or from a dreary round of sordid living. The evils due to alcoholism are too well known to require reiteration. It is no exaggeration to say, however, that alcoholism in either parent undermines the foundations of family life. Its effects are probably worse in the far less frequent cases where the mother is addicted to drink. The degeneration of mind and character which result lead not only to unreliability, loss of efficiency, and increasing poverty, but to the destruction of the sense of security so necessary to the normal development of children.[3] Finally, alcoholism is one of the chief causes of anger, brutality, abuse, and cruelty to children, as many tragic incidents known to social workers bear witness.

means the protracted absence from home of either husband or wife without consent of the other. "Desertion" frequently figures as a cause for divorce, but in most such cases it is a manufactured legal arrangement and not the true reason for seeking divorce, nor, usually, a genuine case of desertion.

[1] Joanna Colcord, *Broken Homes* (1919), pp. 21–23.

[2] In a study of 636 case records of the Jewish Social Service Bureau, and 937 of the United Charities of Chicago, Mowrer found that intemperance occurred in connection with 57% of the problems of domestic infelicity, 30% of desertion, 35% of non-support, and 41% where there was a combination of problems. The factor of intemperance was recorded of 30% of the husbands, 3% of the wives, and 17% of both husbands and wives. *Domestic Discord* (1928), p. 45.

[3] A study made by the Children's Bureau of 2,731 delinquent children, belonging to 2,155 families, between 1917 and 1925, showed 41% of fathers, 7% of mothers and 6% of both fathers and mothers, alcoholic at some time. Repeaters were more likely than first offenders to come from alcoholic homes. *The Delinquent Child*, p. 355.

Treatment of Desertion. Desertion is not unknown in rural communities, but it is much more frequent in cities. Earlier treatment focused attention on the apprehension of the deserting husband and on legal proceedings. It is now realized that such disciplinary measures in many cases destroy the last chance of reconciliation. To secure support of wife and children is important, but family rehabilitation is a more desirable and inclusive end. A number of states now grant aid to deserted wives with dependent children. Intensive social case-work in each family where desertion occurs is the best way of coping with the problems involved.

Effects of Family Disorganization on Children. All forms of family disorganization and disintegration are fraught with dangerous possibilities for children. Behavior problems, ranging from minor maladjustments to the extremes of antisocial conduct, develop where family relationships are inharmonious. All studies show that a high percentage of delinquents come from broken homes.[1] Where the home is broken by divorce, separation, or desertion, children not only are the victims of the discord preceding the actual break, but often suffer a sense of inferiority from the open avowal of their parents' disagreements. Studies of delinquents by age and sex groups reveal two significant facts. The importance of the family in the earlier years of the child's life is attested by the much higher rate of broken homes among the younger delinquents; and the lack of normal family life appears to be a factor of greater influence in the delinquency of girls than of boys.[2]

In cases of desertion many unfavorable conditions are usually combined. It is therefore impossible to estimate how far a parent's desertion itself is a factor in the child's behavior. In the *Natural History of a Delinquent Career*, already alluded to, the father's frequent desertion rendered necessary the absence of the mother at work during much of Sidney's childhood. She had been able to exercise much closer supervision over an older son who showed no tendencies to delinquency. This fact

[1] For a summary of studies see Elmer, *Family Adjustment and Social Change*, pp. 173–199.

[2] Maude Miner, *Slavery of Prostitution* (1919), p. 54, reports that, in a study of 878 homes of young prostitutes, 60% had been broken by desertion, divorce, or death. Juvenile Courts Statistics in 1929 showed 33% of the boys and 52% of the girls were not living with their own parents, while other studies give estimates showing that 60% and 67% of delinquent girls came from broken homes. Estimates given for boys are uniformly lower. Among girls committed for sexual immorality and for larceny, an unusually large proportion came from homes broken by death, more often the death of the mother when the girl is a sexual delinquent.

constituted the most significant difference between the early environments of the brothers.

MOTHERS WHO MUST EARN

The Contribution of Mothers to Family Support. In Chapter XV further consideration is given to the work of women, and to the notable increase in the number of married women in gainful occupations. At this point but one aspect of the situation demands attention: the effect on children where the mother is forced to become an industrial wage earner in order to contribute to family support. Only a very small proportion of married women enter industry because factory work affords companionship, and interests them more than housekeeping. The vast majority work because they *must:* they work to supplement their husband's inadequate wages or because their husbands are unemployed, ill, dead, or have deserted.

A Philadelphia study of 728 *mothers* showed *six* reasons as immediately responsible for wage earning: insufficient wage of the husband, 29%; death of the husband, 22%; illness of the husband, 14%; desertion by the husband, 13%; non-support by the husband, 11%; preference for employment outside the home, 11%.[1] Other studies substantiate the fact that married women-breadwinners include a large proportion of mothers, and that, of these, many have children under five.[2] Dire need and the desperate struggle to make ends meet is the reason which drives most of these women to assume the double burden of outside work and caring for their families.

Infant Mortality and the Employment of Mothers. Miss Wald tells of an unemployed man and his pregnant wife slowly starving themselves, in order that their children might have most of such food as the wife was able to secure, through part-time factory work. She became ill, but insisted "I've got to keep my job till labor pains begin." She did; and the baby died at birth. This is but one of thousands of instances where the extra-domestic employment of mothers was in all probability a contributory factor in causing the death of babies. In the eight cities investigated by the Children's Bureau the mortality rate for infants of mothers who, during pregnancy, had been gainfully employed, away from home, was 1.8 times

[1] Gwendolyn Hughes Berry, "Mothers in Industry," *Annals of the American Academy of Political and Social Science*, Vol. CXLIII (May, 1929), p. 315.

[2] "Family Status of Breadwinning Women in Four Selected Cities," *Women's Bureau Bulletin*, No. 41 (1925) and "What the Wage-Earning Woman Contributes to Family Support," *Women's Bureau Bulletin*, No. 75 (1929).

the rate of those whose mothers had not been employed.[1] Studies both here and abroad show the mortality to be particularly high when mothers work outside up to the period of confinement, and return to work soon afterwards.[2]

Where babies die when their mothers go to work and stop nursing them, it is very probable that artificial feeding has not been undertaken in a sufficiently expert and sanitary manner. The exact effect of the employment of mothers on infant welfare is, indeed, almost impossible to determine; for poverty, ignorance, malnutrition, and lack of sanitary facilities are all likely to be found in the households of mothers who work. A definite correlation has been found between infant mortality and low wages of the father.[3] Where family incomes were more adequate and living conditions better, the death-rate of babies whose mothers were at work was not nearly so high as in communities, such as Manchester and New Bedford, where there was much poverty and many mothers were illiterate and foreign-born.[4]

The Manchester study also showed an unusually high number of stillbirths among mothers working away from home; but nothing definite appears to be known as yet of the effect of mothers' employment on the incidence of stillbirths. A very definite impression is gained, however, from reading the case histories included in these studies, that overwork was at least one cause of the many miscarriages, premature births, and stillbirths.[5] Reports both here and abroad corroborate Katherine Anthony's observation that, among breadwinning mothers, "abortions are common and unsuccessful attempts are even more common."[6]

[1] "Causal Factors in Infant Mortality," *Children's Bureau Publication*, No. 142 (1925), p. 131. For the infants whose mothers were employed at home it was only one-sixth higher than when mothers had not been employed.

[2] In Manchester, N. H., of 110 babies whose mothers went to work before they were 4 months old, 33 died in their first year, a mortality rate of 277.3, as compared to 121.7 for the remainder of a group of 1,389 babies who had survived at least 2 weeks. "Infant Mortality: The Results of a Field Study in Manchester, New Hampshire," *Children's Bureau Publication*, No. 20 (1917), p. 53.

[3] In Manchester, when the chief breadwinner's earnings fell to $450, infant mortality rose to 242.9, almost one death to each *four* births. As the wages of the father increased, there was a consistent fall in the infant-mortality rate. *Ibid.*, p. 45.

[4] "Infant Mortality: Results of a Field Study in New Bedford, Massachusetts," *Children's Bureau Publication*, No. 68 (1920). The infant mortality rate for artificially-fed babies of foreign-born mothers was one and a half times as high as among artificially-fed infants of native mothers; it was highest of all among the illiterate Portuguese.

[5] Take, for example, a mother of 35 in her *fifteenth* pregnancy, who in 13 years had had 14 pregnancies, 6 of which resulted in miscarriages. The doctor attributed these to overwork in the mill. She had also lost three babies from gastrointestinal complaints. *Children's Bureau Publication*, No. 20, p. 94, and see other cases, pp. 84–100.

[6] *Mothers Who Must Earn* (1914), p. 154.

Children Deprived of Their Mother's Care. Social workers tell of the heroic efforts made by wage-earning mothers to keep their homes clean, their children fed and decently clad. But it is often impossible for them to secure adequate care for their young children during the hours they are at work. There are, as we saw, few day nurseries, and such as exist are frequently too far from the working mother's home for her to take advantage of their services. Sometimes a relative or a neighbor helps, or older brothers and sisters provide intermittent care when free from school or work. Cases are reported of babies left by themselves with a bottle of milk tied round their necks, but in general the care provided for children under five is more adequate than for children over five.[1] Miss Addams tells of listening to tragic reminiscences of children maimed and burnt because "I had no one to leave them with when I went to work."[2] "The first three crippled children we encountered in our neighborhood had all been injured while their mothers were at work; one had fallen out of a third story window, another had been burned, and the third had a curved spine due to the fact that for three years he had been tied . . . to the leg of the kitchen table, only released at noon by his older brother who hastily ran in from a neighboring factory to share his lunch with him."[3] A day nursery was early established at Hull House, and it was the death of one of the nursery children which gave Miss Addams "one of the most piteous revelations of the futility of the . . . attempt [made by mothers] to both support and nurture their children." Five-year-old Goosie fell from a roof when handing clothes-pins to his mother at six one morning. When asked after the funeral if anything could be done for her, the poor mother said: "If you would give me my wages for to-morrow, I would not go to work in the factory at all. I would like to stay at home all day and hold the baby. Goosie was always asking me to take him and I never had time."[4]

The health of many of these working mothers is very bad: they suffer from hernia, varicose veins, aching feet, bad teeth, and from the results of frequent pregnancies. The situation

[1] One study reports a definite tendency for mothers to stay at home where there are very young children or where families are large. *Many* women were found to earn during *part* of their married life, rather than a *few* earning for the *whole* of it. "Children of Working Mothers in Philadelphia, Part I, The Working Mothers," *Children's Bureau Publication*, No. 204 (1931).

[2] *Second Twenty Years at Hull House* (1930), p. 67.

[3] *Twenty Years at Hull House*, pp. 167–168.   [4] *Ibid.*, pp. 173-174.

is even worse where mothers work at night so that they may care for their children by day. Not only must the mother be absent in the evening, "the only time when the workingman's household can gather together," but, in most cases, "the failure of the home job is clearly enough evidenced by the typical night-worker's home—the untidy and disordered rooms, the unkempt, neglected, sickly-looking children, the mother a weary and irritable drudge whose task as her vitality fails grows more and more hopeless." Many of these mothers are irritable at the slightest annoyance; "their children are not only not mothered, never cherished . . . , they are nagged and buffeted." The mother is forced to neglect them despite her utmost efforts. The older children run wild while the mother sleeps. The situation is particularly full of hazard for girls. "In other cases the results of the mother's night work is to throw premature and disproportionate burdens on the older children."[1]

An excessive demand on children for services in the home was found, by Hughes, to be also a result of the wage earning of mothers. In several studies, the school records of these children are shown to suffer, children often being kept out of school to help at home. In a Chicago study a clear connection was indicated in some cases between behavior problems and the employment of mothers.[2] In two cities it was found that one-fourth of the delinquent children came from homes where the mother was employed.[3] Altogether it is evident that under present conditions, whole-time employment of working-class mothers is undesirable from the standpoint of child welfare. More adequate wages for the fathers would relieve many from wage earning, as would a more extensive system of mothers' aid.

It must be remembered, however, that the absence of the mother from her home need have no such deleterious effects were adequate substitutes provided; day nurseries, supervised playgrounds, and collective devices relieving mothers of some of the heaviest household labor should make it possible for the mothers of all but the youngest children to work, at least part-time, without harm to their children.

[1] "Employment of Women at Night," *Women's Bureau Bulletin*, No. 64 (1928), pp. 54–55.
[2] "Children of Wage-Earning Mothers," *Children's Bureau Publication*, No. 102, (1922).
[3] *The Delinquent Child*, p. 354.

BAD HOUSING

Prevalence of Bad Housing. The fundamental influence of housing conditions on family life is obvious. Yet, in 1935, 36% of the housing of the United States was definitely sub-standard: 6,000,000 non-farm homes, and 5,000,000 farm homes were of a character "to injure the health, endanger the safety and morals and interfere with the normal life of the inhabitants."[1] Appalling conditions prevail not only in city slums, but in poverty-stricken rural districts, where there are numerous unpainted two-room shacks with broken windows and the walls covered with newspapers.[2] There is great overcrowding and lack of sufficient light and air. Sanitary deficiencies are far more frequent in small towns and rural districts. Frequently there are no sanitary facilities of any kind. Water becomes contaminated, and the possibilities of contagion are obvious. The great prevalence of hookworm in certain areas gives evidence of the degree of soil contamination.

Some of the larger cities, such as New York and Boston, have 100% city water and sewer connections, but most communities still contain areas without city water and with no sewers. Filthy back-yard privies serve two to a dozen families, who must also share the same well or outside hydrant. Even where conditions are not so extreme, the majority of tenements lack adequate bathing facilities and sufficient sanitary toilets. Garbage disposal is frequently inadequate, screens are lacking to keep out flies and mosquitoes, while vermin infest the walls of dirty and dilapidated structures. Characteristic of bad housing in cities are: overcrowding; the lack of light, particularly sunlight; lack of ventilation; and incessant noise. Some families live in dark, damp basement rooms, many more are crowded together in two or three dimly-lit, ill-smelling rooms, some of which are without windows opening to the outer air, while others open on narrow courts or mere cracks between walls.[3]

[1] Edith Elmer Wood, "Slums and Blighted Areas of the United States," *Bulletin*, No. 1, of the Housing Division of the Federal Emergency Administration of Public Works (1935).

[2] Secretary Wallace recently stated that one-third of the farmers of the United States lived under conditions far worse than the peasantry of Europe, and that he had never seen among the latter such abject poverty as exists in the cotton states from Arkansas to the East Coast. *New York Times Magazine*, Jan. 3, 1937.

[3] In 1900, New York City had 350,000 rooms which did not open to the outer air: of these, Edith Wood estimated some 200,000 to 250,000 remained in 1931. *Recent Trends in American Housing* (1931), p. 4.

Effects on the Health of Children. Under conditions such as these, even the best and most devoted parents cannot secure normal home life nor adequately protect the health of their children. As Wood says, "children cannot thrive where flowers have not sunlight enough to bloom."[1] Lack of sunlight causes rickets and facilitates the spread of tuberculosis. Every germ disease spreads most easily where there is overcrowding and lack of cleanliness. The Children's Bureau studies of infant mortality showed that a high rate accompanied specific housing defects. The Baltimore study dealt with a sufficient number of cases to show that the rate rose with increasing congestion. In Johnstown, the infant death-rate was higher where water was carried in by hand, where there were no bath tubs, where there was dampness and uncleanliness, where the babies slept in unventilated rooms, or in a bed with others; and the death-rate also rose in proportion to the number sleeping in one room. The poverty and low standards of living associated with bad housing are undoubtedly contributory factors. Apparently, however, some of the responsibility for infant mortality may be directly attributed to housing conditions.

Only recently have the deleterious effects of noise begun to receive attention. Normal mental and emotional development are impossible when young children are deprived of sufficient quiet and undisturbed sleep. In crowded tenements, where there is no escape from noise coming from neighboring apartments, from factories, street traffic, and elevated railroads, there is never a quiet minute day or night. It has recently been suggested that the great increase in the gangster type in the last twenty years may be due to the nervous and emotional instability of those who all their lives have been bombarded by noise. Significantly enough, some of the highest delinquency rates in New York City, in 1926, were found among children in four small blocks of wretched housing under an elevated railroad structure. On the basis of these and other findings a Crime Commission stated that "the relation of bad housing to delinquency has been clearly indicated."[2]

[1] *Ibid.*, p. 5.
[2] Wood, *op. cit.*, p. 292. Not only is there a definite relation between noise and emotional response in early infancy, but the pressure of the brain is raised by loud noises. Miss Wood points out that, before immigration was restricted, the newly arrived usually took over the worst housing. Only in the past few years have children born in the worst slum areas come to maturity in the same surroundings, with very little likelihood of ever escaping. She believes that this situation may be linked with the increase in crime.

Bad Housing in Relation to Delinquency. In addition to its harmful effects on health and emotional stability, bad housing constitutes a menace to morals, through overcrowding and lack of privacy. A situation of peculiar danger to girls is created where, in addition to parents and children, one or more lodgers are crowded into a few rooms.[1] Many young prostitutes admit to having been assaulted at the age of twelve or thirteen by lodgers or by drunken or vicious relatives, uncles, and even fathers.[2]

Many boys and girls are led into delinquency by the life of the streets to which they escape from wretched home surroundings. Where family connections bring nothing but disgrace, young people are prevented by shame from making friends with others more fortunate than themselves. Even where actual delinquency does not result under bad home conditions, overcrowding and lack of privacy undermine family life; nervous tension is inevitable, and with it discord and strained relationships. Slovenly habits are all but inevitable where there is not even room for all to sit down to meals, where no one has any place of his own in which to keep his property or be alone.

Problems of Housing Reform. Organized agitation for the improvement of housing began in the nineties, and regulative and restrictive laws have done something to eliminate some of the worst features of bad housing; but this is only the beginning: to forbid a bad house does not provide a good one. The housing situation was found by Wood substantially the same in 1931 as in 1917. In 1931 President Hoover's Conference on Home Building and Home Ownership described American housing as "the largest mass of obsolete and discredited equipment" in the country, and reported that no new and desirable types of houses had been built in recent years at a cost within reach of two-thirds of the population. One root of the difficulty is to be found in the fact that only those who can afford to build, if not satisfied with what is offered, are in a position to make an effective demand for good housing. The laws of supply and demand cannot be relied upon to force private enterprise to furnish acceptable housing for any but the favored few. Moreover, as matters now stand, private enterprise cannot possibly furnish new housing in big cities at a cost which the

---

[1] A sudden doubling of the illegitimacy rate for Cleveland, in 1920, was largely attributed to the particularly crowded conditions prevailing in the post-war period.

[2] There has been an actual increase in cases of incest due to overcrowding during the depression. J. Prentice Murphy "Children in the New Deal," *Annals of the American Academy*, Vol. CLXXVI (Nov., 1934), p. 129.

masses can pay.[1] The situation is only susceptible of improvement by means of subsidies from public agencies. Such agencies can cut costs and can borrow money more cheaply. Except for a subsidy, public low-rent housing may be financed very largely by private capital; but the initiative must be public, as are the ownership and operation. Already by 1930 in Europe, notable developments in housing reform had taken place. In England, Germany, Belgium, Holland, Sweden, and Austria, 70% of all new dwellings had been erected through government aid. The best European practice attacks the needs of the lowest and middle economic thirds at the same time; while the worst houses are being vacated and torn down in the course of slum-clearance, the number of those who can live in new and better homes is increased by non-commercial financing schemes under government auspices.

The Development of a Public Housing Program. There have been a number of experiments in this country in new methods of financing housing and in the provision of state or municipal housing, but the needs of the lowest income groups have been, until very recently, utterly neglected. The federal government made its first significant attack upon the housing problem in 1932, when the Reconstruction Finance Corporation was authorized to loan money for low-cost housing. In 1933 the Housing Division of the Public Works Administration made further funds available for slum-clearance and for the building and operating of low-rent multiple dwellings. In the same year the Tennessee Valley Authority embarked on the construction of new housing for rent to workers. In 1934, the Federal Housing Administration was set up to help in the refinancing and construction of housing for those with moderate incomes. In 1935, the Works Progress Administration and the Resettlement Administration were established. The demolition of old buildings is undertaken by the former, while the latter is building low-cost housing in suburban areas adjacent to industrial centers. In 1936 the Wagner-Ellenbogen Bill, creating a permanent Federal Housing Authority, was defeated in the House, but in 1937 the Wagner-Steagall Housing Bill was passed on the closing day of Congress, after Senate and House had agreed upon a compromise measure.[2] The bill authorized a Federal

---

[1] The lowest rent at which this can be done is $11 per room, while $6 a room is the highest that most workers can pay. Evans Clark, "The Subsidy of Low Rental Housing," *Annals of the American Academy*, Vol. CXC (March, 1937).

[2] *New York Times*, Aug. 21, 22, 1937.

Housing Authority, in the Department of the Interior, to issue $500,000,000 in bonds during the next three years. This money is to be used for loans to state and local housing authorities for low-rent dwellings and slum-clearance. In each project, rents are to be kept low by means of an annual subsidy to which the local community would contribute not less than 20%, the government to pay the rest. The local housing authority would also contribute at least 10% of the construction cost, the federal government lending the balance. Construction costs must not exceed more than $1,000 a room, or $4,000 a family unit, except in cities of 500,000 population or more. In these, the limit would be $1,250 a room, and $5,000 a family unit. Not more than 10% of the federal funds may be spent in any one state.

The lead taken by the federal government has stimulated state and city interest in housing. Already, by 1936, twenty states had passed housing authority laws, and municipal housing authorities in a number of cases were enlisting federal aid in housing projects. New York City's first venture in public housing, First Houses, was opened to 120 families on December 3, 1935.[1] An average monthly rental of $6.50 a room is being paid; baths, kitchens, and refrigeration are in modern style, and much of the land on which First Houses is erected has been left open for garden-courts, playgrounds, and walks. Two other low-rental projects are nearing completion, in 1937, in New York, and the experience of tenants in First Houses augurs well for their success. There is a marked improvement in the health of children since they moved to First Houses, and the tenants take great pride in the neatness and cleanliness of their premises. When the PWA's Housing Division concludes its program in 1938, it will have supplied help to fifty-one projects in thirty-five cities. Under the Resettlement Administration, three "green belt" suburban communities have been established near Washington, Cincinnati, and Milwaukee; over 6,000 houses for rural families are built or under construction, and the program for subsistence homesteads, begun under the FERA, is being continued. The first such project was the Reedsville Experimental Community in West Virginia, or Arthurdale, as it is usually called, where the center of community

[1] As Langdon Post, then chairman of the New York Housing Authority, said: "The name First Houses is appropriate, in that these are the first dwellings which are predicated upon the philosophy that sunshine, space, and air are minimum housing requirements to which every American is entitled, no matter how small his income." *New York Times*, Nov. 21, 1935.

interest is an excellent progressive school and the various social and health services tributary to it. A beginning is therefore being made which promises well for the future.

COMMERCIAL AMUSEMENTS

The Enormous Increase in Organized Commercial Amusements. Approximately 40% of the time of most young people under eighteen is spent in leisure-time activities.[1] The potent influence of agencies providing recreation is thus obvious; and growing concern is felt over the dangers inherent in commercial amusements, dangers which are greatest in the case of the socially handicapped: those young people whose home life provides no opportunities for creative activity and imaginative release, for adventure and recreation in its fullest meaning. In the absence of community facilities for recreation, this neglected field has been seized upon by those whose motive is profit, irrespective of social health. There is perhaps no clearer indication of the unsatisfactory quality of contemporary life than the mushroom growth of commercial amusement, whose purveyors are ever alert to profit from the craving for thrills and excitement.[2]

The Influence of Motion Pictures on Children. With the publication, in 1933, of the results of a four-year investigation, under the auspices of the Payne Fund and at the instigation of the Motion Picture Research Council, accurate and detailed knowledge has become available with regard to the influence of movies on children. Results obtained by an earlier study of 10,000 Chicago children, conducted in 1929 by Alice Miller Mitchell, have been corroborated and supplemented, in a manner calculated to disturb all who have the welfare of children or the future of society at heart.

Almost the whole juvenile population is subject to the influence of the movies; 11,000,000 children under fourteen attend weekly. Socially handicapped children are drawn even more irresistibly than others to these moving, talking, illustrated story books.[3] Excessive attendance at movies is characteristic

[1] The uses of leisure are given fuller consideration in Chapter XXIV.

[2] In 1930 it was estimated that $500,000,000 yearly was spent on commercial amusements. Slightly over half of this went for theaters, motion pictures, cabarets, and vaudeville; the rest, on dance halls, pool rooms, amusement parks, carnivals, and steamer excursions.

[3] Mrs. Mitchell found that auto-riding was the only form of recreation having a greater appeal with all the groups she studied; Boy and Girl Scouts, unselected grade and high school boys and girls, and juvenile delinquents. Among the latter group, begging and petty larceny are frequently due to an insatiable desire for the world of make-believe. Two little girls of 12 and 13 prostituted themselves for 15¢ and 20¢,

of groups where children are undirected and left to themselves without other recreational outlets.   The frank preferences expressed by children of all groups for "blood-dripping murderous" movies, for "red-hot romances," for movies which "make your blood surge" and "arouse your senses," are not to be wondered at, when it is realized, as disclosed by the Payne Fund studies, that between 75% and 80% of all pictures deal with love, sex, and crime.

For the most part, it is a sensational, vulgar and tawdry distortion of life which children eagerly drink in, with the apparent sanction of adults.[1]   The majority of characters are young, wealthy, unmarried, absurdly overdressed, with no useful occupation, and lacking in social goals and ideals.   The seriousness of the situation is fully realized, however, only when it is discovered that children absorb correct information and misinformation alike, with an average retention of 70%, more than twice as high as the retention of text-book knowledge; and that the vivid imagery of the screen has an expansive quality which may subsequently bring retention as high as 100%. Moving pictures are thus proved to be one of the most powerful instruments of education, an instrument which, instead of being used to aid in the development of mind and character in accordance with social ideals, is making difficult, if not impossible, of realization the aims which consciously directed educational agencies are striving to obtain.

The definitely deleterious effects on children's sleep, and the emotional overstimulation and the nervous shocks frequently resulting from moving pictures were also studied.   Harmful effects of fright pictures were mitigated by the presence of a parent or sympathetic adult, a finding which makes more significant the fact that so great a proportion of children go unaccompanied by parents, either alone or with companions of their own age.[2] Definite evidence was also secured to prove that moving pictures

in order to acquire the price of admission to a movie theater. Delinquent children, both boys and girls, wander from lobby to lobby to find "de pitchure wid de biggest kick." *Children and the Movies* (1929), p. 58.

[1] In 115 pictures chosen at random, 59 murders or homicides were attempted or committed, 406 crimes committed, and 43 more attempted. In 22, illicit love was the goal of the leading character, and bedroom scenes form the largest single classification under the head of settings.

[2] In the White House Conference study reported in *The Young Child in the Home*, a larger number of children were found to go to the movies with their parents, than was the case in the Payne Fund study. For example, at 8 years old, in the latter, 44% of boys and 57% of girls go with parents; in the former, in the 8 to 9 group, 71% do so. Pp. 261–264.

had both direct and indirect influence on the formation of delinquent patterns of behavior.

Among distorted impressions given by motion pictures, one of the most potentially harmful is the assumption that easy money, luxury, and extravagance are the right of everyone. The appeal of a seemingly glamorous life of ease was shown to have played havoc in the case of many young delinquents and marginal delinquents, and to have been a contributory cause in sex delinquency in the case of girls. In their portrayal of criminal methods, the movies proved themselves to be a veritable crime school. Particularly striking were the results obtained from an intensive study of one of the most deteriorated and overcrowded immigrant sections of New York City, where the dimly lit "dumps," as the cheapest motion picture houses were called, were the scene of a variety of sexual practices, and afforded opportunities for contact between boys and experienced criminals.

At present the finer types of pictures are not the most profitable, and altogether the problem of reform is one of great complexity. Nevertheless vigorous efforts are now being made, not only to censor unsuitable pictures, but to improve the tastes and standards of the public.[1] Progress has already been made in many school systems in improving standards of taste and judgment and in fostering intelligent criticism among boys and girls. Good pictures are shown in many schools, and other forms of community recreation are being developed. The chief safeguard for children is the careful supervision of their recreation by home and school, and the provision of numerous worthwhile leisure-time pursuits. Even so the quality of moving pictures must be improved if even the best-cared-for children are not to suffer in some degree from their influence.

Pool Rooms and Dance Halls. Antedating as they do the more recent forms of commercial amusement, pool rooms and dance halls still play an important part in the lives of less fortunate young people. In 1925, a comparative survey of Chicago's recreational centers disclosed that 2,020 of these were commercial, 881 were private centers such as settlements and clubs, and 263 were public institutions such as libraries and playgrounds. Classified by type, billiard and pool halls

---

[1] The Catholic Church has been particularly active in "a holy crusade against the abuses of motion pictures." A Papal Encyclical, dated June 29, 1936, gave full recognition to the influence of moving pictures and urged that they "be directed towards the noble end of promoting the highest ideals and the truest standards of life." *New York Times*, July 3, 1936.

far outstripped the rest, there being 1,098; boys clubs, including Scout troops, came second, 463; the movies third, 381; and dance halls fourth, 264. The commercial centers claimed an annual attendance of 171,000,000; the public, 44,000,000; and the private, 15,400,000. If well conducted, pool rooms afford opportunities for wholesome recreation, but far too often they are gambling centers, "booze joints," and hang-outs for gangs, where young men between sixteen and twenty-one concoct burglaries and other crimes.

Public dance halls also meet real recreational needs. They offer the only social opportunity for many country boys and girls coming into town for amusement, for many young people at work away from their childhood homes, and for those whose parents through poverty and ignorance make no provision for their social needs. Conditions are by no means always bad. Legislation in more than half the states, and ordinances in a large number of cities regulate the operation of dance halls and provide for their supervision. Sometimes "hostesses" are present, not only to supervise the behavior of the patrons, but to engage in case-work where this is necessary. One of the chief difficulties nowadays is to protect young people from the dangers of the unregulated dance halls and the road-houses situated outside the jurisdiction of city ordinances. The supervision of such places under state laws has proved very difficult. Regulated city dance halls are often used as recruiting places for roadhouses, which have become all too easy of access for those who use automobiles. Difficulty has also been encountered in interesting sufficiently the parents of dance-hall frequenters. Large numbers of mothers were found to be wholly ignorant of their daughters' whereabouts in the evenings.

Only where home, school, and community combine to provide wholesome recreation are young people afforded protection from the temptations inherent in commercial forms of amusement. City recreation programs in charge of specialists now include athletics, dramatics, handicraft, music, and dancing.[1] Emphasis is being placed on active participation in games and sports, a most important matter since commercial facilities provide for so much passive amusement. There has also been a notable development in boys' and girls' organizations. The

[1] The results of programs of supervised play are noteworthy. In Flint, Michigan, for example, in two years of operation, traffic fatalities among young people have been virtually eliminated and juvenile delinquency reduced 70%. *New York Times*, Nov. 29, 1936.

educational value and far-reaching implications of such an organization as the Boy Scouts is obvious. In its first quarter-century of existence, 5,000,000 boys have come under its influence. In 1930 there was still only *one* playground for each 3,000 city children. But recent years have seen a vast expansion in recreational facilities. Statistics gathered by the National Recreation Association show that they have more than doubled in the last ten years.[1] Rural youth on the other hand are limited in their recreational and social contacts. For them, even more perhaps than for urban young people, there is still urgent need for the extension and wider support of public and private leisure-time, character-forming movements.

THE CHILDREN OF IMMIGRANTS

The Peculiar Problems of the Foreign-born and Their Children.[2] Those of foreign birth and parentage form a comparatively small proportion of delinquents and adult criminals. But the situation is apparently reversed for the *native-born* children of *foreign* parents.[3] The conflict between the traditions and standards of an old country and of the new strange land to which the parents have been transplanted leads to added strains in parent-child relationships, to social maladjustment, and to delinquency.

In the decade prior to the World War, well over a million immigrants were being admitted yearly, and an increasing proportion of these were peasants from Southern and South-eastern Europe, drawn by the demand for cheap labor, and by the hope of making a better living and securing greater opportunities for their children. Comparatively little has been

[1] *New York Times*, Aug. 30, 1936. By 1936, over 2,200 communities were supporting recreational programs, as against 748 ten years before. In 1936, there were 21,000 publicly owned baseball diamonds, bathing beaches, golf courses, ice-skating arenas, tennis courts, and recreation buildings available for public use without charge or for a nominal sum. The use of federal emergency funds, first through the Civil Works Administration, and now through the Works Progress Administration, has aided much in the development. Many of the trained leaders have been on the WPA payrolls, there being 45,000 leaders in 1936 as against 17,177 in 1925.

[2] Limitations of space forbid inclusion of the special problems of Negro families and of Negro children, in a white society which discriminates against its colored citizens. It is obvious that so far as Negro children feel themselves inferior the difficulties of social adjustment would be accentuated. Deficiencies in Negro family life are found to be reflected in lower personality-adjustment ratings in the study reported in *The Adolescent in the Family*, p. 304. Several sections of the *Young Child in the Home*, pp. 269–332, are devoted to home facilities and child care among Negro families.

[3] In the Gluecks' study of 1,000 delinquent boys, four-fifths were native-born, but 7 in 10 of these had foreign-born parents.

done to facilitate the adjustment to American life of these vast numbers of aliens, with their differing languages and customs. For the most part, the tendency has been for them to form colonies in the poorer sections of large cities. Very frequently they have been exploited, and their initiation into American life too often comes solely through contact with the disorganized social conditions of the blighted areas in which they have been forced to settle.

In addition to the usual disadvantages of poverty-stricken working-class families, many of the foreign-born are, in Miss Addams' words, "pathetically stupid" in meeting the requirements of congested urban life, accustomed as they are to the life of peasants in rural communities.[1] The mothers are often overburdened with work, particularly where a number of boarders are taken. Among the Serbo-Croatians, for example, the rooms of a married couple are frequently filled with beds for unmarried male lodgers. The women do more laborious work than any other group of foreign-born women, and significantly enough the infant-mortality rate among them was higher than that for any other group.[2]

Strains in Family Relationships. In a disproportionately large number of immigrant families, children are deprived of the conditions necessary for healthy development through the poverty and ignorance of their parents. From the standpoint of mental hygiene the situation presents even greater problems. These children go to the public schools, it is true, but other influences are at work, in the streets and pool rooms, the dance halls and moving-picture theaters, which too often nullify any impressions made by the school. It is impossible for the foreign-born parents to serve as guides and interpreters to their children in the bewildering and complex life of a strange civilization, particularly since they are themselves so frequently the victims

[1] Accounts of the work of both Miss Addams and Miss Wald among the foreign-born are of the greatest interest. Encouragement given to the cultural resources of the immigrants, to their native crafts and skills, helped in revealing foreign-born parents to their children, and in encouraging closer sympathy and understanding between the generations.

[2] The rate was 263.9 as against 171.3 for all immigrant women. In the case of one mother whose six children, including two stillborn, were all dead, the doctor had advised her after the last child's birth to give up her 20 boarders. The baby died of inanition, caused, it was thought, because she had not stopped working soon enough; cutting wood and carrying wood and water and coal and cases of beer on her back had been "a great strain." The father was furious, and showed his disrespect for a woman who could not produce children who would live, by wearing a red tie at the baby's funeral. "Infant Mortality: Results of a Field Study in Johnstown, Pa.," *Children's Bureau Publication*, No. 9 (1915), p. 83.

of its most corrupt aspects. Normal parent-child relationships are, indeed, quite often reversed, and the young people, feeling undue security in their shallow and distorted "Americanism," consider themselves better qualified than their parents to understand and cope with the world about them.

Anxious to escape ridicule and align themselves with American children, sons and daughters who retain some degree of affectionate regard for one or both parents are involved in emotional conflict. Ashamed of their homes and of their parents with their "outlandish," old-world customs,—of the mother, for instance, in her peasant dress,—they easily develop an attitude of scornful superiority to family traditions and ideals. Family unity and integration become impossible; and the gap which always exists between the generations is enormously widened in the case of adolescent children of immigrant families.

The situation of the parents is in many cases tragic. They tend very naturally to adopt one of two courses. Sometimes, finding older methods of control useless, they allow their children to go their own way, with little or no attempt at guidance. More frequently, however, the parents, and particularly the father, endeavor to reassert parental authority and dominate the children by means of repressive or even cruel discipline. Italian and Jewish girls are often strictly guarded until they enter an early marriage arranged by their parents. But in many cases girls rebel against overstrict or harsh parents, with their denial of requests for American clothes, for spending money, freedom, and recreation. Even when boys and girls are earning, their wages are very often claimed as a matter of course by foreign-born parents. Many run away from home or else resort to petty thievery. Unless given intelligent help, the girls frequently become sexual delinquents.

Education is the only service America has been eager to bestow upon the immigrants, the majority of whom are equally eager to avail themselves of these new advantages for their children. Much remains to be done, however, before the schools measure up to their opportunity with children of the foreign-born. The magnitude of the task is of course appalling. In New York City, for example, in 1934, 33% of the population were foreign-born. One of the most urgent needs, according to Berle, is the creation of a corps of teachers who are linguists and so able to get in touch with foreign-born parents in their own tongue.[1] Only in this way can effective coöperation be

[1] "Handicaps in Schools," *New York Times*, Dec. 30, 1934.

secured between home and school; the parents would get accurate knowledge of their children's school experiences; and children could no longer escape the control which parents alone can exercise. Highly successful results were obtained in this way in a Boston school. Through effective case-work begun with children of the foreign-born in their preschool years, it should be possible for the schools to give every child a course fitted to his needs.

CHILDHOOD AND OLD AGE

The Problem of the Aged under Modern Conditions. Frequent strains in family relationships are due to the residence, with the family group, of parents of either husband or wife. The presence of any but the wise, serene, and well-adjusted grandparent may be the cause of marital maladjustments and react very harmfully on the younger members of the family.[1] For this reason, and because the problems of old age are closely bound up with other problems discussed in this chapter, they are given brief consideration at this point.

A number of factors have contributed to render the position of the aged increasingly difficult. Older family members have always been most fortunate when, owing to their possessions, or to the number of children and relatives who contribute to their support, they are not felt to be an economic burden. Particularly is this the case where they have been held in high regard and even reverenced as representing the wisdom of the social group. Where age brings wisdom, and skill in craftsmanship is the fruit of years of experience, the elders are regarded as valuable members of the community.

The contrast is marked between such a situation and the position of most old people in the rapidly changing and predominantly urban civilization of to-day. Far from being reverenced as heads of families and consulted on all important matters, they find themselves regarded as old-fashioned, incapable of comprehending modern problems, and deprived of authority either social or intellectual. The process of increasing estrangement from children and grandchildren is most evident in the case of the foreign-born, where cultural adjustments to life in a new country proceed rapidly for the young, and slowly, if at all, for the old. But, in a lesser degree, the same process is at work with the majority of the aged to-day, though least of all for those who remain mentally alert throughout life.

[1] Most harmful results often follow when grandparents interfere with the discipline of children, which should, within the home, be left entirely in the hands of parents.

Many older people, feeling themselves slighted, are in a state of chronic resentment; feeling themselves unwanted and a burden, they become irritable and self-assertive. This is particularly the case where they are financially dependent on the family of a son or daughter; most of all, where their dependence brings hardship or deprivation to children or grandchildren. Such a situation is hard for the able-bodied and well-adjusted; but a large proportion of the aged are in failing health, if not actually ill; and personality maladjustments become more acute in the absence of useful and interesting occupations and with increasing loneliness and loss of hope.[1]

The psychological difficulties presented by the care of aged people in the homes of their children are much accentuated by economic factors. Families now being so much smaller, there are fewer among whom the burden of supporting the aged may be distributed. Financial assistance to parents hampers the education of the children, deprives them of other opportunities, and may even send them earlier to work. The situation is less acute on farms where the old may still find useful work and where there is often more room for them. In crowded city flats, the presence of an unoccupied, querulous, and often invalid grandparent may prove an intolerable added strain in an already difficult family life.[2] In cases of prolonged illness the care of an aged parent may become a burden so great as to lead to family disorganization. Altogether "there must be a very happy concurrence of a great many favorable factors to make the support of aged parents by children a possibility which should not react in a very harmful way upon the younger family groups."[3] And yet, outside of institutions for the aged, 40% of those over 65 were supported primarily by their children, in 1930.

The problems of the aged have been aggravated by the fact that the number of those over 65 has greatly increased. There has been a *relative* increase due to a falling birth-rate and reduction of immigration, but also an *absolute* increase due to the lengthening of the span of life through the advance of medical science.[4] Not only has *physiological* old age been on the

---

[1] It is probably true that the consolations of religion are to-day far less generally effective in sustaining courage and hope in the last days of life, than they were even a generation or so ago.

[2] Aged women are of greater economic value in a home than are men, with the result that twice as many aged men as women are to be found in almshouses.

[3] I. H. Rubinow (editor), *Care of the Aged* (1930), p. 9.

[4] In the beginning of 1935 there were 6,400,000 persons 65 and over in the United States. It is estimated that by 1970 some 15,000,000 of this age will constitute 10%

increase, but also *economic* old age. With the mechanization of industry there is a general trend to eliminate men at earlier ages. In agriculture older men may continue to work to the limit of their powers. In industry those who fall below a certain level of efficiency are deprived of any opportunity of working at all. The need is for speed and endurance, no longer for the wisdom and skill which come from long experience. Therefore, while the old retain their place among the gainfully employed in agriculture, business, public service, and the professions, they are all but eliminated from the major industrial occupations. Economic superannuation occurs in many cases at forty or forty-five. Willingness to work hard and to save no longer assures a secure and independent old age, even when no disaster overtakes the individual. In 1934 it was established that fully one-half of all those over 65 years of age were in need.

Social Responsibility for the Support of Old Age. Such conditions have forced recognition of social responsibility for the support and protection of old age. Legislation to this end began some half-century ago in the leading industrial nations abroad. In over twenty of them, the worker is guaranteed a secure, independent old age through contributory insurance. Most laws secure against invalidism in old age. In some half-dozen other countries, by a non-contributory plan, the state provides a pension to aged persons with incomes insufficient for self-support. The tendency has been away from gratuitous pensions in favor of contributory insurance.

In the United States, until about a dozen years ago, most of the states made no provision for the needy aged, save through the medium of the almshouses or poor farms. Appalling conditions were disclosed in a survey of these made in 1923 and 1924 by the Bureau of Labor Statistics; and one does not wonder that "black dread clouds the lives of the poor" as old age approaches: a "gripping fear of the poor house."[1] These disclosures, together with the high costs of maintaining the dependent aged in institutions, stimulated interest in non-institutional relief for needy old people. By 1925, only Nevada, Montana, Wisconsin, and Alaska had passed old-age pensions acts, but, by the end of 1935, twenty-nine states, Alaska, and Hawaii had enacted such laws. The functioning of these laws, however, soon made

of the population, and that by 2,000 some 19,000,000 will form close to 13%. At least one in every eight persons will be 65 and over.

[1] Jane Addams, *Twenty Years at Hull House*, p. 155.

it apparent that state action alone could not be relied upon to provide either adequate or universal old-age assistance.

When therefore the Social Security Act was passed in 1935, provision was made both for old-age assistance and for a contributory old-age pension plan. Grants are authorized on a fifty-fifty basis to assist states in caring for those of 65 and over, provided the federal government's share shall in no case exceed $15 a month. A long-range pension system is to be financed by an income tax on employees and a payroll tax on employers, starting in each case at 1% in 1937 and rising each three years till 1949, when each contribution is to be 3%. After January 1, 1942, each qualified worker who retires will receive a pension until his death, the rate of payment varying between $10 and $85 a month depending on the total amount of wages earned by the beneficiary after December 31, 1936, and before he reaches a retirable age.

It is much to be hoped that in this way a measure of financial security will in time be assured to all old people. Difficulties in family relationships would undoubtedly be alleviated; although it would still be inadvisable for the aged to live in too close association with their children's families, unless their character and disposition are such as to make their presence eagerly welcomed by all. The grandparent who has many interests, who remains mentally alert, and, above all, is emotionally adjusted may be a valuable influence in family life.

SOCIAL INSURANCE

The Need for Social Insurance. Without a far greater degree of economic security for families than is at present attained, no consistently sustained progress is possible towards securing for all children the rights enunciated by the Children's Charter. Were the wages of all workers adequate to secure food, clothing, and shelter necessary for "health and decency," even so, families would be unprotected against unemployment, the hazards of sickness and accident and premature death, and the impairment accompanying old age. Costs due to unforeseen misfortunes are the commonest cause of want and can only be met through the use of insurance. The insurance principle involves the distribution of the varying and uncertain costs of losses, sustained by individuals, over a large number and for a long period of time, so that they may be reduced to uniformity and certainty.

The costs of private insurance are prohibitive to most workers. Social insurance, on the other hand, relieves the worker of part of this cost, either by means of contributions from employers or by the use of public funds, and can also make insurance protection universal by means of legal compulsion. Finally it arouses public interest in prevention of the calamities against which insurance is obtainable. The fundamental doctrine underlying social insurance was summed up many years ago by a British official as follows: "a proper regard for the solidarity of each community requires that all classes belonging to the community should be protected by the strength of the community as a whole against the incidents of misfortune on the class or on the individual. . . . It is better that misfortune falling on the individual should be distributed and borne lightly; rather than that the individual should be crushed by the weight of his own misfortune."[1]

The Movement towards Social Insurance. In many European countries, social insurance is now regarded as a normal agency in a modern community.[2]   Experiments have been made in many parts of the world during the last fifty years, and there have been frequent alterations in original plans. While imperfections are still admitted, the consensus of informed opinion is that such legislation has done immeasurable good.

In the United States, no national plan for social insurance was undertaken before the Social Security Act of 1935. The principle of workmen's compensation had been accepted, but there were still four states in 1933 without any compensation laws, and the laws in the remaining states were most of them inadequate and far too limited in scope.[3] Old-age pension laws were passed by a number of states, while, in 1932, Wisconsin, alone among the states, put into effect a measure for dealing with unemployment. In America, the most prosperous country in the world, the mass of the workers have thus been living in appalling insecurity, and it has taken an economic crisis of unprecedented magnitude to stimulate interest in social insurance. The British are fully as individualistic as are Americans,

[1] Quoted by the Secretary of Labor, Frances Perkins, "Basic Ideas behind Social Security Program," *New York Times,* Jan. 27, 1935.

[2] The English worker contributes, each week that he is employed, to social insurance funds to which the employer and the state also contribute. He has workmen's compensation protection, and provision is made through this pooled fund for the costs of medical care, for family support when unemployed or too ill to work, for an old-age pension, and, in the event of his death, for pensions for the widow and minor children.

[3] The first workmen's compensation law in this country was passed in 1911. For a discussion of the need for a standard measure which would correct the shortcomings of existing laws, see B. N. Armstrong, "Trends in Workmen's Compensation Regulation," *Annals of the American Academy,* Vol. CLXX (Nov., 1933), pp. 18–20.

yet, forced by circumstances, they are a generation ahead of this country in social legislation. In America, on the other hand, there was no widespread realization of the effects of industrialism upon the families of workers until the present century. The Department of Labor was created as late as 1903, the one great department of the government all of whose activities deal with human welfare.

The ten objectives of the Social Security Act are: a federal plan of old-age annuities; a federal-state plan of unemployment compensation; three grants-in-aid to states for public assistance of the needy aged, the needy blind, and dependent children; assistance of states in maintaining public-health services, in programs of vocational rehabilitation of the physically disabled, in providing medical care for crippled children, in promoting the health of mothers and children, and in caring for homeless and neglected children. It thus includes a long-range plan for insuring against old age and unemployment, and provisions for immediate assistance to the states in caring for dependent unemployables.[1] In introducing the original measure, Senator Wagner said: "We are breaking the ground for a structure in which economic wisdom and humanitarian impulses shall be blended in perfect proportion to protect millions of our citizens from undernourishment in their formative years, from privation in their prime of life, and from destitution in their old age."[2]

State plans must be federally approved if federal aid is to be received. Notable progress had been made, however, in the fifteen months which elapsed between the placing of the Social Security Act on the statute books and the decision of the Supreme Court, in May, 1937, upholding its constitutionality. In every state at least six of the Act's ten provisions were in operation and in most of them the number of provisions carried out was still higher.[3] By August, 1937, every state and territory had unemployment insurance laws approved by the Social Security Board.[4] No proposal for health insurance was included

[1] For a detailed analysis and appraisal of the federal Social Security Act see Paul Douglas, *Social Security in the United States*, 1936. The text of the act is given in an appendix.

[2] *New York Times*, Jan. 18, 1935.   [3] *New York Times*, May 30, 1937.

[4] A. J. Altmeyer, "Towards the Social Security Goal," *New York Times Magazine*, Aug. 15, 1937. The speed with which state unemployment insurance laws were passed illustrates the need for treating the major problems of social security on a national basis. In the same way, five months after federal funds became available, every state had established maternal and child health divisions under full-time direction, while in 1934, only 34 states had done so. Domestic and agricultural workers are not yet included in the unemployment provisions.

in the Act, although such insurance has long been recognized as a necessary part of any all-round program for economic security. Moreover, alone of social risks, insurance for health would involve no imposition of a new burden, but rather the redistribution of the average family's medical expenses so that regular payment of small sums would replace the risk of occasional overwhelmingly large bills. To be successful, however, health insurance plans must meet with the wholehearted support of the medical profession, and this could not be obtained in the United States. Nevertheless the movement for health insurance is gaining in strength. Already a number of local medical organizations and some national organizations have declared in its favor. The American Medical Association took its first important step in the direction of socialized medicine with the introduction of a resolution before its House of Delegates, on June 7, 1937, urging immediate recognition of the fact that "the health of the people is a direct concern of government and a national public health policy directed towards all groups of the people should be formulated."[1] A series of principles and proposals outlined the development of such a plan under the supervision of the medical profession.

FAMILY ALLOWANCE SYSTEMS IN OTHER COUNTRIES

Rapid Spread of Family Endowment Systems Abroad. In a number of foreign countries systems of family allowances have been introduced since the war. These significant social experiments are expressions of the principle of family endowment defined by Eleanor Rathbone as follows: "that the economic structure of society should include some kind of direct provision for the financial cost of rearing children, instead of leaving it to be met through the ordinary wage system on the assumption that normal wages either are, or should be and can be made to be sufficient to cover the cost of child rearing."[2]

During the war, separation allowances were paid for wives and children of the men in the services, and in most countries war bonuses, made necessary by the rise in prices, were proportioned to the size of the family. The way was thus prepared for the rapid development of plans for paying, in addition to wages, allowances for children and sometimes for wives. The payment of allowances for children of those in the public

[1] *New York Times*, June 8, 1937. The text of the "principles and proposals" of the resolution is given in full.
[2] *The Ethics and Economics of Family Endowment* (1927), p. 9.

service has now become established in most European countries and in Australia. Everywhere, however, these allowances only provide for part of the cost of rearing a child.

France was the first country to engage in a practical demonstration of the system by which family allowances may be paid by employers to married workers, according to the number of children under a specified age. M. Romanet, the managing director of a metallurgic industry at Grenoble, initiated the movement in 1916, and in 1918 took a decisive step in aiding its development by suggesting the device of the equalization fund.[1] According to this scheme, the expense of family allowances is divided among a number of employers, either within a single industry or else within a certain area. The scale of allowances having been agreed upon, the number of children to be covered is estimated, and employers are assessed for their share in proportion to the number of workers employed, or the amount of the wage-bill, or the number of hours of work. This plan guards successfully against the danger of discrimination against married men. So rapid was its spread, that by May, 1929, there were 229 funds in France, covering 25,000 firms and benefiting 1,740,000 workers.

Allowances are usually paid monthly, and, in an increasing number of instances, are paid directly to the mother. This method is of more certain benefit to the children, and also emphasizes the fact that allowances are not additions to wages, but recognition of the service of parenthood. The trade unions, at first hostile, came to accept the plan in principle, but still resented its control by employers and demanded that it be placed on a state-controlled basis. This step was taken in France in the passage of the law of March 11, 1932, providing for a national compulsory system of family allowances, for the benefit of manual and non-manual workers of both sexes, in industry, commerce, agriculture, and the liberal professions.

In France, interest in the movement has been in part due to a desire to increase the population. This is clear from the way the allowances are graded upwards.[2] Apparently this object has been unachieved; but the whole system has had undoubted success in promoting family and child welfare. In Belgium too, progress has been rapid, and family allowances were made

[1] *Caisse de compensation pour allocations familiales.*

[2] In 1927 the rates averaged 27 francs per month for one child, 67 for two, 115 for three, and 181 for four. In some of the leading funds, the rates went as high as 60 francs for one child, 150 for two, and 240 for three.

generally applicable to workers by a liberal law of August, 1930.

In England, despite wide discussion and the efforts of the Family Endowment Society established by Eleanor Rathbone, no important results have as yet been obtained.[1] In two British Dominions, however, significant steps have been taken. In New Zealand, a Family Allowance Act was passed in 1926, and in New South Wales, Australia, a Family Endowment Act was passed in 1927.[2]

Arguments in Favor of the Principle of Family Endowment. Australian experience with minimum wage legislation, and "living wage" investigations in Australia, Great Britain, France, and the United States furnish the advocates of the family endowment system with their most effective arguments. It has generally been assumed that the *living wage* must support in decency the *normal* or *standard* family of father, mother, and three children. Careful investigations have proved that this supposed "normal" family is one of the smallest of actual groupings. Among a sample of 13,475 English working men over twenty, representing some 448,000, it was found that 27% were bachelors or widowers with no children; 24.7% were married, but with no children under fourteen; 16.6% had *one* dependent child; 13% had *two; only 8.8% had three;* while *9.9%* had *more* than three. In this last group of families were included about 40% of all the children. On the basis of the British census figures for 1911, Rathbone estimated that the payment of a living wage based on the needs of a family of five would mean making provision "for 3 million phantom wives and for over 16 million phantom children, while on the other hand, in families containing more than three children, those in excess of that number, over 1¼ million in all, would still remain unprovided for."[3] Accordingly, if the payment of a wage calculated to support a family of five were financially feasible, it would be wasteful, particularly in securing disproportionately high wages to *unmarried* men. On the other hand

---

[1] In the United States, the leading advocate of the family endowment system is Paul Douglas (*Wages and the Family*, 1925). The U. S. Bureau of Labor Statistics published a *Bulletin*, No. 401, "Family Allowances in Foreign Countries" (1926). Otherwise there seems to have been little interest in the matter. As Goodsell points out, there are a few isolated instances of payments of family allowances in this country. *Problems of the Family* (rev. ed., 1936), pp. 235–236.

[2] For the provisions of these acts and subsequent legislation see George Anderson, "Wage Rates and the Standard of Living," *Annals of the American Academy*, Vol. CLVIII (Nov., 1931), p. 173.

[3] From *The Disinherited Family* (rev. ed., 1927), p. 20. By Eleanor Rathbone (London: George Allen and Unwin, Ltd.: New York: Longmans, Green and Co.).

it would be seriously inadequate for the families containing a large proportion of the children.

A system of family allowances, or of direct provision for children, recognizes that the bearing and nurture of children "is the most essential of all the nation's businesses," and offers a hope "of making attainable by every family, even the lowest in the industrial ladder, the material means for healthy living, and of placing the service of motherhood in the position of security and honour which it merits but can never reach under the present system."[1]

Fear of over-population or malpopulation as a result of the system does not seem warranted. Such evidence as exists all points "to the conclusion that direct provision paid to the mother would raise standards of life for the poorer wage-earners, and that orderly and self-respecting living is the best cure for indiscriminate and dysgenic breeding."[2] If family allowances became available in classes with high standards, economic causes for restriction of families would be to some extent removed, and somewhat larger families would very probably result. Moreover, if society takes upon itself the direct maintenance of children, it will for the first time be able to do something "to control the quality and quantity of population . . . by manipulating the amount, incidence and conditions of family allowances."[3]

Rathbone believes that state schemes of family allowances would be preferable in the long run, for they would be "not only the truer expression of the motive idea of the scheme— the value of maternity and childhood independently of all other forms of productive services—but the more economically sound method of distributing national income."[4] She grants, however, that other methods of meeting costs, through equalization funds or contributory insurance, are probably better suited in earlier and more experimental stages in the development of systems. She believes that a scheme which was universal in operation would ultimately prove of most value, since it would encourage a rise in the birth-rate among those who, on the whole, have better hereditary endowment, and can provide their children with a better environment. No great saving

---

[1] *Ibid.*, pp. ix–xi. The condition of the children of the poor in England showed improvement as a result of the separation allowances during the war. In many cases, the purchase of perambulators enabled poor mothers to take their *two* youngest children together into the fresh air and sunshine. Previously, the "ex-baby" almost inevitably suffered neglect and became less and less healthy. *Ibid.*, pp. 57–58.

[2] *Ibid.*, p. 243.   [3] *Ibid.*, pp. 247–248.   [4] *Ibid.*, p. 277.

would result if the scheme were not extended to those with higher incomes; they are relatively few and in any case contribute most largely to taxation. Finally the extension of family allowances to all would place the whole conception "in its true light of an act . . . of recognition of the right of the family to its share in the national dividend."[1]

CHILDHOOD AND SOCIAL RECONSTRUCTION

Enhanced Appreciation of the Significance of Childhood. Defects in human beings are in large part responsible for the gravity and magnitude of present-day social problems. Realization that many of these defects might have been prevented, through the removal of handicaps in childhood, brings heightened perception of the social possibilities of improved nurture. Increasing attention is accordingly bestowed on problems of education, and social arrangements are coming to be judged in terms of educational values and ideals; a fact which may have decisive influence in social and economic reorganization.

From the standpoint of the conservation of childhood, a striking factor of the present situation is the great *decrease* in numbers of children. While from 1900 to 1920 there was a 28% increase in the number of individuals of twenty and under, from 1920 to 1930 there was only an 11% increase, the gain being solely in the age groups five to twenty, with an actual *decrease* in the number of children *under five*.[2] The magnitude of child welfare problems should thus be reduced and high standards of child care should become possible.

Concern for the conservation of childhood has led to explicit recognition of the social services rendered by the family. Emphasis is shifting from paternal authority to the duty of fathers, and mothers, to their children.[3] Under modern conditions, however, this duty cannot be performed without the coöperation of the community. Protection of life and property have long been community functions; so too, in an increasing degree, is the protection of health. Education to supplement home nurture is provided by society, and community provision of recreation is a recent development. Finally, public responsibility for children is being found to involve, at least under

[1] *Ibid.*, p. 289.
[2] *Recent Social Trends*, Vol. II, p. 754. The eugenic aspects of this situation are discussed in Chapter XVII.
[3] This is cogently expressed in the French legal principle: "*Le pouvoir paternel est plutôt un devoir qu'un pouvoir,*" quoted by Westermarck, *Origin and Development of the Moral Ideas*, Vol. I, p. 615.

present economic conditions, the supplementation of family resources in case of need.

Child Welfare as Motive, Means, and Goal. Concern for childhood is one of the most powerful motives for reconstruction. As Frank says: "We are witnessing the emergence of the child as a sensitive indicator of the quality of social life. His status is becoming a measure of the value of the whole complex of economic, political, and social activities as they affect his health, emotional development, education and maturation. . . . This concept . . . , the dominant theme of the White House Conference . . . , may well assume a position of outstanding significance, foretelling the major influence in twentieth century social development."[1] Thoughtful parents long, above all other things, that their children may have the best that life has to offer. They are thus led to increasing sympathy with other children; and also to the realization that the welfare of *all* children must be considered, if they would make the world a better place for their own children to live in.

For there can be no more potent means of social reconstruction than through the better nurture of childhood. In opening the White House Conference President Hoover said: "If we could have but one generation of properly born, trained, educated and healthy children, a thousand other problems . . . would vanish." "If we could put into practice what is now known," said Secretary Davis, "we could in a single generation profoundly improve the whole character of our national life."[2]

Many obstacles remain to prevent improvement of child nurture. And yet, as Miss Wald says, in speaking of our growing "sense of the obligation of a democracy to uphold its people": What has already been achieved "is a challenge to every right-minded person to become interested, to study, to understand and to participate." We can, moreover, stiffen our courage "by a backward look over the way we have come."[3] If these obstacles are to be removed child welfare programs must be broadly conceived. As Frank says: "to the extent that social life is assessed in terms of its decisive influence upon mating and child rearing, the crucial factors of child welfare will be revealed. Out of such an assessment . . . may come the aspiration to seek a social life which recognizes in child nurture both the criterion of its soundness and the instrument of its

---

[1] "Childhood and Youth," *Recent Social Trends*, Vol. II, p. 753.
[2] *White House Conference, 1930*, pp. 7, 29.
[3] *Windows on Henry Street*, pp. 249, 250.

enduring progress. . . . In the longer perspective of history what we are doing to and for our children may prove the most significant of all social trends, because the child is the bridge, biologically and socially, to the future."[1]

The major problem of social reconstruction thus becomes the direction of "social change towards the conditions requisite for wholesome child life." The child becomes the touchstone of social effort; and we must "test all our organizations and activities by the quality of the children they help to produce."[1] In charting its course with the well-being of the child as its goal, the Children's Charter adopts, says Dewey, "the most fundamental philosophy of social order and progress which can be formulated."[2] So far as we direct all the new resources of knowledge and skill which science has placed at our command towards putting in action this philosophy, "we may face the future with confidence."[2]

SUGGESTED READING

Abbott, E., and others, *The Tenements of Chicago, 1908–1935*, 1936.

Anthony, K., ed., *Mothers Who Must Earn*, 1914.

Armstrong, B. N., *Insuring the Essentials*, 1932.

Breckenridge, S. P., *Family Welfare Work*, 1924.

Children's Bureau, *Publication 102*, "Children of Wage-Earning Mothers," 1922.

——, *Publication 125*, "Unemployment and Child Welfare," 1923.

——, *Publication 204*, "Children of Working Mothers in Philadelphia, Part I, The Working Mothers," 1931.

——, *Publication 208*, "Leisure-Time Activities of Rural Children in Selected Areas of West Virginia," 1931.

——, *Publication 231*, "Handbook for Recreation Leaders," 1936.

——, *Maternal and Child Welfare Bulletin 1*, "Grants to States for Maternal and Child Welfare," 1936.

Colcord, J., *Broken Homes*, 1919.

Douglas, P., *Wages and the Family*, 1925.

——, *Social Security in the United States*, 1936.

Elmer, M. C., *Family Adjustment and Social Change*, 1932.

Falk, I. S., *Security against Sickness*, 1936.

Federal Emergency Administration of Public Works, Housing Division *Bulletin 1*, "Slums and Blighted Areas in the United States," 1936.

——, *Bulletin 2*, "Urban Housing. The Story of the PWA Housing Division, 1933–1936," 1936.

——, *Bulletin 3*, "Homes for Workers," 1937.

Forman, H. J., *Our Movie-Made Children*, 1934.

[1] *Op. cit.*, Vol. II, pp. 799–800.   [2] *New York Times*, Apr. 10, 1932.

Frank, L. K., "Childhood and Youth," *Recent Social Trends*, 2 vols., 1933, Vol. II, Ch. XV.

Glover, K., and Dewey, E., *Children of the New Day*, 1934.

Goodsell, W., *Problems of the Family*, rev. ed., 1936, Chs. VIII, IX, XI.

Groves, E. R., and Brooks, L. M., *Readings in the Family*, 1934, Chs. XIV–XVII, XXII.

Hughes, G., *Mothers in Industry*, 1925.

Mitchell, A. M., *Children and the Movies*, 1929.

Murphy, J. P., "Children in the New Deal," *The Annals of the American Academy of Political and Social Science*, Vol. CLXXVI, Nov., 1934, pp. 212–230.

Public Health Report, *Reprint 905*, "Factors in the Mental Health of Girls of Foreign Parentage," 1924.

——, *Reprint 917*, "Factors in the Mental Health of Boys of Foreign Parentage," 1924.

Rathbone, E., *The Disinherited Family*, 3rd ed. rev., 1927.

——, *The Ethics and Economics of Family Endowment*, 1927.

Resettlement Administration, *Greenbelt Towns. A Demonstration in Suburban Planning*, 1936.

Rowlands, D. T., and Woodbury, C., eds., *Current Developments in Housing*, in *The Annals of the American Academy of Political and Social Science*, Vol. CXC, March, 1937.

Rubinow, I. M., ed., *Care of the Aged*, 1930.

Stern, B. J., ed., *The Family Past and Present*, 1938, Chs. VII–X.

United States Bureau of Labor Statistics, *Bulletin 401*, "Family Allowances in Foreign Countries," 1926.

Women's Bureau, *Bulletin 64*, "The Employment of Women at Night," 1928.

——, *Bulletin 74*, "The Immigrant Woman and Her Job," 1930.

Wood, E. E., *Housing of the Unskilled Wage Earner*, 1919.

——, *Recent Trends in American Housing*, 1931.

CHAPTER XIV

CHANGES IN THE STATUS OF WOMEN IN ENGLAND AND AMERICA

WOMEN IN SUBJECTION

The Influence of Women through the Ages. Profound modifications in the traditional pattern of family life have been brought about by the so-called emancipation of women, the result of the "woman's movement" of the last century and a half. To emphasize the great opportunities and the consequent responsibilities of women to-day is not, in any way, to belittle the services and influence of women through the ages. Mary Beard has done well to insist on the focal cultural influence, always and everywhere exercised by women. If we penetrate to the realities of daily life, beneath the military and political events recorded by historians, women appear as an elemental force in human progress; the "eternal feminine being always at the center of things . . . , assuming chief responsibility for the continuance and care of life."[1] The influence of *most* women in the past has been exercised from within family life and the home. But there have been notable exceptions, women who through rank and position, or through their gifts and force of character, have achieved influence as independent individuals. Consider, for example, Joan of Arc.

Eighteenth Century Ideas of the Female Character. In the French salons of the eighteenth century, women were valued for brilliancy of intellect more than for their feminine charms. Yet a number of factors combined to produce at the same time, in England and America, an artificial and pernicious ideal of the "female character." It was against the degrading and debilitating influence of this conception that Mary Wollstonecraft so ardently rebelled, and in so doing launched the movement for the emancipation of women.

In England, the licentiousness of Restoration circles and Puritan attitudes towards sex combined to concentrate attention on woman as a sexual being. With industrial changes, sharper distinctions were made between women who worked and upper-class women as ladies of leisure. It became *genteel*

[1] Beard, *On Understanding Women*, pp. 522, 513.

to be idle, a notion which corrupted not only the women of the upper class, but also the wives and daughters of the middle class, who, with increasing prosperity, aped the manners of the genteel. "A lady to be such, must be a mere lady, and nothing else."[1]

Men regarded women as inferior to and less developed than themselves, and most women acquiesced in this masculine estimate. "Women . . . are only children of a larger growth," said Lord Chesterfield; they may have some wit, but are utterly devoid of "reasoning good sense." "A man of sense only trifles with them . . . , humours and flatters them . . . , but he neither consults them about nor trusts them with serious matters, though he often makes them believe he does both."[2] Dr. Gregory, though not so extreme, since he concedes that his daughters may have good sense, yet warns them to "be ever cautious of displaying it. . . . If you happen to have any learning, keep it a profound secret, especially from the men."[3] Moreover, "We so naturally associate the idea of female softness and delicacy with a correspondent delicacy of constitution," that Dr. Gregory advises his daughters to "never make a boast of good health, but enjoy it in grateful silence."[3] Women are in peculiar need of "the supports of religion" to enable them to be resigned and to bear their "sorrows in silence." "Besides, men consider your religion as one of their principle securities for that female virtue in which they are most interested."[3] Lord Kames points out that, in contrast to man, for a woman "the least doubt of her chastity deprives her of every comfort in the matrimonial state. In the education of females, accordingly, no motive has greater influence than the thought of what people will say of them. . . . This is essential to the female sex, forever subjected to the authority of a single person, or to the opinion of all."[4] No effort is made by these eighteenth-century gentlemen to depict marriage as an idyllic state. "Woman, destined to be obedient, ought to be disciplined early to bear wrongs without murmuring." It is "the chief duty of a woman to make a good wife."[4]

Apart from the protests of a few bold spirits, such as Mary Astell, very much the same view was expressed by the leading

---

[1] Quotation from a diary kept by Margaretta Greg, in 1853, in which she protested against the exclusion of ladies from useful work in their homes or outside them. Pinchbeck, *Women and the Industrial Revolution*, p. 315.

[2] *Letters to His Son* (1774), Letter CLXI.

[3] *Legacy to His Daughters* (1784). Quoted by Langdon-Davies, *op. cit.*, pp. 330–334.

[4] Kames, *Loose Hints upon Education* (1781 ed.), pp. 135–137, 228, 229.

women of the day.[1]   Hannah More (1745–1833), author of
Strictures on the Modern System of Female Education (1799),
was most influential in her insistence on *propriety*, "the centre
in which all lines of duty and agreeableness meet," as the core
of the female character, founded as it was on *religion* and
chastity.[1] Herself a witty member of Blue Stocking circles, and
an extremely popular writer, she believed in education for
women, but chiefly in order "to put an end to those cavils
and contentions for equality which female smatterers so anx-
iously maintain."[2]

A great gulf was thus fixed between men as *human beings*
and women as *females*, subject to and supported by a father,
till they were successful in securing the support of a husband
to whom they must transfer their "whole duty."   Chastity
was the one supreme virtue for women; but they had to be
chaste, debilitated in body, weak and delicate in mind, and
devoted to religion, primarily in order to fascinate men. However much false modesty might obscure its frank recognition,
the capture of a husband was the sole aim of a woman's existence.
Ironically enough, it was Rousseau, champion of the rights of
man and advocate of freedom from artificiality and debasing
social conventions who, failing to extend his principles to
women, gave most explicit expression to the current view.
"The education of women," he says, in Book V of *Émile*,
"should be always relative to the men.   To please, to be useful
to us, to make us love and esteem them, to educate us when
young, and take care of us when grown up, to advise, to console
us, to render our lives easy and agreeable: these are the duties

[1] Mary Astell, 1668–1736, protested against the injustices suffered by women,
and argued that women were what men had made them.   Women should cease
thinking only of pleasing men and turn to a consideration of their own souls. To this
end she proposed a religious institution of learning for women, in order "to expel
that cloud of ignorance that custom has involved us in."   Her chief works were:
A Serious Proposal to Ladies for the Advancement of Their True and Greatest Interest
(1694); *An Essay in Defense of the Female Sex* (1696); and *Some Reflections upon
Marriage* (4th ed., 1730). It is also refreshing to read "The Detached Thoughts of a
Young Lady," *London Magazine*, Oct. 1777, who asked, "Why is sincerity made a
virtue in one sex and a weakness in the other? Female delicacy seems to consist in
acting contrary to our sentiments, by giving the lye to our hearts, and what is something extraordinary, a woman must become a hypocrite to be thought virtuous."
Quoted by Ida O'Malley, *Women in Subjection* (Duckworth, 1933), pp. 63–64.

[2] Quoted by Langdon-Davies, *Short History of Women*, pp. 352–357. "The rights of
man," she says, "have been discussed, till we are somewhat wearied. . . . To these
have been opposed, as the next stage in the progress of illumination, the *rights of
woman.* . . . The world will next have grave descants on the *rights of youth*, the
rights of children—the *rights of babes!*" Totally incapable, therefore, of any sympathy
for Mary Wollstonecraft, she believed the *Vindication* to be a justification of adultery!

of women at all times and what should be taught in their infancy." Men must be bold, active, strong; women timid, passive, weak: bashfulness and modesty are the weapons "with which nature hath armed the weak, in order to subdue the strong." Girls, "formed to please and be subjected to man," should be "early subjected to restraint."

Mary Wollstonecraft and Her Vindication of the Rights of Woman. No wonder Mary Wollstonecraft vehemently attacked Rousseau for his blindness to the full implications of his ideals, and for his injustice in failing to extend them to women.[1] From observation of the life around her, and from tragic personal experience, she knew only too well what eighteenth-century conventions meant for women.[2] Her father was a tyrannical drunkard and spendthrift, her mother died worn-out, thankful "it was all over," her sister made a miserably unhappy marriage, and she herself, denied an education by her father, was obliged to become a despised governess and companion, to support her younger brothers. Intense as were her emotions, she was able to see her own experience as part of a larger life where the results of cruelty and ignorance must be combated by love and enlightenment.

Her *Vindication* was the first part of a larger work she did not live to write.[3] "It is time," she says, "to restore to" women "their lost dignity—and make them, as a part of the human species, labour, by reforming themselves, to reform the world."[4] Women "are almost sunk below the standard of rational creatures."[5] "Mistaken notions of female excellence" have been to blame, and a system of education devised by men who, "considering females rather as women than human creatures, have been more anxious to make them alluring

---

[1] She also criticizes in detail the views of Dr. Gregory and others who wrote in similar vein and is indignant over the arguments of *women* who "follow in the same track as men, and adopt the sentiments which brutalize them with all the pertinacity of ignorance." *Vindication of the Rights of Woman* (1792), Everyman's Library, No. 825, 1929, p. 111.

[2] The coarseness and brutality of this period were glossed over with a superficial veneer of artificiality and elegance. The terrible treatment accorded to women in prisons serves to show the spurious character of masculine "homage." Mrs. Peel states that women criminals were burnt rather than hanged at the end of the eighteenth century because it was *unseemly* for a woman to be strung up so high! *The Stream of Time,* p. 43.

[3] It was preceded by *Thoughts on the Education of Daughters: with Reflections on Female Conduct in the More Important Duties of Life* (1785), and *Vindication of the Rights of Man* (1790), an arraignment of Burke's attitude towards the French Revolution; also translations and adaptations made for the bookseller who gave her ten guineas for her first book.

[4] *Op. cit.,* p. 51.   [5] *Ibid.,* p. 184.

mistresses than affectionate wives and rational mothers."[1] "Trifling employments have rendered woman a trifler."[2] Women should be educated for useful work in society,—for example, as physicians,—and they should study politics. Ignorance, moreover, has prevented women from being good mothers. "Make women rational creatures and free citizens and they will quickly become good wives and mothers."[3] But "children will never be properly educated till friendship subsists between parents."[4] Woman must be educated "to become the companion of man . . . , the friend, and not the humble dependent of her husband."[5]

Hoping she had found such a friend, capable of sharing her ideals, Mary lived in Paris with Gilbert Imlay; but, despite her devotion, he turned to another woman after the birth of their daughter. One of the few in England who sympathized with her and shared her interests was William Godwin. Shortly before the birth of a daughter who was to be Shelley's wife, they married. But Mary died from the effects of childbirth, thus draining to its last dregs the cup of tragic feminine experience. "She was only thirty-eight," says Ida O'Malley, "and probably had not reached the summit of her powers, but the intensity of her emotion and the courage of her thought had given a special value to her experience. . . . In her struggles she had indeed hurt herself, but she had plucked a brand from heaven for the enlightenment of other women: to the women's movement she was a kind of Prometheus: the fire she brought to earth smouldered for several generations, but it broke out at last into a clear flame."[6] "Her book may be said to mark the emergence of the women's movement into conscious life: it did not become an organized effort till many years after her death, but, when it did, it took the *Vindication of the Rights of Woman* as a text book and has been occupied ever since in working out the reforms that are advocated or implied there."[7]

THE EMANCIPATION OF WOMEN IN ENGLAND [8]

Dependent Daughters, Wives, and Mothers. During the first half of the nineteenth century, the vast majority of women, including almost all those in the middle and upper classes,

[1] *Ibid.*, pp. 94, 3.
[2] *Ibid.*, p. 84.
[3] *Ibid.*, p. 197.
[4] *Ibid.*, p. 213.
[5] *Ibid.*, pp. 10, 34.
[6] *Women in Subjection*, p. 175.
[7] *Ibid.*, p. 167.

[8] For the sake of continuity, consideration of the situation of American women in the era of subjection is postponed till the next section.

were utterly dependent on men for the support of themselves and their children. The justification for their existence was to be found entirely in their relationship to men. A book for girls, still popular in the forties, informs them: "There is something unfeminine in independence. It is contrary to Nature and therefore offends. A really sensible woman feels her dependence, she does what she can, but she is conscious of inferiority and therefore grateful for support."[1]

Even when fathers were kind and indulgent, their daughters led idle, irresponsible, and futile lives. Of this state of affairs there is no more scathing indictment than *Cassandra*, written in 1852, by Florence Nightingale.[2] Longing to be of real use in the world, she vainly chafed for years against a system under which the "young lady" never had a moment to herself, but had to devote her life to "company," "visiting," and hours of sitting in drawing rooms "*passing* the time." "So women play through life . . . , *spending* their time . . . , the most valuable of all things," in "conventional frivolities" which are called "duties."[3] "Why," she asks, "have women passion, intellect, moral activity—these three—and a place in society where no one of the three can be exercised."[4] Marriage, which most women hailed as an escape, seemed to Florence to offer but "a continuation and exaggeration of my present life."[5] Moreover, women had no means of learning how to be good mothers, and there could be no "real communion between husband and wife," when young men and women never become well enough acquainted "to justify them in marrying."[6] She scorns the superficiality, dullness, and pettiness of domestic life. "The sacred hearth!" she exclaims, "sacred to their husband's sleep, their son's absence in the body and their daughter's in mind!"[7] Accordingly, because "to put it out of my power even to be able to seize the chance of forming for myself a true and rich life would seem to me like suicide," she deliberately rejected marriage, even with a man she really cared for!

No wonder few women had such courage. Except for the well-endowed, an unmarried woman was apt to be considered

[1] Quoted by Lothrop Stoddard, *Story of Youth*, p. 316.
[2] This fragment was privately printed in 1859 after her return from the Crimea. It was not published in full, however, until its inclusion as Appendix I, pp. 395–418, in Ray Strachey's *Struggle* (1930), published in England as *The Cause*.
[3] *Ibid.*, pp. 402–404. "Women," she writes, "are never supposed to have any occupation of sufficient importance not to be interrupted"; an assumption still too widely prevalent to-day, at least for *married* women, and an obstacle in the paths of women who have exacting work to do in business or the professions.
[4] *Ibid.*, p. 397.   [5] *Ibid.*, p. 22.   [6] *Ibid.*, pp. 410–411.   [7] *Ibid.*, p. 415.

a "ridiculous old maid," forced in many instances after a father's death to support herself by becoming a companion or governess.[1]   Accordingly, despite stirrings of discontent, it remained pretty generally taken for granted that the "two essentials of a woman's being" were to be "supported by," and "to minister to the comfort of men."[2] It must not be forgotten, moreover, that while in *theory* women were sheltered and protected, in actual fact, even for those willing to live in meek submission, life too often brought cruel hardships; and masculine authority was as likely to degenerate into capricious tyranny as to be inspired by wisdom and benevolence. Husbands were autocratic, and sometimes cruel and unfaithful.   Moreover, whatever their character, they had supreme control over the destinies of their children.   Worst of all, most mothers lost several of their children, and many became semi-invalids from repeated childbirth. For not till the middle of the century did medical science begin to alleviate the sufferings of women in childbirth, and to some extent remove its dangers.

The Development of Modern Methods in the Treatment of Women in Childbirth. No account of the emancipation of women is complete, which does not give explicit recognition to one vital aspect of their improved status and comparative freedom from former disabilities. The mothers of to-day need no longer bear numerous children in order that a few may survive. Nor need they be subjected to the unrelieved agony and the dangers which attended childbirth, when the use of anesthetics and aseptic methods were as yet undiscovered. Medical practitioners were more frequently in charge a hundred years ago than they had been earlier.   But there were protests against the extreme damage thus done to female delicacy and modesty.[3] Even more pernicious than such prudery was the idea that any alleviation of the pangs of labor was an impious frustration of the curse of Eve. When, in 1847, Dr. James Simpson first used chloroform for childbirth, the immediate result was violent controversy and a storm of protest, led by the clergy, but participated in by

[1] As Jane Austen says, in *Emma*, the income made all the difference, "a single woman of good fortune is always respectable and may be as sensible and pleasant as anyone else," but "a single woman with a narrow income must be a ridiculous old maid, the proper sport of boys and girls."

[2] A statement in the public press in 1857, quoted by Strachey, *op. cit.*, p. 93.

[3] In 1827, there appeared in the *Pamphleteer*, dedicated to both Houses of Parliament, "An Address to the Public on the Propriety of Midwives instead of Surgeons Practising Midwifery." There was even more intense prudishness in America than in England.

the press and even by physicians.[1] Fortunately Dr. Simpson
was no less skilled in argument than in his profession. In his
*Answers to the Religious Objections against the Employment of
Anesthetic Agents in Midwifery and Surgery*, he pointed out
that every effort of human beings to improve their lot on earth
might, with equal justice, be branded as interference with
divine providence.[2]

Despite the ravages of puerperal fever, which reached epidemic proportions in the hospitals of the seventeenth, eighteenth,
and early nineteenth centuries, it was not until 1795 that its
contagious character was given recognition. None went to
hospitals then but those who had no other means of care;
so poverty-stricken and outcast women were the most frequent
victims of puerperal fever. In 1843, Oliver Wendell Holmes
proved, in his "Contagiousness of Puerperal Fever," that doctors
and midwives were the means of its conveyance to patients;
but not until this fact was independently established by
Semmelweis in Vienna three years later, were any steps taken
to diminish the number of deaths due to this cause. With
Pasteur's germ theory and Lister's development of antiseptic
technique, the way was open for the eradication of one of the
greatest dangers to women in childbirth.

The Participation of Women in Humanitarian Movements.
Although the position of women remained apparently unaltered
for years after Mary Wollstonecraft lived and wrote, the philanthropic movement already gaining headway was destined to
open new vistas to women; enlisting them in increasing numbers
in efforts at social amelioration, and making them aware of

[1] Both in England and America, clergy and ministers have been prominent in their
hostility to the emancipation of women. A large number of illustrations of their
attitude were given in Matilda Gage's *Woman, Church and State* (1893), including
sermons preached against the use of anesthetics in childbirth. There could be no
better evidence of the warping influence of religious fanaticism and ascetic hatred
of sex. When, in the eighteenth century, the invention of obstetrical forceps was
kept secret in order that its inventor and his family might reap the greater profit, an
obstetrician called de La Motte declared that a man who could do such a thing,
"deserves to have a worm devour his vitals to all eternity." In the case of all the
smug, pious, and unfeeling gentlemen who protested against anesthetics, one could
almost wish for them rebirth in the rôle of prolific mothers, *without* benefit of anesthetics.

[2] Many innovations in the past, he added, had in point of fact been opposed on
theological grounds. One is also reminded of the present-day opposition to birth
control. As a matter of fact, Dr. Simpson's arguments had less to do with the acceptance of anesthesia than the example of Queen Victoria, who sent for Dr. Simpson to
give her chloroform at the birth of a son in 1853: her one contribution, even if un-
witting, to the emancipation of women and the alleviation of the lot of ordinary
women.

the obstacles in the way of their assumption of social responsibility. These women pioneers in humanitarian movements were for the most part inspired by Christian principles, particularly by their renewed expression among the Quakers and Methodists.[1]

Paradoxically enough, one of the earliest philanthropists was Hannah More, despite her complacent assumption that the poor had been allotted their dependent and inferior stations by God. It was the "duty" of the "higher class" to be condescending and charitable, and of the "lower" to be sober, industrious, contented with their lot, and overflowing with gratitude for any favors bestowed on them. But the fashion of cottage visiting and the Sunday School movement, both of which Hannah More was influential in starting, laid the foundations for revolutionary changes. Not only were the poor being taught something, however little, but a new sphere was being marked out for the activities of women. The monotony of their days began to be relieved by what Strachey calls "a faint trickle of lady-like philanthropy."

A few exceptional women went much further. Elizabeth Fry, the daughter of a liberal Quaker and wife of another, was married at twenty, ordained a minister at thirty-one, and at thirty-three, after the birth of her *eighth* child, began her work among the female prisoners at Newgate in 1813; thus promoting prison reform throughout the world.[2] It was not till nearer the middle of the century that more women began to take an active part in benevolence. Mary Carpenter, who, educated at the boys' school conducted by her father, started her first "ragged school" in the slums of Bristol in 1846; and Louisa Twining, the originator in 1851 of workhouse reform, were outstanding examples. Florence Nightingale, who at last

[1] Both these sects owed much to the influence of women. John Wesley openly acknowledged his debt to his mother, while the wife of George Fox, Margaret Fell, played a large part in the first Christian sect in which women were accorded complete spiritual equality with men and in which they took their full share both in preaching and in the organization of practical good works. The Salvation Army also accepted sex equality from the first. Catherine Mumford refused to marry its founder until she had won him completely to her position in this matter. Strachey says that the Army exerted "a most tremendous influence on the position of women . . . ; the practical example of sex equality which it displayed did more than millions of arguments to destroy the suspicion and the prejudice of the poor." *Op. cit.*, p. 212.

[2] Conditions among women prisoners were unbelievably terrible. At Newgate, three hundred women with many small children were herded together in filthy and half-naked squalor, the untried with the guilty and those condemned to death. A contemporary journal describes Elizabeth Fry reading the Bible with a woman who was "surrounded by her four children, and only awaiting the birth of another, which she hourly expects, to pay the forfeit of her life." Her husband had already been executed for the crime of forgery. Peel, *The Stream of Time*, p. 59.

succeeded in securing three months nursing training, at a German Deaconesses' Institute, was prepared by this and her subsequent headship of a philanthropic nursing home for her great mission in the Crimea, when war broke out in 1853.[1] Most courageous of all, perhaps, was Josephine Butler, in her espousal of what was then considered an outrageously indecent and utterly shocking cause: protest against the regulation of prostitution. Men might, and did, pass freely over the gulf between the two feminine worlds: that of *fallen* women, outcasts from society for behavior condoned in men; and that of the sheltered *respectable* women who were supposed to ignore the very existence of prostitutes and the problems they created. Josephine Butler was one of the many women pioneers of the nineteenth century, both in England and America, whose work was largely made possible through the whole-hearted help and sympathy of an enlightened husband.

A great impetus was given to the activities of socially minded women by the formation, in 1857, of the National Association for the Promotion of Social Science. In the same year, a group of "strong-minded" ladies issued the first number of the *English Woman's Journal*, which became the vehicle for the new movement. Its earliest practical venture was the establishment of a Women's Employment Bureau.

Women Workers in Mines, Factories, and Domestic Industries. While ladies were considered too "delicate" for the everyday work of life, the women of the poor were living and working under appalling conditions. This was, of course, no new phenomenon; but it was not until the nineteenth century that public opinion was aroused through the revelations made by a series of government commissions. It was reported, in 1833, that "the hardest labour in the worst room in the worst factory is less hard, less cruel and demoralizing than the labour in the coal mines."[2] Most of the women were employed in dragging

---

[1] In spite of her own great success she was discouraged by the attitude of women themselves, their lack of sympathy, of accurate information, and of efficiency. With remarkable psychological insight she diagnoses the difficulty. "When shall we see a woman making a *study* of what she does? Married women cannot; for a man would think, if his wife undertook any great work with the intention of carrying it out . . . , that she would destroy, as it is called, his domestic life." As it is, women are "exhausted with feelings which lead to no action. If they see and enter into a continuous line of action with training constantly kept up to the occupation, occupation constantly testing the training . . . , they are retempered, their life is filled, they have found their work and the means to do it." Strachey, *op. cit.*, pp. 409, 407.

[2] Pinchbeck, *Women Workers and the Industrial Revolution*, p. 243; quotation from a Factory Commission Report.

or pushing heavy loads of coal through narrow and steep subterranean passages. They were described as "chained, belted, harnessed . . . , black, saturated with wet, and more than half-naked, crawling upon hands and feet."[1] Other women carried coal up ladders to the surface, some weeping bitterly, groaning with the excessive weight, trembling in every nerve, with their knees sinking under them. Two tons might be brought to the surface, in from ten to fourteen hours, and the wage was often not more than 8d. Pregnant women worked till labor began, and babies were born in the pits; in many instances there were miscarriages and stillbirths. One woman testified: "I have a belt round my waist, and a chain passing between my legs, and I go on my hands and feet. . . . I have drawn till I had the skin off me; the belt and chain is worse when we are in the family way."[2]

Intense indignation was aroused by this report, and it resulted in the exclusion of women and boys under ten from the pits.[3] But no substitute employment was found and the subsequent destitution was overlooked. Evils in the factories, though less spectacular, were none the less real, before the general regulation of the new system by the state. By the mid-nineteenth century women factory workers were far better off than any other working women. Thousands of women and children were still engaged in domestic industries such as strawplaiting, nail-making, and lacemaking. In the latter occupation 180,000 were engaged in 1831. Fourteen hours of the most skilful embroidery work would earn 1/-. Some lace-runners made no more than 3/- a *week*. Many of the single women were driven to prostitution by such wages. The married women, not having time even to suckle their offspring, "freely administer opium in some form . . . to their infants. . . . A great number of infants perish. . . . Those who escape with life become pale and sickly children, often half-idiotic and always with a ruined constitution."[4]

Women in Agriculture. Among the hardest-driven women workers in the early nineteenth century were the agricultural day-laborers. Some engaged in the heaviest agricultural work, but the majority were employed in setting crops, transplanting, hoeing, weeding, and in gathering fruit and vegetables and

[1] *Ibid.*   [2] *Ibid.*, p. 252; quotation from a report on mines.
[3] Many seem to have been less horrified by the accounts of the heavy labor than by the half-naked state of women mine workers.
[4] Pinchbeck, *op. cit.*, p. 212; a quotation from an 1843 report of the Children's Employment Commission.

carrying them to market. In 1796 a woman was paid 6d for carrying a heavy basket nine miles to Covent Garden. Sometimes they made two trips a day. In 1807, women, working all day in gardens, made 1/- a day in summer, and 10d in winter. The Poor Law Commissioners who investigated the situation in 1843 found that, apart from rheumatism, agricultural day-laborers were healthier than other women workers, but their children were perforce neglected, and there was not "the same attention paid to" the husband's "comforts"; "he may have to wait for his supper."

Domestic Servants and Needleworkers. In 1841 close to 100,000 women and girls were engaged in needlework, the occupation which, with factory and domestic industry, agriculture, and domestic service, claimed the great majority of women workers.[1] Domestic service led all other forms of employment with over 700,000. Although all but those lowest in the social scale employed servants, the supply far exceeded the demand. In London, unemployment was at its worst, for the shortage of situations in rural districts sent large numbers of untrained girls to London. Cases of suicide or death from starvation were frequent. Many of the London prostitutes had been servant girls, who could either find no employment or who had been discharged, without a character, through the caprice of master or mistress.

Except during the fashionable season, there were also multitudes of dressmakers and milliners out of work. At the height of the season, however, there was a tremendous demand for their services, and new victims were continually recruited into this "sweated slavery." Working eighteen to twenty hours, sometimes even for several days and nights without a break, in dark, crowded, and unventilated rooms, they were able to earn 4/6 a week. A few managed to set up in business for themselves, but otherwise their situation was highly precarious. Even those who found employment were usually unable to stand the strain for more than three or four years. Nevertheless, since needlework was considered "genteel" in comparison with most forms of work open to women, it was the sole resource of large numbers of "young females of respectable parents . . . necessitated by the pecuniary misfortunes of their parents to earn a livelihood." Moreover, as was shown by the police

---

[1] An amazing number of occupations are represented in the population returns for 1841, which for the first time were made on an occupation basis. See Pinchbeck, *op. cit.*, pp. 317–321 for the numbers engaged in each occupation.

reports at this period, "many young prostituted females from the polish of their manners . . . must have had a respectable origin."[1]

Governesses and Literary Ladies. Dressmaking was considered "genteel" enough for "young females" of the middle class, forced by "pecuniary misfortunes" to abandon a life of lady-like idleness. But for those of really gentle birth no forms of paid work were conceivable save employment as governess or companion, apart always from the talented few who were able to support themselves by writing. This field too was overcrowded, there being, in 1862, 810 applicants for one position as governess, at a salary of £15 a year. Charlotte Brontë and Anna Jameson describe their own experience when they write of the "dreary solitary work" of "governessing drudgery and slavery." These "ladies," obliged to earn, were in an entirely anomalous position, treated with little consideration by employers and with impertinence by their pupils and the servants. Fiction played a considerable part in leading to the relief of governesses and indirectly to a greater interest in the fate of all working women.[2] And the fiction writers themselves not only described the lot of governesses but showed themselves possessed of talents which were entirely unexpected in women.

Anna Jameson, a governess at sixteen, was not content with writing of the woes of governesses, but was prominent among those who initiated practical reforms. She realized that education was the great necessity, if governesses were to receive better salaries and better treatment. A series of Lectures for Ladies, begun in 1847, developed, in 1848, into Queen's College, which was established to teach "all branches of female knowledge," and to grant governesses certificates of proficiency. From this modest beginning the higher education of English women took its start, as did the development of teaching as a profession.

Women Doctors. Medicine was the one profession besides teaching into which English women were able to make their way in the nineteenth century. A long and bitter fight was necessary, however, before they won the privileges of medical education or the right to practice as doctors on equal terms with

---

[1] *Ibid.*, p. 315, note 2; a quotation from the *Address on the Propriety of Midwives* (1827), already alluded to.

[2] As W. F. Neff points out in *Victorian Working Women* (1929), p. 164, a governess made an appealing "ladylike heroine of delicate sensibility and infinite capacity for forbearance. . . . What a coarse working woman could not feel, was torture to her finer clay."

men. Fortunately they could point to a special need for their services, so that, despite the "indelicacy" of "ladies" engaging in such work, they finally succeeded in penetrating this masculine stronghold. Not until after the World War did the Law open its doors to women by allowing them to practice as barristers and solicitors. The established Church, the Army, and the Navy still remain hopelessly out of reach.[1]

The first woman to have her name placed on the British Medical Register, in 1859, was Elizabeth Blackwell, who, born in Bristol, had been taken to America as a child and there secured her medical degree in 1849. In 1860, the holders of foreign medical degrees were excluded from the register and the chief need was for medical education and degrees for women. In this cause Elizabeth Garrett and Sophia Jex-Blake were pioneers, the former taking a Paris M.D. degree, in 1869, and the latter a degree at Berne, in 1877. Victory came in sight when King's and Queen's College of Physicians in Ireland consented to examine and grant medical degrees for women. Sophia was reëxamined and put her name on the Medical Register. Soon after, the Royal Free Hospital consented to admit students to the Women's Medical School, and London University agreed to admit women medical students to examinations.

Higher Education for Women. The struggle for medical education was closely associated with the movement for higher education. In 1875, the universities were empowered to admit women if they so desired, an enactment which made possible the granting of medical degrees. Long years of struggle had preceded this triumph. The fashionable boarding schools of the eighteenth and early nineteenth centuries were concerned with turning out "accomplished young ladies" of elegant appearance and correct deportment. Several of the most talented women of this time seem to have profited by escaping the artificial influences of such establishments and by conducting their own education. Mary Somerville, after one year at a boarding school where she wore stays with steel busks and an iron collar, taught herself Latin, Greek, and mathematics; and later, after a second marriage with a liberal man, was able, in 1827, to publish the first of her famous books on astronomy. Among other "strong-minded" ladies were Maria Edgeworth, Mary Berry, Joanna Baillie, and Harriet Marti-

---

[1] There have been some distinguished women ministers in the Congregational Church in England.

neau. Elizabeth Barrett Browning and Marian Evans, better known as George Eliot, were self-taught, and were among the notable women who were fortunate enough to win the complete sympathy of enlightened husbands.

George Eliot saw education as the key to all else. The general status of women could be raised only "by women improving their work—ceasing to be *amateurs*."[1] By the middle of the century, there were many girls who wanted both to do some useful work and to know how to do it.[2] Women thronged to Queen's College, and to meet the demand Bedford College opened in 1849. The earliest real secondary schools for girls were founded soon after by women who had attended these colleges. Finally, in 1873, through the efforts of Emily Davies, three young women were admitted to and passed the final examinations at Cambridge University.[3] One of these, Louisa Lumsden, who died, in 1935, at the age of 94, was the founder, in 1877, of St. Leonards School, the first girls' school to resemble closely the great public schools for boys, and the first to send a student to Cambridge who placed ahead of all the men of her year in the final examinations. This was in classics, and before long other women were to perform similar feats both in classics and in mathematics.

There could be no further doubt as to the ability of women to succeed in the most exacting mental work. An attack along other lines was tried: if women cultivated their minds, would it not unfit them for "performing their functions as women"? Even Dr. Elizabeth Garrett Anderson found it no easy matter to reply, in the refined manner then considered necessary if decency were not to be offended. She, and other champions of women's education, very cleverly insisted on physical development as a necessary accompaniment of intellectual activity; and the movement for gymnastics and organized games for

[1] Quoted from an account of George Eliot, by the old friend of Lewes and herself whom she married a few months before her death. A. A. Winter, *The Heritage of Women* (1927), p. 210.

[2] As late as 1865 Ruskin stated as women's function "to understand and perhaps to help the work of men." Even this was an advance on former views.

[3] These girls were members of a small group which formed the nucleus of what is now Girton College. Newnham College came into being soon after, and residence halls were opened before long at Oxford. In 1880, London University granted women full membership, and all the new provincial universities then being established did the same. Oxford and Cambridge, however, would grant *no degrees*, however distinguished the scholastic achievements of their women students. A few years ago Oxford finally granted degrees, and the last privilege was won when degrees in theology were opened to women in 1935. Cambridge alone still refuses to grant more than titular degrees to women.

women not only diverted the attack, but had far-reaching results for the health and all-round development of women.

The Status of Married Women in English Common Law. Late in the eighteenth century Justice Blackstone described the position of married women in English common law as follows: "By marriage the husband and wife are one person in law; that is, the very being or legal existence of the woman is suspended during the marriage, or at least is incorporated or consolidated into that of her husband, under whose wing, protection and cover she performs everything."[1] A married woman possessed no independent legal rights; her person, her property, and her children were owned and controlled by her husband. Nor was she able to escape, for prior to 1857 divorce was not obtainable by a wife.[2] The supposed privileges of a wife were not of much avail in saving her from unusually harsh treatment under criminal law. The murder of a husband was called *Petty Treason* and punished by burning to death. Not till 1790 did hanging become the punishment for both men and women who murdered their partners in marriage. This was the only law determining a wife's position, relative to her husband, to be repealed prior to the middle of the nineteenth century.[3]

Extension of Contractual and Property Rights to Married Women. Significantly enough, the woman who led the fight for the amendment of property laws was the daughter of a liberal father who left to each daughter, as well as to each son, an independent yearly income. Barbara Leigh Smith, later Barbara Bodichon, began by publishing a *Brief Summary in Plain Language of the Most Important Laws concerning Women.* But apart from the two laws, passed in 1857 and 1861, protecting the property of wives who were deserted or abused by their husbands, progress was very slow. In 1870, however, an act was passed which, radical as it was thought at the time, still left the management of a married woman's real estate, and the ownership of all personal property above £200, to her husband. But in 1882 the final step was taken, and every

---

[1] *Commentaries on the Laws of England,* 1765–1769. Quoted by Strachey, *op. cit.,* p. 15. To be sure, as Blackstone proceeds to point out: "the disabilities a woman lies under are for the most part intended for her protection and benefit, so great a favorite is the female sex in the laws of England."

[2] Theoretically it could be obtained by Act of Parliament; in only two cases was it obtained at the instance of a wife.

[3] This was not due to any alteration in attitudes towards women, but simply part of a general development of humane feeling which rendered juries reluctant to convict prisoners of the many crimes punishable by death.

woman married after January 1, 1883, was given the absolute ownership of all property, both belonging to her before marriage or coming to her afterwards, including earnings.[1]

Mothers' Rights of Guardianship. The recognition of the independent legal personality of all women, married as well as single, was an essential step in the emancipation of women, and of utmost significance in the interests of family reconstruction. Of even more crucial significance, however, from the latter standpoint, is the recognition of the mother's full and equal rights in her legitimate children. Until 1839 paternal rights were all but absolute; the first concessions being won in that year by Caroline Norton, herself an anti-feminist, but driven by her own suffering to promote the earliest legislative attempt to improve the position of women. She had left her husband, who thereupon took her three children from her. "I have learned the law respecting married women piecemeal," wrote Caroline Norton, "by suffering every one of its defects of protection. . . . I really lost my young children—craved for them, struggled for them, was barred from them—and came too late to see one that had died . . . except in his coffin."[2]

Not until 1886, however, did the Guardianship of Infants Act grant a mother equal rights in the custody and care of her children with any guardian appointed by the father to act after his death. In his lifetime she still had no legal rights to custody or control. At last, by the Act of 1925, it was declared expedient that the principle of legal equality "should obtain with respect to the guardianship of infants and the rights and responsibilities conferred thereby."

Removal of Inequalities in Divorce Laws. The Matrimonial Causes Act of 1857, the primary purpose of which was to abolish the jurisdiction of the ecclesiastical courts and make divorce possible otherwise than by Act of Parliament, also achieved certain reforms with regard to protecting the property of injured wives. But it perpetuated the old inequalities of rights with respect to divorce. A husband might divorce his wife for adultery, but a wife might divorce a husband only if, in addition to adultery, he were guilty of cruelty or desertion. Despite its limitations, it opened the way for court judg-

[1] The Married Woman's Property Act was passed first for Scotland in 1881, at which time the objection to the bill was succinctly voiced by Lord Fraser as follows: "The protection which has been thrown around a married woman already is sufficient, and why she should be allowed to have money in her pocket to deal with as she thinks fit, I cannot understand." Strachey, *op. cit.*, p. 275.

[2] Quoted by Strachey, *op. cit.*, pp. 37–40.

ments and further acts which gradually undermined the old theory, that in marriage a woman became her husband's property. Not till 1891, however, was a woman's personal freedom safeguarded. A court decision freed a wife whose husband had seized and imprisoned her after obtaining a decree for restitution of conjugal rights. Complete equality between the sexes with regard to grounds of divorce was not established until the Matrimonial Causes Act of 1923.

Beginnings of the Struggle for Suffrage. Educational and economic opportunities might be extended to women, they might be accorded an improved legal status, but without the final step, the *winning of suffrage,* the emancipation of women could never be complete. Mary Wollstonecraft had clearly recognized this fact; but not till seventy-four years after her *Vindication* did John Stuart Mill make his parliamentary speech on the *Admission of Women to Electoral Franchise.*[1] The small band of feminists who had gathered round Barbara Leigh Smith and had founded the *Englishwoman's Journal* eagerly supported the parliamentary candidacy of Mill, and, with his support and that of Henry Fawcett, formed the first Woman's Suffrage Committee in 1866, and presented a petition for the enfranchisement of women.[2] When Mill opened the first debate on this new and popularly distasteful subject, eighty men voted for it. Not until 1870, with the definite blocking of the Suffrage Bill, was the full force of the opposition disclosed. With the defeat of the Suffrage amendment, introduced during the debate on Gladstone's Reform Bill in 1884, a period of delay and discouragement set in.

Suffragists and Suffragettes. In 1893, New Zealand granted woman's suffrage, to be followed the succeeding year by South Australia. Popular sentiment was becoming more favorable; and, in 1897, a national organization came into being under the name of the National Union of Women's Suffrage Societies,

---

[1] In his *Subjection of Women,* Mill says that from his youth he had held an opinion which "had been constantly growing stronger by the progress of reflection and the experience of life, that the principle which now regulates the existing social relation between the sexes—the legal subordination of one sex to the other—is wrong in itself, and now one of the chief hindrances to human improvement." (Everyman edition, p. 219.) He argued that much good might be expected to result were women the equals of men both in rights and in cultivation. Not only would women be much happier, but the quality of family life would be immeasurably improved, and society would gain untold benefit from making use of the abilities and services of one-half of its members.

[2] In the absence of Barbara Bodichon, who was ill, Emily Davies and Elizabeth Garrett took the petition to Mill at Westminster Hall. It was signed by over 1,500 women including Florence Nightingale, Harriet Martineau, Mary Somerville, and Josephine Butler.

with Millicent Garrett Fawcett as president. The Independent Labor Party, then entering the field of practical politics, included equal rights in its program. Among its promoters were Mr. and Mrs. Pankhurst, the latter of whom, impatient for more vigorous action, organized the Women's Social and Political Union and the *militant* suffrage movement. Though united in their final aim, there was now a fundamental cleavage in the suffrage ranks. The law-abiding, constitutional forces, commonly called *suffragists*, belonged to the National Union, and set themselves to the conversion of public opinion. The militants or *suffragettes* adopted the policy of public protest. In season and out, they brought up the question of suffrage, with arrest and imprisonment for "obstruction" as the result. Driven to more violent tactics, they broke the windows of shops and public buildings, set fire to empty houses, and put acid into mail-boxes. When imprisoned, they displayed indomitable courage, went on "hunger-strike," and were subjected to "forcible feeding." Emily Davison became a martyr to the Cause by flinging herself under the feet of the racing horses on Derby Day.

The Winning of Suffrage. With the outbreak of the War all political activities of the suffrage societies ceased at once, and women by the thousands dedicated themselves to the service of their country. In the nursing service, in munition factories, and in innumerable forms of work which had hitherto been reserved for men, women at last had an opportunity to demonstrate their efficiency. The effect on public opinion was profound. As a result, in the early spring of 1918, by the passage of the Representation of the People Act, suffrage was conferred on women over thirty who were householders or wives of householders. A further act made women over twenty-one eligible to be nominated and elected to the House of Commons. Ten years later, the full enfranchisement of women on equal terms with men was secured by the passage of the Equal Franchise Act of 1928.

The Present Status of Englishwomen. The last glaring inequality was thus removed, but many minor inequalities still remain. Particularly in the economic world, as Ray Strachey says, equality is still a "distant dream."[1] With partial enfranchisement attained in 1918, the leaders of the fight for suffrage set themselves to work for a "real equality of liberties, status and opportunities between men and women."[2] An Emancipation

[1] *Op. cit.,* p. 384.
[2] A number of women have been elected to the House of Commons since 1918, and one woman, Margaret Bondfield, has held cabinet office.

Bill which was intended to remove all remaining disabilities failed, but in the same year, 1919, the Sex Disqualification (Removal) Act passed. However, when in 1922 Viscountess Rhondda claimed a seat in the House of Lords on the basis of the laws of 1918 and 1919, her claim was denied. Under her leadership and that of other outstanding women, a series of measures were passed, in the next few years, in which the principle of legal equality between the sexes was translated into actual fact and put upon the statute books.[1]

THE EMANCIPATION OF WOMEN IN AMERICA

Contrasts between the Position of Women in America and England. A fundamental contrast between conditions in the New World and the Old lay in the opportunities afforded by the unappropriated resources of the vast new continent. As the tide of emigration moved westward, and pioneers renewed their struggle for conquest of the wilderness, attitudes were formed which have had profound influence on American life and thought, and which have been an important factor in improving the status of women. Under frontier conditions, it is true, women are dependent on men as hunters and protectors of the family group, and they are bound to their traditional tasks of rearing numerous children and engaging in arduous and unremitting household production. But they share at the same time in the work of men, and their courage and invaluable help in emergencies give them higher value than homemakers usually attain under less primitive conditions. Moreover, there was always a scarcity of women on the frontier; another factor which greatly enhanced the estimation in which they were held. Western influences tended to undermine the traditional attitudes towards women prevalent in the settled life of the East; so that it is not surprising that American women have had on the whole an advantage over Englishwomen in their struggle for emancipation.

As in England, the position of women was not on the whole so favorable in the late eighteenth and early nineteenth centuries as it had been earlier. English attitudes, it must be remembered, exercised a constant influence on American opinion. In spite of the fact that the legal status of colonial women perpetuated the spirit of English common law, women had fuller social and political rights in the colonies than in the

[1] For a brief discussion of these see Erna Reiss, "Changes in Law," in *Our Freedom* (1936), edited by Ray Strachey.

early days of the Republic.   There were no such outstanding women in the early nineteenth century as Abigail Adams, the wife and able assistant of John Adams, or Margaret Brent and Ann Hutchinson, in the seventeenth century.[1]   Independence of spirit and freedom of expression among women seemed to have vanished.   Even in literature women had very little to say, apart from Hannah Adams with her theological and historical works.   In the eighteenth century there had been numerous women journalists, but between 1792 and 1840 there is no record of American women in newspaper work.

Already by the end of the eighteenth century there was a marked contrast between the position of unmarried daughters in America and in England.   The modification of parental authority by means of democratic ideas was particularly noticeable in the case of girls.   De Tocqueville, writing in the thirties, not only remarked this fact, but contrasted the emancipated condition of girls with the continuing subordination of American wives.[2]   The "American independence of woman" he wrote, "is irrevocably lost in the bonds of matrimony."   Not, indeed, till after the Civil War was the traditional subjection of wives modified to any appreciable extent.[3]

[1] Margaret Brent, who came to Maryland from England in 1638, distinguished herself in business and public affairs and was appointed by the Governor of Maryland as his sole executrix. Entering the Assembly in 1648, she "requested to have a vote in the House for herself and voyce allsoe." A. M. Earle, *Colonial Dames and Goodwives* (1895), pp. 47–48. Anne Hutchinson was banished from Massachusetts for her religious views, in 1638, four years after her arrival from England. She had demanded that "the same rights of individual judgment upon religious questions should be accorded to woman which the Reformation had already secured to man." Anne's chief opponent was Governor Winthrop, whose views on women are evident from a letter written in 1840, deploring the loss of her reason and understanding by "a goodly young woman . . . by occasion of her giving herself wholly to reading and writing and had written many books. . . . For if she had attended to her household affairs and such things as belong to women and not gone out of her way and calling to meddle with such things as are proper for men whose minds are stronger, she had kept her wits and might have improved them usefully and honorably in the place God had set her." Earle, *Child Life in Colonial Days*, p. 90.

[2] *Democracy in America* (4 vols., tr. H. Reeve, London, 1835–1840).

[3] In rural districts the corporal chastisement of wives to enforce the husbands' supremacy seems to have been nothing unusual in the earlier nineteenth century. One Methodist exhorter "every few weeks gave his wife a beating with a horsewhip. He said it was necessary, in order to keep her in subjection and because she scolded so much. Now this wife surrounded by six or seven little children . . . was obliged to spin and weave cloth for all the garments of the family . . . , to milk . . . , to make butter and cheese and do all the cooking, washing, making and mending . . . ; and, with the pains of maternity forced upon her every eighteen months, was whipped by her pious husband 'because she scolded.'" E. C. Stanton, S. B. Anthony, M. J. Gage, I. H. Harper, *The History of Woman Suffrage* (6 vols., 1881–1922), Vol. I, pp. 88–89.

The Genteel Female. These emancipated young ladies seem to have spent a wholly disproportionate amount of their time in reading sentimental novels. Those who did so belonged in many cases to the leisure class, whose women in increasing numbers were becoming indolent and self-indulgent ladies of fashion. Artificial standards of gentility became current, in direct opposition to the spread of democratic ideals, and, as always, the leisure class was influential in determining current fashions and standards. Ignorance and uselessness were considered genteel even for women who were not among the "ornaments" of society. On Southern plantations, English aristocratic ideas had been influential from the first. Although wives had little opportunity to be idle, Southern ladies embodied, perhaps better than any others, the current ideals of delicacy and fragility, and were treated with romantic gallantry by men.[1]

American novels, as well as the great mass of reading intended for feminine consumption, the elegant periodicals, anthologies of verse, and gift books, were largely the work of women writers.[2] At first these novels were derivative, offshoots from English fiction which was widely read in America. Of all English women writers, Hannah More was most influential, and her much eulogized "propriety" was absorbed into the ideal of the "genteel female."

Religious interests were considered peculiarly appropriate to genteel females, and a morbid introspective piety was highly esteemed. Ministers exercised great influence, and lost no opportunity in impressing on women the fact of their mental inferiority to men. Christianity, said one of them, in 1822, has

[1] This gallantry and the jealous guarding of the chastity of their women were traits compensating for the actual licentiousness of Southern men, facilitated by Negro slavery and the demoralizing association of white men with colored women. Venereal diseases were common among the colored population, and Calhoun surmises that the proverbial delicacy of Southern women may to some extent have been the result of contracting venereal diseases from their husbands. *Social History of the American Family*, Vol. II, Chapters XI and XII.

[2] The titles of these periodicals and gift books are revealing. *The American Moral and Sentimental Magazine* was one, while *Godey's Lady's Book*, the most successful of all, was edited by Sarah Josepha Hale, whose chief objects were "the elevation of Christian female character and the moral improvement of society." She was a strong believer in "gentility," and "found the key to life in the interpretation of the Bible." Gift books known as *keepsakes* began to appear in increasing numbers from 1826 on. The names of some of these were: *The Golden Chalice, The Angel Visitor, The Token, The Pearl, Gem of the West, Religious Souvenirs, The Ladies Wreath: a Selection from the Female Poetic Writers*. By the middle of the nineteenth century there were so many "female poetic writers" that five anthologies appeared at almost the same time.

"wisely assigned the stations which females may occupy with appropriate dignity. . . . Modesty . . . , while it prescribes a silent and gentle manner, allows and commends in her a powerful and extensive influence. It clothes her with . . . those retired virtues, which render her lovely to the Christian observer, rather than the mental decorations and embellishments by which she might more successfully obtrude herself on the common eye."[1] Furness believes that "it would be almost impossible to overemphasize the importance of this conviction that men were ruled in matters of religion and refinement by the sway of the Genteel Female." She is "the ideal agent of social and moral uplift" or, as an eminent divine put it, in 1837, "The influence of the pious female, in her own proper sphere, is conducive to the best interests of humanity, both for time and eternity."[2] Similar ideas in England were by no means so potent as in America. Here, because of the absence of indigenous masculine standards in popular literature, feminine ideals had peculiar power in shaping the mass mind: one of the chief reasons, Furness believes, for the trend towards feminization in America.

Much attention was paid to etiquette and decorum in dress; such changes in fashion as exposure of elbows or insufficiency of petticoats at once brought charges of immodesty and indecency. The sickly sentimentality of the love poetry is ample proof of the unwholesome effect of artificial standards.[3] The exquisite susceptibility of the truly genteel female was never shown to greater advantage than when she went into a decline induced by unrequited love and died of a broken heart. It was *indelicate* to be too robust. "The slender and ethereal form" was considered the "fitting embodiment of the gentle spirit."[4] "The prevalent conception of gentility," Furness says, "demanded a touch of physical decadence. . . . A touch of tuberculosis added to feminine charms was deemed irresistible."[5] While still exercising an influence in the middle of

[1] Clifton Furness (ed.), *The Genteel Female* (Alfred A. Knopf, Inc., 1931), p. 211.
[2] *Ibid.*, p. xxx.
[3] According to a group of ministers, meeting in 1837, modesty and delicacy would be "consumed, and the way opened . . . to degeneracy and ruin," if females were acquainted with and conversed on "things which ought not to be named." Calhoun, *op. cit.*, Vol. II, p. 98. In this connection it is suggestive that the elegant, but none the less explicit, verses which appeared in a newspaper in 1843, should advertise Lucinda's Cordial or The Elixir of Love for sexual ills, including barrenness. Furness, *op. cit.*, pp. 176–178.
[4] See selections from a funeral sermon, in 1856. *Ibid.*, pp. 46, 47.
[5] *Ibid.*, p. xxxi.

the nineteenth century, such pernicious ideas had fortunately been giving way for some time before a more healthful outlook. By 1832 physical education was being recommended in the form of "calisthenic exercises for females."

Of particular significance is the fact that the sentimental outpourings of female writers bore witness to what Furness calls an "adolescent and therefore exaggerated humanitarianism." It was realized that the mother might lose her child not only by death; her "wandering boy" might become a drunkard or criminal; her overtrusting daughter might meet with "a fate worse than death." Were her "female innocence betrayed" she might be deserted and abandoned as an "irretrievably ruined fallen woman."[1] Poems such as *She Knew She Was Deserted*, or stories of unfortunates who had strayed from the path of virtue, held widespread appeal. Nor were the newly awakened humanitarian sentiments entirely without practical expression. Rescue missions were founded for "abandoned females," and active work in prison reform was undertaken under the leadership of Lydia Maria Child, the foremost literary lady of her day, who in 1833 wrote the pioneer anti-slavery book, *An Appeal on Behalf of That Class of Americans Called Africans*. Interest also became widespread in the care of orphans, one of the first orphanages being founded, in 1827, through the work of Joanna Graham Bethune.

As women gained in actual influence in the world outside the home, and above all when the demand arose for an equal share with men in social responsibilities and for "equal rights," the opposition increased in vehemence and insisted anew on the "magic power" exercised by chaste and pious females within their "proper sphere" as wives and mothers. As late as 1859, W. M. Thayer addressed young girls as follows: "It is more necessary that girls understand what their mission is at the present day, on account of the preposterous claims set up for what are called 'women's rights.' The female character appears to advantage only in its appropriate sphere. Who can respect Joan of Arc . . . ? Her remarkable prowess and brilliant victories do no atone for her breach of female delicacy."[2]

The Participation of Women in Temperance Reform and in the Anti-slavery Movement. Sentimentality reached its height when

---

[1] "Of all the spectacles which meet the eye," admonished the same minister, whose eulogium on female modesty has been quoted, "none, to the virtuous and delicate mind, is more disgusting, hideous and loathsome than that of an abandoned female." *Ibid.*, p. 108.

[2] *Ibid.*, p. xxvii.

women were no longer submerged in the round of daily work, and before it had become possible for them to make effective efforts to ameliorate the sufferings of their own lives and the evils in the world around them. In the absence of the necessary education, independence, and social and political influence they could but take refuge in pious emotions. The core of reality imbedded in the sentimental legend of woman's power, the very potent influence they have exerted within the family, was gradually informed and set free during the nineteenth century, to become effective in social amelioration.

In America, much of the nineteenth-century zeal for reform was absorbed in the movements for temperance and abolition. In both, women were destined to play a leading part. The movement for temperance, in particular, appealed to the missionary spirit, which was such a pervasive aspect of American life; the missionary field being actually included in woman's otherwise closely circumscribed sphere. Men had been working for temperance since the beginning of the century, but women did not take an active part till after 1840.[1] Leaders for women's rights such as Elizabeth Cady Stanton, Susan B. Anthony, and Amelia Bloomer had all been active in organization for temperance reform. It was in the abolition movement, however, that women first began to do public work and to organize. The first woman's club with a political object was the Philadelphia Female Anti-Slavery Society, founded in 1833, of which Lucrecia Mott was corresponding secretary. In 1836, Angelina Grimké, of South Carolina, became agent for the American Anti-Slavery Society, and was one of the very first American women who dared to speak in public.

The Civil War. By the end of the Civil War, the relation between the sexes had been profoundly disturbed, as has so often been the case in times of social upheaval. Women had risen to the emergency, and kept their families together by taking over the work of men on farms, in business, and in government service. The first woman in government service was Clara Barton, who became a clerk in the Pension Office in

[1] Mary Austin in *Earth Horizon* (1932), pp. 140–141, discusses the prevalence of hard drinking and the actual conditions underlying the intensity of the Mid-Western campaign for temperance. This book gives a vivid first-hand picture of the spiritual release from the drudgery of housekeeping and from the caprices of masculine tyranny which came into the lives of women with their membership in the Women's Christian Temperance Union, founded in the seventies. By the end of the century, it became, under the leadership of Frances Willard, the most powerful woman's organization in the United States. Without its unceasing efforts the Eighteenth Amendment would never have been passed in 1920.

1854. During the War, she organized and led corps of nurses on the battlefields, caring for the wounded of both sides alike. She helped abroad in the Franco-Prussian War and, on her return, organized the American Red Cross, for service in the alleviation of all public calamities. Another leader of trained nurses during the War was Dorothea Dix, who had already won world-wide fame for her work for the insane. Nursing was raised to a profession and invaluable experience in coöperation and organization was gained by women. Moreover, self-reliance and independence were inevitable results of even the temporary absence of husbands and fathers. Other women were widowed or remained unmarried, and so were permanently independent of masculine protection and control.[1] The genteel female accordingly became a *woman*. "The shock of the war seems to have awakened American women from ladylike futility. . . . Thousands of women learned contempt for frivolity, gossip, fashion, idleness; learned to consider seriously and fairly the capacities of their sex; and thus laid a strong and practical basis for the advancement of the rights of woman."[2]

Women's Clubs. Before passing to specific aspects of the emancipation movement, one other topic of a more general character deserves mention: the prevalence and influence of those unique institutions, American women's clubs. Apart from church and missionary societies and charitable organizations, the first women's clubs in America were those established in the New England mill towns by the earliest women factory workers; but it was not till after the Civil War that typical women's clubs began to spring up throughout the country.[3]

There were various reasons for this phenomenon. Clubs helped to fill the vacuum left when war work came to an end. And the housewives of the seventies in any case found themselves with more leisure, because of the development of many household aids such as the sewing machine, and the substitution of factory products for those of home production. Finally, middle-aged women were becoming conscious of the limitations

[1] Already in 1855, Margaret Fuller Ossoli in her book, *Women in the Nineteenth Century*, had answered those who deplored the exodus of women from their "proper sphere," by pointing out that for thousands of women no domestic sphere existed, since they were obliged to support themselves. Even more were obliged to assist their husbands in earning the support of the family.

[2] Reprinted by permission of the publishers, The Arthur H. Clark Company from Calhoun's *Social History of the American Family*, Vol. II, pp. 360 *et seq.*

[3] These post-war clubs, it will be noted, had accepted the transition from *female* through *lady* to *woman*. The first club in the modern sense had been the Jacksonville Ladies' Educative Association founded in 1833.

of their education and longed for "culture." These reasons, combined with circumstances peculiar to American life, in particular the absence of sharply defined class distinctions, gave rise to that "spirit which has marked American women ever since—a curious sex-solidarity having in it no sex-antagonism."[1]

The two leading pioneers among women's clubs were both founded in 1868. Sorosis was the result of the exclusion of Mrs. Croly and other women journalists from the Press Club dinner given for Charles Dickens in New York. The programs were at first wholly literary, but in 1869 a committee was appointed to investigate infant mortality in orphan asylums. The New England Woman's Club of Boston engaged from the first in social and philanthropic work. Women's clubs had two main purposes: to achieve broader culture and to work for social betterment. While the study clubs were at first in the majority, as the club movement spread, an increasing number entered the field of social service.[2] In addition to the regular women's clubs, other clubs for special purposes came into being, and, in 1888, there was further organization in two national federations: the National Council of Women, whose leaders were interested in suffrage, and the General Federation of Women's Clubs, composed of groups of women either opposed or indifferent to suffrage. At the two Chicago Fairs, the National Council of Women sponsored a congress of women, but where the women came in 1893 as groups of homemakers petitioning for equal rights and opportunities, they came in 1933 dedicated to further "Our Common Cause— Civilization," by a frontal attack on world problems on the part of organized groups of citizens. Women's clubs, higher education, and the ballot were recognized by the leaders of the congress as the three chief agencies in effecting this significant change in the attitudes of women.

The older type of club, organized for the most part in the General Federation, tends to conservatism, since its membership is largely composed of middle-aged homemakers. Not until 1914 was suffrage endorsed by the Federation. Its endorsement of birth control, in 1935, would seem to indicate the spread of more liberal tendencies among its members. As agencies for adult education and for civic and social reform, women's clubs

[1] Inez Haynes Irwin, *Angels and Amazons* (1933), p. 211.

[2] As high schools and colleges opened their doors to girls the longing for culture lost some of its influence in shaping programs. On the other hand, with increasing participation by women in the life of the world outside the home, more women came to feel an urge to social action.

have a notable record of achievement. Women to-day owe their present freedom and power, not only to the leaders of the emancipation movement, but to the assistance rendered by less articulate women, organized in the women's clubs of the country.

Women Enter Industry. At the close of the eighteenth century, Charles Brockden Brown made a plea for greater opportunities for women. "Women are generally superficial and ignorant, because they are generally cooks and seamstresses."[1] A hundred years later the list of occupations, as given in the 1900 census, contained 303 separate employments in 295 of which women were to be found.[2] The largest occupational group was engaged in domestic and personal service. In this, and in the employment of women—chiefly Southern Negroes—in agriculture, the nineteenth century is responsible for no revolutionary change. The three outstanding occupational events were the entrance of women into the professions and into the field of business, classified by the census as trade and transportation, and, thirdly, the emergence of vast numbers of women from their homes to engage in manufacturing and mechanical pursuits.

Already between 1820 and 1840 more than a hundred industrial occupations were open to women, industries at all stages of development being carried on according to a variety of methods.[3] In some of the early cotton mills the majority of the employees were the daughters of farmers: capable and ambitious girls, unwilling to enter domestic service and with no other employment open to them save the unremunerative occupation of schoolmistress. In factory work they saw the opportunity of acquiring economic independence, or of saving money needed for some cherished purpose: to help their families or to further their own education. Conditions in mill towns such as Lowell, in the forties, are revealed by the *Lowell Offering*, a magazine published by Lucy Larcom and her fellow factory workers. Many of them were eager to avail themselves of every "opportunity," Lyceum lectures, lending libraries, debating clubs, and

---

[1] Extracts from Brown's "Rights of Women" in the *Weekly Magazine*, March 17, 1798, are reprinted in *The Genteel Female*, pp. 241–243.

[2] No women were reported as U. S. soldiers, sailors, or marines, nor as street-car drivers, fire-department foremen, apprentices and helpers to roofers and slaters, helpers to steam-boiler makers, and brass workers.

[3] See Edith Abbott, *Women in Industry* (1909), pp. 64 *et seq.*, for discussion of the misquotation from Harriet Martineau's *Society in America*, to the effect that in 1836 but seven occupations were open to women.

"female circles" of all kinds, including the Improvement Circle made famous by the *Lowell Offering*. Some of the girls attended academies or were schoolmistresses part of the year. As teaching opportunities increased for women, the number of educated operatives steadily decreased.

At no time did most of these girls contemplate permanent employment in the mills. They were therefore content to put up with long hours, insanitary and unventilated mills, crowded boarding houses. Not until the influx of a fairly permanent body of factory operatives were definite attempts made to improve working conditions. But by then most of the women operatives were of foreign origin, easy to exploit. Although the number of women in industry increased to over a million and a quarter by 1900, not until the end of the century were they beginning to achieve effective organization. For the most part they have been all along engaged in low paid and unskilled work.

Women Enter Business. The census of 1870 was the first to list employed persons by sex and occupation. There were *seven* female shorthand writers listed; 355 "employees of telegraph companies (not clerks)"; 943 government clerks; and 6,194 shop girls. At this time, 867,354 women were employed in domestic service, and, of the 571,966 other women working outside their homes, the largest group was employed in factories. The tremendous increase in the number of women "gainfully employed" by the end of the century is to be accounted for, not only by the entrance of women into factories, but also into business. In 1900, 503,347 women were employed in "trade and transportation." The invention of typewriters and telephones had much to do with this situation. From the first, women typists were employed and stenography became a growing field for women's work. In the census of 1880, 147 women were listed as "female employees of telephone companies (not clerks)." Women's entrance into the business field was thus well begun in the nineteenth century.

Women Enter the Professions. While the early mill girls played their part in the long struggle for emancipation, on the whole the results of that struggle had little effect on working women. Its benefits have accrued almost entirely to the well-educated; most of all to women of the professional groups.

Just as in England, though under very different circumstances, teaching was the first profession to enlist the services of women. In the middle of the century they were still ill-paid, and their position unenviable.[1] Already, however, the first women doctors had taken their degrees.[2] Ironically enough the earliest chance for women to study medicine was given by Dr. Samuel Gregory. In 1848, in horrified protest against the practice of obstetrics by men, he had started a school of scientific midwifery in Boston called the Female Medical College. In 1850 an institution of the same name was founded in Philadelphia, designed to give a thorough medical education. Before this time, however, several women had demanded education as physicians; most famous of all being the Blackwell sisters Elizabeth and Emily. In 1849 Elizabeth graduated at the head of her class, the first woman to win a modern medical degree.[3]

By 1864 there were between 250 and 300 women physicians regularly graduated from medical schools. Women's hospitals began to be opened by women doctors, a Woman's Medical School was opened in Chicago in 1869, and in the same year the University of Michigan opened its medical school for women. In 1882, Johns Hopkins admitted women, and finally, by the turn of the century, only seven important medical colleges in the United States remained closed to them.

In both England and America the earliest women's organizations had been established for religious purposes; there had also been a number of American female missionaries. But apart from the Quaker women who preached,—among whom Lucretia

---

[1] At an educational convention held in Rochester in 1853, Susan B. Anthony had the temerity to address the chair. When she was finally allowed to speak to a hostile audience, she said: "It seems to me, gentlemen, that none of you quite comprehend the cause of the disrespect of which you complain. . . . So long as society says a woman is incompetent to be a lawyer, minister or doctor, but has ample ability to be a teacher . . . , every man of you who chooses this profession tacitly acknowledges that he has no more brains than a woman." Quoted by Irwin, *op. cit.*, pp. 25–26.

[2] Since women in all ages had served as nurses and midwives, their entrance into medicine would apparently have been natural enough. And yet, in this step, was involved a complete break from the conception of the lady as of inferior intelligence, but with sensibilities too refined to face the harsher facts of life; also as one whose chastity was best preserved through ignorance. The entrance of women into the medical profession here, as in England, constituted, on this account, one of the most important steps in emancipation. As a sample of the reasons advanced for excluding women from medicine, one physician solemnly pointed out that they would not be able to stay out late at night, nor could women grow moustaches!

[3] The students of the medical department of a small university, at Geneva, N. Y., had voted to admit her as a joke. But when she joined their classes, they treated her with respect; the townspeople, on the other hand, considered her as either a lunatic or a bad character. Women held their skirts aside as she passed on the streets and made insulting remarks. After foreign study, she attempted to practice, but having few patients, she founded, in 1853, The New York Dispensary for Poor Women and Children. Her sister Emily, who had studied with Sir James Simpson in Edinburgh, joined her in this undertaking.

Mott was outstanding,—no woman became an ordained minister in a Christian church anywhere in the world before Antoinette Brown Blackwell, in 1852, was ordained and given the little Congregational Church at South Butler, N. Y., after taking the three-year course in theology offered by Oberlin College. The religious tone of America being predominantly non-ritualistic, women have been able to become ministers in a number of denominations, one of the pioneer preachers being the great suffrage leader, Anna Howard Shaw, who was ordained in the Methodist Protestant Church in 1880.[1]

The census of 1870 listed "four lawyers, female." The first women lawyers met less determined opposition than had the pioneer doctors. To obtain a legal education was easier, however, than to obtain admission to the bar. In 1869, Arabella Mansfield was admitted to the Iowa bar after "reading" in a private office. But many women in other states were not so fortunate. The Wisconsin Supreme Court, in refusing admission, in 1875, to Lavinia Goodell, already admitted to the local bar by the Circuit Court of Rock County, voiced the still prevailing sentiment as follows: "It would be revolting to all female sense of the innocence and sanctity of their sex, shocking to man's reverence for womanhood . . . that women should be permitted to mix professionally in all the nastiness of the world which finds its way into courts of justice."[2] Nevertheless, by 1882, there were fifty-six women attorneys, thirty-one of them graduates from law schools; and by the end of the century there were 1,010.[3]

Education for Women. The Quakers opened their elementary schools from the first to girls as well as boys. In parts of New England girls were allowed to attend the public elementary schools in summer and early in the morning or late in the afternoon, when boys were not using the buildings. By the end of the eighteenth century, however, there appears to have been a disposition on the part of the more liberal to recognize that women as well as men stood in need of "cultivation of the mind," and the rudiments, at least, of higher education. Private

[1] Besides the Congregationalists, there have been women ministers among the Christians or Campbellites, the Unitarians, Universalists, and Methodists.

[2] Quoted by Irwin, *op. cit.*, pp. 174–175.

[3] Not all these women practised. Some took up law as a preliminary to business or else worked on legal periodicals. Among those in active practice were women who made brilliant careers for themselves, such as Belva Lockwood, the first of her sex to be admitted to the bar of the United States Supreme Court, and Ellen Spencer Mussey who brought about changes in laws affecting married women.

schools led the way. Prior to the nineteenth century, there had been only fashionable finishing schools for girls and no academies, the counterparts of the public high schools.[1] In 1802, a Female Academy was established by the Moravians in Salem, North Carolina, and in 1803, Bradford Academy added a "female department," remaining coeducational until 1836, when it became a school for girls exclusively, in order "to afford to young ladies . . . every facility for a thorough education"; it being a matter of the utmost importance, according to the catalogue, to guide and direct the "amazing influence" exerted by women.

By 1836, numbers of Female Academies and Ladies' Seminaries had been established. Associated with these are the names of the pioneer women educators of America, Emma Hart Willard and her sister, Almira Hart Phelps, Zilpah Grant, Catherine Beecher and her sister, Harriet Beecher Stowe, and Mary Lyon, who established the South Hadley Female Seminary, which was to become Mount Holyoke.[2]

The erroneous impression exists that academies, in common with earlier boarding schools, devoted much time to useless accomplishments. It is true that their catalogues list such items as painting, gilding, soirée, conversation, politeness, tambour, filigree, embroidery, and ornamental needlework. But most of their courses were designed to impart "useful communicable knowledge" and "discipline" the "intellectual powers." Bradford Academy in 1837 taught History, Philosophy, Chemistry, Geology, Botany, Astronomy, Rhetoric, and Metaphysics. The Alabama Female Academy in the same year included in "useful female knowledge," in addition to the above subjects, Arithmetic, Geometry, English, Geography, Political Economy, Natural Theology, Ecclesiastical History, Evidences of Christianity, and Female Biography and Mythology.[3] There was

[1] There had been some academies which admitted girls for part of the year, but none gave special attention to the instruction of girls. The finishing schools, both day and boarding, were on the English model, for the purpose of turning out "accomplished" young ladies.

[2] Catherine Beecher (1800–1878) founded with her sister the Hartford Female Seminary, and later, after establishing the Western Female Academy in Oxford, Ohio, became particularly interested in developing high schools with normal departments in Western towns. To assist her, a new organization came into being in New York City in 1852, The American Woman's Association. Miss Beecher also wrote *Suggestions Respecting Improvements in Education* (1829), and *Physiology and Calisthenics* (1850).

[3] An expansion of curricula for women was not accomplished without much opposition. The clergy, in particular, discovered most absurd reasons why each new subject was unsuitable. Geography, for example, might make women dissatisfied with

no suggestion, however, that ladies should be "strong-minded." Women seem to have acquiesced in considering intelligence a predominantly masculine attribute, thus tacitly acknowledging the *weakness* of the "female mind."

The development of academies was paralleled by the gradual opening of public secondary education to girls.[1] In recognition of the growing need for women teachers, the first normal schools opened in Massachusetts in 1839. But before this, in 1833, an event of the greatest importance had occurred. Oberlin College, in Ohio, established a "female department," in which women were to receive the same instruction as men. The purpose of this momentous step was declared to be "the elevation of female character by bringing within the reach of the misjudged and neglected sex all the instructive privileges which hitherto have unreasonably distinguished the leading sex from theirs."[2] In 1837, four young women were accepted for entrance into the collegiate department, and in 1841 the first three arts degrees ever received by women in the United States were granted by Oberlin.[3]

Colleges for women alone came next, but not till 1852, with the founding of Oxford Female College, did a woman's institution appear of coördinate rank with contemporary men's colleges. In the same year Antioch College became the first co-educational college to place women on absolutely equal terms with men. In 1865 Vassar opened: the first woman's college to offer educational facilities fully equaling those offered by the best colleges for men. Three hundred and fifty-three students entered in the first class, and among its first professors was Maria Mitchell, the astronomer.

In the seventies, Smith and Wellesley were founded, and from then on there was no lack of opportunities for college education for women, either in separate institutions, or in the increasing numbers of new Western state institutions which admitted women on an equal footing with men, or in colleges

domestic life and desirous of travel. It is noteworthy, moreover, that traditional taboos operated to exclude subjects such as zoölogy and physiology. In 1844 when Pauline Wright gave lectures on physiology, it was reported, "when she uncovered her manikin, ladies would drop their veils and run from the room, sometimes they 'fainted.'" Calhoun, *op. cit.*, Vol. II, p. 90. Higher mathematics, Latin, and Greek were also excluded, as beyond the grasp of the "female mind."

[1] Worcester, Mass., was the pioneer in opening a high school for girls in 1824. Boston followed, in 1826, but the school proved so "alarming" a success, there being more pupils than could be accommodated, that it closed in 1828.

[2] R. S. Fletcher and E. A. Wilkins, "The Beginning of College Education for Women and of Coeducation on the College Level," *Bulletin* of Oberlin College, New Series 343, 1937.

[3] In 1847 Lucy Stone was denied her diploma, because of bold objection to the rule that young ladies might not read their graduating exercises in public as did the men.

such as Barnard or Radcliffe, established in affiliation with existing universities for men.

The Revolution in the Legal Status of Married Women. In England changes in the law of domestic relations, being enacted by Parliament, affect the whole country uniformly. Under our federal system such changes lie solely within the jurisdiction of the several states. The result is a great diversity of laws, ranging from ultra-conservative to very liberal, even radical enactments. But one hundred years ago there was still at least one field of legislation in which uniformity and adherence to English common law prevailed throughout the country. Married women were deprived of legal personality, their persons and property controlled by their husbands whom they were legally obliged to serve and obey, and who in turn were obliged to support them.[1]

A substantially true picture of the legal status of women in the middle of the century is presented in the "Declaration of Sentiments" framed at the Seneca Falls Woman's Rights Convention in 1848.[2] Listed among other "injuries and usurpations on the part of man towards woman" are the following:

He has made her, if married, in the eye of the law civilly dead.

He has taken from her all right in property, even to the wages she earns.

He has made her morally an irresponsible being, as she can commit many crimes with impunity, provided they be done in the presence of her husband.

In the covenant of marriage, she is compelled to promise obedience to her husband, he becoming to all intents and purposes, her master —the law giving him the power to deprive her of her liberty, and to administer chastisement.

He has so framed the law of divorce, as to what shall be the proper causes, and, in case of separation, to whom the guardianship of the children shall be given, as to be wholly regardless of the happiness of women—the law in all cases going upon the false supposition of the supremacy of man, and giving all power into his hands.

---

[1] Besides the right to support, a wife had certain minor property rights: such for instance as dower rights in her husband's real estate. He was therefore obliged to obtain his wife's concurrence in the sale of any large portion of his land.

[2] The full text of the "Declaration of Sentiments" is to be found in *The History of Woman Suffrage*, Vol. I, pp. 70–71.

Slow changes in public opinion had nevertheless begun to register themselves in legislation in the first half of the nineteenth century. Connecticut led the way, in 1809, by allowing wives to dispose by will of such property as their husbands could not legally claim. Three other states followed suit in 1843. In 1839, Mississippi passed a law allowing married women to own property in their own right, and in the next decade several states granted certain property rights to married women. American legislation here preceded English and was without precedents to guide it. These changes were for the most part not due to any perception of the injustice of common law, but were designed to protect a woman's property in the interests of her heirs. It was indeed explicitly pointed out that they did not destroy "the proper authority of the husband."

More and more laws were enacted in the second half of the century which reveal a growing belief in the equality of husband and wife.[1]   In 1860, New York passed a law which removed almost all the disabilities under which married women had suffered. Although it was subsequently amended to the prejudice of women's interests, yet steady movement towards legal equality was under way. By 1900, married women might, in every state, dispose by will of their own property; in about two-thirds of the states they controlled their own earnings; and in a great majority they might make contracts and bring suit. In only a few states, however, had mothers equal rights with fathers in the guardianship of their children.

Beginnings of Political Action on the Part of Women. Women were not explicitly excluded from the franchise by colonial laws until Virginia in 1699 restricted suffrage to men. Shortly after the Revolution, New York disenfranchised women and was soon followed by all the states but New Jersey, which permitted tax-paying women to vote until 1807. In that year suffrage was restricted to free white males. There seems to have been no feminine protest against these measures, apart

---

[1] As early as the thirties protests were being made by liberal-minded husbands. In 1832 Robert Dale Owen, on his marriage with Mary Jane Robinson, signed a document which concluded: "of the unjust rights which, in virtue of this ceremony, an iniquitous law tacitly gives me over the person and property of another, I cannot legally but I can morally divest myself." In 1855 Lucy Stone and Henry Blackwell entered a similar protest in their marriage contract. They believed "that marriage should be an equal and permanent partnership, and so recognized by law; that, until it is recognized, married partners should provide against the radical injustice of present laws, by every means in their power." This statement was published in the *Worcester Spy.*

from a petition of Hannah Corben for a vote in the Virginia elections of 1778. Not, indeed, until the thirties is there evidence of growing interest in "women's rights," a phrase used by Sarah Grimké in articles for a Boston periodical in 1838. Already in 1836, Ernestine L. Rose had addressed the Michigan legislature requesting the enfranchisement of women.

Certain voting privileges began about this time to be given to women in matters connected with education, and to those women "who had no man to represent them." For example, in 1838, Kentucky "widows with children" were given a voice in school suffrage.

The Seneca Falls Convention. The organized suffrage movement began in protest against the exclusion of the women delegates to the World's Anti-Slavery Conference held in London in 1840.[1] In 1848 Lucretia Mott and Elizabeth Cady Stanton joined with Martha C. Wright and Mary Ann McClintock in issuing a call to a Woman's Rights Convention to be held at Seneca Falls, New York. With James Mott in the chair, and led by Elizabeth Stanton, the "Declaration of Sentiments" was adopted. In addition to the protests against the legal disabilities of married women, the following grievances against man were included in this historic document:

He has never permitted her to exercise her inalienable right to the elective franchise.

He has compelled her to submit to laws, in the formation of which she had no voice.

He has monopolized nearly all profitable employments.

He has denied her the facilities for obtaining a thorough education.

He has created a false public sentiment by giving the world a different code of morals for men and women, by which moral delinquencies which exclude women from society are not only tolerated, but deemed of little account in man.

He has usurped the prerogatives of Jehovah himself, claiming it as his right to assign for her a sphere of action, when that belongs to her conscience and her God.

[1] It was argued, with the evident approbation of the majority, that "all order would be at an end" if "promiscuous female representation be allowed" and "God's clear intention violated." Quoted by C. C. Catt and N. R. Shuler, *Woman Suffrage and Politics* (1923).

In conclusion, the Declaration demanded on behalf of women "immediate admission to all the rights and privileges which belong to them as citizens of the United States."[1]

Wide publicity was immediately aroused and a storm of ridicule and denunciation broke upon the suffrage leaders. But the movement spread rapidly. A National Woman's Rights Association was organized in 1849, and Lucy Stone and Susan B. Anthony joined Lucretia Mott and Elizabeth Stanton as its leaders. Popular prejudice was aroused anew by the temporary adoption of "bloomers" on the part of some of the suffrage supporters; but such progress was made that victory seemed in sight, when, with the Civil War, woman suffrage became "so hopelessly enmeshed in the politics of the negro question as to be inextricable for long years to come."[2]

Years of Struggle. Despite the acknowledged services of women during the War and the determined efforts of suffrage leaders, the Fourteenth Amendment used the term "male" in referring to suffrage, and the Fifteenth omitted the word "sex" in prohibiting the abridgment of the right to vote.[3] Disillusioned but undaunted, the suffragists argued that the Fourteenth Amendment conferred suffrage on all citizens. To put the matter to the test, several women registered, and a few, including Susan B. Anthony, actually voted. Not until 1875 did a Supreme Court decision conclusively demonstrate that citizenship did not confer the right to vote. In 1878, a woman's suffrage amendment, formulated by Susan B. Anthony, was introduced for the first time in Congress.

Meanwhile the suffrage cause was not without some success in the states. Suffrage in school and local elections was granted in some states, and full suffrage was obtained for the first time in the territory of Wyoming in 1869. When Wyoming became a state in 1890, its constitution confirmed the right of women to vote. Three neighboring states soon followed suit: Colorado in 1893, Idaho and Utah in 1896. From 1869 on, the suffrage forces were efficiently organized in two groups, until in 1889

---

[1] *The History of Woman Suffrage*, Vol. I, pp. 70–71. A number of resolutions were forthwith adopted, all of them unanimously, except the ninth which urged women to secure the right to vote.

[2] Catt and Shuler, *op. cit.*, p. 31. Bloomers were invented by a Mrs. Miller in 1852, but derive their name from Amelia Bloomer, a worker for temperance and suffrage, who wore them from 1857 to 1865, finally giving them up for fear her name would be connected with *them*, rather than with her work.

[3] In crushing an amendment to strike out the word "male" in the Fourteenth Amendment, the Senate recorded the first vote on the question of woman's suffrage on Dec. 14, 1866.

they were amalgamated in the National American Woman Suffrage Association. But despite growing strength the suffrage cause met with repeated defeats.[1]

State Victories and the Suffrage Amendment. In 1910, Washington voted for suffrage, to be followed by California in 1911; Arizona, Kansas, and Oregon in 1912; the territory of Alaska in 1913; Montana and Nevada in 1914. Formidable opposition was still encountered in the East, the people of twelve states rejecting suffrage in the years 1912 to 1915. Concentrating all their resources on New York the suffragists conducted an intensive campaign which, in 1917, culminated in victory. In 1918, the woman's suffrage amendment was passed by the House of Representatives, and the national committees of both parties decided to support it. From now on, state suffrage became of less importance than the passage of the federal amendment. But before its final adoption, fifteen states and Alaska gave women full suffrage, fourteen gave women presidential suffrage, and Arkansas and Texas allowed women to take part in primaries.

In drawing up what was to be the Nineteenth Amendment, Susan B. Anthony and her friends had followed the phraseology of the Fifteenth: "The right of citizens of the United States to vote shall not be denied or abridged by the United States, or by any State, on account of sex." No adequate pressure had been brought to bear prior to 1910, when the NAWSA once again opened headquarters in Washington. In 1912, Alice Paul, who had served with the militants in England, took charge, and her tactics caused a rupture in the party ranks. The Congressional Union, organized by Miss Paul, favored "holding the party in power responsible," and, definitely separating itself from the NAWSA, in 1914 became the National Woman's Party. The spectacular activities and unswerving courage of the militants probably hastened the final passage of the amendment by both House and Senate in 1919. This result would, however, have been impossible but for the steady work of the more conservative parent organization. All efforts were

[1] The liquor interests were particularly formidable adversaries. The prohibition societies had endorsed woman's suffrage, foreseeing, as did the liquor interests, that women would vote to curtail or prohibit the liquor trade. Moreover, growing interest on the part of women manifested itself not only in adherence to suffrage, but in active opposition, crystallized in the Association Opposed to the Further Extension of Suffrage to Women. The "antis" worked hard to stem the tide, and were frequently driven into paradoxical inconsistencies, such as persistent appearances on public platforms to prove that "woman's place is in the home."

now concentrated on securing the ratification of the amendment by thirty-six states. By June, 1920, thirty-five states had ratified. In August, Tennessee made the thirty-sixth, to be followed by Connecticut in September. Women throughout the country voted in the presidential elections of 1920.

SUGGESTED READING

Abbott, E., *Women in Industry*, 1909.

Abbott, G., "The Changing Position of Women," *A Century of Progress* (ed. Beard, C. A.), 1932.

Beard, M. R., *America through Women's Eyes*, 1933.

Breckenridge, S. P., *Women in the Twentieth Century*, 1933, Part I.

Calhoun, A. W., *Social History of the American Family*, 3 vols., 1917–1919, Vol. II, Chs. IV, V, IX, XIV; Vol. III, Chs. V, VI.

Furness, C., ed., *The Genteel Female*, 1931.

Goodsell, W., *A History of Marriage and the Family*, rev. ed., 1934, Chs. X, XI.

Groves, E. R., *The American Woman*, 1937.

Groves, E. R., and Brooks, L. M., *Readings in the Family*, 1934, Ch. VI.

Haggard, H. W., *Devils, Drugs, and Doctors*, 1929, Chs. IV, V.

Irwin, I. H., *Angels and Amazons*, 1933.

Mill, J. S., *The Subjection of Women*, 1869.

O'Malley, I., *Women in Subjection*, 1933.

Pinchbeck, I., *Women Workers and the Industrial Revolution*, 1930.

Stern, B. J., ed., *The Family Past and Present*, 1938, Ch. V.

Strachey, R., *Struggle*, 1930.

——, ed., *Our Freedom*, 1936.

Wollstonecraft, M., *Vindication of the Rights of Woman*, 1792.

Woody, T., *A History of Women's Education in the United States*, 2 vols., 1929.

CHAPTER XV

THE OCCUPATIONS OF WOMEN IN AMERICA

OCCUPATIONAL TRENDS

Women in Gainful Occupations. Between 1870 and 1930, the female population over sixteen has increased less than fourfold. At the same time there has been a sixfold increase in the number gainfully employed.[1] Out of every 1,000 women in 1930, 253 were working outside the home, constituting 21.9% of all occupied persons. The rapid influx of women into gainful occupations began to attract notice at the beginning of the century. Since the problems of women in industry appeared the most crucial, and added attention was given to them owing to the need for efficiency in war time, the first federal organization to be concerned with women's problems was established, in 1918, within the Department of Labor. So effective did it prove that, in 1920, it was put on a permanent basis as the Women's Bureau, under the directorship of Mary Anderson.[2]

By 1930, women were represented in large numbers in seven of the ten major occupational classifications employed by the Census Bureau: domestic and personal service, 3,438,000; clerical occupations, 1,970,000; manufacturing and mechanical industries, 1,860,000; the professions, 1,526,000; trade and agriculture, each less than a million; transportation and communication, something over a quarter million. Comparing 1870 percentages of employed women with those in 1930, decrease is shown for agriculture, 21% to 7%; manufacturing, 20% to 18%; and domestic and personal service, 53% to 33%; increase is shown for the professions, 6% to 12%; clerical

---

[1] In 1870, 1,836,288 females over 10, of whom 1,701,000 were over 16, were gainfully employed. Corresponding figures for 1930 were 10,752,116 and 10,546,000. One marked change for the better is the distinctly smaller proportion of girls under 16 who have been drawn into labor. In 1920, 56 out of 1,000 little girls, 10 to 15, were at work; in 1930, only 29. There were also considerably more girls, 16 to 20, working in 1920 than in 1930.

[2] It was originally called the Woman in Industry Service. While most of its investigations are still concerned with women in industry, it has broadened its sphere to include studies of women in domestic service, laundries, agriculture, and also in business and the professions. Its work has been of incalculable value; both as a scientific fact-finding agency in these varied fields, and in its formulation of standards of hours, wages, and working conditions for women.

occupations, 0.4% to 19%; and trade and transportation, 1% to 12%.[1] Altogether there has been a continuous shift from the older agricultural and industrial pursuits towards office, store, and professional work; while, despite the decline in percentage, there has been greater stability in the numbers employed in domestic and personal service.

Married Women and Gainful Employment. From the standpoint of the family, no trend is of greater importance than the tremendous increase in married women among the gainfully employed. In 1900, there were 769,000 married women workers; in 1930, 3,882,143. While the number of all employed women doubled, the number of employed married women increased fivefold and constituted well over one-third of all women in gainful employment. Over 450,000 of the employed homemakers, or well over one-eighth, were the *only* wage earners in their families. One-third of them were making homes for four persons or more (including themselves), and 132,000 represented families of at least *eight* persons. Of these women, 80% were employed outside their homes. One-fourth were in domestic and personal service, under one-fifth in manufacturing, one-tenth in the professions, one-tenth in agricultural pursuits, and a smaller proportion in sales occupations. One-sixth of them took in lodgers. A heavy burden is thus imposed on the majority of employed homemakers.[2] The old adage, "woman's work is never done," acquires a new and sinister significance when applied to mothers who must care for their families before and after long and exhausting hours spent in laundry, field, and factory; hours spent to earn a mere pittance, which, however small, is yet essential if their families are to be fed and clothed.[3] Many of these women work at night, cleaning offices and stores. Others who earn while staying at home engage in industrial home work, making or finishing articles with the help of daughters or young children, to earn a few cents an hour. Home workers are subjected to all the worst industrial evils: extremely long hours, very low pay, irregular employment, and working conditions which constitute a menace to the health of the workers and the public.

To speak of the "emancipation of women" in connection with the majority of working women is sheer mockery. It is

[1] See *Recent Social Trends*, Vol. I, p. 717.

[2] "The Employed Woman Homemaker in the United States," *Women's Bureau Bulletin*, No. 148 (1936).

[3] A particularly vivid picture of working women is given by Grace Hutchins, in *Women Who Work* (1934).

true, of course, that few men of the working class are *free* in any effective sense. But the lot of the working-class woman is far harder. Beginning usually to work in her teens in order to contribute to her parents' household, she marries young and bears children. Even if not forced to earn, but "supported" by a husband, her life as a working-class housewife is over-burdened with work and harassed by anxiety. For women such as this there is no equality of opportunity or of actual status.

WOMEN WHO WORK

Women in Domestic and Personal Service. Besides those engaged in the old domestic occupations of cooks, servants, and waitresses, this group includes janitors, elevator operators, and all those working in hotels, restaurants, and boarding houses, in laundries, in cleaning, dying, and pressing shops, and in beauty parlors. There is a noticeable drift, of recent years, from pursuits carried on independently and in the home, to similar work carried on in establishments; or, as in the case of power laundries, in what is in reality a machine-equipped factory. Domestic service, both in private houses and in hotels and restaurants, remains the most backward and unregulated of all pursuits in which women engage.[1] Beauty culture, on the other hand, is becoming a business with rising requirements for special training.

Women in Manufacturing and Mechanical Industries. Women outnumber men in clothing industries, in silk and knitting mills, in cigar and tobacco factories, and as operatives in candy factories. Relatively few women are found in skilled operations except in dressmaking, millinery, and tailoring, and in these their numbers have greatly decreased, probably because of the transfer of this work from the home or small shop to the factory. Relatively, too, the number of forewomen and officials in manu-facturing industries has decreased. Men continue to replace women where elaborate and heavy machinery has replaced simpler processes; and women continue to do the work which requires little training and strength, but in which quick, agile fingers and speed are assets. Despite the ability shown by women during the war in taking up new lines of work, in particular ma-chine-shop manufacture, they have apparently been unable to maintain the opportunities opened up to them at that time.

---

[1] More than a third of the women employed in this way, and in power laundries, are Negroes. Excessive heat and moisture, combined with long hours of high-speed work, make employment in laundries particularly exhausting.

On the whole, therefore, women work in less skilled and less well-paid occupations.[1] Not only are women's wages very low when measured by demands for health, decency, and comfort, but "different scales of pay usually exist for so-called women's and men's jobs and different scales often exist for individual men and women when the occupational equipment is alike and the quality and volume of work substantially identical."[2] Although, as a rule, women fill the unskilled jobs, this is by no means the sole cause for lower pay. Prejudice exists against women workers, and they are assigned less importance as wage earners than men; it being for the most part unrecognized that they frequently have others partially or wholly dependent upon them. It is true, of course, that women's opportunities are limited to some extent by their own attitude to work; it is often regarded as temporary, lasting only until marriage, or until the family has been tided over a difficult period. They are then unwilling to take the time for training or to assume a fully responsible attitude as wage earners. These circumstances combine to limit the bargaining power of women and to impede effective organization among them.

Long hours of work have been the rule for women. The studies of the Women's Bureau prove that the majority of women have worked in excess of forty-eight hours a week. As a matter of fact, most of the states where eight-hour laws have been passed are not important manufacturing states. Even where laws have been effective in limiting working hours, the result has been an intensification of labor known to the workers as the "speed-up" in its various forms. The laws are violated constantly, and overtime work is usually compulsory if the worker is to hold her job.

Physical breakdowns are common. There may be no actual disease; simply malnutrition and overfatigue due to the strain of long hours of high-speed work, seated very likely on a backless stool, in an ill-ventilated and badly lighted room. But there are also certain diseases from which women workers suffer more frequently than men. Chief among these is tuberculosis, to which *young* women are particularly subject. Four common hazards are apt to be contributing factors: faulty air conditions, fatigue, dust, and poisons or irritants affecting mucous membranes. Lead and benzol poisoning both attack women more

[1] Foreign-born white women are as a rule less fortunate than natives, and Negroes suffer worse exploitation than any other women workers.

[2] Sophonisba Breckenridge, *Women in the Twentieth Century* (1933), p. 215.

frequently and more severely than they do men, and have disastrous effects on the reproductive organs of women. All these health hazards are peculiarly injurious to expectant mothers, and render girls less fit for future child-bearing. Industrial accidents which kill or maim women are also on the increase, particularly among the younger workers. Very soon, however, the woman who remains at work grows old; and she can often find no work after she is over thirty. The need for social security is thus even more pressing for women than for men. Illness and accident are a more serious menace, old age is as hopeless, and there are the added hazards of maternity. Unemployment has been, relatively, even more widespread among women than among men.[1]

When women have organized they have shown themselves fully capable to secure substantial gains. A number of women have been outstanding labor organizers and leaders of strikes. Yet comparatively few women have been organized. Trade unions have been most successful among experienced and skilled workers, whereas most women workers are semi-skilled, or unskilled, and relatively young. An attitude of impermanency towards their work prevents many women from developing a consciousness of themselves as a permanent group in industry. And the superior and prejudiced attitude of working men towards women workers has been another obstacle. The National Woman's Trade Union League, founded in 1903, gathered together not only working women, but also some professional women and women of leisure.[2] It has a long record of achievement, and throughout has tended towards conciliation, endeavoring to settle industrial conflicts without strikes. Once

[1] In urging social security legislation, Senator Wagner attacked industrial discrimination against women. So long as present conditions persist, he said, their political liberation will be "an illusory blessing and their social equality a meaningless slogan." Deploring the extensive unemployment among women, and the fact that when employed they are underpaid "cheap material for the labor market," he described them as "stepchildren of industry in times of sunshine," and "the first orphans of the storm" when the depression came. *New York Times*, March 29, 1935. For a summary of data on unemployment among women, see the recent publication of the Women's Bureau, *Women in the Economy of the United States of America* (1937), Part I, Ch. 2.

[2] Its avowed purpose has been "to assist in the organization of women wage-earners into trade unions, and thereby to help secure conditions necessary for healthful and efficient work and to obtain a just return for their work." Seven points were included in its platform: organization of all workers into trade unions; equal pay for equal work regardless of sex or race; 8-hour day and 44-hour week; an American standard of living; full citizenship for women; the outlawry of war; and closer affiliation of women workers in all countries. For a brief account of its activities see Irwin, *op. cit.*, pp. 313–321.

industrial war has broken out, however, the League has supported strikers with both personal service and funds.

The Desirability of Special Legislation for Women in Industry. The National Woman's Party preserved its organization intact after the passage of the Nineteenth Amendment, which it regarded, not so much as an end, but as a tool for attaining "perfect equality between the sexes both by law and custom." To this end, its members have been working since 1921 for the passage of the Lucretia Mott Amendment: "Men and women shall have equal rights throughout the United States and in every place subject to its jurisdiction." In this way, they assert, the principle of equal rights would be established once and for all, because it would "override all existing legislation which denies women equal rights with men, and would render invalid every future attempt on the part of legislators or administrators to interfere with their rights." It would thus prove "the most effective and the surest, quickest, and least expensive method of securing equality to men and women before the law."[1] Since the passage of the amendment would profoundly affect, if not wholly nullify, all laws designed to protect women in industry, a consideration of this proposal is apposite at this point.

In *Towards Equal Rights for Men and Women*, Ethel Smith, of the League of Women Voters, presents a masterly analysis of the issues involved. As against the claims made by its proponents she holds that "any such blanket proposal for the removal of inequalities between men and women under existing law would be probably the least effective, the most uncertain, the slowest, and the most expensive method that could be devised for the purpose of securing the ends desired by the proponents themselves, while it would almost certainly be destructive to the purpose of other advocates of equal rights."[2]

The amendment is based on doubtful assumptions. It takes for granted that *equal rights* are something specific and determinable which can be decreed by law, thereby establishing equality in fact. But where there is actual *inequality* of social

[1] *Equal Rights by National Amendment* (National Woman's Party), p. 3. Quoted by Ethel M. Smith, *Towards Equal Rights for Men and Women* (1929), p. 58. A wider application of this proposal takes the form of a treaty first presented at the Sixth International Conference of American States at Havana in 1928. *Op. cit.*, pp. 59, 60, 81 *et seq.*

[2] *Ibid.*, p. 59. Even before the ratification of the Nineteenth Amendment the NAWSA had transformed itself into the National League of Women Voters whose central purpose was the education of women as full citizens. It also engages in active work for policies and measures upon which its membership is agreed.

or economic opportunity, as in the case between men and women, legal equality tends to aggravate rather than remove such inequality.   It could scarcely prove the *surest* means of securing equal rights, for legal authorities are divided in their opinion as to its results.   Its ends could not be accomplished without further detailed legislation which could, if desired, be enacted independently.   Far from being the "most effective, quickest and least expensive method," it would involve unnecessary delay, complication, and expense.   Worst of all, while "it is doubtful whether the amendment would remove, *ipso facto*, more than a few of the inequalities it is intended to remove . . . , it is virtually certain that it would create others . . . , that it would destroy or seriously impede the operation of valuable legislation affecting millions of women who are already subject to great hardships."[1]

Laws which protect women in industry are, with other labor laws, the product of "a new philosophy of social responsibility and coöperation" which "superseded the old theories of individual rights and free competition."[2]   This requires a new principle in law, "not the old arbitrary equalitarianism, but a classification of citizens for purposes of providing equal protection of the law."[3]   Special classes have different legislative needs which can only be met by special legislation.   Women, in their capacity as mothers, constitute a special class, and hence social legislation frequently differentiates between men and women.   The proponents of the equal rights amendment, retaining an individualistic point of view, see all differentiations as discriminatory.   Their opponents, interested primarily in social justice, regard *some* differentiations as discriminatory, but others as making for social and economic equality.   "Where the labor laws affect women only, they are based on the economic fact of women's peculiarly weak bargaining position, as compared with that of men, plus the physiological considerations of potential motherhood in its relation to public health."[4]   Such laws therefore are in the interests of public health and social welfare, and in accord with the constitutional principle of equal protection of the laws.

For women as wage earners the sex-equality issue intersects

---

[1] *Ibid.*, p. 85. Mothers' aid laws would be open to challenge, and even if the court decision was ultimately in their favor, the resulting delay and interference with their operation would have disastrous effects.   Non-support laws applying to wives of deserting or neglectful husbands and labor laws for women would not only be thrown into court, but almost certainly invalidated.

[2] *Ibid.*, p. 54.   [3] *Ibid.*, p. 54.   [4] *Ibid.*, p. 32.

with the class-equality issue; and the principle of *less* restriction for women as a means to equality and freedom, applicable to the solution of the former problem, conflicts with the principle of *more* restriction at the lower economic levels as a means to equality and freedom, applicable to the solution of the latter problem. Ultimate equality and freedom would be best secured by approaching some problems as sex problems, and others as labor problems. The theoretical approach, with its demand for equal rights, is wholly inadequate to cope with the complexities of the actual situation. A realistic and pragmatic approach is needed, which examines each law where differentiation occurs between men and women, with a view to discerning "the purposes underlying existing provisions, the appropriateness of such provisions to present-day conditions, the bearing of social forces as well as the law upon those present-day conditions, the function the law can and should serve for the remedy of injustice and inequality."[1]

The Effects of Protective Legislation for Women. On very few questions at present are final and undebatable answers obtainable as to what constitutes equality. With regard to protective legislation, most laws *prohibiting* occupations for women are obsolete, and handicap rather than safeguard. But, in the matter of night-work laws, such serious issues of health and welfare are at stake that the issue of sex-equality pales in significance. Regulation of hours and wages is first and foremost a *labor* issue and concerns women not as a sex, but as "forced underbidders in a competitive labor market, where not only women themselves, but their own husbands, brothers, fathers and sons are the sufferers by their competition."[2] Industrial equality between men and women can only be brought about by equal bargaining power, to attain which there are two accepted methods: trade union agreements and law. In the former, men have hitherto been more widely successful, while women have gained more through law, because of the feasibility of securing laws for women on the basis of their special needs, where similar laws would be unattainable by men.

In 1928, the Women's Bureau published the results of its first inclusive attempt to discover the actual effects of special legislation.[3] Limitation of working hours was found to tend towards equalization of hour schedules and of bargaining power

[1] *Ibid.*, p. 57. [2] *Ibid.*, p. 43.
[3] "The Effects of Labor Legislation on the Employment Opportunities of Women," *Women's Bureau Bulletin*, No. 65 (1928). For a summary of data relating to the experience of women under labor legislation, see *Women in the Economy of the United States of America*, Part II.

between men and women. Economic equality was in these ways *increased* through special legislation. Gains such as these, as well as the direct gains in health and happiness to individual women workers, would all be lost if the proponents of an abstract legal equality were to have their way. A chief reason for the stand taken in this matter by the National Woman's Party is the fact that its members belong almost entirely to the business and professional classes, and thus have no firsthand experience of the effects of these laws, as have industrial workers. The economic problem of the individualized business or professional woman is entirely different from that of a woman in industry. She competes as an individual and is handicapped in relation to the men in her field by any discrimination against her as a woman. Hence the demand for equal rights at all costs, which to her class would mean greater equality of opportunity.[1] For the masses of women workers, *laissez-faire* and free competition with men would be disastrous and bring even greater inequality of opportunity. These millions of unskilled or semi-skilled workers must be considered as a group, for as individuals they can gain no recognition, one being easily replacable by another as mere "hands," units of cheap labor material. In face of this situation, to insist on individualistic sex-equality is short-sighted indeed. Most significant of all is the fact that not only those whose aim is social justice rather than abstract equality, but also *the women to whom the laws apply*, have always demanded such legislation.[2] Noticeable also is the fact that opposition to protective legislation for women comes not only from upper-class women unaffected by these laws, but also from employers, chiefly men, who want unregulated competition in order to secure a plentiful supply of cheap labor.

[1] In July, 1937, the equal rights amendment was enthusiastically endorsed by the convention of the National Federation of Business and Professional Women, despite the plea of some of its members, such as Mary Van Kleeck of the Russell Sage Foundation, that all women should be united for the advancement of all, including the less fortunate. An international women's charter sponsored by Mary Van Kleeck and a number of women prominent in the Women's Bureau, League of Women Voters, Woman's Trade Union League, and other organizations was rejected because of its inclusion of protection for women in industry. *New York Times*, Dec. 28, 1936, and July 24, 1937. In March, 1938, after two tie votes, the Senate Judiciary Committee reported the equal rights amendment without endorsement.

[2] Not only the League of Women Voters, The Consumers' League, and the subcommittee of the Women's Joint Congressional Committee oppose the amendment, but also the Women's Trade Union League and organizations of working women. It would surely appear as though working women are not only peculiarly fitted, but also entitled to decide what *equality* means, as applying to the laws governing the terms of their employment.

Women in Agriculture and Farm Life. In 1930, the Census listed as employed in agriculture 910,268 women, only 8.5% of all women gainfully occupied.[1] The Census enumerators were instructed, in making their report of the gainfully occupied, to exclude women who work "only occasionally or for a short time each day at outdoor farm or garden work, or in the dairy, or in caring for live stock or poultry." Accordingly the majority of hard-worked farm wives were omitted, most of whom carry on certain important by-industries not only for home consumption, but also for money-making purposes: market gardening, poultry raising, and dairy work.[2] In addition they do all their housework, including cooking, baking, cleaning, sewing, and the particularly difficult and heavy laundry work, and also care for their children. For the majority, all this work must be undertaken under primitive conditions; there is little or no labor-saving machinery in farm homes even when such machinery is used for field work, and in 1932, only 15.8% of the farms of the United States had piped water. Comparatively few farms have bath tubs and even fewer have indoor toilets. Electricity is comparatively infrequent, and old-fashioned kerosene lamps, needing frequent filling, are in common use. Cookstoves, and, in winter, stoves used for heating, must also be tended by the farmer's wife. The average hours of work are eleven, while thousands work from dawn till long after darkness falls.

Very seldom do farmers' wives get rest or a change; year in and year out they carry on the same ceaseless round of daily drudgery. Many lead lives of great isolation, for they are too busy even to visit neighbors a few miles away.[3] Competent observers believe that one of the reasons for the shift of popula-

[1] Of these 495,000 were Negroes in the Southern states. Of the whole number 171,323 were wage-earning farm laborers, 262,645 were owners and tenants, the majority of them poor or middle-class farmers, while 475,000 were "unpaid family workers."

[2] Much of this work, particularly the handling of cans of milk, is as heavy, backbreaking work as any work done on the farm.

[3] Although farm women have little time for organized activities, one of the first women's clubs was the still existing Mutual Improvement Association, founded in 1857, at Sandy Springs, Maryland. For the most part, farm women's participation in organizations has been through farm movements, such as the Grange, and Farmers' Institutes and Clubs, which include the whole family. In the Grange, ever since its organization, women have been admitted on a basis equal to men. In 1930, 26 out of 128 major offices were held by women. Organization among farm women has been noticeably stimulated by the Smith-Fess Act appropriating federal money for extension work in home economics and agriculture. In 1930, 646,340 women were engaged in extension work.

tion to the cities has been the growing dissatisfaction of farmers' wives over the hardships and deprivations of their lot.

WOMEN WHO HAVE LEISURE

Women and Leisure. The lives of many women are wrecked by the strain of overwork, but there are others whose lives are wrecked "by leisure strain and underwork."[1] Some of these are women who do no real work of any kind; many more have part-time work in the home. Since productive labor is irksome, it has always in the past been performed by those who were considered inferior, women, servants, or slaves. The possession of leisure, of conspicuous abstention from labor, became, as Veblen pointed out in his well-known *Theory of the Leisure Class* (1899), the distinctive mark of the powerful and superior to whom the inferior many are subjected. For centuries the chief evidence of noble birth and breeding and of gentility has been the possession of leisure, made manifest in dress, manners, accomplishments, and occupations giving evidence of a non-productive consumption of time. Nothing bears more conspicuous witness to superiority than the maintenance not only of an elaborate household, but of subservient individuals, a wife and domestic retainers, largely exempt from the production of goods, but waiting on the person of their owner and adding to his prestige by their vicarious leisure. So long do traditional customs and attitudes survive that, even where, with changing social conditions, the man of the upper classes has become a worker, it is still a mark of superior status to be able to support wife and daughters in idleness, and to clothe them in the conspicuous manner which makes clear their function as the "chief ornaments" of his household.

The Idle Woman as Parasite. In *Woman and Labor* (1911), Olive Schreiner was one of the first to call attention to the fact that under certain social and economic conditions women, because of their sex functions, have been maintained in idleness and have become parasites. Instead of the hard-working mother and homemaker, there has arisen, in her place, "the effete wife, concubine or prostitute, clad in fine raiment, the work of others' fingers; fed on luxurious viands, the result of others' toil; waited on and tended by the labor of others. . . . Finely clad, tenderly housed, life became for her merely the gratification of her physical and sexual appetites, and the appetites of the male, through the stimulation of which she could maintain

[1] Lorine Pruette, *Women and Leisure* (E. P. Dutton & Co., Inc., 1924), p. xiii.

herself. And whether as kept wife, kept mistress or prostitute, she contributed nothing to the active and sustaining labors of society." The type is essentially the same whether in Eastern harems, in the Roman Empire, or in modern centers of fashionable life; "the 'fine lady,' the human female parasite—the most deadly microbe which can make its appearance on the surface of any social organism."[1] The decay of a class or race is inevitable when the majority of its women belong to this type, for parasitic women do not nurture virile men and women of character. Many, indeed, remain childless; others who have children, leave their care to servants. Yet the kept wife who performs no useful work of any kind assumes herself entitled to support, in view of her satisfaction of her husband's sexual demands and her mere potentiality for motherhood, a potentiality she tends to confuse with its actual fulfilment.

In the eighteenth century, events conspired to produce large numbers of these ladies of fashion, whose only business it was to gain and keep the attention of eligible men. Seeking power through beauty, dress, and display, they made manifest their entire uselessness as conspicuous consumers of vicarious leisure: high heels, pinched waists, trailing skirts, amazing semi-permanent coiffures, not to speak of delicate slenderness, small feet, and soft hands, all bespoke their complete exemption from vulgar toil. Each class, as Veblen has pointed out, emulates the standard of consumption of the class above, so that "all canons of reputability and decency, and all standards of consumption, are traced back by insensible gradations to the usages and habits of thought of the highest social and pecuniary class—the wealthy leisure class."[2] Wherever wealth flowed, men tended to exempt their women from work and to support them in genteel idleness.

The results of this situation have already been discussed in the last chapter; the dependence, artificiality, and idleness of upper- and middle-class women, and the rebellion and restlessness which gave rise to the woman's movement. But, despite all that has been gained, traditional attitudes are still widely prevalent. Whenever a woman considers herself entitled to support by men, first by her father and then by a husband, wholly ignoring any correlative social responsibilities on her part, her attitude is that of a sex parasite. The contemporary situation is serious, moreover, because, in contrast to past ages, when only a comparatively small group have suffered

[1] *Op. cit.*, pp. 79–81.　　　　　　　　　　　　[2] *Op. cit.*, p. 104.

from the parasitism of their women, there are to-day not only many idle so-called "society women," but enormous numbers of women who are semi-idle for the greater part of their lives.

Semi-idleness among Women To-day. Many a woman to-day lives in luxurious ease supported by a hard-working husband and ministered to by servants. She is preoccupied with the supervision of her establishment, her dress, entertainments, and other social "duties." Among these duties, it is true, some society women include their support of various charitable enterprises; but as yet it is only the few who in any way realize the opportunities and responsibilities of their privileged position.

Since the great majority of American women do their own housework, and look after their own children with little or no help, it might appear that idleness among women would be a less frequent phenomenon here than in countries where domestic help is more readily available. But the fact remains that homemaking can only occupy the full time of an able-bodied woman during the early childhood of her children, and that for the greater part of their lives, women who have no other serious occupation have too much leisure. It is true that available facts indicate that, for the majority of women, homemaking is not a part-time job, judged by the hours actually spent.[1] But there are innumerable women whose incomes allow of labor-saving devices and perhaps domestic help, and who have small households and no young children, for whom homemaking, even without any help, is by no means a full-time job. Moreover, such hours as are spent are often needlessly long and could with efficient management be very much reduced. Some to fill their time indulge in all sorts of unnecessary elaborations in housekeeping; although it is true that, as standards of living rise, more time is required to maintain family life at a desired level.

Social waste is obviously involved where the community is losing a large part of its potential labor power. According to Lorine Pruette, these women on part-time jobs "from the social standpoint form a social menace. By the thousands they wander up and down city streets, looking for something to fill the idle lonely hours. They are a mark, not only of their husband's ability to keep them in comfort, not only of 'vicarious consumption,' but of social inefficiency, of society's failure ade-

[1] See Hazel Kyrk, *Economic Problems of the Family* (1933), Chapter VI.

quately to make use of its human material."[1] For the most ominous aspect of the social waste involved is the soul-destroying effect of idleness on the women themselves and through them on their families, their children in particular. Some among them are efficient housekeepers; though where the only interest is in the routine details of daily life, a fussy over-insistence on order and cleanliness is often the result, which may be as destructive of home atmosphere as the inefficient home management which is so often the corollary of an unsupervised, unstandardized performance of household tasks. These are the women who gossip and "window-shop," who become "movie-fans," and "bridge-fiends." Deprived of the discipline of purposeful, efficiently-performed work, they become contented with their lot, in proportion as they grow soft in body and flabby in mind.

And yet the very restlessness of most of these women bears witness to their profound sense of frustration. The main thesis of Dr. Myerson's book, *The Nervous Housewife*, is "that the neurosis of the housewife has a large part of its origin in the increasing desires of women, in their demands for a fuller, more varied life, than that afforded by the lot of a housewife."[2] It is obvious that, in spite of all that has been accomplished in women's struggle for emancipation and worthwhile occupation and social responsibility, multitudes of women are still leading frustrated, semi-wasted lives; a state of affairs of the greatest menace to the well-being of children, and an undoubted factor in the instability of family life at the present time.[3]

[1] *Op. cit.*, p. xiii.

[2] *Op. cit.* (1920), p. 75. In his *Subjection of Women*, pp. 276–277, John Stuart Mill found want of a worthwhile occupation to be a chief cause of women's "nervous susceptibility." Much of it, he said, is "the mere overflow of nervous energy run to waste, and would cease when the energy was directed to a definite end. . . . Moreover, when people are brought up . . . a kind of hot-house plants, shielded from the wholesome vicissitudes of air and temperature, and untrained in any of the occupations and exercises which give stimulus to the circulatory and muscular system, while the nervous system, especially in its emotional department, is kept in unnaturally active play, it is no wonder [they show] morbid characteristics." In *The Family* (1934), pp. 287–310, Folsom discusses suggestions looking towards the reorganization of women's work. He seems, however, somewhat to underestimate the profound satisfaction of worthwhile work, suited to *individual* capacity and interest, for women as well as for men.

[3] Dr. Bikoff, assistant pediatrician of the Jewish Hospital, Brooklyn, reported that numbers of young middle-class mothers refused to nurse their babies, and that 80% of their children had behavior problems. These mothers live in good apartments, buy good food, employ domestic help, read child health booklets, and attend child hygiene lectures, but they have little to do, are highly neurotic, and smoke cigarettes to excess. *New York Times*, June 9, 1937.

450 NEW HORIZONS FOR THE FAMILY

WOMEN AS CONSUMERS

Women as Buyers and Controllers of Consumption. Stuart Chase has pointed out that, from an economic point of view, not only idleness and domestic inefficiency, but also over-consumption and unintelligent consumption are chief sources of waste and friction in the time and activities of women.[1] As matters now stand, women with leisure are responsible for a great part of the flagrant overconsumption of to-day; and they are also largely influential in setting standards for the buying of women in general. And it has been estimated that, if home-makers who control the family income are included as well as women who control personal incomes, women are responsible for two-thirds of the national expenditure for consumers' goods.

Standards of living are rising, not only in matters of comfort, but in what are now realized as necessities for health and for the adequate nurture of children. To meet these growing needs, an extraordinary proliferation of goods is forced on the attention of consumers by competing business interests. While it is true that production depends, in the long run, on the choices of consumers, yet the determining factor is not so much the necessity of the average consumer as the manufacturers' need for profit. Accordingly, pressure is aimed primarily at the more favored income groups; and an unexampled increase in advertising gives evidence of the endeavor to induce the consumer to buy, irrespective of actual need.[2] But, quite apart from these coercive influences, wise selection of the best article for any given purpose is impossible without information such as is possessed by very few. For most people, buying becomes, in Hazel Kyrk's words, "a gigantic grab-bag performance." Increasing attention is now being paid to the problems of buyer and consumer; nevertheless, according to Lynd, "it is an open question whether factors making for confusion . . . are not actually outstripping the forces making for effective consumption."[3]

[1] "Wasting Women," *Survey,* Vol. LVII (Dec. 1, 1926), pp. 268–270. The very phrase "activities of women" brings to mind the pages or sections of newspapers and magazines devoted to what are supposedly, and too often actually, women's chief interests: shopping, largely in the interests of personal adornment or elaborate household decoration; entertainments, clubs, and other "social" activities.

[2] In 1929, 2% of the national income, or $1,782,000,000 was spent in advertising. The purchase of more expensive commodities has been made possible for those with smaller incomes by the increase in instalment selling and in the availability of consumer credit.

[3] "The People as Consumers," *Recent Social Trends,* Vol. II, p. 911. Expenditures for 1929 in terms of billions of dollars are given on p. 889. *Buying* has been defined as "the technology of consumption." *Consumption* involves the more fundamental

Recognition of the influence of women as potential buyers is evident in the volume of advertising specially designed to appeal to them. It is essential therefore that women should realize their responsibilities as consumers and buyers. In their choice of goods on which their income is to be spent, and in their market-selection of specific articles, they not only determine to a large extent the quality of individual and family living, but throw the weight of their vote for the production of certain goods rather than others.[1] While the influence of the individual consumer may be, in most instances, negligible, through organization it should be possible for women to exert a deliberately beneficial influence. So significant might be the social results, that women's "power as buyers of goods gives them a strategic position in the unfolding of modern civilization."[2]

Fashions in Dress and Cosmetics. By way of illustration, no topic is more appropriate than that of fashions in dress and cosmetics; a matter of the greatest importance in relation to the status of women. As Ross has pointed out, fashions spring ultimately from a desire for self-individualization. The connotations of *distinction* and *distinguished* are significant. For the savage the most common marks of distinction are trophies indicating power and position, ornaments decorating the person and sometimes involving mutilation, and ornamental dress.[3] Social leaders, such as the leisure classes, the specially privileged or wealthy, have always differentiated themselves by their *style* of living, and the *fashion* of their dress. The less fortunate, where not restrained by sumptuary legislation as in a caste society, imitate the leaders.

In America, with its nominal abolition of class distinctions, financial disabilities alone prevent imitation of social leaders by the masses. The current tendency to measure progress by acquisition of material possessions, and the enormous production of comparatively cheap imitations of clothing, and other posses-

---

problems of setting a standard of living and of the choice of the best means for realizing this standard so far as is possible. *Buying* means the final step of concrete market-selection. Hazel Kyrk, *op. cit.*, Chapters XIX, XXII.

[1] Further consideration is given to the problems of buying the family living in Chapter XXI.

[2] Charles A. Beard and Mary Beard, *The Rise of American Civilization* (one vol. ed., 1930), p. xiii.

[3] Women who constrict their waists, pinch their toes and distort their posture with high heels, and mutilate themselves by having their ears pierced, still use barbaric methods of ornamentation. It has been estimated that 80,000,000 Americans, mostly women, suffer from some form of foot trouble, due to their footwear. W. B. Pitkin, *Take It Easy* (1935), p. 83.

sions of the wealthy, combine to stimulate competition along the line of fashion to an unprecedented degree. Fashion now extends to an immense number of objects; its latest dictates pass immediately down the social ladder, and its changes grow ever more rapid.[1] The *latest* fashion is the thing: the *exclusive* mode; distinction from the common herd being attained not only by *costliness* but by *timeliness* in style. As has been aptly said: "Style is mass chasing class, and class escaping mass."[2] This mad scramble to secure the latest fashions is deliberately encouraged by industrial interests which profit when styles are soon discarded and new articles must be purchased.

Nowhere are these generalizations more true than in fashions in women's dress. The latest models in automobiles, radios, and electric refrigerators usually embody genuine improvements. Considerations of utility and beauty are both involved. Not so with fashionable dress, though on occasion its designers are forced to take such considerations into account, as in the provision of sport clothes, and in the use of color. There is no more obvious method of self-individualization and assertion of status than dress. Men are, of course, not wholly immune from this common usage.[3] And fashions change for men. But, as compared to women, men are indifferent to fashionable dress. In a democratic and industrial age they have come to depend far less on the superficial distinction conferred by clothes, and have devoted themselves to becoming distinguished by their achievements. Other factors may be involved in the feminine urge to fashionable dress, but the root of the matter is found at this point. Despite present freedom and opportunity, comparatively few women are conscious of the inherent distinction conferred by a developed, well-integrated personality and a life full of interests and responsibilities. Assertion of distinction and status in terms of clothing and possessions is a sign of spiritual

[1] Ease and rapidity of communication and transportation have contributed largely to these results. Outstanding personages, be they royalty or screen stars, adopt some new style of dress or coiffure or personal accessory, and the "news" is flashed round the world. Moving pictures soon make it graphic to the masses, and goods to meet the demand for this latest style make their way to all but the remotest parts of the country.

[2] Quoted by W. Rauschenbush, "The Idiot God Fashion," *Woman's Coming of Age* (ed. Schmalhausen and Calverton, 1931), pp. 424–446.

[3] America is deprived of the pageantry of dress and decoration inseparable from an aristocratic hierarchy in other countries, although the members of the army and navy remain as examples of men whose rank is made manifest by their dress. The extreme popularity of fraternal orders with their distinctive dress and insignia bears witness to the fact that men are not immune, even in a democracy, from the allure of distinctive dress.

emptiness. Those who are oriented to *things*, as Mumford says, "have every sort of possession except self-possession."[1]

Nothing can, of course, be more natural and legitimate than for women, and men as well, to be anxious to make the best of themselves. And to this end clothing may contribute much, when it is becoming to the wearer, suitable to the occasion, and beautiful in color, line, and texture. The arbiters of fashion care little, however, for designing clothing which is suited to individual needs, either aesthetic or utilitarian. Fashion would, indeed, compel change even for those who had found the perfect means for authentic self-expression. As it is, "right clothes" give self-confidence to those who feel themselves insecure, so that it is no wonder that adolescents, both girls and boys should be susceptible to the compulsions of fashion. But that these standards exercise a tyranny over older women is an indication that they too are restless and insecure and their lives empty and unsatisfying, however much they may be filled with the pursuit of pleasure, prestige, and possessions.

Clothes still remain for many women the chief weapon with which they compete for the attention of the other sex.[2] And the situation seems aggravated by the instability of family life and the obsolescence of traditional standards. The dependent married woman, who has relied on her charms to "hold" a husband, is in competition to-day not only with so-called "adventuresses," but with divorcees, widows, other married women, and with hosts of independent unmarried women who work and can afford to dress well. In addition to being formidable rivals, because they have more money and time to bestow on making themselves attractive, many of these women, having shared the pursuits of men in the world outside the home, are also more interesting companions.

[1] Quoted by Rauschenbush, *op. cit.*, p. 444. The waste and extravagance in women's clothes is quite appalling. For example, in a recent newspaper discussion of the best-dressed women in the world, it was stated that they were not necessarily *very* wealthy, although to be among the best-dressed they were obliged to spend $10,000 to $40,000 a year on their dress. Every year, moreover, 14% of all purchases at department stores in this country are returned, thus canceling $1,500,000,000 sales. The woman buyer of clothes is very largely responsible for this waste of time and money. *New York Times*, Apr. 30, 1931.

[2] An instance of this is found in the expensive clothes worn by girls in high school. The Lynds noted in *Middletown* a "feverish preoccupation on the part of the younger women with this activity of personal ornamentation. . . . Girls fight with clothes in competition for a male." Pp. 163, 166. Sometimes all the money which had been saved by parents for a college education had to be used for clothes. In other cases, young people, boys as well as girls, left school because they were unable to wear the right clothes.

The prevalent use of cosmetics is not only symptomatic of the tendency to confuse a superficial glamour and glitter with genuine charm and distinction, but is also indicative of the present emphasis on *allurement*. Prostitutes in all ages have practised the arts of seduction by making themselves conspicuous by their dress, the color of their hair, potent perfumes, and facial makeup. Ladies of fashion have time and again adopted much the same arts, and now, once again in this era of overpreoccupation with sex, young girls, their mothers, and grandmothers alike flaunt scarlet mouths and finger-nails and even toe-nails. The expenditure for cosmetics and beauty parlors in this country in 1929 reached a staggering sum, nearly equal to one-third of the total expenditure for public education.[1] The great majority of women who frequent beauty parlors are not interested in securing the services of a qualified skin specialist. They prefer "beauticians" who provide the flattery which brings self-assurance and the short-cuts to a supposed charm which is more often than not an entirely artificial veneer.[2]

What constitutes good taste in cosmetics? To correct defects and make the most of natural looks is not only legitimate, but from the aesthetic standpoint incumbent on all. Surely, however, a happy mean can be found between pale, chapped lips and those of a livid and sensuous vermilion. Good taste demands good health and the elimination of any conspicuous and unnatural adornments.

There are certain indications that in time the tyranny of fashion may be overcome. An increasing number of women conform tardily to the dictates of fashion, simply in order not to be conspicuous, and altogether refuse to adopt the extremes of fashion. The more active life led by women, their interest in athletics, and their need for business clothes, all tend to the adoption of simple and standardized clothes suitable for the occasion. Apparently, too, the point has been reached where

---

[1] $700,000,000 was spent on cosmetics and beauty parlors, while the costs of public education were about $2,250,000,000. Many cosmetics have been proved to be definitely injurious, and the cost of harmful and harmless alike often goes as high as twenty or fortyfold the cost of the ingredients. M. C. Phillips, *Skin Deep* (1934).

[2] Advice on beauty culture in leading women's magazines explicitly assures women that they can *remake* their *personalities*, by adopting a new style of coiffure or undergoing a specific facial treatment or by the use of some cosmetic preparation or what not. Of interest in this connection is the fact that the word personality is derived from *persona*, a mask! Some writers therefore use the word *individuality* to indicate what is unique and intrinsic in a human being, reserving *personality* to describe a type. Others, however, use these terms in a manner diametrically opposed to the above.

fashion-makers can no longer force changes in opposition to fundamental trends. A recent effort to introduce trailing and flounced skirts, for daytime wear, met with utter failure.

Agencies for the Education of the Consumer. There has been increasing emphasis in recent years on the need for consumer education. Home economics departments in the public schools are now endeavoring in many ways to meet this need, and much is to be hoped in time from the guidance of young people in their choice of standards and in a wise use of money. At present, however, there are almost insuperable obstacles placed in the way of fully intelligent buying. Women who buy for family needs lack the experience, information, and judgment of the expert purchasing-agents employed by commercial concerns. The federal Bureau of Standards is the outstanding example of the possibilities inherent in expert buying. Its findings have meant vast savings to the government, and it has been estimated that, if the results of its researches were made available to the public, consumers at large would be enabled to save at least a billion dollars annually.[1]

Despite the difficulties of the present situation, consumers can affect consumption standards if they organize in urging further legislation, better standardization, and the provision of more accessible sources of information. Moreover, much fuller use might be made of such reliable information as has already been made available by professional, technical, coöperative, and commercial agencies as well as by the government.[2] Federal legislation with respect to standardization of goods benefits the consumer, and direct assistance has been forthcoming through the Bureau of Home Economics of the Department of Agriculture. Writing in 1933, Lynd summarized the situation as follows: "A coherent and active policy as regards the consumer does not exist throughout the government bureaus at Washington at the present time. . . . The primary concern . . . is whether the government is prepared to give to the spending of the national income the same degree of concern that it at present bestows upon the earning of that income. Such coherent leadership is needed, if schools and other agencies are to educate

[1] Stuart Chase and C. J. Schlink, *Your Money's Worth* (1927), p. 203.

[2] For example, the American Medical Association, The American Home Economics Association, Consumer's Research, The Metropolitan Life Insurance Company, and the National Consumers' League. The last-named organization was established, in 1899, with the object of directing the attention of the consumer to insanitary and sweated conditions under which certain goods were made or distributed, and, in this way, bringing pressure to bear towards the improvement of conditions of production.

the individual consumer in the practice of the fine art of spending money."[1]   A first attempt at providing such leadership was made under the NRA, culminating in the creation, in 1935, of a Consumer's Division.[2]

WOMEN IN BUSINESS AND THE PROFESSIONS

Women as Telephone Operators and Workers in Stores and Offices. A great proportion of the rapidly increasing numbers entering the business field are concentrated in a few occupations. Of women classified under transportation and communication, 94% were telephone operators, and of those in trade almost four-fifths were clerks in stores. Of the close to 2,000,000 in the clerical group, 39% were stenographers, 36% were clerks, and 24%, bookkeepers and cashiers. For the first time, in the 1930 census, more women were engaged in clerical occupations than in industry. To rise into the "white-collar" class is considered a distinct advance in social status, and clerical occupations are favored by girls who have been able to get the necessary training.[3] For those who have no special training there is little chance of anything but a routine job, without opportunity of promotion to higher levels. Comparatively few women secure high-grade clerical positions, and the masses work for long hours at low wages. Unemployment was very frequent even before the depression, there being, in 1929, some 300 to 500 applicants for every 100 jobs available in New York State.

Recent studies indicate that women workers at the lowest levels of business possess little advantage over factory workers. Women in stores must stay long hours on their feet, often not allowed to use the stools or chairs which may have been provided when required by state laws. In telephone exchanges, the introduction of the automatic dial system has displaced many operators, and those who remain have been subjected to more

[1] *Recent Social Trends*, Vol. II, p. 911.

[2] *New York Times*, Sept. 8 and Oct. 11, 1935.

[3] There is a generally recognized stratification of the different groups of working women based on the desirability and prestige of the occupation in which they are engaged. "Domestic service and the less desirable types of factory employment vie with each other for bottom place. The poorer kinds of store work usually come next, followed by the skilled factory work and ascending through telephone and selling positions to the clerical occupations. The less desirable forms of clerical work, however, are often on a level in public esteem with those in the telephone exchanges and stores, while the office positions requiring the most skill reach a level recognized usually by those concerned as equal to that of the less skilled professional positions." G. L. Coyle, "Women in Clerical Occupations," *Annals of the American Academy*, Vol. CXLIII (May, 1929), p. 181.

intense speeding up.   In offices, too, machines are displacing workers, and the work of those who are retained tends to become specialized and mechanical.

The Widening Range of Business Opportunities for Women. Perhaps the most noticeable feature of women's business activities is their widening range.   Women are entering the fields of radio and commercial aviation, to mention two recent developments; while in some of the older fields they occasionally achieve the more important executive positions.   There are larger numbers of women bank officials and inspectors, and more real-estate and insurance agents.   Numbers of women are proprietors of specialty shops, or heads of departments, buyers, and personnel directors in large stores.   Many own and manage tea-rooms, restaurants, or cafeterias.   An amazing variety of activities is listed by Miriam Leuck in a study of "Women in Odd and Unusual Fields of Work."[1]   Some women have reached outstanding positions entirely through their own efforts, others have taken the place of fathers or husbands and have thus gained an opportunity of demonstrating their capacity.   It would certainly appear that there is no field of endeavor in which specially qualified women, if given the chance, may not be successful.

As early as 1918 there were a number of notably successful business women, some of them executives earning as much as $50,000 a year.   This is proved by the records of a conference called by Lena Madesin Phillips, a lawyer who was organizing war work for the YWCA.   This meeting had as its result, in 1919, the permanent organization of the National Federation of Business and Professional Women's Clubs.   This organization engages in investigations and issues a magazine, the *Independent Woman.*[2]

---

[1] *Annals of the American Academy,* Vol. CXLIII (May, 1929), pp. 166–179. Numerous instances are listed of women who have risen to the highest executive posts as presidents, treasurers, and sales managers of large companies, one woman being a railroad president, and another, president of a gas company.   Other women are experts in foreign trade, one woman being chartering manager for a firm of ship owners. Women have been particularly successful in running stock farms, and in many cases where they have themselves built up a business, such as one in educational toys, they have shown marked originality as well as business ability.   There is a marked tendency for women who enter unusual fields to specialize in work for which they possess special aptitude as women.   During the depression many women showed great ingenuity in turning such assets as they possessed into new ways of earning a living. See *Women Workers through the Depression,* ed. L. Pruette (1934), Chapter V.

[2] As a result of the extension of the work of this organization to foreign countries, The International Federation of Business and Professional Women was formed in 1930, with branches in some 19 countries and European headquarters at Geneva.

Teachers in Schools. In 1930 there were 1,526,234 professional women and 1,727,650 professional men in the United States, the increase being much the same since 1920, 50.6% for men, 49.6% for women. The teaching profession claims the greatest numbers of both men and women, but where 57.7% of all professional women were teachers, and 56% were in schools, only 14.1% of all professional men were teachers, and 11% were in schools.[1] There has, however, been a relative decrease in the proportion of professional women engaged in teaching; but, while the proportion of women school teachers has declined, there has been a considerable increase in the numbers of women who are college teachers.

In the public and private elementary schools of the country the proportions of women to men were 90.2% to 9.8%; in the secondary schools, 64.8% to 35.2%. Nursery schools and kindergartens have been in the hands of women from the first and the elementary grades very largely so. The elementary school principalship is coming to be a woman's position, but apart from this the numbers of women in administration or positions of responsibility was very small, considering their numerical preponderance in the profession. Women principals and superintendents have shown marked executive ability, but the tradition against women administrators remains strong.[2]

In the larger cities there has been a tendency towards equality of salaries for men and women, but in general women receive salaries of about a quarter less than men of equal training or experience.[3]   Neither men nor women are paid proportionately to the cost of their training, and although there has been improvement, the general run of salaries remains low. Insecurity of tenure remains another chief cause of dissatisfaction among teachers, whose difficulties were much accentuated by the depression.[4]

[1] There were 880,409 women teachers and 244,111 men. In the schools there were 853,967 women and 190,049 men; in the colleges 20,131 women and 41,774 men.

[2] Women have held important positions in the U. S. Office of Education and in the Federal Board of Vocational Education. In 1928, women were at the head of the Departments of Education in six Western states. There were 900 women county superintendents, also for the most part in the West, 45 city superintendents, 169 secondary school principals, and 1,866 elementary school principals.

[3] One study in the Minneapolis schools found that the women teachers were no more likely to work only temporarily than were the men, and that women had nearly as many dependents as men.

[4] It was estimated by the American Federation of Teachers that in October, 1933, 25% were unemployed. Salaries were sharply cut 10% to 25%, and many teachers were forced to contribute "voluntarily" 1% to 5% of their reduced incomes to relief funds. Chicago teachers were not paid at all for one period of eleven months.

Teachers in Colleges and Universities. In 1930, in the universities and colleges, only 26.7% of the faculty members were women; in professional schools, 4%.[1] Of the 226 institutions approved by the American Association of Universities, only 18% of the faculty were women: 1% in forty-seven men's institutions, 16% in 143 co-educational institutions, and 68.5% in thirty-six women's colleges.[2] In all three types of institution women are found in greater numbers in the lower ranks. Meanwhile, the numbers of women in student bodies have steadily increased, as have the numbers taking higher degrees.[3] But in the ranks of college teachers women are still severely handicapped. A study of 844 women in 122 institutions in 1929 indicated a low correlation between rank and training, and between rank and years of experience. Promotion beyond the rank of instructor or assistant professor was hard to achieve, while only 17.8% reported that they received a salary equal to that of their male colleagues. Although women were found teaching in nearly every field, they tended to concentrate in English, modern languages, home economics, and physical education.

Women as Trained Nurses. In only one other profession are women represented in very large numbers. There were, in 1930, 228,737 graduate trained nurses, 18.9% of all professional women.[4] Relatively more women are going into nursing, a fact of significance, in view of the decline in the number of untrained midwives and nurses at one end of the scale, and of the women doctors at the other.[5] Large numbers were also listed in the semi-professional groups of doctors' and dentists' assistants.

Women in the Fields of Music, Drama, Literature, and the Arts. There has been a decline both in the actual numbers and in the proportion of professional women engaged in the field of music, either as music teachers or musicians. While there has been an absolute increase in the numbers of women artists and

[1] In 1910 no women were employed in professional schools.

[2] Breckenridge, "Women's Activities outside the Home," *Recent Social Trends*, Vol. I, p. 726.

[3] The proportion of men to women in colleges was 65.4% to 34.6% in 1900 and 58.6% to 41.4% in 1930. In 1900 women received 20 of the 342 Ph.D. degrees; in 1910, 44 out of 409; in 1920, 93 out of 532; in 1930, 332 out of 2,024. *Recent Social Trends*, Vol. I, p. 352.

[4] These numbers do not include the undergraduate nurses, in training while they work in the hospitals. There were 5,452 men working as trained nurses, only 0.3% of all professional men and by far the smallest group.

[5] Women also seek irregular and unorthodox opportunities for work related to the care of the sick, there being, in 1930, 7,866 "healers" and 9,203 chiropractors.

art teachers, actors and showmen, authors, editors, reporters, designers, draftsmen, and photographers, there was a relative decline in the fields of art, acting, and photography. Women are only beginning to enter the field of architecture, there having been 379 women architects, in 1930, as against 21,621 men. As composers, too, they have only recently begun to make their way, but in painting and sculpture they already have noteworthy achievements to their credit. In the development of modern poetry and the novel they have had a significant share, while as singers and actresses their success fully equals that of men.

Women in Social Work and as Ministers. In the 1930 census, the 24,592 women and 6,649 men, engaged in social work, constituted a new classification on the professional list, having hitherto been included in the semi-professional group of welfare workers.[1] Although women have had a major share in the development of social work, much the same situation obtains as in teaching. If a well-paid administrative position is to be filled the men are always considered first.[2] Of recent years, however, women have occupied a number of important positions in the public service.

There were 3,276 women ministers in 1930 as against 145,572 men. In 1926, out of sixty theological schools, 70% admitted women and would grant them degrees, but forty of the sixty indicated that either the school or the denomination opposed the ordination of women.

Women in Medicine, Dentistry, Science, and Engineering. Only one group of professional women, besides musicians and music teachers, showed an actual decrease since 1910, the physicians, surgeons, and osteopaths. These now number 8,388 as against 8,882 in 1920, and 9,015 in 1910.[3] This decline has

[1] In this new group, women accordingly constitute 78.7% of the total number. Librarianship also has been and remains largely a woman's profession. In 1920 women constituted 88.4% of the total, and in 1930, 91.3%. In 1920, 13 out of 1,000 professional women were librarians, in 1930, 17 out of 1,000.

[2] Grace Abbott, "The Changing Position of Women," *A Century of Progress* (ed. C. A. Beard), Chapter X. She points out further that the National Conference of Social Work had met annually for more than thirty years before it elected, in 1919, its first woman president, Jane Addams, for many years its most distinguished member. About the same time, the National Education Association elected Ella Flagg Young as its first woman president.

[3] In 1910 and 1920, 59 out of every 1,000 doctors were women, now the number is 52. There were 151,532 men in this group, 8.8% of all professional men. In 1920 there were nearly 1,000 fewer men doctors than in 1910; but between 1920 and 1930 they increased by more than 10,000. In 1910 there were 1,576 men doctors for every hundred women; in 1930, 2,154.

occurred in spite of enormously increased opportunities for medical training.   But women still encounter difficulties in securing internships in the best hospitals.   Less than half of these are open to women in approved hospitals, and to many of them women are rarely appointed.

There is no doubt of the ability of women physicians.   Despite all handicaps they have numerous outstanding achievements to their credit; for example, the work done by the American Women's Hospitals in establishing hospitals and clinics during and after the war in France, the Balkans, and the Near East. In 1931, fifty-eight women were fellows of the American College of Surgeons, and twenty-five of the American College of Physicians, while sixteen states had women directors of maternity and infancy work.   There are also a number of women physicians who have become well-known authorities in their chosen fields.[1]

There were but 1,287 women dentists as against 69,768 men in 1930, a slight increase since 1910, though a decrease since 1920. A greater number, 1,905, were listed as chemists, whereas there were only 113 women in engineering, the profession which includes more professional men than any other but teaching.[2] Even in engineering, however, individual women have shown marked ability.[3] Increasing numbers of women are now engaged in scientific research. Some among them are attached to the staffs of museums, others to colleges; some are in the public service or connected with industrial organizations, others are doctors.[4] The largest number are laboratory technicians.[5]

[1] For example: Dr. Josephine Baker, formerly Director of the Child Hygiene Division of the Department of Health in New York City; Dr. Rachelle S. Yarros, Associate Professor of Obstetrics and Professor of Social Hygiene at the University of Illinois; Dr. Alice Hamilton, specialist in industrial diseases, and first woman to occupy a professor's chair at the Harvard Medical School, and only woman member of the health committee of the League of Nations; Dr. Florence Rena Sabin, first woman elected to full professorship in an American medical school of the first rank, first and only woman member of the National Academy of Science, and first to be a full member of the Rockefeller Institute of Medical Research.

[2] 226,136 or 13.1% of professional men were engineers. The number of women engineers is slowly increasing, however, there having been only 11 in 1910 and 41 in 1920.

[3] For example: Lilian Gilbreath, well-known as an industrial engineer, and Edith Clarke, transmission expert for the General Electric Company.

[4] For example: Margaret Mead is engaged in anthropological research and Delia Akeley collects specimens of big game in Africa. At Harvard, Dr. Annie Cannon is in charge of a corps of women who for many years have been preparing a catalogue of stars. Dr. Maud Slye at the university of Chicago has made an exhaustive study of the relation of heredity to cancer.

[5] In 1935, eighteen women's colleges canvassed the scientific records of their graduates. Women had only had opportunities for basic scientific training in the

Women Lawyers. In 1930, there were 3,385 women lawyers, judges, and justices as against 157,220 men, twenty-one in a thousand lawyers being women as against fourteen in 1920. According to Breckenridge, "the professional path trod by them is a rough and often not an ascending path."[1] Nevertheless they are making places for themselves on the bench and in connection with the administration of justice. Mabel Walker Willebrandt was appointed assistant attorney general, in 1921, and Judge Florence Allen was elected, both in 1922 and 1928, as Justice of the Supreme Court of Ohio. A number of judgeships are now held by women, many in juvenile courts.

WOMEN AND GOVERNMENT

Women in Civil Service and Appointive Political Office. Women have found regular employment in the civil service since 1862, although even in the fifties a few women were government employees. Not until 1919, however, were all competitive examinations for the civil service thrown open to women. By the end of 1930, there were 595,456 government employees in the civil service, and of these 94,163 were women. A large number are employed in the District of Columbia, others throughout the states. At least 18,000 of the positions were of a professional character, many of them in scientific work, others in health and social welfare, library work, and teaching. Few women reach higher grades of the service, however, and advancement comes slowly, making it evident that "women workers in government have not been freed from the occupational disability of their sex."[2]

There are also positions outside the classified service to which incumbents are appointed by bureau chiefs or department heads or by the President.[3] The appointment of a few women to positions of responsibility preceded the granting of suffrage to women, the first major appointment being that of Julia

last thirty years and already they were found in research laboratories everywhere. In the last ten years as large a proportion of girls at Smith, Wellesley, and Vassar, as men at Harvard, Yale, and Princeton, had majored in science. Eunice Fuller Barnard, "Woman's Rise in Science," *New York Times Magazine*, Oct. 27, 1935.

[1] *Women in the Twentieth Century* (1933), p. 203.

[2] Breckenridge, *op. cit.*, p. 305. The principle of equal pay for equal work was written into the law regulating government employment by the Reclassification Act of 1923, but not even then was the principle generally applied.

[3] In the case of some of these, postmasters for instance, the Civil Service Commissions give examinations to test the qualifications of the candidate for appointment. So far as the postal service is concerned, while in 1919 only a little over one-tenth of all postmasters were women, in 1930 this proportion had increased to nearly one-fifth, 940 out of 5,338. No large city postmastership had gone to a woman.

Lathrop as head of the Children's Bureau. In 1922 the first woman was appointed to the diplomatic service; and since then some half dozen women have represented the United States in the Foreign Service. In 1933 Ruth Bryan Owen was appointed Minister to Denmark, the first American woman to hold a major diplomatic post, and the second woman anywhere.[1] President Roosevelt also made history by appointing Frances Perkins as Secretary of Labor, the first woman to become a cabinet member in the United States.[2]

Women in Elective Office. With the ratification of the Nineteenth Amendment, women became eligible to elective offices hitherto closed, and since that time they have been elected to Congress, to governorships, to state legislatures, and to offices of judge, sheriff, and mayor. A number of the earlier women representatives "inherited" their membership from father or husband whose death had left a vacancy. In 1931, however, of the six women members, all but one had owed their election to no influences other than their own capacity and service. In 1936, five women were elected to the House of Representatives. Apart from Rebecca L. Felton of Georgia, who served for one day in 1922, no women sat in the Senate until 1931, when Hattie Caraway was first appointed temporarily and later elected to serve out her husband's unexpired term. In 1932, she won election to a full term.[3]

In state and local governments, women have made more substantial advances. Women were active in state governments long before they had any part in the federal government. There have been women governors in Wyoming and Texas both of whom inherited their places from their husbands. Between 1920 and 1930, however, thirteen women have held the office

[1] When Mrs. Owen married a Danish officer in 1936, it was announced that she would retain her official position. Not long afterwards, however, she resigned. Brilliant records have been made by women career diplomats, but by April 15, 1937, all but two had married and resigned. Frances Elizabeth Willis is third secretary of the legation at Brussels, and Constance Ray Harvey is vice-consul at Milan. On April 19, 1937, Florence Jaffray Harriman was nominated as Minister to Norway by President Roosevelt.

[2] Since then he has appointed Josephine Roche, economist, philanthropist, and coal magnate to be Assistant Secretary of the Treasury, and more recently Executive Chairman of the National Youth Administration; Nellie Tayloe Ross, former Governor of Wyoming, to be Director of the Mint; and Mary Dewson as a member of the Social Security Board.

[3] Rose Long served in the Senate from Jan. 31, 1936 to Jan. 3, 1937, appointed to fill her husband's place; and Dixie Graves was appointed by her husband, the Governor of Alabama, in August, 1937, pending the election of a successor to fill the unexpired term of Hugo L. Black, appointed to the Supreme Court. She served until Jan. 10, 1938.

of secretary of state, and women have served as state treasurers, deputy or assistant attorney general, and as clerks of state supreme courts. Since enfranchisement, as before, the most usual state governmental activity is membership on state boards.[1] There were women in state legislatures before 1920, but there has been a notable increase in their numbers since that time. In 1937, a total of 135 women, sixty of whom were reëlected, served in the legislatures of forty-three states, an increase of five over the 1936 total. The substantial advances made by women in city and local government have been largely ignored, according to Breckenridge. Of a number of women mayors only one has held office in a large city, but women have held a number of important offices in city governments.

Some Results of Woman's Suffrage. Breckenridge points out that, among the arguments for suffrage, were three having reference to public employment. In the first place there were positions for which the experience of women particularly well qualified them, and women should therefore transfer to a wider platform the services they render in the home. Secondly, women should be admitted to legislative bodies for the same reason, in order that their experience and judgment should be embodied in legislation. Thirdly, women's general opportunity for employment would be widened were they to hold positions not previously open to them. Hitherto the results seem rather disappointing, although a larger number of women in state legislatures have a special interest in what is generally called women's legislation.[2] And if we consider the work women are doing as policewomen, probation officers, juvenile court judges; as heads of Divisions of Child Welfare or Hygiene in state boards of health, or as State Superintendents of Instruction; as chiefs and their co-workers in the Women's Bureau, the Bureau of Home Economics, and the Children's Bureau; we can confidently affirm that the special interests and experience of women are being given an increasing opportunity to make themselves effective on the wider platform of national development.

[1] It must be noted that by October, 1937, there were still fourteen states in which women were not eligible for jury service.

[2] Breckenridge makes the interesting suggestion that, if suffrage had been won earlier, women might have shown greater interest in the problems of government. Economic independence came first, however; young women of training accept earning a living as their first responsibility, and increasing numbers of married women have jobs. Leisure for politics, which women would have had a generation earlier, is now wanting; recognition in other fields is perhaps easier to secure; and other interests compete with political interests.

It is, of course, far too early to form any conclusive estimate of the results of woman suffrage. At first women seem to have been even more remiss than men in going to the polls; but by 1927 Carrie Chapman Catt stated her belief that they were voting in larger numbers. Existing data are inadequate to serve as a basis for judgment. In the four Western states which adopted suffrage more than a generation ago, women appear to have voted, in 1908 and 1912, about five-sixths as frequently as men. A study made, in 1909, in Colorado, indicated that women were more independent of party organizations than men and that by means of the vote they had been able to exercise a beneficial effect on legislation in support of the reforms advocated by women's organizations.[1]   In the same way, the ballot now provides women throughout the country with a powerful instrument for the promotion of causes in which they have long been interested.

The struggle for equal rights for men and women absorbs the attention of the National Woman's Party. The League of Women Voters, on the other hand, while pursuing its policy of educating women voters, is actively engaged in the promotion of certain major interests. These include legal equality, wherever this is in the interests of all women, child welfare, international coöperation to prevent war, the welfare of women in industry, social hygiene, efficiency in government. In addition to the League and the Woman's Party, the Women's Joint Congressional Committee engages in direct political action. This committee endeavors to promote the programs of federal legislation endorsed by a large number of national organizations of women, including the General Federation of Women's Clubs and the National Council of Women. Through its subcommittees it works for measures which very generally have social betterment as their aim.[2]

In 1895, Anna Garlin Spencer declared the "liberation from bondage of the moral and intellectual initiative of women" to

[1] Helen L. Sumner, *Equal Suffrage: The Results of an Investigation in Colorado* (1909). She found that the participation in political activities enlarged the interests of women, quickened civic consciousness and not only provided them with wider opportunities for service, but in many cases developed ability of a high order. Her conclusions are summarized as follows: "The Colorado experiment certainly indicates that equal suffrage is a step in the direction of a better citizenship, a more effective use of the ability of women as an integral part of the race, and a closer comradeship and understanding between men and women." P. 260.

[2] Such, for example, as passage of the Child Labor Amendment; entrance of the United States into the World Court; adequate appropriations for the Children's and Women's Bureaus; continuance of federal work for social hygiene; the creation of a federal department of education. Recently the American Association of University Women has been active in following and promoting legislation at Washington.

be "the greatest institutional reform of the century just closing," a reform, moreover, which was indissolubly linked with the solution of some of the most pressing problems of family life. The twentieth century has seen further progress in the removal of legal barriers and the bestowal of rights and opportunities, and it has seen many women, *though by no means all*, making effective use of their newly acquired freedom and assuming a greater share of social responsibility. In certain quarters, however, we are now witnessing a reaction; and, even apart from such retrogressive tendencies, we are realizing more and more that the effect of all these changes is to create *new* problems. The most crucial of these center in the relationship of the emancipated woman to family life.

SUGGESTED READING

Boothe, V. B., ed., *Women in the Modern World*, in *The Annals of the American Academy of Political and Social Science*, Vol. CXLIII, May, 1929.

Branch, M. S., *Women and Wealth*, 1934.

Breckenridge, S. P., *Women in the Twentieth Century*, 1933.

——, "Women's Activities Outside the Home," *Recent Social Trends*, 2 vols., 1933, Vol. I, Ch. XIV.

Groves, E. R., and Brooks, L. M., *Readings in the Family*, 1934, Ch. VIII.

Hutchins, G., *Women Who Work*, 1934.

Johnsen, J., ed., *Special Legislation for Women*, 1926.

Lynd, R. S., "The People as Consumers," *Recent Social Trends*, 2 vols., 1933, Vol. II, Ch. XVIII.

Myerson, A., *The Nervous Housewife*, 1929.

National League of Women Voters, *Towards Equal Rights for Men and Women*, 1929.

——, *Survey of Women in Public Office*, rev. ed., 1937.

Pruette, L., *Women and Leisure*, 1924.

——, ed., *Women Workers through the Depression*, 1934.

Rauschenbush, W., "The Idiot God Fashion," *Woman's Coming of Age* (eds. Schmalhausen, S. D., and Calverton, V. F.), 1931, pp. 424–446.

Schreiner, O., *Woman and Labor*, 1911.

Veblen, T., *The Theory of the Leisure Class*, 1899.

Women's Bureau, *Bulletin 30*, "The Share of Wage-Earning Women in Family Support," 1923.

——, *Bulletin 41*, "Family Status of Breadwinning Women in Four Selected Cities," 1925.

——, *Bulletin 65*, "The Effects of Labor Legislation on the Employment Opportunities of Women," 1928.

Women's Bureau, *Bulletin 75*, "What the Wage-Earning Woman Contributes to Family Support," 1929.

——, *Bulletin 77*, "Study of Two Groups of Denver Married Women Applying for Jobs," 1929.

——, *Bulletin 108*, "The Effects of the Depression on Wage Earners' Families: A Second Survey of South Bend," 1936.

——, *Bulletin 115*, "Women at Work, A Century of Industrial Change," 1933.

——, *Bulletin 117*, "The Age Factor as It Relates to Women in Business and the Professions," 1934.

——, *Bulletin 120*, "The Employment of Women in Offices," 1934.

——, *Bulletin 132*, "Women Who Work in Offices," 1935.

——, *Bulletin 135*, "The Commercialization of the Home through Industrial Home Work," 1935.

——, *Bulletin 137*, "Summary of State Hour Laws for Women and Minimum-Wage Rates," 1936.

——, *Bulletin 144*, "State Labor Laws for Women," 1937.

——, *Bulletin 147*, "Summary of State Reports of Occupational Diseases, with a Survey of Preventive Legislation, 1932–1934," 1936.

——, *Bulletin 148*, "The Employed Woman Homemaker in the United States," 1936.

——, *Women in the Economy of the United States of America*, 1937.

CHAPTER XVI

CONFLICTING VALUES IN WOMEN'S LIVES

EMANCIPATED WOMEN AND THE FAMILY

The Outward Freedom of Modern Women. The women of to-day are the inheritors of all the gains of the emancipation movement. Girls of the more fortunate classes may now look forward to a thorough education and to a wide range of opportunities for a self-directed life of individual expression and social service. The contrast between the women of to-day and those of even fifty years ago is, perhaps, best symbolized by the outward freedom achieved by women: their physical freedom of movement, their freedom from hampering and constricting clothing, their freedom to engage in sports and to go independently where they will, alone or with men. Other factors besides the women's movement have, of course, contributed to this result: the growing popularity of athletics, the invention of the bicycle, the automobile, the airplane, and all the liberating influences of war-work.

Not until the nineties was the movement for physical freedom well under way.[1] The protected young lady of earlier days had been appropriately concealed in voluminous trailing garments, swathed over tightly laced corsets. While fashion frequently permitted an exaggeration of bust and hips with a corresponding constriction of the waist, and extremely low-necked evening attire, there might never be any *open* suggestion that an adult female possessed legs.[2] No wonder Jane Austen spoke of *one-half* mile as "a distance eminently suited to elegant female walking." Croquet could be indulged in, it is true, while fashionably clad, and horseback riding could be enjoyed on a side-saddle, with a skirt sweeping the ground. Even tennis in its earlier stages appears, from contemporary illustrations, to have been an elegant pastime requiring no freedom either for breath

---

[1] See T. Woody, *A History of Women's Education in the United States* (2 vols., 1929), Vol. II, Chapter III, for an account of the early advocates of exercise and dress-reform for women.

[2] The bloomer dress *did* suggest such a possibility, with its bifurcated garment gathered at the ankle and its skirt as much as six inches from the ground; and very probably this is what made it so *shocking,* so *mannish.* In the fifties and sixties, its temporary adoption by certain notoriously "strong-minded" ladies caused a great scandal.

or movement.[1] With the gradual introduction of gymnastics and more strenuous games for girls, the bloomer dress was revived in modified form, to be worn on appropriate occasions in exclusively feminine society.

But then came the bicycle, an invention not only necessitating sensible dress for women, but making it easy for them to venture farther from their homes. Bicycling costumes and bathing suits mark the beginning of sport clothes in the modern sense. With the growing popularity of swimming, bathing suits, which at first covered their wearers to the ankle, gradually allowed the legs to be revealed almost to the knee.[2] The era of physical freedom and of dress appropriate to its use was only fully inaugurated by the years of war-work.[3] Bobbed hair, short skirts, riding breeches, overalls, and, last of all, shorts are now commonplace, as are the most abbreviated of backless bathing suits. And there is no segregation of these scantily clad modern girls. Far from it. Where, a hundred years ago, a young lady could hardly speak to a young gentleman unchaperoned, the boys and girls of to-day are companions in work and play; while the automobile allows them to travel far from home, and makes impossible any close supervision by their elders. No longer is the wearing of shorts, or trousers, regarded as mannish or detracting from the femininity of the wearer. It is realized that the modern young woman is not aping man, but is simply wearing the clothes suitable to her occupation.[4]

Women can now, if they so desire, engage in almost all the same physical activities as men, even in those which require the greatest endurance and skill and the most intrepid daring: they may swim the English Channel, may be explorers and big-game hunters, they may fly over continents and oceans, alone or with men. A hundred years ago, Harriet Martineau was asked, "is it possible you think women have the same duties and rights as

[1] Not indeed until 1894 was experimental evidence forthcoming in disproof of the theory that women breathed *costically*, in distinction from men who breathed abdominally. It is not surprising, then, to find an authority on dress writing, in 1895, that corsets were a necessity, women always had worn them and *"they always will."* Quoted by the Lynds, *Middletown*, p. 159.

[2] Earlier in the century it was considered *unfeminine* to be able to swim. The lady should rather *wait to be saved* from drowning. H. Ellis, *The Psychology of Sex*, Vol. VI, p. 45.

[3] The yardage in a woman's apparel was reduced from 18½ yards to 7 between 1913 and 1928.

[4] As a typical instance, the case may be cited of the American tennis champion who played in shorts at Wimbledon in the afternoon, and appeared that same evening, to be presented at Court, clad in the traditional sweeping satin, and with ostrich plumes in her hair.

men?" She replied, "I think her powers ought to settle the question." [1] Upon the basis of their "powers," women have already proved conclusively that they cannot with justice be excluded from any opportunity open to men. There is no feat of skill or daring, nor any field of artistic or intellectual or practical endeavor, in which some woman has not proved herself able to hold her own with men. Moreover, women may now, without social disapproval, remain unmarried; self-reliant and dependent upon their own ability alone for a successful career.

The Dilemma of Marriage. Marriage and motherhood remain, however, of central importance in most women's lives. Here, then, is the crucial dilemma of modern women. One phase of the emancipation movement is drawing to a close. Women have shown themselves capable of becoming individualized human beings and responsible members of society. A new phase of the women's movement is beginning: the coördination of women's new interests and new opportunities, for self-fulfilment and social service, with their enduring functions as wives and mothers. There is, of course, no one solution for this problem of the integration of family responsibilities with work outside the home and with wider social responsibilities. Individual solutions adapted to individual circumstances can only be reached through actual experiments. Knowledge of the issues involved is, however, essential to the successful conduct of such experiments.

Some of the most successful marriages on record, significantly enough, were those made by many of the leaders of the nineteenth-century humanitarian and emancipation movements. Women such as Elizabeth Fry, Josephine Butler, Lucretia Mott, Lucy Stone Blackwell, and Millicent Fawcett, all were devoted mothers, and had made marriages in which love and comprehending friendship were combined. Their husbands belonged to the small group of liberal-minded men who, both in America and England, ably seconded women in their struggle for independence and opportunity.[2] Others among these women leaders, for example, Florence Nightingale, Susan Anthony, Mary Lyon, and Dorothea Dix, never married, apprehensive of interference with whole-hearted devotion to their work. And in recent years, it must be confessed, many of the greatest women have to some extent owed their success to the fact that they have devoted

[1] Quoted by Furness, *The Genteel Female*, pp. 240–241.

[2] This should be remembered when confronted with statements, such as Ludovici's, that the unrest of women has been largely due to the embitterment of spinsters and unhappily married women.

themselves with a single mind to their work and to the service of humanity. In general, however, it is impossible to accept a solution of women's problems which excludes from actual motherhood any considerable proportion of the ablest women.

Much depends, therefore, on the modern women who marry: the future, not only of the women's movement, but also of the family, will be determined by them. Before turning to a more detailed consideration and evaluation of the issues involved, let us briefly examine the legal status of married women in America. It at once becomes evident that a married woman, even now, is only beginning to be considered as a fully distinct personality apart from her relation to her husband.[1]

THE LEGAL STATUS OF MARRIED WOMEN

Property and Contractual Rights of Married Women. In the majority of the states, by 1930, married women had acquired a status nearly equal to that of their husbands.[2] In twenty-three states a married woman had an absolute right of contract; in the remaining states limitations of this right ranged from minor restrictions, to the Texas law, whereby a wife had practically no right to contract free from the consent of her husband. In regard to property rights, husband and wife had an equal interest in each others' real estate in thirty-one states. These included five of the eight community-property states, in which all property owned by either husband or wife before marriage, or coming to either through gift, devise, or descent, belongs to his or her separate estate.[3] On the other hand, all property acquired after

[1] Women's loss of independent identity through marriage is clearly indicated in customary usage, when a married woman is spoken of as the *former* so-and-so. The implication here goes beyond a mere matter of names, and is, of course, quite natural so long as women take their husbands' surnames, a matter of custom rather than of law. It is now becoming customary for women who have made distinguished contributions, in any field, to retain their own surnames (although these to be sure are their *fathers'* surnames) usually prefixed by Miss. Frances Perkins and Amelia Earhart are well-known examples. Since 1920, the Lucy Stone League has led in a movement to have the surnames of women retained even when they have not made a name for themselves. As pointed out by Ruth Hale, in *The First Five Years of the Lucy Stone League* (1925), there is a great body of legal opinion supporting a woman's legal right to her own surname. The League has succeeded in establishing a number of precedents for the transference of real estate in the so-called maiden name, also for its use on library cards, insurance policies, charge accounts, in hotel registry, and on passports. In a number of cases husband and wife have adopted a hyphenated surname, combining their individual surnames.

[2] For a detailed analysis see *A Survey of the Legal Status of Women in the Forty-eight States* (League of Women Voters, 1930). An up-to-date survey is being undertaken by the Women's Bureau. It will probably be completed in 1938.

[3] Arizona, California, Idaho, Louisiana, Nevada, New Mexico, Texas, and Washington.

marriage by the joint efforts of husband and wife is *community property, owned* jointly, although the husband is given its *control* during his lifetime. In all but Nevada, the wife could dispose of her half of the community property by will, whereas in Nevada a widower took it all, and a widow only half. In Arizona, California, Louisiana, New Mexico, and Washington, the community property was held to include the *wife's earnings* if she was living with her husband, and these, therefore, became subject to his control. She could only secure the right to manage her own earnings if separated from him, or if he deserted her or became insane. In all other states except Georgia, where a wife owned her earnings only if separated from her husband, a married woman owned the wages earned outside her home. This matter of control of the wife's earnings is obviously of increasing significance, as more and more married women enter the ranks of the gainfully employed.

In nine states a husband still retained some authority, however slight, over his wife's separate estate. In no state did a wife receive by law any portion of the family income free from the dictation of her husband, unless she had earned it outside the home; nor could she in any state collect for services performed in the home. In forty-five states mothers had equal rights with fathers in the inheritance of a deceased child's estate, but in only thirty did the mother share equally in the earnings of minor children.

Mothers' Rights of Guardianship. Marked changes have occurred in guardianship laws since the beginning of the century. Only eight states in 1930—Alabama, Georgia, Kentucky, Louisiana, North Carolina, Oklahoma, Texas, and Vermont— still gave the father sole rights of guardianship over the children.[1] In this way they perpetuated common law, according to which, in Blackstone's words, "the mother is entitled to no power but only to reverence and respect." In Georgia, the father might even will away from the mother the custody of the child, *without her consent.*[2] In ten states this was possible, but only with the mother's

[1] In Pennsylvania the wife's equal share in guardianship was dependent on her fitness and her contribution to the maintenance and support of her minor children.

[2] Of all laws discriminating against women those which permit a father to deprive a mother of her children are the most unjust and cruel; yet women were given property rights long before they were given mothers' rights. In 1855, Margaret Fuller Ossoli in *Women in the Nineteenth Century,* pp. 32–33, stated that she knew of scores of cases where husbands had robbed their wives of the children. "I have known these men steal their children, whom they knew they had no means to maintain, take them into dissolute company, expose them to bodily danger, to frighten the poor woman, to whom, it seems, the fact that she alone·had borne the pangs of birth and

consent. In thirty-seven states he could not do so under any circumstances. One aspect of the patriarchal family has as yet remained unchallenged. Legitimate children legally take the surname of the father. Illegitimate children alone bear a mother's surname. So long as an exclusively patronymic system persists in the identification of the family group, mothers cannot be said to stand on a complete legal equality with fathers in relation to their children.[1]

Towards Legal Equality. The case is theoretically won for the recognition of the equality of husband and wife as legal personalities. But the confused state of public opinion with regard to family relationships is reflected in law, which, in any event, lags behind opinion; and the statutes of most states reveal an inconsistent mingling of new with traditional attitudes. For example, despite the increasing numbers of gainfully employed married women, the law still treats wives as *economically dependent*, without taking into consideration the services performed by the wife within the home. The wife is everywhere entitled to support by her husband, but, unless the case is taken to court, the extent of support is left in the husband's hands, and bears no relationship to the wife's services performed in the home. In Pennsylvania, a mother is entitled to an equal share in her minor children's earnings only when she contributes to their support, thus putting a premium on work outside the home, and underestimating the value of services in the home. One other striking illustration of the way in which economic considerations have influenced the law is the fact that in no state, by 1930, was a wife entitled by law to determine the choice of the family domicile.[2]

In the nineteenth century, among the Quakers alone, marriage implied equality between husband and wife. All the colonies except Connecticut had discriminated in favor of the husband in cases of separation or divorce. Even in the middle of last century,

---

nourished their infancy, does not give an equal right to them." When Kansas, at an early date, incorporated, in its constitution, the right of a mother to her children, it did so with the express purpose of attracting women emigrants.

[1] In comparison with certain other issues, a matter of names may seem unimportant. Many mothers would, however, be glad to have their own family names perpetuated in the surname of their children. A hyphenated surname is one way out of the difficulty, but leads to complications in the succeeding generation. Perhaps children of one sex might take the surname of the parent of the same, or opposite, sex. In Russia the matter is settled by agreement between husband and wife.

[2] Even in the eight states where the wife had, for certain purposes, been authorized to establish a separate domicile, the general principle was that her husband's domicile is hers.

when a wife secured a divorce because of her husband's infidelity, she lost her home, property, and children.[1] To-day, except in some states, with regard to support on the part of husbands, and as concerns mothers of illegitimate children, the statutory grounds for divorce, widely as they differ from state to state, are the same for husband and wife.[2]

Prior to 1922 an American woman who married a foreigner took the nationality of her husband, and an alien woman was naturalized through marriage with a citizen of the United States. The Nationality of Women Act, of 1922, granted married women citizenship status independent of their husbands.[3] A 1931 amendment removed a last restriction, in permitting women who had lost their citizenship by reason of marriage to ineligible aliens, prior to the amendment, to be naturalized. The act gives rise, it is true, to certain difficulties for those foreign women who by marriage to Americans forfeit their nationality under the laws of their native countries. But all American women are now assured of nationality rights.

SOCIAL AND ECONOMIC CONDITIONS AFFECTING THE WORK OF MARRIED WOMEN OUTSIDE THE HOME

Marriage and "Careers." No just estimate can be formed of women's position, either in society or within the home, without realization of the fact that *as mothers* they are *ipso facto* incapable of competing on equal terms with men. The word "career," should not be used in too narrow a sense: it should include not only intensive work demanding long unbroken hours year in and year out, but also all the many forms of work in which the individual woman may put her gifts and training to profitable use. The use of the word "career" is significant, how-

[1] Conservative opinion long upheld traditional views. As late as 1880, a Philadelphia minister declared: "wifehood is the crowning glory of womanhood, in it she is bound for all time. To her husband she owes the duty of unqualified obedience. There is no wrong which a man can do which justifies his wife in leaving him. It is her duty to subject herself to him always and no crime he can commit can justify her lack of obedience." Ida H. Harper, *Life and Work of Susan B. Anthony* (3 vols., 1899–1908), Vol. I, p. 79.

[2] Fourteen states, in 1930, granted a wife separation or divorce for her husband's failure to support, and two states did so where the husband was a vagrant. In fifteen states a husband could obtain a divorce if the wife had been before marriage the mother of a child born out of wedlock, or was, at the time of marriage, pregnant, without the husband's knowledge or responsibility.

[3] For a discussion of the independent citizenship rights of a married woman see Breckenridge, *The Family and the State*, pp. 152 *et seq.*; also *Marriage and the Civic Rights of Women* (1931). The Cable Act, as it is called, was one of the first two federal legislative victories to be gained largely as a result of women's efforts, after they won the right to vote, the other being The Maternity and Infancy Act.

ever, indicating as it does that the conflict between homemaking, in particular the nurture of children, and independent work is most acute for educated women in the professions and more creative lines of business. Nor is this strange. Throughout the women's movement, small groups of women of this type have led the way, have roused other women to awareness of their problems, and have set standards for the future. Now with so many of their former objectives won, they find themselves confronted with the most baffling problem of all. While these leaders agree that every opportunity should be open to women to achieve success and financial reward in the world of outside work, that, to paraphrase Dewey, nothing but the richest and fullest experience possible is good enough for *women*, there is far less certainty as to the content of this richest and fullest life, and as to the means by which it may be achieved.

This is no academic problem. There is, as we saw, a marked trend towards the increasing employment of married women, in spite of all obstacles, whether due to social disapproval and actual restrictions on their work, or to the intrinsic difficulties of combining homemaking with outside work.[1]

Restrictions on the Work of Married Women. If the trend continues towards the participation of married women in work outside the home, legal restrictions will doubtless in time be removed. The rights of a married woman to contract for her services, to work when and where she pleases, to consider her earnings her own property are still subject to limitations in a number of states.[2]

The most obvious instance to-day of rulings restricting the work of married women is afforded by the by-laws of school boards which discriminate against married women.[3] Where the

---

[1] According to the occupation statistics of the 1930 Census, the increase in the percentage of married women between 1920 and 1930 in the different groups was as follows: manufacturing and mechanical industries, 30.2%; domestic and personal service, 73.8%; public service, 110.3%; trade, 115.2%; transportation and communication, 125.1%; professional service, 137.9%; clerical occupations, 184.4%. Of all gainfully occupied married women, .2% were in public service; 2.3% in transportation and communication; 9.2% in agriculture; 9.6% in professional service; 11.3% in trade; 11.8% in clerical occupations; 19.8% in manufacturing and mechanical industries; 36.1% in domestic and personal service.

[2] M. P. Smith, "Legal and Administrative Restrictions affecting the Rights of Married Women to Work," *Annals of the American Academy*, Vol. CXLIII (May, 1929), pp. 255–264.

[3] A survey of 1,500 cities, made by the National Education Association in 1930–1931, showed that 77% did not employ married women as *new* teachers, and only 37% allow women who marry to continue after marriage, a number of these retaining only such women as have been elected for permanent service.

validity of these by-laws has been tested in the courts of certain states, decisions have tended to break down some of the restrictions. Before the depression, a beginning was being made in securing full opportunity for married women to contribute their services to public education. In many instances, however, such gains have now been lost, owing to the need for retrenchment and the view that one wage earner in a family is sufficient, particularly in times of widespread unemployment.[1]

There are also numerous instances of rulings imposed by business concerns discriminating against married women. During the recent financial crisis, many married women who had hitherto been allowed to hold their positions were dismissed to make way for men or unmarried women; dismissed simply because they were married, irrespective of their actual situation, their need for work, or the number of their dependents.

Discrimination against women is much more marked in the case of married women, and inevitably so. "So long as marriage is regarded as an alternative to gainful employment, so long must women find their economic opportunity restricted and subordinated to what is regarded as their real vocation." [2] While the single woman is now coming to be accepted as a worker, the central issue in the economic problems of women stands clearly revealed in the opposition to the gainful employment of married women, and the discriminations to which they are subject.

But while conservatives stubbornly and blindly insist on woman's sphere within the home, where she is "supported" by a husband and supposed to find ample outlet for her abilities, radicals no longer help matters by their demand that women shall at all costs be fitted into the man-made world outside the home. Neither are willing to embark on the long road of reconstruction, to the end that social and economic institutions may better serve their functions in present-day society.

As an encouraging example of a constructive approach to the problem we may cite the attitude of several women's colleges, among them Bryn Mawr, Bennington, Sarah Lawrence, and Barnard, towards the employment of married women, or both husbands and wives, on their faculties. Many colleges and

---

[1] It is encouraging, therefore, to note that, on July 16, 1935, married women in London, England, won, after twelve years of struggle, their claim to be employed as teachers and doctors by the London County Council. *New York Times*, July 17 and Aug. 6, 1935.

[2] E. J. Hutchinson, "The Economic Problem of Women," *Annals of the American Academy*, Vol. CXLIII (May, 1929), p. 136.

universities, it is true, employ married women, but a common ruling very frequently prohibits the employment of both husband and wife by the same institution.[1] Most significant is the recent action of the Trustees of Barnard College. In her annual report for 1932, Dean Gildersleeve said: "We have felt for many years that a women's college was a peculiarly appropriate place in which to experiment with solutions of the new problems faced by women, and to attempt to arrive at some wise adjustment. Our observations have shown that the combination of rearing children and carrying on college teaching is a difficult one, but in some cases certainly very desirable. It is of the greatest importance that our teachers should be normal and interesting human beings with as full and rich lives as may be." In accordance with this enlightened point of view the Trustees resolved: "That a woman member of the administration or instructional staff of Barnard College, on Trustee appointment for full time, who is expecting a child, be granted a leave of absence for a half year on full salary, or for a full year on half salary."

Equal Pay for Equal Work. Nowhere are the conflicting and confused attitudes prevailing to-day more evident, than in the discussion which centers on the principle of *equal pay for equal work.* According to Sylvia Anthony, this "essentially implies not merely payment for work done irrespective of sex, marriage, family obligations or any other individual idiosyncrasy of the worker, but also the equal liberty of citizens to apply for work, or for the preliminary training necessary to secure it."[2] And the fact remains that, in business and the professions, as well as in industry, the tendency is everywhere for women to occupy subordinate and less well-paid positions. "There runs throughout the field of employment the attitude that men have the actual as well as the legal economic responsibilities of the home upon their shoulders, and they have therefore a vested right in higher

---

[1] This is particularly unfortunate since the marriage of two college instructors is of fairly frequent occurrence, and because it precludes what would otherwise be a happy means of overcoming one of the gravest obstacles in the way of a wife finding employment: the fact that, except in big cities, it is frequently very hard, if not impossible, for husband and wife to find work in the same locality. If the home is not to be broken by husband and wife living apart, it is the wife, in almost all cases, who must relinquish paid employment.

[2] *Women's Place in Industry and Home* (1932), p. 195. Breckenridge emphasizes the fact that "the question is not only one of getting the same pay if one has the same job, but of getting the opportunity to do the interesting and important work at any scale of pay." This statement is made in connection with work in the civil service and in teaching, where the principle of equal pay for equal work is most widely put into practice. *Women in the Twentieth Century,* p. 230.

wages than women." [1] Women are accordingly obliged to establish their right to work against an opposition which grows stronger the higher they are in the social scale. Those who do not *have* to work, are accused of taking work from those who need it.

As a matter of fact men's remuneration is never fixed relative to the number of their dependents, but it is always taken for granted that the normal man is supporting a family. Rarely is the fact taken fully into account that many women too have dependents, unmarried women sometimes being the sole support of elderly parents or younger brothers and sisters, and married women being, in increasing numbers, obliged to supplement the family income. There can be no such clear-cut distinction: many men have no dependents to support; many women have. The current assumption is, however, based on the obvious fact that a salary which is sufficient for a family is relatively large for an unmarried man or woman *without dependents*. And it is, of course, true, that in certain lines of work such as school teaching, most of the men are married, most of the women unmarried.

Since there is a tendency to discriminate against all women, because of their actual or potential relationship to family support, it is very natural that the tendency should be most marked in connection with married women. Yet, from such studies as have been made of the earnings of married women in business and the professions, it would appear that economic necessity operates here too, as one, at least, of the chief reasons for combining gainful occupation with homemaking. [2]

The most hopeful solution of the dilemma would seem to be the proposal of Eleanor Rathbone, Paul Douglas, and other proponents of family allowances, that these should be used to supplement a system of strictly equal pay for equal work, irrespective of sex. Only then could the question of equal wages be disentangled from that of the support of the family. [3]

[1] E. J. Hutchinson, *op. cit.*, p. 133. For a summary of data relating to the compensation of women and women's share in the support of their families, see the recent publication of the Women's Bureau, *Women in the Economy of the United States of America*, Part I, Chapters 3, 4, and Appendix A.

[2] Chase G. Woodhouse, "Married Women in Business and the Professions," *Annals of the American Academy*, Vol. CXLIII (May, 1929), pp. 325–329.

[3] So long as the present situation continues, men will undoubtedly endeavor to keep women from the skilled and better paid positions, whereas, as Douglas says, "The provision of an equal minimum wage for both sexes based on the cost of living for a single person and with allowances made for dependents would prevent the undercutting of the men's rate by women and would protect them from the competition of cheap labor." *Wages and the Family*, p. 273; see too Rathbone, *The Disinherited Family*, Chapter IV.

The Development of Part-time Work.   In a study of 100 women who have successfully combined professions with homemaking, Virginia Collier reaches the conclusion that "a woman can hold a job, a full-time, well-paid job, and run a comfortable contented happy home besides." *But,* there "are four important, almost necessary elements in the situation." One of these is "short and flexible hours of work." [1] There are some forms of work which women may carry on successfully at home within call of their children. The writer, painter, sculptor, musician, or consultant of any kind can arrange her own hours of work, so that she may care for her children, particularly if they have reached school age. Other women, such as actresses, occasional lecturers, physicians, and part-time workers, can absent themselves from home for short periods and still keep in close touch with the children. If below school age, the children must of course be left under competent and responsible supervision either in a nursery school or at home.

Mothers who are bent on full-time careers, which necessitate their absence all day from home and in which they must compete for success and position with men, cannot possibly be in as close touch with their young children as mothers who are more often at hand when needed. Most professionally trained mothers, however, are no more willing to accept this solution of their problems than they are to allow themselves to become wholly absorbed in the daily routine of homemaking. Women who will not surrender any of their unique prerogatives as mothers, but who yet wish to work, must turn for guidance rather to those women who are combining the close supervision of their children with careers in the broader sense of satisfying, creative, and gainful work.

Part-time employment is the obvious solution for many women who wish to combine motherhood with professional work. But so ingrained is the alternative of whole-day employment or no employment at all, that the idea of part-time work has been slow in winning acceptance on the part of employers or of the public. In all forms of business where the heaviest demands are made at certain hours, the employment of part-time workers at these periods is entirely feasible. There have also been numbers of instances where women workers have been paired, each working half the time in the same position.

It would seem as though agencies should exist throughout the country for bringing applicants for part-time positions into

[1] *Marriage and Careers* (1926), p. 113.

touch with employers who can make use of their services. The success attending the Bureau of Part-time Work, established in New York in 1922, shows both the need for such agencies and the valuable services they perform.[1] In the first ten years of its existence, 15,277 part-time positions had been found for qualified women. Since the early experimental work of the Bureau, part-time work has made for itself a recognized place in many fields, and opportunities have been slowly increased by research and field work. Not only have the problems of thousands of women been solved, but a reliable body of evidence has been secured showing that much of the world's work can be accomplished in a shorter working day. A large proportion of the applicants for positions are married women, and one of the chief accomplishments of the Bureau has been its provision of gainful employment for highly trained married women who had business or professional interests before taking up family responsibilities. Through part-time work they can keep a close grip on these interests, and so facilitate reëntry into their former field when home and children no longer make such heavy demands upon them.

COMBINING MOTHERHOOD WITH A PROFESSION

The Professionally Trained Woman's Dilemma. Bacon said, "he who hath wife or children hath given hostages to fortune, for they are impediments to great enterprise, either of virtue or mischief." In commenting on this, Mary Wollstonecraft remarked, "I say the same of women." [2] But with how much more force must it be said of women! For a father can certainly pursue a career with a single-mindedness impossible for a mother. An unmarried woman, or perhaps a married and childless woman, may achieve such single-mindedness, but at the expense of sacrificing the experience of motherhood. The intelligent mother is aware that the earliest years of childhood are all important for future well-being, the fabric of character being woven in the give and take of daily living. Realizing then what their relationship to their young children may mean not only for their own

[1] The Bureau was established by Eleanor Adler in coöperation with a group of representative men and women. Its New York headquarters are at 105 West 40th St. A similar Bureau was opened shortly after in Philadelphia. Progress was slow at first. Few employers were sympathetic and those who had positions to offer, had hitherto had no agency through which they could register their calls. In the first year, 2,374 women registered, while only 691 employers called for workers and 521 were placed. By 1929, with a registration of 2,776, there were 2,810 calls and 2,542 placements.

[2] *Vindication of the Rights of Women,* p. 70.

happiness, but for the children themselves, many women are unwilling to surrender into other hands any part of their care prior to the nursery school age, save perhaps for the *very few* purely routine duties which are involved. What then if these women are doctors, lawyers, teachers, engineers, or business women? It is for women such as these that the dilemma is most acute and the "antinomy" in women's interests most obvious.

The difficulties of such women are accentuated, in America, by the fact that efficient domestic help is both scarce and expensive. In many cases, therefore, a mother who foregoes adding to the family income must do much, if not all, the housework, as well as care for her children. It was estimated, in 1910, that about two-thirds of the married college women in America were included in the class of the "educated American drudge."

Factors Which Favor Individual Solutions. Turning again to Collier's study, the three other important, almost necessary, elements making for success were: (1) good training and experience before marriage; (2) good health; (3) sympathetic coöperation from the husband.[1] It was also found that not only were short and flexible hours indispensable, but that there was a much better chance of securing and holding an appropriate position in a large city. If the husband is employed in a small community, there is much less chance that the wife will be able to find work in the same place: one of the very real and most frequent obstacles in the way of both husband and wife engaging in work outside the home. In a large city, moreover, the element of critical public opinion, frequent in smaller communities, is largely removed.[2]

It is, of course, fairly obvious that the well-trained woman, and, even more so, one who had already been actually engaged in an occupation, would find herself better able to combine work with marriage. But two women, among the hundred, actually both began and completed a medical course after marriage. Good health is of supreme importance.[3] Some, however, only achieved good health through finding congenial work. Although,

---

[1] In Chapter XIX detailed consideration is given to the marital tensions which arise when a husband is unsympathetic with his wife's desire for work. Discussion of the results of the work of married women on marital relationships is, therefore, almost entirely omitted in the present chapter.

[2] An instance is cited of a woman criticized for writing during the mornings while the children were at school. Her critics spent the same period playing bridge in boudoir caps and negligees!

[3] Several women commented on the almost insuperable difficulties in their way when health was temporarily impaired, from the effects of childbirth or from overstrain owing to the illness of members of the family.

under present conditions, women who combine work with home-making may be in danger of nervous overstrain, they escape that sense of frustration which so often leads to pathological conditions and ill-health.

Most significant of all is the fact that so many of these women attributed their success to the sympathetic coöperation of their husbands. "At least fifty-six of the husbands, themselves lawyers, business men, editors, college professors and scientists, do one or many of the following chores. They help cook the dinner, set the table, wash dishes, give the baby his early morning bottle, start breakfast while the mother dresses the children, help between cooks, 'do' one child while the mother does the other, do the marketing regularly, and, in short, work along with their wives until the job is cleaned up. Sharing the care of the children seems to be a welcome privilege in many cases."[1] Unfortunately the attitude of these husbands is hardly representative of prevailing masculine opinion.[2]

Proposed Solutions to the Problem: Conservative. Gina Lombroso holds a medical degree and has written many books. Nevertheless, in *The Soul of Woman* (1923), she analyzes with the utmost skill the psychology of women whose lives have been molded to dependence, and in them discovers the unalterable prototype of *Woman*. On this basis she advises women to make the most of their traditional rôle and to accept their tragic position. Despite the violence and prejudice revealed in Anthony Ludovici's books they make stimulating reading. He would solve all the world's problems through a masculine renaissance, which shall put woman *back in her place* and restore to her the serenity of a dependent existence.[3]

---

[1] Collier, *op. cit.*, p. 85. Count Keyserling considers coöperation of this kind to furnish conclusive evidence of the "psychological subjection" of American men to the "predominant American woman" (*America Set Free* (1929), p. 402). His statements are thought-provoking, but throughout conditioned by the fact that he hypostatizes patriarchal traditions as the eternal law of nature, and conceives of himself as the perfect embodiment of the masculine ideal. The father's authority must be preserved through the *distance* he places between himself and his children who respect and reverence his haughty aloofness! Quite naturally Count Keyserling cannot imagine himself caring for a baby, and so considers it incompatible with virile masculinity to engage in this or any other occupation which "nature demands of women."

[2] For a study of masculine opinion see Pruette, *Women and Leisure* (1924), Chapter VI and Appendix I. Out of 354 men applying for work at a commercial employment office: 57.6% believed married women should devote their time to the home; 27% believed married women should work outside if they desired, except where young children demand their time; 3.5% held more radical views. The younger, unmarried, and less well-educated tended to be more conservative.

[3] A brief summary of his views is to be found in *Lysistrata* (1924). One wonders if Ludovici has ever been psychoanalyzed. He is, of course, a disciple of Nietzsche's,

Extreme anti-feminists are too reactionary to afford any assistance in solving the problems of modern women. More helpful are those conservatives who, while they desire to restrict women very largely if not altogether to the home, yet realize the individualization of modern women and are eager that they should take their full but *appropriate* part in a changing social order. Alarmed by the depreciation and devaluation of the work of women in the home, on the part of more radical feminists, several writers seek to emphasize the supreme values inherent in family life and the all-important social services rendered by the mother and homemaker. Among such writers are Ida Tarbell, Ellen Key, C. Gasquoine Hartley, and Meyrick Boothe.[1]

Much that they have to say is excellent; but, if it be admitted that women, as human beings, should be educated in such a way as to discover and develop their individual aptitudes, it must also be admitted that a considerable number of women could not possibly find within the home fully satisfactory outlets for their special abilities. Nor, indeed, could performance of their functions as intelligent consumers and their participation in social service help matters much. Conservatives betray themselves by their tendency to generalize about a chimerical entity *Woman*, rather than to discuss the problems of *women*, who as human beings are possessed of as wide a variety of interests and capacities as men.

Take, by way of example, a woman whose profession would be of the utmost assistance in contributing to homemaking: the pediatrician or child psychologist. She would certainly make use of her profession in her family life, but how could she be expected to be satisfied with so limited a scope for her abilities. The case is even more obvious for women whose professions are not connected in any way with home activities; lawyers or archaeologists, for example. Ethel Puffer Howes has made clear the persistent fallacy underlying so many of these arguments, a fallacy

---

but it may be of some significance that he was educated chiefly by his mother. Among his concrete suggestions for securing a race free from physical degeneracy and feministic tendencies is the advocacy of infanticide. All but the mentally and physically perfect would be weeded out and the population kept within desirable limits *without* the use of contraceptives.

[1] Tarbell, *The Business of Being a Woman* (1912); Key, *The Renaissance of Motherhood* (1914); Hartley, *Motherhood* (1917); Boothe, *Woman and Society* (1929). It may be surprising to find C. Gasquoine Hartley, and still more Ellen Key, characterized as conservatives, in view of their radical beliefs about sex relationships. But their strong conviction of the supreme value of motherhood leads them to believe that mothers must for a time at least relinquish any other occupation but motherhood.

which confuses the application of knowledge to a single concrete use with the normal practice of a science or art in itself. Strangely enough some of the arts most prized in the home come nearest to escaping from this current misconception. It is seldom, if ever, suggested that women highly gifted in music, literature, painting, or sculpture should find "the proper and sufficient use of their talents within the home." Yet, no less specific and far more frequent are executive, scientific, and intellectual gifts.

Meyrick Boothe, the most recent of these moderate conservatives, concedes that much good has come of the emancipation movement and that women should not be debarred from entering any sphere of work. It should *not*, however, be regarded as *normal* for them to have any wider social functions, save as these are derived from their central mission of maternity. Very logically he stresses the need for radical alterations in women's education to embue them with truly feminine and racial ideals. We must get *back*, he insists, to "the eternal truth that men and women are complementary opposites. Accordingly man's primary function is to create food and wealth for the community, while woman's primary function is to bear and rear the children of the community."[1] His constructive suggestions are thus vitiated by the fundamental assumption of all conservatives: that we already have adequate and final knowledge of "woman's nature and her social functions." It is surely far too soon to turn our backs on all the new possibilities opening for women and to abandon the experimentation which is necessary, if women are to discover new ways of achieving harmonious and socially valuable lives: lives, moreover, in which, for the majority, marriage and motherhood will be the central and possibly all-pervading interest, but in which there is also room for a wide range of other interests, including the ability to engage in a gainful occupation.

Proposed Solutions to the Problem: Radical. The moderate conservatives are, of course, very right in their rejection of extreme feminism, with its over-individualistic and exclusive insistence on independence and equality of opportunity in securing positions hitherto held by men. They do not always realize that such a one-sided point of view is the inevitable result of the long-protracted and increasingly bitter struggle of women, to win full status as independent and socially responsible human beings.

One of the greatest of feminist leaders, Olive Schreiner, in no

[1] *Woman and Society*, pp. 66–67.

way deserves to be classed as one-sided or ultra-radical.[1] She states the central issue with the utmost clarity. "We claim all labor as our province," she announced, "yet more especially do we claim those fields in which the difference in the reproductive functions between man and woman may place male and female at a slightly different angle with regard to certain facts of life." That they may fully contribute to social well-being, women must have "an equal share in the control and governance of national life."[2] She demanded that all occupations should be open to women, not in order that women should fit into a man-made world, far less that they should grasp at privileges hitherto denied. But because she believed that otherwise injustice would be done to individual women, in the diversity of their capacities, and because she realized, in a truly experimental spirit, that freedom of opportunity was necessary, for "at present we have no scientific data from which to draw any conclusion, and any attempt to divide the occupations in which male and female intellects should be employed, must be to attempt a purely artificial and arbitrary division."[3]

Charlotte Perkins Gilman was, perhaps, the outstanding radical feminist. In her *Woman and Economics* (1899), she combined a brilliant analysis of the evils arising from the economic dependence of women with radical suggestions for the reorganization of family life. If women could achieve complete economic independence and equality with men, and share equally in the work of the world, this would make possible a higher development of social life, a higher sex-life, and a better motherhood. Monogamy is "the form of sex union best calculated to serve the interests of the individual and society."[4] But all industrial processes should be taken from the home, and the former services of wife and mother be replaced by the organized services of "experts." The care of children too would be very largely in the hands of trained specialists.[5]   Charlotte Gilman's

---

[1] Only conservatives would now consider Olive Schreiner as a radical; her views were wholly constructive and the expression of what liberals now regard as fundamental truths.

[2] *Woman and Labor*, p. 184. Even Meyrick Boothe concedes that the author of what he calls "the leading text-book of feminism" was possessed of "insight much superior to that of most present-day feminists." *Op. cit.*, pp. 85 and 12 *et seq.*

[3] *Op. cit.*, p. 164.   [4] *Op. cit.*, p. 25.

[5] She very rightly condemned the "doting and gloating" mother as too intensely personal to have a good influence on her child. She also maintained that not every woman has the special qualities or the education and experience necessary to give her child expert care. As Ellen Key pertinently remarks, Charlotte Gilman's whole program rests on assumptions which "emanate from a comparison between the

suggestions with regard to the impersonal aspects of housework are valuable and anticipate modern tendencies. But one wonders where could be found all the "born educators" and experts in child care, on whom extreme feminists rely for taking the place of mothers; particularly since increasing stress is now laid on the need of little babies for individualized fostering care most naturally bestowed by mothers. Experts in child care are at work, to-day, on educational experiments in group care which are valuable as *supplements*, but as supplements *only*, to the individual care afforded by the home. Fortunately, as Sylvia Anthony points out, women of modern outlook tend to take more and more interest in the rearing of children. "Rather than give up child care for the sake of independence, they are often inclined to do the opposite, not through undervaluation of independence, but through revaluation of child care."[1]

The Coördination of Women's Interests. The typical feminist solution is altogether too one-sided and does not take into account the actual complexities of the situation. It is now known, as Ethel Puffer Howes points out, that "what mothers must provide, beyond milk, orange-juice, spinach, and cod-liver oil, right habits of feeding and bathing and behaving, is a firm foundation for the child's universe. Affection, security, order, continuity, justice, sympathy, freedom must flow from her." What is more, "the scientific students of child nature have now made it possible for every mother, if she be sincere and humble-minded, to learn to guide herself aright in dealing with tender souls, as she could once learn only how to deal with tiny bodies. . . . Now that it is possible, it is surely the duty of every woman who brings a soul into the world to school herself to cherish it aright."[2] Convinced that "the child whose mother is not *on call* is bound to lose" Ethel Howes has devoted much thought and actual

present untrained mother and trained educators, and between all the dark sides of the home and the light sides of collective upbringing." *The Renaissance of Mother-hood*, p. 131.

[1] *Women's Place in Industry and Home*, p. 222. Nevertheless, views very similar to Charlotte Gilman's are still held by prominent feminists. Alice Beal Parsons, for example, devotes the second half of *Woman's Dilemma* (1926), to a consideration of "Will the Home be Endangered if the Mother Has an Outside Job?" She agrees that children need "that refuge of the spirit which during centuries men have called home"; but, since "children, like automobiles and cauliflowers, thrive best under the care of specialists," a crèche, under the care of trained nurses and supervision of a doctor, "is probably a safer place for the day-time hours of little children than the majority of homes." The "element of maternal solicitude and love has ample opportunity to function, when the mother takes her baby home each day." Pp. 249, 264, 256.

[2] "The Mother in the Present-Day Home," *Concerning Parents* (1926), pp. 24–25.

experimentation to the problem of securing *continuity for women*.

The Institute for the Coördination of Women's Interests was established at Smith College in 1925, with Ethel Howes as its director, and with the definite purpose of assisting the modern college woman "to work out a philosophy of life and a technique of living that shall include all her main interests."[1] A full-time career, according to Ethel Howes, is incompatible with motherhood; but, both from the standpoint of mental health and from the social and economic standpoint, mothers with trained capacity should be given effective outlets beyond the sphere of the home. Constructive social changes must be preceded by a period of exploration and experimentation.

Results of Present-day Experiments. Already there are many families in which marriage is viewed as a coöperative venture, with no hard and fast distinctions between the husband's work in the outside world and the wife's in the home; where the wife is principal homemaker but also has her own work, and the husband, in turn, helps in the home. There are cases, too, where husband and wife have been in the same professional field, in which particularly successful combinations of home and work have been devised.[2] One of the most striking aspects of the Collier study was the evidence gathered to show that "happiness is the chief result from this extra-activity of woman; happiness for herself and hence happiness for those she loves and cherishes."[3] To be sure, these women had all but eliminated the usual afternoon social engagements on which most women spend so much of their time. But they found their curtailed social life, which they now shared much more frequently with their husbands, far preferable.

Interesting work is conducive to mental health. But it must be admitted that where there is strain involved in combining professional interests with homemaking, it may be hard to achieve the serenity and poise essential in a homemaker and most of all in a mother.[4] Amid the bewildering perplexity of

[1] In addition to the coöperative nursery school, an organization for home assistance was established. Methods for releasing women from wasteful occupations in the home were investigated, and research undertaken with a view to exploring professional opportunities and opening new possibilities for productive and satisfying occupation in conjunction with family life.

[2] Outstanding examples were Mme Curie and her husband, and now the Curies' daughter, Mme Joliot-Curie, and her husband.

[3] *Op. cit.*, p. 121.

[4] This is particularly the case where little or no help is available in the routine work of the household. On the other hand, the dissatisfaction engendered by unrelieved domesticity may be even more destructive of poise.

modern life, the need for a restful home, if it be but "a room of one's own" grows more imperative for both adults and children; somewhere to be alone, or in easy and peaceful association with one's own immediate family.

In the Collier study it appears that the children were particularly happy in their relations to their parents. Only twenty-nine of the 100 mothers had children under three; and all admitted that the combination of work with motherhood was far more easily made when children are of school age. However, even where mothers worked full-time, there was no evidence of neglect of the children.[1] These families were well-integrated, harmonious groups, and the *fathers* took more than the usual share in the care of the children. These facts alone would go far to guarantee the happiness and well-being of the children. Moreover, the children were encouraged to become resourceful and independent individuals living their own lives, while retaining the closest ties of affectionate friendship with their parents.

The continuation of their outside interests on the part of married women has one further result of the greatest benefit both to their children and to themselves. There can be no question at all that these mothers find it easier to overcome possessiveness in themselves and to foster independence in their children: a matter of the utmost importance for the emotional and social adjustment of young people. The happiness and mental health of middle-aged women is, indeed, very largely dependent on their pursuit of interesting work.[2] Fortunate, indeed, are those women who, never having wholly given up the work for which they are specially trained, can now take full advantage of their "second leisure." Moreover, only those mothers who are emotionally well-adjusted are able to be the sympathetic, understanding, and helpful *friends* of their grown-up children.

And finally, the broader and enriched experience of women who are wives and mothers is often of great value in professional work. Seventy-five of the women in the Collier study felt sure of the enhancement in value of their work. Even in professions where the experiences of marriage and motherhood have no

[1] They were, of course, left with relatives, or nurses, and well cared for. It would be impossible, probably, to estimate what effect such a procedure would have on the relationship between mother and child. Many mothers, however, are unwilling to relinquish the supervision of the earliest years of childhood to others, and this choice quite definitely precludes *full-time* professional employment for a number of years.

[2] Of recent years increasing study has been devoted to the new adjustments necessary for middle-aged women. See, for example, Sarah Trent, *Women over Forty* (1934), Grace Louck Elliott, *Women after Forty* (1936), W. Beran Wolfe, *A Woman's Best Years* (1934).

direct bearing, broader perspective and a more balanced view-point are indirectly valuable.[1] Several of these women were led to take up their professions because of their endeavors to pro-vide a richer content for their children's lives. Some, for ex-ample, started schools in order to provide their children with a satisfactory education. In another case, a leader of mothers' clubs was so successful that she was persuaded to become head of the State Mothers' Aid Board of Massachusetts. Mothers such as these give, Collier says, "a hint of a new attitude" in women towards wifehood and motherhood.

In most cases where monetary reward was one motive for work, these mothers desired money in order to give their children additional advantages. Financial *necessity*, in the sense of need for essentials, motivated less than 10%. More than half worked because of need for an outlet. In the group of 568 married col-lege alumnae studied by Chase Going Woodhouse, economic reasons for working were far more prominent, particularly in the case of those with children. With this larger group, also, reasons listed under "desire to work" came second. These were not a selected group of brilliant women, yet Woodhouse believes, "The indications are that the day of the old style feminist is passing and that of the trained woman who works as a matter of course is arriving." [2]

The Need for Further Experimentation. Undoubtedly there is much need for further experimentation. Further studies are needed along the lines suggested by Ethel Howes and more studies such as Collier's and Woodhouse's.[3] Most important of all, however, is the adoption of an experimental attitude on the part of women towards their own lives. Obviously the difficul-ties in the way of combining motherhood with a profession are

---

[1] One woman said: "To my mind, a woman who does not have babies has almost as great an interference with her best creative work in trying to find adequate sub-stitutes for her normal sexual outlet, as the woman with the actual babies themselves." *Op. cit.*, p. 46.

[2] "Married College Women in Business and the Professions," *op. cit.*, p. 329.

[3] There is no intention here to minimize the importance of all experiments which look to the reduction of what Ethel Howes calls "the present feudal proportions and absurd overstressing of household mechanisms." Of particular interest, therefore, is the experiment, begun in 1933, under the auspices of Columbia University, with the families of twenty of its junior officers, in an apartment house remodeled for this purpose. Group activities are directed to common problems which may be at-tacked by joint action without destroying the individuality and privacy of each family. Experts are bringing science and management to bear to rid the small house-hold of "the remorseless routine which abbreviates leisure, deprives parents of social and cultural opportunity, and complicates the upbringing of children." *New York Times*, Oct. 15 and Nov. 19, 1933.

not due solely to present social conditions. There is a real conflict in the interests of women who are absorbed in some line of work and yet fully realize their parental responsibility and the supreme opportunity, possessed by mothers, for guiding the development of mind and character through companionship with their children. Each woman who is successful in integrating these conflicting values, in a harmonious pattern, is conducting a valuable experiment which should be of help to other women, and which should also serve to modify public opinion, so that, in time, social conditions may facilitate rather than hinder such efforts at integration. Before attempting to outline certain principles which may be of assistance in the conduct of such experimentation, it seems desirable to gain a fuller perspective on the problems of modern women, from a brief survey of their present position in other countries.

WOMEN IN OTHER COUNTRIES TO-DAY

Women in Soviet Russia. In Russia an experiment has been under way, which has had as one of its conscious purposes complete equality between the sexes and the participation by women in all forms of work. As Fannina Halle points out, the experiment is being tried "for the first time in human history, of according to both sexes the same right to mould our life." [1] What the most advanced advocates of the emancipation of women in other countries have so long struggled to attain, equal rights and equal responsibilities with men, has been part of the accepted Soviet policy since the October Revolution of 1917.

A number of influences have contributed to this result. Foremost among them have been Russia's retarded industrial progress, and the intimate connection between the women's movement in Russia and revolutionary movements for wider social reform. The radical wing of the women's movement was early permeated with revolutionary ideas, combining as it did the desire for education and opportunity with aspiration to serve and help the downtrodden masses. Women revolutionaries worked side by side with men, taking their full share in the campaign of terrorism, and with undaunted courage suffering imprisonment and death.[2] In the Russian labor movement, also, women occupied a prominent place from the first, and were

---

[1] *Woman in Soviet Russia* (1933), p. 396. At this point we consider only the effect of Soviet policy on the status of women. In Chapter XX, further consideration is given to its effect on family life.

[2] See Vera Figner, *Memoirs of a Revolutionist* (English tr., 1929).

accustomed to work with men.   And again, during the war, masses of women were forced from their narrow home environments, and already desperate with the added sufferings and privation's imposed on them by the war, became fully roused to a sense of their economic importance.   It thus happened that "the international women's day, in February, 1917, was the first great historic day of the Russian Revolution, which . . . paved the way for Red October." [1]

The Bolsheviki had all along championed the rights of women. In the spring of 1917, Lenin demanded, from the central executive committee, their support of freedom and responsibility for women.   "Unless women are drawn into taking an independent part, not only in political life generally but also in daily social service, obligatory to everyone, it is idle to speak not only of socialism, but even of complete and stable democracy.   Certain 'police' functions, such as the care of the sick, of homeless children, pure food supervision, etc., will never be satisfactorily discharged until women are on a footing of perfect equality with men, not only on paper, but in reality." [2]   The greatest emphasis has been laid, moreover, on the need for increased production, in the hope of overtaking, in a few decades, a century of industrial progress in other countries.   Hence the factory more than any institution has become the center of Soviet life, and women were valued most highly in their capacity as workers.   Every opportunity was accordingly given them to take their part in the service of the state, and as the *economic* partners of men. [3]

Historical and industrial forces have thus combined to secure for Russian women their present status: "Political and civil equality regardless of sex is fully provided. . . . No profession and no society is closed to them. . . . Equal pay for equal work, without discrimination based on sex, limits the worst aspect of women's exploitation as wage earners.   The full legal rights of childbirth regardless of marriage, remove the foundation of unequal social responsibility attached to sex relations.   The woman,

---

[1] Halle, *op. cit.*, p. 90.

[2] Quoted by S. M. Kingsbury and M. Fairchild, *Factory, Family, and Woman in the Soviet Union* (C. P. Putnam's Sons, 1935), pp. xxi–xxii.

[3] The Soviet government has all along given support to the lowest economic classes, a fact of great advantage to women workers, hitherto economically weak and correspondingly oppressed.   There has been a steady increase in the numbers of women workers.   By 1934, they were reported to constitute 35.4% of all salary and wage earners.   The largest number were to be found in the traditional women's trades, but they are to be found too in all types of industry and in almost all forms of occupation. Particularly significant has been the steady infiltration of women into the upper grades of industrial pursuits.

before the law, is given full recognition of her status as a citizen and as a person, not less than the man.[1] According to Kingsbury and Fairchild, opportunity for promotion to responsible positions, both in and out of industry, seems to be "extraordinarily available." And women are to be found in comparatively large numbers in important posts. Not only in industry, health, and education, but in such fields as finance, foreign affairs, commerce, transportation, and the administration of justice.[2] Kingsbury and Fairchild concluded that "Women in positions of authority . . . may be taken as indicative of an inclination and tendency to utilize their capacities, a tendency that promises to be permanent." [3]

In the new Russian Constitution, adopted in 1936, women are once again guaranteed equal rights in all branches of economic, cultural, public, and political life. But there has also been an increasing emphasis on women's functions as mothers which may, conceivably, if continued, seriously conflict with women's opportunities for work. From the first, it is true, Soviet policy has recognized that women were not only workers, but also the mothers of future workers. Now, however, the emphasis has fallen on the need for future *soldiers* and every effort is being bent to increase the size of families.

The Soviet government early concerned itself with the protection of childhood and motherhood, and has undertaken to facilitate the performance by women of their dual rôle as workers and mothers. In the first place, certain restrictions have been placed on the work of women and of young people. Secondly, the Soviet system of social insurance includes provisions which cover all the special needs of married women workers. Insurance for pregnancy and childbirth cover the mothers' needs for a period before and after confinement. Free medical attention is provided, and a money allowance for the baby's layette and for special food for mother and child. Mothers have a legal right to retain their positions during the insured period after confinement, and must be granted time to nurse their infants, without

[1] Kingsbury and Fairchild, *op. cit.*, p. x.

[2] A despatch from Moscow to the *New York Times* (March 9, 1935) reported that a national check-up had been ordered to see that women were promoted to leading positions on the basis of equality with men. It was further announced that women were particularly active at this time in preparation for national defense; 2,380,000 belonging to the National Air and Chemical Defense Society. There are 100,000 crack markswomen and 460,000 are in training, while there are hundreds of women airplane pilots.

[3] *Ibid.*, p. 265; for a detailed analysis of women's work in the Soviet Union see G. N. Serebrennikov, *The Position of Women in the U.S.S.R.* (1937).

loss of pay. As the numbers of crêches increase, it becomes more and more possible for mothers to leave their babies in expert hands during their working hours. Finally, to assist women in becoming economically independent, a variety of attempts were made to set women free from "the old household slavery." [1] This involved the establishment of commercial kitchens, public dining rooms, wash-houses, and mending centers, in addition to crêches, kindergartens, and other educational institutions. According to Kingsbury and Fairchild, "the overwhelming tendency in the Soviet Union is for society through state and municipality to supplement the home by every kind of public service."[2] The essential purpose is to replace by organized public service the physical aspect of family care. Peculiar difficulties have been encountered in replacing the traditional home because of the acute housing shortage.

Prior to the advent of renewed emphasis on the value of the individual family, it was even hoped that in time a new type of family feeling on the part of members of a commune would replace the old family relationships. Lunacharsky, for many years Commissar of Education, even prophesied that in time the phrases "*my* parents," "*our* children" would fall out of use. Individuality would then be developed through work and leisure-time activities. Advocates of such extreme suggestions do not seem to realize to what an extent the individual ties between parents and children have been responsible for the development of social sentiments. The weakening or elimination of these ties might have serious consequences for social progress. That it might also be detrimental to the development of independent and individual thinking, would not probably disturb the Soviet leaders. Indoctrination with what is, to all intents and purposes, the religion of communism is undoubtedly facilitated by mass methods of nurture and education.

Women in Germany. In striking contrast to the position of women in the worker's state is the deliberate effort to check all tendencies making for the emancipation of women in both Germany and Italy; states which are organized primarily for

---

[1] Lenin repeatedly emphasized the importance of liberating women from domestic slavery. "Women's domestic life is a daily sacrifice amidst a thousand insignificant trifles." Not only should women share in the economic development of the country, but, from the political point of view, exclusive domesticity is undesirable; "the domestic milieu dulls a woman's wits." Quoted by Halle, *op. cit.*, pp. 364–365. Soviet workers call the individual kitchen, " that little penitentiary," and it has been declared that "the separation of the kitchen from marriage is an event of greater historical importance than the separation of church and state."

[2] *Op. cit.*, p. 269.

military purposes. The contrast is all the more striking in Germany, since the Third Reich, inaugurated through the rise to power of the National Socialists, in 1933, immediately succeeded the republican period, in which, under the Constitution of 1919, women had been accorded full citizenship rights, and a number of women had been elected to the Reichstag. In no other country, indeed, had so many women served in the highest governing body. This is of particular interest, because not only had the women's movement developed relatively late in Germany, but it had always had as its central goal the needs of women as mothers. The German women leaders desired freedom and opportunity, but sought not so much equality with men as standards of their own.[1]

Ironically enough, the central emphasis in Nazi Germany, so far as women are concerned, is still on motherhood; not, however, on motherhood with the aim of nurturing free and developed personalities, but simply as a means to the production of pure-bred and vigorous warriors. Von Papen publicly advised women "to exhaust themselves in producing soldiers to die in battle." [2] Women's cultural task is to bring up children in Spartan simplicity to a "cultural soldierliness"; a subsidiary task is to provide "recreation for tired warriors."

In this dictatorship, by and for soldiers, women ideally would have no functions which would not subserve their central rôle.[3] While they are severely discouraged from engaging in any but domestic work, as a matter of fact 10% more women were employed in Germany in 1935 than in 1932. Everywhere they are being excluded from the better-paid and more interesting positions. They are still to be found in elementary education, offices, stores, and factories, but the increase in their numbers is very largely in unpaid or small-paid domestic service, in service in the large labor camps, and in *munition factories.*

[1] *The Bund für Mutterschutz*, founded in 1905, soon became a powerful force in behalf of all mothers, unmarried as well as married. When, therefore, the Constitution gave equal rights to men and women, special provisions were included such as laws providing maternity benefits and regulating the work of women in the interests of motherhood.

[2] Every woman is urged to bear and rear the "normal five-child family." Characteristically, when mothers bear *more* than four, it is the *father* who wears a badge and appears to take the credit. Various inducements in the way of financial assistance and opportunities for employment are offered to the fathers of many children.

[3] Mary Beard has pointed out that the Fascist movement in Germany is "essentially a dynamic of unmarried males." In an hour of economic chaos, Hitler gathered other ex-soldiers of sadistic temper around him. In many of its aspects, the similarity is striking between Nazi Germany and ancient Sparta. "The Economic Background of Sex Life," *The Sex Life of the Unmarried Adult* (ed. I. S. Wile, 1934), pp. 155 *et seq.*

Opportunities for secondary education, and even more for work in the universities, are being severely curtailed; while labor service on the land is encouraged for girls as well as for young men. In the labor camps they are trained in domestic work and in rendering assistance to men in settling on the land, and, above all, are prepared physically and mentally and morally for their career of motherhood. The organization of these camps is being directed by the Women's Working Service, one of the five main divisions of women's interests and work which are co-ordinated under the *Deutsches Frauenwerk*, or Federation of Women's Organizations.[1] Under the auspices of Nazi women detailed plans for "Mothers' Schooling" have been worked out. Paradoxically enough, this elaborate organization staffed entirely by women, working *outside* the home, has as its central purpose keeping women *in* the home. While many women are finding means for self-expression through these organizations, on the whole the women of Germany have suffered an astounding degradation of status and have seen the hard-won gains of years swept away by an overwhelming tide of reaction.

Women in Italy and Other Latin Countries. In Italy, too, women have been deprived of much, although they had never secured voting rights as had the German women. In 1934, it was reported that Mussolini planned to take all women workers out of industry.[2] An editorial in his newspaper *Popolo d'Italia* asserted that "the working woman creates the problem of population decrease as well as that of unemployment. Work, even when it is not a direct impediment interfering with propagation, foments independence and consequent physical and moral habits antagonistic to conception." Obviously women in Italy are not supposed officially to have any sphere but the home, and are regarded not so much as individuals as instruments for the production of fighting males.

Women in Latin and Catholic countries, both in Europe and the Americas, were slower to become interested in suffrage and other aspects of the women's movement. At the time of the Spanish revolution of 1931, women were granted suffrage by the new Constitution, and in 1937, in view of their signal services on behalf of the loyalist government, they were granted absolute equality of status with men.[3] In South and Central America

[1] The others are the National Socialist Women's Organization, through which women express themselves politically; a group composed of surviving women's organizations, such as the YWCA and the Association of University Women; the Labor Front, handling problems of women in industry; and the Red Cross.

[2] *New York Times*, Sept. 5, 1934.   [3] *New York Times*, Feb. 5, 1937.

new interest has been aroused, and on September 1, 1935, all Mexican women workers were granted equal voting rights with men.

Women in France. The case of France is peculiar.[1] After the war, the leading nations, with the exception of Italy and France, accorded the suffrage to women. Yet French women have long been successfully engaged in medicine, law, newspaper work, business, and even finance. Moreover, in the individual family and small business, the French wife is frequently the more powerful partner. On the other hand, the French Civil Code still discriminates against the married woman, her position being one not only of political, but civil inferiority.[2] The depression of the thirties, and the menace of fascism, with its reactionary attitude towards women, aroused the women of France to new interest in suffrage. Since 1934 determined efforts have been made under the leadership of Louise Weiss, who, after serving as a war-nurse, rose to prominence as a peace advocate and founder of the weekly *L'Europe Nouvelle.* Three times the Chamber of Deputies has passed a bill granting suffrage. Three times the more conservative Senate has rejected it. Even their staunch supporter Léon Blum did not succeed in securing the vote for women. He did, however, appoint three distinguished women to junior posts in his first ministry.[3]

Women in Turkey. Most dramatic of all is the recent change in the status of women which has occurred in Turkey under the leadership of Mustapha Kemal Pasha.[4] Turkey, wishing to take a place among modern nations, has endeavored to give women equal opportunities with men. Not so long ago, women went abroad only if veiled and enveloped from head to foot in the black folds of the *charshaf.* Peasant women, working in the fields, alone were exempt. Now polygamy is abolished; and women have equal rights in marriage and divorce. Girls have equal educational opportunities with boys, and the professions are open to

[1] For a detailed discussion see Frances I. Clark, *The Position of Women in Contemporary France* (1937).

[2] Joseph Barthélmey, the noted jurist, has said that the woman who marries in France enters the class of minors and lunatics. See A. M. Jungmann, "French Women Leap a Barrier," *New York Times Magazine*, July 12, 1936. Many reforms in the status of married women, including independent legal status, were secured by a bill which passed both Chambers in Febuary, 1938.

[3] Mme Irene Joliot-Curie, Under-Secretary of State for Scientific Research; Mme Cecile Brunschvicg, Under-Secretary of State for Technical Education; Mlle Suzanne Lacore, Under-Secretary of State for the Protection of Children.

[4] For a detailed discussion, see sections on Turkey in *Moslem Women Enter a New World* (1936), by Ruth Frances Woodsmall.

women.   Already there are women doctors, lawyers, judges,
teachers, and police officers.   Both men and women vote in legislative elections at the age of twenty-three and may become
deputies at thirty-one.   Seventeen women took their seats in the
Turkish Assembly in 1935.

Women in Asia.   In Asia, too, women are beginning to emerge
from their age-long seclusion.   Throughout the Moslem world
the status of women is changing, though in some parts more
rapidly than in others.[1]   In India, women have taken a leading
part in political developments; and there is a definite women's
movement, not only directed towards removing the disabilities
of women, but concerned with social reform.[2]   In China, as we
saw, the forces of revolution, combined with Russian and Western influences, are rapidly changing the status of Chinese women.
The Japanese, however, well aware that feminism would in the
long run prove subversive of their military ambitions and of the
existing order in general, are endeavoring to suppress its doctrines in common with all other "dangerous thoughts."   Except
for poor families, after the fourth child, birth control is officially
interdicted, despite the efforts of Baroness Shidzue Ishimoto,
who sees, in the enormously high birth-rate, mass production of
soldiers and prostitutes.

Countries Which Have Granted Suffrage to Women.   New Zealand took the lead in granting voting rights to women.   This
was in 1893, and since that time New Zealand has been prominent as a laboratory of social experiments and noted for its
legislation on behalf of motherhood and childhood.   The same
has been true of the Scandinavian countries.   Finland granted
suffrage in 1906, Norway in 1913, Denmark in 1915, Sweden in
1919.   In a marriage law of 1920, Sweden gave legal recognition to the new status of women as economically independent,
and to the new concept of marriage as a coöperative venture.[3]
Holland granted suffrage in 1919, to be followed shortly by
Austria, Esthonia, Czechoslovakia, and Lithuania.

---

[1] *Ibid., passim.*

[2] All aspects of the life of women in India, and the problems which confront them,
are discussed in a symposium written by Indian women, *Our Cause* (1936), edited by
Shyam Kumari Nehru.

[3] "The spouses are under obligation, each according to his capacity, whether by
supplying money, by household work, or by other means, to contribute to the maintenance of the family on a scale of living in reasonable accordance with their position.
The term maintenance of the family shall be understood to include what is necessary
for the household, for the education of the children, and for meeting the special requirements of each of the spouses." *International Woman Suffrage News*, May–June,
1923, p. 135; quoted by Anthony, *op. cit.*, pp. 226–227.

The Menace of Reaction. In spite of the gains made in so many countries, women leaders are alarmed at the wave of reaction now sweeping over the world. Wherever economic depression has made itself felt, women have been the first to lose their positions. Ellen Wilkinson, British feminist and labor member of Parliament, believes that women's position will remain precarious so long as there are periodic crises and periodic wars. So long as economic interests take precedence over military, a country like Great Britain can afford to give women equality, but only as a luxury, something which Wilkinson believes may be dispensed with if economic crises again lead to war. Women's equality can be firmly established only where it is based on their social services in the interests of giving to every individual the best life possible.

In Russia the equality of women was secured in response to economic needs. It must always be remembered, however, that popular rights in the U.S.S.R. are subject to the dictatorship of a minority. There, just as much as in Germany, women, and men too, are not so much ends in themselves as units dedicated to the service of the state. Altogether, the present situation of women is seemingly far less secure than in the years preceding the economic crises and international tensions of the thirties. One thing alone seems fairly sure: that women will be accorded a fuller share in the world's work in proportion as there is progress in promoting international understanding, and as nations are enabled to concentrate attention on the welfare of all elements of their population.

GUIDING PRINCIPLES

Women at the Crossroads. The central note of the women's movement was struck by Ibsen when, in *A Doll's House*, Nora says, "Before all else I am a human being . . . , or at least I should try to become one." Never before have so many women been accorded the opportunity of becoming individualized and responsible human beings. Never before have so many women in some measure achieved that status. And yet, even in America, masses of women have scarcely emerged from the stage in which they may still with justification be considered not so much as individuals as groups; no longer, certainly, as "females" or "the sex," but as housewives, for example, or society women. Large numbers of women, chiefly of the working classes, are still deprived of opportunities through no fault of their own. But it is not they who retard women's advance. Rather is it all those women who are willing to remain immature dependents, to be lazily lapped in security, to let others shoulder their responsibilities, and to accept special privileges without making an adequate return. Many others, more independent, yet accept as a matter of course all the opportunities which have been won for them, but realize vaguely, if at all, the responsibilities inherent in their improved status.[1]

There Can Be No Turning Back. Divergent paths lead from the crossroads. Already certain groups of women have pressed far ahead; others are being pushed back or are turning back of their own accord. But, for all those who believe women are potentially as fully individualized human beings as men, there can be no turning back. And indeed, apart from temporary retrogression, turning back is impossible, unless all the social changes of the last few centuries are swept away. Conservatives who insist on women's sphere within the home, fail to realize the curtailment of women's work in the home, with the limitation in size of families and the transference of the greater part of home production to outside industry. Others, such as Boothe, are more abreast of actual facts, when they suggest that women should follow their former home responsibilities into the outside world, to the extent of engaging in work which is appropriate to women. But to predetermine women's sphere, in this way, is to assume a knowledge of feminine psychology which we are very far from possessing. In the interests not only of women's individualization and self-realization, but also of securing their full contribution to social well-being, they must be free to experiment and adventure, unhampered by premature and unscientific assumptions as to feminine psychology.[2] With growing knowledge of the extreme malleability of human nature, it is obvious that so-called feminine psychology is, to some extent at least, the result of social conditioning. Margaret Mead accordingly inquires whether civilization could not achieve a richer culture by weaving "a less

---

[1] The ambiguous attitude of many women, wanting both "to eat their cake and have it," is well symbolized in so-called *sports* clothes, which are often so costly and elaborate as to preclude their use by participants in actual sports.

[2] Boothe has much to say along the lines made familiar by Count Keyserling. Feminine psychology is determined by the "eternal truth that men and women are complementary opposites." A metaphysical statement so general and ambiguous as this simply begs the question. The derived concept of "sex polarity," and of men and women being related to one another as foci of an elliptical field of force, may very well be used to symbolize the differing functions of fatherhood and motherhood; but, far from indicating that women's work and men's work are mutually exclusive, would rather imply that the whole field of men's work and interests is also that of women's, although approached from a different perspective.

artificial social fabric, one in which each diverse human gift will find a fitting place."[1] Fully as true to-day as when it was first written is John Stuart Mill's remark: "There are no means of finding out what either one person or many can do, but by trying. . . . One thing we may be certain of—that what is contrary to women's nature to do, they never will be made to do by simply giving their nature free play. . . . Women's services . . . are most wanted for the things for which they are most fit; by the apportionment of which to them, the collective faculties of the two sexes can be applied on the whole with the greatest sum of valuable result."[2] "How much longer is one form of society and life to content itself with the morality made for another. We have had the morality of submission, and the morality of chivalry and generosity; the time is now come for the morality of justice."[3]

The Need for Freedom from Artificial Restrictions. Were society more fully convinced of the need for a morality of justice, women's advance would be much facilitated. Gains can be consolidated, and the women who have fallen behind be helped forward, only in proportion as opportunities are open to women and they are free to develop their capacities and interests and to make use of them in remunerative work. Only when education and social conditions produce such a situation will it be possible fully to discover the fields for which women have special aptitudes and the ways in which they may most effectively cooperate with men in the world's work. Even then there should be no strict line of demarcation between men's work and women's work, and no field of endeavor should exclude women. Every woman, as well as every man, should be enabled to work in the field for which she, as an individual, is best fitted.

The Avoidance of Negative and Extreme Attitudes. Under modern conditions it is absolutely necessary that every woman should be *prepared* to support herself. She needs a skilled occupation, in the first place, as an insurance against reverses. She needs it, moreover, in order that she may be a thoroughly efficient and responsible human being, not a mere amateur, but one prepared to share expertly and intelligently in the world's work. This does not necessarily mean, however, that women should aim at duplicating men's achievements, and fitting themselves and their lives into a predominantly man-made world. Necessary as it doubtless was to demonstrate that women could

---

[1] *Sex and Temperament*, p. 322.
[2] *The Subjection of Women*, pp. 243–244.   [3] *Ibid.*, p. 259.

hold their own with men in every field, the time has now come for a less extreme and more constructive outlook. Above all, nothing can now be gained by the aggressive attitudes and antagonism to men, which were the natural result of stubborn masculine opposition to emancipation. Only in this sense, however, is it correct to speak of the *decline* of feminism, as certain otherwise liberal men writers on the family are doing to-day.[1]

We have now reached a stage where a more balanced estimate is possible of the values involved in the conflicting interests of women. It becomes apparent that, if a woman chooses to become a mother, her primary responsibility lies within this most significant of all human relationships. Despite her insight into the needs of children and her wise advice on parenthood in a recent book, Lorine Pruette earlier attacked what she called the "dogma of the child": the dictum "that the child must be first in all the interests of the mother, which operates as the greatest check upon experimentation by women."[2] Surely this expresses realization of the full implications of human relationships rather than dogma; and experimentation which ignored this fact could have little constructive value. Women must indeed be prepared to earn their living, and it is well if they have experience in doing so before marriage, and at least part-time in the early years of marriage before there are children. But although in some cases work can be continued when the children are young, yet it very often will be best for a mother to interrupt for some years the pursuit of a gainful occupation, although by no means relinquishing her interests, in order to concentrate her attention on the science and art of expert motherhood. Once again, when her children are growing up, such a woman may look forward to returning to her former occupation, either as a salaried worker or else in some unsalaried position of wider social service for which her interests and experience particularly well fit her. While each

[1] The word *feminism* is of course ambiguous: it may be used in the broadest sense of the women's movement, or else to connote extreme and negative attitudes. There is some suspicion that these writers and many others are assuming that women have had their fling, and having found out what their "ambitions" were worth, are now contented to settle back into predominantly "feminine" pursuits. In view of these facts, the significance of the homage recently accorded by both England and America to great feminist leaders is not entirely clear. In 1936, a statue of Mrs. Pankhurst was erected in London, and a Susan B. Anthony stamp issued in America.

[2] *Women and Leisure*, p. 208. In her more recent book, *Parents and the Happy Child* (1932), she speaks of the conspicuous success being achieved by women who are experimenting with new kinds of motherhood; who move slowly, however, because they *do not wish to hurt their children*. As a result of women's activities outside the home, fathers are being given an opportunity within the home, and mother-love is less likely to be "smother-love." Pp. 54–55.

woman must experiment for herself, guiding principles such as these may prove helpful as a general policy.[1]

Women in Coöperation with Men. In relinquishing a more aggressive policy and a demand for a full-time career for all women, there is no slightest relinquishment of the goal of full individualization as human beings for women as well as for men. Rather is life viewed in terms of human relationships and the opportunities afforded for self-fulfilment and social service. In her *Art of Being a Woman,* Olga Knopf well expresses this constructive attitude: "Women can trust themselves and believe in their value; and the way to do it is by contribution, the one evidence that they are worthwhile. . . . And if they are assured of their value men will agree with them; for men are brought up by women and they form their opinion of women's value from the guidance they receive from women in childhood. . . . It is women who must change the cultural position which women are given; and it is women who must change the opinion men have of them. They cannot do it by claiming more than their share. They cannot do it by any of the thousands of ways of going on strike. They can do it only by acting as equals and accepting the responsibilities of equals. . . . The Art of Being a Woman can never consist in being a bad imitation of a man. It can consist only in being equal, independent and coöperative; in understanding human nature and human capacities and in applying the knowledge first of all to oneself."[2]

Graham Wallas said of women: "If they do more work, think more thoughts, and offer a larger contribution of skilled organization than they do at present to the grievously insufficient personnel by which the Great Society is held together, we shall be drawing a larger dividend from the same body of human capital."[3] Human well-being can best be served by what Gid-

---

[1] It is significant to note that this is very much the attitude being adopted by thoughtful young women in the leading women's colleges, where full opportunity is given for women to explore vocational opportunities. Quite definitely the majority of girls make marriage central in their plans, but they hope to be able to combine some form of occupation with marriage, or at least work before marriage and again later in life. Increasing numbers of college graduates, moreover, are managing to coördinate marriage and work. Recent classes are marrying sooner after graduation; and this fact may partly account for the comparative indifference of college girls, in 1937, to the increasing number of available jobs. Some personnel workers feel, however, that the former "career" motive is being supplanted by a desire for work with a definite view to comparatively short-time employment. See Eunice Fuller Barnard, "The College Girl Puts Marriage First," *New York Times Magazine,* April 2, 1933; and *New York Times,* June 13, 1937.

[2] *Op. cit.* (Little, Brown and Company, 1932), pp. 295–296.

[3] *The Great Society* (1914), p. 348.

dings calls "a continuing selection of intelligence and sympathy." Where women coöperate more fully with men the gain is not only in quantity of intelligence and sympathy, but in the quality of sympathy which has been best described as *motherliness*. Already indeed, what Ellen Key called "social motherliness" has made itself increasingly manifest in public affairs.

Beatrice Hinkle sums up women's new responsibility as follows: "Through her maternal impulses of love and service, woman possesses an instinctive basis for the evolution of a new humanity in which the principles of understanding, love, and altruism shall supersede the principles of power and greed." Woman "gives birth to the new generation in the physical realm. The responsibility is upon her to bring forth the new humanity in the spiritual realm . . . , a task which requires the greatest self-consciousness and a voluntary effort of the highest order. . . . The new humanity needs . . . a new mother with unfettered capacities to bring it to birth and nourish it."[1] Modern women, accordingly, in Jung's words, confront "a great cultural task, which means perhaps the beginning of a new Era."[2]

SPECIAL PROBLEMS IN THE EDUCATION OF WOMEN

The Need for the Fullest Educational Opportunities for Women. In addition to the earlier discussion of educational aims and methods, a few points need emphasis as bearing on the education of women as distinct from men. In order that they may be fully equipped for their "cultural task," their nurture and education is a matter of special importance from earliest childhood. Above all, there should be no artificial restriction of the educational opportunities of girls and women. At present most girls are subjected to a subtle conditioning from infancy, molding them into conformity with traditional ideas of feminine psychology and hampering the development of independence and responsibility.[3] To further limit their education because of their supposed inherent qualities would be a fatal mistake. If anything, there should be enlargement and expansion of present curricula if the special needs of women are to be fully met.

The present tendency to include household arts and education in child care, in curricula for boys as well as for girls, is an important step in the right direction, facilitating understanding

[1] "The Chaos of Modern Marriage," *Harper's Magazine*, Vol. CLII (Dec., 1925), p. 13.

[2] *Contributions to Analytical Psychology* (1928), p. 188.

[3] Fuller discussion of the differential treatment accorded boys and girls is included in Chapter XXIV.

and mutual coöperation in family life. Moreover, whether men
and women marry and have children or not, experience with
children is invaluable in broadening their sympathies and affording insight into social problems. It would seem advisable that
some education of this kind be obligatory not only for girls but
also for boys.

Yet criticism is still directed to-day against the higher education of women, which, as at present conducted, is supposed to be
socially wasteful, since men and women have different functions
in life. As we saw, many experiments are being conducted in
colleges, including a number which are designed to educate
women to become expert in their traditional rôles as homemakers
and mothers and in the wider social services related to these
rôles.[1] This is excellent; but there is a definite danger that the
current revulsion from curricula which were designed primarily
for men may operate to *limit* women's educational opportunities
and to *handicap* rather than help them in achieving a harmonious integration of love, marriage, children, and the development
of expert knowledge and skill in a chosen field.

A Human Relations Program Designed for College Women. To
insist that the *central* aims of education are the same for men
and women, as human beings, does not preclude the possibility
of sequences designed specially for women or for men. One
promising line of educational experimentation is the devising of
integrated curricula in human relations. For both men and
women the specific aims of such curricula might be: (1) to promote understanding of and insight with regard to the social
relationships involved in everyday life, in the family, local community, and nation, and internationally; (2) to promote understanding of and insight with regard to the relationships and responsibilities involved in the specific profession, vocation, or
field of work selected on the basis of interest and ability; (3) to
provide some degree of further preparation along lines of vocational and professional interest.

While primarily cultural or pre-vocational in aim, such a
program would merge with further professional and vocational
education. It should, indeed, afford unrivalled opportunity for
the discovery of interests and aptitudes in such a way as to bring
to light their intellectual and social meaning.

[1] For example, at Vassar, the so-called major sequences of child welfare, nutrition,
physical welfare, and public health are offered as electives. Recognition has recently
been accorded to the experiment in consumer education conducted at Stephens College, through the establishment there of a national center for research and education
in consumer's problems. *New York Times*, Feb. 6, 1938.

Within a more general program of this kind, education designed to develop the special interests of women and prepare them for their responsibilities in the modern world finds a fitting place. Special emphasis would be laid on women's concern with nurture and with the provision of conditions making for health, growth, and fulness of life; and, secondly, on the promotion of harmonious social relationships and of the art of living. The tendency would probably be to concentrate on the vocations and professions in which the majority of women engage: education, nursing, public health, social work. Stress would naturally be laid on family life and expert motherhood. But it must be made convincingly clear that the responsibilities of a modern educated woman do not end within her home and family.

Educational experiments along these and similar lines are vitally necessary to-day. So too are individual experiments in living carried on by intelligent and far-sighted women. In these ways, we may hope to find constructive solutions for present conflicts, and to hasten the day when the women's movement will merge with a coöperative movement, integrating the activities of men and women in their common enterprise of living and working together.

SUGGESTED READING

Anthony, S., *Women's Place in Industry and Home*, 1932.

Boothe, V. B., ed., *Women in the Modern World*, in *The Annals of the American Academy of Political and Social Science*, Vol. CXLIII, May, 1929.

Breckenridge, S. P., *The Family and the State*, 1934, Sections II–V.

——, *Marriage and the Civic Rights of Women*, 1931.

Clark, F. I., *The Position of Women in Contemporary France*, 1937.

Collier, V., *Marriage and Careers*, 1926.

Gilman, C. P., *Woman and Economics*, 1899.

Groves, E. R., and Brooks, L. M., *Readings in the Family*, 1934, Chs. VIII, XVIII, XIX.

Hale, B. F-R., *What Women Want*, 1914.

Halle, F. *Woman in Soviet Russia*, 1933.

Howes, E. P., "Accepting the Universe," *Atlantic Monthly*, Vol. CXXIX, Apr., 1922, pp. 444–453.

——, "Continuity for Women," *Atlantic Monthly*, Vol. CXXX, Dec., 1922, pp. 731–739.

Kingsbury, S. M., and Fairchild, M., *Factory, Family, and Woman in the Soviet Union*, 1935.

Knopf, O., *The Art of Being a Woman*, 1932.

National League of Women Voters, *A Survey of the Legal Status of Women in the Forty-eight States*, rev. ed., 1930.

National League of Women Voters, *The Economic Status of a Wife Working at Home*, 1924.
——, *The Married Woman and Her Job*, 1937.
Pankhurst, S., "Women under Fascism," *Hibbert Journal*, Vol. XXXIV, Jan., 1936, pp. 219–234.
Parsons, A. B., *Woman's Dilemma*, 1926.
Reuter, E. B., and Runner, J. R., *The Family*, 1931, Ch. XIV.
Vernier, C. G., *American Family Laws* (5 vols. 1931–1938), Vol. III.

CHAPTER XVII

POPULATION AND BIRTH CONTROL

TRENDS OF POPULATION

The Decline of Population Growth in Industrial Nations. The increasing prevalence of family limitation is a matter of fundamental social significance. The practice of contraception is instrumental in dissociating sexual intercourse from its natural outcome in reproduction; and effective control is being made possible over the number of offspring in a marriage. As with all other instruments for interfering with or controlling natural processes, the consequences effected by birth control may be beneficial or the reverse, depending on the purposes for which it is used, and the total situation within which it operates.

To place the practice of birth control in its social setting, accurate information is necessary with regard to trends of population. Since Malthus wrote his *Essay on the Principle of Population*, in 1798, all discussions of the growth of population have been profoundly influenced by his theory that "the power of population is infinitely greater than the power of the earth to produce subsistence for man." Nor is this surprising, considering the unprecedented increase in population which has taken place during this period.[1] And this actual increase of population has continued even in those countries where the decline of the birth-rate has been most marked. This is due to the fact that the falling birth-rate has been accompanied by a no less remarkable decline in the death-rate, especially in the infant death-rate. A number of students of the subject, such, for example, as East and Pearl, were thus led to believe that the menace of over-population is still very real and that there is a likelihood, even in the United States, of a severe pressure of population on food supply.

Of recent years, however, it has become apparent that such prognostications are not only based on inadequate statistical methods, but do not sufficiently take into account the enormously increased power over nature which modern science makes

---

[1] It has been estimated that the population of the world increased from less than 850 millions in 1800 to more than 1,700 millions in 1900; that is, it has taken but one century to double the number of the world's inhabitants.

possible.[1] There is no longer any justification for the assertion that the food supply must inevitably limit population growth. And new refinements of statistical method have invalidated earlier forecasts of the future growth of population. They show that, while there is still increase, the growth capacity of a majority of civilized communities is changing in such a way that a considerable *decrease* is inevitable, provided fertility and mortality remain unchanged. This apparent paradox is explained by the fact "that the balance of births over deaths gives us no indication of the capacity of a population for further growth, unless its age and sex composition is also known."[2] Kuczynski has shown that the clearest indication of the capacity for future growth in a population is the average number of female children who will be born to every newly born girl. This gives the rate at which the female population is regularly replacing itself, and is called the Net Reproduction Rate. If every mother is replaced by one mother and no more, this rate is unity, and a population will become stationary in the long run, if current fertility and mortality rates *do not change*. Similarly, a rate of more than unity signifies eventual increase, and a rate of less than unity, eventual extinction.

The decline in the birth-rate began in France, made itself felt in England about 1878, and from then on spread to nearly all the countries of Western and Northern Europe, to Australia, and to America. In 1926, the net reproduction rate was 0.93 in Western and Northern Europe. In 1933, it was only 0.75 for England and Wales. In 1920 the United States had an average rate of 1.13, but even then it was tending towards a rate of less than unity, a figure which it reached in 1926. Almost all industrial nations, therefore, including England and America, are destined, if present tendencies continue, to decline in population.[3]

[1] According to Enid Charles: "a technical revolution has taken place in less than a generation. . . . It would hardly be an exaggeration to say that the world's food production could be increased many times without increasing the area of cultivation, if mankind exploited to the fullest extent all the scientific knowledge already available." *The Twilight of Parenthood* (1934), pp. 29–30; and see too O. W. Willcox, *Reshaping Agriculture* (1934), for an account of the revolution in agriculture which will be as momentous for mankind as the industrial revolution. The author states that no well-informed agrobiologist can see any reason why one square mile of well-managed land should not feed at least 15,000 people at a subsistence level. On this basis the present population of the United States could be fed at this level on little more than one-sixth of the plow-land now cultivated in Illinois.

[2] Charles, *op. cit.*, p. 40.

[3] Conditions in Eastern and Southern Europe are far more diverse than in the West and North. In several of these countries, such as Italy, which in 1928 showed

The Decline of Population Growth and Differential Fertility in the United States. From 1920 to 1930 there was an increase of 17,000,000 in the United States, the largest total increase ever recorded in one decade. Nevertheless, the rate of increase has been declining with striking rapidity since 1923. The decrease in numbers of young children, already noted in Chapter XIII, is of particular significance, indicating, as it does, that the sources of future population are being contracted.[1] Lorimer and Osborn estimate that "population increase will presumably cease absolutely somewhere from twenty to forty years from now with a maximum population of some 150 millions or less. This event may be followed by some decline in total population for several decades; but there are so many uncertain elements in the picture that it is idle to speculate far into the future."[2] They believe, therefore, that the immediate concern should be not so much over the prospect of a declining population as over the large *differentials* in fertility among different groups in the United States, a fact denoting that forces are at work which may have far-reaching consequences. Some groups are rapidly expanding, others are declining; and, although some of these differentials may be temporary, "others are grounded in fundamental differences in ways of living and are likely to persist indefinitely unless means are found for their social control."[3] Not only the hereditary capacities, but the different culture-levels in the future population may thus be profoundly modified by the differential increase or decrease of groups, varying in their biological and social heritage.

There is, in the first place, an extreme rural-urban differential, involving a constant tendency to accumulate a surplus population in the rural areas, which is likely to continue indefinitely although in a reduced degree. Its economic effects alone are serious, for "the highest fertility is now found among large rural

a positive rate of increase, there has since been decline. In Russia and in Japan the growth of population presents exceptional features. In Russia the birth-rate was higher than any found in the rest of Europe even before the present propaganda for larger families. In Japan, while the population "is certain to increase rapidly for some time, analysis of changes in fertility and mortality suggests the possibility that Japan is destined eventually to travel the same road as North-Western Europe or the United States of America." *Ibid.*, p. 96.

[1] Despite the great increase in population, the number of births in the United States was practically the same in 1925 as in 1915. In 1920 the birth-rate was 23.7, and, by 1935, it was only 16.9, according to the Census Bureau.

[2] From *Dynamics of Population* (1934), p. 19. By permission of The Macmillan Company, publishers.

[3] *Ibid.*, p. 20.

groups whose economic status is already that of a poor peasant class."[1] No important differences in reproductive tendency are found among large groups classified by race or country of origin, when considered apart from the more inclusive problem of differential fertility among regional and social groups.

Large differentials in the fertility of social groups, classified by occupation or by economic status, are almost as universal, though less extreme, than the rural-urban differential. "Clearly throughout the last few decades and during recent years, births have been most frequent among families of low economic status and least frequent among families with superior educational advantages and superior occupational ratings."[2] A generally negative relationship is thus evident between reproductive tendency and social status.

THE SOCIAL CONSEQUENCES OF PRESENT TRENDS

Their Significance for the Social Heritage. Realizing that *intelligence* as measured by tests is a function not only of heredity but of environment, Lorimer and Osborn believe measurable characteristics to be best described by the phrase *cultural-intellectual development.* With few exceptions, studies reveal a marked correlation between cultural-intellectual development and superior social and occupational status.[3] From the standpoint of the social heritage alone this situation is very serious, for "the cultural level of each generation determines in high degree the environmental factors which will affect the intellectual development of the next generation."[4] Several generations, moreover, would be required, before the effects on a given group of a serious initial handicap were overcome, even with the greatest possible improvement of environment. As matters stand at present, in certain groups a vicious circle is involved: "Retarded development fosters the maintenance of excessive fertility; and excessive fertility tends to retard economic and cultural development."[5] For example, accumulation of surplus population in agricultural areas, with limited natural resources, prevents a rise in levels of living, including levels of health and education. If present trends continue, there will be a disproportionate spread of the social heritage of groups show-

---

[1] *Ibid.*, p. 37.　　　　　　　　　　　　　　　　　　[2] *Ibid.*, p. 342.

[3] There is, it is true, much overlapping of *individual* abilities in these classes, but there is "a relatively high frequency of persons of unusual ability in the upper social groups," and "a relatively high proportion of mental defectives, or persons with very inferior intellectual ability in the lowest social groups." *Ibid.*, p. 179.

[4] *Ibid.*, p. 179.　　　　　　　　　　　　　　　　　　[5] *Ibid.*, p. 185.

ing low cultural-intellectual capacity, inasmuch as a disproportionate share of successive generations will inevitably come from these groups.[1] While the lowest economic and occupational groups, in the country and in towns and cities, are more than replacing themselves, "there is hardly a single urban group, in which the majority of the young people enjoy the advantages of high school education and in which many continue their education through college, that is now replacing itself from one generation to another. . . . The negative association between fertility and cultural-intellectual level in the population of the United States reveals a powerful force that is working against our most cherished national ideals and that threatens to defeat the aim of the whole public education movement. If this force remains unchecked, its eventual political and social repercussions may be tremendous."[2]

The Effect on Hereditary Capacity. The situation may be even more serious from a long-range point of view, if differences in cultural levels reflect differences in hereditary capacity. According to Lorimer and Osborn the best evidence available "indicates that the usual negative correlation between fertility and social status involves a gradual decline in average hereditary capacity for intellectual development."[3] On the other hand, Thompson, Charles, and other opponents of eugenics challenge the assumption that membership in the upper classes gives proof of innate superiority.[4] There is undoubtedly greater overlapping in hereditary capacity than in apparent cultural-intellectual levels among individuals in different classes.[5] Nevertheless, Lorimer and Osborn believe it probable that present tendencies, if "continued for many generations, would result in a serious lowering of capacity for cultural-intellectual progress by the American

[1] "The only groups in the United States which are at present reproducing at rates far above actual replacement needs, are located in certain rural areas, and predominantly in communities that are at the lowest economic levels and most remote from those educational and cultural influences which are held typical of social progress in this country. And within the towns and cities, the lower occupational groups, characterized by low ratings as regards cultural-intellectual development, are commonly found to have birth-rates somewhat above replacement needs and far above the birth-rates characteristic of neighboring groups with superior advantages." *Ibid.,* p. 199.

[2] *Ibid.,* pp. 199–200.   [3] *Ibid.,* p. 344.

[4] W. S. Thompson, "Eugenics as Viewed by a Sociologist," *Publications* of the American Sociological Society, Vol. XVIII (Dec., 1923), pp. 60–72; Charles, *op. cit.,* Chapter IV.

[5] "The overlapping in capacity for intellectual development among children derived from different social groups must be even greater than the overlapping in apparent intelligence among adults in these groups, because of the environmental influence of different social situations on intellectual development, and because of variability in inheritance due to the operation of recessive genes." *Ibid.,* p. 344.

people."[1] "Present reproduction tendencies seem to be having especially serious effects at both extremes of the scale of intellectual development, tending disproportionately to reduce the number of individuals with unusual ability to be expected from any given number of births, and significantly to increase the proportion of individuals of low-grade intelligence."[2] While it may be possible through educational endeavor "to outweigh the depressing effects of population trends in their purely environmental aspects," there can be no compensation if these trends involve "the dying out of any large proportion of people with superior capacities for education."[2]

FACTORS AFFECTING FERTILITY

Physical and Medical Factors. Understanding of factors affecting fertility is a prerequisite to social control. Although physiological sterility and limited fecundity are important factors in determining reproduction rates, there seems little evidence for a decline in reproductive capacity among civilized peoples.[3] Other influences must be responsible for the conspicuous decrease in the birth-rate. For example, it is known that the fecundity of women begins to decline in the late twenties. Age of the wife at marriage, therefore, has definite influence on fecundity. Accordingly, among groups in which late marriages are frequent, part of the decline in size of family may be involuntary, although it is also known that there is more voluntary limitation of fertility on the part of couples who marry later. Lorimer and Osborn conclude that "the frequency of childless or one-child families in groups with superior education is due in large part to involuntary sterility and other influences connected with late marriage; but the scarcity of very large families in this group is due largely to voluntary limitation."[4]

An increasing body of data on variations in contraceptive practice, as affecting fertility, yields clear indication of the fact "that contraception is used much more extensively at the upper economic levels in American urban society than among groups that are more handicapped economically and socially."[5] In

[1] *Ibid.*, p. 344.   [2] *Ibid.*, p. 346.

[3] See, however, F. H. Hankins, "Does Advancing Civilization Involve a Decline in Natural Fertility," *Publications* of the American Sociological Society, Vol. XXIV (May, 1930), pp. 115–122. Grounds are here given for the thesis that the psychophysical optimum for fertility is realized less frequently nowadays, owing to the intensity of modern life.

[4] *Ibid.*, p. 279.

[5] *Ibid.*, 273. Moreover, "there appear to be significant differences in the availability to different social classes of accurate contraceptive information; and such

addition to contraceptive practices, resort to sterilization and abortion affect the size of families. Sterilization has as yet had a very limited application, but abortion is alarmingly prevalent at the present time.[1] No certain conclusions can be reached, however, as to the frequency of abortions in different social classes. The increase in the number of induced abortions has two-fold influence on the birth-rate, because of its relation not only to foetal, but to maternal mortality.

Spread of the Family-limitation Pattern. The basic factors influencing fertility are the social and economic conditions and the personal motives which have produced a situation, where, as the data show, "no groups with a high standard of living and with a knowledge of birth control methods can expect to be permanently self-replacing, unless influenced by social conditions which are distinctly favorable to fertility."[2] The prime sources of "the spread of the family limitation pattern through different sections of American life" have been rising standards of living, and the "development and diffusion of new attitudes towards all human affairs and particularly towards reproduction."[3] This main current in the vital changes now going on has run most rapidly in the urban centers and especially among the most highly educated, while it has been retarded or checked in certain other groups. Further diffusion of the family-limitation pattern may, however, be expected in the near future. The very large variations in fertility which obtain at present are thus in part "the expression of an incomplete social process, which has perhaps run its full course in some sections of our population, but not in others."[4] While, therefore, considerable modifications in group differentials may be expected in the course of a few generations, the fact remains that "the well-educated urban groups . . . have been characterized by a drift toward patterns of living which are incompatible with family replacement."[5] These pat-

---

differences affect the relative efficacy of contraceptive practices in different social groups. In part, however, the high fertility of handicapped groups may be due to difficulties inherent in the effective use of the most reliable contraceptive methods now available." *Ibid.,* p. 279.

[1] Taussig estimates that out of every 1,000,000 human beings conceived, between 300,000 and 400,000 perish in the first six months of their intrauterine existence. Abortion may be spontaneous (miscarriage), therapeutic, or criminally induced. The last of these is by far the most common, particularly in the large cities where from 75% to 80% of abortions are induced. *Fetal, Newborn, and Maternal Morbidity and Mortality* (White House Conference, 1933), pp. 446–470.

[2] Lorimer and Osborn, *op. cit.,* p. 326.

[3] *Ibid.,* p. 325.   [4] *Ibid.,* p. 326.   [5] *Ibid.,* p. 327.

terns, moreover, are the outcome of conditions which are not likely soon to disappear.[1]

Major Motives Tending to Lower Fertility. Two major motives for family limitation are concern for health and economic pressure. The proper spacing of births is now known to be highly desirable for the sake of both mother and child. Health considerations include desire for optimum health of children, concern over the effects of childbearing on the mother's health, and anxiety over assuming the risks of maternity, particularly on the part of older women.

Families with high standards of living tend to limit families because of economic pressure, a tendency running counter to the general negative correlation between size of family and income.[2] When parents are anxious not only to maintain a high standard of living, but to assure it for their children, family limitation is inevitable, except in cases of unusual economic security.[3] High standards of child care are the most significant of all items in a high standard of living. "Young professional and business class families with slender means may be content with inexpensive housing, food and clothing, but unwilling to accept inferior obstetrical service or inadequate health protection for the children, and they may regard expensive higher education as essential. Such conditions make large families seem impossible to persons with high standards of living and small income."[4]

Social Conditions Tending to Limit Fertility. Urban housing conditions are definitely unsuitable for the nurture of children. In metropolitan areas the family dwelling unit is growing smaller; either because of the diminishing size of the family, or because families with several children tend to move to the suburbs. But restricted housing, planned with no concern for the needs of children, may well accentuate a trend towards family limitation among persons with superior standards.[5]

If taken in isolation from other variables, religion is probably

[1] Such, for instance, as "differences in age at marriage and frequency of marriage, in standards of living, in ideals, and in personal factors which affect resort to and efficacy in attempts at birth control." *Ibid.*, p. 326.

[2] "Below a certain level, an accentuation of poverty seems to cause a rise rather than a decline in fertility rates." *Ibid.*, p. 292.

[3] One hopeful aspect of the present situation is the fact that among certain very limited groups with high educational background and unusual economic security the rate of reproduction may be sufficient for replacement.

[4] *Ibid.*, p. 297.

[5] For those with low standards, on the other hand, slum conditions tend to produce "attitudes of indifference, despair and neglect that usually seem conducive to high fertility." *Ibid.*, p. 307.

a minor factor in the determination of fertility trends. It can be definitely shown, however, that there exists a negative association between full-time gainful occupation for women and fertility.[1] This fact, however, involves a two-way relationship, and the more important causal sequence is very probably from low fertility to gainful occupation. But the causal sequence in the other direction is marked in the case of women in responsible and fairly lucrative positions, who are more likely to postpone childbearing.[2]

The Fertility of College Graduates. The families of college graduates as a class are known to be small. Two distinct variables must be taken into account as influencing their fertility; marriage frequencies by sex, and age at marriage. Certain general conclusions are possible on the basis of a number of studies. In the first place, married women who are college graduates have about as many children as married college men or others with similar status and interests. In so far as they have somewhat fewer children than their married non-college friends and relatives, this difference may be attributed entirely to one factor, age at marriage. College women marry, on the average, somewhat later than non-college women.

There is, however, a large difference in fertility between men and women college graduates, because a far larger proportion of the men marry. The proportion of men who marry is about the same whether they are college graduates or no. "On the other hand, relatively low marriage frequencies are universally reported as characteristic of college women as a class. The percentage of college women who never marry ranges in reliable studies from 50% or less to about 75%."[3] Apparently, however, considerable changes are now taking place in the direction of increased fertility among women who are college graduates. Recent studies of Smith, Vassar, and Bryn Mawr graduates show a definite trend towards earlier and more frequent marriages. And this trend towards early marriage does not seem to be associated with avoidance of childbearing. "Nevertheless,"

[1] "Gainfully employed wives are more frequently childless and have on the average fewer children than wives of similar background who are not gainfully employed." *Ibid.*, p. 310.

[2] It is possible, Lorimer and Osborn believe, that "a new adjustment between professional activities and effective reproduction may still be achieved." At present, however, "whatever may be the causal interpretation of the situation, the fact remains that full-time gainful occupation of women has not yet been found compatible with effective reproduction in any group—although many striking exceptions may be cited." *Ibid.*, p. 312.

[3] *Ibid.*, p. 323.

Lorimer and Osborn conclude, "in spite of the recent tendency to earlier and more marriages among college women, advanced education still tends somewhat to delay, if not to hinder marriage." However, "except for the higher frequencies of celibacy and of late marriage among women pursuing advanced education, higher education as such does not exert any depressing effect on fertility."[1]

THE SOCIAL CONTROL OF POPULATION

Genetics and Eugenics. Modern interest in eugenics took its rise from the investigations of Galton.[2] Striking examples were discovered of the transmission of unusual intellectual ability in certain families. On the other hand, other family histories showed that the inbreeding of bad stock almost invariably produced numbers of mental defectives and individuals who became criminals or social outcasts. It seemed obvious that the improvement of the human race depended on the sterilization of the unfit and the encouragement of marriage and reproduction on the part of the fit. The establishment of the Mendelian principles of heredity, and their successful application in plant and animal breeding, gave further encouragement to those who placed their hopes on eugenics as the most potent means for race betterment.

With the discovery of the hereditary characters called *genes*, and the development of genetics as an exact experimental science, it became apparent that the whole matter is infinitely more complex than had hitherto been suspected. Human heredity is particularly difficult to study for several reasons. In the first place so many genes are involved.[3] Then again, there is "the intrinsic difficulty of dealing with a species which breeds slowly, has few offspring and cannot be mated by the investigator at will."[4] Most important of all is the fact that, in dealing with human beings, nature and nurture can never be treated as independent variables and that environmental influences are of a peculiarly subtle and complex character. According to Hogben, "no statement about a genetic difference has any scientific

[1] *Ibid.*, p. 325.

[2] Eugenics, according to Galton, is "the science which deals with the influences that improve the inborn or native qualities of the race, also with those which develop them to the utmost advantage." The first of the publications in which he laid the foundations for such a science was *Hereditary Genius* (1869).

[3] The individual gene complex in human beings in composed of 48 distinct groups of genes called chromosomes, 24 of which are derived from the egg-cell of the mother, and 24 from the sperm-cell of the father. These genes are linked in ways which are as yet only partially understood.

[4] L. Hogben, *Nature and Nurture* (W. W. Norton & Company, 1933), p. 10.

meaning unless it includes or implies a specification of the environment in which it manifests itself in a particular manner. Characteristics of organisms are the result of interaction between a certain genetic equipment in the fertilized egg and a certain configuration of extrinsic agencies which include the conditions of life in the uterus and the external environment in which social existence is carried on."[1]

Differences between individuals are due both to different equipment of genes and to differences in uterine and postnatal environment. There are, moreover, two types of genetic difference, those which are recognizable in any environment and those which are only manifest within a fairly restricted environment.[2] In the first type alone can there be fairly confident prediction as to the rate with which affected individuals might be eliminated by interference with parenthood. Finally, it must be noted that "one and the same gene substitution may be responsible for many and various manifestations, depending upon the environment in which development occurs"; also that "the effect of the gene substitution depends on all the other genes with which it is combined."[3]

The sociological significance of these facts becomes evident when it is realized that the framework of environment includes the uterus, the family, and larger social units as well; and that "families belonging to one social level are more alike with respect to hygiene, diet, access to sunlight and culture than families belonging to different social levels."[4] This stratification of society at different social levels is thus intimately related to the distribution of genetic differences. Present knowledge can set no limits to the changes which *might* be brought about by regulating the environment. Imperfect coördination of human effort is to blame for the most formidable problems of civilization, and

[1] *Ibid.*, p. 14.

[2] Hogben points out that, while differences of the second type are less easy to detect, this does not mean they are less numerous. A good example is mongolian idiocy. Whatever gene differences are involved, they appear to require a special prenatal environment to make them recognizable, for mongolism occurs most commonly among children of mothers who have nearly reached the limit of the child-bearing period.

[3] *Ibid.*, pp. 16, 17. In human genetics, accordingly, the concept of *ancestry* should only be used with full awareness of its actual meaning. If it connotes what an individual shares with or derives from his ancestors, it must include: "(i) a system of genetic relations, (ii) a system of developmental relationships determined by the uterine environment but correlated with the preceding, and (iii) a framework of social and physical environment also related to the genetic 'ancestral' relationship." *Ibid.*, p. 110.

[4] *Ibid.*, p. 118.

Hogben concludes that, "If with its present endowments mankind lacks the capacity [to] discover forms of organization which will guarantee the continued development of our present civilization, . . . the application of genetic knowledge can only offer a very remote prospect of producing a race which will."[1]

Possibilities of Selective Breeding. With further advances in medicine and genetics, eugenic selection will probably assume increasing importance. Even now beneficial results may be expected from the application of genetic principles. But any considerable improvement of the human race through the elimination of pathological traits will necessarily be very slow, for such traits are in large part *recessive*, that is, they appear only in individuals receiving a double inheritance of the gene phase tending to cause the trait, and are accordingly carried in the majority of cases by *apparently normal* individuals.[2] For example, if all albinos were sterilized in every generation it would probably take many centuries to halve their present number.[3] There are, however, a number of diseases and disfigurements which might be eliminated in a generation, were all individuals suffering from them not allowed to reproduce. Each of these is due to a rare *dominant* condition in individuals who nearly always possess the gene determining it on one chromosome only.[4]

In the crucial case of mental deficiency, the matter is far more complex than it was formerly supposed to be. Hogben fears that over-emphasis on the genetic aspect of mental deficiency may discourage research into the rôle of environment. There is no

[1] *Ibid.*, p. 9. With regard to feeble-mindedness, for example, Hogben believes that "the selfishness, apathy and prejudice which prevent intellectually gifted people from understanding the present crisis in civilization is a far greater menace to the survival of culture than the prevalence of mental defect in the technical sense of the term." *Ibid.*, p. 33.

[2] Since an individual who exhibits a recessive condition must receive it from both parents, he or she must be the offspring of one of three types of marriage: (1) between two recessives; (2) between a recessive and an apparently normal carrier of the gene; (3) between two carriers neither of whom exhibit the trait. Marriages of the last type are far the most common. Consanguineous parentage is more common among parents of recessives than in the general population for evident reasons: the chances of a carrier of a recessive condition marrying another carrier being greater, when a proportion of the genes in each have been derived from a common source.

[3] On the other hand, since recessive conditions tend to turn up among several brothers and sisters in a family, prevention of further reproduction on the part of parents who have produced a child exhibiting a recessive condition, would prevent further spread of defective genes. And in the case of sex-limited recessive characters, in which, unless special environmental conditions are essential for their manifestation, all males who carry the recessive gene exhibit the recessive trait, sterilization would halve the proportion of persons affected in each generation.

[4] A trait is *dominant*, if it is recognizable when the individual who shows it has received a particular gene from one parent only.

doubt, however, as to the concentration of mental defects in certain inbred stocks. And recent research in England indicates that hereditary mental deficiency is due to a series of recessive genes, which would render its eradication even less possible than if it were determined by a single recessive gene phase.[1] Even if the latter were the case and all feeble-minded individuals were sterilized, their proportion would be reduced by 11% in the first generation, and thereafter with increasing slowness.[2] Moreover, the sterilizing of mental defectives would prevent the birth of individuals of mediocre and even superior intelligence.[3] It must not be forgotten, however, that these apparently normal or superior individuals come from a stock producing defectives, and, further, that the mentally deficient are obviously unsuitable as parents from the standpoint of the nurture they give their children. Prevention of reproduction on the part of the feeble-minded would thus appear advisable from the *social* point of view even if the rapid elimination of mental deficiency cannot be hoped for by these means.

Sterilization as a Negative Means of Control. Already by the end of 1935, sterilization laws were in force in twenty-seven states.[4] There has been much litigation regarding sterilization laws, and the disposition of the courts has been to declare unconstitutional laws which have been punitive in purpose, on the basis that they constitute "a cruel and unusual punishment." The decision having most far-reaching influence was that of May 2, 1927, when for the first time the Supreme Court passed on the constitutionality of a state law providing for compulsory

[1] In an English study, 103 mentally deficient parents produced 338 offspring, of whom 110 were mentally deficient. Of the 228 normal persons, 150 were mediocre in intelligence and 78 supernormal. In a group of normal families, 626 parents produced 1,032 offspring, of whom 86 were mentally deficient. The study indicated, Hurst concludes, that all forms of mental deficiency, except those caused by injuries before or at birth, "are due to the *cumulative* action of a series of recessive genes when the dominant gene for normality is absent; and the more recessive genes there are, the lower the grade of deficiency. When the dominant normal gene is present, the individual is normal and the recessive genes are inactive." "Germany's Sterilization Law," *New York Times*, Aug. 5, 1934.

[2] Fisher has calculated that only 11% of the feeble-minded are the offspring of feeble-minded parents, 89% coming from matings of the carrier group. "Elimination of Mental Defect," *Journal of Heredity*, Vol. XVIII (1927), pp. 529–531.

[3] According to the English study cited above, sterilization of defectives would prevent the birth of 3 superior and 6 mediocre individuals for every 4 defectives.

[4] Also in two Canadian provinces, in Denmark, Norway, Sweden, Finland, Germany, the Canton of Vaud in Switzerland, and the state of Vera Cruz in Mexico. The first law in this country was passed in Indiana in 1907, in which state, since 1899, sterilization operations had been performed with the consent of the patient. Since then over sixty different laws have been enacted in the United States.

sterilization. The test case was that of a feeble-minded woman whose mother was feeble-minded and who was the mother of an illegitimate feeble-minded child. In delivering the opinion which declared the Virginia law constitutional, Justice Holmes remarked, "three generations of imbeciles are enough." [1]

Comparatively few individuals have as yet been sterilized under the laws of any state, save California, where the cause of eugenic sterilization has been promoted by the Human Betterment Foundation headed by E. S. Gosney and Paul Popenoe.[2] Under its auspices an intensive study was made of the first 6,000 cases, in order to determine the actual effects of the law. The California law is compulsory and applies only to the insane and feeble-minded committed to state institutions. Very rarely, however, is the operation carried out against the wishes of those most nearly concerned. Nevertheless, the Human Betterment Foundation maintains that the compulsory provision has been found desirable for several reasons.[3] Sterilization in many instances makes possible the release of patients from institutions, and enables handicapped persons to marry and, freed of the responsibility of children, to earn enough for self-support.

Contraception as a Negative Means of Control. If, with the further progress of genetics, it becomes possible to recognize the apparently normal carriers of defective genes, eugenic measures could be made far more effective. In the meantime, sterilization, wisely administered, is of great social benefit, and may be used to reduce the incidence of hereditary defects. More may be

[1] The Virginia law provides that the superintendents of state institutions for incompetents may advise vasectomy or salpingectomy for the best interests of the patient and society, and that the operation shall be performed at the prescription of a board of experts after the patient has had the opportunity of defending himself or herself. Vasectomy is the minor operation, practically painless with the use of local anesthesia, commonly used for sterilizing a man. Salpingectomy, which sterilizes a woman, is a major operation since it involves an abdominal incision. These operations do not unsex the patient, their only effect being prevention of parenthood.

[2] Up to January 1st, 1938, 27,869 persons had been sterilized in the United States, 16,241 women and 11,628 men. In five states, numbers ranging from 1,218 to 2,916 had been sterilized, while in California the number was 12,180: 5,910 women and 6,270 men.

[3] For example, a woman with manic-depressive insanity and a family history of mental disease already had 7 children. She and her husband decided against sterilization before her release, because, with *two more* children, they would be able to live, without working, on the money given them by the state in the form of "half-orphan aid." In spite of cases such as this the Committee of the American Neurological Association for the Investigation of Eugenical Sterilization were very critical of compulsory laws. They also recommended that sterilization laws should apply as well to patients in private institutions and in the community at large, in order to avoid group or class discrimination. Abraham Meyerson and other members of the Committee, *Eugenical Sterilization* (1936).

hoped, however, from the spread of the family-limitation pattern to the lower levels of society. Economic and educational levels of handicapped groups would be raised and the incidence of mental deficiency decreased as inferior strains became less fertile. A considerable reduction in the fertility of the large group of dull-normal or borderline individuals would have a greater influence on the frequency of mental deficiency, than the sterilization of all actual mental defectives. As Lorimer and Osborn put it: "effective genetic selection for intelligence must be applied all along the line, not only at the extremes." [1] This means also that selection on the basis of intelligence would be best effected by an increase of fertility on the part not only of those of highest ability, but also of the far larger group of superior individuals.

Positive Aspects of Social Control. The eradication of environmental evils is perhaps the most urgently needed of all measures of social control. Were every child born and nurtured in an environment which would foster optimum mental and physical growth, there would be marked advances in cultural-intellectual development and it would also become more possible to determine which pathological traits were due primarily to defective genes and which to adverse environmental influences. [2] Changes along socially desirable lines would also constitute the most effective means for modifying present differentials in fertility. Excessive fertility due to ignorance or indifference would undoubtedly be decreased due to such changes, and the spread of the family-limitation pattern would be facilitated. On the other hand, greater economic security and increased opportunities for early marriage would tend to bring about a release of fertility among families at superior levels of cultural-intellectual development.

Dublin has estimated that with current infant mortality and marriage rates a population can only maintain itself if every woman bears, on the average, three children. To maintain such an average many must bear four or five. Therefore, as Lorimer and Osborn put it: "one of the essential conditions of a stable

---

[1] *Op. cit.*, p. 251. Studies made in certain cities in Sweden and Germany, where it is known that all social and economic classes practice contraception, indicate that when the lower classes reduce the number of their children, there is a tendency towards a larger number in the upper classes. See *Proceedings* of the World Population Conference (1927), pp. 205–206, and *Bulletin* of the International Population Union, Sept., 1930, p. 12.

[2] Considerations such as these lead to the great caution shown by geneticists like Hogben and Jennings. Enid Charles and Warren S. Thompson go further, and consider that under present conditions there is little reason to suppose that the selection of superior stock is possible.

and improving social order, must be the development of patterns favorable to family replacement or natural increase among those who are able to control their own destinies to a high degree. . . . This must involve a widespread preference for families with three, four, five or more children. Such a development will involve social changes and educational changes tending to give greater emphasis to the value of family life, to ways of living which promote physical vigor, and to conditions which guarantee a large measure of economic security, especially to young couples during the early reproductive years. . . . Eventually, if our dream of human progress is to be realized, rational social action must replace the operation of blind forces in this as in other fields." [1]

It is not surprising, considering the recency of the birth-control movement, that as yet so little has been accomplished in the way of encouraging reproduction at the higher levels of cultural-intellectual development. As McIver says: "like every assumption of control over nature within or outside him, this new power presents civilized man with new tasks, new responsibilities, new risks and new prospects. . . . If its potential benefits are to be won it must evoke the mores of a new responsibility, especially on the part of those members of the community who are most highly endowed." [2] There are numerous indications to-day of the development of new and informed attitudes towards family life. These attitudes are largely inspired by a new realization of the value of childhood, and inevitably involve a sense of responsibility with regard to reproduction.

But greater economic security must be combined with these newer attitudes if they are to result in larger families among those with highest standards. Otherwise, either early marriage is impossible, or else childbearing is postponed while both wife and husband work; and the family will be strictly limited to the number of children who can be nurtured in accordance with these standards. Lorimer and Osborn are emphatic on this point: "The combination of early marriages and the financial security of young couples must constitute the foundation of any practical program of positive eugenics." [3] To secure such a state of affairs for all young people, but especially for young intellectual workers, they advocate several changes, including *parental*

---

[1] *Op. cit.*, p. 348.
[2] From R. M. MacIver, *Society: Its Structure and Changes*, pp. 461–462. Copyright, 1931. Reprinted by permission of the publishers, Farrar and Rinehart, Inc.
[3] *Op. cit.*, p. 331.

endowment of marriage and fellowships for advanced students of superior ability with automatic adjustment to size of family. The desirability of a system of family allowances to include all classes of the community is again evident. It has also been suggested that systems of taxation might be devised by which the childless should contribute a larger share to the support of children.[1] Financial security combined with high standards of parenthood should prove conducive to racial welfare. Freedom from defect, vigorous health, and superior intelligence are as eagerly desired by enlightened parents for their children, as they are necessary for eugenic progress.

THE BIRTH-CONTROL MOVEMENT

The History of the Birth-control Movement.[2] Interest in the prevention of conception is known to have existed in Egypt as early as 1850 B.C., and Greek and Roman physicians considered contraception to be a legitimate phase of their work. The modern birth-control movement, with its social emphasis, had its inception in 1823 in the educational campaign of Francis Place, an English working man. Convinced from personal experience that family limitation alone could solve the problems of the poor, he sought to inform the working masses through the distribution of leaflets, the "diabolical handbills," as they were soon called.[3] Influenced by Place's work, the American birth-control movement began in 1828. In 1830, Robert Dale Owen published his *Moral Physiology* and, in 1832, the first American treatise on conception control, written by a physician, was published by Dr. Charles Knowlton: *Fruits of Philosophy, or The Private Companion of Young Married People.*

[1] Ellsworth Huntingdon suggests and discusses several methods for encouraging birth release at the higher levels in *Tomorrow's Children* (1935). He lays particular stress on the great need for eugenic education.

[2] The phrase "birth control" is variously used. Some believe it to be better usage to regard birth control as denoting all voluntary practices tending to limit births, even including abortion, and to use the term contraception for conception control. However, as originally coined by Mrs. Sanger (and as used in this chapter) "birth control" applies exclusively to methods for limiting the number of offspring by preventing conception. Strictly, it applies only to artificial methods of preventing conception, as opposed to abstinence from intercourse, or even intercourse during the so-called "safe period."

[3] Married very early and very happily, he was the father of fifteen children and had been bitterly poor. Place won support from such men as John Stuart Mill. Thinkers of the utilitarian school had been deeply impressed by Malthus' theory; and, while Malthus himself refused to countenance the notion of deliberate limitation of offspring, James Mill, writing in the *Encyclopaedia Britannica*, declared, "the grand practical problem, therefore, is to find a means of limiting the number of births." His son and some of the other utilitarians agreed with him.

For forty-three years the latter book sold in England at the rate of about 700 a year and then its right to publication was contested in the notorious Bradlaugh-Besant trial in 1875. In the three months before the trial, 125,000 copies were sold, and public interest in contraception was greatly increased.[1] The decline in the English birth-rate which began in 1880 was undoubtedly due in part to these events, although other factors contributed. Another book which had much influence was the *Elements of Social Science* (1854), by Dr. George Drysdale, who was also instrumental in founding the Malthusian League, of which his brother was president for many years. At the time of the Bradlaugh-Besant trial, this League came into prominence and helped the cause of birth control in England and on the Continent, notably in Holland, where the first birth-control clinic in the world was opened by Dr. Aletta Jacobs.

In the United States, concern over the falling birth-rate was manifest soon after the Civil War. Both Emerson and Ingersoll advocated control of population, but bitter antagonism was aroused by the radical experiments in eugenic mating and control of procreation made in the Oneida Community between 1848 and 1881.[2] The prevailing temper was one of violent prejudice, and, as a result of agitation on the part of Anthony Comstock of the New York Society for the Suppression of Vice, the New York legislature in 1869 included contraceptive information and supplies in an obscenity act; and a federal law was passed in 1873 declaring the giving of information concerning contraception to be illegal and obscene, and prohibiting the distribution of such information or of contraceptive devices through the mails. All the states save North Carolina and New Mexico then passed similar, though varied, laws.[3]

---

[1] The defendants did not, indeed, wholly approve of the book itself, and, when its publication was no longer contested, Mrs. Besant issued her own *Law of Population* in 1879. This was widely sold until withdrawn from circulation on its author's conversion to theosophy. Reprinted by Johnsen in *Selected Articles on Birth Control* (1925) is an extract from Mrs. Besant's autobiography in which she tells how Mme Blavatsky persuaded her to relinquish her advocacy of birth control as being inconsistent with occult views. Though feeling forced to agree, Mrs. Besant was very unwilling to forego this means of alleviating the miseries of the poor. Pp. 98–102.

[2] Ingersoll declared that "science, the only possible savior of mankind, must put it in the power of a woman to decide for herself whether she will, or will not become a mother." Quoted Johnsen, *op. cit.*, p. 17.

[3] Much confusion has resulted from the interpretation of these laws. In 1932 there were 31 states where physicians might legally give information on the prevention of conception. In 11 others they might give it, but not publish it. In two, information might only be given for the prevention and cure of disease. In four states the matter was in doubt, and in one of these, Connecticut, the *use* of contraceptives was de-

Margaret Sanger's Fight for Birth Control. No other name is so closely connected with the birth-control movement as that of Margaret Sanger, leader of the movement in America and a world-wide crusader in the cause. Her autobiography, *My Fight for Birth Control* (1931), gives a vivid description of the experiences which gave her insight into the tragic lives of poverty-stricken mothers.[1] From 1912 on, she worked unceasingly, at first alone, to make effective methods of contraception available to the poor. In 1914 she founded the American Birth Control League and in 1916 the first Birth Control Clinic. In 1917 the *Birth Control Review* began publication. Repeated efforts were made to curtail her activities and those of her husband and other co-workers; as a result they all suffered frequent arrests and imprisonment. In 1922, Mrs. Sanger made her first world tour in the interests of birth control and was later instrumental in organizing the World Population Conference at Geneva in 1927.[2]

In her earlier efforts at legislative reform Mrs. Sanger emphasized state rather than federal legislation. Later, however, she organized the National Committee on Federal Legislation for Birth Control. Mary Ware Dennett had founded, in 1919, the Voluntary Parenthood League, with the aim of repealing the federal laws that dealt with information or supplies pertaining to the prevention of conception.[3] Mrs. Sanger worked not for repeal, but amendment, in order to permit the dissemination, by recognized medical agencies, of contraceptive information and supplies.[4] In 1930 and 1932 bills were introduced in Congress only

clared illegal. Only in Mississippi were physicians *prohibited* from giving information. Seldom, however, is any effort made to enforce these statutes. Nevertheless, when in 1930–1931 a "doctors' bill," supported by the best medical talent, was proposed in Massachusetts, it was defeated by the legislative committee; and a Connecticut bill presented at the same time was also unsuccessful.

[1] As a trained nurse, she stood one night in 1912 by the bedside of a dying mother, and came to the determination that something radical must be done to alleviate the misery caused by incessant pregnancies, and to save poor mothers from the added suffering and death which all too often followed their desperate efforts to induce abortion.

[2] She has estimated that over a million men and women wrote to her for advice between 1916 and 1928.

[3] The laws in question are Sections 211, 245, 311, and 312 of the U.S. Penal Code, adopted in 1873 and in 1909; further legislation was included in Section 305 of the Tariff Act of 1922. Violation involves fines of $2,000 or $5,000, or imprisonment for five years, or both fine and imprisonment.

[4] Under the proposed amendments, the prohibitory sections of the law would not be construed to apply to "any book, information, article, drug, medicine or thing designed, adapted or intended for the prevention of conception, for use (1) by any legally licensed physician, or by his direction or prescription; (2) by any legally chartered medical college; (3) by any druggist in his legitimate prescription business; (4) by any licensed hospital or clinic." *New York Times*, April 24, 1934.

to be "smothered" in the Senate Judiciary Committee. In 1934 the Senate Judiciary Committee reported favorably, but in 1935 the House Committee voted against the bill.

The hearings in these committees at which the advocates and opponents of the amending bill argued their cases make instructive reading.[1] A marked contrast is apparent between the attitude of the doctors, sociologists, and religious leaders who supported the measure and the bitterness and prejudice of their opponents. These were for the most part Roman Catholics, including priests, laymen, and doctors. Other determined opponents were John Sumner of the Society for the Suppression of Vice, Canon Chase as representative of the World's Purity Federation, and Ralph Burton, vice-president of the National Patriotic League.[2]

Meanwhile, despite the anomalous situation created by this delay in legislation, the number of birth-control clinics has been rapidly increasing. The New York Birth Control Clinical Research Bureau, conducted entirely by physicians, began systematic work in 1923, and by 1930 had received over 12,000 visits. When, in 1929, this clinic was raided, the case was dismissed, the phrase "prevention of disease" being interpreted in a very liberal sense. In 1930 there were still only some fifty clinics; by 1935 there were 150; and in that year more than 70,000 new patients were received, 41% of whom were on whole or partial relief. The number of clinics doubled in the next two years, and by 1938, there were 374 in the United States, Hawaii, and Puerto Rico. Much remains to be done, however, before clinical service is available even to all urban women, while the movement has only begun to penetrate outlying rural districts. Several state birth-control leagues are considering the inauguration of traveling clinics.[3]

[1] *New York Times*, May 13 and 20, 1932; and Jan. 19 and 20, 1934.

[2] Canon Chase denounced the proposed measure as a "crooks' bill," charging that it was "loosely drawn in such a fashion as to assist those who are in the business of pandering to vice." Mr. Burton feared it would facilitate the importation of "the communistic doctrines of the Soviets, including free love, abolition of the home and destruction of home ties." The representatives of the Roman Church marshaled a wide variety of arguments in support of their dogmatic conviction that the bill was, in Dr. Ryan's words, "intrinsically and everlastingly immoral." Catholic women, including a representative in Congress who is the mother of only one child, actually accused Mrs. Sanger of commercial interest in contraceptive devices and professed disbelief in her concern for downtrodden mothers.

[3] There has also been a wide development in clinical services abroad. In England Marie Stopes opened a London clinic in 1921, and another was opened by the Malthusian League in 1922. Birth control has been a public-health measure since 1930, when the Ministry of Health urged local maternal- and child-health authorities to

There have been great changes in public opinion in America in recent years. Hornell Hart analyzed the enormous volume of discussion to be found in periodical literature from 1930 on, and found the opinions expressed to be predominantly favorable.[1] The years 1936 and 1937 were to mark the turning point in the birth-control movement in America. In 1933, a package of contraceptives imported from Japan by Dr. Hannah Stone was seized at the Customs. On the initiative of Margaret Sanger the case was contested, and, in November, 1936, the United States Court of Appeals reaffirmed the favorable decision of the lower court, and stated the opinion that the design of the Comstock Act of 1873 "was not to prevent the importation, sale or carriage by mail of things which might intelligently be employed by conscientious and competent physicians for the purpose of saving life or promoting the well-being of their patients." In January, 1937, it was announced that there would be no appeal to the Supreme Court. This decision brings to a successful termination a sixty-year struggle to make clear that federal obscenity laws do not apply to the legitimate activities of physicians. An amendment has become unnecessary, since the purpose of Mrs. Sanger's National Committee for Federal Legislation is accomplished. Another significant event was the Conference on Contraceptive Research and Clinical Practice held in New York at the end of December, 1936.[2] And finally, in June, 1937, the American Medical Association gave official recognition to birth control.

Birth Control and Social Welfare. Among the opponents of birth control some are alarmed at the rapid decline of the birth-rate and advocate increase in numbers irrespective of the quality of those who are born.[3] Others insist that improvement of

set up contraceptive clinics. By the beginning of 1937, 196 of the 423 such authorities in England and Wales had done so. (See Mabel T. Wood, "Birth Control's Big Year," *Current History*, Vol. XLVI, Aug., 1937.) Birth-control centers are also operating in a number of European countries, and a series of international conferences has been held. On the other hand, France (1920) and Italy (1924) and the Irish Free State (1930) have all passed laws against contraception.

[1] *Recent Social Trends*, Vol. I, p. 415. In 1935, despite the vigorous opposition of the representatives of Catholic clubs, the General Federation of Women's Clubs gave its endorsement to birth control.

[2] Medical and biological investigations in contraceptives are of the utmost importance, since upon them depends the possibility of discovering reliable biochemical means for rendering women temporarily immune to conception. This chapter should make obvious the far-reaching benefits which should result from such a development.

[3] This is particularly the case with those who are concerned by a decrease in man power for use in future wars. Such a point of view is held most strongly by militaristic nations such as the Italians and Germans and Japanese.

social and economic conditions is the *only* great necessity.[1] It is evident, however, that unrestricted propagation at the lower economic levels is a contributory factor in all the most pressing social problems of the day.[2] Primary problems of poverty, unemployment, and public health, and derivative problems, such as delinquency and child labor, would all be more capable of solution were the numbers involved less overwhelming. A study of the birth-rates among families on relief was made by the Public Health Service with the help of the Milbank Memorial Fund. In almost every case the greatest number of children was born in families least capable of assuming the responsibility.[3]

What all this means in terms of mental and physical suffering, particularly for mothers, it is almost impossible to exaggerate. No wonder some poor mothers have been driven to call children the "curse of God." Why should those whose lives are a ceaseless round of unremitting drudgery wish to add to their burdens, by bringing children into the world for whom they can hope no better fate than their own? Yet it is to mothers such as these that reliable contraceptive information, even to-day, is least accessible.

Birth Control and Health. A valuable body of data is accumulating, through the work of the clinics, and by means of studies fostered by the National Committee on Maternal Health, organized in 1923. Evidence has been gathered which refutes the commonest allegations of the opponents of birth control; proving, as it does, that modern contraceptive techniques possess a high degree of reliability, that they are not injurious, and that they do not cause sterility. Such statements are true, however,

---

[1] There could be no disagreement, of course, as to the urgent necessity for social amelioration. But there are some who seem to believe that the improvement of social conditions will, of itself, tend to restrict fertility, without recourse to deliberate family limitation. Father Cox, for example, says: "It is a known fact that the fertility of women decreases in an improved economic and cultural environment. Raise the standard of living, increase education and nature automatically decreases the birth-rate. All this will come with the new era of social justice." *New York Times*, Jan. 14, 1935.

[2] The director of the classification clinic and health service at Elmira reformatory testified before the House Judiciary Committee that he had found large and unwarranted families to be a major factor in the cause of crime: 55% of the prisoners came from families of over five, 10% from families of from ten to twenty-one children. The first, second, and third children in these families accounted for 63% of the prisoners. They had left school before 15, the majority in order to help support their parents' increasing families. *New York Times*, Jan. 19, 1934.

[3] *New York Times*, March 10, 1935. From October, 1929, to October, 1933, 1,612,891 babies were born in families on relief rolls. These babies formed 12.7% of the total relief-roll population, while in the general population children of the same age formed only 9.6%.

only for those patients who have received medical advice and treatment suited to their *individual* cases, and where *approved* methods have been used. It is only too true, on the other hand, that most commercial contraceptives are *unreliable*, and that among them are drugs and devices which have caused injury and even an occasional death.[1]

Because of the unreliability of commercial contraceptives, large numbers of unwanted pregnancies result among both unmarried and married women, and resort is all too frequently had to abortion. Available data indicate that the number of induced abortions is increasing yearly; and a similar condition has been found to exist in a number of European cities. Data obtained from the clinics show that the great majority of abortions to-day take place among married women, and the increase is noted primarily among women with three or more children. Numbers of women have had six or seven abortions, a few have had as many as fifteen, while one woman has had thirty-two. While abortion is very common among the poor, it is far more frequent than usually supposed among women of the upper levels of society.[2]

Quite apart from the ethical questions involved, the increasing prevalence of abortion is responsible for an appalling toll of maternal death and injury. Taussig estimates the annual death-rate at 15,000, and states that deaths from puerperal sepsis following abortion are relatively seven times as frequent as those from sepsis after childbirth.[3] In addition to the deaths directly attributed to induced abortions, in many other cases the result is permanent sterility or chronic invalidism. Therapeutic abortions are recognized as necessary where a woman's life is endangered by pregnancy. But the *prevention* of pregnancy is infinitely preferable in all cases of serious disease.[4] There are, in

[1] An enormous volume of advertising is now devoted to "feminine hygiene" products, and millions of dollars worth of contraceptives are sold annually. Such facts corroborate the data obtained by the clinics as evidence of the widespread and insistent desire for family limitation. When scientific information is not readily available, recourse is had to commercial contraceptives, in ignorance as to their reliability and irrespective of their suitability to individual need.

[2] Katherine Davis, *Factors in the Sex Life of Twenty-Two Hundred Women* (1929), p. 20.

[3] *Fetal, Newborn, and Maternal Morbidity and Mortality*, p. 470.

[4] In reviewing the study of maternal deaths made by the New York Academy of Medicine, Dr. Taussig gave it as his opinion that "429 or ⅓th of the deaths due to induced abortions, therapeutic abortions, chronic nephritis, cardiac disease, tuberculosis, Caesarian section, fibroid tumors, could have been prevented by the use of contraceptive measures." *Birth Control Review*, Jan., 1934; quoted by Dorothy Dunbar Bromley, *Birth Control, Its Use and Misuse* (1934), pp. 156–157.

fact, a number of chronic conditions which make pregnancy a decided risk. Even more imperative is the avoidance of pregnancy where, as in the case of venereal diseases and tuberculosis, the child may suffer serious effects. Sterilization might be preferable in all cases where for eugenic reasons or for reasons of maternal health pregnancy is permanently contra-indicated.

Even for the strong and healthy woman, too frequent pregnancies should be avoided. Health may be undermined, and the ability of mothers to care for their children may be lessened, if a due interval does not elapse between a birth and a subsequent conception. In the Children's Bureau study of the *Causal Factors of Infant Mortality* it was shown that an infant's chance of life is influenced by the length of time which has elapsed since the next preceding birth. Children born only a year after another birth had the highest mortality rate (146.7), and those born after an interval of four or more years had the lowest (84.0). There was a marked difference between the mortality rate of babies born after one year and those born after two years (98.6). For those born after three years the rate was 86.5.[1] Undoubtedly other factors are involved which may be as significant as the amount of time elapsed since the preceding birth. Nevertheless, inadequate spacing is evidently harmful. Moreover, the new-born infant is not the only sufferer. It has been found that a baby is three times as likely to die when another is conceived before he is one year old. His nursing is interrupted and he suffers loss of care from the drain on the mother's energy.[2]

Altogether, therefore, it is of the utmost importance that children be spaced, that each conception be planned "with a view to the best time and season for both mother and child. . . . The wise mother and father will plan to have as many children as can be safely carried, safely born and adequately reared."[2] Medical advice is essential to enable a woman to determine the number of her children, the best time for their births, and the rest periods needed between them. Intervals of two, two and a half, and three years are those most frequently recommended, and the youngest child should, as a rule, be born before the completion of the mother's thirty-fifth year.

---

[1] It was also found that after the fourth pregnancy the infant death-rate steadily mounts, until with the tenth child the risk is almost double what it is for the second, whose chances for survival are the best. This study was, of course, based on infant deaths in families in poor circumstances, and the later-born infants may have been less well-nourished and cared for. But this probably does not wholly account for the markedly greater mortality among the later-born.

[2] Frederick C. Holden, "Child Spacing," *Birth Control Review*, March, 1931.

Voluntary, intelligent parenthood involves control of conception. There are many who would agree with this statement and yet oppose all artificial contraceptive practices, advocating in their place abstinence from marital intercourse. There is a growing body of evidence to show that abstinence within the framework of marriage often has injurious results. Abstinence within marriage, being an entirely different matter from continence for the unmarried, is "impracticable, undesirable, and in most cases impossible." [1] Continued abstinence has been shown to be the cause of nervous disorders and depression, and of emotional conflict and domestic discord.

Despite the seemingly obvious case for birth control from the standpoint of health, the medical profession has been slow in reaching a unanimous judgment. [2] Although birth control was publicly endorsed by certain leading physicians in England and America as early as 1912, few doctors dared to help Mrs. Sanger in the early days of her campaign. Only very recently has the American Medical Association given any recognition to contraception as a medical problem, although in 1925 the Section on Obstetrics, Gynecology, and Abdominal Surgery recommended "the alteration of existing laws, wherever necessary, so that physicians may legally give contraceptive information to their patients in the regular course of their practice." Yet not until 1935 was the Association willing to appoint a committee to study the question of birth control. In 1937 unanimous approval was given to the recommendations of this committee, outlining a con-

[1] James F. Cooper, *The Technique of Contraception* (1928), p. 112. In England the medical inquiry conducted by the National Birth-rate Commission reported that "in the close relationship of married life the effects of continued abstinence may be grave for persons of certain temperaments," and that "it is impracticable for the majority of young married people." To this, Lord Dawson of Penn added the following statement: "If this harmful restraint succeeds in preventing conception, there eventuates the inevitable prevalence of sex excitement followed by abortive and half-realized satisfaction, and the enhanced risk of the man or woman yielding to outside sex temptations. No! birth control by abstention is either ineffective, or, if effective, is pernicious." Quoted by Bromley, *op. cit.*, p. 43.

[2] In 1931 a report of a special committee of the New York Academy of Medicine very rightly branded, as mediaeval, the absence of education of the public in sexual matters by physicians, and urged a change of attitude on the part of physicians. Nothing indeed so clearly indicates the strength of traditional taboos. That prejudice dictates the utterances of medical opponents of birth control is very evident from the language employed by their leaders in congressional hearings. An emeritus professor of gynecology, aged 76, and the father of nine children, assailed the whole controversy as "inconceivably distressing and disgusting," and declared the proposed bill was "infinitely degrading to women." Another physician of 72, the son of a minister and himself unmarried, said that birth control would change the Ten Commandments to say: "Thou shalt covet thy neighbor's wife" and "thou canst now commit adultery." *New York Times*, Feb. 15, 1931; Jan. 20, 1934.

structive program to forward the progress of contraception in research, in clinical service, and in medical school education.[1]

The Organized Opposition of the Roman Catholic Church. The motives underlying the implacable hostility towards birth control, on the part of those who oppose artificial restriction of births, are most clearly evident in the attitudes of religious bodies, most of all in the stand taken by the Roman Church. The Encyclical *Casti Connubii*, issued by Pope Pius XI, on December 31, 1930, gives authoritative reaffirmation to the opposition of the Catholic Church to "pernicious errors and depraved morals," as well as to the "false principles of a new and utterly perverse morality," which "have begun to spread even among the faithful" and whereby the "divine institution" of matrimony is "on every side degraded."[2] The "very source of these evils . . . lies in this, that matrimony is repeatedly declared to be not constituted by the author of nature nor raised by Christ the Lord to the dignity of a true sacrament, but invented by man." The faithful are warned against "the overrated independence of private judgment and that false autonomy of human reason"; nor must they "imagine that the Church, sent by God to teach and guide all nations, is not conversant with present affairs and circumstances. . . . A characteristic of all true followers of Christ . . . is to suffer themselves to be led and guided in all things that touch upon faith and morals."

Christian law permits continence in marriage where both parties consent, but, "since the conjugal act is destined primarily for the begetting of children, those who in exercising it deliberately frustrate its natural power and purpose sin against nature and commit a deed which is shameful and intrinsically vicious. . . . Divine Majesty regards with greatest detestation this horrible crime. . . . Onan . . . did this, and the Lord killed him for it."

Aside from the "shameful arguments" put forward to justify "the evil use of matrimony, . . . others false and exaggerated are put forward. Holy Mother Church very well understands and clearly appreciates all that is said regarding the health of the mother and the danger to her life. . . . We are deeply touched by the sufferings of those parents who, in extreme want,

---

[1] For full report of the recommendations see *New York Times*, June 9, 1937.

[2] For full text see *New York Times*, Jan. 9, 1931, or *Current History*, Vol. XXXIII (Feb., 1931), pp. 797 *et seq.* It is most important for all those interested in the development of a new family pattern to be familiar with the position of the Roman Church, the only contemporary organization which consistently endeavors to uphold the traditional point of view.

experience great difficulties in rearing their children." However, "no difficulty can arise that justifies the putting aside of the law of God which forbids all acts intrinsically evil; there is no possible circumstance in which husband and wife cannot, strengthened by the grace of God, fulfil faithfully their duties and preserve in wedlock their chastity unspotted." It is, however, granted that "in matrimony as well as in the use of the matrimonial rights there are also secondary ends, such as mutual aid, the cultivating of mutual love, and the quieting of concupiscence, which husband and wife are not forbidden to consider, so long as they are subordinated to the primary end and so long as the intrinsic nature of the act is preserved." Accordingly, those are not "considered as acting against nature who, in the married state, use their right in the proper manner, although, on account of natural reasons either of time or of certain defects, new life cannot be brought forth."

In this last statement the limitation of offspring is authorized not through continence alone, but by regulating intercourse so that it occurs at a time when the fertility of a woman is low. Ever since the eighties, the Roman Church has viewed the progress of "the heresy of contraception" with alarm. There is much evidence to show, moreover, that many Catholics, while not breaking away altogether from the Church, are not allowing it to control their marital lives.[1] Accordingly, as has been explicitly admitted, the Church is endeavoring to find "a way out of the difficulty without a compromise of principle."[2] Several books have made their appearance in recent years, bearing titles such as *The Rhythm of Sterility and Fertility, The Sterile Period*

[1] The records of birth-control clinics reveal that large numbers of their patients are Catholic women. The records of the fifty clinics established by 1931 showed that of the patients 33% were Protestants, 32% Catholics, and 31% Jewish. In *My Fight for Birth Control*, Mrs. Sanger tells of cases where mothers had come to feel that their visits to the clinic were none of the priests' business. "When I was married," said one, "the priest told us to have lots of children and we listened to him. I had fifteen. Six are living. Nine baby funerals in our house. I am thirty-six years old. Look at me! I look sixty!" (p. 157). Another highly significant fact is the number of abortions among Catholic women. Out of 5,010 patients of the Birth Control Clinical Research Bureau in New York who admitted having had abortions, 28% were Protestants, 26% were Catholics, and 43% were Jewish. After the fifth pregnancy the Catholics led all the others. It must be remembered that the Roman Church severely condemns even *therapeutic* abortions. In the words of the 1930 Encyclical: "however much we may pity the mother whose health and even life is gravely imperiled in the performance of the duty allotted to her by nature, nevertheless, what could ever be a sufficient reason for excusing in any way the direct murder of the innocent?"

[2] Father Reiner in the introduction to *The Rhythm of Sterility and Fertility* (1933), by Dr. Leo J. Latz; quoted by Bromley, *op. cit.*, p. 47.

of Family Life, and *Legitimate Birth Control according to Nature's Law.* It is argued that there is an *obvious* moral difference "between interposing artificial deterrents to conception in the act itself and using marriage naturally, but only when nature itself makes a woman sterile." To those unsympathetic with the Catholic point of view, this distinction would seem to adhere to the *letter* rather than to the *principle.*[1]

Only in recent years has research been directed towards verifying the common belief that there exists a sterile period, and towards ascertaining its incidence and duration. Up to the present time all studies point to the fact that a sterile period *does* exist in the menstrual cycle, but most investigators believe that the theory cannot be given unqualified endorsement nor can reliance usually be put upon it in practice. Even if, in time, it became possible exactly to determine the "safe period" in the case of each individual woman, intercourse would have to be limited to that period, in order to prevent conception. As Dr. Matsner of the Clinical Research Bureau has pointed out, this method would offer no relief whatever for the large numbers of women whose husbands will not coöperate in preventing conception.

The advocacy of contraception as a means for lessening social problems and improving the economic status of workers has been violently denounced by the Catholic Church.[2] In a recent controversy with thirteen Protestant and Jewish clergymen over the suggestion that birth-control information should be given to families on relief, Cardinal Hayes actually condemned those who differed with him as "irreligious, unscientific, and disbelievers in a moral law."[3] The bitter hostility and emotional language

[1] For the Catholic argument, see Wilfred Parsons, "Is This 'Catholic' Birth Control?" *America, A Catholic Review of the Week,* Vol. XLVIII (Feb. 25, 1933), pp. 496 *et seq.* Note the following passage: "It was never limitation of offspring that was forbidden by the Church, but only artificial interference with the natural end of the act itself, since it is an act whose end is not subordinated to man, being a function of the race, but one to whose end he is himself subordinated. This makes it different from all other 'interferences' with nature." For fuller treatment see E. R. Moore, *The Case against Birth Control* (1931).

[2] A group of Bishops, acting as members of the administrative committee of the National Catholic Welfare Association, recently decried the "promotion of the Godless, selfish and inhuman propaganda of birth prevention," a "repellent doctrine" which finds in economic conditions a "justification for a criminal marital life." The Catholic Daughters of America characterize the sponsors of movements advocating dissemination of birth-control information as "the Herods of the twentieth century," who would "cut off the heads of the poor and unemployed rather than feed the hungry, clothe the naked and shelter the homeless." *The Literary Digest,* Vol. CXX (July 20, 1935), p. 20.

[3] *New York Times,* Dec. 9, 16, 19, 1935.

evoked by what Catholics believe to be a "diabolical and damnable doctrine," based on "pure animalism," can be very readily understood. Led by a celibate priesthood, and adhering to unchanging dogmas permeated through and through with an ascetic horror of sex, they find themselves fighting a losing battle. Till recently, moreover, the Catholics had the support of other religious bodies, whereas more and more of these are now relinquishing their traditional stand.

Changes in the Attitudes of the Other Churches. As late as 1920, the Lambeth Conference of the Bishops of the Anglican Church uttered an emphatic warning against artificial means for the control of conception; while at the 1930 Conference there was recognition of the need for family limitation, and the use of contraceptive methods was deemed, under certain conditions, not incompatible with Christian principles. The Protestant Episcopal Church in America first took decisive action in 1934, when its Bishops, by a vote of forty-four to thirty-eight approved the following resolution: "We endorse the efforts now being made to secure for licensed physicians, hospitals and medical clinics, freedom to convey such information as is in accord with the highest principles of eugenics, and a more wholesome family life, wherein parenthood may be undertaken with due respect to the health of mothers and the welfare of their children."[1]

In the other Protestant churches, also, opinion is now divided. While freer from the authority of ecclesiastical tradition than are Catholics and Episcopalians, they are, on the other hand, profoundly influenced by the Puritan attitude towards sex. Such liberal action as has been taken is very recent, by far the most important pronouncement, reflecting a new attitude, being that contained in the 1931 report of the Committee of the Federal Council of the Churches of Christ in America. A majority of the Committee, twenty-one against three, believed that "the careful and restrained use of contraceptives by married people is valid and moral."[2] As was to be expected, this report was immediately repudiated by a number of Protestant groups, including the Lutherans and one section of the Presbyterian Church, despite the fact that the Presbyterian Special Commission on Marriage, Divorce, and Remarriage had approved the use of con-

[1] *New York Times*, Oct. 21, 1934. Bishop Huston, in advocating the measure, remarked: "We have had a lot of pious twaddle from celibate clergymen who are about as far from knowledge of the realities of life as the man in the moon. The underprivileged should have access to information which others can so readily obtain."

[2] *Current History*, Vol. XXXIV (April, 1931), p. 99. The full text of the report is published here, pp. 97 *et seq.;* also in the *New York Times*, March 21, 1931.

traceptives "for worthy objectives, . . . and only . . . in fidelity to the highest spiritual ideals of the Christian home."[1]

Of recent years there has been a striking adoption of the liberal attitude on the part of Jewish religious leaders, a fact of particular significance in view of the high value always placed by Jewish orthodoxy on motherhood and on family life. In February, 1935, the Rabbinical Assembly of America adopted a resolution favoring legal change and maintaining that "proper education in contraception and birth control will not destroy, but rather enhance, the spiritual values inherent in the family, and will make for the advancement of human happiness and welfare."[2] That liberal Christian opinion is in agreement with this point of view was made evident by the united stand taken by eleven Protestant clergy and two Jewish rabbis in the recent controversy with Cardinal Hayes. The discussion it evoked has made very evident the fact that those who oppose birth control take their stand on a "revealed," absolute, and eternal moral law, while its advocates are actuated by humanitarian ideals of social justice.[3]

Ethical Aspects of Birth Control. The first step towards building a constructive ethics of family and sexual relationships must be their reintegration within the field of an ethics of social justice. The extraordinary significance of sexual relationships as the most intimate and complex of all human relationships must be accorded full recognition. Nevertheless, they must be subject to the guidance of ethical principles alone. This means their complete release from the entanglements of superstition and outworn tradition, above all, as MacIver puts it, from "the unclean superstition of the uncleanness of sex."[4]

Positive ideals of social justice demand that human relationships be viewed, by each individual involved, in the light of the well-being of all concerned, their richest experience and fullest and freest development. From the standpoint of such ideals birth control at some periods of married life is for the vast majority a moral necessity.

[1] *New York Times*, March 21 and April 27, 1931.

[2] *New York Times*, Feb. 7, 1935. The resolution continues: "As rabbis we are deeply concerned with the preservation and extension of the human values inherent in the institution of the monogamous family. Careful study and observation have convinced us that birth control is a valuable method for overcoming some of the obstacles that prevent the proper functioning of the family under present conditions."

[3] As stated by this group of thirteen: "a program or policy such as birth control, which reduces the death-rate of children, preserves and prolongs the life of mothers, and which mitigates misery and distress, must be judged . . . as profoundly ethical both in essence and in social action." *New York Times*, Dec. 30, 1935.

[4] *Society*, p. 140.

Undoubtedly birth control may be used unwisely, and for *genuinely* immoral purposes. Certain of its occasional harmful consequences must be accorded brief consideration, because they are used as arguments against birth control under *any* circumstances. In the first place it is stated that the availability of birth-control information will lead to an increase in promiscuity and extra-marital relationships. Secondly, that the use of contraception within marriage undermines moral self-control and encourages the dominance of physical passion over the spiritual aspects of marriage. Further, it tends, it is said, to the selfish pursuit of pleasure and the shirking of the responsibilities of parenthood.

With regard to the first of these arguments, it may at once be admitted that the removal of the fear of pregnancy, through contraception, probably tends to bring about some increase in sexual irregularities, particularly among girls of the more favored classes. This topic meets with discussion in the next chapter. For the present it may be pointed out that publicly sanctioned birth control, under medical direction, would facilitate early marriage and so tend to reduce the number of irregular unions. It must not be forgotten, however, that extra-marital relationships have at all times been widely prevalent, and that fear of pregnancy and of the social opprobrium attaching to unmarried motherhood has never served as an effective check on promiscuity. The thousands of illegitimate births yearly make this only too obvious. Indeed, one of the most powerful arguments in favor of the dissemination of adequate contraceptive methods lies in the hope that the incidence of illegitimacy would be materially decreased thereby.[1] For all but the traditional moralist, this would be so great a good as to outweigh a possible increase in sexual laxity.

Not only would adequate contraceptive methods prevent the birth of illegitimate children, but they would diminish the great and growing evil of abortion. Indeed the only possible way of controlling abortion is by the substitution of birth control. So menacing is the present situation, that some authorities believe a more liberal policy should be adopted in performing therapeutic abortions. Others go so far as to advocate the legalizing of abortion for reasons other than those of health.[2] There

---

[1] Harold Cox in *The Problem of Population* (1923), pp. 165–166, gives figures to show that both the rate and volume of illegitimacy has decreased in England since birth restriction has been practised.

[2] Dr. Rachelle Yarros argues that, in certain cases, social, economic, and psychological grounds may equal in importance the grounds of health which make it inadvisable to bring a child into the world. *Modern Woman and Sex* (1933).

would probably be sharp differences of opinion here, even among those who are freed from traditional prejudices. Each individual case would have to be considered on its own merits. But the need for such painful decisions should be in large measure obviated with the widespread use of reliable contraceptives.

The alleged evil effects of contraception within marriage are: overemphasis on sex, to the loss of friendship, companionship, affection, and love; the degradation of marriage through selfish indulgence, to the detriment of chivalrous self-control; childlessness, as a result of absorption in selfish pleasure. With regard to the last accusation it is doubtless quite true that certain couples are childless from selfish motives. But such couples would hardly be desirable as parents, for the unwanted child of selfish, pleasure-seeking parents is severely handicapped. As to the degradation of marriage, there is not the slightest evidence of low standards of morality in middle- and upper-class families where birth control is known to be practised. On the contrary, it is well established that in large numbers of these families, those, for instance, of doctors, lawyers, educators, and clergymen, high moral standards are combined with intelligence, foresight, and high standards of living. On the other hand, abundant testimony has been obtained by the birth-control clinics, that in many families where no means are taken for preventing conception, license rather than self-control has been the rule: incessant indulgence on the part of husbands and a veritable sex slavery on the part of wives. Women who have had a rapid succession of pregnancies thrust upon them come to feel themselves helpless victims. Fear of pregnancy entirely precludes the harmonious physical relationship between husband and wife so necessary in a satisfactory marriage, and sometimes results in driving the husband to seek sexual satisfaction elsewhere. Yarros reports cases where the use of contraceptives made both physical and psychological adjustments so much more satisfactory, that the frequency of intercourse had actually been diminished.[1]

Obviously the ascetic attitude is at the root of all fears as to the degradation of marriage into "legalized vice." For those who still believe men and women to be primarily "spiritual" beings, who must be freed from "animal passions," sex is undoubtedly a formidable obstacle in the way of perfection. For those, on the other hand, who seek the good in the direction of human impulses towards spiritual ends, sexual union becomes

[1] *Ibid.*, p. 152.

not only the means of reproduction, but the supreme expression of mutual love.[1] The practice of contraception, through its dissociation of the satisfaction of sexual impulse from its natural consequences, has introduced for the first time, *within the family*, a distinction between its sexual and reproductive functions. Accordingly it makes more possible the adequate fulfilment and reconciliation by the family of two of its central and essential functions: procreation and nurture of children, and a satisfactory love life for their parents. It thus facilitates the emergence of a new pattern of marriage; a pattern which can only be maintained by the acceptance of new responsibilities for the intelligent direction of the sexual impulse as the instrument of a two-fold spiritual purpose: voluntary parenthood, on the part of those between whom there is enduring mutual love.

Voluntary Parenthood. An ethics of social justice is committed to the consideration of each human being as an end in himself or herself. Where "souls" alone are given absolute value, as in the traditional ideology of the Christian Church, there is all too wont to be neglect and depreciation of the individual life, and a tendency to treat individuals as instruments in the service of authoritatively determined ends, external to themselves. Such a view is utterly incompatible with the principle of voluntary parenthood, implying, as it does, that society and humanity are best served where the promotion of the well-being of their children is realized as the primary and central responsibility of parents.

Despite the fact of excessive family limitation among some of those best qualified to be parents, and despite the theories of hostile critics who envisage a growing revolt of women against childbearing, birth-control clinics furnish abundant testimony to the natural desire of women for children. As Mrs. Sanger says, the mothers who come to clinics do so, "not because they do not love children, but because they do love them, and to give those children they already have a fair chance in life and health."[2] She calls attention, as does Yarros, to the large families of a number of mothers in comfortable circumstances who have carefully planned for each child.

The use of birth control is a necessity for the growing number of parents who hold sacred the individual life of the child, and

[1] As the Rev. Oliver M. Butterfield says, in his widely distributed pamphlet on *Marriage* (1932): "Because proper sexual intercourse does contribute so much toward the growth and development of mutual love, it would be unfortunate indeed if it had to be limited to those relatively few occasions when children are desired."

[2] *New York Times*, Feb. 14, 1934.

would substitute voluntary and intelligent parenthood for accidental and indiscriminate reproduction. No more potent means for achieving the ideals of social justice could be devised, than that each and every child should be *well-born:* his birth eagerly desired and planned for, so that he is assured of a healthy heritage and an environment favorable to his optimum development. John Haynes Holmes has well said: "Birth control or voluntary parenthood, rightly understood, is only one more chapter in the history of man's emancipation as a spiritual being, by which we mean his dedication to spiritual uses."[1]

SUGGESTED READING

Baber, R. E., "Birth Control: A Balance Sheet," *Forum*, Vol. LXXXVIII, Nov., 1932, pp. 294–299.

Bromley, D. B., *Birth Control: Its Use and Misuse*, 1934.

Charles, E., *The Twilight of Parenthood*, 1934.

Dublin, L., ed., *The American People*, in *The Annals of the American Academy of Political and Social Science*, Vol. CLXXXVIII, Nov., 1936.

Folsom, J. K., *The Family*, 1934, Ch. IX.

Goodsell, W., *Problems of the Family*, rev. ed., 1936, Chs. XII–XV.

Gosney, E. S., and Popenoe, P., *Sterilization for Human Betterment*, 1929.

Groves, E. R., and Brooks, L. M., *Readings in the Family*, 1934, Chs. VII, XIII, XX.

Himes, N. E., "Birth Control in Historical and Clinical Perspective," *The Annals of the American Academy of Political and Social Science*, Vol. CLX, March, 1932, pp. 49–85.

Hogben, L., *Genetic Principles in Medicine and Social Science*, 1932.

——, *Nature and Nurture*, 1933.

Holmes, S. J., *The Eugenic Predicament*, 1933.

Huntingdon, E., and others, *Tomorrow's Children*, 1935.

Jennings, H. S., *Genetics*, 1935.

Johnsen, J., ed., *Selected Articles on Birth Control*, 1925.

Landman, J. H., *Human Sterilization*, 1932.

Lorimer, F., and Osborn, F., *Dynamics of Population*, 1934.

Kopp, M. E., *Birth Control in Practice*, 1934.

Muller, H. J., *Out of the Night*, 1935.

Myerson, A., and others, *Eugenical Sterilization*, 1936.

Reuter, E. B., and Runner, J. R., *The Family*, 1931, Ch. XVII.

Sanger, M., *My Fight for Birth Control*, 1931.

Thompson, W. S., and Whelpton, P. K., "The Population of the Nation," *Recent Social Trends*, 2 vols., 1933, Vol. I, Ch. I.

[1] Quoted by Cooper, *Technique of Contraception*, p. 17.

CHAPTER XVIII

THE INSTABILITY OF THE MODERN FAMILY

THE REVOLT AGAINST TRADITIONAL MORALITY

The Prevalence of Pre-marital Sex Experimentation. Bewildering conflicts in social usages and ethical standards are nowhere more acute than in the realm of sex. On the one hand, there is actual or nominal adherence to tradition and consequent repression of frank discussion; on the other, there is continual overstimulation of interest in sex through agencies such as moving pictures and sex-adventure magazines, not to speak of the suggestive advertisements to be found to-day in so many periodicals. Widespread discussion of sex, in books and magazines, with the prevailing overemphasis on its physiological aspects, the popularization of Freudian theory, and the publicity given to radical views, such as those of Bertrand Russell, have only augmented the confusion in the minds of those unprepared to separate the wheat from the chaff.

It is, therefore, not to be wondered at, that the older standards of sexual morality are losing their hold over increasing numbers of the younger generation. This is happening, moreover, at a time when, with the increase of recreational facilities outside the home, and above all, with the use of the automobile, young people have escaped, as never before, from the supervision of their elders. They have thus acquired unprecedented freedom when few are prepared for its wise use. There are no generally recognized standards; and education for self-direction is inadequate.

Although boys have also acquired greater freedom, the revolutionary change has, of course, been in the freedom accorded to girls. Where they are educated to self-support, as are their brothers, they can no longer be held to the submissive rôle of dependents. In proportion as women are regarded as responsible and independent, complacent acceptance of the "double standard" becomes impossible. The old hypocrisies and subterfuges of traditional morality are repudiated: the supposed necessity for buttressing monogamy with prostitution and casual relationships, on the part of men; and the hard and fast distinction between *good* and *bad* women, the good being defined as those with no sex experience, or with sex experience wholly within marriage, and the bad as those damaged beyond restoration through extra-marital experience.

Under such circumstances, and in view of the fact that, in certain of its phases, the women's movement involved a grasping at all privileges which had hitherto been reserved for men alone, it is no wonder that many women and girls should claim the same freedom for sex experimentation as had always been tacitly allowed to men. The increasing effectiveness of contraception, and the spread of information on this subject, facilitated the acceptance of such an attitude. Definite evidence is available in support of the impression that sexual experience on the part of girls and women, before and outside of marriage, is a striking feature of to-day. Definite evidence also exists as to a marked increase in experimentation among young people. There is, of course, danger of exaggeration; there has always been a certain amount of sexual laxity, but until very recently most of the older people have been entirely ignorant of what has been going on. To-day, however, there is such frank interest in sex on the part of the young, such freedom of conversation and of association with the other sex, that those who are still bound by the old taboos interpret the situation as a complete abandonment of all restraint.

Frequency of Sex Experimentation According to Available Studies. The studies hitherto made have been very largely based on the experiences of the better educated, more self-conscious, and sophisticated members of the community, those who answer questionnaires and consult gynecologists and psychiatrists.[1] But, as case histories of clients of the birth-control clinics are analyzed, data are being obtained which are more representative of the general public.[2] Nor can we overlook the evidence obtained by Judge Lindsey on the basis of his twenty-seven years' experience as a juvenile court judge in Denver.[3] He concluded that at least

[1] For example, Hamilton's study made for the Bureau of Social Hygiene, in 1927, covered 100 married men and 100 married women, all belonging to cultured urban groups. Results of this study were published in *A Research in Marriage* (1929), and also in popular form in collaboration with Macgowan, *What Is Wrong with Marriage* (1929).

[2] Moreover, as Yarros points out on the basis of her wide experience as medical director of birth-control clinics, "the sentiments and ideas," of the intelligent and cultivated, "gradually trickle down to the culturally inferior strata of society." *Modern Woman and Sex*, p. 29. Many agencies to-day disseminate at least a "half-knowledge" among the general public, and patients at birth-control clinics are demanding definite information on all these matters, so that the tendencies noted among the sophisticated minority may be more significant than is at first apparent.

[3] Presented in popular form with the collaboration of Evans in *The Revolt of Modern Youth* (1925). See too "The Promise and Peril of the New Freedom" in *Woman's Coming of Age*, and "Wisdom for Parents" in *Sex in Civilization*, both edited by

one high school girl in every ten has her "feet set on more or less perilous paths." As to high school boys, he believed at least 50% had had sex experience, chiefly in the last two years of school. Definite figures have been obtained from a number of questionnaire studies. In summarizing the results obtained from ten such studies, six of the sex conduct of men, and four of the sex conduct of women, Harvey found the approximate percentage of pre-marital intercourse to be 35% for men and 15% for women.[1] In Hamilton's study 54% of the men and 35% of the women reported pre-marital intercourse. About a third of both the men and women reported pre-marital intercourse with their future marriage partners, but only fourteen of the women as against twenty-four of the men had had relations with individuals other than those they later married. Hamilton's analysis of sex behavior, according to date of birth, suggests that illicit relations among women are on the increase, while there is a decrease for men.[2] Increasing freedom of experimentation among women is also indicated by Dickinson's comparison of three groups of patients. Of a group studied in 1895, 20% had had sex experience before marriage; of a group in 1929–1930, $33\frac{1}{3}\%$; and of a group in 1934, 50%.[3]

"*Petting.*" There is some divergence of opinion as to the propriety and desirability of "petting," even in its "lighter"

Schmalhausen and Calverton. In one two-year period, for example, 769 girls between fourteen and seventeen consulted him, and altogether he won the confidence of thousands of high school boys and girls. Through these he heard of many more who did not come to him, either because illicit sexual relationships had not involved them in trouble, or because they were sophisticated and self-reliant enough to cope with the situation themselves. Many of the girls who did not seek his advice had recourse to abortion. Judge Lindsey estimated that about 5% of the girls who entered into irregular relations became pregnant.

[1] "Some Statistics Derived from Recent Questionnaire Studies Relative to Human Sexual Behavior," *Journal of Social Psychology*, Vol. III (1932), pp. 97–100. The studies made by Peck and Wells of two groups of college graduate men, of median age 23, showed percentages of 35 and 37; *Mental Hygiene*, Vol. VII (1923), pp. 697–714 and Vol. IX (1925), pp. 502–520.

[2] It appears from this and the other studies that, owing to the increasing laxity of girls, young men engage in sex experimentation far more with girls of their own status, and a decreasing number have recourse to prostitutes.

[3] R. L. Dickinson and Lura Beam, *The Single Woman: A Medical Study in Sex Education* (1934). A significant difference was found in pre-marital experience according to social status. "Girls and women in personal service tend to have a relation brief and physical, with undue proportion of pregnancy and venereal disease. Among clerical workers there is a considerable frequency of unfortunate outcome, but a longer period of constant devotion than in the first group and less demand for medical treatment or abortion. With the professional women and students, it is almost altogether a case of the one-and-only man, . . . with venereal infection absent and conception rare." *Sex Life of the Unmarried Adult* (ed. Wile, The Vanguard Press, 1934), pp. 200–201.

forms.[1] Judge Lindsey is emphatic in his condemnation, pointing to the harmful mental and physical effects of over-stimulation, and the fact that petting so often leads to further intimacies, and in a large number of cases to intercourse.[2] There are others, including college students, who defend the "lighter" forms of petting as providing sublimation for sexual impulses. Floyd Dell further contends that petting is desirable as a form of experimental courtship, an educational process which should eliminate many marriage failures, for courtship is "the private search for and finding of a mate, . . . a person with whom one can be deeply enough in love to warrant the begetting of children."[3]

Dell's advocacy of petting has been widely criticized. It has been pointed out that sexual desire may become fixated at this level, and that the emotional barrier against carrying petting too far may later be hard to overcome. In so far as this is the case, petting, far from providing a preparation for normal sex coöperation, may make it difficult for the individual to find physical and emotional satisfaction in marriage. In the absence of decisive knowledge, the constructive policy suggested by the Harts offers undeniably wholesome advice to young people: "Concentrate, in your social relations with persons of the opposite sex, upon joint activities which are keenly enjoyable, but not sentimental, slushy or erotic. Refuse to engage ever, with anybody, in spooning, petting, or necking for the mere sake of the physical thrill. . . . The thrill, adventure and creative stimulus of friendships between men and women, when the element of physical sex is held under voluntary self-discipline, make the allure of exclusively physical exploration seem crude and curtailed." Accordingly Mr. and Mrs. Hart very wisely advise postponing any form of caress until it may be the wholehearted expression of deep feeling for a real comrade.[4]

[1] This term seems susceptible of different interpretations; sometimes it means kissing; and sometimes it covers various stages of more intimate caresses, stopping only short of actual intercourse.

[2] It is particularly difficult for young people to exercise control over their conduct if they have been drinking. Petting is then definitely dangerous.

[3] *Love in the Machine Age* (1930), p. 55.

[4] Hornell Hart and E. B. Hart, *Personality and the Family* (D. C. Heath and Company, 1935), pp. 81–82. In the same way, Harrison S. Elliott and Grace Loucks Elliott, in their counseling manual, *Solving Personal Problems* (1936), suggest "that in their relations with the opposite sex, adolescents should engage in sexually releasing rather than sexually stimulating activities." In the former type, attention is focused on the activity and their enjoyment in sharing it; in the latter, "the whole attention of the couple is focused upon themselves, and they are engaged in practices with each other which set off the sex emotions." Pp. 153–154. Dancing, it is pointed out, may be of either type.

THE INSTABILITY OF THE MODERN FAMILY 545

It is to be hoped, indeed, that the present prevalence of casual physical intimacies between young men and women may prove to be a passing phase, natural enough in view of past restrictions and the absence of adequate sex education and preparation for marriage. Moreover, as women and girls become more conscious of their responsibility for formulating constructive moral policies, it should be possible for them to take the lead in upholding a single standard; not in the sense of imitating the sexual freedom which was formerly the prerogative of men alone, but through their serious and intelligent attitude towards sex, as intimately bound up with the richest and most precious of life's experiences. To lay stress on the peculiar responsibility of women for the upholding of high standards of sexual behavior in no way indicates any return to traditional sentimentality in reference to the superior "purity" and "goodness" of women. Sex has greater *fundamental* significance for women than it has for men, because it is they who bear children. Upon them, therefore, rests the greater responsibility for the development and maintenance of constructive codes, all the more so since, in general, the physical urge of sex is less likely to be insistent in women, and self-control is therefore less difficult for them than for men.

Pre-nuptial Mating. It must not be imagined that the younger generation is without its own codes.[1] There are many signs of the development of responsible feeling among college students, both men and women, that augurs well for the future; provided pre-parental education becomes more adequate and widespread.[2]

Every effort should be bent not only to make of marriage a positive goal, but to facilitate early marriage. This does not mean hasty marriage, but it means that young people should not have to face indefinite postponement. Dell believes that marriage should take place when the partners are emotionally fit for it, independent of their economic circumstances. Under present conditions many young people find themselves unable to marry for a long time after they have become engaged. During the depression the decline in the marriage rate from 1930 to 1934, compared with 1925 to 1929, indicated the indefinite post-

[1] Noticeable in the present attitude of girls is their tolerance of sexual experimentation on the part of their friends, even when they themselves think it undesirable. P. Blanchard and C. Manasses, *New Girls for Old* (1930), Chapter V; several unpublished studies of college girls are in agreement on this point as is the study of college students by Dorothy Dunbar Bromley and Florence Haxton Britten, which is to appear before long in book form.

[2] The assumed sophistication of many young people to-day is no sign of their enlightenment, but rather, in many cases, of a superficial and distorted half-knowledge.

ponement of marriage on the part of at least 2,000,000 young people.

It is, therefore, not in the least surprising that there has apparently been a marked increase in pre-nuptial mating, and that the developing codes of the day draw a distinct line between promiscuity and pre-marital intercourse, as a prelude to the more permanent arrangement of matrimony.[1] Dr. Dickinson finds from his records of pre-marital sex practice that the full marital privilege is adopted on the average only after a full year of increasing demonstration of affection. He holds that this "pattern of progressive youthful solution of sex life" contrasts very favorably with the traditional standard procedure. Such young couples, he adds, feel themselves fully justified, but "grieve at the need of furtive love-making."[2]

Everything points to the desirability of marriage for young people deeply in love and well adjusted to one another, at the time when they reach the natural climax of their relationship.[3] A relationship which is publicly sanctioned, even if carried out in opposition to the wishes of parents or relatives upon whom the young people are dependent, will escape the many undesirable features of clandestine pre-nuptial mating. Love-making which must be furtive is less secure. Not only must pregnancy be avoided at all costs, but it is less easily avoided than in the settled and favorable circumstances of married life. Fear of social disapproval may bring with it a sense of guilt which is destructive of the stability of the relationship. When marriage is long delayed, the emotional energy of the earlier stages of intimacy may subside when not followed, as in normal marriage, by a growing absorption in the shared interests of family life.

[1] Yarros finds that there is a "growing willingness of engaged couples to indulge in sexual intercourse. The phenomenon is not entirely new but . . . the spirit surrounding it is radically different." These young people are not radicals, they believe in marriage and intend to marry when it becomes possible, but "they do not think it morally wrong to cohabit prior to marriage." *Op. cit.*, p. 30.

[2] *Sex Life of the Unmarried Adult* (ed. Wile), p. 205. It would appear, from these accounts, that the younger generation of men no longer feel that a woman willing to cohabit before marriage has put herself outside the class of "decent women." On the other hand, Dr. Olga Knopf states that the attitudes of the past still persist to so great an extent, that engagements are far more likely to culminate in marriage where a woman has refrained from pre-nuptial intercourse with her lover. *Women on Their Own* (1935), p. 123. It is suggestive too that, in Hamilton's study, those men and women who had had pre-marital intercourse with their future partners were below the average in happiness.

[3] At present, if they married, most young people would be severely penalized economically or through the loss of educational, business, and professional opportunities. Suggestions made in the last chapter for the facilitation of early marriage for eugenic reasons are equally apposite here.

Under such conditions it is not to be wondered at that prenuptial mating frequently has an unfortunate outcome.

Circumstances Accentuating Present Trends. A number of circumstances have conspired in recent years to accentuate the breakdown of traditional morality. Not only have large numbers of young people been forced to postpone marriage indefinitely, but for many others, in particular young women, there seems no certainty of future marriage. When, in addition, such young people, already out of accord with their parents' attitudes, are uprooted from their home surroundings and live in single rooms in the crowded loneliness of the cities, where nobody knows them and they are free from the pressure of local opinion, unconventional sex behavior is likely to be very frequent.[1] There is, in any case, an accentuation of present trends in the more sophisticated groups in urban communities, and it is probably of these that Dr. Wile is speaking when he notes "a growing acceptance of sexual rights and practices among the older group of the unmarried."[2] Olga Knopf's discussion of the desirability of "complete love affairs" for older unmarried women not only bears witness to their frequency, but to a revolution in social attitudes.[3]

Extra-marital Relations on the Part of the Married. Among the married as well as the unmarried the revolt against traditional morality has been pronounced in its effects. Hamilton's study disclosed that not only 28% of the men, but 24% of the women had committed adultery. It is perhaps even more significant that in this group of 200 married men and women, only ten men and sixteen women considered adultery absolutely unjustifiable.[4] Dell's criticism of what he calls the "polite adultery, indulged in by sophisticated would-be ultra-moderns," is interesting. Far from being a new adjustment necessitated by changed conditions, he holds that a great majority of such extra-marital liaisons, often carried on with the knowledge of husband or wife who pride themselves on their absence of jealousy, are simply "stale old patriarchal compromises," relics of the time when marriages were arranged; "only when biological love is a social

[1] An extreme case is the casual promiscuity to be found among the thousands of young transients who were rendered homeless by the depression; see Thomas Minehan, *Boy and Girl Tramps of America* (1934).

[2] *The Sex Life of the Unmarried Adult*, p. 51.

[3] *Women on Their Own*, pp. 131–133.

[4] *What Is Wrong with Marriage*, p. 24; 5 men and 16 women considered it very hard to justify, while 69 men and 55 women considered it justifiable under some circumstances, and 16 men and 13 women believed it needed little or no justification.

crime, is adultery poetic." The genuine modern, Dell holds, cannot be satisfied with "such evasive and irresponsible relationships, such tame substitutes for the realities of love, such patchwork arrangements to console people for the emotional deficiencies of unsatisfying marriages." They conform to the patriarchal pattern by making possible the continuance of unsatisfactory marriages. Extra-marital relationships *may* be justified, but only when they are serious in affording "an experimental approach to permanent, socially recognized mating."[1]

PROSTITUTION AND VENEREAL DISEASE

Changes in Public Opinion with Regard to Prostitution. The revolt against traditional morality has many undesirable and dangerous features, but it also involves a wholesome resentment against hypocrisy, and a total rejection of the so-called morality which held that the "protection" of the virtuous woman, within legal marriage, was of such paramount importance as to be worth the ruin of countless other women, reviled and outcast from society because of their use as instruments of sexual gratification.

There are many who still hold this view, which ironically enough has been that of official Christianity, at least since the time of St. Augustine.[2] Even in Lecky's famous passage, written in 1869, the *necessity* of the sacrifice of many women is still taken for granted; but traditional convictions are obviously in conflict with a more humanitarian standpoint.[3] Lecky goes so far as to criticize the severity of the English attitude towards

[1] *Op. cit.*, pp. 70–85.

[2] According to St. Augustine, society would be overwhelmed with capricious lust, were prostitution suppressed. St. Thomas Aquinas said: "Prostitution in towns is like the sewer in the palace; take away the sewers and the palace becomes an impure and stinking place." In Protestant England the same argument was restated by Bernard de Mandeville in his *Remarks to Fable of the Bees* (1714), pp. 93 *et seq.* "If courtesans and strumpets were to be prosecuted with as much rigor as some silly people would have it, what locks or bars would be sufficient to preserve the honor of our wives and daughters. . . . It is manifest that there is a necessity of sacrificing one part of womanhood to preserve the other, and prevent a filthiness of a more heinous nature. From which I think I may justly conclude that chastity must be supported by incontinence, and the best of virtues want the assistance of the worst of vices."

[3] To appreciate to the full the change of attitude which has occurred, this passage should be read in full. It concludes as follows: "But for her, the unchallenged purity of countless happy homes would be polluted, and not a few who, in the pride of their untempted chastity, think of her with an indignant shudder, would have known the agony of remorse and despair. On that one degraded and ignoble form are concentrated the passions what might have filled the world with shame. She remains, while creeds and civilizations rise and fall, the eternal priestess of humanity, blasted for the sins of the people." *History of European Morals*, Vol. II, pp. 282–283.

"female frailty." His remarks on the transmission of venereal diseases by guilty husbands to innocent wives and offspring are, to the modern mind, tragically ironical, in view of his earlier statement as to prostitution saving the "purity" of homes from pollution.

Schopenhauer was quite right in speaking of prostitutes as "human sacrifices on the altar of monogamy," if by monogamy is meant the traditional form of patriarchal marriage, bound up as it has been with ideas of property, with the deferring of marriage for men and the strict protection of "virtuous" women. As an offset to this system, irresponsible relationships of men with their social inferiors are very generally condoned, and prostitution is taken entirely for granted as providing an outlet for the sexual needs of unmarried men, and as affording diversion and variety for married men, whose virtuous and often frigid wives do not satisfy them. Public opinion had begun to change among enlightened people long before the recent more spectacular revolt. An event of the highest significance occurred in 1875, when the first Congress of the International Federation for the Suppression of the State Regulation of Prostitution met in Geneva. Josephine Butler was one of the leading promoters, and for the first time sexual problems were openly discussed by men and women, and women openly rebelled against the injustice of visiting contempt on the prostitute alone when her male client is exempt. It was agreed that regulation of prostitution for hygienic reasons was too one-sided to be effective.

Developments in America. Another landmark in the movement for modification of the double standard was an international conference held in Paris in 1902. It was stated at that time that continence was entirely compatible with health. An international agreement with regard to the prevention of diseases connected with prostitution was signed by thirteen nations in 1904, and later by others. The American delegate to the Paris conference, Dr. Prince Morrow, returned to this country convinced of the need for sex education. He was influential in the formation, in 1910, of the American Federation for Sex Hygiene, which, in 1914, merged with the American Vigilance Association to form the American Social Hygiene Association with its comprehensive interest in the problems of prostitution, venereal disease, sex education, and preparation for marriage.

Between 1910 and 1917, forty-three investigations, in American cities, revealed the shocking prevalence of organized vice, protected as it was by the police and other officials who shared in its profits. Public indifference was in some measure dispelled. Another influential factor in the formation of enlightened attitudes was the publication of Flexner's book, *Prostitution in Europe*, the result of a survey made under the Bureau of Social Hygiene, organized in 1911 for the study of conditions in America and Europe.[1] The movement against non-toleration of commercialized vice was given even greater impetus by the campaign to prevent venereal diseases in the army during the World War. Shortly before the entry of the United States into the War, the American Medical Association declared continence to be compatible with health and the most effective preventive of venereal disease. Partly to keep the soldiers fit, and partly to reconcile parents to conscription, the government accepted this principle, and the Commission of Training Camp Activities made the following announcement, endorsed by the Surgeon General: "It used to be thought that the sex organs had to be used if they were to be kept healthy. This is a lie."[2]

The Campaign against the International Traffic in Women and Children. The twentieth century has also seen a concerted movement for the suppression of the international traffic in women and children for immoral purposes. Josephine Butler long ago pointed out that the licensing of prostitution in segregated districts created markets for the white-slave traffic. At the turn of the century concerted action began to be taken for its suppression, and an international congress was held in London in 1913. Meanwhile an investigation by the Immigration Commission revealed that large numbers of girls were brought into the United States for immoral purposes, and the Mann Act or White Slave Traffic Act was passed, in 1910, forbidding the international or interstate transportation of females for immoral purposes. When the League of Nations came into existence in 1920, Article 23 (C) of the Covenant stated that members "will entrust the League with the general supervision over the execution of agreements with regard to the traffic in women and children." An international conference was held, and an agreement was ratified by thirty-four states. In 1927, the results

[1] "Prostitution," Dr. Flexner pointed out, "is a concept involving two persons. Logic and justice alike require that both parties alike be considered as equal partners in the act; and in no respect is it more completely impossible to omit either of the two essential factors from the reckoning than in the matter of disease. Society has chosen to overlook the man; but nature has righted the balance by impartially distributing disease and suffering; nor will she permit herself to be outwitted by any one-sided scheme, even though it be far more extensive and efficient than regulation has thus far anywhere been." *Op. cit.* (The Century Company, 1914), p. 264.

[2] Quoted Breckenridge, *Women in the Twentieth Century*, p. 207.

of an expert two-year investigation were submitted to the League.[1]

One result of this investigation was the corroboration of the contention that the existence of licensed houses provided an incentive to the national and international traffic. The situation with regard to licensing has improved in the twentieth century. At the beginning of the century the cities of France, Belgium, Austro-Hungary, Russia, Italy, Spain, Portugal, of two Scandinavian countries, and of most of Germany tolerated licensed houses of prostitution, as did most cities in the Orient where there is more open acceptance of prostitution than in Europe or America. By 1930, there were thirty countries including Great Britain and the United States which had no system of licensing. In Great Britain, Holland, Switzerland, and the United States, there is no registration or examination of prostitutes, and public health is more effectively protected by means of venereal clinics.

The Effect of the Prevailing Sexual Laxity on Prostitution. The decline in brothel prostitution has been brought about not only through the growth of humanitarian attitudes, but also through the greater freedom in sexual relationships in which no commercial considerations are involved. No longer does the extreme stigma fall on women and girls who engage in extra-marital relationships; it is reserved for the single type who indulge in sex intercourse promiscuously with strangers for an obvious cash payment. Where the great majority of prostitutes were formerly of this one type, there is now no hard and fast line between the prostitute and women who are socially accepted. Reitman distinguishes eleven categories of women who should technically be called prostitutes because they profit economically, either directly or indirectly, from illicit sexual relationships.[2] Reckless

[1] This investigation was financed by the American Bureau of Social Hygiene. At the first meeting of the League of Nations Commission on the Traffic in Women and Children, Grace Abbott, Chief of the Children's Bureau, had requested that such an investigation be made and had offered to secure funds for its prosecution in the United States. Her work at Hull House as superintendent of the Immigrant's Protective League and four years in charge of the state Immigration Bureau had made her familiar with the dangers threatening the immigrant girl. The investigators visited some of the chief cities in twenty-eight countries, in Europe, Northern Africa, North and Central America and on the Atlantic coast of South America. South America has become the main objective of the traffic from Europe, the headquarters of which appears to be France. The Argentine is a party to none of the international agreements, and there is a constant flow of prostitutes to Buenos Ayres and every part of the Argentine. Brazil agreed to the conventions and in its modified penal code makes procuration and brothel-keeping an offence. Nevertheless, ostentatious brothels abound in Rio de Janeiro.

[2] *The Second Oldest Profession* (1931). These eleven categories are arranged in slightly modified form by Mabel Elliott and Frances Merrill in *Social Disorganization* (1934), pp. 182–183, and quoted by Joseph K. Folsom, *The Family* (1934), p. 400.

describes the decline in brothel prostitution as accompanied by the rise of the cabaret, road house, and night club and by the increase in the class of independent, clandestine prostitutes who want the life without its stigma and hardship.[1]   Numbers of such semi-professional girls can be reached by telephone from resorts, many of them being nominally engaged in other occupations.[2]

Dr. Dickinson presents a rather more hopeful angle of the situation when he attributes the decline in prostitution in part to the fact that contraceptives have put the control of childbearing in the hands of the wife, who need no longer refuse her husband for fear of pregnancy. For the same reason and because of the greater freedom customary, a young man unable as yet to marry his fiancée is less likely to resort to a prostitute.[3] Dr. Yarros, after visiting European clinics and prisons in 1925, reported keener desire to suppress prostitution, but deplored the lack, both in the United States and abroad, of fundamentally constructive work looking towards the removal of underlying causes and towards the rehabilitation of girls who have gone in for promiscuity.[4]

The Control of Venereal Diseases. Unfortunately, in spite of the development of effective methods for coping with venereal diseases, and the combined efforts of public health agencies and organizations such as the American Social Hygiene Association, the prevalence of these diseases is appalling.[5] Dr. Thomas Parran, Surgeon General of the United States Public Health Service, has estimated that 10% of the inhabitants of the United States have been infected with syphilis at some time, while gonorrhea is at least twice as prevalent.[6] Syphilis disables half a million a year, and ranks with cancer, tuberculosis, and

[1] *Vice in Chicago* (1932).

[2] In commenting on the driving of prostitution underground in Middletown by 1925, the Lynds report a remark of the juvenile court judge to the effect that the "automobile has become a house of prostitution on wheels." In *Middletown in Transition*, pp. 162–164, they say that the automobile was, ten years later, playing a more and more important part in the informal type of prostitution which had become even more prevalent in the depression years. But they found, as well, that they had much underestimated the extent of prostitution in Middletown in their earlier study in 1925.

[3] He reports that on a visit to fourteen countries, in 1926, he heard everywhere of the dwindling business of the prostitute, her chief remaining clients being old unmarried men. *Sex Life of the Unmarried Adult* (ed. Wile), p. 208.

[4] In Chapter XX the efforts at rehabilitation being made in Russia are given brief consideration.

[5] The discovery of the cause of syphilis, in 1905, resulted in the development within the next six years of exact methods of diagnosis and of methods of treatment which, if begun early enough and continued long enough, would make the disease rare and perhaps lead to its eventual extinction.

[6] "The Next Great Plague to Go," *Survey Graphic*, Vol. XXV (July, 1936), pp. 404–411. The conservative estimate of the American Social Hygiene Association is to

pneumonia as one of the four great killing diseases. Adequate treatment in the first stage effects a cure in about 86% of the cases, while only a short delay causes a drop in cures to about 65%. As always, however, the great obstacle to the spread of information, and to the use of modern methods in the control of venereal diseases, is the "conspiracy of silence" with regard to them. Fortunately within the past two years there has been marked progress in this respect.[1] It is essential that the whole problem be brought into the open as a major problem of hygiene.

Great Britain and the Scandinavian countries have demonstrated what may be accomplished towards the eradication of syphilis. In the Scandinavian countries, all cases must be reported and must take treatment, which is available *free* to *all*. If desirable for the protection of others, they must be hospitalized. There is abundant publicity as to the venereal clinics, and everyone realizes the nature of the problem. As a result syphilis has been virtually eliminated. In Great Britain there is no compulsion, the emphasis being placed on abundant free treatment, and there has been a 50% decrease in the prevalence of syphilis since 1920. It is quite obvious, then, that *immediate* humane treatment is the essential, which can only be secured by making free clinic service of high quality available to all.

Educational measures are of primary significance; all young people should know the truth about syphilis and gonorrhea, know how to avoid them, and what to do if they become infected. It should be made very clear that risk of infection is *always* entailed by promiscuous relationships. It is generally known that very few prostitutes escape infection, but the risk involved in all forms of sexual freedom is often overlooked.[2] The rate of venereal diseases remains higher for men, indicating that pros-

the effect that 2% of children, 7 to 12% of men, and 4 to 6% of women have syphilis. See M. J. Exner, *What You Should Know about Syphilis and Gonorrhea* (American Social Hygiene Association, 1937).

[1] The newspapers now print accounts of conferences, and the word syphilis is used in headlines, which was never the case before. An anti-syphilis campaign was launched early in 1938, February 2 having been designated as National Social Hygiene Day. Perhaps few now would fully endorse the policy of the Boston dispensary, in 1796, when it announced that it excluded from treatment "persons suffering from venereal diseases or from the effects of alcohol, as being victims of their own sensual indulgences." (*Recent Social Trends*, Vol. II, p. 1072.) But the old moralist tradition of disease as a punishment for sin is undoubtedly still strong in the case of venereal diseases, irrespective of the hideous injustice so often involved.

[2] Venereal clinics and physicians in private practice report that many of their patients become infected through association with clandestine prostitutes, girls who though not professionals are not reluctant to indulge in promiscuity, sometimes for pay, sometimes simply for the sake of pleasure or temporary companionship.

titution, whether professional or not, is still the chief source of infection. But the further spread of venereal infection among unmarried women may be expected if there is an increase in sexual irregularities.[1] At present venereal disease is most frequently pre-marital in men, but *post-marital* in women, indicating that most women are infected innocently.[2] With fuller knowledge of facts and the far greater frankness which now prevails among young men and women, it should become a matter of course for an engaged couple to be fully cognizant of each other's physical fitness for marriage and procreation. A sense of shared responsibility in these vital concerns renders utterly impossible the older attitudes of indifference and evasion in connection with so great a menace to successful family life.

The Causes of Prostitution. All measures which diminish promiscuity, and in particular those which reduce prostitution and commercialized vice, operate towards the eradication of venereal diseases. Legal and protective measures can only become efficient in so far as they are directed towards the elimination of the causes of prostitution, and are concerned not with the punishment, but with the rehabilitation of its victims. These causes are fundamentally the same as have already been discussed in connection with juvenile delinquency and with unmarried motherhood. Not only is sex delinquency very largely due to factors operative in childhood and youth, but the majority of prostitutes are young, most being in their early twenties.

In Miner's study of 1,000 prostitutes over a period of nine years, she found the following reasons for prostitution, given by the girls: influence of procurers, 25.6%; bad home conditions, 21%; amusement and bad companions, 18.7%; economic and occupational factors, 17%, and personal reasons, 17%.[3] Bad home

[1] It has been estimated that a young woman who "picks up" a stranger as a sex companion in an American city takes one chance in twelve of exposing herself through association with a man under treatment for venereal disease. Hart, *Personality and the Family*, p. 59.

[2] Undoubtedly many men who infect their wives believe themselves cured, particularly in the case of syphilis, where infection may persist for years even with treatment. In the case of gonorrhea there may be ignorance of the fact that its results are far more serious for women than for men. On the other hand, there have been innumerable cases where the diseased husband "takes a chance," and where under the seal of professional secrecy a doctor aware of his condition has refrained from revealing it to the bride or her parents. Needless to say that by modern ethical standards such conduct is utterly inexcusable.

[3] *Slavery of Prostitution*, pp. 2–7. All of these factors receive abundant illustration in case studies of delinquent women, such, for example, as the Gluecks' study of *Five Hundred Delinquent Women* (1934), and the cases so conveniently assembled in the chapter on the demoralization of girls, in *The Unadjusted Girl* (1923), by W. I. Thomas.

conditions were the fundamental factor in most cases, it was found. Many girls admitted to having been assaulted or seduced at the age of twelve or thirteen by men lodging with their families. In even more tragic cases, an uncle, older brother, or father had victimized a girl. The situation is most dangerous when fathers and, even worse, mothers are vicious or criminal. Young girls accustomed from their earliest days to drunkenness, obscenity, and immorality have no chance to develop wholesome attitudes and habits.

In numbers of cases the parents may not be bad in the usual sense, but they are overstrict and fail to understand their children. As we have seen, such a situation is common among foreign families who wish their daughters to conform to Old World standards. Many of these girls, who have been driven into rebellion and waywardness, have been cast off by their parents and easily led into a career of prostitution. Over three-fifths of the girls in Miner's study were of foreign parentage.

One-fifth, who were of native parentage, had drifted to the city from poor homes in small communities. And in the fact that such numbers of girls come from the country or small towns to seek employment in the cities is to be found one of the reasons for the magnitude of urban prostitution. They may fail to find any job at all, or if they do they may be very poorly paid or employed in one of the trades full of danger for young girls, such as those of waitresses in cafés, chambermaids in hotels, manicurists, models, chorus girls. Home influences no longer restrain them. No one knows them, and they are lonely and longing for gaiety and romance. Even more lonely are the girls who go into domestic service, an occupation whose dangers are evident from the fact that between 37% and 60% of professional prostitutes have been servant girls.[1]

The problems of urban prostitution are also due to the fact that all conditions dangerous to the welfare of youth are more prevalent in the teeming life of the cities. Moreover, the anonymity of city life enables girls to escape detection, particularly when their promiscuity is of the clandestine type. Actual want or hunger is rarely reported as a reason for entering prostitution; but very low wages are a contributory factor since they deprive the working girl of the only things which seem to her to make life worth while: pleasure, gaiety, excitement, and romance, and most of all the pretty clothes, the silk stockings, and finery

[1] Thomas, op. cit., p. 118.

which she feels essential to her prestige.[1] Although there are exceptions in the case of some over-sexed girls, the consensus of expert opinion is in agreement that prostitutes are "not usually impelled to their life by motives of sensuality."[2] Finally, all studies of delinquent women reveal that a considerable proportion are mentally subnormal, many so retarded as to be feeble-minded. Low mentality is, however, not so much a *cause*, as a contributory factor taken in conjunction with other factors. It is also significant that the majority of prostitutes have had scarcely any educational opportunities.

Obviously the measures already discussed as necessary for child welfare would go far towards the elimination of prostitution, since more and more girls would be prevented from entering upon a life so repugnant to the normal woman. The same measures should also decrease the demand for the services of prostitutes, a matter of great importance, since demand, here as elsewhere, creates supply. So long, however, as obstacles are placed in the way of early marriage, and monogamous marriage fails to satisfy men, sometimes through no fault of the wife, but because of a desire for sexual variety, the demand will persist for women who are willing to enter into transient, even casual relationships. Whatever the future may bring, it is much to be hoped that prostitution in the old sense will disappear, and the mercantile element will entirely vanish from sexual relationships, which, even when irregular and extra-marital, need not involve exploitation of the less fortunate and that denial of personality to the woman which is the worst travesty of love.

Commercialized Vice. Meanwhile commercialized vice in the great cities still presents well-nigh insuperable problems. The recent depression is believed, indeed, to have led to an increase in vice. Investigation in New York and Brooklyn led to the disclosure, in 1936, of an organized "vice ring" which employed between one and two thousand women in some 200 houses, in operations involving at least $12,000,000 a year.[3] Such facts

---

[1] After examining 3,000 girl delinquents Thomas concluded: "The beginning of delinquency in girls is usually an impulse to get amusement, pretty clothes, favorable notice, distinction, freedom in the larger world which presents so many allurements and comparisons. . . . Their sex is used as a condition of the realization of other wishes. It is their capital." *Ibid.*, p. 109.

[2] Havelock Ellis, *op. cit.*, pp. 261 *et seq.* The young girls examined by Thomas had usually become "wild" *before* the development of sexual desire, and sex feeling was not aroused by their casual relations: "intercourse is something submitted to with reluctance and embarrassment, and something [they are] glad to be over with." *Op. cit.*, p.109.

[3] *New York Times*, Feb. 3, 1936. A number of men operated a system whereby the women were shifted weekly from place to place. Girls were both recruited in New

would seem to substantiate the contention of Magistrate Anna M. Kross of the New York Women's Court, when, in an official report to the Mayor in March, 1935, she denounced the whole system of combating vice as wrong. The Women's Court, established in the hope of protecting New York from the moral and physical danger of commercialized vice, had become, she contended, the focal point for racketeering and corruption growing out of prostitution. Even those lawyers and bondsmen who are honest at first cannot resist the pressure of the system. The prostitutes themselves never get a square deal; and the whole criminal-legal handling of prostitution is futile, proceeding as it does against the victims rather than against the structure of commercialized vice. Magistrate Kross therefore recommended the abolition of the Women's Court and the treatment of prostitutes on a medical-sociological basis.[1]

The League of Women Voters believes that commercialized vice can be eliminated only if *three* laws are passed in all states and public opinion demands their enforcement: *Anti-Prostitution* laws which provide for the arrest and trial of those who *profit* by the business of prostitution, and also for the arrest of *men* as well as women who commit acts of prostitution; *Injunction and Abatement* laws which provide a tool for the use of citizens, if officials will not enforce the Anti-Prostitution law; and *Ouster* laws, providing for the removal of officials who neglect their duty.[2]

York and imported from other cities in a number of states. Their earnings averaged from $150 to $300 a week, but they kept only $30 to $50. The balance went in exorbitant payments to managers, to maids, and for board and lodging. Many girls lived in their own homes reporting to managers between 11 A.M. and 3 P.M. and remaining twelve hours for six days a week. One doctor connected with the vice ring admitted to having received between $20,000 to $30,000 a year; he performed two or three illegal operations every week. On July 7, 1936, the conviction of the head of the ring and of his henchmen was secured through the efforts of a special committee headed by Thomas Dewey, now District Attorney of New York County.

[1] This should involve "an informal tribunal consisting of a doctor, a psychiatrist and a lawyer," and the adoption of individualized hospital and institutional care for prostitutes instead of prison sentences. "Socially trained, well-paid medical workers" should be "empowered to apprehend all persons engaged in the practice of prostitution, and, therefore, liable to have contracted venereal diseases." There should also be "intensification of the propaganda for the prevention of venereal disease, intelligent sex and mental hygiene guidance for the entire community, with especial attention to the needs of young people." Finally, she recommended the adoption of "a scientific modern viewpoint which will seek the fundamentals of the problem, and make an honest endeavor to reach the causative factors of this social manifestation as well as treat the symptoms." *New York Times*, March 8, 9, 1935.

[2] Ann Webster, *Three Laws* (League of Women Voters, 1926).

MARRIAGE TRENDS

A brief statement of recent marriage trends is a necessary preliminary to a discussion of divorce, since each divorce indicates public recognition of the failure of a marriage. Ogburn's study of the census figures, from 1890 to 1920, showed a steady increase in marriage where all ages are considered together.[1] With lowered birth- and death-rates there had been an increase in the groups over twenty-five years of age, where the majority are married, relative to the groups fifteen to twenty-four where marriage is less frequent. The married percentage of the whole population over fifteen would therefore be higher, even if there had been no actual increase in marriage. But such an actual increase was found in the percentage married at any given age in the lower age levels. These two factors accounted for the increase and were sufficient to offset an opposing tendency, namely a decrease in the percentage of married among the older age groups. When the figures of the 1930 census were subjected to similar analysis by Thompson and Whelpton, they too were found to show that the increase in marriage has been mainly at the lower age levels, and that in groups over thirty-five the trend was either stationary or downward.[2]

A suggestion is made by the authors of both these analyses as to the influence of birth control on the tendency to earlier marriage, which has taken place concomitantly with the rapid spread of contraceptive information. A study of 170 cities showed that those with lower birth-rates also had, on the average, larger percentages of young persons married. It seems probable, therefore, that birth control encourages early marriage. Ogburn found, on the other hand, that the employment of women tended slightly to delay marriage and perhaps to discourage it. City life was found to discourage marriage, there being a much higher percentage of women married in rural areas and a larger percentage of single women in the cities. Altogether, however, as Folsom puts it "the United States is a much and an early married country."[3]

[1] E. R. Groves and W. F. Ogburn, *American Marriage and Family Relationships* (1928), Chapter XI.

[2] *Population Trends in the United States* (1933), and *Recent Social Trends*, Vol. I, Chapter I.

[3] Reprinted by permission from *The Family* (p. 327), by J. K. Folsom, published by John Wiley and Sons, Inc. Comparing the United States with European countries, it is found that, not only are there more divorces here than anywhere in Europe exclusive of Russia, but that marriage tends to be earlier in the United States than in Europe, including even France and Italy. In this country the romantic marriage

Nevertheless, nearly a third of the population, fifteen years or over, have never married. The 1930 figures are about 60% married, 8% widowed, 1.2% divorced, and 30% never married. The percentage of single is, of course, much less for the groups over twenty-five, but altogether about one in ten persons who live to be old never marry. An added social importance is given to these data by the fact that there is less death, crime, insanity, and pauperism among the married than among the unmarried, or even the widowed and divorced. Some selection of the more healthy and stable for marriage, or remarriage, may be operative, but on the whole statistics reënforce the common opinion as to the desirability of marriage.

DIVORCE TRENDS

The Increasing Divorce Rate. The largest number of divorces ever granted in one year in the United States was in 1929, when there were 201,468 divorces, or about one every two minutes. Apparently more than one in six marriages end in divorce, and over half a million men, women, and children are directly affected every year by divorce. The common practice is to state a divorce rate in terms of 1,000 population or else to compare the number of divorces in any year with the number of marriages. Cahen points out that, in the first case, no account is taken of age composition of the population, and, in the second, there is no logical connection, since extremely few marriages end in divorce the same year. The ideal statistical unit is *divorce per thousand married population*, a refined rate which in 1929 was 4.05.[1]

In spite of annual fluctuation there has been a steady increase in the divorce rate in every decade since the Civil War. Over a period of sixty-three years the divorce rates increased about five times as rapidly as the married population, being compounded annually at about a 3% rate of increment.[2] All evidence seems to indicate a continuing upward trend.

Changes in Grounds for Divorce. Contrasting the percentages

of free choice is favored, whereas in Europe marriages tend to be made only with the consent, and often at the initiative, of parents.

[1] *Statistical Analysis of American Divorce* (1932). The cruder rates must frequently be used for purposes of comparison with data formulated in terms of such rates.

[2] There have, however, been wide variations in rate between different parts of the country. The Pacific Coast states in 1929 had three times the divorce rate of the Atlantic seaboard; while the central states are intermediate in their rates. These variations are undoubtedly due to a large number of influences to whose effect the West has been particularly subject. Differences in divorce laws do not alone offer sufficient explanation.

which indicated the leading grounds for divorce, in 1928, with those in 1867, the earliest year recorded in American divorce statistics, Cahen found that the principal changes concerned adultery and cruelty. The former ground is only one-fourth as frequent, whereas cruelty is four times as frequent, 47% of divorces in 1928 being granted for cruelty. This change, however, is not due to diminishing unfaithfulness, or to increasing cruelty, or to legal changes, but simply denotes increasing judicial leniency in the interpretation of mental cruelty, so that where it is a permissible ground the publicity of a trial for infidelity is no longer necessary. Most of the states allow cruelty and desertion as grounds, and they are alleged for more than three-fourths of all divorces. On the other hand, New York, the District of Columbia, North Carolina, and Louisiana have such strict laws that practically all their divorces are granted for adultery. In these states the divorce rate is only 20% of the national rate; and Cahen concludes that in all probability about 20% of divorces throughout the country are actually due to adultery, the 9% figure existing merely because it is easier to charge cruelty or desertion where these grounds are permitted.

Concerning the other really *valid* grounds for divorce, in the strict sense of the word, drunkenness would be included with 2%, long-time desertions with 8%, and minor grounds with 3%; making with the 20% for adultery, 33% or one-third of the total divorces. The remaining two-thirds are listed under cruelty, desertion, and neglect to provide. They predominate in the liberal Western regions, are almost always uncontested, and are undoubtedly the result of what is usually termed "mutual incompatibility" in marital life.[1] The legal terms used in divorce suits in no way reveal "the overwhelming prevalence of mutual consent in American divorce."[2]

Differential Divorce Rates. Urban divorce rates appear to be almost double the rural rates. The disparity would moreover be far greater were it not that the cities of industrial states include large numbers of Catholics and also of foreigners, among whom divorce rates are low relative to the native-born, and that the laws of some of these states, such as New York, are stringent. These mitigating factors account for the higher rates in the pre-

---

[1] Only 12% of all divorce suits are contested, the majority of these contests being technical matters concerning questions of alimony and disposition of children, and not being genuine attempts to prevent divorce.

[2] Cahen, *op. cit.*, p. 43.

dominantly agricultural West. In cities all the complex factors undermining the unity of the family are intensified.[1]

The evidence is inconclusive for a relation, either positive or negative, between divorce and the increased employment of women. There has, however, been a definite decrease in the number of wives demanding and receiving alimony.[2] The common opinion that the emancipation of women from dependence on their husbands is a cause of divorce is borne out by the fact that, by 1932, 73.5% of all divorces were granted to wives.[3] It is probably true that women are more ready to dissolve unsatisfactory marriages when they have other means of supporting themselves.[4]

Of particular interest are conclusions drawn by Folsom, from data on college graduates, combined with evidence from the census occupational data and Mowrer's study of family disorganization. Divorce, he says "is not a characteristic of the highest social and educational stratum. It is not prominent among the class which initiates social changes in general. It does not behave like traits which start at the top and gradually filter downward through the social scale. Neither is it a characteristic of the farming class, nor of the immigrant, largely Catholic, laboring classes. It seems to characterize rather that vague area which we call the 'middle classes.' It characterizes persons engaged in domestic and personal service and occupations involving exhibition of the person, frequent absence from home, and close contact with the opposite sex."[5]

[1] Lichtenberger believes the differences in urban and rural rates very likely indicate a greater degree of marriage instability under city conditions, but does not consider the statistics give conclusive evidence when so many other factors are involved. *Divorce* (McGraw-Hill Book Company, 1931), pp. 121–123.

[2] From 1867 to 1886 these figures were 16% and 12%; from 1887 to 1906, 13% and 9%; whereas latest available data give 9% as requesting alimony, and 6% receiving it.

[3] The number has grown steadily through the years since 1867 when it was 64%. In estimating the significance of these figures, it may be noted that in the Pacific states, in the period 1867–1886, the percentage granted was already 74.5%, and that it had only increased to 75.9% in 1929.

[4] There are other causes for the preponderance of wives among those who seek divorce. It is easier to prove cruelty against a man than a woman, and cruelty is the actual ground for 44% of divorces granted to wives and for only 32% granted to husbands. Possibly husbands furnish more occasions for divorce. There are in any case more legal grounds on which a wife may seek divorce, non-support for example. And, finally, since children are usually awarded to the mother, fear of separation from their children would deter more men than women from seeking divorce. That this is the case is indicated by the fact that, while wives obtain somewhat over two-thirds of all divorces, where children are concerned they obtain over three-fourths.

[5] Reprinted by permission from *The Family* (p. 386), by J. K. Folsom, published by John Wiley and Sons, Inc. Statistics from a number of college alumnae offices show

Children and Divorce. Statistics make clear that the chances for divorce are much less where there are children.[1] In 1928, for 63% of all divorces, no children were involved; one child for 20.5%; two for 9.5%; three for 3.9%; four for 1.7%; and five or more for 1.4%. On the basis of these figures, and using Lotka's estimate that 17% of all American marriages are sterile, Cahen shows that 71% of childless marriages end in divorce, while only 8% of couples with children are eventually divorced: 20% of these divorces come from one-child marriages, and only 7% of all divorces are granted to couples with three or more children. Divorce appears therefore as more of a *marriage* than a *family* problem. The annual quota of children of divorced parents is less than one-third the number of divorced persons. Although deprived of a fully normal environment they are probably better off with one parent than in the strained atmosphere of parental incompatibility.

While it is quite certain that "the more children the less divorce," the causal connection is not fully clear. Does the presence of children make parents less desirous of divorce, or does it keep those who do want divorce from securing it? Or it may be that people who get divorced are to a large degree the same people who do not want children, because in both cases they want to retain a larger measure of freedom. Since the larger share of divorces are in the earlier years of marriage, it is evident that "the majority of American divorces actually represent Lindsey's companionate marriage pattern: trial and error without children, then a marriage with much higher probability of permanence after there are children."[2]

Divorce and the Duration of Marriage. The increasing divorce rate has been concomitant with a decrease in the duration of married life. Unrefined computations overstate the number of divorces taking place in the earlier years of married life, yet Cahen found that the third and fourth years of marriage show

divorce rates among graduates to be ⅛th to 1/20th of rates for the states in which the colleges are located. Some recent figures are included in a study made by John Tunis of the Harvard class of 1911 in *Was College Worth While?* (1936). Of the class, 87% have married and only 7% are divorced; 34% married college girls and seemingly doubled their chance of happiness, for the college wives average only one divorce in thirty, as against one in fourteen for the class at large.

[1] Between 1915 and 1929 the birth-rate declined from 25.1 to 18.9; in the same fifteen years divorces increased from 2.45 to 4.05 per thousand married population. Ogburn found a marked negative association between birth-rate and divorce rate in the 170 cities studied.

[2] Reprinted by permission from *The Family* (p. 383), by J. K. Folsom, published by John Wiley and Sons, Inc.

the highest number of divorces. For the first five years divorce outranks death as a breaker of the home; after that death steadily increases, while divorce declines, during the later years of married life.

Comparison with the Divorce Rates of Other Countries. Strict comparison of statistical data in different countries is often difficult. It appears established, however, that the divorce rate is higher in the United States than in any other country.[1] Also it appears that divorce has been increasing in every country where records are available except in Japan.[2] This may indicate an accelerated tendency on the part of the family to disintegrate. But it may also mean simply a more liberal attitude towards divorce, so that more maladjusted families solve their difficulties in this way. So many factors are involved that conclusions with respect to the relative amount of family disintegration, based on differences in divorce rates alone, cannot be relied upon. Low divorce rates give no assurance of marital adjustment, for they may be entirely due to religious or legal restrictions. America's high rates do not therefore prove that family disorganization is more prevalent here, but simply that, in a larger number of cases, legal sanction is given to a discontinuance of married life. It seems generally recognized, nevertheless, that the problem of family disorganization is particularly acute in America.

INTERPRETATIONS OF THE INCREASING DIVORCE RATE

Inadequate Explanations: Divorce Laws and the Divorce Rate. For those who are determined to preserve the traditional pattern of marriage, the emphasis falls on divorce as an evil in itself, something which must be suppressed at all costs. To the scientifically minded on the other hand, the increasing prevalence of divorce is first of all a symptom calling for diagnosis. The emphasis shifts from divorce to an investigation of underlying causes of family disorganization. For in this way alone is there hope of discovering the means whereby marriage may be given greater stability.

Certain popular explanations are obviously inadequate. In

---

[1] In Soviet Russia the divorce rate was the same as the United States in 1926 (*Recent Social Trends*, Vol. I, p. 693).

[2] In Japan, the divorce rate exceeded the American rate until 1915, but it has been progressively falling. The code of 1897 made divorce more difficult to obtain than formerly, when marriage was easily terminated at the whim of a dissatisfied husband. It is possible however that a further development of Western influence may in time lead to a renewed upward trend of divorce.

the first place it is sometimes believed that legislative tendencies have been instrumental in increasing the divorce rate. A survey of these tendencies shows one thing clearly: the futility of endeavoring to suppress divorce by law. For forty years the main tendency has been in the direction of stringency. Both Cahen and Lichtenberger analyze the correlations between specific types of marriage and divorce legislation and find that, while undoubtedly a certain number of bad and hasty marriages could be prevented by better marriage laws, yet there is no substantial evidence that such reforms could do much to stem the advancing divorce rate. With regard to divorce laws there is even less reason to hope anything from their reform. All that they accomplish, in Mowrer's words, is to provide "the molds into which the discord arising in family relations must be made to fit before the state will sanction a discontinuance of that relationship." [1]

In the period in which divorce has increased fivefold there have been surprisingly few major legal changes, and an analysis of these shows their influence on divorce rates to be negligible. It is true, of course, that Nevada's reduction of its residence requirements to six weeks was followed by a rapid increase in divorce rates in that state; also that Arkansas and Idaho followed suit in reducing the term of residence. The only other states which differ significantly from the fairly uniform lenient laws of the remaining jurisdictions are South Carolina, which permits no divorce; New York and the District of Columbia, which permit divorce only for adultery; and North Carolina and Louisiana, where the laws are so strict that practically all their divorces are granted for adultery. The divorce rate is lowest in New York and the District, but it is also fairly low in several states which allow numerous grounds.

Inadequate Explanations: Migratory Divorce. Two other common assumptions may also be shown to be erroneous. In each case popular judgment rests on exaggeration of the facts due to the newspaper publicity given to the individuals most commonly involved. It is not true that any large number of persons seek divorce in order to remarry, nor is it true that migration to more lenient states accounts for a large part of modern divorce. As a matter of fact Cahen shows that only 3% of divorces are strictly migratory. Normal migration accounts for by far the greater number of divorces granted to persons in states other than those in which they were married. It is not at all surprising that mi-

[1] "The Variance between Legal and Natural Causes for Divorce," *Social Forces,* Vol. II (March, 1924), pp. 388–392.

gratory divorce is most common for inhabitants of New York and the District of Columbia, with strict laws and cosmopolitan populations whose attitudes are radically different from those responsible for the laws. In the District, about 40% of divorces are obtained by deliberate migration; in New York only about 20% are purposely obtained in this way, most often in contiguous states, but also in Nevada, and, rarely, in Mexico or in Paris.[1] South Carolina's refusal of any grounds for divorce must fairly represent the attitude of its population, for the divorce rate is only one-twelfth of the average American rate, most divorces being obtained in the neighboring states of North Carolina and Georgia.

Inadequate Explanations: Divorce and Remarriage. Although about one-third of all divorced persons remarry, there has been no great acceleration of remarriages. In some cases where a divorce is immediately followed by remarriage, there has been a long period of separation. Divorce is then secured when remarriage is contemplated, and dissolves a union which had for some time been nominal only. There is in any case no warrant for the popular opinion that large numbers divorce in order to remarry.

Divorce and Alimony. While it is unnecessary to dwell at any length on what Lichtenberger calls the "negligible but noisy minority," whose marital disharmonies, trips to Reno, and frequent divorces and remarriages are featured in the headlines, yet certain aspects of these scandals are significant because they make clearly evident the current confusion with regard to women's status in relation to marriage. Suits for breach of promise and what has been called the "alimony racket," both make it very evident that numbers of women who consider themselves respectable are yet sex-parasites, believing themselves entitled to a comfortable living once they have secured husbands, even after separation from these husbands. The extreme examples of women of this type are the regular "gold-diggers" who figure in breach of promise suits and seek separation or divorce from mercenary motives.

The word alimony is derived from *alere*, to nourish; and originally means nourishment or sustenance, showing very clearly the original purpose of alimony statutes. When matrimony was the only vocation for a woman, it was necessary to protect those

[1] In the chief divorce market, Nevada, only 2,553 divorces were granted in 1929, only 1.3% of all American divorces, while a few hundred only were obtained in foreign countries.

who might be driven from their homes by a husband's misdeeds. Still to-day, in a certain number of cases, and notably where there are children, the court very rightly awards alimony to a wife. Alimony is granted whether divorce is limited or absolute and without regard to whether the wife is plaintiff or defendant. She is also allowed temporary alimony for her maintenance and to enable her to bring suit. The law is only beginning to take into account economic changes which make it possible for women to earn. Already, however, some fifteen jurisdictions allow alimony to a husband, and, in a number more, the court is permitted to award him part of his wife's property. Moreover, there is a growing belief that, while alimony should be awarded to a wife with young children, the childless and able-bodied young wife, or the woman with property, is not entitled to support.

Even to-day, however, there are spectacular cases in which a sentimental court awards huge sums to the wives of wealthy men to enable them to live in idle luxury. In some cases wives refuse their husbands a complete divorce which would enable them to remarry; in others men spend long periods in gaol at the expense of the taxpayers, because they are unable to pay the sums demanded, being, of course, far less able to do so if kept in gaol and not allowed to work.[1] Of recent years, however, there has been growing dissatisfaction on the part of judges with alimony laws, which have been described as "the greatest curse in America," and as instrumental in turning too many wives into "parasites, liars, cheats, intriguers, money-grabbers and contributors to immorality."[2]

There has been, as we saw, a great decrease in demands for alimony, but this may be accounted for by the increasing employment of women, and may not indicate any decrease in a class of women whose continued tolerance by society is a menace to family stability. For while the alimony hunters may be com-

[1] Alimony imprisonment is the sole survival of imprisonment for debt, although, since this is illegal, the defaulting husband is imprisoned not on the charge of owing money to his separated or divorced wife, but on the charge of contempt of court in refusing to pay. A number of cases illustrating different aspects of the alimony situation are assembled by Apstein, *The Parting of the Ways* (1935), Chapters XII and XIII. In one instance, not included here, the daughter of a policeman, who became an actress and married an orchestra leader, complained that $400 a month was insufficient for her maintenance. In asking for $7,450 *monthly* she provided an itemized list of her needs; these included the monthly expenses for five servants, each at $100; for clothes $2,000, for medicine, recreation, and groceries $1,000; $200 for a private secretary and $150 for a masseuse.

[2] The opinions of a number of judges are summarized in *The Literary Digest*, Vol. C (March 16, 1929), p. 26.

paratively few, they exhibit, in extreme form, the attitudes of vast numbers of idle or semi-idle and pleasure-loving women whose lack of any sense of social responsibility greatly diminishes the probability of their contracting permanent or successful marriages.

The Churches and Divorce. The divorce rate would undoubtedly have been higher save for the unswerving adherence of the Roman Church to traditional dogmas.[1] It has never surrendered its absolute moral and spiritual dictatorship over its members, and unconditionally denies to them the right to use the civil law of divorce.

Although civil jurisdiction over marriage replaced ecclesiastical through almost the whole of Western civilization during the nineteenth century, the Protestant churches have consistently sought to shape civil legislation and have upheld their own standards through ecclesiastical legislation binding on their members.[2] During the period in which divorce has been steadily increasing, all churches have viewed this "deplorable" state of affairs with mounting alarm.   On the whole, however, their efforts have been reactionary.   But few changes have been made in legislation, and these have been, almost without exception, in the direction of increasing the restraints of ecclesiastical control. Undoubtedly the attitudes of the churches have a restraining influence over their loyal members.[3] Yet in the same period in which divorce rates have been mounting, there has been no indication of religious decline as indicated by church membership figures. It must be admitted, apparently, that the churches have spent most of their energy in a protest which in the last analysis is proving itself impotent.   Cruelty, the leading ground of divorce, is not allowed by any church.   While the majority of

[1] In the words of the Papal Encyclical, *Casti Connubii*, the sacrament of marriage carries with it "a perpetual and indissoluble bond which cannot be dissolved by civil law. . . . Christ, by virtue of His supreme legislative power . . . restored the primeval law in its integrity by those words which must never be forgotten: 'What God hath joined together, let no man put asunder.'"

[2] The leading Protestant churches allow divorce on scriptural grounds, which in most cases is limited to adultery, while desertion is allowed by some.   In 1931, the Presbyterians abolished desertion as a rightful cause, and, in 1930, the Lutherans repealed an earlier regulation which had permitted extreme cruelty in addition to adultery and desertion.   The Protestant Episcopal Church has recently endeavored to ease the ban on the remarriage of the "guilty" person in a divorce. A storm of controversy has been aroused by the suggestion that remarriage shall be at the discretion of Bishops.

[3] In 1929, an extensive investigation of the frequency of divorce, among the members of a number of leading churches, disclosed that the problem of divorce was not serious where both husband and wife were regular attendants at church.

active church members obey ecclesiastical legislation, there has been a decline in the prestige of the churches.[1] The sanctions of traditional religion are being replaced by scientific sanctions, and enlightened opinion is turning to the findings of psychologists, psychiatrists, and sociologists, as offering more effective guidance in dealing with divorce and the problem of family instability.

Growth of Liberalism within the Churches. While a considerable number of Protestant clergy decry divorce as a sign of moral decadence, there is at the same time a growing number of liberals who seek to revitalize religion by a reinterpretation of its essentials in terms of a practical ethics, designed to cope with contemporary social problems. Christ's ideal of marriage, they hold, does not find full expression in the ecclesiastical position with its overemphasis on adultery, as the only ground of dissolution, and its insistence on the letter rather than the spirit. A true marriage is a genuine physical and spiritual union, indissoluble in its very nature. Where there is no true marriage, divorce, in the words of Joseph Fort Newton, is "a necessary measure of moral sanitation." [2] It is at times the only possible means for realizing a new spiritual ideal, by giving a second chance to those who have been the victims of mistaken choice. Some of the leading churches, even when adhering to uncompromising attitudes on divorce, are also engaged in constructive efforts to educate young people for family relationships. Far more substantial results might be expected, were the energy of the churches turned from attempts at compressing human relations within the outworn molds of ecclesiastical dogma, and directed towards social experimentation undertaken in the spirit of the teachings of Christ.

The Lessening Control of External Social Influences. The changes recently undergone by the family have involved the removal of certain of its former functions from the home to outside social agencies. There is, accordingly, less necessity for mutual dependence among the family members. This is most obvious in the case of the economic compulsions which formerly held the family together. In America, where marriage has all along been less concerned with considerations of property, it has been more easily dissolved than where property settlements serve as a cement. But here, as everywhere, economic produc-

---

[1] Hart shows that there has been increasingly less approval of ecclesiastical control over marriage in the opinions expressed in leading periodicals in recent decades. *Recent Social Trends*, Vol. I, pp. 402–408, 421.

[2] "What God Hath Not Joined," *Atlantic Monthly*, Vol. CXXXI (June, 1923), p. 724.

tion within the family exercised coercive influence in holding its members together. Industrial development has largely removed such economic control. The family members, all but the youngest children, may become economically independent, and so need no longer submit to conditions from which formerly there was no escape.

Economic forces have thus relaxed their pressure, and religious sanctions have lost much of their former power. Finally, with the mobility of modern life, the control exercised by local public opinion has been weakened. City life in particular is a great solvent of custom.[1] A general liberalizing of opinion is, indeed, bound to follow increasing movement of families from place to place. In this way social attitudes are more rapidly influenced by modern trends; an important matter in connection with divorce, for the removal of public censure undoubtedly leads to an increase in divorce.

Civil and ecclesiastical laws governing marriage and divorce were the product of social and economic conditions which no longer obtain. As the control of external influences is undermined, legal efforts to force conformity to an earlier pattern become ineffective. With the weakening of the external framework holding marriage together, internal tensions and strains produce effects hitherto held in check. Causes previously dormant now come to light and may lead to divorce.

The Readjustment of Marriage to the New Social Order. A further reason for the instability of the modern family lies in the fact that new tensions and strains are developed in the course of the readjustment of marriage to the changing social order. Modern conditions favor democratic and coöperative family relationships, yet many men cling to obsolescent patriarchal prerogatives, and seek to dominate wife and children in a manner wholly incompatible with the growing individualization of women and the newer attitudes towards childhood. So far as wives are concerned, it is those who lag behind who are most apt to be restless and discontented, clinging to the comforts of semi-idle dependence on one hand, but asserting their rights as individuals on the other. It is women such as these, rather than the genuinely emancipated and individualized women, who are in the main

---

[1] Mowrer has shown that divorce in Chicago is definitely correlated with high mobility of population. "With the breakdown in neighborhood control in the city, resulting from the constant movement from one situation to another, the individual is freed from the usual social restraints which function so effectively in the country and upon which much of the stability of social organization in the past has been built." *The Family* (University of Chicago Press, 1932), p. 206.

responsible for the exaggerated individualism which is so disruptive of the coöperation necessary in marriage. As Ross said long ago, "When independence and the assertion of rights are in the air, there are sure to be some who become acutely aware of their rights before they realize their duties."[1]

The Trend towards Individualism. It cannot be gainsaid that the modern trend towards individualism has made both women and men more intent on finding personal happiness in marriage and less tolerant of social restraint. In America, the "democratic spirit of self-determination" has had fewer obstacles to encounter than in older countries. This is one reason for the more rapid rise of the divorce rate in America. Moreover, democracy has meant an increasing popularization of law, and many people now have access to divorce courts who formerly felt recourse to the law was beyond their reach. The spread of individualism to all classes and both sexes will undoubtedly lead to greater confusion in social life and most of all within marriage, until, through the development of the ethics of personal responsibility, the new freedom comes to be more wisely used.

In the meantime the newer ethical ideals themselves may serve as a disruptive factor in marriage. Loyalty to an institution is being replaced by a valuation of marriage in terms of the well-being of the family members. There is far greater readiness to dissolve marriage when its consequences are disappointing. But this is no sign of a breakdown of morality or of a decline in standards. Rather does it indicate an increase in moral sensitiveness and a raising of standards. Lichtenberger says: "the divorce trend in certain of its aspects . . . may be only the visible evidence of a struggle towards a higher ethical consciousness in regard to sexual and other marital relations. . . . The basis of marriage as a personal relation is shifting from necessity to free choice, from the formal to the ethical, from a relation preserved by external pressure to one maintained by internal attraction."[2] Under such circumstances uncongeniality and incompatibility are much more likely to disrupt marriage. In the long run, changes such as these should prove wholly salutary. In the meantime, they throw the burden for the maintenance of marriage on the affectional relationship between the family members; and many to-day are ill-prepared indeed for any such responsibility. For, as Goodsell points out: "Serfs cannot be

---

[1] "The Significance of Increasing Divorce," *Century Magazine*, Vol. LXXVIII (May, 1909), pp. 149–152.

[2] *Op. cit.*, pp. 322 and 249.

transformed into self-directing freemen merely by striking off their shackles. . . . A prolonged period of education is essential if men and women are to learn to substitute moral sanctions of their deliberate choosing for the old external compulsions."[1]

Divorce as the Terminus of a Disintegrative Process. It thus becomes apparent that, in the last analysis, the increase in divorce can be accounted for only in terms of tensions and strains within the family. There is almost certainly more maladjustment within marriage than formerly; and, when present, maladjustment and discord are much more likely to lead to divorce. Divorce is, therefore, the culmination of a process of disintegration, in which discord grows as strains develop within the complex reciprocal interrelationships of marriage. Some episode in this process is usually adduced as the "cause" for which divorce is sought, but only in rare cases does some single event destroy marriage. And usually no *one* factor is the underlying cause of divorce, though one factor may be, as it were, the focus of the disturbance.

THE REFORM OF MARRIAGE AND DIVORCE LAWS

The Need for Marriage Law Reform. Far more attention has been paid to divorce laws than to marriage laws, although the elimination of "bad marriages" is obviously more important in preventing divorce than any form of divorce legislation. Frivolous, mercenary, ignorant, and physiologically bad marriages are the cause of many divorces, although Lichtenberger believes undue emphasis has been placed on bad marriage laws as a cause of divorce, by authorities such as Howard. The reform of marriage laws which can be shown to facilitate "bad marriages" is, in any case, highly desirable in itself. And yet, until recently, there has been almost complete neglect of marriage laws by those interested in family problems.

Child Marriages. Interest in marriage laws has been increased through the work of the Russell Sage Foundation. One of its studies dealt with child marriage, which proved, on investigation, to be a far greater evil than had been anticipated. Very youthful marriages are far more prevalent among girls than boys, and very young girls frequently marry much older men. It is true, of course, that these marriages require parental consent. The common-law ages of marriage were fourteen for a boy and twelve for a girl, an inheritance from Roman law, based on the usual ages for puberty in Rome two thousand years ago. Yet, in 1937, in

[1] *Problems of the Family*, p. 405.

nine states marriage is still allowed at these ages.[1] In the other states statutory ages now vary with few exceptions from sixteen to eighteen for boys, and fourteen to sixteen for girls. New Hampshire, with twenty for boys and eighteen for girls, has the highest limits. At the time of the 1920 census there were 5,554 married girls under fifteen in the United States, a number reduced in 1930, according to census records, to 4,241, at which time there were 761 married boys under fifteen.

The weight of expert opinion is against marriage for girls before the completion of the rapid growth of adolescence.[2] Before some reserve of vigor is stored up, childbearing is not advantageous, and it was found by the studies of the Children's Bureau that the children of very young mothers have less chance of living. Many youthful marriages are of very short duration, ending either in annulment or divorce. They are often hasty marriages, the licenses having been obtained without parental consent by means of false affidavits of age. Many parents, however, consent to the marriage of mere children.

Richmond and Hall believe that parental consent still serves a useful purpose in marriages of girls under eighteen and boys under twenty-one, and that it *could* be made to serve this purpose effectively, if marriage licenses were never granted without adequate evidence of age and of parental consent. All efforts for better control of marriage must center, they hold, in a more socialized use of the administrative device of the marriage license.[3] They advocate the raising of the minimum for girls to sixteen in all states where it is lower, but with the power to grant exceptions in individual cases vested in certain designated judicial officers.[4]

Hasty Marriages. A considerable proportion of marriages are hastily contracted. Some are the result of a sudden attachment; others are even more lightly and frivolously entered into, perhaps as the aftermath of some drinking party. The occasions for undue haste range from a jest to a crime; in bigamous mar-

---

[1] According to a table made public by the Children's Bureau and reported in the *New York Times*, June 22, 1937; public interest having been aroused by the recent marriage of a nine-year-old girl in Tennessee.

[2] Richmond and Hall, *Child Marriages* (1925), pp. 24–26.

[3] *Marriage and the State* (Russell Sage Foundation, 1929), Chapters II, III.

[4] *Ibid.*, p. 146. The trend towards raising the age of marriage has met with much resistance because of a possible increase in pre-marital sex relations and the fact that young girls who become pregnant would be debarred from marriage. Such cases should be treated as exceptions and, in any case, Richmond and Hall found that the problem of pre-marital pregnancy entered into youthful marriages in only a small minority of instances.

riages, for example; in marriages where secrecy or concealment is desired by one or both partners; and in the "large and ill-assorted" group known as "forced marriages."[1] In order to prevent the worst evils of hasty marriage, a number of states have passed laws requiring advance notice of intention. There are two types of such laws, only one of which is effective; where the license may not be issued till a stated number of days, usually five, after the time of application. Illegal unions may often be prevented in this way, and time is given for reconsideration to those who are entering marriage impulsively without sufficient thought.

Unfortunately, where one state requires advance notice, or in other ways reforms its laws, and neighboring states do not, there are many who evade the law by out-of-state marriages.[2] The demand for hasty marriages has led to the existence of numerous "marriage-markets," or so-called "Gretna Greens," easily accessible to nearby states, in states where marriage laws are weak or where license issuers do not ask awkward questions.[3] Complete advance notice laws seem the only effective check to this commercialization and debasement of matrimony.[4]

Medical Certification for Marriage. Though obviously desirable, the control of mental defect and transmissible disease by means of marriage laws encounters the greatest difficulty. Most of the states specify that no marriage license be issued to the feeble-minded and insane, but some of the laws seem to assume

[1] The phrase "forced marriages" should be limited to those marriages where one or both parties enter the marital relation unwillingly, because of pressure from without, usually because the woman or girl is pregnant or has had sex relations with the man or boy in the case.

[2] So great has been the financial loss both to county treasuries and to business concerns when marriage and honeymoon profits are lost to nearby, but out-of-state, "Gretna Greens," that reform in marriage laws is apt to meet with determined opposition. The Wyoming, 1931, "gin-marriage" law, in reality a law requiring advance notice of five days before issuance of a license, was repealed in 1935, because of its detrimental effect on public revenues.

[3] Richmond and Hall found 57 of these in 29 states. Interested in this form of exploitation are not only the too obliging license issuers and the marrying parsons or justices, but also business men, such as jewelers, and taxi drivers who meet incoming trains and drum up business for those officially connected with the local marriage mill. Newspaper publicity is welcomed by such a town, although the names of couples can often be kept out of the news, by payment of a double fee.

[4] In an effort to reduce evasive out-of-state marriages, several states have adopted marriage evasion acts, which declare marriage of a resident null and void in that state, if it violates the requirements of the state and was contracted in another state in order to evade those requirements. Richmond and Hall believe that the most effective method of handling this problem would be the adoption of a *double license* system. Candidates, applying for a license in a state where both were non-residents, would be required to present a license obtained in the state of residence and marriage license district of the prospective bride. *Op. cit.*, pp. 208–209.

that mental disease is easy to detect, and certain of them actually require an affidavit of freedom from disqualifications from the person in question.[1] There is, however, a marked tendency towards requiring a medical certificate of one or both parties before a marriage license is issued. By the end of 1935 some dozen states had enacted such laws.[2] But they have not proved very effective, for the medical examination is often superficial, whereas exacting tests are necessary for an authoritative statement as to freedom from venereal diseases. Nevertheless their educational value cannot be questioned, particularly in regard to the menace of venereal diseases.

Common-law Marriages. Most authorities believe that common-law marriages should be abolished.[3] They are still frequent in America to an extent unknown elsewhere in the civilized world. There was considerable justification for the continuance of this Old World custom under frontier conditions. Now, however, no valid excuse remains. Nearly half the states still recognize common-law marriages, and the courts must decide whether a given pair, who have dispensed with a marriage ceremony, are legally married or no. Courts are at variance in their decisions, and the resultant confusion makes possible many evils.[4] The toleration of common-law marriages is, moreover, a deterrent to the education of public opinion: a matter of greater importance than any direct results expected from legislative reforms. At present, however "bad" a marriage may be, however risky, hasty, or frivolous, someone can be found to "solemnize" it. A long process of social education is obviously necessary before public opinion will be ready to pass and enforce better marriage laws.[5]

[1] In one such affidavit the male applicant must swear: "I am not feeble-minded, imbecile, epileptic, insane, a common drunkard, and am not afflicted with pulmonary tuberculosis in its advanced stages, nor with contagious venereal disease." Richmond and Hall, *op. cit.*, p. 60.

[2] In 1933 North Carolina repealed her requirement for a health certificate, because of the pressure exerted by the *border* counties on account of their annual loss in license fees. By May, 1938, nine states had laws requiring pre-marital tests for syphilis.

[3] "A common-law marriage," according to Richmond and Hall, "is a marriage not solemnized in any particular form but based on a mutual agreement between persons legally capable of making a marriage contract, to enter into the relation of husband and wife. The state is given no part in the arrangement, has no record of it, and no opportunity beforehand to pass upon the qualification of the parties to it." *Op. cit.*, p. 26.

[4] Opportunities are created for exploitation and blackmail, and the protection of common-law wives and their children is often inadequate.

[5] Folsom suggests that the law should do more than merely restrict the rights of individuals to marry; if it created new agencies providing for expert investigation and guidance of marriage candidates, and if courses of pre-marriage instruction were made compulsory, then the law might indeed have a more constructive influence on marriage.

The Desirability of Divorce Law Reform. Divorce law reform may have no effect in diminishing the divorce rate, but nevertheless it is desirable that the laws be brought into touch with social realities. The discrepancy between the real reasons for divorce and the technical grounds on which it is granted necessitates frequent manipulation of evidence. And while most divorces to-day are the result of mutual agreement, the law still treats a suit for divorce as an action of an injured party against an offending party.[1] Technically, therefore, in countless instances *collusion* takes place, and evidence is either fabricated or concealed for the purpose of obtaining a divorce. Hypocrisy, subterfuge, and perjury are prevalent in divorce courts. The frequency of collusive agreement is particularly obvious in the ease with which evidence of infidelity may be obtained.[2] Marshall and May, on the basis of an intensive study in Maryland and Ohio, sum up the matter as follows: "The final outcome is this: a divorce decree will be duly issued to anyone who has a certain amount of time and money—and a coöperative spouse."[3]

Divorce by Mutual Consent. Increasing numbers of judges grant divorce where they think it justified. So liberal an interpretation is given to "cruelty," that divorces are really being granted for "incompatibility," although no such ground is legally allowed. These are, to all intents and purposes, divorces by mutual consent, which contravene the whole tenor of the law, to the effect that when *both* parties want a divorce it should not be granted.

If laws were to be revised to conform with this frequent practice, they would have as precedents the laws already prevailing in certain other countries, notably Denmark, Norway, and Sweden. Married partners, who agree to disagree, go before *civil* authorities and are given a private hearing at which they explain the details of the understanding they have reached, with regard to children and division of property and payments to be made by the husband. When infidelity is proved by the testi-

[1] This is true even of Nevada, although the 1931 law provides that, "when both husband and wife have been guilty of a wrong or wrongs, the court shall in its discretion grant a divorce to the party least in fault."

[2] According to Apstein, an entirely new profession of divorce-aiders has come into existence in New York, where adultery is the only legal ground for divorce. Men and women hire themselves out for the evening as professional corespondents. They go to a chosen hotel bedroom and meet the husband, or wife; whereupon, as previously arranged, detectives and house-manager arrive. They then receive $25 to $50 and depart. *Op. cit.*, pp. 127–128.

[3] Leon C. Marshall and Geoffrey May, *The Divorce Court* (2 vols., 1932–1933), Vol. II, p. 23.

mony of the third party, immediate divorce is granted; otherwise a legal separation is granted, and a waiting period decreed before divorce becomes absolute. The whole proceedings cost between $8 and $10; there is no scandalous publicity, mutual vilification, hypocrisy, and perjury. In Scandinavian countries, divorce by mutual consent accounts for some 75% of divorces, the remaining divorces being granted by courts where the judges have great latitude of discretion. Although the divorce rate has been raised, it yet compares very favorably with the American rate.[1]

The Results of Repressive Laws. Repressive laws undoubtedly diminish the prevalence of divorce, but only at great cost. Even in England where, prior to January, 1938, divorce has only been granted on the ground of adultery, a premium has thus been put on perjury. More liberal recommendations were made by the 1909 Royal Commission on Divorce and Matrimonial Causes. But ecclesiastical influence prevented any change until July, 1937, when A. P. Herbert won his long battle to liberalize the law. Under the new Matrimonial Causes Act, divorce may be obtained not only for adultery, but for desertion without cause for three years, cruelty, and incurable insanity.[2]

When no divorce is allowed, as among Catholics or in South Carolina, there are more illegitimate unions, more separations, and more annulments.[3] Particularly significant is the fact that South Carolina laws do not make adultery an indictable offense, and are unique in limiting the amount of property which may be left to an extra-legal "wife." Extra-marital adjustments are thus tacitly accepted for men.

---

[1] In Denmark, with its larger urban population, there is only one divorce to every twelve marriages, while in Norway and Sweden the rate is much lower. The actual rates in 1926 were 0.57 divorces per 1,000 population in Denmark; 0.29 in Sweden; 0.21 in Norway as against the American rate of *1.52.* Divorce is most frequent in the sophisticated city of Copenhagen, and there Dorothy Dunbar Bromley noted one distressing effect of divorce by mutual consent: the frequency with which divorces among the middle-aged result from the husband's desire to marry a younger woman. There are, however, far fewer extra-marital liaisons than in England where divorce has been difficult to obtain, or France where, although the divorce law is liberal, there is a strong sentiment in favor of the family as an institution, not only for rearing children, but for preserving the family name and maintaining property intact. "Where Divorce is a Simple Formality," *New York Times Magazine*, Oct. 2, 1932; and "Civilized Divorce," *Nation*, Vol. CXXVIII (May 22, 1929).

[2] For further details see *New York Times*, July 24, 1937.

[3] Annulment is a decision by the courts that a marriage never existed. Most states determine the grounds on which annulment may be secured. In some states children are expressly declared legitimate, in others they are left illegitimate through annulment. In 1929, 4,408 marriages were annulled, the greatest numbers being in California (1,476), where the legitimacy of children is protected, and in New York (1,029), with its strict divorce law.

Constructive Divorce Reform. Repressive divorce laws exercise no remedial effect on the underlying causes for marital disaster, and their result is moral confusion. Yet American divorce laws have consistently tended towards greater stringency, except in the matter of grounds and in the few states which have made a thriving business out of migratory divorce.[1] This blatant and vulgar commercialization of divorce is highly deleterious to the formation of wholesome public opinion. Otherwise it plays a minor part in the divorce problem.

Although the one hopeful method of approach is to transfer interest from divorce to the diagnosis and constructive treatment of the causes for marital instability, yet Lichtenberger stresses the need for adapting divorce laws to modern requirements. Divorce must be recognized as a remedial measure, when there is complete disorganization of marriage. It should therefore be liberalized so as to eliminate all hypocrisy and subterfuge, and its procedure should be so modified as to "obviate the spreading before the gaze of the morbid public the salacious details of marital scandals."[2] Legal separations, with their immoral consequences, should be abolished.

Uniform Marriage and Divorce Laws. As early as the eighties efforts were made to secure greater uniformity in the marriage and divorce laws of the states. Some advocated state coöperation, others a federal amendment. In 1922, urged by the General Federation of Women's Clubs, Senator Capper introduced in Congress a sample marriage and divorce bill in the form of an amendment to the Constitution. With minor revisions this bill has been reintroduced at every Congress since, but has never come to a vote.

As Lichtenberger points out: "the crux of the federal amendment issue is the diverse status of married and divorced persons and of their children, created by their removal from one jurisdiction to another."[3] Undoubtedly this problem would be solved by an amendment, and the evasion of beneficial marriage and divorce laws through migration would be avoided. But such

[1] In 1927, Nevada reduced its residence requirement from six months to three, and in 1931 Arkansas and Idaho, anxious to grab their share of the profits, decreased their residence requirements to three months. Alarmed at the prospect of a decrease in their $3,000,000 to $4,000,000 "divorce business," the Nevada legislators promptly reduced their requirement to *six weeks.*

[2] *Op. cit.*, p. 449.

[3] *Op. cit.*, p. 203. He continues: "Marriage is a civil contract, but it differs from other contracts in that it creates a status, and because it does so, may neither be entered into nor dissolved at will, except by compliance with laws and procedures laid down by the state of residence."

a law would probably create more problems than it would solve.

Richmond and Hall contend that, where marriage and divorce laws are combined in a single program, divorce gets all the attention. Marriage provisions are treated as a minor matter during the struggle between those who want to make divorce easier and those who want to make it more difficult. The Capper bill does not include details which are absolutely necessary to the good administration of marriage laws, and thus proves how "difficult, if not impossible, it will be to draft a federal measure that will not materially lower the present administration of higher standard states." [1] Far more desirable is the natural, if slow, growth of uniformity through better state laws and a gradual development of interstate coöperation.

So far as divorce is concerned, its reduction could not be hoped for by any such proposal as that of the Capper bill, which is a composite code of state legislation. It names six grounds for divorce, and would probably lead to slight increases in the states with more conservative laws. Thus the Capper bill is far from satisfactory to the conservatives, who form a large proportion of the proponents for uniform legislation. [2]

As long ago as 1894, Elizabeth Cady Stanton pointed out that the adoption of a uniform law would restrict experimentation: "As we are still in the experimental stage of the question, we are not qualified to make a perfect law, that would work satisfactorily over so vast an area as our boundaries now embrace. . . . By leaving the states free to experiment in their local affairs, we can judge of the working of different laws under varying circumstances, and thus learn their respective merits." [3] This is almost as true to-day as in 1894. As Cahen says: "Divorce in America is still a flexible and changing problem, unready for a standardized legal solution. . . . A federal divorce law would deprive the country of forty-eight experimental laboratories in social legislation, which provide the primary source of improvement." [4]

[1] Richmond and Hall, op. cit., p. 199; and see pp. 198–213 for detailed discussion.

[2] As a matter of fact, the diversity of opinion with respect to divorce makes it doubtful that any federal amendment could be framed which would embody a sufficient consensus of opinion to ensure its successful administration and enforcement. Even if an amendment were passed, it would, according to Lichtenberger, "have little effect, if any, in diminishing the divorce rate, for the simple reason that the causes which determine the divorce trend lie outside the domain of law and are neither produced by it nor are they subject in any considerable degree to its control." Op. cit., p. 208.

[3] Quoted by Julia E. Johnsen, Selected Articles on Marriage and Divorce (1925), pp. 275–276.

[4] Op. cit., pp. 95–96.

SUGGESTED READING

Blanchard, P., and Manasses, C., *New Girls for Old*, 1930.

Breckenridge, S. P., *The Family and the State*, 1934, Sections I, IX.

Cahen, A., *Statistical Analysis of American Divorce*, 1932.

Dell, F., *Love in the Machine Age*, 1930.

Ellis, H., *The Psychology of Sex*, 7 vols., 1899–1928, Vol. VI, Chs. VI, VII.

Folsom, J. K., *The Family*, 1934, Chs. XI–XIII.

Goodsell, W., *Problems of the Family*, rev. ed., 1936, Chs. VII, VIII.

Groves, E. R., and Brooks, L. M., *Readings in the Family*, 1934, Chs. XIV, XVII, XIX.

Groves, E. R., and Ogburn, W. F., *American Marriage and Family Relationships*, 1928.

Haggard, H. W., *Devils, Drugs, and Doctors*, 1929, Chs. X, XI.

Hamilton, G. V., *A Research in Marriage*, 1929.

——, and Macgowan, K., *What Is Wrong with Marriage*, 1929.

Hart, H. H. and E. B., *Personality and the Family*, 1935.

Howard, G. E., *A History of Matrimonial Institutions*, 3 vols., 1904, Vol. II, Ch. XVI; Vol. III, Chs. XVII, XVIII.

Johnsen, J., ed., *Selected Articles on Marriage and Divorce*, 1925.

Lichtenberger, J. P., *Divorce, A Social Interpretation*, 1931.

Lindsey, B. B., and Evans, W., *The Revolt of Modern Youth*, 1925.

May, G., *Marriage Laws and Decisions in the United States*, 1929.

Mowrer, E., *Family Disorganization*, 1927.

——, *The Family*, 1932.

Parran, T., "The Next Great Plague to Go," *Survey Graphic*, Vol. XXV, July, 1936, pp. 404–411.

——, *Shadow on the Land*, 1937.

Reuter, E. B., and Runner, J. R., *The Family*, 1931, Chs. VIII, XV, XVI.

Richmond, M. E., and Hall, F. S., *Child Marriages*, 1925.

——, *Marriage and the State*, 1929.

Stern, B. J., ed., *The Family Past and Present*, 1938, pp. 351–393.

Thomas, W. I., *The Unadjusted Girl*, 1923.

Vernier, C. G., *American Family Laws*, 5 vols., 1931–1938, Vols. I, II.

Westermarck, E. A., *The Future of Marriage in Western Civilization*, 1936.

CHAPTER XIX

MARITAL ADJUSTMENTS

THE OBSOLESCENCE OF THE PATRIARCHAL FAMILY PATTERN

The Patriarchal Principle of Coercive Control. In the patriarchal family the pattern of relationships between husband and wife, parents and children, was relatively fixed and taken for granted. The family organization was maintained intact through the subservience of all members to the typical pattern of masculine dominance. Family coherence, stability, and strength were maintained at the cost of the development of its members, in general, and of women and children, in particular. The accord existing between the family members was primarily that of a pre-existing pattern, irrespective of the deeper ties of sympathy and affection.

In so-called civilized countries the *form* of the family is still patriarchal, but among more progressive peoples, and particularly in America, the patriarchal pattern is in process of dissolution. The whole present emphasis is psychological; it falls on personal relationships and the delicate adjustments and readjustments necessary for successful family life. And such a change of emphasis is inevitable, for, as McIver puts it, "the family, no longer strongly, if rudely, cemented by extraneous functions, has to surmount in its own strength the psychological tests of its cohesion." [1] The *inner substance* of the family organization is being laid bare by what Beatrice Hinkle calls the "disintegration of the outer shell." This, she says, "is producing the modern disturbance; the substance has long needed reorganization." [2]

The patriarchal family pattern is thus obsolescent. The patriarchal principle of coercive control has outlived such usefulness as it may formerly have possessed. Nevertheless, traditional attitudes derived from this principle, ill-adjusted though they be to modern social and economic conditions, are yet extensively approved and deeply embedded in public opinion, in

---

[1] From R. M. MacIver, *Society: Its Structure and Changes*, p. 139. Copyright 1931. Reprinted by permission of the publishers, Farrar and Rinehart, Inc.

[2] "Marriage in the New World," in *The Book of Marriage* (ed. Keyserling, 1926), p. 226.

custom, in religion, and in law. One source of the present confusion is to be found in this fact. Not only do frustration and maladjustment result from clinging to the older attitudes, but their persistence makes more difficult the emergence of constructive new ideals. Too often the modern attitude remains negative, one of protest or revolt against the old. And never was there greater need for clearly defined attitudes and ideals, based on understanding of the essential character and functions of the family.

The Psychological Principle of Coherence through Integration. An adequate psychology of marriage must conceive of the family in terms of the *reciprocal responsiveness* of its members. The unity of the family is a "unity of interacting personalities," involving an integration of complex relationships.[1] Patterns of relations must be developed between partners in marriage, involving mutual accommodation and a degree of accord sufficient to maintain a fundamental unity of feeling and emotion in the family group. No two marriages present exactly the same problems, for no two personalities are exactly alike, nor can the integration of relationships between one couple be achieved by exactly the same means as between any other couple. Nevertheless, certain general principles are emerging: certain types of maladjustment occur over and over again, and certain frequently recurring attitudes are found to be harmful, while certain others are wholesome.

Fuller understanding is conducive to a gradual emergence of new ideals, which, difficult as they may be to achieve as yet, presage the coming of a coöperative and democratic family; a pattern of relationships designed to secure the fullest and freest development of each member of the family; where love and companionship between a man and a woman lead to voluntary parenthood within a *home*, as a physical, social, and spiritual environment, deliberately created and directed for the purposes of family life.

Voluntary parenthood must be central in a complete pattern of family life; but the fundamental determinant of the pattern is found in the relation of intimate responsiveness of husband and wife to each other: the enhancement of experience to be achieved through shared sensations and emotions, shared interests, aspirations, and ideals. The desire for response has to-day become a dominant, very often *the* dominant, motive for mar-

---

[1] E. W. Burgess, "The Family as a Unity of Interacting Personalities," *The Family*, Vol. VII (March, 1926), pp. 3–9.

riage: the desire for love, affection, appreciation, sympathy, and understanding; "for the satisfactions which grow out of a mutual integration of individual behavior, such that the reactions of one person are supplemented and enhanced by those of the other." [1]

The situation to-day is paradoxical, even tragic. Never probably has there been so insistent a desire for genuine companionship and comradeship between husband and wife. [2] "People do not marry with less craving for affection than formerly, but with more." Modern matrimony as it now exists in American culture, is "predominantly an expression of the profound need of men and women to find their highest happiness in the close, character-developing experiences of marriage and the family." [3] And yet, to-day, the confusion and strain of an era of transition, the conflicting tendencies and the complexities of modern life, and, finally, the very stress on individuality and on personal emotion and feeling, all accentuate the difficulties of marital adjustment.

THE RESULTANT CONFUSION AND ACCENTUATION OF MARITAL TENSIONS

The Romantic Complex. There is real danger in the assumption, on the part of those who have "fallen in love," that the fusion of personalities they experience will endure unchanged, that it will solve all their problems, and that they "will live happily ever after," if once united in marriage. Even to-day, when the prevalence of marital discord should be obvious to all, this "fairy-tale" or romantic view still plays the dominating rôle in American marriage. [4] In extreme form the romantic ideal is that of love at first sight between predestined affinities, and of marriage as

[1] From Mowrer's *Personality Adjustment and Domestic Discord* (1935), p. 150. Copyright. Used by permission of the American Book Company, publishers.

[2] The derivations of the words *companionship* and *comradeship* are significant in this connection. Companions, literally, are those who share bread together, while comrades are those who share their dwelling place.

[3] Groves and Ogburn, *American Marriage and Family Relationships*, p. 29. Many factors combine to produce this result. Individualization leads to emphasis on human relationships, on sympathy and understanding. Yet present-day mobility separates many individuals from their parental family, their relatives, friends, and childhood environment. Life is difficult and in many ways insecure. As Frank puts it: "successful mating has become so much more important in marriage. . . . Men and women require more affection and fuller sex realization to compensate for the loss of other activities and satisfactions, and to sustain them under strain and anxiety." "Social Change and the Family," *Annals of the American Academy*, Vol. CLX (March, 1932), p. 101.

[4] In Middletown, romantic love was theoretically held to be the only basis for marriage, and children were assured, "You'll know when the right one comes along." Pp. 114–115.

the institutional form of romantic love, involving perpetual courtship and the endurance of the "excited" love characteristic of the early stages of "falling in love."

Since this excited, or "cardiac-respiratory" love, as it has been called from its typical manifestations, depends to a large extent on the novelty of the situation, it is necessarily transitory and cannot endure unchanged. To recognize this fact is not in any way to belittle romantic love as the source of intense and incomparable joy. "The flowering of this sentiment," says MacIver, "is one of the great experiences of life. It involves an integration of sex with the whole personality of the individual. Nevertheless, by itself, it cannot normally sustain the family through the changes it inevitably undergoes. In the course of time it has to be supplemented and in part replaced by other sentiments."[1]

Meanwhile popular literature, moving pictures, and the inescapable barrage of current "song hits" all conspire to impress an exclusively romantic, and therefore wholly inadequate, conception on the minds of the young, with consequences disastrous to family life. According to Mowrer, "this romantic conception of the marriage relation . . . becomes the focal point in marital discord at the present time." [2] It is responsible for many ill-advised marriages and for many an unnecessary divorce. For it leads to marriages where compatibility is impossible, and it prevents the formation of realistic attitudes on the part of those who might otherwise have been well suited to one another. When marriages are made on "the assumption that love is a mysterious visitation," there is complete failure on the part of the lovers "to realize that compatibility is a process and not an accident, that it depends on the maturing of instinctive desire, by adaptation to the whole nature of the other person and to the common concerns of the pair of lovers." [3]

Those who make romantic love an end in itself, rather than a prelude to love of a more enduring quality, are in love with *love* rather than with their marriage partner. They are intensely monogamous only so long as romantic love endures. When it fades they leap to the conclusion that marriage has failed and make no serious efforts to preserve the relationship on any other basis. As Lippmann well says: "Lovers who have nothing to do but love each other are not really to be envied; love and nothing else very soon is nothing else. The emotion of love in spite of the romantics is not

---

[1] *Op. cit.*, p. 144.   [2] E. D. Mowrer, *Family Disorganization* (1927), p. 162.
[3] From Walter Lippmann, *A Preface to Morals* (1929), p. 310.   By permission of The Macmillan Company, publishers.

self-sustaining; it endures only when the lovers love many things together, and not merely each other. It is this understanding that love cannot successfully be isolated from the business of living, which is the enduring wisdom of the institution of marriage."[1]

Unaware that such is the case, the disillusioned romantic tends to seek the realization of his, or her, ideal elsewhere. Women, particularly those with leisure time and no other interests outside marriage and the home, are more likely than men to cling to the romantic glamour of the days of courtship and to demand a constant demonstration of affection. Under such circumstances it is fatally easy to develop an infatuation for a third person. In America, romanticism and puritanism combined are responsible for the belief that any infidelity, even if it is but a passing disturbance and does not seriously weaken permanent married love, is yet wholly destructive of marriage. Such a situation is difficult, often tragic, but many students of family life now hold that infidelity, occurring in a moment of passion, should not be allowed to disrupt an otherwise harmonious marriage. Jealousy on the part of the injured partner is not only ineffective, but may cause what would otherwise be a passing infatuation to develop into something far more serious.

Romantic attitudes are responsible for many such infatuations. Indirectly, because they prevent the adjustments necessary in a successful marriage, directly because they lead to a shift of partners in the vain hope of remaining perpetually in love. Accordingly, at the very time when there is an idealization of permanence in love and of life-long companionship between lovers, the popular emphasis placed on the "love-life" of individuals leads to a desire for romantic novelty which undermines the stability of marriage.

Prevalence of Sexual Maladjustments. The desire for full responsiveness in marriage, and the current emphasis on sex, have combined to concentrate attention on the part played by sexual maladjustment in rendering success in marriage difficult and sometimes impossible of attainment. There is general agreement that sexual maladjustment is an underlying cause in most cases of marital friction.[2] But it is important to realize that it is the sex relationship in its *emotional* as well as its physical aspects which plays a major part in married life.[3] Sexual maladjustment

[1] *Ibid.*, pp. 308–309.
[2] See, for example, statements by Paul Popenoe, *The Conservation of the Family* (1926), p. 80; and Hamilton and McGowan, *What Is Wrong with Marriage*, pp. 88, 279–280.
[3] *Factors in the Sex Life of Twenty-two Hundred Women*, Chapters III and IV.

in most cases is not primarily a physical matter, but due to psychological causes. Except in abnormal cases, physical adjustments can be worked out satisfactorily, provided husband and wife persist in consideration for each other, and in an endeavor to understand each other's feelings and attitudes.[1]

Causes for the Prevalence of Sexual Maladjustment. The prevalence of sexual maladjustment is due to a number of causes. It must be remembered, of course, that not only does every marriage involve sexual adjustment, but that the sexual relationship provides in most cases the earliest occasion where the need for mutual adjustment is made evident to lovers. Conflict is very likely either to originate in, or to be thought of, in terms of sexual incompatibility, even where it is actually a far more complex matter. The whole realm of mutual responsiveness, with its exclusiveness and intimacy, comes to be symbolized for husband and wife by the sexual relationship. On the basis of her wide experience as a consultant, Harriet Mowrer says: "While it is true that sex conflict is usually found in domestic discord cases, sometimes even appearing in disguised form, the conflict is in most cases so complex as to involve every phase of the marriage relationship. Sex cannot, therefore, be considered the basic factor any more than any other of the factors which make up the conflict pattern."[2]

There are certain features of the present age which serve to accentuate the problems of sexual maladjustment. We live in an era of "moral and intellectual ferment with regard to sex relations."[3] Traditional attitudes are being undermined, as science takes the place of superstition. When sex is regarded as a natural impulse of fundamental biological and social significance, the emphasis falls on normal sex expression as beneficial to physical and mental health. And this new appraisement of sex applies not only to men, but also to women. No aspect of present attitudes is more subversive of tradition than the realization that women, also, are beings with sexual potentialities and needs, rather than passive instruments for providing children and for relieving the sexual tensions of men.

The current preoccupation with sex is further intensified by the fact that men and women associate far more freely and famil-

---

[1] Chase Going Woodhouse found that relatively little stress is laid on sex problems by happily married people. The essential determinants of happiness are held by them to be the fundamental attitudes of the family members towards each other. "A Study of 250 Successful Families," *Social Forces*, Vol. VIII (June, 1930), pp. 518–532.

[2] *Op. cit.*, p. 149.

[3] Lichtenberger, *op. cit.*, p. 358.

iarly with one another to-day, irrespective even of marital status. Wider and more varied opportunities are thus afforded for sex-stimulation: a fact particularly evident during the war, when the abnormal tensions it created had a drastic effect in sweeping away the inhibitions of the older morality and in causing widespread sex experimentation. War conditions so accelerated the passing of prudery that the pendulum has undoubtedly swung too far in the direction of an exaggerated eroticism.

Such a course of events was probably inevitable in the absence of wholesome attitudes towards sex. Few, even of the present generation, have escaped the influence of unwholesome attitudes and mistaken notions. In this fact is found an underlying cause of the present obsession with sex, and an underlying cause in most cases of sexual maladjustment. Hamilton's study left him with the impression that "most husbands and wives have been so thoroughly warped by the training and environment of their childhood that they can do very little to-day to better their condition." [1]

Men have been taught by tradition to make an altogether too rigid distinction between impure lust and a higher form of love to be anticipated in marriage. But rarely have they realized the need for consideration in initial marital behavior. Women have very frequently been kept in ignorance of the physical aspects of sex, and have almost universally been conditioned in childhood in such a way that over-modest and inhibitory attitudes are deeply ingrained. Under such circumstances it is not to be wondered at that the first experience of marital sex relations so often has injurious psychological effects, particularly for women. [2] Shock, horror, resentment, and profound sexual antagonism may be the result. And matters are not improved by mothers who tell their daughters that "men are like that," or "women must make the best of it," or words of similar import.

Shock and resentment in the early days of marriage are among the causes for the high frequency, among women, of the varied conditions which are popularly grouped under the term "frigidity,"

---

[1] *Op. cit.*, p. 287.

[2] The Davis study of 1,000 married women made very clear the fact that there was a greater chance for subsequent happiness when this first experience was attractive, not repellent. These more fortunate women emphasized the sense of spiritual and emotional agreement which accompanied physical pleasure, and stressed the consideration and self-control of their husbands. Exactly the opposite qualities were emphasized in the other group. The wife, ignorant and shocked; the husband, inconsiderate and uncontrolled. If attempts at adjustment failed, there was unhappiness for both. Of those who had no preparation for marriage, 58.6% believed that adequate instruction would have helped them in adjusting their lives. *Op. cit.*, pp. 65, 69–70.

meaning not only incapacity for complete intercourse, but sexual unresponsiveness, apathy, and antagonism. According to Havelock Ellis, in many cases where a woman is considered frigid, her husband is responsible, for, "while in men the sexual impulse tends to develop spontaneously and actively, in women, however powerful it may be latently and more or less subconsciously, its active manifestations need in the first place to be called out."[1] Obviously, not only mutual consideration, but also understanding of the divergence in sexual needs and desires of men and women would facilitate sexual adjustment. In addition to the distinction just noted, the desire for indirect sexual response, for caresses and affection, is much more diffuse and constant in women, while in men it is more closely connected with the direct and relatively localized sexual response. Husbands are accused of being cold and insufficiently affectionate, when absorbed in other interests and sexually unroused; while many wives are considered cold, because of their inability to respond fully to the husband's aroused sexual impulse.

Disharmony is almost inevitable when there is lack of sexual satisfaction on the part of both husband and wife. The negative conditioning of girls results in many cases not so much in repressing desire as in blocking a complete emotional response. In Hamilton's study, 46% of the women were unable to experience the climactic orgasm. Psycho-neurotic difficulties were frequent, and marital infidelity much more common among these women, since sexual desire is often more imperative where intercourse is incomplete. The resulting tension may drive such women to renewed efforts to reach satisfaction in extra-marital relationships.

There is evidence, to-day, of the spread of wholesome attitudes among young men and women. Yarros tells of the numbers who come to her clinic, before marriage, seeking not only advice on contraceptive methods, but preparation for making satisfactory sexual adjustments. As already pointed out, when fear of an unwanted pregnancy is removed through the use of contraceptives, possibilities for successful marital adjustment are increased. There is no longer any difficulty in securing information on the physiology and psychology of sex. There is, indeed, an almost overwhelming mass of literature on these topics. The difficulty now lies rather in the selection of books in which the presentation is entirely wholesome, straightforward, and scientific.[2]

[1] *The Psychology of Sex* (1933), p. 309.

[2] As an excellent example of a reliable book, see *A Marriage Manual* (1935), by Hannah M. Stone and Abraham Stone. Others which may be recommended appear at the end of the chapter under the head of Suggested Reading.

The Complexity of Marital Interaction. A beginning is being made in the scientific understanding of marital adjustment. One fact emerges more and more clearly: the extreme complexity of marital relationships. In marriage, two personalities are brought into a wholly new and exceedingly intimate relationship with one another. Each personality must be considered dynamically, as in process of change and growth, and as exhibiting traits and behavior patterns which are the result of hereditary influences as these have been molded by a particular environment. Mutual integration of the behavior of two disparate personalities can never be a simple matter, and a certain measure of conflict in attitudes, interests, and desires is inevitable. The more so, since marital adjustment is not static, it cannot be effected once for all, but must be a continuous process, as the personalities of husband and wife are modified by their relationship with one another and by outside influences.

This situation may be most adequately described as a dynamic whole of interrelationships in which equilibrium can be maintained only by renewed adjustments. Certain adjustments are of fundamental importance to harmony, such, for example, as the sexual. Whenever, on the other hand, there is an unresolved conflict of attitudes, tensions and strains develop. Studies of marital maladjustment have revealed a number of *type-tensions*, or typical situations which give rise to marital discord. In each individual case, one such type-tension is usually found to be dominant, although others may also be present. Indeed, one tension leads to another, until a whole configuration of tensions is operative, some of which have cumulatively become more intense while others play a subordinate rôle. It must not be forgotten, of course, in speaking of type-tensions and so emphasizing the total social situation, that in the last analysis we are concerned with the experiences of two human beings. From this point of view it may be more helpful to describe type-tensions in terms of the specific interferences or frustrations with the wishes of the individual.[1]

---

[1] This suggestion is made by Folsom, who translates Mowrer's type-tensions into terms of three categories of frustrations. (1) Non-interpersonal frustrations: frustrations of wishes which normally find satisfaction through the individual's relation to the environment, such as the desire for financial security, for an intellectual life, for higher living standards, etc. (2) Interpersonal frustrations, which are divided into (a) love frustrations, (b) inferiority frustrations. *Op. cit.*, pp. 468 *et seq.* Mowrer considers the four major type-tensions to be: (1) incompatibility in response; (2) economic individualization; (3) cultural differentiation; (4) individualization of life patterns. *Family Disorganization*, pp. 196 *et seq.* Other classifications are those by Burgess and Krueger. Burgess finds seven spheres of marriage in which there may be

Numerous attempts have been made to classify type-tensions and specific causes of discord, and some of these analyses undoubtedly contribute to an understanding of marital maladjustment. Yet they tend to oversimplify the situation, and, as Kirkpatrick says: "One wonders . . . concerning the relationship of a cause to a tension, and is rather inclined to suspect that at times there has been a mere naming and renaming of things rather than the provision of conceptual tools for the analysis of any particular case."[1]

The Relative Positions of Husband and Wife. All that can be attempted, in this chapter, is a brief survey of the chief factors which have been found productive of marital discord. One of these factors is frequently not accorded the full significance it deserves, although reference is often made to *ascendance-submission* conflicts. The equivocal psychological relationship between men, as men, and women, as women, is not only one of the most pervasive but also one of the subtlest sources of tension between husband and wife at the present time. Where a wife's desires for wider opportunities for self-expression come into conflict with traditional attitudes on the part of the husband, tension is inevitable. But this is not simply a matter of conflict between traditional masculine attitudes and a newer outlook, or even over-assertiveness, on the part of women. Most women are restless and unsure of themselves; thwarted by traditional estimates of women, and most of all by a subconscious sense of their inferiority to men. Most men, on the other hand, find self-assurance in a conscious or subconscious sense of their superiority.[2] As Schmalhausen points out: "one of the most incorrigible tendencies of the human mind is the quite unconscious revaluation of differences as constituting in actuality a relationship of superior-inferior. . . . Differences are construed from the point of

either accord or discord: economics, sex, health, respect, culture, temperament, pattern of life. Krueger admits that his classification of thirteen items loses somewhat in the matter of exclusiveness, yet believes that it permits the location and description of tensions in a greater variety of situations: economics; occupation; response (sex); control (positional relationships of members to each other); status (positional relationship of the family in social participation); culture; philosophy of life; temperament; health; individual capacities or abilities; appetites and habits; personal behavior patterns; age. "A Study of Marriage Incompatibility," *The Family*, Vol. IX (April, 1928), pp. 53–60.

[1] "Techniques of Marital Adjustment," *Annals of the American Academy*, Vol. CLX (March, 1932), p. 180.

[2] Miss Rathbone has used the apt phrase, the "turk-complex," to describe the assertion of superiority over the members of his family on the part of a man who feels his insignificance in the larger social order. Such a man has often been subject, as well, to the dominance of his father, and has been in this way made to feel inferior.

view of advantages and superiorities. Nothing, absolutely nothing, within the whole range of human thought and conduct is so difficult as the acceptance and practice of genuine equalities."[1]

And yet it is this reciprocal acceptance of the equal human worth of men and women by each other that is indispensable to full marital adjustment to-day. Only so may men and women reach the sympathetic understanding of one another which alone can provide a sure foundation for an integrated and harmonious relationship.[2] This will take time; attitudes operative in human experience for thousands of years cannot be eradicated in a few decades. Nor can they be eradicated save through educational influences, operative from earliest childhood, and through the achievement of emotional maturity on the part of both men and women.

A satisfactory adult relationship is indeed impossible where there is any attempt of either man or woman to dominate, or on the other hand where either is dependent or irresponsible. Traditionally, of course, man has dominated, and so been held superior; woman has been dependent and supposedly subservient, and so held inferior. These accepted rôles of men and women have been determined fundamentally by just one factor—the consequences entailed for women by sexual intercourse. It is no accident that women are now, at last, achieving a measure of equality with men at the same time when they are gaining control of their function of motherhood.

There is no longer any excuse for the age-long prejudice that adjustment in marriage is not so much a mutual matter as it is subservient adjustment of wife to husband. Stability has been attained, it is true, in this way, but only where, as Hinkle says, "the woman had no ego, no self, but patterned herself after the style or type desired by the man and the environment which he created." Now, however, women are beginning to awake "from

[1] "The War of the Sexes," *Woman's Coming of Age* (Liveright Publishing Corporation, 1931), pp. 263–264.

[2] In this way alone, is there hope of alleviating the sex-hostility and antagonism between the sexes of which so much has been written since the development of psychoanalysis. Take, for example, Van der Velde's *Sex Hostility in Marriage* (1931). In spite of the authority given to this author's books by his wide experience as a gynecologist, his interesting discussion of the psychological differences between men and women, due to their disparate sexual functions, is rendered less valuable by his assumption of certain culturally conditioned traits as *innately feminine*, others as *innately masculine*. In the same way, practical advice is given primarily with a view to the adjustment of women to the traditional institution of patriarchal marriage, with its predetermined pattern for the relationships of husband and wife.

their long sleep—a sleep in which they were unconscious of themselves as individuals."[1] The whole conflict, indeed, is not so much between men and women as between older and more modern ideals.

Disharmony between the sexes, to-day, can only be understood if it is realized how far the attitudes engendered by tradition and prejudice still cast their shadows over any endeavor of men and women to achieve mutual understanding, and a fuller measure of spiritual companionship. Alfred Adler, who, more than any other student of human nature, explored the consequences for personality of feelings of inferiority or superiority said: "The fallacy of the inferiority of woman, and its corollary the superiority of man, constantly disturbs the harmony of the sexes. As a result, an unusual tension is introduced into all erotic relationships, thereby threatening, and often annihilating, every chance for happiness between the sexes. . . . Comradeship is the characteristic index of a true reconciliation with the sexual rôle, of a veritable equilibrium between the sexes."[2]

The Changing Status of the Modern Man. The actual responsibilities of husband and father have been altered. His tasks of protecting and providing for and educating his family have been in some measure taken over by social agencies. And the share of wife and mother in these responsibilities has been profoundly modified as she has followed her former occupations into the world outside the home. Women, far more than men, have been forced to break loose from their ancient moorings, although, as we saw earlier, there still remain far too many women who "want to be treated as equals and also as irresponsible, petty and indulged tyrants."[3] Accordingly they "oscillate moodily between the older pattern of the spoiled child (complacently at home in the Doll's House) and the newer pattern of the full-statured adult."[4] The problems already discussed in Chapter XVI are closely allied to much of the domestic discord of the day.

So too is the prevalent lag in masculine attitude, men's unwillingness to acknowledge women's right to full intellectual development and a responsible share in the world's work. The change between past and present has not been so obvious and direct for men. Their occupations are still regarded as of greater dignity and importance than any activities going on in the

---

[1] *Op. cit.*, p. 227.
[2] *Understanding Human Nature* (1927), pp. 145–146.
[3] *The Nervous Housewife*, p. 13.
[4] Schmalhausen, *op. cit.*, p. 296.

home; they earn most of the money income and are still held to "support" wife and family.[1] Altogether women are commonly supposed to have a rôle which is different from and secondary to that of men. No wonder that all but the most thoughtful and liberal men are bewildered, if not resentful, at the restlessness of modern women, at their invasion of the men's world with its prerogatives, and their conviction that coöperation between men and women should involve provision for the individual development of wife as well as husband.

Marriage has undoubtedly been made harder for men. Most men, it is true, still marry the less individualized type of woman, the woman with allure, who flatters their vanity and ministers to their sense of superiority.[2] But such a woman is incapable of full companionship and tends nowadays to become restless and discontented. If, on the other hand, a man marries an educated, individualized woman, new and difficult adjustments are demanded of him. He has lost much of the glamour which formerly surrounded men, as free and superior beings, and he must measure up to higher standards as a human being. The easiest way to assuage his pride is to blame his wife for departing from traditional ways, for neglecting her housekeeping, or for following new-fangled fads and spoiling the children.[3]

As Beatrice Hale well says, the greatest need is for increasing numbers of *new men*. "The new man is a human being before he is a male, and counts a woman human before female. . . . Every male instinct of domination and sovereignty has to be bred out of the individual before he can attain the status of the new man and be a fit mate for the new woman. He has to understand deeply that the woman is half of the human whole and that there can be no more question of either sex dominating the other than of one half of a circle preponderating over the other half. When he realizes this fundamental equality of the sexes, and not before, he begins to understand that women, having as much humanity as men, need equal freedom for its de-

---

[1] For a striking picture of currently accepted attitudes see *Middletown*, pp. 116–120, and *Middletown in Transition*, pp. 176–180 and 410.

[2] See p. 157, note 1.

[3] In a study of 115 cases of marital discord in terms of frustrations, Folsom found a far greater proclivity on the part of men towards what he calls "inferiority" frustration, while there was a marked preponderance of "non-interpersonal" frustration on the part of women. Marriage to-day interferes far more with women's desires for a fuller, freer life than it does with men's. Women's dissatisfactions tend to translate themselves into a "freedom frustration" or rebellion complex. Men, on the other hand, more definitely associate inferiority frustrations with the behavior of their wives. *Op. cit.*, pp. 467–472.

velopment."[1] The emergence of the new pattern of family relationships, and the alleviation of one of the fundamental causes of marital maladjustment to-day, will come about with the development of "a new chivalry of equal and independent beings."[2]

Conflicts Due to Divergences in Cultural Background. In view of the central importance of mutual sympathy and understanding, it is no wonder that definite dissimilarities between husband and wife in their attitudes towards life should frequently cause conflict. One cause for such dissimilarities is divergence in cultural background, a source of conflict which is accentuated in America, where association is frequent between those of different social classes, religions, nationalities, and even races, and where the romantic American attitude diverts attention from the seeds of discord inherent in cultural differences. For example, the disparity between Catholic and non-Catholic convictions with regard to marital relations obviously imperils mutual accord; and, again, those of different nationality frequently find themselves in conflict over the treatment of the children, or the relative status of husband and wife, or the use of money. Quite often, indeed, less fundamental matters of food, habits, dress, or mannerisms may lead to discord; but, as Harriet Mowrer points out, these are, not so much obstacles in themselves, as symbols of a lack of identification of interests and attitudes. The same is true of the even greater difficulties to be found in marriages between those of different social classes. Differences in standards of living, refinement of manners, tastes, and attitudes may be overlooked in the glamour of a romantic attachment, but are apt eventually to create tension, in view of the almost universally accepted "superiority" of one class to another. Social disapproval aggravates the difficulties of individual adjustment.

The Influence of Personality Patterns. The hidden springs of behavior in both husband and wife are to be found in the personality patterns developed in childhood. Marriage maladjustment presents the same problem as other forms of inability to make successful life adjustments, but in a unique and crucial manner; for family behavior, more than any other form of human conduct, "reveals the influences born of the past and the unconscious in the individual. . . . Domestic interaction provides

[1] *What Women Want*, pp. 254–256. This was written in 1914, when in some ways, the situation was more promising than it is to-day. At that time she said, "At present there are only a few: their numbers are increasing yearly, but still fall far short of the number of new women, particularly in the older countries."

[2] Winifred Holtby, *Women* (1934), p. 110.

rare opportunity for past frustrations, wishes, fantasies, fears and conflicts to reappear. The emotional quality and the concentration characteristic of family experience provide fertile soil for the sprouting of these seeds of the past."[1] It is true, of course, that husband and wife may bring with them not only impediments to marital adjustment, but wholesome influences as well. Few to-day, however, have been so fortunate in family background as to have become emotionally mature, considerate of others, forbearing, tolerant, and imbued with a sense of justice. In the measure in which husband and wife are thus well equipped, modern marriage offers, Groves says, "a rare opportunity for happiness, but it also forces upon the men and women who enter matrimony an ordeal which lays bare any serious handicaps of personality."[2]

The psychoanalytic point of view has thrown much light on the way unconscious factors in personality operate in marital interaction. Much overt conduct has been found to be symbolic of underlying desires for sympathy and understanding, for attention or power. Social psychology, on the other hand, supplements the somewhat one-sided view of many psychoanalysts, by stressing behavior as the product of social interaction. Using what has been called "socioanalysis," marital interaction may be interpreted in terms of the *rôles* of the individual, those patterns or coördinations of habits and attitudes through which the individual maintains status in a particular group.[3] In this way, personality can be sufficiently understood without probing the depths of the unconscious.

At marriage, not only do both husband and wife bring fairly definite ideas of the rôles they are to assume to one another, but they may also seek the fulfilment of desires which are the result of their childhood rôles. In general, where there has been identification with a family situation in childhood, the mature individual more or less consciously seeks its reproduction; as when a marriage partner is chosen who resembles the parent of opposite sex. When, on the other hand, there has been antagonism and frustration in childhood, the tendency is to seek in marriage that which makes good the deficiencies of the family situation; as

[1] E. R. Groves, *The American Family*, p. 185.

[2] *Op. cit.*, p. 259.

[3] The term *status* refers both to the position recognized by others and that occupied by the individual himself. One rôle is usually a dominant rôle, while the others differ in degree of importance. The fundamental pattern, or patterns, of personality are determined by the rôle, or rôles, of the child in interaction with the other members of the family group; such, for instance, as the spoilt-child rôle, the father-antagonistic son, or mother-dependent son or daughter, to mention a few of the most typical.

when an emotionally starved child later makes exaggerated demands for emotional response.[1]

In *Personality and Domestic Discord*, Harriet Mowrer presents evidence of the way in which patterns of domestic discord are shaped by elements characterizing the unadjusted life patterns of one or both of the partners. Particularly illuminating are the cases illustrating the effect of the tendency to avoid difficulties or responsibilities on the part of either husband or wife. Marriage is found by such individuals to be the most difficult experience of all, particularly in cases where a woman has used marriage itself as an escape from some situation; an unhappy home or unsuccessful love-affair or tiresome work. Many women then use *illness* as an escape mechanism, which allows them to retain their status as wife and mother, without assuming its unpleasant responsibilities. Society allows women to escape responsibilities far more easily than men, for whom there are "no conventionally sanctioned exits." Very rarely does a man become ill to escape his problems; far more often does he turn to drink—the most typical masculine form of escape. In this way he overcomes his feelings of inferiority and is conscious of an enhancement of status. Since, however, drunkenness is no longer socially acceptable, those who overindulge find, on recovery, that their difficulties have increased, and that they have suffered still further loss of status.

Obviously, warped personality patterns place serious obstacles in the way of marital adjustment. These obstacles become insuperable, where the defective personality patterns of *both* husband and wife come into conflict with each other, as it is almost inevitable that they should. Adjustment is, on the contrary, made much easier, not only when both partners are well balanced and emotionally mature, but when their personality patterns are somewhat similar. Not that *difference* in pattern or in individual traits necessarily leads to conflict. As Folsom says, "it is never the fact of difference which causes the trouble, but the *interference* of some specific wish, attitude, or habit of one partner, with some specific wish, attitude, or habit of the other."[2]

---

[1] Hamilton found, as the *only* incontrovertible result of his research, that "the proper attitude of the parent towards the child is the only sure cure for the ills of matrimony." *Op. cit.*, p. 287. Even among his 200 cases, a startling number exemplified the danger to a son of possessive love on the part of his mother, and to a daughter of over-dependence on her parents or of having an unworthy father. Those who had married partners with qualities similar to those of the parent of opposite sex, were quite definitely happier than the others.

[2] Reprinted by permission, from *The Family* (p. 441), by J. K. Folsom, published by John Wiley and Sons, Inc.

The Influence of Ill Health. Certain defects of personality almost inevitably cause interference with the wishes of the marriage partner and so lead to conflict. It will suffice merely to mention pathological disabilities such as feeble-mindedness and the various forms of mental disorder. It is now being realized that *incipient* cases of mental disease are very prevalent and that there are many more non-asylum cases than there are cases in the advanced stages of mental breakdown necessitating asylum care. Domestic discord is very frequently caused by the fact that either husband or wife exhibits the often misunderstood symptoms of a mild case of mental disease.

Physical health has also been found to exercise a deleterious influence on family life. It need scarcely be said that venereal disease is disastrous to marital success. But quite apart from this obvious case, there are a number of diseases, particularly those of a chronic character, which complicate marital adjustments. Once again, it is not so much the acute cases which cause trouble as those where ill health manifests itself in irritation, nervousness, lowered vitality, discontent, and depression.

The Influence of Specific Habits, Traits, Attitudes, and Interests. There are a number of habits or tendencies which are always dangerous: violent temper, alcoholism, homosexuality, and various abnormal tendencies. Quite apart from these, there are numerous traits which, while normal enough in themselves, may be incompatible with the traits of a partner in marriage. In Hamilton's study the most common cause of marital dissatisfaction, for both husbands and wives, was the temperament of a partner as expressed in certain qualities and traits. Apart from the traits most closely allied to sexual response, a definite difference was found in the fact that so many men complained of the talkativeness of their wives, while so many women complained that their husbands were not talkative enough.[1] In view of the fact that differences in temperament so often lead to antagonism, it is interesting to note that there is some evidence to show that people of like temperament do not tend to be specially attractive to each other. It appears, on the contrary, that those of unlike temperament tend to be mutually attracted.[2]

In other phases of personality, however, and notably in attitudes and interests, there is a strong tendency for those who

[1] *Op. cit.*, pp. 65, 145, 146.

[2] See Folsom, *op. cit.*, pp. 449 *et seq.*, for a brief survey of studies in this field; also Ernst Kretschmer, "Physical and Spiritual Harmony in Marriage," in *The Book of Marriage*, pp. 305–328, for an account of the findings detailed in his book, *Korperbau und Charakter*.

think and feel alike to be drawn to each other. This is natural. Those who differ profoundly in their tastes, who disagree in fundamental matters, and do not accept somewhat the same standards and philosophy of life, can scarcely hope for successful coöperation in family life. It must be admitted, however, that many couples, who at marriage seem fairly well suited to each other, may in their further development diverge so widely in their interests that they drift apart.[1] Disparities in education and in intellectual and cultural pursuits make for divergent interests. Hamilton found that couples whose formal education had been equal in amount were far above the average in happiness.[2]

The Influence of Age at Marriage and of Differences in Age. Possibilities of divergent individualization are much greater in the case of those who marry very young, and this is probably one reason for the lack of success in many youthful marriages. Fairly early marriage has undoubted benefits; and there is some disagreement as to how far marital unhappiness is associated with early marriage.[3] Undoubtedly those who marry very young are inexperienced, and may lack judgment and self-control, or be more likely to be dominated by a passing "sex-spell." Hart and Schields compared 500 cases before the Philadelphia Domestic Relations Courts with the age distribution of 500 marriage license applications selected at random, and found, statistically, that marriages under the age of twenty-two are more likely to fail than those between twenty-two and twenty-nine. The greatest risk appeared to be when both bride and groom were under twenty-two. The marriage of a very young bride to a much older man was also found to be particularly hazardous. Prospects were best when a bride between twenty-two and twenty-nine married a man a few years older.[4]

Too great discrepancy in age is undoubtedly undesirable, and it is significant that in Hamilton's study none of the husbands

---

[1] A typical case is that in which the wife's attitudes and interests remain wholly domestic, while the husband develops under the stimulus of professional and public life.

[2] A recent study indicates that the higher the educational level at the time of marriage, the greater the chances of successful adjustment in marriage. The wife's educational achievement is, apparently, even more important than the husband's. E. W. Burgess and L. S. Cottrell, Jr., "The Prediction of Adjustment in Marriage," *American Sociological Review*, Vol. I (Oct., 1936), pp. 737–751.

[3] Compare, for example, Popenoe, *Modern Marriage* (1925), p. 51; Davis, *op. cit.*, p. 45; Hamilton and McGowan, *op. cit.*, p. 75.

[4] "Happiness in Relation to Age at Marriage," *Journal of Social Hygiene*, Vol. XII (1926), pp. 403–407.

or wives were happy where the husband was seven to ten years older. Strangely enough the highest percentage of happy men, 62%, were in the group where the wife was one to three years older, and 60% of the husbands and 73% of the wives who had married partners of the same age were happy. But no definite conclusions can be drawn in the absence of further studies. In any case, the factor of age differences is so closely bound up with other factors that its influence is hard to determine.

Conflicts Due to Financial Tensions. If marriage is to be successful, harmonious coöperation must be achieved in all the varied aspects of daily experience. Certain of these aspects are of such importance as to give rise to problems which occur in nearly all marriages. Specific adjustments must be made in each such sphere of interaction between husband and wife, and it is therefore not surprising to find that there are certain focal points of conflict in marital relations. The most crucial of these, the basic relationship of sex, has already been discussed. Second only to sex in the frequency with which it figures in marital discord is the financial and economic factor in marriage. Other focal points are to be found in differences over the use of leisure time, over relatives, and over the children.

It must be borne in mind, however, that, whenever irreconcilable conflict occurs in any of these spheres, it is almost always of psychological origin, and is due in far less degree, if at all, to the intrinsic difficulties of the situation. This was, as we saw, the case with sexual maladjustment, and the same is true with regard to tension over the financial and economic matters with which so much of married life is in some way related. "Friction over money," says Hamilton, "is usually a symptom of something wrong with marriage. It is not necessarily the cause of the trouble. . . . The man—or woman—whose nature has been distorted . . . will be unhappy in married life and will be fatally impelled to look for pegs on which to hang his dissatisfactions. He won't even see the fault in himself. He will look for some fault in his wife. Differences of opinion about how to use the family income are some of the handiest pegs available."[1]

Mowrer found that financial tension was the major situation in from 30% to 40% of 466 divorces he investigated.[2] In a study

[1] *Op. cit.*, pp. 69, 70. A husband may accuse his wife of extravagance or of incompetence in housekeeping, while a wife may criticize her husband for his inability to earn a larger income, or resent his "selfish" expenditures for cigars, say, or club dues, while she is compelled to engage in domestic "drudgery."

[2] *Family Disorganization*, pp. 61–69. This investigation was undertaken in a deliberate attempt to discover the *natural* causes for divorces granted on the legal grounds

by Woodhouse, 51% of the husbands gave the management of money as a chief source of worry.[1] In Hamilton's study the wives showed themselves to be far more sensitive to financial difficulties than the men.[2]

Friction over the Use of Leisure Time. Lack of mutual recreational interests may sometimes lead to discord. The proverbial tired husband who wants a quiet evening at home, while his wife is eager for an evening out after her absorption in household routine, is fairly typical. Where women have too much leisure time and too few worthwhile interests, they easily become absorbed in a restless search for pleasure. Lacking the companionship of their husbands, they may seek the society of other men with more time for recreation, a situation fraught with danger to marital stability. Apparently, there is little tendency to-day for married couples to engage in joint leisure-time pursuits. Apart from card-playing and trips in automobiles, there is no evidence of widespread sharing of recreational interests by husbands and wives.

Friction over Relatives. Friction over relatives has also become proverbial, and for good reason; particularly where there is interference on the part of relatives of either husband or wife with the affairs of the newly married couple, or criticism of either of the partners by their relatives-in-law. The situation is most hazardous of all where relatives share the family home.

The establishment of a new family, as a unit independent of both the parent families, involves, even under the most auspicious circumstances, a series of delicate readjustments. Bride or groom may become jealous of the long-established ties of affection which seem to threaten exclusiveness of response with the partner in marriage. For the parents too the situation is difficult. They must relinquish their earlier and long-accustomed close relationship with son or daughter in favor of this new and intimate alliance. Such an adjustment is particularly hard for the mother, most of all where son or daughter has been over-dependent or where, with no interesting occupations of her

---

of desertion, cruelty, and adultery. Mowrer found that the same type of situation might lead to suits on any one of these grounds. Infidelity and financial tension each accounted for from 30% to 40% of the divorces. Alcohol, cruelty, and personal habits accounted for at least 20%.

[1] "Does Money Make the Marriage Go?" *Survey*, Vol. LXVII (1932), pp. 355–358.

[2] *Op. cit.*, pp. 66–82. Hamilton's results give evidence of the complications introduced into the financial relationships of husband and wife by the changing economic position of women, and the consequent close relationship between financial and economic tensions and more deep-seated causes for discord. The easiest way, judging in terms of happiness, was to let the husband take full charge of finances.

own, she has narrowly concentrated all her interests on her children. Hence the notorious difficulties encountered by a newly married couple owing to the interference of mothers-in-law. And it is hard indeed for a mother-in-law in close contact with the household of her son or daughter not to endeavor to give them the benefit of her experience. The relationship is most difficult between mother-in-law and daughter-in-law, because the wife inevitably to some extent supplants the mother.

Rarely is every characteristic of a marriage partner wholly pleasing. Parent or parents are then blamed—and very often quite justly—for the defects of their child. Every trait in which an individual resembles his own family may in time evoke antagonism. All such factors make for hostility towards relatives-in-law, and also jeopardize marital harmony. Moreover, except in rare cases, adjustments between the new family and parent-families are necessary in every marriage.

Friction over the Children. Finally, if they would avoid serious conflict, and disaster to their children, husband and wife must agree on family discipline. Fortunately this should become less difficult, now that there is a growing body of expert knowledge as to the nurture of children. But where there is ignorance or rejection of this newer medical and psychological knowledge, conflict is very frequent. American fathers often play too little part in their children's lives; and there is, as we saw, a tendency for women to become better educated than men with regard to children. A father with traditional ideas of discipline may accuse his wife of spoiling the children, particularly where such criticisms provide a convenient outlet for some deep-seated sense of inferiority or of grievance. On the other hand, mothers who really spoil their children are all too numerous, and among them are many wives who have sought compensation for their marital dissatisfaction by concentrating their affections on their children. All such situations, in common with marital discord in general, are highly injurious to the children, and may lead to the complete disorganization of the family.

THE RECENT DEVELOPMENT OF A SCIENTIFIC APPROACH
TO PROBLEMS OF MARITAL MALADJUSTMENT

Constructive Methods for the Prevention and Treatment of Marital Discord. A considerable amount of data has been amassed which throws light on the problems of marital maladjustment. There is, of course, little exact scientific knowledge as yet: the recency of a scientific approach and the subtlety and complexity of the subject matter have precluded more substantial results. One thing, however, is clear: the future of marriage and the family very largely depends on the development of methods for the prevention and treatment of marital discord. Until recently almost all proposals for the reform of marriage were concerned with its sociological rather than its psychological aspects. It is now realized that economic and social reforms, however much they may strengthen the family and facilitate the performance of its functions, would not of themselves guarantee wholesome and harmonious family relationships.

Among the innumerable suggestions which have been made are many of great value, particularly where emphasis is laid on education for family life, and upon marital clinics and domestic courts. But there is still far too much implicit adherence to tradition and too much reliance on exhortation, such for instance as the promulgation of "ten rules for happy wedlock," or "ten suggestions for wives (or husbands)": attitudes far removed from the experimental approach, by which alone there is hope of discovering means for the promotion of marital harmony and family stability.

The Treatment of Discord as a Process. To be successful, treatment must rest upon an accurate analysis of the situation. Concepts derived from psychoanalysis, socioanalysis, and social psychology may all contribute to a description of the factors and causal sequences involved in a case. There is much discussion to-day over methods of analysis and techniques of treatment. The Mowrers show very conclusively that the older and simpler procedures of agencies, dealing with domestic discord cases, have been inadequate in bringing about reconciliation.[1]

For purposes of diagnosis and subsequent treatment, Harriet Mowrer stresses the importance of seeing discord as a process, to be understood in terms of its genesis in the sequence of events, in the earlier lives of husband and wife and in their subsequent interaction with one another, which culminates in discord. "The most significant aspect of sequences in domestic-discord cases is the circular nature by which one element passes into another, which in turn directly or indirectly modifies or aggravates the first element." In this process certain elements become *symbolized* in other phases of the relationship. There are indeed "almost unlimited ways in which covert phases of

[1] *Domestic Discord* (1928).

602 NEW HORIZONS FOR THE FAMILY

conflict express themselves overtly, all of which are significant from the standpoint of analysis and treatment."[1]

The problem of the social therapist is to get below the level of overt behavior and discover the fundamental elements and patterns. Diagnosis thus emerges in the course of an analysis, thorough and penetrating enough to yield interpretation which may be made use of as a basis for treatment. An objective clinical approach involves not only a definite conception of the essential data required, but also a definite procedure for securing these data in the course of interviews with both husband and wife. Interviews may be conducted in such a way as to take the form, not only of diagnosis, but also of treatment.

The Central Significance of Attitudes. The purpose of treatment is not so much to get the client to perform certain overt acts as to bring about *change in attitudes.* For the treatment to be successful, marital adjustments must be worked out in the attitudes of husband and wife. During the interview, elements may be introduced "into the situation which . . . change its significance and meaning so that the conflict is modified or dissolved. Fundamentally, treatment becomes a process of changing through socio-psychic therapy those attitudes constituting the basic conflict pattern."[2] Husband and wife must be helped to reinterpret their individual experience and to redefine the situation on a rational rather than an emotional basis. Instead of an emotional approach with its usual moralistic explanations, husband and wife are given an *objective interpretation* of their conflicts. And the efficacy of this *displacement technique,* as the Mowrers call it, "lies in the fact that, if successful at all, it tends

---

[1] From Mowrer's *Personality Adjustment and Domestic Discord,* p. 217. Used by permission of the American Book Company, publishers. Folsom believes additional concepts are needed for fuller analysis of the interaction process, such, for example, as Groves' classification of marital discord into *concealed, acute,* and *chronic,* or, as Folsom himself suggests, *progressive* conflict, *acute* conflict characterized by sudden onset, and *habituated* conflict, usually chronic, which continues indefinitely without getting worse. *Op. cit.,* pp. 477–478; and Groves and Ogburn, *American Marriage and Family Relationships,* pp. 79, 85–87. Krueger enumerates seven points which should be brought out in a thorough analysis, based on a detailed life history of the pre-marriage social background of each of the partners, and a social record of their marriage relationship. These are (1) the entire configuration of tensions operating in the case; (2) the tensions which cumulatively have gradually become more intense; (3) the circular interplay of tensions which intensify each other; (4) the sequential relationship of tensions in which one or more tensions lead to others; (5) the rise and disappearance of tensions; (6) the combination of certain tensions which decisively interplay to dominate the process (*primary tensions*); (7) the tensions playing a minor or subordinate rôle in creating conflicting attitudes (*secondary tensions*). *The Family,* Vol. IX (April, 1928), pp. 53–60.

[2] Harriet Mowrer, *op. cit.,* p. 6.

to modify both overt and covert behavior at the same time, by breaking down the barriers of inner tensions and antagonisms."[1] With understanding, the disposition to blame is dispelled. Husband and wife are then prepared to decide *for themselves* on a future course of action consonant with their real desires.

Analysis, diagnosis, and treatment may all be subjected to testing in terms of outcome. The process of therapy thus constitutes the nearest available approximation to experimental control. When there is adjustment, as shown by change of attitudes in the direction of accord, treatment has been in so far successful, and analysis and diagnosis are in so far adequate. A sufficient number of detailed records of cases should, in time, make possible the working out of typical diagnoses with suggestions as to treatment. As a rule, however, family case-work agencies, as at present constituted, are under such pressure for immediate action and results as to seriously handicap research under their auspices. The Mowrers accordingly advocate the establishment of special clinics for the analysis and treatment of cases of domestic discord. If these were competently staffed and able to command the services of specialists, "Sufficient results should soon be available which might be taken over by departments within case-work agencies, courts and other institutions interested in the social control of domestic discord."[2]

A wealth of data should in time be attained in this way; and also through the establishment of clinics where pre-marital advice is available. Case histories might be accumulated in pre-marital clinics and further data compiled through follow-up work. The latter approach to the whole problem is considered by Kirkpatrick by far the most promising from the standpoint of research.[3] And from the practical standpoint, it is also the most promising, for, after all, *prevention* of domestic discord is the fundamental problem, even though the present situation has tended to concentrate attention on treatment.

Prevention of Discord through the Adoption of a Socio-psychiatric Attitude. From the standpoint of prevention, it is fortunate indeed that the central clue to marital maladjustments is found to be a matter of attitudes. If certain attitudes can be fostered through home nurture and formal education, the incidence of domestic discord should be considerably lessened. Folsom suspects that "there is one trait which is more or less a master key to

[1] *Domestic Discord*, p. 250; and see Chapter V; also Harriet Mowrer, *Personality Adjustment and Domestic Discord*, Chapter II.

[2] *Op. cit.*, pp. 252–253.   [3] *Op. cit.*, p. 182.

all the personality factors which favor marital adjustment. This suspected key is primarily intellectual. It is favored, but not guaranteed, by general intelligence and by the generalized attitude of compassion for suffering. Essentially this 'magic secret' is an intellectual emancipation from the whole ideology of 'blame,' this being replaced by a habit of viewing oneself, one's family, and all human beings from a socio-psychiatric point of view. . . . Intellectual understanding is not a sure cure for all marital problems, but among all *general* remedies known to us to-day, it offers the greatest hope."[1]

Education for family life, supplemented, if need be, by premarital clinics, should eventuate in such widespread understanding of the realities of married life, that young people would approach marriage forewarned, and so forearmed, to meet its challenge, and to secure for themselves the best it has to offer. "There is no doubt," says Bjerre, "that preknowledge and an anticipation of the difficulties is the best means of dealing with their power to inflict damage."[2] In time, then, we may hope that, from the chaotic conditions of the present period of transition, there may eventuate "the remaking of marriage into an inner experience."[2]

The Development of Agencies Offering Guidance for Marriage and Family Life. A wide variety of agencies and individuals are now engaged in offering guidance on family problems. A comprehensive survey of this work in the United States, prior to 1932, has been made by Bridgman.[3] The need for guidance is being realized to-day, both by those in need of counsel, and by social workers, clergy, doctors, judges, and educators, who either as individuals or through the medium of special agencies, are contributing to this work.

The practice of social case-work has in recent years come to include guidance for marriage and family life. Professional social workers within family-welfare agencies have found that sexual and marital maladjustment must be taken into account in dealing with family problems. Sometimes an ordinary case

[1] Reprinted by permission, from *The Family* (pp. 545–546), by J. K. Folsom, published by John Wiley and Sons, Inc.

[2] *The Remaking of Marriage* (1931), p. 200.

[3] "Guidance for Marriage and Family Life," *Annals of the American Academy*, Vol. CLX (March, 1932), pp. 144–164. In Europe too there has been a development of family consultation centers. In pre-Nazi Germany alone, 200 marriage-advice stations were listed. Most of these served as reference bureaus, from which clients were sent to physicians, birth-control clinics, and welfare offices. A-M Durand Wever, "Marriage Advice Stations for Married and Engaged Couples," *The Family*, Vol. XI (May, 1930), p. 85.

worker is expected to offer marital advice, recommending recourse to specialists where necessary. In other agencies, marital advice is made available through a special department, or through reference to a marriage-guidance clinic.

The Catholic Church has long provided guidance for family life through the confessional. Its function is, however, strictly limited by its dogmatic and reactionary attitude. And the same is true of the advice offered by many Protestant clergy. But some ministers have developed reasonably effective procedures; either keeping abreast themselves with the literature in this field, or organizing clinics or bureaus in their churches. The Commission on Social Service of the Federal Council of Churches of Christ in America and six of the larger denominations have all recommended that ministers be qualified to provide instruction and guidance to young people at whose marriages they officiate. The Protestant Episcopal Church has made such instruction obligatory.

As Folsom points out: "It is to medicine and social work that we must look mainly for adequate solutions of individual problems. . . . The physician is peculiarly the servant of modern individualism and liberalism." Being "independent of any great institution with cultural values to defend, . . . the physician and some kinds of social workers may give their prime loyalty to human beings as individuals." On the other hand, ministers, lawyers, and educators must all "observe a certain loyalty to an institution."[1] In spite of their privileged position, Bridgman found that few family physicians had equipped themselves to offer marriage guidance. Certain gynecologists include sex hygiene and marriage guidance in their practice, one of the pioneers in this field being Dr. Robert L. Dickinson.[2] New emphases are also emerging within the birth-control movement, and there is increasing interest in the expansion of the services of clinics to include sex-hygiene instruction and guidance in marital relationships. Child guidance clinics also find it necessary, for the sake of the children, to offer guidance to the parents

[1] Reprinted by permission, from *The Family* (p. 542), by J. K. Folsom, published by John Wiley and Sons, Inc.

[2] As early as 1890, Dr. Dickinson began to collect data on the sex lives of his patients, and by 1925 he had accumulated clinical records of 8,000 cases. "In 1915 he began to persuade his colleagues of the unique opportunity of the physician for preventing serious disorders and unhappiness by the practice of preventive gynecology and marriage relationship guidance." (Bridgman, *op. cit.*, p. 153.) Since 1925 all his time has been devoted to the Committee on Maternal Health, which became, in 1930, the National Committee on Maternal Health, Inc., acting as an advisory service to the medical profession on all aspects of preventive gynecology.

in their marriage relationship. Psychiatrists on the staff of such clinics, and some others in private practice, have come to include marriage guidance as a regular procedure.

Most lawyers, according to Bridgman, have "apparently concluded that it is professionally unethical for them to offer clients marital and family life guidance." Some courts, however, "are developing social philosophies and socialized procedures more rapidly than the legal profession as a whole."[1] Domestic-relations courts are, as we saw, an innovation in legal institutions, depending as they do on case-history data secured by probation officers, social workers, psychiatrists, and clinical psychologists. Decisions are private and judgments are considered as a step in treatment. Some of the courts have established domestic-relationship adjustment bureaus or departments of conciliation. The term adjustment used by courts varies widely from the giving of advice to protracted family case-work equal to that done by the best family agencies.[2]

Interest in education for family life is making its way through educational institutions at all levels from nursery schools to adult education. What more natural than that those who are students of marriage and family life should be asked for guidance? Yet, as Bridgman points out, "educators who offer marriage and family life guidance do so with a wealth of general knowledge about family life seldom found in the other professions, but with relatively little training for or experience in giving personal assistance through the interview. For the most part they carry over into their guidance work the points of view and assumptions of teachers of subject matter: that telling people what they need to know helps them to feel differently about and behave differently in their marriage and family relationships; and that what they need to know can be more or less accurately ascertained by comparing results of psychological tests with findings in the study of a thousand or more typical cases. These assumptions stand in sharp contrast to the generally accepted professional standards of social case-work and of medicine: that the guidance of human relationships is an art

---

[1] *Ibid.*, p. 156.

[2] For example, the Milwaukee pre-divorce court, established in January, 1935, had, according to Judge Hennessey, "mended" 40% of the 4,000 cases coming before it by May, 1936. *New York Times*, May 24, 1936. In the 1937 annual report of Justice Hill of the New York Domestic Relations Court, it was pointed out that, due to the extension of the system of personal interviews and adjustments, there had been a rise in the number of conciliated cases. Of 21,705 applicants interviewed, fewer than half, or 9,332, pressed their cases through to trial, while 75% of the adjustments remained permanent. *New York Times*, July 23, 1937.

which can be practiced safely and effectively only by those who have served apprenticeships in clinical work under supervision; that the most important factor in the process of guidance is the use made by the clinician of the personal relationship that develops between himself and his client; and that the kind of information given and the form in which it is couched is less important than the meaning it holds for the client and the use he makes of it." [1]

The newest and most significant type of agency offering guidance on family problems is the marriage or family relations consultation center. A number of these have been established in recent years by universities, churches, courts, and other social agencies. Outstanding among them is the Institute of Family Relations in Los Angeles, which represents the first organized attempt in the United States to bring the resources of science to the promotion of successful family life.

Founded, in 1930, on a much broader basis than any similar institution in Europe, it has become a leader in this movement. Incorporated as a non-profit enterprise, its services are available to the public at a minimum cost. The work falls into three main divisions: public education, research, and personal service. [2] The educational department arranges for lectures and courses and conferences, in collaboration with other organizations in related fields, and with state and local educational agencies. The research department is engaged in the investigation of factors making for success or failure in marriage. [3] Since, during four and a half years, the Institute assisted 13,000 people, it is amassing a wealth of material. The department of personal service has hitherto found itself called upon most frequently for advice in a wide range of family maladjustments. Special emphasis is laid, however, on its work in pre-marital preparation. This includes a study of personal and family history, a physical examination, and personal instruction according to the client's needs.

Bridgman believes that the practice of marriage and family life guidance will in time be reabsorbed into the professions from which it is now emerging. It is much to be hoped that in time all young people will be prepared for marriage and family life in the regular course of their education, and that specialists in

[1] *Op. cit.*, p. 160.

[2] Its general director is Dr. Paul Popenoe, and the staff includes medical, educational, and research directors, directors of personal and psychological service, and medical and family relations counsellors and lecturers.

[3] Dr. Roswell Johnson, director of personal service, has in preparation a book, shortly to be published under the title of *Happy and Unhappy Marriages*.

guidance will have developed within the professions. In the meantime, organizations such as the Institute of Family Relations are indispensable, both because the service offered is comprehensive enough to escape the limitations of present attempts at guidance within the special professions, and because of the opportunities afforded in this service for experimentation in the development of guidance techniques, and for research in the field of marriage and family life.

SUGGESTED READING

Bridgman, R. P., "Guidance for Marriage and Family Life," *The Annals of the American Academy of Political and Social Science*, Vol. CLX, March, 1932, pp. 144–164.

Davis, K. B., *Factors in the Sex Life of Twenty-two Hundred Women*, 1929.

Dickinson, R. L., and Beam, L., *A Thousand Marriages*, 1932.

Ellis, H., *The Psychology of Sex: A Manual for Students*, 1933.

Folsom, J. K., *The Family*, 1934, Chs. XIV–XV.

Groves, E. R., *Marriage*, 1933.

——, and G. H., *Sex in Marriage*, 1932.

——, and Brooks, L. M., *Readings in the Family*, 1934, Chs. XVI, XXIII.

Hamilton, G. V., *A Research in Marriage*, 1929.

——, and Macgowan, K., *What Is Wrong with Marriage*, 1929.

Hart, H. H., and E. B., *Personality and the Family*, 1935.

Mowrer, E., *Family Disorganization*, 1927.

——, *The Family*, 1932.

——, and H., *Domestic Discord*, 1928.

Mowrer, H., *Personality Adjustment and Domestic Discord*, 1935.

Schmalhausen, S. D., "The War of the Sexes," *Woman's Coming of Age* (eds. Schmalhausen, S. D., and Calverton, V. F.), 1931, pp. 260–297.

Stone, A., and H. M., *A Marriage Manual*, 1935.

Stopes, M., *Married Love*, 1918.

Van der Velde, Th. H., *Ideal Marriage*, 1930.

Wright, H., *The Sex Factor in Marriage*, 1931.

Yarros, R., *Modern Woman and Sex*, 1933.

CHAPTER XX

THE EMERGENCE OF A COÖPERATIVE FAMILY

RADICAL THEORIES OF REFORM

Freedom in Love. The rapidity and extent of changes in attitude, towards the problems of sex and marriage, are made clearly apparent by reading some of the books which, at the beginning of the century, were considered dangerously iconoclastic and subversive of morality.[1] True that Edward Carpenter's proposal of *freedom in love* and similar proposals made by Ellen Key, and by Bertrand Russell at a later period, are radical even to-day; but it is impossible now, for those who did not experience it, to imagine the startling impression created by frank discussion of the problems of sex and love and marriage.[2]

The revolt against the restrictions and repressions of marriage, according to the patriarchal pattern, was the product of several influences. Socialists and feminists both attacked contemporary marriage, and so reënforced the efforts of those whose chief interest lay directly in its reform.[3] While Carpenter's central emphasis lay on freeing the full potentialities of love, Ellen Key, influenced by Nietzsche's dreams for the future of the race, advocated "freedom for love's selection." Carpenter maintained that the reality of marriage is to be found in the living bond which unites lovers, and that liberty is needed to keep this living.[4] According to Ellen Key, the creative force of love should accept

[1] For example, Edward Carpenter's *Love's Coming of Age* (1906), written in the nineties, had to be privately printed after being refused by every publisher to whom it was submitted. By 1911 it had been translated into many languages, and in Germany had reached its fourteenth edition.

[2] Many of Carpenter's proposals are now accepted by all liberals, such, for instance, as the freedom of women and sex education, both of which Carpenter considered essential steps in reform; also his plea for "a humaner, wiser, and less panic-stricken treatment" of the subject of marriage. *Op. cit.*, p. 82.

[3] Limitations of space preclude any account of the penetrating criticisms made of marriage. See, for example, August Bebel, *Woman under Socialism* (1893); Mona Caird, *The Morality of Marriage* (1897); Grete Meisel-Hess, *The Sexual Crisis* (1916).

[4] While formal contracts would probably continue to be made for some time, they should "lose their irrevocable and rigid character and become in some degree adapted to the needs of contracting parties." In spite of his idealism, Carpenter admits that "love is doubtless the last and most difficult lesson that humanity has to learn." *Ibid.*, pp. 114, 119.

no standard but "enhancement of life." "The new sexual morality," she says "—where the light . . . will radiate from the child—may, however, continue to uphold single love as the ideal for the highest happiness and development both of the lovers and of their children." [1]

The Post-war Revolt against Sex Restrictions. The earlier advocates of greater freedom in sex relations were idealists, profoundly in earnest, and must be sharply distinguished from the majority of those who have broken loose from social and moral restraints in sexual matters: the thoughtless, the undisciplined, the over-sexed, cynics, sensualists, and hedonists. The chaos of the World War was succeeded by an era of disillusionment in which traditional attitudes, already undermined, crumbled and were swept away. Radical opinions, hitherto held only by small groups of intellectuals, came to be openly expressed. The views of Bertrand Russell, based on his own experiences, were typical in their mingling of justification for extra-marital relationships with constructive criticism, and even idealism, in regard to marriage.[2] He was so influential that Catholic writers speak of him as "the most dangerous man living."

It was probably inevitable under the circumstances, that license should have accompanied the sexual revolution. No serious leader of radical opinion has condoned, far less advocated, promiscuity. Its consequences in disillusionment and devaluation of life have been only too obvious. But, during the war, multitudes of young people lived under the constant menace of death. The value of life was condensed into the passing moment, and sexual relationships became casual affairs, offering momentary solace and release as a means of escape from actual life. Something of this cynical attitude persisted through the disappointments of the post-war years, but its force is apparently diminishing, wherever more normal conditions have come to prevail.

---

[1] *Love and Marriage* (1911), p. 155.

[2] Sex morality, according to Bertrand Russell, must be derived from two principles: "that there should be adequate care of children, physical and psychological," and "that there should be as much as possible of that deep serious love between man and woman, which embraces the whole personality of both and leads to a fusion by which each is enriched and enhanced." *Marriage and Morals* (1929), p. 315. Yet, "I think that where a marriage is fruitful, and both parties to it are reasonable and decent, the expectation ought to be that it will be lifelong, but that it will not exclude other sex relations." *Ibid.*, p. 142. For "to close one's mind in marriage to all approaches of love from elsewhere is to diminish receptivity and sympathy and opportunities of valuable human contacts." *Ibid.*, p. 141. The duty of controlling jealousy should be substituted for the duty of conjugal fidelity.

Criticism and Reconstruction. Sexual relationships can only be treated as trivial by those for whom life is devoid of profound significance; for example, by those selfish individuals who spend their days and nights in a restless and futile search for pleasure and excitement. Those who are wiser have learned from experience that happiness is not to be won by means which threaten personal integrity. To identify *self-expression* with giving a free rein to powerful impulses which human beings share not only with all other human beings, but also with animals, is evidence of impoverishment, and of lack of well-developed individuality.[1] Life cannot be enriched, nor experience enhanced, where the satisfaction of sexual impulse becomes a casual physical matter, detached from the full significance it may have in human experience.

A constructive morality demands, therefore, that sex be integrated with the whole of life. "The wise individual," says Tufts, "instead of abdicating control over passion, so organizes his life as to make passion and emotion contribute to its fullness. To this end he has to commit himself and undertake responsibilities. Fullness of life and the more lasting joys are not attained by a casual dependence upon whatever allures. And the gratification of sex makes its finest contribution when it is associated with the refining influences of art, the dignity of intelligent guidance, a 'partnership in the whole of life,' as the Roman jurist defined marriage, the grace of affection, and, for many, the sacredness of a religious institution. It suffers by isolation."[2]

Constructive freedom never means untrammeled freedom. Free choice of a way of life means acceptance of its attendant responsibilities and the resignation of alternative ways. The one-sided exaltation of freedom in love is thus self-defeating, since it renders impossible a complete integration of love with an enduring relationship between a man and a woman. Radical theories, whether actuated by visionary idealism or cynicism,

[1] Such behavior, according to Dewey, is better described as *self-exposure. Art as Experience* (1934), p. 62. In *Sex and Culture* (Oxford University Press, 1934), as the result of an exhaustive study, J. D. Unwin reaches the conclusion that the energy displayed by a society has depended upon the degree of *restriction* of sexual opportunity. He concludes accordingly: "If . . . a vigorous society wishes to display its productive energy for a long time and even for ever, it must re-create itself . . . ; first, by placing the sexes on a level of complete legal equality, and then by altering its economic and social organization in such a way as to render it both possible and tolerable for sexual opportunity to remain at a minimum for an extended period, and even for ever. In such a case, the face of society would be set in the Direction of Cultural Process; its inherited tradition would be continually enriched; it would achieve a higher culture than has yet been attained." P. 432. By permission.

[2] Dewey and Tufts, *Ethics* (Henry Holt and Company, rev. ed., 1932), p. 505.

are, as Floyd Dell points out, characteristic products of a period of transition in which the patriarchal pattern, though obsolete, still impedes adjustment to modern conditions. "Ideological compensations" for this "cultural lag" are in the nature of emotional propaganda, of religious consolations, and aesthetic wish-fulfilments, and cannot be treated as embodying constructive plans for future action.

Bertrand Russell's discussion of the supplementation of marriage and parenthood by other "love" relationships cannot, of course, be dismissed as dealing with the merely theoretical. He is in fact describing a state of affairs which is very frequent to-day, and suggesting its acceptance as part of the "new morality." It must be admitted, also, that, with freer conditions of life for women as well as men, very few escape being attracted in greater or less degree to members of the other sex besides their marriage partners. There is, indeed, always the possibility that friendship between a man and a woman will ripen into love. Since this is so, must such friendships be abandoned, unless shared by both husband and wife? This would surely be to return too far in the direction of narrow possessiveness.

Friendships with the opposite sex are least dangerous when they involve a sharing of impersonal interests. Sexual attraction is more likely, where the relationship becomes too personal, where the desire for response, mutual sympathy, and understanding becomes strong.[1] Perhaps, with fuller psychological wisdom and better preparation for marriage, husbands and wives will more frequently be able to achieve such a degree of mutual responsiveness, that friendships with others of the opposite sex may enrich experience with less danger to marital ties. The course of such friendships may, moreover, be subject to control, which does not of necessity mean their complete abandonment.

In all the deepest and most significant relationships of life, suffering, even tragedy, is occasionally inevitable. In the relationship of marriage, there would probably be more suffering and tragedy and less chance of achieving success, were men and women to enter marriage in the expectation of supplementary sexual relationships. An invaluable safeguard would then be removed, the determination on the part of both husband and

---

[1] As Bertrand Russell remarks, "love is the principal means of escape from the loneliness which afflicts most men and women throughout the greater part of their lives," op. cit., p. 122. Psychiatrists, and in some cases doctors, are obliged in order to help their patients, to show so much sympathetic understanding that what psychoanalysts call "transference" is all but inevitable.

wife to overcome all obstacles in the way of achieving an *enduring mutual* relationship.[1]

COMPANIONATE MARRIAGE

On the foregoing fact is based the chief criticism of the concrete proposal for marriage reform known as "companionate marriage."[2] In his advocacy of the legal and social recognition of "companionate marriage" as a distinct form, Judge Lindsey has in mind not only the legalization of contraception, which makes possible avoidance of parenthood in the earlier years, but also the facilitation of early marriage between young couples, who for economic and social reasons should not yet assume the responsibilities of full family life. Divorce would be by mutual consent for childless couples and with no payment of alimony. Young people who had been educated for family life would thus be enabled to marry, "under conditions that would best insure the success and permanence of marriage, but which would also afford a line of retreat in case the marriage failed."[3] Lindsey holds that companionate marriage differs in spirit and intent from *trial* marriage, and would tend "towards stable relationships rather than towards reckless promiscuity."[4]

From the educative standpoint Judge Lindsey's proposal has

[1] Esther Harding well says of marriage, "its very essence implies permanence. The man and woman who marry declare their intention of taking this one relationship of all possible relationships in order to work on it and make it permanent. . . . The difficulties and dangers of any close relationship demand the mobilization of all our forces. It is a well known psychological fact that if the attitude be secretly taken, 'we can always turn back,' it is impossible to mobilize all our forces. . . . The adventure is all but doomed at the outset, if a back door of escape be left open." *The Way of All Women* (Longmans, Green and Co., 1933), pp. 172–173.

[2] The term *companionate* was first used by Knight, in 1924, in pointing to the prevalence in modern society of deliberately childless marriages: "we may call the state of lawful wedlock, entered into solely for companionship, and not contributing children to society, the 'companionate,' using the term 'family' in its true historical sense, as the institution regulating reproduction, early education, property inheritance and some other things. . . . The companionate is one of our community institutions and we have been dealing with it as though it were the family, which it is not." "The Companionate and the Family," *Journal of Social Hygiene*, Vol. X (May, 1924), pp. 257–267.

[3] Lindsey and Evans, *Companionate Marriage* (1927).

[4] *Ibid.*, p. 191. Interestingly enough, "trial marriage," as advocated by Elsie Clews Parsons in her book, *The Family* (1906), is substantially companionate marriage, and thus antedates Lindsey's proposal by twenty-one years. After pointing out that "truly monogamous relationships seem to be those most conducive to emotional and intellectual development," she says that "it would therefore seem well from this point of view to encourage early *trial* marriages, the relation to be entered into with a view to permanency, but with the privilege of breaking it, if it proved unsuccessful and in the absence of offspring, without suffering any great degree of public condemnation." Pp. 348–349. A storm of protest greeted this proposal.

value as an honest endeavor to readjust marriage to present-day conditions. After all, however, the chief change proposed is not in marriage but in divorce law; and divorce by mutual consent for childless couples could be legalized without making so radical a distinction between the two forms of marriage.

The source of its chief weakness has been pointed out by Lippmann: "at best it is frankly an attempt at a compromise between marriages that are difficult to dissolve and clandestine relationships which have no sanction whatever."[1] It is, therefore, inspired rather by the "pathology of sexual relations," and designed as a cure for "corrupt marriage on the one hand and furtive promiscuity on the other." It points out a way "of escape from the bad life," but does "not define the good life in sex."[2] As such, it is not constructive in the fullest sense, and might tend to encourage less serious attitudes towards marriage.

THE RUSSIAN EXPERIMENT

Purposes of the Experiment and Conditions of Its Inauguration. An experiment in family relationships has been in progress in Russia since 1917. There has been a deliberate endeavor to determine sexual ethics, and the forms of marriage and the family, solely through considerations of social welfare, and quite uninfluenced by irrational traditions of the sinfulness of sex. In the earlier years it looked very much as though the family would disappear. The "social function of motherhood" was accorded full recognition, since a plentiful supply of healthy children was necessary. But motherhood was valued very largely in its physiological aspects. Domestic and educational functions of the single household were to be transferred to the community; women would then be free for economic production, and the training of young communists would be performed more efficiently through state institutions than in isolated families, where the collectivist spirit is compromised by individual interests and aims. The family, moreover, was regarded by many with contempt as a relic of the bourgeois regime.

"Bourgeois morality" became, indeed, a synonym for all codes, customs, and conventions which had to be utterly rooted out if the new way of life were to prevail. The sexual anarchy of the years following the Revolution was thus in part due to an iconoclastic revolt from bourgeois tradition. Very largely, however, it was the result of chaotic social conditions. In Russia the

---

[1] *Preface to Morals*, p. 298.   [2] *Ibid.*, pp. 307–308.

war was followed by revolution, counter-revolution, civil war, and famine. But unrestrained license was never countenanced by Soviet leaders. Far from being an integral part of communism, the "new sexual morality" was denounced by Lenin as "a phenomenon of decadence" and "an extension of the bourgeois brothel."[1]

Legal and Social Measures. Ecclesiastical marriage and divorce were abolished, and civil marriage recognized, by Lenin's decrees of December, 1917. A tentative marriage law, of 1918, made of marriage a contract based on the principles of complete equality, separate property, and mutual responsibility for support; a contract, moreover, which could be dissolved by the wish of only one partner. All distinction between legitimate and illegitimate children was abolished, both alike having rights to support and inheritance from both father and mother. Proved paternity gave the mother a right to one-third of the father's earnings. A new code was adopted and put into force in 1927; the most important emendation being the placing of *factual*, non-registered marriages on an absolute equality juridically with registered marriages. Apart from children, both marriage and divorce were private affairs. In case of any dispute over the support of children, judgment was to be determined by the interests of the children.[2]

The welfare of children is regarded as a matter of primary significance to the state. *Protection of Motherhood and Childhood* has become one of the most important parts of the Soviet program and is carried on under the direction of the State Scientific Institutes for the Protection of Mothers and Infants, in Moscow

[1] During these turbulent years the rising generation was much influenced by the "glass-of-water" concept, according to which sexual relations had only physiological significance, and should be indulged in as casually as the drinking of water when thirsty. According to Lenin, such a view was *unsocial*. "Drinking water really is an individual concern. . . . But will a normal person under normal conditions lie down in the dirt on the road and drink from a puddle? Or even from a glass with a rim greasy from many lips? Love, however, has a social aspect; it involves two, and a third, a new life, may come into being. That implies an interest on the part of society, a duty to the community. . . . Communism is not meant to introduce asceticism, but the joy of life and vital vigor, attained partly through the fulfilment of love. . . . The hypertrophy in sexual matters, which we often observe now, does not produce the joy of life and vital vigor, it detracts from them." Quoted from Clara Zetkin's *Reminiscences of Lenin* (1927), by Halle, *Woman in Soviet Russia*, pp. 113–114.

[2] As a rule, a mother receives custody, and a father pays one-third of his earnings till the child is eighteen. If there are more children he pays more, but never more than half his earnings. Sometimes such rulings are reversed, the father keeping the child and the mother paying. If there are no children and both are in good health, there is no alimony.

and Leningrad. Everything possible is done to prepare mothers for their task and to help and protect them in its performance. Breast-feeding is stressed, and babies are given hygienic care in crêches while mothers are at work, passing later to the nursery school, kindergarten, and school, in all of which really sound health education is given to the children. From the earliest awakening of consciousness the child is made to feel himself a part of the community, and is trained in the communist way of life.[1]

Finally, the Soviet state has been unique in the official sanction accorded to voluntary motherhood. Not only were birth-control propaganda and research in contraception sanctioned by the state, but, from 1920 to 1936, legal sanction was given to abortions performed by government surgeons in government hospitals. This step was taken in an endeavor to diminish the widespread evil of clandestine abortion with its risks to life and health. Apparently these dangers were reduced to a minimum, there having been but one death in 25,000 legal cases; and it was claimed that, despite its legalization, abortion was not so prevalent in Russia as in other countries.

When the Soviet government came into power, immediate steps were taken to suppress commercialized vice and to combat prostitution. The emphasis has been placed on prevention and on the removal of economic causes leading to prostitution. Most significant of all has been the treatment accorded prostitutes in prophylactoria. These are combined clinics, rest homes, and trade schools in which venereally diseased and untrained women are received for medical treatment and vocational education. A position and living quarters are found for inmates upon their discharge. At no time are they treated as sinners; but rather as victims of economic conditions, and every effort is made to give them self-confidence as responsible members of the community.[2]

Estimate of Results. A generation has now come of age which was born into the new social order and accordingly accepts its institutions, customs, and standards as a matter of course. Some observers are enthusiastic over the result. Frankwood Williams,

---

[1] For details see Alice W. Field, *The Protection of Women and Children in Soviet Russia* (1932); and Vera Fediaevsky and Patty Smith Hill, *Nursery School and Parent Education in Soviet Russia* (1936).

[2] In 1931 there was held in Moscow a First Conference of Former Prostitutes Now Workers. An account of this meeting, at which she made an address, is given by Fannina Halle, *op. cit.*, pp. 244 *et. seq.* Statistics from a number of sources indicate a gradual decrease in prostitution in Russia.

for example, described the fearless and realistic attitude of a typical couple of young parents with unqualified approval. From an early age they have accepted the Russian code that only those things which injure the group are wrong, and that matters essential only to individuals shall be left to those concerned. Boys and girls are constantly together and accustomed to comradeship. Sex has never been a secret, and no feelings of guilt or degradation are associated with it. Both husband and wife in all probability had sexual experience before their marriage. "With the neuroticism out of sex not only is energy freed for other interests, but by-products such as pornography and perversion and the like drop rapidly to a minimum."[1] There has been a marked decline in the rate of incidence of nervous and mental diseases, for the social order is such as to eliminate to a large extent the feelings of inferiority, fear, insecurity, and guilt which are the cause of so many mental ills.

There are, however, other aspects of the situation. Love still involves tragedy; and suffering is often accentuated, owing to the prevalence of pre-marital and extra-marital relationships. Halle notes a further fact which has recently become apparent: the difference between the attitudes of men and women towards sex and love. Young women in Russia are the equal comrades of men, objective, practical, and seriously interested in social questions; they wholly repudiate "petty bourgeois sentimentality in love"; but they are far less contented than are men with the devaluation of romantic love and of the personal inner aspect of sexual life. There are also, Halle states, a constantly increasing number of unmarried mothers. Sometimes, as the result of bitter experience, women are unwilling to bind their lives to those of men; in other cases, the clash between social activities and love leads to a renunciation of regular family life.

There was indeed much discussion, in the fall of 1934, among members of the League of Young Communists, as to whether they should not forego marriage because jobs, social work, and study occupied so much time. The letters published in *Komsomol Pravda*, organ of the League, with its 5,000,000 members, reveal a feeling of responsibility towards marriage, but also the great difficulties in the way of a satisfactory home life, because of lack of time and because of the housing shortage. This discussion was the occasion for a pronouncement in favor of serious and lasting marriage on the part of a prominent Bolshevik, head of the League of Militant Atheists, Yaroslavsky.

[1] *Russia, Youth, and the Present Day World* (1934), p. 48.

The Reinstatement of the Family. For some years, the League of Young Communists has taken a leading part in the movement towards the rehabilitation of monogamous marriage as a new form, based upon economic, political, and social equality of the sexes, and "upon the common ideas and mental concord of two people who love one another." Various plebiscites indicated that three-quarters of the young people were in favor of the maintenance of lasting marriages and condemned fortuitous, transient, and irresponsible relations.[1]

Observers such as Halle and Kingsbury and Fairchild stress the new life put into personal relationships through the equal sharing in all responsibilities on the part of men and women. In his article in *Pravda*, Yaroslavsky advocated the work of husbands *in* the home, as an aspect of the equality of husbands and wives. "Creation of the family is the most important and responsible step in life," and light-minded and irresponsible relations are to be condemned. They leave nothing but disappointment, foster an "attitude of irresponsibility," and sometimes result in "vulgarizing the family relationship."[2]

The year 1935 was marked by a series of official pronouncements and official measures designed to strengthen the family. In June, *Pravda* declared: "Never before could man love as freely, fully and richly as now," equality of the sexes having been established and the financial dependence of woman on man abolished. "Love is the whole foundation of the Socialist family. Without it, the family cannot exist. Young Communists must be capable of this noble feeling. Those who are not are selfish and parasites. We demand that public opinion persecute them and hold them up to contempt." Moreover, since women not only study and work as do men, but must also be valued as mothers, man is put "under the obligation to care for the woman with special knightliness."[3]

In August changes in the divorce law were announced.[4] Divorces had reached their peak in May, there being 44.3 divorces registered for every 100 marriages. It was revealed, moreover, that 500,000 alimony cases had passed through the

---

[1] Halle, *op. cit.*, p. 200.

[2] *New York Times*, Oct. 19, 1934; and see Milly Bennett, "Soviet Russia Discovers Home, Sweet Home," *New York Times Magazine*, Nov. 10, 1935.

[3] *New York Times*, June 10, 1935; and *Literary Digest*, July 13, 1935.

[4] *New York Times*, Sept. 22, 1935. Divorce was not so common among the young as among those over 30, chiefly petty employees and persons in unskilled work. The divorce evil was found to be largely due to hasty marriages and marriages of convenience, the latter often being contracted by persons needing somewhere to live.

courts in the preceding three years, in the majority of which parents had attempted to shirk their responsibility to their children. Registration of a divorce could be effected, thenceforth, only with the knowledge of both parties.[1] Alimony-dodging became an offense punishable by two years in prison. Finally, in June, 1936, a new family law went into effect. Those who broke marital ties were to be heavily taxed: a law resulting in a 90% decrease in divorces.[2] Abortions were prohibited except for therapeutic reasons, and provision was made for the extension of services to mothers and children and for the establishment of state aid to large families. In every possible way publicity is being given to the new Soviet advocacy of "A happy childhood and a happy and strong family life."

Early in 1937, it became apparent that the elaborate plans to double the population, within twenty-five years, were succeeding beyond all expectations and so rapidly that facilities of all kinds were proving entirely inadequate to care for the 100% increase in babies. The birth-rate was already high in Russia, between 35 to 50 per thousand, but for the first five months of 1937, it was found to have almost doubled over the corresponding period of 1936.[3] Many of the planned-for maternity hospitals, nurseries, and kindergartens have not been completed. The shortage in hospitals is proving particularly serious, it being found almost impossible to cope with the deluge of cases. Moreover, maternity leaves have heavily depleted the personnel of the factories and there is a great shortage of agricultural workers.

The new insistence of Soviet leaders on strict life-long monogamy is defended as based on fundamental Communist doctrines. In the early years of the new regime it was necessary to destroy the patriarchal family with its ties based on economic considerations rather than on love, and also to create new material conditions which would eliminate economic calculations in marriage. Full economic equality of husband and wife will, they believe, facilitate the development of complete monogamy for men, since women will no longer tolerate infidelity as they are forced to do in bourgeois society.[4]

[1] This put an end to "post-card divorces," where notification of a divorce received by one partner was sent to the other by mail.
[2] *New York Times*, July 26, 1936.
[3] *New York Times*, June 28, 1937, and March 7, 1937. Very early marriage and parenthood are customary in Russia, unmarried motherhood is sanctioned, and birth control is not widely practiced. Under these conditions the new law, particularly the abolition of abortions, has achieved startling results.
[4] *New York Times*, Nov. 18, 1936. It is interesting to note that, as late as 1929, observers questioned whether children could ever again become a powerful and bind-

For a time it seemed that Soviet Russia was putting into practice a modern counterpart of Plato's suggestions, and radicals in other countries claimed that events were proving the validity of their contention, that sex was a private and personal matter, except with regard to children. Now, however, as Duranty points out, the Bolsheviki have discovered that the "ancient folkways," such as "mutual love of man and woman and for children," are not products of capitalism, but on the contrary the outcome of the lives and experience of countless generations.[1] Marriage, they find, cannot be treated as the merely personal affair of individuals, but is of utmost concern to the state. All this would be encouraging indeed, seeming, as it does, to presage the emergence of a new and improved pattern of family life, were it not for one factor: that the fundamental motive for the strengthening of family stability is the mass production of Communists; not of individuals considered as ends in themselves, but as units in the population race with Germany and Italy. For every Nazi and Fascist produced, Russia hopes to raise two Communist fighting men!

THE COUNTER TREND TOWARDS THE REËNFORCEMENT OF PATRIARCHAL PRINCIPLES

Our earlier discussion of the position of women in Germany and Italy will have made clear the fact, that the approved pattern of the family in both these countries in strongly patriarchal. In both countries, moreover, all efforts are bent on increasing the population. In this, however, in contrast to Soviet Russia, they are both failing, and neither country has succeeded in checking the trend towards smaller families.[2] In Italy, a variety of measures have been employed for the last ten years. Abortion and birth-control teaching are penalized; special taxes are levied upon bachelors and upon married couples with less than two children; preference is given for government positions to the fathers of large families, and various rewards have been

ing force in the Soviet family, reduced as it was to a skeleton and a shadow of the old family. The young at that time spent almost all their time away from "the narrowing influences of home." See Maurice Hindus, *Humanity Uprooted* (1929). *Individual* family life is now insisted on, as is evident from the condemnation by *Pravda* of a kitchenless apartment house as a "leftist attempt artificially to introduce communal living."

[1] "Liberalism Advances in Soviet Russia," *New York Times Magazine*, July 19, 1936.

[2] Apparently, however, the steady decline of the Italian birth-rate has now been arrested. In 1938, there were 281,629 births in the first three months, as compared with 257,030 for the same period in 1937; a rate of 25.8, instead of 23.8, per 1,000. *New York Times*, April 21, 1938.

devised for the prolific. Finally, the state has established a National Institution for the Protection of Motherhood and Infanthood which has built up-to-date maternity hospitals all over Italy.[1] But since fascism came into power, in 1922, marriages have decreased 30% in proportion to the population, there having been, except for 1930, a steady decline. In 1927 the birth-rate was 27 per 1,000, by 1936 it was 22.2.[2]

In Nazi Germany, there are even more numerous measures for the promotion of marriages and births, and even more insistent propaganda for "larger families and better babies in the Third Reich." From 1932 to 1934 marriages rose from 7.9 to 11.1 per 1,000 population, and births from the post-war record low of 14.7 per 1,000 in 1933, to 18.9 in 1935. But in 1935 the marriages declined to 9.7 and by 1936 once more reached the level of 1932. During the second half of 1935 the birth-rate began to drop and in 1936 ran below the level of the preceding two years.[3] The most recent step towards turning women into machines for breeding cannon fodder is the propaganda advocating the same "respect and protection" for unmarried mothers and illegitimate children as for mothers of legitimate children.[4]

COÖPERATION AT SUCCESSIVE STAGES OF FAMILY LIFE

Principles of Successful Coöperation. For the development of a democratic or coöperative family we must look primarily to those in the highest social and educational stratum of society.[5]

[1] "Dictatorships of Europe Strive to Build Up Their Populations," *New York Times*, Aug. 30, 1936.

[2] *New York Times*, Nov. 14, 1936.

[3] "Dictatorships of Europe Strive to Build Up Their Populations," *op. cit.* In Germany there is advocacy of the old midwife system and of children being born in the home, a significant reversal of modern trends.

[4] *New York Times*, Feb. 12, 1937, and Walter Brockman, "Illegitimacy in Germany," *Current History*, July, 1937. The maternity wards of public hospitals are overcrowded, and a high percentage of the patients are 15 years old, a condition brought about in part by the practice of sending young girls away to work on farms and in labor camps.

[5] It will be remembered that divorce is not characteristic of this class. Recent studies show that not more than one in 75 marriages of those who meet in co-educational colleges result in divorce. *New York Times*, July 21, 1932. Judge Sabath of the Chicago divorce court pointed out that, when rightly mated, college women make less trouble than all other classes of women put together, only an infinitesimal proportion of divorces being granted to educated women who marry educated men. *New York Times*, July 8, 1934. In this connection a study made by Ray Erwin Baber, "Mate Selection," is of interest (*Modern Medicine*, March, 1936, pp. 76–78). Women were found less willing than men to marry those beneath them in economic status, family, morals, health, and intelligence. The greatest emphasis was laid on intelligence. Only 18% of 321 women, as against 76% of 321 men, were willing to marry one less intelligent. This indicates both the endurance of patriarchal principles and, perhaps, also that women are more aware than men of newer attitudes.

Popenoe's study of 3,000 marriages, of at least five years dura-tion, between the college-educated, is therefore of particular interest. In theory they should all have been democratic co-partnerships. As judged by near relatives and close friends, only 37% were actually of this type, while in 35% the man was the dominant partner and in the remaining 28% the woman. Very significantly, however, of the co-partnership marriages, 87% were happy, as against 61% where the husband was dom-inant and only 47% where the wife was dominant. "It appears then that only a minority of educated marriages succeed in reaching the status the theory prescribes for all, but that this minority represents a much greater proportion of successful marriages than the rest." [1]

How then may the number of genuinely coöperative marriages be increased? Husband and wife must "recognize that even in a co-partnership there must be a difference of function and a division of labor"; otherwise "it will be hard for them to operate as a unit, and the result will inevitably be either chaos and a broken home, or else definite assumption of leadership of one or the other." [2] Possibilities of coöperation should be carefully studied by each couple within the principal areas in which the activities and interests of husband and wife overlap: the areas of sex, of finance and economics, of homemaking and housework, and of the nurture of children.

Where attitudes conflict, the ideal solution is an integration of the viewpoints of husband and wife, so that something results better than either had anticipated. This involves patience, intelligence, and, above all, an emotional balance and maturity which most people lack. Far more feasible for most couples is a working agreement as to the sphere in which one or the other is to be the leader and may count on willing coöperation. A reciprocity of services is, however, not enough. Harmonious interdependence of the activities of husband and wife is scarcely possible without a fundamental agreement as to the goals they accept at the outset of marriage; the common objectives to the attainment of which they dedicate themselves.

In order to achieve common purposes a continued endeavor

---

[1] "Coöperation in Family Relations," *Journal of Home Economics*, Vol. XXVI (Oct., 1934), p. 483. As Popenoe points out, social and economic conditions facilitate masculine domination, while woman-dominated marriages usually represent an abdication of the man, and neither husband nor wife is likely to be satisfied with a situation in which the husband does not respect himself and is not respected by his wife.

[2] *Ibid.*, p. 484.

toward what Mr. and Mrs. Hart well call *creative accommodation* is necessary, a process going beyond coöperation, because personalities and purposes in the process of accommodation re-enforce, enhance, and promote each other. Essential to creative accommodation in marriage are genuine mutual consideration, based on sympathetic insight of each partner into the purposes and possibilities of the other; and a definite determination "that the other person shall find fulfilment of personality to the utmost extent possible."[1] Folsom points out that even generosity is not enough to awaken gratitude and reciprocal generosity, if mates differ widely in their attitudes and valuations and lack "insight" and "empathy." He defines insight to mean, "ability to see one's own behavior or personal relationships from the viewpoint of the disinterested psychologist-observer. Empathy is the ability to value another's feeling toward something as that other actually values it, rather than according to one's own feeling toward the same thing."[2] Empathy means literally feeling into the emotional life of another. This is companionship in the fullest sense and the surest foundation for successful family life.[3]

The Pre-nuptial Stage: Courtship and Choice of a Mate. Accommodation must be continuous, and the relationship between husband and wife be flexible and dynamic if it is to survive successfully the "changes and chances of this mortal life." From the standpoint of the partners in marriage, there are four stages in the history of every normal family: the pre-nuptial; the nuptial before children are born; the period of child-rearing; and the stage where the children no longer need parental care.[4]

The whole personality is the background for "falling in love," the overwhelming desire for an exclusive, supremely beautiful personal relationship with a member of the opposite sex, for an enduring fellowship in which loneliness is overcome through sympathetic understanding and affectionate response. This experience in each case has its roots in readiness for mating and in

[1] *Personality and the Family*, p. 321.

[2] Reprinted by permission, from *The Family* (p. 491), by J. K. Folsom, published by John Wiley and Sons, Inc.

[3] In her "Study of 250 Successful Families," *Social Forces*, Vol. VIII (June, 1930), pp. 511–532, Woodhouse found that both husbands and wives mentioned companionship as the chief factor producing happiness. The second factor mentioned by the husbands was mutual understanding and accommodation, while the wives, significantly enough, mentioned interesting work, freedom of personality, and outside interests. This indicates that not only did the wives find satisfaction in the use of their capacities and their development as individuals, but that their husbands were sympathetic and considerate.

[4] See MacIver, *op. cit.*, p. 111.

all the influences which have molded the personality pattern of the individual who "falls in love." When conditions are auspicious for the gradual transformation of romantic love into conjugal love, it provides invaluable aid to success in family life.

The time to face all doubts and consider obstacles to future happiness is before marriage; yet, for lovers, this is difficult, since clear objective judgment is incompatible with the strength of their emotion.[1] As Groves points out, the part intelligence plays best in the mating experience is preparatory: "the opportunity for judgment lies in the building of a background which will have a decisive influence upon sex interest, directing it in its beginning before it becomes finally fixed upon any individual."[2] As a further safeguard against undue attraction to the first possible partner, young people should have wide opportunities for companionship with many members of the opposite sex, and for association with each other in the experiences of everyday life.

Everything which makes for equality of the sexes during courtship, for straightforward honesty and emotional sincerity, is valuable, if this period is to fulfil its functions as a time for experimentation and testing. Courtship serves as an apprenticeship in accommodation, a time during which young people may test their mutual adaptability and congeniality, as they progress in their knowledge of and adjustment to each other. Courtship has increasing significance with higher ideals of marriage, and becomes more and more of a necessary preliminary to the selection of a suitable partner.

When a young man and woman have definitely chosen each other as marriage partners, they are *engaged*, whether or no this step is formally announced. Courtship merges almost imper-

---

[1] The Harts accordingly suggest a technique for meditating over love perplexities which will open the way to constructive solutions. Physical, mental, and emotional calm must be achieved, before there can be effective concentration on all aspects of the situation and perception of the most promising course of action. *Op. cit.*, pp. 121–125.

[2] *Marriage* (1933), p. 65. It should, for example, be clearly understood, that serious risks are incurred by those who choose a partner with bad health either physical or mental, or a partner who is chronically jealous, over-addicted to alcohol, has an ungovernable temper, or any one of a number of personality defects. As a measure of precaution, it is wise to become acquainted as soon as possible with the family of an individual for whom strong attraction is felt. Personality can be far better evaluated when seen in relation to family background. For fuller discussion of the problems of courtship and choice of a mate see Chaps. V–VII, IX, X; also N. Carpenter, "Courtship Practices and Contemporary Social Change," *Annals of the American Academy*, Vol. CLX (March, 1932), pp. 38–44; H. H. and E. B. Hart, *op. cit.*, Chaps. V–VII; and the following *Publications* of the American Social Hygiene Association: No. 502, "Love in the Making"; No. 596, "Choosing a Home Partner," both by N. D. Edson.

ceptibly into engagement, yet the latter, even when secret, constitutes a new stage in their relationship: a stage where uncertainty is all but removed, but which still affords opportunity for further testing before the final commitment involved in marriage. There is apt to be greater freedom and frankness when a couple are definitely engaged; and this is a period in which there should be full discussion of plans for married life, and agreements, so far as these can be made in advance, as to the division of work and responsibility between husband and wife, whether the wife shall work outside the home, the number and spacing of children, the family home, and standards of living. Since the period of engagement fulfils a definite function, it should probably be of at least three months' duration. But an over-long engagement has obvious disadvantages.

The Nuptial Stage before the Coming of Children. There are still many women who want to make a brilliant social event of their wedding, to be, as brides, the center of attention and to be assured of publicity. Conformity to social conventions is doubtless largely responsible, although it is noticeable that an elaborate wedding appears to many men as an unwelcome and unnecessary ordeal. In this they show greater maturity of feeling. The formal wedding ceremony of to-day is a patriarchal relic, derived both in its ritual and in its traditional conventions from the days when a bride was literally *given* by a father to a husband, and marriage was not only the decisive but also the crowning event of a woman's life. As such, therefore, it is an anachronism, a fact which is being recognized by the numbers of young couples who prefer their marriage to be as informal and simple as possible. Privacy rather than publicity is desired by those whose whole attention is concentrated on their mutual relationship. The legal ceremony, which gives social authorization to the full "consummation" of their union, has significance for them simply because it affords the fullest opportunity for strengthening and deepening their fellowship in complete mutual intimacy.

A less formal and public wedding trip or honeymoon is also becoming frequent. While it is undesirable that the establishment of a new home be too long delayed, the honeymoon, which is a modern convention, is distinctly advantageous. It is consonant with natural impulse for the newly married pair to go away by themselves, and it has the definite function of effecting an auspicious transition from courtship to the realities of married life. The honeymoon program should then be framed with the aim of providing the most ideal environment possible for the critical earliest stages of married life.

During these first days the process of full mutual adjustment is begun. Central in this process is the working out of a mutually satisfactory sexual adjustment. Here, as indeed in all aspects of matrimony, the fundamental need is for unselfishness; an intense regard for the other's welfare and the conviction that marriage is a coöperative partnership to which in all its aspects both must contribute to the full. Satisfactory sexual adjustment gives stability and security to marriage, not alone because of its central importance, but also because attitudes which make for sexual adjustment are conducive to adjustment in all other aspects of married life.

To preserve attitudes of sympathetic understanding and full mutual responsiveness is no easy achievement; nor is it possible at all for those who, once they are "safely" married, relax their efforts to please and conciliate. Such individuals may tolerate their subsequent disillusionment for reasons extraneous to the personal aspects of the marital relationship; if not, they are soon involved in conflict. Only those who realize the need for continuance of mutual adjustment, through the changing experiences of life, can hope for a deepening and strengthening of their emotional bond.

The Period of Child Nurture. The relationship between husband and wife is of fundamental importance to their children. It is accordingly essential that satisfactory mutual adjustments be achieved before the conception of the first child. Planned parenthood further demands not only good health on the part of both parents, but also the most auspicious conditions possible for pregnancy, birth, and the early environment of the child. Too long a delay is generally inadvisable, for the normal development of the family demands that the mutual love of husband and wife be both strengthened and enlarged by including love for their children.[1] Only the immature and thoughtless can fail to realize the indissoluble linking of the lives of the father and mother of a new and unique living being.

With the pregnancy of the wife, a new stage begins in the

[1] Sooner or later there comes, not only to most women, but also to most men, the realization that there is no complete substitute for parenthood; that it is part of the process of attaining individual maturity, and that life falls short of fulfillment for most of those deprived of this experience. Frequently, when no child is born, infertility may be found due to some remediable condition. In many cases of sterility on the part of either husband or wife, the adoption of a child or children has been the prelude to a normal and happy family life.

relationship of the married pair, a stage demanding continuing readjustments. Both husband and wife should be aware of the crucial importance of adequate pre-natal care for the future well-being of child and mother. The supervision of an experienced obstetrician through pregnancy, childbirth, and convalescence is invaluable, both to ensure the safety and physical welfare of mother and child, and also from the standpoint of mental hygiene. Confidence in the skill and competence of a doctor, and reliance on his, or her, understanding and judgment alleviate, if they do not entirely remove, the mental and emotional strain of this critical period.

The understanding care of a husband is invaluable. But the wife, absorbed though she be in the maternal process, must guard against becoming self-centered and neglecting her husband, to whom indeed the whole period is likely to be one of anxiety. While undue physical, mental, and emotional strain should be avoided, it is best for a pregnant woman to go on as far as possible with her usual occupations.

From every standpoint hospital delivery is to be preferred. Not only is there less risk for mother and child, particularly in case of complications, but the routine of the household is far less disturbed, and the mother may pass the early days of convalescence in freedom from responsibility for her home and her baby. At the hospital the baby is given skilled care, and a daily routine is being established in which the mother is instructed before going home. The difficulties of the period immediately succeeding the mother's return to her home must not be underestimated. In her convalescent condition the responsibility and work connected with caring for a baby, particularly a first child, may seem overwhelming.[1] Under these circumstances, the husband's help is most welcome and most valuable. Not only is the mutual relationship between the parents strengthened, but the father is thus enabled to assume from the start his full and active share in the life of the child.[2] Where the earliest experience of a child includes companionship with both parents, there is the fullest opportunity for wholesome parent-child relationships.

[1] It is assumed here that there is no nurse, which is the case in the vast majority of American homes, and, with the possible exception of the earliest period, is a situation more favorable to a fully developed parental relationship on the part of both husband and wife.

[2] There is also less likelihood of the husband feeling himself neglected in favor of the child. In some cases there is justification for such a feeling, and a wife should make very sure that her relationship with her husband does not suffer in consequence of her devotion to her baby.

With the birth of the first child and for a number of years the life of the home centers in the nurture of the children. While a far greater expenditure of time is involved in the preschool years of each child, yet the continued preoccupation of the parents is required from the birth of the oldest child until the youngest has achieved independence. For full coöperation in the nurture of their children, it is essential, as we saw, that husbands as well as wives should be educated in the scientific principles of child care.

When the Children No Longer Need Parental Care. The final stage of married life is reached when all the children are grown. It is preceded by a period of transition during which the parents, while encouraging their children to independence, are thrown back on their relationship to one another and on such resources and interests as they possess in addition to their love for their children. This may be a very difficult and trying period, most of all where there has not been continued adjustment in the mutual relationship of husband and wife, and where a wife's interests have been too exclusively centered in the children. The difficulties of this period of transition may be accentuated by its frequent coincidence with the climacteric, the period when physical and emotional changes accompany the cessation of sexual potency and the decrease in sexual desire.

In women this change is more definite and comes earlier, as a rule, than for men. The most usual age for its onset is between forty-five and fifty, and there is usually some degree of physical discomfort and of nervous and emotional disturbance.[1] In men the waning of sex vitality comes much more gradually and a degree of potency may be retained to an advanced age.

Some of the emotional disturbance and depression of this period in the case of many women is due to erroneous ideas. There is no truth in the belief that, having lived beyond the period when she can fulfill her biological purpose, a woman must inevitably become a neutral being devoid of charm. Sexual desire does not usually disappear with the menopause but may persist for many years. Moreover, for those women who have wide and varied interests, and work they want to do, for which they have found little time in the years of concentration on

---

[1] Of recent years methods of treatment have been devised which afford alleviation of these symptoms. The supervision of a gynecologist is of importance, not for this purpose alone, but because it ensures the detection of more serious conditions which sometimes ensue at this time, the earliest symptoms of which are frequently mistaken for manifestations of the menopause.

home life, a new period of creativeness and achievement may now begin.[1]

The relation between husband and wife at this stage may be put severely to the test, not only through emotional instability on the part of the wife, but through the strong attraction often felt by middle-aged, even elderly men, for young women. In an endeavor to recapture the emotions and passions of youth before they entirely vanish, or sometimes due to a revival of strong sex desire, there is the temptation to form a new alliance.[2] It is usually to be deplored if a marriage which has brought satisfaction to husband and wife through many years is disrupted because of what is probably a temporary episode. An enduring relationship, between those whose lives have been interwoven through the shared experiences of married life, is, after all, the one sure foundation for comradeship in old age.

TOWARDS MONOGAMY

Freedom and Monogamy. Freedom implies deliberate and intelligent choice of ways of action, undertaken in view of foreseen and desired ends. It therefore involves the relinquishment of incompatible ways of action. Nowhere is this more true than in the choice of monogamy as the ideal form of marriage: the form which embodies the deepest and most enduring values. It must be realized, moreover, that, where so great a good may be won, possibilities of suffering, loss, and tragedy are also great. Keyserling's conception of marriage as a vocation, to be chosen only by those who wish to lift their lives to higher levels, gives striking expression to the fundamental issues involved in marriage. Marriage is a state of "tragic tension," in which man and woman, "fundamentally different, incompatible and essentially solitary," can never fully merge with one another, even though "love requires a blending . . . , ranging from physical intercourse right up to intellectual and spiritual comprehension." But by means of this "tensile state of marriage . . . regenera-

---

[1] The psychiatrist, Béran Wolfe says, "The sane and normal woman may find her happiness in the pursuit of the goal of being *both* a womanly woman . . . *and* a worker. . . . In my experience the woman who is either all housewife and mother, or all careerist, is not a happy woman." She finds at about forty that "she has missed something essential in life." However, "a woman is never too old to be a complete human being. . . . Nothing is impossible to the woman who wants to lead a full life and courageously proceeds to do so." He admits, however, the very great advantage possessed by women who are fully prepared to "use constructively the leisure of the future years." *Woman's Best Years*, pp. 177–179, 184, 186.

[2] This state of affairs is more frequent for men, but many older married women are by no means immune to the attractions of men younger than their husbands.

tion and new growth are possible. On the physical plane this is represented by the birth of children. On the spiritual and mental plane it is exemplified by the partners' inner development, as a result of their fully accepting and discharging the obligations of life as laid down by marriage."[1]

Bjerre is right in saying that there are "two ways of dealing with the world; we may add to its values or reduce them. We may deepen or superficialize life." The average man "turns his back on sorrows, forgets hardships, and allows himself to be carried along with the tide with no thought of resistance, and still less of giving the tide a new direction. . . . But the strong meaningful chords of life are likewise drowned in the whirl of manifold superficial things. The average man is not tragic, neither is he very happy." The other attitude to life is the *heroic* attitude, for "we cannot at the same time live a profound life and escape life's tragedy."[2]

Something of this heroic attitude is always implicit in the experience of men and women who deeply love one another, but it is hard indeed to maintain amid difficulties and disillusionments. For not only the tragedies of life, but its trivialities must be faced with courage: the worries and anxieties and the dreariness and seeming insignificance of everyday life which too frequently quench all sense of adventure and of enhancement of experience. Yet it is through daily experiences of living together that the texture of creative relationships is woven, relationships through which development of character and spiritual growth are won.

Since monogamous marriage is a means for spiritual growth, it will, Keyserling predicts, continue to grow in importance with the further development of humanity. But less than ever, he believes, will it be the only form of relation between the sexes. It would seem unwise, however, to follow his suggestion of reserving monogamous marriage as a counsel of perfection for the few. If every means is taken to fortify family life, it is to be

---

[1] "The Correct Statement of the Marriage Problem," *The Book of Marriage*, pp. 17, 18, 22. It is not necessary to agree with the details of Keyserling's treatment of marriage in order to appreciate its suggestiveness. As already indicated, his patriarchal perspective is a determinant of his otherwise profound psychological insight. For example, he is led to believe that attraction is most likely to develop between those who should *not* marry, those who as comrades find adventure and stimulation in their mutual friendship. Marriage, on the other hand, should be, not with a comrade, but with a woman of the mother type, or a man of the father type.

[2] *The Remaking of Marriage*, pp. 139–141. In marriage, as in all significant phases of experience, Matthew Arnold's warning holds good, "And if I drink oblivion for a day, so shorten I the stature of my soul."

hoped that successful monogamous marriages will become more frequent.[1] Even so there will undoubtedly continue to be other forms of sexual relationship, very likely more openly engaged in than in the past. Particularly will this be the case for those in whom the desire for variety and fresh stimulation is particularly strong, romantics who, when the first beauty of a love relationship fades, seek a new embodiment of their dreams, artists and individualists for whom the enhancement of their experience through sex remains an end in itself in isolation from other ends.[2] Those whose ideal is the enhancement of experience through a vital, steady, and deep relationship would do well to avoid anything beyond friendship with such as these.

And after all, as Dewey says, "there is something deep within human nature itself which pulls towards settled relationships. . . . That happiness which is full of content and peace is found only in enduring ties with others, which reach to such depths that they go below the surface of conscious experience to form its undisturbed foundation."[3] If what Lippmann calls "the convention of marriage" survives, it will do so because "it correctly interprets human experience," and embodies "a dominant insight into the reality of love and happiness." He believes that "the convention of marriage, when it is clarified by insight into reality, is likely to be the hypothesis upon which men and women will ordinarily proceed. There will be no compulsion behind it except the compulsion in each man and woman to reach a true adjustment to life."[4]

Man and Woman. Modern family life is rooted in a developing psychological relationship between a man and a woman: "Psychological marriage," says Sapir, "is the cornerstone of the

---

[1] Where so little has yet been done in the way of constructive reform, where so many hopeful possibilities lie open, disheartenment as to the future of monogamous marriage and the family is, to say the least, premature. It might even be that, in time to come, the characterization of marriage in Chaucer's *Merchant's Tale* will no longer appear so incredibly naïve as it does at present:

"Non other lyf, said he, is worth a bene
For wedlock is so esy and so clene."

[2] For an expression of this point of view see Max Eastman's humorous and sarcastic criticism of "Floyd Dell's Double Life" in his *Art and the Life of Action and Other Essays* (Alfred A. Knopf, Inc., 1934), pp. 134–157. He concludes by saying "the beginning of any life wisdom which is to rest upon scientific foundations is to recognize the vital rôle that can be played by intelligence—by intelligent individual choice—in liberating us from the exact clutch of biological patterns or any patterns whatever, and enabling us to build new great adventurous and beautiful lives of innumerable different kinds."

[3] *The Public and Its Problems* (1927), pp. 213–214.

[4] *A Preface to Morals*, p. 312.

new family."[1]   The most suggestive contemporary contributions towards fuller understanding of the complexities and subtleties of the psychological relationship between lovers are being made by Jung and his co-workers.[2]   Very clearly they show the far-reaching significance for spiritual development immanent in this relationship; meaning, by spiritual development, the process in which human beings are drawn beyond the collective attitudes they share with others, towards more fully conscious individualization, and also beyond impulses and personal desires towards disinterestedness and the recognition of supra-personal values. As Hinkle says, "Only within a close relationship, voluntarily entered into, can there be found those opportunities for the development of an individual integrity, of an adaptation to reality, and of those higher human attributes without which there is no such thing as real happiness for the individual or for the world."[3]

Jung points out that those who fall in love are dominated largely by unconscious motives, and that there is the tendency to be attracted by a type rather than by an individual, this tendency being more marked in men than in women. A woman's love is more differentiated, if only in the sense that she chooses the man fitted to father her children. Men, on the other hand, idealize motherhood, a function common to all women and in no way differentiating one potential mother from another. Unconsciously both men and women are attracted to a mate resembling the parent of opposite sex. And such a choice is conducive to happiness through the security obtained, when a man is assured of a tender and maternal responsiveness in his wife, and a woman can look to her husband for the sustaining strength and understanding protectiveness of a father; when *each* can trust and look up to the other with respect. But for full spiritual growth this is not enough; there must be mutual development of their potentialities, not only as man and woman, but as individualized human beings.

Husband and wife cannot be independent of one another, but

---

[1] "What Is the Family Still Good For?" *American Mercury*, Vol. XIX (Feb. 1930), p. 150. Sapir's discussion of the purposes for which the family is still needed presents an excellent interpretation of the essential functions of the family in contemporary terms. These purposes are summed up as follows: "first to give the sex relationship its greatest emotional value; second, to rear children in an atmosphere of intelligent affection; third, to prepare the individual for the give and take of society; and fourth, to prepare the child unconsciously for satisfactory mating in the future." P. 151.

[2] See C. G. Jung, *Two Essays in Analytical Psychology* (1928); also Beatrice Hinkle, *Re-creating the Individual;* and Esther Harding, *The Way of All Women.*

[3] *The Book of Marriage*, p. 239.

neither must either be entirely *dependent* on the other.[1] The full
potentialities of their relationship are only reached through the
interdependence of equals. Obviously psychological interdependence implies monogamy as an ideal. What then of infidelity on
the part of those who genuinely aspire to monogamy? The ideal
relationship is undoubtedly destroyed through infidelity.[2] But
a union may fall short of the ideal in greater or less degree and
yet be worth preserving; also, infidelity is of various kinds and
degrees. Husbands and wives, whose genuine desire is for life-
long union, must in each case decide for themselves whether the
crises which threaten the integrity of marriage have irrevocably
dissolved their relationship, or whether its inherent strength
warrants its survival.

It is an interesting fact that the words used in marriage services
which now read "till death us do part," represent an alteration
effected in 1661 from the original form, "till death us depart."
It is of the very essence of marriage that it be conceived as exclusive and enduring, and, unless it is so conceived, its fullest
potentialities can never be experienced.

Monogamy and Social Values. Only those men and women
whose relationship to one another provides the spiritual atmosphere conducive to the well-being of their children, are, in
Nietzsche's words "entitled to desire a child. . . . Beyond thyself thou shalt build, but first of all must thou be built thyself,
rectangular in body and soul." As in marriage, so even more
inevitably in parenthood, are human beings drawn beyond
themselves through creative identification with another life.
And, further, in the measure in which fathers and mothers
realize the full meaning of parenthood they are led once more
beyond themselves and their own children to a more *kindly* and

---

[1] Carpenter pointed out how oblivious to realities were those who chose, as an ideal
symbol for marriage, the graceful vine clinging to the sturdy oak. The ivy, it is true,
is incapable of self-support, but it suffocates the oak and hinders its healthy development. This symbol, however, is accurate enough for the patriarchal family, where
the wife sacrifices her own development to her husband's supposed superior importance. In so doing she may not so much minister to his spiritual growth as bring
about its atrophy.

[2] Briffault says "When the man and woman association comes to be transferred to a
psychological basis . . . , mutual sexual fidelity comes to be accounted of the essence
of the relation, because it is implied in that psychological basis. . . . Infidelity is not
a legitimate ground for the dissolution of that relation . . . ; it constitutes
that dissolution." *Sin and Sex,* p. 208. Hamilton found an interesting distinction between men and women in their attitude towards infidelity, in those
cases where they *both* accepted it as reasonable on *intellectual* grounds. Men did
not find it hard to tolerate adultery, whereas women found it impossible to accept
emotionally.

generous interest in humanity, a deeper compassion with other human beings.[1]

It has always been true that "the welfare of society depends upon marriage and the family far more than on anything else. Therefore, as Hinkle points out, "a new ideal and a new reality attained by individuals in marriage is the first step towards new world relations."[2] The developing psychological relationship between husband and wife demanded by the emerging pattern of a coöperative family is thus of strategic social importance. For, as Lippmann says, it is in the "urgent, vital, inescapable issues between lovers," more than anywhere else to-day, "that modern men and women are compelled . . . to transcend naïve desire and to reach out to a mature and disinterested partnership with their world."[3]

It was no accident that John Stuart Mill, the champion of justice for women, should have been the first man to stress the supreme social significance of the psychological relationship of men and women. "With the profoundest conviction," he maintained that the "ideal of marriage" involves "that best kind of equality, similarity of powers and capacities, with reciprocal superiority in them—so that each can enjoy the luxury of looking up to the other, and can have alternately the pleasure of leading and of being led in the path of development. . . . The moral regeneration of mankind will only really commence, when the most fundamental of the social relations is placed under the rule of equal justice, and when human beings learn to cultivate their strongest sympathy with an equal in rights and in cultivation."[4]

The ideal of monogamy thus involves a new vision of love, marriage, and the family as an adventure in spiritual discovery, and as an unexcelled opportunity for experiments in ways of living through which a wider social justice may be brought into being.

SUGGESTED READING

Bjerre, P., *The Remaking of Marriage*, 1931.
Briffault, R., *The Mothers*, 3 vols., 1927, Vol. III, Ch. XXX.
Carpenter, N., "Courtship Practices and Contemporary Social Change," *The Annals of the American Academy of Political and Social Science*, Vol. CLX, March, 1932, pp. 38–44.

[1] The words "kindly" and "generous" are derived from the roots of *kin* and *gens* meaning one's own people, a significant indication of the origin of social sentiments in the sympathetic relationships of family life.

[2] *Op. cit.*, p. 240.   [3] *Op. cit.*, pp. 312–313.

[4] *The Subjection of Women* (Everyman's Library 825), p. 311.

Dell, F., *Love in the Machine Age*, 1930.

Goodsell, W., *Problems of the Family*, rev. ed., 1936, Chs. XVIII, XX.

Groves, E. R., *Marriage*, 1933.

——, *The Marriage Crisis*, 1928.

——, and Brooks, L. M., *Readings in the Family*, 1934, Chs. XII, XIII, XVIII, XXIV, XXV.

Halle, F., *Woman in Soviet Russia*, 1933.

Harding, M. E., *The Way of All Women*, 1933.

Hart, H. H., and E. B., *Personality and the Family*, 1935.

Keyserling, H., ed., *The Book of Marriage*, 1926.

Lippmann, W., *A Preface to Morals*, 1929, Ch. XIV.

Neumann, H., *Modern Youth and Marriage*, 1928.

Popenoe, P., *Modern Marriage*, 1925.

Sapir, E., "What Is the Family Still Good For?" *American Mercury*, Vol. XIX, Feb., 1930, pp. 145–151.

Spalding, C. A., ed., *Twenty-four Views of Marriage*, 1930.

Stern, B. J., ed., *The Family Past and Present*, 1938, pp. 393–411.

Woodhouse, C. G., "A Study of 250 Successful Families," *Social Forces*, Vol. VIII, June, 1930, pp. 518–532.

HOME LIFE

CHAPTER XXI

HOUSEKEEPING AND HOMEMAKING

THE RELATION BETWEEN HOUSEKEEPING AND HOMEMAKING

The Sphere of Homemaking. Family life is lived at *home:* the material and social environment created and maintained by husband and wife, in which they may live together in privacy and nurture their children and in which provision is made for primary needs of shelter, food, and clothing and also for cultural and aesthetic needs. The satisfactions of home life come, moreover, not only from consumption, from the enjoyment of the *outcome* of our own activities and those of others, but also from these activities themselves. Many, if not all, of the activities which go into the creation of home, all that is comprised under the terms housekeeping and homemaking, may provide satisfaction as affording outlet for ingenuity and skill, for constructive and aesthetic ability.

Housekeeping and homemaking together comprise the sphere of what Andrews defines as "household economics . . . , the science and art of planned family living."[1] Three main functions may be distinguished as comprised within the scope of family economics, the administration, management, and work of the home. Administration means the formulation of the policies for the coöperative partnership of husband and wife. When these have been determined in their broader outlines, management is required, in order that a pattern may be established for family living and for the efficient organization of the household work. No hard and fast distinction can be drawn between housekeeping and homemaking, but it may prove suggestive to point out that efficient housekeeping does not of itself create a home, whereas good homemaking involves the essentials

[1] From *Economics of the Household* (rev. ed., 1935), p. 1. By permission of The Macmillan Company, publishers. As a social ideal, Andrews says, "The American household is an institution in which two adults form a partnership with equal responsibilities, make equal contributions to its support and draw out equal returns not only in the daily physical services of food, clothing, and shelter, but as well in the broadening of experience and in all the satisfactions of life. As junior members enter the group, they are advanced as rapidly as possible to a full partnership relation. At its best the group provides for its members, adult and child alike, broad opportunity for the development of individual personality." P. v.

of good housekeeping, the provision of the physical needs upon which health and welfare depend. Homemaking is to housekeeping as spirit to letter, as art to technical skill, as creation to routine. The fundamental distinction thus appears to be between those aspects of household economics which are definitely expressive of the personality of the homemaker, and those which are impersonal, even mechanical. As illustrations we may contrast the care of a child, intimately bound up as it is with unique psychological relationships, and, at the other extreme, all the various cleaning processes, which may be done equally well by anyone who is thorough and skilful.

Here, then, is a principle, a standard by which it is possible to judge, in any particular case, between those aspects of family living which are essential parts of homemaking and which cannot be delegated to others without loss, and those aspects which, wherever circumstances permit, may be delegated to paid assistants, outside agencies, or, indeed, to machinery, in or out of the home. But, even where it is possible to delegate some or all of the housework, homemaking still involves economic aspects. As Amey Watson says, "There should be acceptance of the fact that homemaking, while having elements of a social and spiritual partnership of the deepest significance, also includes a *business partnership* of the husband and wife together."[1]

Coöperative Homemaking. What, then, are the respective shares of men and women in homemaking? Although details must be worked out according to circumstances in each family, some general principles are clear. In the coöperative family the administration of the home is the business of *both* husband and wife, although now one, now the other, rightly takes the lead in certain decisions: the wife in planning for children and the husband in those decisions which depend on the necessities of his work, if, as is usually the case, he is the chief provider of the money income. Because he is the chief earner outside the home, and also because a mother is bound closely to the home for many years, home management usually devolves on the wife. But the husband may share in greater or lesser degree in management and also in the actual housework.

To make our discussion of home life more definite we must confine ourselves, for the most part, to one of the many varying types of families. We shall accordingly consider *the family of moderate income established by parents who have received a college*

---

[1] "The Reorganization of Household Work." *Annals of the American Academy,* Vol. CLX (March, 1932), p. 170.

education or its cultural equivalent. It is in families of this type, not wealthy, yet belonging to the higher levels of cultural-intellectual development, that coöperative family life finds its most successful embodiment.

PROBLEMS OF HOUSEHOLD ECONOMICS

The economic significance of the modern family and of the work carried on in the home is often underestimated. In the family, it is true, the work is "largely done *for love* and not for money."[1] But this should not prevent realization of the fact that the family still retains economic functions of central importance, not only to the well-being of the members, but to the livelihood activities of society. Indeed, in Bigelow's words, "the American family is the biggest business in the United States."[2] It is of interest to remember that, as Andrews points out, "the modern science of economics . . . , which is the study of general business problems in terms of their social significance, began as household or agricultural economics."[3] The very term *economics* is derived from οἶκος, meaning household property or estate, and νόμος, meaning management.

In contrast to former days, when the family was in large measure economically independent, it is now, from the economic standpoint, dependent upon a vast network of complex forces over which it has no immediate control, and which largely determine the character of shelter, food, and clothing. But there are great gains to offset the loss of direct control over production. The new exchange economy is infinitely more productive and has resulted in a raised standard of living for all. The improvement and cheapening of a growing variety of goods has made common the use of what were formerly luxuries reserved only for the privileged few. Working hours have been reduced, and leisure is more available in which the family may enjoy its increased resources.

All these changes have modified the economic functions of the family. With regard to *production*, the creation of useful commodities and services, the family is concerned most of all with the *end-processes* of production: the preparation and service of food, and the other activities listed under the work of the home, all contribute to making the individual household the *final agent*

---

[1] Amey Watson, *op. cit.*, p. 169.

[2] *Family Finance* (1936), p. vii. "Every year it handles the entire national income, and in addition it turns out billions of dollars' worth of goods and services that statisticians have never discovered."

[3] *Op. cit.*, p. 2.

of production. And the household is also the *final agent of economic distribution.* It is within the household that money income is turned into goods, and the *real* income of the family thus depends upon the efficiency with which this function is performed.[1] Further, within the family, goods must be distributed in such a way as is conducive to the well-being of each of the family members. Finally, the family has now become the *chief agent of consumption,* of the use of wealth for the satisfaction of human needs.[2] By its direction of the wealth-using process, the household profoundly influences individual and social well-being. The quantity and quality of the satisfactions afforded the family members are dependent on the efficiency of the household as an agent of consumption, and the whole course of production is ultimately controlled through its choice of goods and services.

SELECTION OF A STANDARD OF LIVING

Planes and Standards of Living. The problem for each family is to provide by careful management, with the means at its disposal, the richest possible life for all its members. The question at once arises as to how far the good life depends on *quantity* of material goods, how far on *quality* and on the use of material things as instrumental in the promotion of spiritual well-being. The first step must be an analysis and critical evaluation of wants and desires in order to select for satisfaction those which are most worthwhile, those which minister not to ease and comfort alone, but improve the quality of living: there must be choice of a *standard of living.* For clarity, a distinction is now made between *planes* and *standards* of living. A plane of living, or scale or manner of living, all mean the way in which an individual or family actually does live, whereas a standard means all those things an individual or family insists, if possible, upon having: the controlling, even though indefinable force behind all its choices.[3]

[1] Real income, as will shortly become more apparent, includes all the goods and services available, whether purchased by means of money income, or produced in the household or contributed by social agencies.

[2] As Andrews says: "the determining of how wealth and services shall be used, in what variety, in what combinations, by what persons, and in what times and places, is a central responsibility of household economy." *Op. cit.*, p. 50.

[3] In addition, every individual and family has an *ideal* standard which includes all things hoped for in the future, but which extends beyond the present realizable standard. Still another phrase, *norm* of living, has been proposed as the ideal scale of expenditures, determined according to the most recent findings of science to achieve approved social ends. L. L. Bernard, "Standards of Living and Planes of Living," *Social Forces*, Vol. VII (Dec., 1928), pp. 190–202.

Standards of living thus embody attitudes of evaluation towards given modes of life. Nevertheless, one of the most frequent means of classifying standards is in terms of those customary for families at different levels of income.[1] As a matter of fact a complete picture of a standard of living embodies description in terms of underlying valuations, and of the specific commodities and services considered appropriate, and also of the particular ways in which these are used. With rising standards there is greater insistence on this third aspect: on the refinements of living and on that which is *de rigueur;* in clothing for different occasions, for example, or in the service of food.

Characteristics of a High Standard of Living. A clear distinction may be drawn between a high standard and an expensive standard. "The high standard," says Bigelow, "always emphasizes intrinsic rather than pecuniary values, enduring rather than temporary satisfactions, quality rather than quantity of living."[2] A high standard is not necessarily expensive, but may be maintained on a moderate income. Unfortunately, at present, American standards of living tend to be expensive rather than high.[3] There is emphasis on physical comfort, on constant acquisition, on raising the standard in a quantitative sense; and there is remarkable similarity in consumption habits at different levels, differences being not so much in kind as in degree. Throughout, stress is laid on conformity rather than on individual preference. Cleanliness, protection of health, and education are, it is true, rated high. But a low estimate is placed on privacy, on quiet, on beauty.

[1] Levels such as poverty, subsistence, health and decency, comfort, moderately well-to-do, and well-to-do. Any endeavor to characterize these by size of income, or to formulate them in terms of goods and services, is soon out of date, because of price fluctuations and changes in ways of living.

[2] *Op. cit.*, p. 42.

[3] Hazel Kyrk's analysis of the American standard is particularly illuminating. It has "the attributes of a *nouveaux riches* standard with its emphasis on quantity rather than quality and upon display of wealth." She quotes most aptly from C. W. Ferguson "High Class," *Harper's Magazine*, Vol. CLXIV (March, 1932), p. 450, "From the severity and thrift of pioneer life the great mass of our people passed over into elegant circumstances with all the abandon of a crowd of country men coming noisily into the possession of unimagined splendor. Only as we appreciate this epic occurrence can we understand our highly over-stuffed society." *Economic Problems of the Family* (Harper and Brothers, 1933), p. 381. Reprinted by permission. James Truslow Adams has expressed fear that the "American dream" of a richer, fuller, and more satisfying life may be warped into "the false notion of making an up-to-date department store of . . . home and life," due to "a desire for ostentatious luxury based on what I may call the standard of the professional interior decorator." "What of the American Dream?" *New York Times Magazine*, May 14, 1933.

Intelligent choice of a standard of living is thus no easy matter. Patterns of value are acquired unconsciously in childhood from the home environment, and every family is also under constant compulsion to conformity with the standards of the social group to which it belongs. Finally, in America, powerful mass influences oppose not only independence of choice but also the very creation of standards of high quality. Few indeed deliberately think through their range of preferences; most accept as good that to which they are accustomed, or imitate others. Here, however, is the opportunity for husband and wife to achieve a conscious philosophy of life, a matter fundamental to · family well-being, and of educational value to their children, and possibly to others. There is a natural tendency to emulate others in an endeavor to raise the standard: a social force which operates either for evil or good, depending on whether the emulation is primarily pecuniary, or whether it results in reaching genuinely higher levels through the development of a broader range of interests and the deliberate cultivation of taste.[1]

Hazel Kyrk's statement of the essential ends to be sought and the interests which should be fulfilled by a high standard of living is particularly helpful.[2] "Wise uses of time and money," she says, "are those designed to secure in appropriate amounts:

(1) The goods necessary for optimum health and physical vigor and in the case of children maximum growth

(2) Facilities for the formal education and training of children and for the continuing education of adults

(3) Means for furthering such specific individual interests as painting, drawing, music, sports, dancing, handicrafts, dramatics, gardening, research, imaginative writing . . .

(4) Means of enhancing beauty of the surroundings, inside and outside the house, and in personal appearance

(5) Means of securing social intercourse for the sake of friendliness and affection, or for the sake of mental stimulation and experience

(6) Means for securing fun or amusement—the satisfaction of the play interest

(7) Means of securing new experience, aesthetic or otherwise, in connection with peoples, places, things and ideas

---

[1] Conformity to external standards is more necessary at lower levels of society; and in this connection Hazel Kyrk quotes a significant remark made by Mrs. Simkhovitch in her book *The City Worker's World in America* (1917), p. 32: "The simplicity of ignorance of need and the simplicity of indifference to purely external standards are two very different things. One is at the beginning and the other at the end of a long chain of experiences. . . . We learn to discard rather than to do without." *Op. cit.*, p. 397.

[2] *Ibid.*, p. 393.

(8) Means of securing rest and relaxation other than the above

(9) Means of securing order and harmony in the routine of consumptive activities and for reducing the time cost of non-
pleasurable activities incident to consumption

(10) Housing and equipment that will provide facilities for the activities and social intercourse that go on in the home and afford
opportunity for individual privacy"

PROBLEMS OF CONSUMPTION

The importance of consumptive choices and the difficulties in
the way of intelligent consumption were briefly discussed in
Chapter XV. It was also indicated that consumption includes
more than buying; although it is in the process of buying that
the problems of consumption are given concrete embodiment in
the market-selection of specific articles. Buying is the *technology
of consumption*, it is the *final* step and should be preceded first
by a consideration of standards, and secondly by consideration
of means for their realization. Only then is the consumer fully
prepared for actual buying which, to be fully efficient, must be
"the selection of the best article available for the purpose with
a minimum expenditure of time, energy and money."[1] Hazel
Kyrk, accordingly, distinguishes between consumer education
and education of the buyer as follows: "Education of the consumer concerns itself with the character of . . . desires; it
undertakes to modify standards of living, to cultivate tastes, to
form new concepts of need and new valuations. Education of
the buyer upon the other hand concerns itself with the skilful
use of market facilities and with the technique of finding the
best articles available for a given expenditure."[2] In spite of all
the difficulties of the present situation, education in consumption and in buying should have markedly wholesome effects: "a
buying public more certain of what it wants consumers' goods
for, better informed concerning the qualities that make them
suitable for their purpose, more certain in regard to its aesthetic
standards, more zealous in searching for information already
available, more intelligent concerning the market and its activities, more discriminating in weighing advertising and selling
claims, less credulous, less impulsive, less snobbish, could vastly
improve selection even under prevailing conditions."[3] Here are
suggestions which should prove definitely conducive to family
well-being; since so large a part of the family living is in most
cases bought.

[1] Kyrk, *op. cit.*, p. 435.   [2] *Ibid.*, p. 492.   [3] *Ibid.*, p. 493.

PRODUCTION FOR USE IN THE HOME

Although so many goods and services are now obtained through purchase, production still occupies in most households a large proportion of the time of the family members, particularly of the wife.[1] There are, of course, wide variations in the amount of time given to household labor, the hours being longest where income is low and where there are a number of young children, particularly where standards of child care and home-making are high. It is difficult, as we saw, to draw a distinct line between the activities of the family members as unpaid producers and the activities which are the outcome of personal relationships. For practical purposes, however, household production may be limited to what we earlier designated as the less personal and more mechanical activities, or as Kyrk puts it, "those activities carried on by and for the members, that may be delegated to some one outside the family group or replaced by goods bought on the market if income, market conditions and personal inclination permit."[2]

The difficulties experienced in defining the field of household production, because, in the home, production and consumption intermingle, and because it is impossible wholly to differentiate management from performance, make it evident that household production is of a different order from commercial production. Its chief distinguishing feature is that it remains outside the price system: the housewife's services do not come on the market, and, "since it is of their very essence that they are available to only one group of consumers—her own family . . . , they must remain literally priceless."[3] Unfortunately, the very fact that this work is non-pecuniary and non-competitive has lowered its prestige and deprived it of certain powerful incentives to efficiency. In any case, efficiency is not so readily obtainable in household production which is small-scale, decentralized, and unspecialized, household workers being "jills of all trades," in comparison with workers in professions, business, or industry outside the home.

---

[1] *Housewives* comprise the largest occupational group, and in 1930 about *half* as many women gave their full working time to household production as there were persons engaged in *all* gainful occupations. In that year the Census recorded *for the first time* the number of women who were responsible for the care of home and family. Besides the 3,923,516 homemakers engaged in gainful occupations there were 24,481,778 who had no other occupation. As Kyrk says, "activities engaging the labors of so large a group are obviously of no little economic significance," *op. cit.*, p. 43.

[2] *Op. cit.*, p. 46.

[3] Hildegarde Kneeland, "Woman's Economic Contribution in the Home," *Annals of the American Academy*, Vol. CXLIII (May, 1929), p. 33.

It is difficult, moreover, to measure the results of household production, for these results are far less tangible now that so few of the necessaries of life are actually *made* in the home. Preparation, service, and clearing away of meals is the outstanding task, but in this and in the other household tasks it is end-processes and the amenities of existence which engage the time of the homemaker, rather than primary activities essential to existence.

Production for use in the home is unique from still another standpoint: it is a by-product of marriage, being concentrated almost wholly to-day in the hands of wives. Yet so long as we value family life in a private home, certain productive activities must remain in the household. Where consumption immediately succeeds production, as in the case of the end-processes of food preparation, they must occur in the same place. If food is prepared outside, it must be consumed outside, except in so far as services for the transportation of cooked foods can be established which are efficient and not too costly. Care of the house and all its contents are also processes which in large part must, for obvious reasons, take place in the household. The productive services of the housewife have, therefore, a definite place in the economic world. For those women who are without very special abilities or professional interests, who, if they worked outside the home, would be engaging in clerical or industrial work, it can be shown that in almost all respects, and even from the strictly *economic* standpoint, engaging in home production compares very favorably with a program in which the mother works outside the home and delegates her tasks to others.[1]

COLLECTIVE EXPENDITURE

Family wants are satisfied not only through purchase and home production, but also by means of collective expenditure. In this way consumption is socialized and goods and services are enjoyed by a group whose members contribute to the cost. Where collective expenditures are public, payment is made by means of taxation and is compulsory, and the services provided are those which no individual or family could secure so well for themselves: public schools, parks, libraries and museums, water-supply, health, police and fire services, highways, and the postal service. In the case of water and postage, individuals pay

[1] See M. H. Abel, *Successful Family Life on the Moderate Income* (1926), Chapter VIII, for a comparison of housework with outside earning, from the standpoint of the housewife's contribution to the family income. Also see Kyrk, *op. cit.*, Chapters IV–VI.

in proportion to what they get. But in general, taxes are levied in accordance with ability to pay, and so the tax-supported public services tend to reduce wide variations in income by providing services for all, largely at the expense of those best able to pay.

There are also a number of private organizations in which wants are satisfied by collective expenditure: private social welfare agencies, schools, churches, societies, clubs, and smaller groups of many kinds, by means of which individuals and families spend together for goods and services enjoyed by all.

The socialization of consumption has its limits. All the wants of individuals and families cannot be satisfied by collective expenditure, as at present developed. For satisfaction is dependent in many cases on private possession and exclusive use. Take, for example, a family garden. Its chief value would be lost if it did not provide privacy and seclusion and opportunity for creative and artistic activities for the family members. This fact does not detract from the value of public gardens, parks, and forests as supplements to private gardens. Undoubtedly there are many ways, not yet devised, in which satisfactions could be procured for individuals and families by a combination of private with socialized consumption, as, for example, in the case of garden cities. There is need here for experiment; for the devising of ways in which the privacy of family life may be preserved, and integrated within wider schemes of coöperative living.

THE FINANCIAL ASPECTS OF FAMILY LIFE

Sources of Real Income. It is important to realize that there are other sources of *real* income than the *money* income, essential as that is in a pecuniary society; and that contributions to real income are therefore made by family members in other ways than wage earning. "A comprehensive view of family real income," says Andrews "shows at least three general sources— the economic contributions made by members of the family or by family property, securing *money income outside* the household; the economic *services rendered inside* the household which create wealth there, both of materials and services, for family use; and the *social contribution* both of materials and of services by community and state to the family's living."[1]

Contributions of Family Members to Real Income. The complexities of the problem of economic coöperation in the family

[1] *Op. cit.,* p. 68.

have already been apparent in several connections.[1]   In most families the husband's earnings at all times constitute the bulk of the money income and he usually carries the burden of wage earning unaided for a number of years, even if the wife and, later, sons and daughters also earn.   Issues of importance are involved in the wage earning of sons and daughters and in the disposal of their earnings.   More and more the principle is being accepted that children should be supported by their parents for as long a period as they can benefit by education.   When, however, they are no longer being educated, daughters as well as sons should undoubtedly meet the expenses of their own support.[2]   Usually a daughter can "carry her own weight" only through gainful employment, although under some circumstances she can do so by her productive services in the home. In general, sons and daughters who live at home should pay not only their personal expenses for clothing and so on, but also their *proportionate share* in the family expenses.

Although children should not contribute to money income while continuing their education, this does not mean that they may not, with profit to themselves and the family, contribute to the real income of the household through their share in household production.   Since it is almost always desirable and sometimes necessary for the husband to be the sole contributor to money income at certain stages of family life, it is also desirable that he should be the chief and regular wage earner.   Accordingly, it is but just that the wife's contribution to real income through her services as homemaker should be greater than his.   Even where the household labor is performed by paid assistants, the home manager makes a genuine economic contribution, her services being essential to family well-being, although this value is hard to estimate accurately in terms of money.[3]   It is manifestly not

[1] It may be remembered that farm women almost all make financial contributions to family income from by-industries carried on in connection with production for use. Also that, in the 1930 Census, 62.1% of families included only one wage earner, while others had two, three, and four or more. At any one time in one-half to three-fifths of city families the husband is the sole wage earner.

[2] Kyrk states the matter excellently when she says: "no sound reason can be brought forward why adults, either male or female, should not provide the equivalent of their own food, clothing and shelter. . . . Parents who support non-earning daughters are no more justified either from the social standpoint or from the standpoint of the welfare of daughters than they would be in the case of sons. Both grown sons and daughters must assume the responsibility of earning their living, that is of rendering to society a return for the goods and services they consume." *Op. cit.*, p. 129.

[3] It may be pointed out, however, that, where money income is derived from investments, these have often been made possible through savings due to the wife's home management.

only absurd but unjust to designate as economically *dependent*, and *supported* by their husbands, those women who, although they do not earn outside the home, yet make a full economic contribution as home managers and household workers. Such phrases describe only the semi-idle and parasitic, and are most misleading as indications of the status of wives who, through economic *interdependence* with their husbands, coöperate with them in family support.

EXPENDITURE AND THE HOUSEHOLD BUDGET

The Apportionment of Money Income. Expenditure in the broad sense should cover the use of time, money, and goods in the realization of the family's standard of living. Owing to the dependence of family life on money income, the theory of expenditure has been largely concerned with the apportionment of money income: the central phase of the process whereby money income is turned into real income. The choices determining what the family wants can only be made an effective guide to market selection through the intervening process of *budgeting*, or planning expenditures.[1]

The family budget is a guide to intelligent spending through the provision of a balanced pattern of expenditure. The principle of proportion must be expressed in three ways: the pattern for family spending must do justice to the needs and wants of each of the family members; it must provide for proportionate distribution of income between varied needs and wants; and, finally, there must be a balance between the satisfaction of present needs and provision for future security. The budget may then be described as a device " to make sure that income will cover essentials over a period of time."[2] Moreover, because money does not always accrue in even amounts at regular intervals, and because few family expenses are uniform and regular, there is need for planning beyond the day and even the month. The year is, therefore, the time unit usually chosen in planning a budget.

In its strictest sense, the budget means a detailed, written plan of expenditure. There are certain times when the making

---

[1] In actual experience these three phases in the process of turning money income into real income are not mutually exclusive. For instance, the working out of a spending plan, making necessary, as it does, further choice between alternative goods, inevitably involves fresh consideration of needs and wants, sometimes even of the standard of living itself. The actual money income available limits the realization of wants and forces the formulation of a practical pattern of expenditure, which, in turn, serves to restrain impulsive buying.

[2] Kyrk, *op. cit.*, p. 398.

of a formal budget is particularly important. A new family, without experience to guide its expenditure, has far greater need of careful budgeting than a family with well-established habits of expenditure. A revision of the budget is also necessary with increase or decrease of income, or with variations in need, which are bound to occur at different stages of family life.

The Household Budget. The only adequate basis for a budget is a record of past expenditures. Where this is lacking as in the case of a new family, the experience of other families must serve as a temporary substitute. All possible needs must be anticipated, and the total estimated expenditures compared with total expected income. Standard budgets afford a measure of guidance in this process, but cannot be relied on to tell a particular family what it ought to spend.

It is customary to classify expenditures under certain headings, the more general of which appear in all standard budgets: savings; housing or shelter; food; clothing; operation or housekeeping expenses; and the group of expenses which are called personal, advancement, or development expenses. The subheadings under each of these should reflect as far as possible a family's actual expenditure and so furnish a guide to its particular spending problems.[1]

To check the adequacy of a budget and to provide a basis for improvement, account-keeping is necessary—the provision of daily, monthly, and yearly records which furnish data as to the general outlines and the details of the spending plan. The value of household accounts is to be found in their reproduction of the family's financial history over a certain period, the primary purpose being to facilitate analysis of expenditures. Household accounting thus differs from business accounting, and too close an analogy is misleading, tending as it does to an over-cumbersome technique and exaggerated emphasis on completeness and accuracy.[2] At critical or transitional periods meticulous ac-

---

[1] Experts in budgeting have interesting suggestions to make of methods for building budgets. See, for example, Donham's "graphic circle chart" which may be used to detect lack of balance. *Spending the Family Income* (1923). Also Bigelow's suggestive comparison of the "make-life-what-I-like-it" method with the "live-within-your-income" method. The latter, while valuable for beginners, is too negative, he believes, for a family with well-established standards and constructive long-time aims. *Op. cit.*, pp. 345–356. See Andrews, *op. cit.*, p. 572, for a table of approximate percentage budgets for different income levels.

[2] A detailed plan for the keeping of household accounts is suggested by Andrews, *op. cit.*, pp. 554–567. In stressing the fact that classification of expenditure is more important than an exact balance, he reassuringly advises, "Do not unbalance your mind by trying to balance your personal accounts to the last penny." *Op. cit.* (ed.

counting is valuable; at other times records as simple as those furnished by canceled cheques may provide sufficient data for study.

FINANCIAL MANAGEMENT

The Need for a Long-time Plan. No family can be confident of its future security, far less can it hope for an abundant life, unless it builds for itself *sound financial foundations.* Not only for this year and the next, but for all the years to come the family income must be sufficient to provide for all expenditures. Therefore, although *specific* emergencies cannot be foreseen, their possibility must be taken into account and prepared for. Accordingly, a first and indispensable step in providing for the future is found in the setting aside of part of the present income for future needs. All standard budgets, even those for low incomes, now record savings as their first item.

Just as an annual budget is required to direct the spending of the month, week, or day, so a long-time plan is needed to give perspective to the annual budget. Wherever possible there should be a forecast of probable fluctuations in future income and in family expenditures, due to changes in the family situation. For example, even when a secure income is anticipated, apart from unforeseen emergencies, the retirement period must ultimately come, in which no further income will be available from work outside the home. Expenditures at that time should be at a minimum, it is true, since in most cases the children will have become self-supporting. But in the preceding years expenses rise rapidly through the child-bearing and earlier school periods, until they reach a peak in the later stages of education, before a gradual decline as, one by one, the children become financially independent.[1]

Anticipating Future Income by Means of Credit. When expenditures are too heavy to be met by current income, they may be met by the use of *credit.* By means of borrowing power we make use of *future* income to meet *present* needs. The risks of

of 1923), p. 521. Various types of record are discussed by Chase Going Woodhouse, "Planning and Recording Family Expenditures," Department of Agriculture, Farmers' *Bulletin*, No. 1553 (1927).

[1] Several estimates have been made of the cost of maintaining families of varying sizes at successive periods. A summary of these is given by Bigelow, *op. cit.*, Chapter XVI. Also see *The Home and the Child* (1932), for a summary of studies undertaken to determine the cost of adequate provision for children. It has been estimated by the Metropolitan Life Insurance Company that, for a city family in the $2,500 income class, it costs about $7,238 to rear a child to eighteen years of age, including the expenses of maternal care at birth.

incurring debt are obvious; nevertheless, a wise use of credit forms part of sound financial policy.[1]

Credit may be secured in two ways: the family may use *trade* credit, and purchase goods to be paid for at some future time; or it may use *money* credit, by borrowing from some organization which makes a business of lending. The cost of credit is determined by the risk and by the expenses involved and also by the interest charged for the use of capital. But the convenience of credit is often well worth its cost. Take, for example, one of the two forms of trade credit, the use of *charge accounts*. Even when it is entirely possible to pay cash, charge accounts offer great advantages in saving time, in providing a record of expenditures, and in establishing a customer's credit if accounts have always been promptly paid when due at the end of week or month.[2] For the careful buyer, charge accounts at food and department stores, where regular or frequent purchases are made, are an invaluable aid to household and financial management.

The other form of trade credit, purchase on the instalment plan, presents far greater risks even to the wary.[3] Yet the method of partial payment which makes it possible for many to buy homes of their own cannot be condemned outright. And there are other commodities of such value, both in the present and future, that their purchase on the instalment plan is justifiable: labor-saving devices which may be put to productive use, business equipment, and automobiles when they are really necessary.[4] Where possible, however, it is usually safer to

[1] As Andrews puts it: "Credit is dynamite—rightly used it is constructive; wrongly used it is destructive." *Op. cit.*, p. 223. Credit may be of the greatest mutual benefit to both borrowers and lenders, its fundamental purposes being: (1) to allow "people who want things more in the present to use the funds already accumulated by other people who want things more sometime in the future," and (2) to allow "people who want things more in the future to get more in the future than they would otherwise have been able to obtain." Bigelow, *op. cit.*, p. 419.

[2] Checking accounts at banks not only facilitate the keeping of accounts, but, even though small, serve to establish credit.

[3] Interestingly enough, this form of buying on credit, with payments extending over a considerable period, first came into common use with the sale of sewing machines. Houses, musical instruments, and books have also been sold in this way for some time. In the years preceding the depression there was a tremendous increase in the volume of instalment buying, particularly for automobiles, furniture, labor-saving devices, pianos, radios, phonographs, jewelry, and clothing.

[4] There are great disadvantages to instalment buying; its actual costs are extremely high and are apt to be underestimated by the buyer. Instalment *selling* is characterized by "high-pressure salesmanship" which is far too often successful in overcoming "sales-resistance," and tempting the consumer, by means of the easy-payment plan, to spend beyond his means and jeopardize his financial future.

accumulate savings and pay cash, and it is often sounder practice to finance purchases by direct credit through loans rather than by indirect credit on the instalment plan.

Borrowing money from commercial banks or loan agencies of various kinds is exceedingly common.[1] When there are no savings and no insurance policies, borrowing is made absolutely necessary in the case of emergencies. Another frequent reason for borrowing is the liquidation or consolidation of debts. Those who own homes may place a mortgage upon them, or, if they have life insurance, they may borrow up to the fixed loan value. Those who have neither must use their chattels as security, or their expected future earnings. While necessary under certain conditions, the use of credit calls for cool deliberation and greater firmness of character than any other aspect of financial management.

Providing for the Future by Means of Invested Savings and Insurance. Even were every family assured of minimum essentials through social insurance, there would still remain the need for each family to provide as far as possible for its own future, if it is to attain anything beyond a very low standard of living. The chief methods of making provision for the future are *investment* and *insurance*. Present income may be set aside and allowed to accumulate in funds which may be used in case of emergencies, or of heavy demands, or else to secure definite objectives such as a house, or travel, or college education for the children. Through use of the insurance principle a fund or income is forthcoming under certain specified contingencies. Both of these methods should be included in any long-time financial plan.

Saving should not mean hoarding, but the entrusting of a portion of present income for use by others, in return for which interest is received. Opportunities for safe *investment* are therefore essential. Deposit in a strong bank is the safest and simplest form. Investment may also be made in building and loan associations or through the purchase of securities.[2] All young people would do well to start an insurance program as soon as they begin to earn.[3] The earlier life insurance is bought, the lower the annual premium; and a valuable start is thus made in constructive saving. "Every family," Andrews says, "is in-

---

[1] See Bigelow, *op. cit.*, pp. 427–433; Andrews, *op. cit.*, pp. 225–231.

[2] Competent advice on investments is not always easy to obtain, although it is essential for the average family to secure such advice. Criteria by which investments may be judged are discussed by Andrews, *op. cit.*, pp. 190–198, and by Bigelow, *op. cit.*, pp. 454–471.

[3] The varied types of insurance which offer protection against future contingencies are surveyed by Andrews, *op. cit.*, pp. 199–217, and by Bigelow, *op. cit.*, pp. 471–496.

terested in life insurance upon the lives of its income producers, and in fire insurance upon its house furnishings and home if owned; and in addition often in other types." [1]

Financial Policies at Successive Stages of Family Life. The savings and insurance program is an individual problem to be worked out in each family as part of its whole financial policy. Certain general principles are provided by the characteristic needs of families at successive stages. In the early years of married life, before the birth of children, expenses are at a minimum. It is well to accumulate at that time as much permanent equipment as possible and to start a fund which may be used later to purchase a home. Savings are needed to help in meeting the expenses involved in the birth and care of children. Life insurance becomes of far greater importance as soon as a child is expected. With the birth of each child, more life insurance should be secured, if possible. During the early years of each child's life it is also most desirable to accumulate a fund to devote in each case to the heavy educational expenses of the last few years of dependency.

Current expenses will increase as the family grows, and, unless income also rises, the savings program will have to be reduced for a time. When the peak of expenditures is passed some of the insurance carried while all the children were dependent may be dropped, and where there is a cash-surrender value this sum may be invested to provide for the retirement period. The chief hazard of these later years is no longer that the father and mother will leave dependents unprovided for, but that they themselves will become dependent in old age. To provide against such a contingency, all available funds may be used to purchase the largest possible joint annuity.

Coöperation in Family Finance. Financial policies should be discussed fairly thoroughly before marriage. The advantages of beginning to plan as soon as possible are made even more obvious by a realization of the considerable sums of money which in the course of years actually pass through the hands of an average husband and wife.[2] A yearly income of $2,500 for

---

[1] *Op. cit.*, p. 200.

[2] In his exceedingly practical little book *Making the Most of Your Income* (1933), Blodgett suggests ten fundamental rules which will not only clarify thinking, but which should often be consulted as tests of progress. These rules are: "Decide to become independent; Think straight and plan; Master the art of saving; Master the art of spending; Guard against waste; Cultivate the habit of industry; Go into debt wisely; Be a regular bank depositor; Use saved capital for profit; Conserve your capital after getting it." P. 39.

forty years means the management during that period of $100,000.

One aspect of sound financial policy has not yet been mentioned. Both husband and wife should make wills in order that the property in money, real estate, and personal belongings of which each has the legal disposal may be distributed in the exact manner which seems best. The property of those who die intestate is disposed of according to state law, which occasionally works much hardship.[1] Competent legal advice should always be secured when making a will, and there should be a periodic review in order to adjust the terms of a will to changes which have occurred since its last revision.

Centralized control of finances is highly desirable, but it may be exercised in a democratic way by means of family conferences in which even the children participate. The essential matter is coöperation between husband and wife. "In making plans for a home of their own, a man and a woman can do no one thing which will more insure its success than by adopting the principle of the common family purse and its administration in a democratic way. The adjustment of personal habits and points of view as regards finance to a common plan of action, jointly determined, may well be the first expression of abiding ethical and personal unity. Agreement in financial relationships will react in agreement in all their living." If the husband is the sole wage earner, he should recognize that his earnings are "returns made to the partnership, and not to him alone, for work done. . . . The man's earnings in a real sense are the home's earnings." Accordingly, "the man's share for personal spending cannot in right take precedence over the shares of other members of the family." The "only fair standard" which, if "generally adoped, would tend to greatly increase the satisfaction and comfort of living" is to consider the family purse as "a partnership fund held in common, and its distribution [a] matter of joint consideration and decision."[2]

As in all conferences where a genuine effort is being made to reach wise decisions, greater weight must be given to the judgment of those who possess special knowledge or experience. Special competence in any field should be used for the common good. While delegating responsibility in this way, both husband

---

[1] A child or children may obtain twice as much as their mother; or a second wife may inherit the personal property of a first wife, though the latter would certainly have wished her own children to possess it.

[2] Andrews, *op. cit.*, p. 574.

and wife should hold themselves equally responsible for final results. Mutual confidence is essential, and the wife should be as fully informed as the husband with regard to all details of the family's financial situation. Wherever financial coöperation is real and intelligent, a joint bank account, open equally to checking by husband and wife is the one desirable means of access to the family funds.

SUGGESTED READING

Abel, M. H., *Successful Family Life on the Moderate Income*, 2nd ed. rev., 1927.

Andrews, B. R., *Economics of the Household*, rev. ed., 1935.

Bigelow, H. F., *Family Finance*, 1936.

Chase, S., and Schlink, F. T., *Your Money's Worth*, 1927.

Donham, S. A., *Spending the Family Income*, rev. ed., 1933.

Kneeland, H., "Woman's Economic Contribution in the Home," *The Annals of the American Academy of Political and Social Science*, Vol. CXLIII, May, 1929, pp. 33–40.

Kyrk, H., *Economic Problems of the Family*, 1933.

Macdonald, E., and Macdonald, F., *Homemaking, A Profession for Men and Women*, 1927.

Watson, A. E., "The Reorganization of Household Work," *The Annals of the American Academy of Political and Social Science*, Vol. CLX, March, 1932, pp. 165–177.

CHAPTER XXII

HOUSEKEEPING AND HOMEMAKING
(*Continued*)

HOUSING AND THE HOME

The Fundamental Importance of Housing. Food, clothing, and shelter are the fundamental necessities with which every family must be provided. Housing exercises a determining influence on the quality of family life: the health, safety, and contentment of all members of the family, and particularly the children, being in large measure dependent on their dwelling place. The house provides shelter and protection from heat and cold, wind, rain, or snow. In this way it safeguards health, as also by providing access to light, air and sunshine, and pure water, and by the adequacy of its sanitary facilities and the facilities it affords for sleep, rest, privacy, and recreation. Each member of the family should be assured of a measure of privacy, and the house should provide an appropriate setting for group living and for individual development. Finally, the house is also a storehouse and a workshop.

In accordance with the earlier discussion of standards, housing may be considered adequate in proportion as it safeguards health; as it provides means for furthering education and the individual interests of family members; as it affords opportunities for craftsmanship and artistic expression; and as it facilitates a harmonious ordering of daily activities and the reduction of effort and the time cost of housework.

The choice of even a rented home is thus no simple matter; it involves consideration not only of the house and its immediate setting, but also of the location and neighborhood. Where a family buys or builds a home, such considerations are of crucial importance. The type and location of a house not only conditions family living, but materially affects other expenditures. Some houses cost more to operate than others, and the costs for regular transportation to business or school, being dependent on location, should be included in the costs of shelter.

In deciding upon a location the relative importance of a number of factors must be considered; the proximity of good schools, and the distance from stores, doctor, dentist, cultural and recreation centers, and transportation facilities. It should be ascertained whether a neighborhood is reasonably free from smoke, dust, fumes, noise, and heavy traffic; also that land is well-drained, that there are no difficulties in sewage disposal and that protection is adequate in case of fire. A residential neighborhood should be chosen, wherever possible, for there is then room for children to play in gardens or at least in a playground or park. It is also essential to remember that the choice of a neighborhood very largely determines the children's playmates.

Open space around a house is of great value, because it allows all rooms to receive direct sunshine and natural lighting. Every room should also have adequate natural ventilation. It is obviously desirable, of course, that the house be fire-resistive, and well-designed and well-built. It should provide a sleeping room for each child, and, if possible, a common play-room. Later this may be turned into a workshop, studio or music room, or an additional living room for the younger members of the family. There should always be a living room with a fire-place as the center of family life.[1]

Types and Costs of Housing. Housing costs usually take one-tenth to one-quarter of the family income. Larger absolute amounts are spent where incomes are larger; but, at the lower levels, with rise of income the proportion spent for rent decreases. And, as families increase in size, food costs perforce rise and rent expenditures must fall, where income is strictly limited.

There is a decided trend towards living in multiple family dwellings, particularly, of course, in the larger cities.[2] Housekeeping responsibilities are much reduced. Rent is high, but it centers, in one definite monthly charge, payments for a number of items which would vary in ordinary housekeeping. But there is lack of privacy, both because of the crowding of many families in one building and because of the limited size of all but very high-priced apartments. Only recently, moreover, have any apartment houses been built with the interests of children in view. But, even where special facilities are provided for children, an apartment house is a most unsatisfactory environment for growing children. There can be no question at all that the

---

[1] The use of the phrase living room instead of drawing room is significant. It is not so common now for ladies to *withdraw*, leaving the gentlemen at the dinner table. Nor do many find time to sit long hours in their drawing rooms waiting for visitors. The principal room is now one in which the family live together.

[2] In 1930, 76.4% of families still lived in one-family dwellings; 11.6% in two-family dwellings and 12.1% in dwellings for three or more families.

single-family detached house in a garden provides the optimum environment for normal family life. Freedom and privacy are secured, and access to sunshine and the open air. With a safe playground of their own where they may garden, keep pets, and engage in varied constructive pursuits, children are provided with educational essentials for which there is no adequate artificial substitute.

Fortunately for the future of family life there are certain incipient tendencies to-day which run counter to the concentration of population in city apartment houses: the development of greenbelt and of subsistence homestead communities, for example. Most hopeful of all is the fact that, in proportion as electric energy is more widely and cheaply distributed through the country, it will become for the first time possible to separate the production of goods from the production of energy. The complete electrical intercommunication of modern life, through radio, telephone, telegraph, and power transmission, makes possible a general decentralization of industry and life. The typical community of the future is already envisaged by far-sighted architects as one in which some 1,400 families, each with at least an acre of land, will live in a self-contained manner with small farms, small factories, decentralized schools, safe traffic, and simplified government.[1]

Home Ownership. It is to be hoped, then, that in the future it may be possible for the majority to own their homes and to create for themselves a setting conducive to the well-being of family life. Nothing can take the place of a home of one's own as a medium of expression for the family members and as the abiding center of family life. At present, however, it is impossible for many to own even the humblest home, and modern conditions frequently render home ownership inadvisable. Those who are not tied to any one locality possess an advantage in bargaining power when selling their services to employers. If a job or position is lost, another may be sought at once in a more favorable locality. But the home owner can very seldom effect an immediate sale of his property except at a great sacrifice, and he may even be unable to find suitable tenants.[2] The probable

---

[1] A model of such a community, designed by Frank Lloyd Wright was exhibited at the Industrial Arts Exposition at Rockefeller Center in April, 1935. *New York Times*, March 27, 1935.

[2] Home ownership has decided disadvantages as an investment when a family wishes to move, or when, in an emergency, it must turn property into cash. House ownership is in any case an insecure investment when there is depreciation either in land values or in the house itself, owing to lack of repairs or obsolescence. On the other

permanency of the breadwinner's job should always be considered before deciding on home ownership. For farm families the question of home ownership is further complicated by being involved in the larger question of farm ownership. As it becomes harder for farm operators to make the transition from tenancy to ownership, conditions here too are in favor of renting.

Altogether, about half the population to-day lives in rented houses. No obligations are incurred beyond a definite period; there is no responsibility for property, taxes, or repairs, no danger of loss of capital put into a house. Adjustments can readily be made to changes in income, in size of family, in opportunities for employment and other local conditions. Also the actual cost of home ownership is often greater than the cost of renting. Of course, once the home is owned, clear of debt, the current outlay for shelter is less than in the case of the renter: taxes, repairs and improvements, and fire insurance are the only remaining items of expense, but to these must also be added the loss of interest which would have accrued had the same amount of money been invested otherwise than in a home.

The total costs of ownership are commonly calculated at from 10% to 12.5% of the investment. On this basis no family should pay more for a home than from two to two and a half times their annual income.[1] Financing its purchase is a great incentive to thrift and the natural desire for a "real home," not "just a place to live in," is one of the most potent motives for acquiring habits of saving. Home ownership also affords other opportunities for saving. Every member of the family can add to real income by taking part in the upkeep and improvement of house and grounds. Part of the food supply may be obtained where there is sufficient space for raising vegetables and fruit, for keeping poultry, bees, or a goat, or even a cow. All such activities have educational as well as economic value. And there is greater incentive to the development, not only of individual initiative,

hand, there are many cases where home ownership is a secure investment. It is particularly valuable in old age, by taking care of a considerable part of the costs of living.

[1] At an annual income of $2,500, not more than $5,000 to $6,250 can safely be invested in a home. The current outlay of those who are financing the purchase of a home is large compared with the costs of actual ownership, and often as compared with renting. In addition to taxes, insurance, and repairs, regular payments must be made upon the reducing mortgage or instalment contract. Since with a larger down payment far better terms can be secured for financing the balance, the down payment should never be less than 25% of the total cost, and should be as near 50% as possible. A young couple may begin by building a three-room unit so planned that two, three or more rooms may be added to it afterwards.

but of civic responsibility, since the family owning its home is bound to take interest in community affairs.[1]

FOOD AND THE FAMILY

Food and Health. "Our newer knowledge of the relations of food to health," says Sherman "is one of the major revelations of modern science, and perhaps it is outstandingly the one on which each of us can act every day for the lifelong welfare and happiness of ourselves and our children."[2]. The very concept of health is actually being changed by this knowledge, health being now conceived as a positive quality in the life of the individual, as meaning not merely freedom from disease, but "a more buoyant youth of efficient development, a higher level of adult vitality and accomplishment, and an extension of the prime of life farther into the advancing years."[3]

We are, each one of us, "the transmuted substance of the food we eat."[4] Something like three-quarters of a ton of food is necessary each year to the maintenance of a human being. Obviously, the chemical composition of such an amount must have significance for health. It is now known that for organic well-being daily food must provide at least thirty-seven nutrients in appropriate quantitative relations.[5] Food requirements are also determined by age, size, and amount of muscular activity expended. Throughout childhood, food requirements are high, because of the needs of growth and because of the vigorous activities of all healthy children. Wide agreement has now been reached with regard to dietary standards, which may be confidently used in daily practice. But much yet remains to be discovered of the intricate and subtle processes of biochemistry, and in particular of the relation of food to the endocrines. Discoveries of the greatest importance may be made concerning the relation of food to personality and to mental and emotional traits.

---

[1] It is not implied that family life in a rented house is devoid of similar opportunities. They should indeed be provided as fully as possible, even when the parents realize the impermanency of their environment. The years pass much more slowly for children, and the disadvantages of moving from place to place may be offset through the secure atmosphere of home life and the opportunities afforded for expression and development.

[2] *Food and Health* (1934), p. 1.

[3] *Op. cit.*, pp. 196–197. Already food habits are being revolutionized. This fact is made more evident when present habits are compared with those of a generation ago. See *Middletown*, pp. 156–158.

[4] Gove Hambidge, *Your Meals and Your Money* (1934), p. 85.

[5] These include eleven mineral elements, six vitamins, eighteen of the known twenty-two amino acids or digestive products of proteins (the other four being synthetized in the body), glucose, and linoleic acid.

Sherman summarizes the present working knowledge of nutrition in terms of six "pillar concepts . . . upon and around which the twentieth century science of nutrition is being built."[1] Food must provide the *fuel* and *energy* needs of the body; the *proteins* necessary for body tissue; *minerals*, and in particular a liberal supply of calcium;[2] and nutrients grouped together under the name of *vitamins*.[3] A fifth outstanding concept is found in the interrelationships among the different factors in nutrition; for example, that which obtains between the behavior in the body of calcium and phosphorus and the functioning of vitamins A, C, and D. Finally, Sherman stresses the principle that "our most significant concern is with the nutritional reactions of the living body as a whole."[4] If dietaries are planned to meet all known nutritional needs, and these are supplied by reasonably natural foods, they "will almost certainly furnish us any substance which may be essential to our nutritional well-being, though still scientifically unknown to us."[5]

In order that individuals and families may have the full benefit of the science of nutrition, experts must translate their findings into terms of everyday foods and work out such combinations of foods as will ensure good diet. The simplest plan, according to McCollum, is to build the family diet around approximately a quart of milk a day for each individual.[6] In addition there should be two salads a day, making use of whatever raw vegetables and fruits are in season, and a daily serving of at least one green vegetable. Since this diet will make good the deficiencies of whatever else is eaten, the rest of the meals may

---

[1] *Op. cit.*, p. 101.

[2] To be normal and healthy the body must be richer in calcium than in any other mineral element; yet it is born calcium poor, because the flexibility of the infant's bones has had survival value in facilitating birth. A liberal calcium intake is essential to optimum development and health, and is best assured by the use of milk, not only in infancy, but also thereafter. Milk, being a natural food, also supplies the protein mixture best suited to the body's needs.

[3] In the case of vitamins A, C, and G, it has recently been established that nutritional well-being is enhanced if food supplies a considerably larger amount than is demonstrably necessary.

[4] *Op. cit.*, p. 101. It has also become evident that "some of nature's wholes may be expected to bear nutritional relations to each other because of the connections in which they have evolved, the one subsisting on the other." From such a standpoint, milk is seen as one of nature's wholes, "whose sole function in nature is to serve as food, and to nourish animals of the mammalian type—including us." P. 157.

[5] *Ibid.*, p. 160.

[6] The approximate equivalent to one quart of fluid whole milk in milk products may be substituted in whole or in part. These are: 17 ounces evaporated milk; one quart fluid skim milk and 1½ ounces butter; 5 ounces American cheddar cheese; 4½ ounces dried whole milk; 3½ ounces dried skim milk and 1½ ounces butter.

be planned to suit the appetite and growth needs of the family members, provided, however, that the consumption of sugar is in most cases *reduced*.[1] Sherman makes substantially the same suggestion when he says: "let at least half of the needed food-calories be taken in the form of the 'protective foods'—milk and its products, fruit, vegetables and eggs."[2] A second suggestion is that at least half the cereal products eaten should be in whole-grain form. One of the easiest means of giving the right degree of prominence to different types of food is to budget in advance the money to be spent for each. Sherman suggests that at least as much should be spent for milk (including cream and cheese, if used) as for meats, poultry, and fish; and at least as much should be spent on fruit and vegetables as for meats, poultry, and fish.[3]

Food Costs and Food Economy. The national expenditure for food is more than twice that for any other item. Food, being essential to existence, is more nearly a fixed requirement than any other item of the budget, so that the smaller the income the greater the *proportion* which must be spent on food. With larger incomes more money is spent, but only up to a certain point is there increase in amount of food consumed; the change is rather away from the consumption of exclusively cheap foods, such as sugar, potatoes, dried peas, beans, and fruits, cabbage, carrots, and canned tomatoes, and towards increased consumption of meat, poultry, butter, eggs, cakes, fresh fruit and vegetables, and other more expensive and palatable foods.

There are many ways in which food costs may be cut while the food supply remains entirely adequate to family needs. In no other class of expenditures are constant small economies so important. Food should be bought in season, in economical quantities, and in the most economical form. Great economies may be effected where the family produce some of their own

[1] The annual consumption of sugar in America amounts to 115 lbs. per person, an excessive amount for any but very active males over 15.

[2] *Op. cit.*, p. 182.

[3] The most thorough attempt to make nutritional principles available in a form in which they can be easily used by the ordinary housewife is that embodied in *Circular 296* of the Department of Agriculture (1933). In "Diets at Four Levels of Nutritive Content and Cost," Stiebeling and Ward, of the Bureau of Home Economics, present four diet plans to fit four income levels. The depression made evident the importance of applying nutritional principles to the feeding of those on relief or with very restricted incomes. Only the liberal diet can be considered wholly adequate; the minimum and moderate cost adequate diets provide some margin of safety, but the restricted diet for emergency use provides only the minimum requirements with little margin for safety. These four plans are discussed, from the standpoint of the consumer, by Hambidge in *Your Meals and Your Money*.

food supply and are able not only to spend less, but to consume more of the perishable and expensive, but invaluable, protective foods. The avoidance of all waste is essential to food economy.[1] Waste can be avoided if no food is allowed to spoil through exposure to heat or dust or insects. Refrigeration and adequate storage facilities are most important. Poor cooking spoils much food, but even where there is no lack of skill in cooking there may be much waste in preparation, as in the unnecessary or unskilful peeling of fruits and vegetables. Portions served at table should never be greater than can be eaten, and the leaving on the plate of broken bread, lettuce, or other edible parts of food, should be definitely discouraged in all families.[2] The greatest opportunity for skilful economy arises however in the transformation of left-over food into nourishing soups and appetizing new dishes.[3]

Values of the Family Table. In time it is much to be hoped that nutritional principles will have become matters of common knowledge. At present the responsibility for the formation of intelligent food habits rests almost entirely on home managers who choose, buy, and prepare the food for the daily needs of their families. In countless homes, the significance of proper feeding has first been realized in connection with the care of babies and young children. Some progress is being made, therefore, particularly in families with sufficient income who appreciate the value of scientific child care.

The practice of eating together round the family table possesses hygienic, educational, social, and aesthetic values. In the first place it provides the opportunity for the development in children of good food habits and intelligent attitudes towards food.[4] Once food habits are learned they are modified only with difficulty. Hence the importance of being accustomed from earliest infancy to eating foods which possess nutritive values necessary for health and growth. As soon as the baby is old

[1] In 1917 the Department of Agriculture estimated that the annual food waste in homes amounted to $700,000,000, or $31 per family.

[2] One beneficial result of the food economies necessitated by the World War was the discouragement of the American customs of lavish serving and *leaving* of food on the plate as an accepted aspect of good table manners.

[3] Not only may much money be saved when every scrap of food is used in some way, but, through keeping water in which vegetables are cooked and using this for soups and gravies, valuable nutrients are saved from going to waste. Further economies are effected where scraps can be fed to poultry.

[4] At present, the family table more often develops whims and prejudices, but this situation is entirely remediable and depends on the parents. If both are "nutrition-minded," and *calmly* take for granted that the food which is served will be acceptable to all, there is usually little difficulty.

enough to sit in his high chair, it is of the utmost importance that all influences should combine to reënforce good feeding habits which have already been acquired.

The stress laid on table manners makes clear the opportunity which exists for learning, not only *manners* in the limited sense, but courteous consideration for others and cheerful sharing in each other's experiences. Meals at which parents and children assemble should be times for good humor and interesting conversation, peaceful and refreshing interludes in the day's activities, from which emotional tension is banished and where no dispute or wrangling ever finds a place. Meals may be of the simplest and table appointments need not be elaborate, yet the whole situation may have aesthetic value to which cleanliness, order, tasteful service, a bowl of flowers or fruit, all contribute.

Hambidge discusses the possibility of simplified and standardized meals. From the nutritive standpoint it would be possible to live on a diet of whole milk, brown bread, and tomatoes. But without going to any such monotonous extreme, there is no good reason why breakfast and the lighter of the two remaining meals should not be to a considerable extent standardized, while the heaviest meal still allows room for greater variety. Cookery best contributes to nutritional well-being, Sherman points out, by making attractive a simple dietary of reasonably natural food. A plan such as this might contribute to health and prove economical both in cost and in time and labor.

Since the service of food at home secures privacy and adjustment to individual needs, it seems unlikely that it will be generally displaced by centralized systems of eating. There have been a number of experiments in the establishment of depots for the delivery of hot cooked foods to the home. So far they have not been very successful, the chief difficulty being the cost.[1] This plan suggests attractive possibilities of supplementing the prepared foods which already do so much to lighten the labor of food preparation.

[1] Andrews points out that raw food materials, bought by a family, cost from one-fifth to half of the income. If prepared in a central kitchen and delivered at home the cost of meals would be two or three times the cost of the raw foods. Apparently a solution of this difficulty has been reached in Budapest, Hungary, where food is in any case cheap. An extensive new business has developed in which five-course meals are delivered by messengers on bicycles for a cost of 25 cents a person. *New York Times*, Nov. 29, 1936. It may be noted that prepared foods are already provided by canning industries, bakeries, and delicatessen stores, at costs little, if at all, in excess of those for home production.

THE CLOTHING OF THE FAMILY

Clothing Costs. From one-tenth to one-fifth of the income of American families goes for clothing.[1] In lower-income groups the husband spends more on clothing than the wife, while this situation is usually reversed in upper-income groups. In all groups, the clothing of children under fifteen costs less than the clothing of their parents, but sons over fifteen spend more than their fathers and girls over fifteen more than their mothers. The unmarried daughter over fifteen spends more for clothing than any other member of the family.

Clothing expenditures present problems to all but some five, or possibly ten, per cent of the population. Not only is there the temptation to spend too large a proportion of income in order to appear "well-dressed," but expenditures are irregular, come at unexpected intervals, and are particularly heavy at certain seasons. It is, accordingly, best to budget the family's clothing expenditures for as much as three years in advance. Costs may then be spread more evenly; and, in anticipation of future needs, full advantage may be taken of sales and opportunities for buying at less cost.[2]

The purchase of ready-to-wear clothing has now become customary. Tailored garments are still made to order for those who can afford them, but piece goods are being less frequently bought for the home manufacture of clothing. Yet, provided there is time available which would otherwise be unproductive, certain kinds of clothing are still most advantageously made at home.[3] Skill in the alteration or making over of garments is also of importance in reducing the cost of clothing.

Clothing Standards. Plans for clothing the family are further complicated by the disparate purposes served by clothing and the consequent confusion in standards. At the lower levels of

---

[1] At lower-income levels there is a steady increase in the proportion spent for clothing with increase in income. There comes a point, however, where the percentage spent for clothing declines, though there is increase in actual expenditures.

[2] The temptation to buy unnecessary clothing at a bargain is also eliminated, where a definite plan is available as a guide, and buying is always deliberate and never impulsive. Shopping intelligence is all too rare in the purchase of clothing. In Middletown, for example, many women were found to depend entirely on the counsel of the selling agent whose primary object was to make money. They bought on the basis, not of quality, but of looks and price, buying higher-priced stylish garments where able to do so, even if the quality were no better than in those of lower price. *Middletown*, p. 166.

[3] For example, where a desired style or quality or size is not available on the market, or is only available at a high price. Children's clothing, women's dresses, underwear, and knitted garments are the forms of clothes most frequently made at home.

income the protective function of clothing determines its purchase, but with increase in income the decorative function rules, even though finding expression through the cheapest materials. The high costs of dress in adolescence are not only natural but justifiable, since, if seeking social recognition and self-confidence through dress is ever to be condoned, it is at this period. But it is most unfortunate that fashion rather than aesthetic standards should receive the greater emphasis.

Clothing for women as well as men should promote health by protecting from heat and cold, by keeping the body dry and clean, and by allowing unimpeded freedom of movement. Good taste in dress implies in addition the selection of clothing which, while appropriate for occasion and occupation and becoming to the individual, possesses intrinsic aesthetic quality.

The Significance of Intelligent Clothing Habits. The significance of clothing habits lies in the fact that attitudes towards clothing involve not only considerations of health and beauty, but are influential in the formation of character. Particularly is this true of little girls, in whom unwholesome concentration on themselves and the adornment of their persons often goes unchecked and is even encouraged by fond but foolish parents. The development of good clothing habits is at present more important in girls than in boys, although both should be educated in the selection of appropriate and tasteful dress.

Scientific study of the relation of clothing to physiological and psychological health is now in its initial stages.[1] Approved designs for tiny children are simple and attractive, allowing for wholesome exposure to sunshine and for temperature regulation. Openings are so placed and fastenings are of such a kind that the child may learn to dress and undress himself, and so develop manipulative skill and habits of self-help. Children derive much enjoyment from attractively colored clothes, and, through pride of possession, begin to learn the rudiments of their care. From six to twelve there is opportunity for practice in selection of clothing, and, in the earlier stages of adolescence, a clothing allowance is of great educational value. In these ways boys and girls are better prepared for the period when clothes assume such importance for the expression of individuality.

[1] *The Home and the Child*, pp. 153–161. *The Bureau of Home Economics* has issued a number of leaflets dealing with the clothing of little children and giving patterns for such articles as rompers, sun or play suits, little girls' dresses, and little boys' suits.

HOUSEHOLD OPERATION

Items and Costs of Household Operation. The house and its furniture and equipment must all be kept clean and in good repair; there must be supplies of water, fuel, and light; and adequate facilities for the disposal of wastes.[1] Supplies must be at hand for all these processes, and for the repair, cleaning, and laundering of clothing. The expenses of household operation include the cost of all these items and also all payments made to employees or outside agencies rendering assistance in the work of the household. In spite of all this variety of items the costs of household operation remain relatively constant at different income levels.[2] About 15% of moderate incomes are spent in this way, while as much as one-fourth or one-fifth of large incomes are required to meet costs which include the wages of large numbers of employees.

Reducing the Burden of Housework through Efficiency and Time Economy. Time spent in housework might be much decreased, "if all worked with maximum efficiency and zeal, that is, if all possessed superior equipment, had knowledge of the 'one best way' and a strong incentive to reduce working time."[3] The desirability of economy in money and resources is evident to most homemakers, but the value of economy in time is fully realized only by those who have work to do which is more vital to them than housework; the mother who grudges time for mechanical routine which she might give to her children; and women with other interests or occupations. This fact tends to delay the development and spread of systematic and scientific household management and performance. Some women waste time and effort in over-meticulous or over-elaborate housekeeping. Others are inefficient in a way which is not only unwholesome for family life, but may have deplorable social results. In a New York suburb it was found that the excessive speed of

[1] The economic utilization of materials which might otherwise go to waste fosters valuable social attitudes. In addition to food wastes, every household discards clothing, newspapers and magazines, worn-out furnishings, bottles, tin cans, and ashes. Nothing which has economic value should be burnt or given to the garbage collector. Welfare agencies now salvage and use in their industrial departments everything but tin cans and broken glass.

[2] National expenditures for fuel and light are always among the leading items. In the figures given in billions, for 1929, they were 4.8, exceeded only by food (17), clothing (8), shelter (8), automobile purchase and insurance (6.5), and taxes (6.4). Home furnishings accounted for 4 billions. *Recent Social Trends*, Vol. II, pp. 887–890.

[3] Kyrk, *op. cit.*, p. 60. Efficiency is well defined as "a reduction in the time, energy or resources expended in securing a given result, or what is equivalent, securing a better or greater product for the same expenditure." P. 94.

delivery trucks was largely the result of the incessant and unreasonable demands of inefficient housewives. Three or four trips a day to many houses were a regular custom, and seven to nine were not unknown.[1]

Efficiency and Increased Household Production. If time is set free from the ordinary housework, women have more time for their children, and for outside work and interests, or, as a third possibility, they may engage in increased household production. An outstanding advocate of increasing household self-sufficiency is Ralph Borsodi.[2] There is no doubt that, for certain people under certain conditions, increased household production possesses great economic and educational and vocational advantages, and would bring about an increase in the satisfactions to be derived from craftsmanship. But, as a wholesale solution for the problems of household economics and of women's work, it involves the time-honored fallacy that every woman, irrespective of her specific abilities, must find a sufficient outlet in household production.

Ways of Reducing the Time Spent in Housework. There are three chief means of lightening the burden of housework: (1) the transference of housework to machinery, either operated outside the home by service companies, or introduced into the home in the form of labor-saving equipment; (2) the employment of paid household helpers; (3) the systematic coöperation of all members of the family. Two additional means may also be pointed out. Simplicity in homemaking may be combined with good taste in such a way as to reduce to a minimum the problems of cleaning and care. And, finally, efficient planning is one of the

[1] *New York Times*, May 16, 1936. Inquiries at grocery and meat markets elicited the fact that elsewhere also there are numbers of households to which deliveries are always made several times daily, a practice which is responsible not only for exceeding the speed limit, but for a great increase in overhead costs and higher prices. Some housewives come themselves to shop before almost every meal, not even having planned their daily meals in advance, far less ordered their supplies for some time ahead. Women who are content to spend their days shopping around and gossiping with others, equally inefficient and empty-headed, certainly still belong in the class of rudimentary and undeveloped human beings to which, a century ago, it was customary to consign all women.

[2] *This Ugly Civilization* (1929) and *Flight from the City* (1933). A subsistence type of homestead properly organized would, according to Borsodi, lead to so great an increase in household production that it would absorb the energies of women and children and part of the working time of men. It would, he believes, increase the economic function of the family, give added security to families, raise standards of living, strengthen family ties through close association in common tasks, give children a natural education, provide occupation for the aged, and solve the problem of careers for women. In the case of certain activities, several families would combine as economic units, but regular factory production should only be retained for the relatively few goods best produced in factories. Borsodi has himself demonstrated the feasibility of such a plan as director of the School for Living at Suffern, N. Y.

best ways of saving time, as well as resources and energy. With written plans for every detail of management and performance, the homemaker is not only in a position to guide intelligently her own daily tasks and those of others, but is better able to evaluate her work and subordinate non-essentials to essentials.[1]

The Transfer of Housework to Outside Service Industries. When income allows the transfer of housework to outside agencies, it is not difficult to decide what should be taken out of the household as non-essential to home life. All cleaning processes may with great advantage be eliminated from the work of family members. Laundry and the cleaning and pressing of clothes can be transferred to outside agencies, while cleaners may be hired either individually or from outside agencies to care for windows, floors, furnishings, and household equipment. Industrial progress and better homemaking should result from the transfer of all such mechanical tasks.[2]

It must not be forgotten, moreover, that electricity, gas, and water are services supplied to the home by outside agencies, all of which result in a notable lightening in the burdens of housework.[3] Most of all is this true of electric power, which makes possible the development of labor-saving machinery in the home.[4] Electricity

[1] Much of this planning takes no extra time, for it may be done while one is occupied with routine tasks, mending, washing dishes, making beds, preparing vegetables. Even when there is no planning to be done, nowadays, household drudgery may be combined with symphony concerts or opera, thanks to radio. The hours which must be spent over what would otherwise be monotonous tasks, such as mending, thus become hours of rest and refreshment.

[2] The introduction of electric washing machines and ironers into the home has slowed up the trend of laundry work out of the home to large-scale commercial interests. The Lynds point to this fact as an illustration of the haphazard processes of social change. The purchase of a costly washing machine, whether justifiable or not from the standpoint of the individual family, "tends to perpetuate a questionable institutional set up—whereby many individual homes repeat common tasks day after day in isolated units—by forcing back into the individual home a process that was following belatedly the trend in industry towards centralized production." *Middletown*, pp. 174–175. It is true, of course, that few families can afford high grade finished laundry work at its present costs, but a considerable lightening of housework is effected by some of the less expensive types of laundry service.

[3] The telephone too belongs in this group and in a different way lightens housework. The efficient homemaker who values time will do the greater part of the ordering of supplies by telephone.

[4] Comparing electric with steam power, it is evident that the latter is not practicable for use in the home. It cannot be transported far from its source and is adapted for use only in larger units of production. Its introduction thus led to the transfer of industry from the household to factories concentrated near the source of power. Electricity, on the other hand, can be transported long distances and applied to the small machines used in domestic production. It makes possible decentralized, large-scale production and the increase of household production. With the widespread installation of mechanical refrigerators in homes, the manufacture of ice is already being transferred from factory to household.

presents, according to Andrews, "the greatest single opportunity
for progress in housework."[1] The present water-power policy of
the federal government and the work of the Rural Electrification
Administration is therefore of utmost significance to the future of
family life, designed, as it is, "to spread the benefits of electric
energy at as low rates as possible, over the widest possible
area."[2]

Machinery in the Household. Machinery may also be brought
into the home to lighten and make more agreeable the remaining
tasks. As income permits, it is highly desirable to invest in more
adequate equipment in tools, utensils, and machines. Of the
latter a mechanical refrigerator, a vacuum cleaner, and an electric
iron are most valuable. Next to a good stove, a mechanical refrigerator has proved itself as the most essential of all aids to
good housekeeping. The kitchen as work-center should, where-
ever possible, be planned as a unit. The floor area should not be
too restricted, for it should allow room for several members of
the household working together, or for young children playing
under the supervision of their mother. Already, inexpensive and
attractive small houses are being designed by leading architects
to fit the needs of households where the family members cooperate in all phases of home life.[3]

The Changing Status of Household Employment. Although only
about 5% of all private households in America employ help, this
means that a very large group of women, about 1,400,000 in
1930, are working in private homes. But for families with a
moderate income it is now almost impossible to find efficient help
at prices they can afford to pay.[4] Since the nineties there has
been growing interest in the problems of household employment.
While it still remains an unstandardized occupation, far-reaching
changes are under way, tending to make of domestic service a

[1] *Op. cit.*, p. 471.

[2] Delbert Clark, "An Engineer Blueprints a New America," *New York Times
Magazine,* Nov. 15, 1936.

[3] In some of these, usually summer homes, each member of the family has a bedroom, and the living center of the house is a large kitchen-living room. For most
families in all-year homes, a separate living room is desirable, but cooking and eating
arrangements may be combined to advantage. Separate dining rooms were appropriate only when hired domestic service was the rule for all upper-class families. It
is noticeable that, so long as a menial class performed the housework, very little attempt was made to lighten its burdens: in the cities, servants worked in dark base-
ments and climbed long flights of stairs to serve the meals.

[4] In Middletown, in 1925, it was about half as frequent as in 1890 for housewives
to hire full-time servants. Wages then were $3 as against $10 or $15 a week in 1925,
so that a day's housework, performed by a woman "coming in" cost as much or more
than a full week's work in 1890. *Middletown,* pp. 169–171.

definite contractual relation as to hours and working conditions, like other modern occupations.[1] To make of domestic service a standardized vocation, it is essential that its stigma be removed and that it should develop into a skilled pursuit. The encouragement of the employment of workers who live out should also tend to raise the status of household employment.

The Desirability of Part-time Assistance by Household Workers. When the prejudice against housework as menial is finally overcome, many of the young women who now go into offices may be attracted to household assistance. In the meantime the situation is usually unsatisfactory. Even where, with liberal incomes, traditional leisure-class patterns of living survive, it is to be questioned if this provides as educational an environment as one in which all members of the family share in some degree in household processes. Where one domestic worker lives in a household, family privacy is invaded by the presence of a stranger with different tastes and social standards, usually of a lower intellectual and sometimes of a lower moral level. Even where a well-adjusted individual, fond of children, is employed, parents should realize that she exerts a definite influence on their children's nurture.[2] This is even true in cases where a girl receives board and lodging and a small salary, in exchange for household help while living in the family circle. Apart from its invasion of family privacy, this arrangement may be advocated as a form of apprenticeship in homemaking.

The most promising solution, however, would seem to be the development of agencies supplying trained workers, either for general work or for special tasks by the hour or the day, or more permanently by week or month for specified hours. Some of these should be men, specializing in the heavier forms of work, and occupying the same status as plumbers, carpenters, gardeners, house painters, window cleaners, and all workers who come for a specified time to work in a household.[3] Unorganized part-

---

[1] See Andrews, *op. cit.*, Chapter XIX for a survey of the movement.

[2] For example a child sometimes acquires a fear of the dark or of thunder through the influence of a servant, even when he is cared for almost wholly by his parents. In many cases association with servants has had definitely harmful effects upon children.

[3] An experiment along these lines was conducted by the Household Aid Company in Boston from 1903 to 1905. The results secured were negative, owing largely to the critical attitude of the public and their unwillingness to pay more for a skilled worker; also to the varied standards, making part-time work in different homes difficult. According to Andrews: "The Household Aid Company has important lessons for anyone desiring to inaugurate service by the hour." *Op. cit.*, p. 192. Copies of the report of this experiment may be obtained from the *Journal of Home Economics*, Baltimore.

time work is already very widely employed and does much to alleviate the burdens of housework.

The most satisfactory situation would, in general, be that where everything that could be done better outside the home was transferred to outside agencies, where labor-saving devices and adequate equipment were available, and where skilled part-time help could be hired for any work which was not undertaken by members of the family. Routine tasks would be the first to be turned over, then, perhaps, the whole preparation, service, and clearing away of the chief meal of the day. Family circumstances would in each case determine the amount and kind of help employed to supplement the work done by the family members.

Values of Systematic Coöperation in Housework on the Part of All the Family Members. Coöperation in the daily activities going on in the home may prove of the greatest educational value to children. Where both boys and girls take some part in household processes from an early age, they may acquire habits, skills, and attitudes of far-reaching importance. Learning to live and to work with the other members of the family, boys and girls are being educated for family life and as responsible and competent members of society. Every boy and girl should be able to care for his or her own property and have acquired the rudiments of cookery. In this way they become independent of the service of others and may be brought to realize that no form of work well done is degrading, and that there is no inherent superiority in one sex or class, which bestows the right of being waited on or served by others.[1]

Systematic coöperation between the family members is not only of educational value, but a means of lightening the home-maker's burden as the children grow older. Much careful planning is needed, and much patience with the unskilful work of children. Although the assistance they can give is very slight at first, later they may become a very real help. A home where little children and their parents work together at the daily tasks or at gardening, or preparing for some festive occasion, presents most of the educational advantages of a nursery school in a natural rather than artificial form. But the success of such a plan depends entirely on the prevailing atmosphere of home-life. There must be calm and good-humor and lack of fussiness over

---

[1] The otherwise obvious desirability of independence has been obscured by the association of drudgery with a dependent sex or a subservient class.

small details, if family life is to be a coöperative enterprise shared in by parents and children.[1]

THE SIGNIFICANCE OF DEVELOPMENT EXPENDITURES

Development Expenditures as an Item of the Budget. The final item of the budget makes provision for the *personal* life of the family members; for their physical, mental, social, and spiritual *development* or *advancement.* Even at the minimum income levels some provision, usually 12%, is made for these personal expenditures, and, as income grows, an increasing share is spent in this way; 18% to 20% of moderate incomes, and 22% or over of liberal incomes.

As we saw, expenditures for food, clothing, and shelter should all be guided with a view to the supreme value of good health. But there are still other expenses necessary to the *maintenance* of *health:* for recurrent medical examinations; for dental attention; for oculists and opticians; and in the event of illness or accident, expenses which may be very heavy indeed. All of these are included under personal or development expenditures. Vacations and many forms of recreation may also be considered as contributing to the maintenance of health, but expenditures for *recreation* are usually grouped together to include expenses for travel, for games of all kinds, theaters, concerts, music, and musical instruments.[2] Some of these expenditures might also be listed under *education*, but it is customary to include here chiefly expenses connected with attendance at school or college, and those for books and magazines. *Vocational* expenditures and all contributions to *social, civic, political, religious*, and *philanthropic enterprises* are also included under development expenditures, as are the costs of *hospitality* and *gifts*, and finally the individual *expense allowances* for each member of the family.

Health as Essential. There can be no accurate estimate of the unpredictable and sometimes very heavy expenses necessary for health. Most families must rely on their savings or on insurance to tide them through emergencies. What this actually means,

---

[1] Nothing perhaps is so utterly destructive of this atmosphere than solemnity over trifles, so characteristic of those "small souls" who make a ritual of means, with little or no consideration and appreciation of the ends these means should serve.

[2] One particularly heavy item of expense, which in most families must be regarded as primarily a recreational facility, is the automobile. The question of ownership of an automobile should be carefully considered from many points of view in framing a budget. For a discussion of the costs and issues involved, see Bigelow, *op. cit.*, Chapter XII.

however, is that "each year nearly one-half of persons in the lowest income group receive no professional or medical attention of any kind, curative or preventive."[1] It is very evident then, as we saw in Chapter XIII, that there is urgent need for "some plan whereby the unequal and sometimes crushing burdens of medical expenses can be distributed."[1]

It is much to be hoped that before long the insurance principle will be successfully applied to alleviating the financial burden of the family in time of illness. The present situation should operate meanwhile as an added incentive for families to use every endeavor to reduce their illness and accident hazards to a minimum. Without laying undue stress on ill health, children may be led to feel that it is their duty to conserve and promote their own good health and that of others.[2] In the case of preventable illness, children may be brought to realize that the money which is saved through the conservation of good health becomes available for recreation and other items of development expenditures. This fund may indeed be thought of as a reward, both for avoiding expenses for illness, and also for thrift and careful management of expenses for necessities.

Development Expenditures as the Expression of Family Standards. The quality of family life is most fully expressed in development expenditures, for they represent, more fully than all others, the "region of choice." With expenses for health deducted from the development fund, it should be distributed in such a way as to conduce to the best interests of each member of the family, from the father and mother to the youngest child. Development expenditures are thus made expressive of creative homemaking, through providing each family member with what he or she needs for education, recreation, and individual development.

[1] *New York Times*, Nov. 30, 1932. Quoted from the *Final Report of the National Committee on Costs of Medical Care* (1932). This situation obtains, it was pointed out, "in spite of the large volume of free work done by hospitals, health departments and individual practitioners, and in spite of the sliding scale of charges." It was found that more than $3,650,000,000 was spent by the people annually for medical care, but of this amount 78.5% went for the treatment of illness, 17.4% for dental care, 2.7% for eye care, and *only 1.4% for prevention.* This report was the result of five years' work involving twenty-six extensive studies in all aspects of the problem. It was underwritten by a group of philanthropic foundations.

[2] A family atmosphere where the duty of conserving health is taken for granted is far removed from the hypochondriacal atmosphere of families where fear of disease, preoccupation with prescriptions, patent medicines, and medical folklore combine to produce a situation disastrous to mental health. Definite tendencies to hypochondriacal complaints are frequently found in the children of such families.

SUGGESTED READING

Abel, M. H., *Successful Family Life on the Moderate Income*, 2nd ed. rev., 1927.

Andrews, B. R., *Economics of the Household*, rev. ed., 1935.

Bigelow, H. F., *Family Finance*, 1936.

Hambidge, G., *Your Meals and Your Money*, 1934.

Kyrk, H., *Economic Problems of the Family*, 1933.

Rose, M. S., *Feeding the Family*, 3rd ed., 1929.

———, *Foundations of Nutrition*, 3rd ed., 1938.

Sherman, H. C., *Food and Health*, 1934.

Stiebeling, H. K., and Ward, M. M., "Diets at Four Levels of Nutritive Content and Cost," *Circular 296* of the Department of Agriculture, 1933.

Watson, A. E., "The Reorganization of Household Work," *The Annals of the American Academy of Political and Social Science*, Vol. CLX, March, 1932, pp. 165–177.

———, "Employer-Employee Relationships in the Home," *The Annals of the American Academy of Political and Social Science*, Vol. CXLIII, May, 1929, pp. 49–60.

White House Conference, *Growth and Development of the Child*, Part III, *Nutrition*, 1932.

———, *The Home and the Child*, 1931.

Women's Bureau, *Bulletin 93*, "Household Employment in Philadelphia," 1932.

———, *Bulletin 106*, "Household Employment in Chicago," 1933.

———, *Bulletin 112*, "Standards of Placement Agencies for Household Employees," 1934.

———, *Bulletin 138*, "Reading List of References on Household Employment," 1936.

CHAPTER XXIII

HOMEMAKING AND THE CHILDREN

HOME AS THE ENVIRONMENT OF CHILDHOOD

The Fundamental Significance of Nurture in the Family. In its opening sentences the Children's Charter gives explicit recognition to the fundamental significance, for every child, of the security and understanding and love which home alone can provide. The scientific study of childhood is a very recent development, yet already we may discern limitless opportunities for the progressive improvement of human nature, if the love of parents for their children may be transformed through intelligence into a constructive social force: a force, moreover, which is cumulative, since, in every home where parents realize their responsibility and are willing to be guided by the best available knowledge, children are growing who should, in the future, prove even better parents themselves.

The Essentials of an Ideal Home. In an ideal home the social environment would so supplement the physical environment as to be conducive to the optimum all-round development of children. As a first essential the birth of the child must be wholeheartedly desired and planned for by both parents.[1] He must be sheltered so far as possible from all adverse influences and provided with all conditions necessary to physical and mental health and sturdy independent growth. Socially responsive from the first, the child must be given recognition as a unique individual, and treated in such a way that he may remain secure and free from feelings of inferiority.[2] This, however, is not enough. Love and encouragement are essential, but they must be balanced by a willingness to allow the child to meet difficulties, in order that he may develop self-reliance and courage and learn to adjust himself to reality.

[1] Recent studies have made evident the instability of environment and inconsistency of handling to which children are subjected who are unwanted and the victims of *maternal rejection*. See H. D. Newell, "The Psycho-dynamics of Maternal Rejection," *The American Journal of Orthopsychiatry*, Vol. IV (July, 1934), pp. 387–401 and *Smith College Studies in Social Work*, Vol. II (March, 1932).

[2] As Flügel says: "in adopting his attitude towards the members of his family circle, a child is at the same time determining to a large extent some of the principal aspects of his relations to his fellow men in general." *The Psycho-analytical Study of the Family* (3rd ed., 1929), p. 4.

Unremitting attention to the developing needs of the child is essential, if he is to be provided with a widening and appropriate range of activities and experiences, and if parents are to be fully aware of the changing quality of their relation to him. For they must learn not only to protect, but to stimulate, and to be guided in general by the principle of never doing *for the child what he can do for himself*.[1]

Both father and mother are needed as the child's companions and as interpreters of life. Their active and harmonious coöperation is essential, if the home is to be an ideal agency for realizing the central aims of education. Home nurture may secure optimum individual growth and development through providing physical and social environments which both sustain and stimulate: it may foster social insight through coöperative daily living; it may cultivate good habits of thinking through providing opportunities for learning by doing and for the progressive enrichment of experience with meaning.

ASPECTS OF CHILD DEVELOPMENT

Personality in the Making. Each child is a unique being, differing from every other: a new personality in the making, as inborn impulses encounter the selecting and stimulating influences of the environment. Parents must accept each child for what he is and must endeavor to provide the nurture appropriate to his capacities.[2] This means, moreover, the sympathetic evaluation of the interests and aptitudes of those who are in no way superior, who may even be in some way handicapped, as well as of those who are gifted. It is natural indeed for parents to overrate their children and to be bitterly disappointed if they fall short of expectations. But here, as elsewhere, reality must be faced if children are to be helped to make the most of inborn capacity.[3]

The necessity for considering each child as an individual is all

---

[1] Conscientious parents must realize, however, that, if they become over-anxious and too fearful of making mistakes, this in itself is a threat to the child's security.

[2] This implies, on the negative side, that parents should never "project" their own unfulfilled ambitions on the child, nor endeavor to mold him along predetermined lines. See Kimball Young, "Parent-child Relationships: Projection of Ambitions," *The Family*, Vol. VIII (May, 1927), pp. 67–73.

[3] Systematic record keeping is of the greatest assistance to understanding. It becomes more possible to discover causes of behavior and to judge of the success of methods of treatment. To the intrinsic interest of a full and accurate record of the earlier years of childhood may be added the value of an objective case-history, which can be made use of in a later study of the individual in order to correct specific difficulties. The Blantons suggest that a day-by-day diary should be preceded by a systematized personality study. They present a trait chart and an outline for personality study in Chapters XVII to XX of *Child Guidance* (1927).

the more necessary because of the prevalent overemphasis on *average* standards. As Kugelmass says, averages are "no criteria of normality so far as the development of an individual child is concerned. They are first approaches but not final indices in the developmental diagnosis of the individual."[1] It must also be realized that there is no marked series of developmental levels, or stages of growth, although, for purposes of study, it is convenient to use terms and phrases such as infancy, early, middle, and late childhood, and adolescence. Development is characterized by *continuity;* any and every event, "even birth itself should be regarded as only a conspicuous incident in the developmental process of the human being." In studying a child, say Goodenough and Anderson, "we have to deal with a very complex phenomenon of an organism whereof the different parts are growing at different rates and which is at the same time extremely sensitive to many environmental influences.[2] However, "although children vary greatly in rate of development, the order of development as marked by the successive appearance of various developmental events varies but little from one child to another."[3]

Physical Development. While physical, mental, emotional, and social development are inseparable aspects of the growing organism, yet the physical instrument of life must often, for purposes of theory and practice, be considered in comparative isolation. Amazingly rapid developmental progress takes place between conception and birth, but birth is "life's greatest hazard. It involves an abrupt transition from Nature's soil and care to man's hazardous life."[4] Unremitting care and medical supervision are thus essential in the earlier stages of adjustment to the new environment.

The growing child still manifests *maturation,* or the kind of growth which shaped him before birth, and which is chiefly due to inborn factors. The main trends of maturation comprise "three springing-up periods and three filling-out periods."[5] Rapid growth from birth until two is followed by a slow preschool period until six; rapid growth during the period of second dentition, marked by the coming of the temporary molars, is followed by slower and fairly uniform growth till about ten in girls and twelve in boys; rapid growth in pubescence, a period marked by the coming of the second molars, is followed by slower

---

[1] *Growing Superior Children* (1935), p. 244.
[2] *Experimental Child Study* (1931), p. 21.
[3] *Ibid.*, p. 24.   [4] Kugelmass, *op. cit.*, p. 21.   [5] *Ibid.*, p. 77.

growth in adolescence. The wisdom teeth, coming at about twenty-four, usually terminate the third growth period.[1] There are many individual variations, particularly as regards the onset of puberty and growth during adolescence. And girls tend to be in advance of boys and to end their growth earlier.

As already indicated, food is the most important factor in promoting physical growth and positive health. Essential, too, is a regime providing an appropriate balance between activity and rest, and sufficient sleep. While the benefits of fresh air and sunshine are obvious, it is to be noted that a reasonably changeable climate is conducive to robust health, which demands capacity for adjustment to changes in temperature and atmospheric conditions.

The close interrelation of physical and mental development is made obvious by the fact that good food, air, sunshine, and facilities for rest, sleep, and play can only contribute to health through the acquisition of a number of habits: habits of eating and sleeping, of regular elimination, of cleanliness, of posture and muscular control, to mention a few which are basic. As sense-organs, muscles, brain, and nervous system mature, the child learns from experience, and establishes those regular connections between stimulus and response which are called habits.[2]

Mental Development. In forming habits the child is acquiring a predisposition not only to specific patterns of behavior, but also to ways and modes of responding. Accordingly, the process of habit formation in infancy and early childhood lays the foundation for the later development of complex intellectual, emotional, and social dispositions. All these aspects are properly included in mental development, although the term may be narrowed to cover primarily sensori-motor and intellectual development.

The infant responds to his environment with increasingly intricate behavior patterns. Sensory skill and perception of relationships are developed as he responds to sensory stimuli and learns to coördinate muscular movements with touch and vision. Sensori-motor development means the acquisition of increasingly complex coördinations and skills. In so far as the child

[1] The time at which teeth erupt, and their condition, are now known to be a readily observable index, not only of growth, but of health and usually of nutrition.

[2] At birth all the more than twelve billion brain cells are present, and the brain itself is about half as large as it will ever be. By the sixth year, and sometimes as early as the fourth year in better-nurtured children, the brain has attained its full size. From the moment of birth and during this period of rapid brain and mental growth, habits and behavior patterns are being formed which underlie all future development.

observes, manipulates, and explores with a purpose, and notes the results of his efforts, intellectual development also takes place. Intellectual development is intimately bound up with behavior and most of all with the mode of behavior called language. A baby delights in making sounds, which later become language when he uses them as symbols to represent or obtain some object, or to express ideas. In learning to talk a child absorbs ideas and attitudes, and thus tends to reproduce the intellectual caliber and cultural level of those with whom he is in close contact.[1] Parents possess an unrivalled opportunity for promoting intellectual development by means of the answers they give to a child's questions.

Emotional Development: General Characteristics. Emotion is a form of response which, like others, adjusts the individual to stimulating conditions, but which "differs from other types of response in that it involves a massive unpremeditated reaction of the entire body."[2] Any form of sudden stimulation, if sufficiently strong,—loud noises, dropping, or restraint—produces at first only aimless muscular activity and crying, although very early indeed patterns of *withdrawal* or *aggression* are developed. In contrast to these two forms of adaptive reaction in which there is *rejection* of the stimulus, there is *acceptance* of stimulating conditions such as feeding or soothing, resulting in passivity, relaxation, and lessening of muscular tensions. The different emotions develop as the child learns to differentiate between various situations and to establish different responses to them. Considering the complete dependency and helplessness of the new-born, it is no wonder that the handling he receives should establish his underlying emotional patterns, as emotions are *conditioned* through the transference of emotional responses to new stimuli.[3]

[1] A number of studies have substantiated the fact that intellectual development is related to the social and cultural environment. Of particular significance in this connection is the work of Newman and his associates with twenty sets of identical twins who had been brought up in different environments. It was found that 50% of the total difference between twins of a set, in Stanford-Binet I.Q. ratings, was due to education; 10% to differences in social environment; 12% to joint social and educational differences; 9% to physical health; 19% to causes probably prenatal. The positive correlation between social environment and ratings indicates, Newman believes, the influence of cultural elements in the social environment. See H. H. Newman, F. N. Freeman, K. J. Holzinger, *Twins: A Study of Heredity and Environment* (1937).

[2] M. Sherman and I. C. Sherman, *The Process of Human Behavior* (1929), p. 144.

[3] The word *conditioning* describes the following process: a new stimulus is presented along with the original stimulus which evokes a certain reaction. Presently, this reaction comes to be elicited by the new stimulus alone. In many cases, conditioning takes place only when there is frequent repetition of the situation in which the old and new stimuli are associated. A single instance or intense experience may, however, be sufficient, and this is particularly true in the case of *fear*.

Emotional Development: Fear. The emotional response specific enough to be described as *fear* is aroused in an infant of six months by a loud, sudden noise or by loss of bodily support. Darkness, on the other hand, is not an original source of fear, this being only too easily acquired through conditioning. A loud noise waking a child in a dark room is sufficient to give him a terror of the dark, which without *reconditioning* seems ineradicable.[1] Fear also becomes attached to objects associated with pain, and many fears are aroused through suggestion when those around show fear, say, of thunderstorms or snakes.[2] Although unnecessary fears must be prevented, children must learn caution, although not at the expense of loss of security or reasonable self-confidence. Courage, caution, and self-control are best learnt in actual situations where achievement demands such qualities; and parents should not show fear for their children's safety as they climb trees, swing, slide, or learn to ride or swim.

Apart from specific fears, feelings of insecurity develop very readily when a child believes himself in some way inadequate. Much may be done, not only through the removal of handicaps, but also through the discovery of definite ways in which a child can achieve success. Feelings of insecurity and inadequacy may lead later to serious maladjustments. But they are less likely to develop where a child is assured of the affection and understanding of his parents.

Emotional Development: Anger. In an infant of six months, an emotional pattern, definite enough to be called anger, is aroused when restraint is put upon freedom of movement. Before this, however, a baby subjected to excessive or rough handling or to overmuch stimulation is likely to become aggressive and irritable.[3] These are the earliest manifestations of resentment against interference with self-assertive tendencies. Anger, at first aroused through physical restraint, soon becomes

[1] Ingenious methods have been devised for the removal of specific fears through reconditioning. For example, games are played in the course of which a ball is rolled into a dark room. The child is encouraged to find his way towards a phosphorescent glowing pendant attached to the light pull-cord. Fear of the dark is lost as the child comes to realize he can light the room without aid.

[2] Kugelmass points out that most fears are caused by suggestion, carelessness, and deliberate terrorization. *Op. cit.*, p. 420. Needless to say, all endeavors to influence children's behavior by threats of punishment, of bogey-men, policemen, hell, or God's anger, are utterly condemned by modern principles of nurture.

[3] Dr. Margaret Fries has reported the discovery of three major behavior patterns which may be observed in the first ten days of life: the over-active, moderately active, and under-active. If the child is to become well adjusted, handling and methods of treatment should be appropriate to type. *New York Times*, May 14, 1937.

aroused by psychological limitations, criticism, ridicule, or the control and regulation of behavior.

Any one of a number of incidents in the baby's daily routine may be the occasion of anger, particularly where he is hungry or sleepy or suffering a digestive upset. If he discovers that upon a display of anger his difficulty is at once removed, or his wish granted, he may make a habit of temper tantrums, violent outbursts characterized by a wide variety of behavior.[1]

Each tantrum calls for individual treatment, although, since its object is to center attention on the child and enforce compliance with his wishes, the most effective general means is never to fulfill a wish sought by this method, nor to appear at all concerned. If possible, the child should be left alone, and so deprived of an audience until calm, when the cause of the difficulty may be ascertained.

As with other emotional responses, the goal of nurture is not suppression or eradication, but the control and utilization of the zestful energy characteristic of anger in socially acceptable ways, such, for example, as persevering effort to overcome obstacles and difficulties.

Emotional Development: Affection. Gentle and rhythmic stimulation of an infant's sense organs or body surfaces, such as patting, stroking, rocking, or singing have a soothing, pleasing effect. Cooing and smiling responses are made, and in older infants the arms are stretched to the stimulating object and other expressions of pleasure occur. The earliest responses of affection are for those who soothe, rock, and care for him. Naturally the mother who nurses the infant and meets his wants is the object of strongest attachment, but his affection is capable of extension to others of his immediate circle.

Passing from the earliest stage of self-love and absorption in bodily needs, the normal development of affection proceeds through extension, first of all to those who minister to these needs, the family members; and then to friends, usually, though not always, of the same sex, and, finally, to an interest in the opposite sex.[2] It is of the utmost importance that such develop-

---

[1] Such outbursts are most frequent in the later part of the second year, and after two years are more frequent and intense with boys than girls. As children grow older, the more violent manifestations may be replaced by sulking or whining.

[2] Psychoanalytic theory includes suggestive analyses of the stages of development in the affections of boys and girls. For the boy, the mother-phase is supposed to continue until 7 or 8, after which attention and interest are centered on the father till about 12, when the play-mate or school phase supervenes, with loyalty to friends of his own sex. With puberty he becomes increasingly interested in persons of the opposite sex, until the mating-phase involves specific attachments with eventual choice of

ment should not be thwarted and arrested. Wholesome emotional growth demands experience of the emotions appropriate to each stage. *Fixation*, or arrested development, occurs either when there is no opportunity for living through an experience at the normal stage, or where such an experience is over-emphasized or unduly prolonged. Lack of normal love and affection is just as harmful as excessive affection.

Earlier attachments do not wholly disappear, but persist in the tone and quality given to later stages of development: for example, where the devotion of little children to parents is transformed into affectionate trust and friendship which in no way interferes with mature heterosexual love. Arrested development is an entirely different matter. It means persistence of undue self-love, or undue dependence on a mother or father, or undue affection for companions of the same sex.

Criteria of Emotional Health. In the normal development of the love impulse is found one criterion of emotional health. Happiness is another. As Pruette says: "Happiness is health: emotional health. Happiness belongs to the independent, the competent, the courageous. Happiness belongs to those who have resources within themselves to combat ill-fortune, to those who can inhibit anger over trivialities and release it for just cause, to those who have few fears or none, to those who can love unselfishly and give pleasing expression to this love. . . . The parent with a true concern for the child will build up emotional stability, courage and hope in the child as the protection against the trials of later life."[1]

Nowhere, indeed, can parents more profoundly influence their children than through establishing a home atmosphere conducive to emotional health. They are able to do this in proportion as they are themselves emotionally stable and mature, and treat their children with objective kindness and consistency. As already indicated, there should also be provision of experiences in which children may learn to meet difficulties with persistence, and face reality with equanimity. In the ability to meet situations

a mate. There is less agreement with regard to girls. Flügel notes a father-phase, but Crichton-Miller believes the second phase to be the school phase. Flügel, *op. cit.*, Chapter II; H. Crichton-Miller, *The New Psychology and the Parent* (1922), Chapters IV and V. While there is obviously some truth in such descriptions, the whole matter is probably far more complex. Interestingly enough, the findings of the White House Conference study of 3,779 children under 13, in 2,758 families, do not fully substantiate psychoanalytic theory. Half the children have no favorite in the home, slightly more boys than girls, and more children of *both* sexes prefer mothers to fathers. *The Young Child in the Home* (1936), pp. 227–234.

[1] *Parents and the Happy Child* (Henry Holt and Company, 1932), pp. 226–227.

realistically is found still another criterion of emotional health.

Many marked abnormalities develop as the result of conflicts which the individual is unable to solve in a satisfactory manner. Children may have temper tantrums, they may escape reality through phantasy and day-dreaming, or they may escape through illness, or blame others for their own failure. Most children show symptoms of such tendencies, and parents require all the skill they can command to prevent their further development.

Social Development: General Characteristics. The socially adjusted adult is described as "one whose behavior has successfully carried him through childhood and adolescence, from the pretense life of the little child to an independence of coddling, to an independence in controlling his emotions, and to the ability to be considerate of people's opinions. His behavior shows him to be one who has attained self-support, a heterosexual attitude, and a philosophy of life which are to stand him in good stead as he engages in the trials of maturity and old age."[1]

Although all normal children are socially responsive, there are differences in social sensitiveness, and certain typical attitudes have been observed as early as six months.[2] Even so, if the prevailing atmosphere in the home is one of mutual courtesy and consideration, the child generally learns to conform to the wishes of others through the pleasure he feels in gaining their commendation. In learning to achieve a balance between self-expression and subordination to group standards, children experiment in a wide variety of reactions to social situations. They are friendly with familiar people, shy with strangers, and aggressive where there is interference with their desires for possession and power, or from motives of rivalry. Aggressive behavior is a promising early response, for social adaptation is far better secured through positive attitudes, aggressiveness, friendliness, joyousness; while negative attitudes such as shyness, exclusiveness, fear, and suspicion hinder social adaptation.[3]

---

[1] *Growth and Development of the Child*, Part IV, p. 145 (White House Conference publication).

[2] Charlotte Bühler believes that her studies of infants, of 6 to 18 months, show three primary social attitudes which develop independently of environment: (1) the socially *blind* who pay no attention to other children; (2) the socially *dependent* who are either inhibited or stimulated in their activities by the presence of other children; (3) the socially *independent* who, though aware of the presence of other children, are neither intimidated nor inspired. "Social Behavior of Children," *Handbook of Child Psychology* (ed. Murchison, rev. ed., 1933), p. 393.

[3] The development of *negative* attitudes may usually be traced to defects in the social environment, particularly in the parent-child relationship. Stubbornness and persistent obstinacy may also develop through faulty disciplinary methods.

Children should have the opportunity for acquaintance with a larger social sphere than is provided by the home. Between two and five there is a marked change in the relationship of children with each other. The two-year-old is interested in others, but plays independently. *Parallel play* gradually disappears, however, as *coöperative play* takes its place and becomes characteristic by five. Larger groups of children tend to play together, now one, now the other taking the lead. Guidance in choice of playmates is best given indirectly through the atmosphere and social standards of the home, for it is of the utmost importance that a child should learn to live with others through wide social experience.

Social Development: Valuable Attitudes. Consideration for others and willingness to coöperate are fundamental social attitudes. They are best secured through an *orderly* home routine, designed in such a way that, as early as possible, the child begins to help himself and to engage in communal tasks, in order that he may feel responsible for "pulling his own weight in the boat."[1] Gradually he learns the rudiments of consideration and of respect for the needs and interests of others. But this demands the development of honesty of attitude. Full coöperation is possible only between individuals who are *trustworthy*, who respect one another's property, and may be relied upon in their communications with one another.

Honesty involves a scrupulous regard for property rights and also *truthfulness* or honesty towards facts. Both can be satisfactorily learned only through constant practice in specific situations. Much depends on the response made by parents to early instances of pilfering or misstatement of facts. Quite naturally the tiny child tries to appropriate a coveted object. But, if provided with a sufficiency of possessions of his own, he is easily led to distinguish between his own belongings and those of others. Even so a child of six or seven, usually honest, may impulsively take something from a store, or appropriate some money to spend on candy. Such incidents should *not* be branded as stealing and severely punished. The child should, however, be helped to make restitution without public humiliation. A child who steals habitually is, almost without exception, the victim of an unfavorable home environment.

Learning truthfulness is a more complex matter. The emphasis should fall on the desirability of obtaining accurate knowledge of facts and on the value of truthful responses out of

---

[1] A child may, for example, learn to dress himself between three and five.

consideration for others. If the emphasis falls wholly on truth *telling*, it is harder for the child to learn to refrain from literally accurate, but tactless and inconsiderate remarks. At the outset a little child does not differentiate between imagination and reality, but he can gradually be led to distinguish between a "good story" and an actual account of facts, labeled "truth." When he has opportunities for satisfying achievement, there is less temptation to indulge in fanciful and highly-colored accounts of his activities in a desire to win admiration. The majority of lies are the result of fear—where punishment is feared, for example, and the consequences of an act can be avoided by shifting the blame to others.[1]

Parental example is the first essential. Parents must prove themselves absolutely trustworthy and must show their trust in their children. There must be scrupulous care that the child is never misled in any way: for example, by being led to believe his parents are close by, when in reality they go out after he has gone to bed.[2] Valuable lessons are learned when a child observes the scrupulous accuracy of parents in discharging debts: when, for example, the mistake is at once pointed out if a conductor neglects to collect carfare, or a storekeeper tenders overmuch change.

AUTHORITY, DISCIPLINE, AND FREEDOM

Authority without Domination. The absolute dependence of the tiny child on his parents endows them with *natural authority*. Inevitably it is through their behavior that social controls become effective in the child's development. Much therefore depends on the use of authority. Discipline must mean wise guidance of children's behavior, in order to promote healthy emotional growth, the development of social attitudes, and the gradual acquisition of self-control. But only the emotionally mature and integrated personality can be trusted to make wise use of authority. And, unfortunately, it is precisely those who are least capable of constructive discipline who conceive of themselves as law-givers and judges, justified in their righteous wrath and moral indignation at any infraction of their commands. As Pruette aptly remarks, "A great many parents, particularly

---

[1] The work of Hartshorne and May (*Studies in Deceit*, 2 vols., 1928, and *Studies in the Organization of Character*, 1930) has proved conclusively that deceit and untruthfulness are widely prevalent among children. Deceit was found definitely related to home conditions and the treatment accorded by parents to their children.

[2] From this point of view, the traditional Santa Claus stories are unwise, though not so dangerous as the prevalent "stork" and "doctor's bag" evasions.

perhaps fathers, seem to confuse themselves with God."[1] Yet only those who are ignorant of the findings of psychology can assume that severe discipline and the domination of children are conducive to their welfare. It is, at times, convenient if children are "seen, but not heard"; but exemplary conduct is very apt to be due to intimidation, and, if so, is probably symptomatic of maladjustment.[2] The use of authority is safe only with those who can be completely honest with themselves, who can analyze their own motives and be sure of their freedom from any trace of wounded self-esteem and enjoyment of power for its own sake. Disciplinary measures must have but one controlling motive, the welfare of the child.

Traditional methods of despotic discipline are still prevalent. But there are to-day many would-be modern parents who have gone to the opposite extreme and encouraged their children in unrestrained self-expression. This abdication of all responsibility for parental guidance, far from securing the freedom which comes from self-discipline, is likely to render the child the slave of his own impulses. Such children are frequently over-protected as well, and so have no opportunity of learning restraint through the consequences of their behavior. They become spoiled, selfish, self-indulgent, indolent, and remain emotionally immature.

Autocracy and anarchy alike prevent the family from fulfilling its disciplinary function. But, if democratic leadership is to prove successful, there must be perfect accord between parents in their use of authority, and absolute consistency in discipline.[3] For full coöperation in authority there must be a common understanding of motives and purposes, an understanding which may be more readily achieved where scientific attitudes are combined with sympathy for the child. In the last analysis, the possibility of discipline through coöperation rather than compulsion is determined by the quality of family relationships: the mutual relationship of the parents, and the relationship between them and their children.

Genuine coöperation is only possible where there is mutual respect and courtesy, both of children towards parents and each

[1] *Op. cit.*, p. 121.

[2] Excessive severity may lead to a variety of difficulties: submissiveness, lack of confidence, fears, stuttering, boasting by way of compensation. Thom remarks, "the parent who is quick-tempered and erratic in dispensing discipline is equally responsible for the personality deviations of his children as if he had crippled them by physical force." *Everyday Problems of the Everyday Child* (1927), p. 37.

[3] One of the fundamental rules, says Thom, "is that the parents should present a united front to the child. If differences in judgment occur let them be settled in private." *Op. cit.*, p. 46.

other, and of parents towards each other and *towards their children*. It is of the utmost importance that no one be made to feel in any way humiliated or inferior to the others. Even the youngest should be treated with consideration and politeness as an *equal*.[1] Within a family group of this kind social control resides in the common understanding between the family members. The pattern of family life persistently selects certain responses and eliminates others, and effective discipline is operative through daily experience. It is essential of course that the behavior of the children should be diagnosed in terms of its underlying causes. Parents must not respond to symptoms or to disturbing effects of behavior alone, but be guided by ability to imagine the child's point of view.[2] Children should be able to count on their parents as companions and confidants, who will always understand and sympathize with them, even when they also warn and criticize; who can always be trusted and will never fail; who are, in a word, their children's best and most faithful friends. In this way a developing relationship is established, which endures long after the children have left the parental home.[3]

Freedom through Discipline. The function of authority is primarily positive and constructive: discipline is the means whereby the individual is helped to make the most of life, to achieve progressive release of capacity and the degree of maturity appropriate to age and level of development. In a secondary sense, of course, discipline is negative, in the sense of eliminating hindrances to the achievement of its goals. Significantly enough, however, the word discipline may be used to describe both goal and method; the results and the means whereby they are brought about: for without *self-discipline* there can be no effective freedom.

Freedom through self-direction is a continuing process, and, as such, is best brought about if parents provide for their children every possible opportunity for experimental living through which they may grow in responsibility and power of self-direc-

---

[1] Even in a thoroughly happy family it is often difficult to avoid hurting the feelings of tiny children through the natural amusement resulting from their mistakes; in the misuse of words, for example.

[2] Thom says "a mother who is too busy to bother with a little child's nonsense will never be bothered by his real problems." *Op. cit.*, p. 45.

[3] Where parents and children are *friends*, there need be none of the disillusionment which is bound to come when children find their dominant and would-be superior parents to be fallible; and none of the breaking away from the possessiveness of parents who are unwilling to allow children to grow into the control of their own lives.

tion.[1] Protection and guidance of children may be combined
with a large measure of freedom, of experimentation with their
own powers, and with the people and things in their environment. This does not mean a *free* rein, but it *does* mean a *loose*
rein, accompanied by unobtrusive observation and guidance
when necessary. It means, as has been well said, giving a child
plenty of rope, but always keeping fast hold of the rope's end.
Discipline must of course be adjusted to age, but its general
purpose is at all times to foster progress towards self-determining
maturity. It thus returns to its original meaning: the treatment
accorded to those who *learn*.[2]

Methods of Discipline. When discipline is viewed as an educative experience, psychological principles are obviously applicable.
Learning eventuates most readily where practice is attended
by satisfactory results. The acquisition of socially valuable
habits, skills, and attitudes is thus facilitated through successful activity, and through encouragement and praise bestowed
by those in authority. While it should never be extravagant or
indiscriminate, praise for specific actions should be bestowed
whenever possible. The reverse is true of disapproval, blame, or
punishment. Much should be overlooked, and reproof should
be as gentle and punishment as slight as they can possibly be
made. Some have held that the very word punishment should
become obsolete, and many would agree if corporal punishment
is meant. But the term may be retained to describe methods by
which undesirable tendencies may be overcome, and also the
unfortunate or painful natural consequences which attend certain forms of behavior. A very young child may be discouraged
from certain actions by mild punishment such as a little rap on
the finger. But a parent's "no" may be equally effective, if
sparingly and judiciously used, and there is then less danger of
other undesirable attitudes being acquired at the same time.
Physical punishment may deter from a specific act, but at the
same time it may generate fear and hinder the development of
confidence and social adequacy. All the more severe physical

[1] Kilpatrick says: "we wish children to grow in intelligent self-direction or . . .
grow in the integration of self, as the self is increasingly adapted to the control of this
shifting world. . . . I think then of our discipline as helping the child to increasing
self-control, so that he can make his own decisions and thus increasingly become a
strong self-directing personality that takes proper account of others, that they too
may grow into such strong self-directing personalities." "Newer Meanings of Discipline," *Concerning Parents* (1926), p. 201.

[2] The disciple originally meant the learner, the term being derived from *discere*, to
learn. Owing to ascetic influences the connotation of disciple was narrowed, and discipline came to be regarded as synonymous with repression and punishment.

punishments must, without question, be ruled out, in families where mutual respect obtains and where every effort is made to avoid humiliation for the child.[1] As a matter of fact, corporal punishment is very often indicative of a breakdown of discipline and of parental lack of emotional control. The same is true too of violent scolding and of a prolonged show of displeasure.

Failure to approve, or a restrained use of disapproval, are often sufficient deterrents; in other cases the isolation of a little child for a short time, or depriving him of some small pleasure, prove efficient methods. But treatment of this kind should be attached *immediately* to *specific* actions, and should be understood by the child as a natural consequence of his conduct. Very little punishment may be necessary if the parents patiently explain at every step the reasons for desirable conduct. Reasoning is, of course, not possible when a child is too young to understand. And there are other occasions too when safety depends on prompt obedience. Hence obedience is still a *means* to discipline, but must never be regarded as an end in itself. Self-direction and self-discipline are not learned through habits of passive compliance with prohibitions. Implicit, prompt obedience should be required only in the very few types of situations where it is necessary: for example, the tiny child should learn to stop at once when told to do so, or to be quiet, and to come when called. The child can early understand the value of this kind of automatic obedience, as affording him protection and support sufficient for the development of self-reliance. All obedience to family regulations and social laws and customs must be interpreted in such a way as to bring about acceptance of standards and of ideals, which will later serve as guiding principles.

[1] As a result of corporal punishment the very first moral experience of many children has been a sense of *injustice*. See F. C. Sharpe, *Ethics* (1928), pp. 212–218; also Hart and Hart, *op. cit.*, pp. 267–268; also, for present practices, *The Young Child in the Home*, pp. 210–221. From this survey it is evident that the better educated parents and those with better social background resort least to "spanking." But it is still very prevalent, particularly between two and five, and most of all at three. Boys of school age are more frequently spanked than girls, and although spanking decreases as children grow older, there are actually many instances at twelve years old, the age limit in this study. There is also much evidence to show that spanking means poor discipline, for the incidents leading to punishment included temper tantrums, quarreling, running away, disobedience, fighting, crying, wetting clothes, screaming, playing with mud, spilling soup and coffee, running into the street. In the study made by Joseph Miller, Director of Guidance of the Wilkes-Barre schools, among 30 particularly happy well-adjusted high school graduates, three girls and one boy had *never* been punished in any way; fifteen more had never been spanked, and of the eleven others only one had been spanked more than very rarely. *New York Times*, Dec. 2, 1934.

LEARNING THROUGH FAMILY LIFE IN THE HOME

Home as a Laboratory for the Children. In the first two years of life, and longer unless there is attendance at nursery school, the home must take the whole responsibility for providing the child with a fully educative environment, one which should afford a well-equipped laboratory for his earliest ventures and first experiments in living. Apart from routine requirements the little child's time is spent in *play*. Absorbed in present interests and purposes he pursues them into wider fields, manipulating, exploring, and gradually noting more fully the results of his activities. Play merges into work, and through both the child is effectively "learning by doing."

The ideal home, accordingly, provides full facilities for learning by doing both indoors and out. The home should be planned with the little child's needs in view. There should be certain safeguards, such as a gate at the head of stairs, and special equip-ment is needed to allow him to share in the activities of others, his high chair at meals, for example, and dishes and utensils of the right size. He should have a room of his own with furnishings appropriate to size and needs, and either there, or in a separate playroom, space in which to store toys and equipment, and for use on rainy days. There should be garden spaces in which to play, sand-piles, swings, and see-saws, also a plot of his own to dig in and cultivate, a playhouse, and later on a workshop and laboratory. There should also be pets, for whose care and feeding he becomes responsible as he grows older. Ideally, too, the house and garden should be situated so as to give easy access to fields and woods. For a child is deprived of his full birthright if he has not grown up in intimate companionship with nature. Nothing can equal the joy of these early experiences: the eager search for the first spring flowers, for berries, or nuts; peeping at eggs and little birds in nests; watching or playing with tadpoles and frogs and snails and butterflies; wading brooks, climbing trees, romping in the hay. Excursions or summer holidays may bring wonderful experiences of farm and countryside, lake or sea; and at other times there are playgrounds and parks. But the *ideal* environment allows close contact with nature through all seasons of the year.

Play, Playthings, and Playmates. The fortunate child who plays in a wide natural environment with sand, water, stones, sticks, flowers, and animals has less need of artificial toys. For children who have little outdoor space in which to play, toys and equipment of various kinds are essential, as tools for self-education through play.[1] Babies and little children should not be overstimulated. It is better never to interfere with the absorbed activity of a little child unless absolutely necessary. With appropriate environmental conditions and a minimum of guidance, learning keeps pace with maturation.

The educational significance of play is best appreciated if its three leading *motifs* be distinguished, although they frequently mingle in actual play or in the uses to which a particular plaything is put. Play may be *motor*, or *dramatic*, or *creative*. Throughout childhood play follows along the line of the child's muscular development; vigorous outdoor play of all kinds being essential to optimum sensori-motor development. As the ball is the typical toy for motor play, dolls or substitutes for dolls have in all lands and ages provided the typical toy for dramatic play. Alone or in groups little children learn, in the happy land of make-believe, how to live with others in the real world. Through reproducing in their play the life around them, they come to participate in social attitudes and develop appreciation of inherent meanings and values. Not only dolls and their clothes, but sets of dishes and equipment for housekeeping and toy animals and live pets may play a part in dramatic play. Much of the equipment for motor play may also be put to use. Big boxes, for example, may be used as houses or stores.

In general, play equipment will have fullest educational value where it requires something of the child, where it must be fashioned and given form, and so serves both to stimulate imagination and to provide for creative expression. Over-elaborate mechanical toys, which operate when wound up, often prompt not so much to constructive efforts as to destruction, in efforts to find out what makes them go! To give full scope to creative play a wide variety of materials is necessary—paper, chalk, paints, clay, scissors, paste, blocks, wood, carpenter's tools, materials for sewing, weaving, and basketry, and musical instruments.[2]

[1] For detailed discussion of children's play at various ages, and the toys and equipment which are appropriate, see Josephine C. Foster, *Busy Childhood* (1933), and Rose H. Alschuler, *Two to Six* (rev. ed., 1937). The latter is an excellent brief handbook of suggestions for parents of young children.

[2] The recent enormous development of the American toy industry has been guided in part by a recognition of the educational value of toys. There seems to be, however, a marked tendency towards over-elaboration: for example, reproductions of the latest models of streamlined cars, trains, and steamers, and doll-replicas of movie-stars. Such standardization, and insistence on the expensive and on being up-to-date, has its sinister aspects. The modern toy store is bewildering to parents and its effect

Many of the newer playthings, such as electrical and chemical sets, serve as introductions to serious study, and games involving numbers and the use of language may play an important part in intellectual development. Most children eagerly collect all sorts of trash, but, with suitable encouragement, interest in bottle tops or broken automobile horns may be superseded by collections of stamps, shells, wild flowers, bird's eggs, beetles, and butterflies.

Children should have ample opportunity for interesting solitary occupations and also for group activities. After the earliest years the most important of all play-needs is *playmates*. As we saw in discussing progressive education, learning to live and work with other children of approximately the same age level is of the utmost importance for socialization. A child's playmates may profitably include his brothers and sisters and parents. Parents who not only unobtrusively guide their children's play, but on occasion join in the fun, find it easier to maintain the friendly atmosphere so essential to coöperative family living.

Responsible Participation in Family Life. Homes are happiest where all have their *fair* and *appropriate* share in play, in work, and in responsibility. At birth, children "should enter a life that is already being lived and in which there is a place and a part for them. . . . It is better, too, for children to enter the family life as sharing rather than as receiving members; [to be] from the beginning a part of the adventure of living. Just as we plan for them from the beginning, so let them be an integral part of living from the very moment they begin to be. Live with them, but not for them."[1] In these words Lilian Gilbreath expresses the spirit underlying the successful adventure which she and her husband, both industrial engineers, shared with eleven children.

Each family member, she believes, should be given the chance for leadership and responsibility in proportion to his or her ability to assume it. Few parents realize the unequalled educational opportunities to be found in little children's earliest efforts to do things themselves, to be of genuine service, to share responsibly in the life of the household. What may seem dull routine tasks are of absorbing interest to the little child. First, equipped with appropriately sized implements, he may work

cannot be wholesome on children, being indeed one aspect of the larger problem created by the current overemphasis on material possessions. It is reassuring to learn that one plaything remains unchanged and as popular as ever, the Teddy bear. See E. F. Barnard "Toyland Goes Ultra Modern," *New York Times Magazine*, Dec. 13, 1936.

[1] Lilian Gilbreath, *Living with Our Children* (1925), pp. 46, 60, 66.

with mother and father, may sweep and dust, mow and rake leaves, but gradually he may be made responsible for specific tasks, not only those associated with his own belongings, but some of value to the family group. Where a spirit of service and a desire for efficiency have been encouraged, children recognize as only fair that they take a competent share in the household routine.

To ensure an atmosphere of good sportsmanship, fair play, and impartial justice, each child should as soon as possible become an active participant in all family problems and share in deciding matters of importance to the group as a whole.[1] Plans for a new home or new furnishings, the use of holidays, even the financial affairs of the family, in particular the spending of the development fund, may be profitably discussed by the family in council. All these matters may also be subjects of informal conversation at meal-times or whenever the family gathers together. Such discussions, however, can only be fully successful where parents are their children's companions, are capable of self-criticism, and are never didactic or solemn.

Valuable lessons are learned through conversation. Courtesy and consideration for others is required if all are to contribute, and there is practice in the clear expression of ideas in accurate language. At the same time, the parents are afforded valuable opportunities to serve as interpreters of life and to guide their children in the formation of tastes, attitudes, and standards.

Parents who live with their children and share with them in at least some of the household occupations foster their social development through adjustment to the realities of work and life. There can, moreover, be no more effective preparation for future homemaking than full opportunity to learn, within the parental home, how to live and work with other members of the family.

Bringing Fathers Back into Family Life. If a father coöperates with a mother in child care, as fully as his other obligations permit, he finds it far less hard to be his children's friend and companion as they grow older. Many mothers shut fathers out through assuming sole responsibility for every detail of a child's care and assigning to the father the rôle of law-giver and disciplinarian, or of aloof head of the family to be treated with special deference when at home, because he is in need of rest

---

[1] Lilian Gilbreath describes the formal family councils held in her family, at which each child freely and frankly expressed his or her opinions and shared in family decisions.

from the all-important business of making the family living. But, as Pruette remarks, "children need a father who is more than a pocketbook and a threat of punishment."[1]

In other cases, where fathers do help with child care, they more or less consciously resent being forced into what they consider a non-masculine rôle. Subconscious factors have been found by psychiatrists to contribute to such resentment, and the possibility of these conflicts must be taken into account in all effort at educating fathers.[2] Fathers may be brought to realize that "child study is not merely a discipline for mothers, but a way of understanding human nature. They will begin to recognize a new importance in family life and its attendant problems, for they will see that a family is, indeed, a bold adventure in human relationships."[3]

The companionship of parents, and particularly of fathers, is welcome to both boys and girls: a fact not only fully observable in harmonious happy families, but attested to by the Lynds, who secured, from Middletown high school students, ratings of the traits most desirable in fathers and mothers. Of 369 boys and 415 girls, 61.5% of the boys and 66.5% of the girls considered the quality most desirable in a *father* to be, "spending time with his children, reading, talking, playing with them."[4] The White House Conference survey revealed that, in the families of higher status, the fathers spend more time than do those in families of lower status, in caring for their children, playing with them, and in studying about them. As Anderson points out: "This indicates that the more intelligent and the better educated the father, the more likely he is to take his responsibilities to his children seriously."[5] Nor is this surprising, for the more we learn of the influences shaping personality the more evident does it become that every child needs *two* parents, and that every boy and every girl needs the guidance and companionship of both father and mother.

[1] *Op. cit.*, p. 53.

[2] See, for example, L. Blumgart "Conflict and Growth," *Child Study*, Vol. IX (Feb., 1932), pp. 162–163. Unconscious envy may be felt by the father, or else jealousy, even enmity, towards the child who has deprived him of an exclusive hold on his wife's affections. He may also feel a certain protest against parental obligations since he is without the profound gratification which compensates the mother.

[3] E. Lindeman "Bringing Father Back into the Family," *Child Study*, Vol. IX, p. 162.

[4] *Middletown*, Table XV, p. 524. In the case of mothers this was *second* choice for both boys and girls, the first choice being that she should be a good cook and housekeeper.

[5] *Happy Childhood* (1933), p. 283.

Fathers and Mothers as Interpreters of the World outside the Home. When women have work and responsibilities outside the home, they should be able to share more fully with fathers in the orientation of their children towards life in the larger world.[1] To interpret contemporary life is no easy task for either fathers or mothers. Even the most thoughtful may find it hard to develop a philosophy of life, which is coherent enough to reassure and yet flexible enough to provide guiding principles in a changing social order. Standards which are over-rigid, and too much at variance with those of the world outside, hinder the social adjustment of children, who tend, in this case, either to the dogmatic reproduction of these standards or else to rebellion and wholesale rejection. Yet no thoughtful parent would be willing to allow children to be subjected to the influences of the outside world without some effort at interpretation and orientation, particularly to-day, when it is so much harder to protect children from premature exposure to these influences.

The atmosphere of home, and the attitudes of parents as expressed in their actions, are more potent an influence than any merely verbal adherence to ideals and standards. Yet conversation plays an important part, and explanations may be made which help children to interpret their experience more fully in its relation to the wider social group. While premature exposure to outside influences is to be deplored, children must not be over-shielded, but must be given understanding of the actualities of life. Experiences of success are invaluable in developing self-confidence. But experiences of failure are also valuable if children are to learn their limitations and be guarded from illusion. Nothing, perhaps, is harder for parents than to allow their children to learn the bitter lessons of experience. There is, however, no other way in which they may achieve maturity and strength of character.

The Influence of Family Life in the Formation of Intellectual Attitudes and Standards. There is paramount need to-day, as we have seen, for the development of the scientific habit of mind, for scientific attitudes and objective methods of thought. Intellectual honesty demands self-criticism, in an effort to eliminate prejudice and emotional bias; accurate observation; and an experimental attitude which continually retests conclusions. All this

---

[1] Frank says: "Probably the dominance of the father in forming the ego-ideals and ambitions of his children (both boys and girls) explains why the more socialized values and idealistic aims of the woman count for so little in the careers of her sons and daughters." "The Father's Rôle in Child Nurture," *Child Study*, Vol. IX, p. 169.

is implied in helping children to learn to think for themselves, one of the chief educative functions of the family in present-day society. Unfulfilled though this function may be in most families because of ignorance and prejudice, yet unique opportunities are afforded in home nurture for the development of intellectual integrity and independent thinking; a matter of vital importance when mass influences are so widespread and potent.

With the first dawnings of curiosity, parents may encourage intellectual interests and an experimental attitude. Questions should be answered in a way suited to the child's level of understanding, but also in such a way as to invite further investigation. Some questions receive a sufficient answer in words, others are best answered by observation or simple experiment. When parents do not know the answer, they may set themselves to find out, together with the children. All the methods being successfully developed in progressive schools are methods already devised by intelligent parents in their children's nurture.

The Influence of Family Life in the Formation of Aesthetic Taste and Standards of Appreciation. Children very early respond with interest to certain elements of aesthetic experience, to rhythm, movement, sound, and color. Responses to form, design, symmetry, and balance develop later in childhood. Here then are tendencies which if afforded appropriate stimulation may lead to a wide variety of aesthetic interests. It has also been discovered that children, when furnished with essential tools and encouraged freely to express their artistic impulses, are often capable of quite amazing results in painting and sculpture, poetry, drama, and music. From the success attending the efforts of progressive schools in stimulating spontaneous artistic expression, it is apparent that almost all children may experience the joy of creation in one or more of the arts.[1] These talents should not, however, be overestimated and made the basis of false expectations. Only the few possess artistic gifts of a very high order.

If all children were given opportunity for artistic expression, not only might more with unusual gifts be discovered, but all would be afforded joyful experiences in childhood which might provide a basis for worthwhile leisure-time interests in later life.

[1] For descriptions of some of the work which is being done, see H. Rugg and A. Shumaker, *The Child-Centered School* (1928), Chapters XI–XX; S. N. Coleman, *Creative Music for Children* (1922); H. Mearns, *Creative Youth* (1925), and *Creative Power* (1929); G. Hartman and A. Shumaker, eds., *Creative Expression* (Progressive Education Association, 1932); F. W. Nicholas, N. C. Mawhood, M. B. Trilling, *Art Activities in the Modern School* (1937).

It is very probable, too, that aesthetic appreciation is enhanced through experience in artistic expression.

Fortunately the appreciation of beauty is not only less specialized in one field, but is also far more capable of development in most people than is capacity for production. Long ago Plato emphasized the importance of surrounding children with beauty from their earliest years. And to-day, if a child grows up in a tastefully decorated, even if modest, home, if the house is set in a garden, and there are wide views over the countryside, conditions are ideal for the development of a love of natural beauty and the beginning of interest in the arts.

Even under less favorable circumstances parents who are keenly aware of the beauties of nature may reveal them to their children: the glories of sunset, of sea and mountains, of forests and fields of flowers; and all the exquisite details of natural objects, the tracery of bare twigs, the graceful flight of birds, the patterns and colors of leaves and flowers and butterflies. There are also many and varied opportunities for artistic expression in homemaking, and all these afford opportunity for the development of aesthetic taste in children who participate in family plans. In their own rooms and their own part of the garden they should be able to experiment, and they should also have some share in planning for house and garden; in selecting color schemes, textiles, and furniture. In the ideal home the standard of living and the choice of concrete means for its embodiment, however subject to financial restrictions, are yet guided throughout by considerations of health and beauty.

Children may be accustomed to listen to music from an early age, and songs and nursery rhymes serve as an introduction to poetry. Illustrated books and pictures may be chosen with a view to experiences in color, form, and design. As manipulative and constructive capacities develop, a variety of materials may be provided to give encouragement to creative expression. Here, as in the case of intellectual interests, parents may well be guided by the principles and procedures of progressive schools.

Even when everything possible has been done, there is frequent difficulty in developing discriminating taste. This is partly due to the fact that the standards of parents may be too mature, too highly developed for the children; but also because it is impossible nowadays to protect children from a veritable barrage of mass influences which constantly expose them to the cheap, trivial, banal, and vulgar in the way of popular so-called art. The influence of the movies has been discussed. But in the home itself children eagerly pore over the "funny" papers, and are now in increasing numbers exposed to the influences of radio with its vast potentialities in the way of recreation and education, and its mixed and dubious effects on the development of taste and appreciation, not to speak of interests and social attitudes and standards.[1] Never before have such marvelous opportunities been afforded for the development of musical appreciation through hearing the finest music. But there is even greater opportunity for children to listen to jazz orchestras and the latest song hits.

In order that children should outgrow absorption in the catchy, trivial, and crude, they should be exposed as fully as possible to the influences of good music, literature, and other forms of art. But it is most important that no attempt should be made to *force* these finer appreciations, nor to prohibit or even to disparage too severely the children's choice of entertainment. If this is done, the child's protest may take the form of a greater insistence on his preference and a rebellion against family standards.

There seems real cause for alarm, however, now that children everywhere are being exposed not only to the products of crude and debased aesthetic taste, but are in danger of what Glover and Dewey call the "mental adulteration" and "moral contamination," emanating from so much of the "commercial depredations on children's play" through ready-made amusements.[2] Popular music to-day is too often an appropriate vehicle for words in which false sentimentality is only one of many influences subversive of wholesome attitudes.[3] And it is beyond question that many radio programs are objectionable in their sensationalism, and in the reënforcement they afford to the commercialism and

[1] In the survey reported in the *Young Child in the Home*, 56.9% of the homes studied owned radios, the highest percentage being in the semi-professional or managerial group, 79.2%. In a New York study by A. L. Eisenberg, *Children and Radio Programs* (1936), radios were found in 91% of the homes in the metropolitan area; in 87% of homes at low-income levels, 88% at the next higher level, 95% of middle class homes, and 98% of those at high-income levels. See throughout for detailed discussion of the influence of radio on children; also S. M. Gruenberg, "Radio and the Child," *Annals of the American Academy*, Vol. CLXXVII (Jan., 1935), pp. 123–128.

[2] Katharine Glover and Evelyn Dewey, *Children of the New Day* (1934), p. 247.

[3] Long before the days of radio, Jane Addams deplored the dangers to youth from "blatant and vulgar songs . . . , the trivial and obscene words, the meaningless and flippant airs" which "run through the heads of hundreds of young people." *The Spirit of Youth and the City Streets*, pp. 18–19. To-day they run through the heads of hundreds of thousands.

love of publicity already so unfortunately prevalent in American life.[1]

The Influence of Family Life on Manners and on the Formation of Social Attitudes and Standards of Conduct. The concept of the *well-bred* individual, including as it does habits of correct speech and intonation of voice and also good manners, bears witness to the fact that these desirable qualities are very largely the product of early associations. Manners, it is true, are far too often conceived of as concerned with trivial and non-essential matters of etiquette, of exact customary usage in the social group; in particular, in the highest levels of society. Good manners, even in this superficial sense, are useful, for they make for ease of association in groups; but become of genuine importance when they are also the expression of that politeness, tact, and courtesy which spring from genuine consideration for others. In this sense manners have been well called *minor morals.* Table manners are a good example: apart from trivial niceties as to the use of table utensils, polite usage demands that habits of eating should be inoffensive to others, and so conducive to a pleasant social atmosphere.

Parental example is the most potent influence in the acquisition of good manners, but a certain amount of instruction is necessary which may, as the child grows older, be made a vehicle for inculcating consideration. In this way children learn that, while details of etiquette may change, social attitudes which facilitate group life have been found of enduring value.

It is often pointed out that one of the psychological functions of home life is to afford an oasis from the strain of formal social relationships. But the rest and relaxation afforded by feeling at ease in the friendly and informal atmosphere of home need not mean the relinquishing of courtesy and consideration in family relationships. Indeed from the standpoint of the children it is essential that the prevailing atmosphere be one of courtesy, even though there be much greater informality and less restraint of speech and opinion than in less intimate social groups.

Through living and working and playing together, in conversations at table and by the fireside, the attitudes and standards of

---

[1] It is too early, as yet, to assess the actual enduring effects on children of the radio. In 1933 a joint committee was formed representing the American Library Association, the Progressive Education Association, and the Child Study Association. Under the chairmanship of Sidonie M. Gruenberg it has been devising methods of coöperation between those interested in the welfare and education of children and commercial interests, including broadcasting companies, advertising agencies, and program sponsors.

parents effectively influence their children. Even so, it is hard to counteract the subversive social attitudes prevalent in contemporary American life. Many influences combine to delude young people into imagining that the way to happiness lies in becoming rich and famous. More and more the good life is interpreted in terms of financial success, of material possessions, publicity, comfort, idleness. If, in addition to the pervasive influence of such standards, there is emphasis in the home on social emulation, on the external aspects of family living, however well ordered or even beautiful these may be, the home atmosphere but reënforces other influences detrimental to wholesome social attitudes.

Parents should, on the contrary, provide every opportunity for children to discover for themselves that the enduring satisfactions of life lie in creative activity, suited to individual capacity, and in harmonious human relationships. While every opportunity should also be afforded for the concrete embodiment of desirable social attitudes and standards of conduct in daily living, parents may, at the same time, so interpret the child's social experience as to develop a sense of responsible participation in widening social circles; a sense of membership not only in the family, but in the larger society, and in the life of humanity.

SUGGESTED READING

Alschuler, R. H., *Two to Six*, rev. ed., 1937.

Anderson, H. H., *Living with Children in the Family*, 1937.

Anderson, J. E., *Happy Childhood*, 1933.

Blanton, S. and M. G., *Child Guidance*, 1927.

Blatz, W. E., and Bott, H., *Parents and the Preschool Child*, 1929.

Cameron, H. C., *The Nervous Child*, 4th ed., 1929.

Child Study Association, *Parent's Questions*, 1936.

Children's Bureau, *Publication 4*, "Prenatal Care," rev., 1930.

——, *Publication 8*, "Infant Care," rev., 1929.

——, *Publication 30*, "The Child from One to Six," rev., 1931.

——, *Publication 143*, "Child Management," rev., 1937.

——, *Publication 202*, "Are You Training Your Child to Be Happy," 1934.

Deering, I. E., *The Creative Home*, 1930.

Faegre, M. L., and Anderson, J. E., *Child Care and Training*, 4th ed. rev., 1937.

Fisher, D. C., and Gruenberg, S. M., eds., *Our Children*, 1932.

Foster, J. C., *Busy Childhood*, 1933.

——, and Anderson, J. E., *The Young Child and His Parents*, 1930.

Gesell, A., and Thompson, H., *Infant Behavior: Its Genesis and Growth*, 1934.

Gilbreath, L. M., *Living with Our Children*, 1928.

Glover, K., and Dewey, E., *Children of the New Day*, 1934.

Goodsell, W., *Problems of the Family*, rev. ed., 1936, Ch. XIX.

Groves, E. R., and Brooks, L. M., *Readings in the Family*, 1934, Chs. IX–XI.

Kugelmass, I. N., *Growing Superior Children*, 1935.

Langdon, G., *Home Guidance for Young Children*, 1931.

Lucas, W. P., *The Health of the Runabout Child*, 1923.

Nimkoff, M., *The Child*, 1934.

Pruette, L., *Parents and the Happy Child*, 1932.

Rand, W., Sweeny, M., and Vincent, E. L., *Growth and Development of the Young Child*, 2nd ed., 1934.

Richards, E. L., *Behavior Aspects of Child Conduct*, 1933.

Stern, B. J., ed., *The Family Past and Present*, 1938, Ch. XIII.

Stuart, H. D., *Healthy Childhood*, 1933.

Thom, D. A., *Everyday Problems of the Everyday Child*, 1927.

Van Alstyne, D., *Play Behavior and Choice of Play Materials of Pre-school Children*, 1932.

White House Conference, *The Home and the Child*, 1931.

——, *The Young Child in the Home*, 1936.

CHAPTER XXIV

ASPECTS OF FAMILY EDUCATION

ACHIEVING INDEPENDENCE OF PARENTS AND HOME

The Adolescent in Modern Society. Adolescence means, literally, growing into maturity. From the biological standpoint adolescence extends from puberty to cessation of growth. But this cessation does not occur all at once. Physical, emotional, and intellectual maturity—each is a complex phenomenon. And from the psychological standpoint there are no well-defined beginning and end of the transition from childhood to maturity. Certain characteristics of pubescence are, of course, clear. The boy or girl becomes possessed of the capacity for procreation, and there is a period of accelerated growth and development followed by slower growth to maturity. Correlative changes occur in mental and emotional life, and these in part account for some of the characteristics of turbulent adolescence. But only in part, as becomes apparent if adolescence in primitive societies is compared with adolescence in a complex civilization such as ours.[1]

In primitive groups, the individual mates when physiologically ready; and independence of parents and recognition as an adult member of the social group are achieved with the requisite emotional and intellectual preparation; this emergence from family tutelage into the wider social life being given definite public recognition. In civilized society, the social adjustments required of the mature and responsible adult are beyond the capacity of the pubescent boy or girl. An intervening period of preparation is necessary, during which the adolescent remains dependent on parents, and the exact age at which he or she achieves independence is left to private discretion and particular circumstances. Although eighteen for a girl, and twenty-one for a boy are generally accepted for *legal* coming of age, the confused state of public opinion is shown by lack of uniformity in laws designating adulthood.[2] The pattern of civilization thus ac-

---

[1] As is done by Margaret Mead in *Coming of Age in Samoa*, and *Growing Up in New Guinea*.

[2] For example, there are wide divergencies, between the states, in fixing maximum age for compulsory school attendance or for receiving public pensions as dependent

centuates the difficulties of adolescence as a period of transition.

Emphasis falls, accordingly, on the guidance afforded the adolescent; and it at once becomes apparent that the unwise treatment of adolescence is responsible for most serious cases of maladjustment. It is also apparent that, while adolescence is prophetic of adult destiny, it is, at the same time, the "early harvest period of childhood."[1] The adjustments of the adolescent years will be made most easily by those who are self-reliant and secure in their relationship to their parents. The insecure and those who cling to immature ways of meeting difficulties are inevitably handicapped. Nurture in the pre-adolescent years may thus be made the means for avoiding or at least mitigating the conflicts of adolescence.

The Pre-adolescent Years. Parents should be aware of the importance of normal psychological *weaning;* of how necessary it is for their children to achieve emotional and intellectual independence, and of the possibility of facilitating this process through treatment in the pre-adolescent years. In discussing the prevention of the anxieties and fears of adolescence, Bronner says: "Here, as in all matters concerning adolescence, begin long before adolescence arrives; guide, rather than force; be an intelligent observer of the child; anticipate and try to prevent, rather than wait and attempt to cure."[2] Parental attitudes are fundamental, here as elsewhere. Those who view their children not as possessions, but as independent individuals in the making, will endeavor to foster self-reliance. They will trust their children, and allow them to assume greater responsibilities and to become increasingly independent, making sure always that they are as fully prepared as possible to meet their new experiences with confidence.[3]

The years from about eight on are full of opportunities which are frequently neglected. The boy or girl is no longer a little child, gives comparatively little trouble, and is usually occupied with groups of friends and varied interests. Actually, however, he is still very dependent on home influences as he makes his first ventures into the outside world. Intellectually he is eagerly

minors, also with regard to minimum age for marriage, for culpability for unlawful behavior, for entering industry, and receiving an automobile license. And further, within any one state, the ages fixed in these different cases do not coincide.

[1] E. R. Groves and G. H. Groves, *Wholesome Parenthood* (1929), p. 278.

[2] "Adolescent Anxieties," *Child Study*, Vol. XIII (April, 1936), p. 208.

[3] Sex education, already discussed in Chapter X, is a good example of such preparation. When sex problems have been discussed as matters of scientific and social interest, long before they become personal problems, adolescents are afforded the best available safeguards in their relations with the opposite sex.

reaching out for information, seeking to understand the world he lives in; socially he is adjusting himself as a member of groups of his own sex; emotionally "the very essence of this age is its steady, though often imperceptible, weaning, a progress from dependence to independence."[1] This process is facilitated where parents keep in sympathetic touch with the interests and friend-ships of their children, give them a fuller share in family respon-sibilities, and encourage every effort at emancipation.

Adolescent Needs. The two essential needs of adolescence, as Frankwood Williams has pointed out, are emancipation from home, and the establishment of heterosexuality. The second need is met with the development during adolescence of be-havior patterns leading towards the selection of a mate. The first need is for psychological weaning: detachment from the fam-ily "in the emotional life, to such an extent at least, that there shall remain no crippling bondage to interfere with legitimate personal choice and achievement of what counts most for adult happiness, vocation, mating and attitude towards life."[2] Earlier habits of dependence on parents and the home environment must be superseded by confident and responsible self-direction.

But, in civilized society, readiness for marriage and emotional and intellectual autonomy are not enough. Independence also means capacity for self-support; so that the biologically appro-priate time for mating and independence is no longer the socially appropriate time. Mating must be postponed, with resultant physical stress: self-support is postponed, with enforced depend-ence for subsistence on parents. Moreover, present economic con-ditions justify the anxieties of the adolescent over his chances of achieving self-support in a field of work suited to his capacities. Young people look forward, to-day, with no certain assurance that their dominant impulses will not be thwarted, and their needs for congenial work and family life be left unsatisfied.

There is yet another factor which makes for conflict. The adolescent needs to achieve a mature point of view which will integrate experience and give it meaning. But the adult world, to-day, offers youth no compelling philosophy of life, no widely

---

[1] S. M. Gruenberg, "Half-Way Up the Stairs," *Child Study,* Vol. XI (Oct., 1934), p. 4.

[2] Leta S. Hollingworth, "Getting Away from the Family: The Adolescent and His Life Plans," *Concerning Parents,* p. 73. Frankwood Williams' well-known dis-cussion of adolescence was also first published in this volume (pp. 137–159), which is a record of the proceedings of a 1925 Conference on Modern Parenthood. It also appears in *Intelligent Parenthood* (1926), pp. 195–214, and as a chapter in his book, *Adolescence* (1930), pp. 101–120.

accepted religious integration of experience, but rather a confusing multitude of conflicting standards. Painful emotional conflicts are frequently involved when the adolescent accepts an explanation of the meaning of life which he later finds impossible to believe on intellectual grounds.

Symptoms of Adolescence. It is not surprising then that adolescence is a period marked by strange and even distressing symptoms, particularly when the tendencies natural during these years meet with much resistance. Adolescents are found eager to conform to the customs and standards of others of their own age: they follow fads and fashions of the moment, and make every effort in doing so to be socially successful and popular. They critically appraise themselves, their physical and mental prowess, their appearance and clothes, eager to be well-dressed, attractive, and prominent. They make greater demands for money, for the use of an automobile, and for the control of their time without parental supervision.[1]

At home, the adolescent's attempts to maintain his newly emerging self may find expression in more vigorous opposition to restraint, in irritability, rudeness, carelessness. He may be argumentative, even dogmatic; and very shortly afterwards change his opinions. Emotional instability may be shown by an alteration between buoyancy and depression. He critically appraises his home and family, and comes to realize that his parents are far less important and wise than he had hitherto believed. On this account, and also in his eagerness for independence, he resents advice, scoffs at sentiment, and becomes secretive and given to day-dreaming. His ideas and ideals are thrillingly important to him and he becomes conscious of new ambitions. Among superior adolescents, in particular, this may be a period of altruistic idealism, of revolt against the evils of the world and ardent interest in social service and social reform.

Sources of Friction between Adolescents and Their Parents. Certain of these symptoms of adolescence play a predominant part in disagreements between boys and girls and their parents. In *Middletown*, the Lynds found that frequency of late hours and actual hours of return led all other sources of disagreement with both boys and girls. Grades at school came as the third source for both, though considered more important for boys. Spending

[1] A study of the written wishes of 400 adolescent boys and girls, made by Washburne, in 1932, showed that these are preponderantly for material possessions. The desire for *material wealth* led all others, over 65%, followed closely by autos, 61%; next came clothes, 42%; 11% wished to "help humanity" and 2% wished to "improve humanity." See *Handbook of Child Psychology*, pp. 896–897.

money, use of the automobile, and choice of friends are the other three leading sources of friction for both sexes.[1] Case studies bear witness to the fact that unwise parents tend to deal directly with symptoms and to overlook the normal tendencies of which these symptoms are the expression.[2] It goes without saying that parents often have very real reason for anxiety when their children stay out late, associating freely with the opposite sex, and speeding about in automobiles, particularly where there is drinking.[3] But unwise treatment of all manifestations is very rarely due to legitimate anxiety alone; almost always it is rather the result of one or more typical attitudes on the part of parents: for example, reluctance to relinquish power over their children, which may express itself in an irksome censorship of their daily lives, or in an endeavor to impose the standards of the parents' own youth through a rigid patterning of adolescent conduct. Emotional possessiveness is another typical attitude, expressing itself in overprotection, and unwillingness to trust young people with responsibility; and, lastly, unwholesome attitudes towards sex are still widely prevalent.

Pruette believes that "the stress between the parent who does not wish to relinquish power and the adolescent who is determined to take power is actually the most significant aspect of the adolescent picture."[4] Parental concern over late hours *may* be due to genuine anxiety for health and safety; but quite often it is motivated by resentment at the adolescent's emancipation from parental control. The use of the automobile, in particular, facilitates the severing of home ties, through affording opportunity for privacy and freedom and a wide variety of social contacts. Often when parents find fault with friends, or with school grades, an underlying motive is a desire for control of the adolescent's time, his recreation and associations. And a struggle for power is sometimes the real source of friction over money, although it may on the other hand be due to need for

[1] Table XIII, p. 522. In this study of 348 boys and 382 girls, in addition to these most frequent sources, others ranking fairly high with boys were smoking and drinking; and with girls, going to unchaperoned parties, dress, home duties, also cigarettes and petting parties. Other studies are in close agreement. See, for example, A. B. Auerbach, "Freedom and the Latch Key," *Child Study*, Vol. XIV (April, 1937), pp. 203 *et seq.*

[2] See, for example, the case studies reported in Chapters III, VII, and VIII of Averill's *Adolescence* (1936).

[3] At the present time, parental fears of automobile accidents are well founded, and there is reason too to fear sexual misadventure, particularly for daughters, and the formation of habits of over-indulgence in drinking or gambling.

[4] *Parents and the Happy Child*, p. 258.

economy and the desirability of reliable habits of using money.[1] It is particularly hard for an only child or the youngest child to achieve independence, and it is harder for girls than for boys: facts largely due to possessiveness on the part of mothers. That late hours, use of the automobile, and choice of friends are leading sources of friction is undoubtedly accounted for by the fact that parental love of power, possessiveness, and unwholesome attitudes towards sex frequently combine in the efforts of parents to censor the social activities of their sons and daughters.

Conflict is rendered more acute because the adolescent appears before a critical public as a representative of the family. Not only the parents themselves, but others too may observe "the results of parental craftsmanship."[2] Far too often parents are concerned primarily with what others will think if their children "disgrace" them, instead of having their thoughts centered on the well-being of the children themselves. As in all human relationships, the greater part of the difficulty arises from selfishness and lack of understanding. Parents who believe that love and respect are their right as parents, whether they have earned them or not, grow increasingly critical of the self-absorbed and seemingly unresponsive adolescent. Such selfishness not only betokens lack of insight into the functions of parenthood, but also emotional maladjustment; the principle source, as we have abundantly seen, in all family difficulties: difficulties which often reach a crisis in friction between parents and adolescent boys and girls.[3]

There are, finally, some parents who are so preoccupied with their own affairs that they quite definitely neglect their children, and take, at most, a superficial interest in their problems. Such parents inevitably fail to provide the secure environment and sympathetic guidance needed by young people until independence is achieved.[4]

[1] The use of money is discussed in a later section, but it may be pointed out here that the management of a definite allowance to cover incidentals, clothes, recreation, gasoline, and other regular expenses is of the utmost importance in fostering responsible independence.

[2] Pruette, op. cit., pp. 246–247. Adolescence, she says, "is the Nemesis of the bad parent, and since no one is as good a parent as conceivably he might be, it is reasonable enough for us all to dread adolescence. . . . Adolescence-time is judgment-time, is harvest-time for the parent, when the parent is compelled to judge the results of his past efforts." P. 245.

[3] Averill says: "A parent who has failed to evolve emotionally becomes a disagreeable center of contagion whence diverse emotional viruses emanate throughout the home, contaminating all those who come beneath their evil power." Adolescence, p. 249.

[4] When "the great home securities are lacking the adolescent finds himself either plunging blindly into life in order to escape from home, or furtively turning aside from the encounter and shrinking into himself, hopelessly negatived and introverted." Ibid., p. 85.

Constructive Attitudes on the Part of Parents. If the family atmosphere is one of mutual consideration, it is less difficult for parents gradually to relinquish authority and be content to remain simply friends, treating their children tactfully and politely as responsible and independent and *mature.* Guidance is still needed, but, as Thom says, "frequently this guidance must be delicately passive rather than forcefully active."[1] The parent's rôle now is, as Pruette says, "the hard rôle . . . of standing by night and day, always ready to answer any call, always keenly interested in the adolescents' interests but never forcing a way into the other's life . . . , according a full privacy to the adolescent" and "the right of different tastes, different purposes and different life-patterns."[2]

Unless there seems real danger, it is better to remain tactfully blind to many of the symptoms of adolescence; in other cases, matters may be treated lightly and with humor, particularly where dealing with what is probably a passing phase; extravagances in dress and appearance, or the interest in pornography so openly prevalent to-day. A parent who refuses to be shocked and react emotionally, but instead discusses such interests with critical detachment is far more likely to have influence. This is also true with regard to adolescent ventures in drinking and gambling, where the best safeguard is thorough understanding of the dangers involved, if self-control is undermined.

Never should parents subject their children to ridicule, a practice far too common in the levity with which adults treat adolescent love affairs. They should treat seriously whatever is serious to the adolescent. Censoriousness must be checked and ordering and forbidding eliminated. The essential thing is to help the adolescent to find wholesome and constructive outlets for his urges and desires, and to encourage him to substitute these outlets for others which may be dangerous.

Successful parenthood in the adolescent years means, on the one hand, acceptance by parents of the separate individuality of their children, and, on the other, appreciation on the part of children of their parents as interesting, wise, and mature friends, with whom they may exchange experiences with full assurance of sympathy and understanding. The establishment of a "happy relationship of independent and trusting friendship" is, as Pruette says "the final challenge of parenthood, the final test of a good parent."[3]

[1] *Normal Youth and Its Everyday Problems* (1932), p. 13.
[2] *Op. cit.*, p. 260.   [3] *Ibid.*, p. 266.

RELATIONSHIPS BETWEEN CHILDREN IN THE SAME FAMILY

Differences in Environment for Children in the Same Family.
Our discussion, hitherto, has been oversimplified by the assumption that the home environment is the same for all the children
in a family. This is, of course, never the case, save conceivably
for certain pairs of identical twins. Hitherto, also, insufficient
recognition has been given to the frequency of jealousy, antagonism, and discord, and the inevitability of conflict, bickering, and
childish quarrels. Of recent years case-work has made evident
the fact that "There is no such thing as an identical environment for any two individuals. What is apparently the same environment is modified in each case by the individual's sex, age
and order of birth. . . . Every child has stood in his own individual dynamic relation to his parents, his brothers and sisters, to
the general family situation and to whatever outside influences
enter into the family life."[1]

In the first place the responses made by each child, even to the
same environment, would differ. But the *social* environment
never *is* the same for one child and the next. The parents grow
older, more experienced, their mutual relationship alters somewhat; and the only or oldest child responds to a very different
family pattern from the second child or later children, who must
adjust themselves from the first to the presence of another child
or other children.

Conflict between Children in a Family. Quarreling is natural
among children. Sharing and coöperation between dissimilar
individuals is no automatic affair, but requires continual readjustments and tactful guidance on the part of parents. But
valuable lessons in social adjustment may be learned through
the sometimes stormy process of give and take between brothers
and sisters. Moreover, childish resentments "are soon outgrown
and soon forgotten—other things being equal," to quote Josette
Frank. "It is only when other things are *not* equal that family
sharing becomes a focal point of potential danger, involving not
only the relationships of the brothers and sisters to one another
but their individual development as people and as members of
the larger society."[2] The one fundamental problem is the share
of children in the love of their parents; the subtle but determining factors in relationships between brothers and sisters being
the treatment accorded them by their parents.

[1] Blanche Weill, *The Behavior of Young Children of the Same Family* (1928), pp. 5, 4.
[2] "Share and Share Alike," *Child Study*, Vol. XIII, p. 6.

One of the chief sources of jealousy and behavior problems is differential parental treatment of children, differences in affection, appreciation, approbation, and expectation. Differential treatment of boys and girls is discussed in the next section. But invidious distinctions between children may be based on a number of factors besides sex. One child may be brilliant, and fit into the family pattern of family achievement; another may be comparatively dull and his capacities along what the family considers inferior lines. One boy is handsome and athletic, another homely and awkward. One girl is pretty and socially successful, another plain and shy.

The Influence of Order of Birth. Also, as already indicated, position in the family hierarchy tends to modify parental treatment in a characteristic way. Although there is some disagreement as to the exact results which may be expected, a tentative statement may be made of some of the possibilities inherent in the situation of an only child and in the ordinal position of the other children. The disadvantages of being an only child have probably been over-stressed, although they are very real where parents over-protect and fail to provide an only child with numerous companions of his own age. The recent study made by the White House Conference found that only children have closer emotional ties with parents and are more dependent on them, but that they rank as slightly *superior* in personality adjustment, tending to be more thoroughly integrated into the social group and to follow social codes more closely.[1]

The oldest child is for a time an only child, but his environment is profoundly altered with the birth of the second child. Adler, who, more than anyone, has stressed differences in "psychic development" of the first, middle, and last-born children, held that the "*first-born* possesses a sort of conservative tendency. He takes the element of power always into consideration . . . ; he regards his superiority over his brothers and sisters as his inviolable possession. The *second-born* always has before and behind him someone who can do more, of more importance, who generally possesses greater liberty of action. . . . If a second-born child is capable of any development he will unquestionably live in a condition of continuous endeavor to surpass his elder brother. . . . In the attitude of the type perhaps most prominent among the *last-born*, we find something infantile . . . ; he learns to expect to have everything done for him by others. There is no need of his developing his powers, for, as a

[1] *The Adolescent in the Family* (1934), pp. 239–243 and Tables 81–83, pp. 389–397.

baby, he is automatically forced into the center of his environment." But there is also another type of last-born: "Restlessly pushing forward, they surpass everyone by their initiative, frequently transcending the normal and becoming pathfinders."[1]

Like so many psychoanalytic hypotheses, this offers a suggestive partial explanation of the facts. It is evident that the factor of ordinal position operates in different ways according to the varying factors with which it interacts in the family pattern: factors of sex, age, relative ability, and differing personality traits; even perhaps factors of economic and cultural status.[2] It seems fairly evident, however, that the middle child or children are apt to receive less concentrated attention. The White House Conference study found them to be the most independent and to have more social contacts than the first- or last-born.

The last-born is never dethroned from his position as baby of the family; a crucial experience for which a child should be carefully prepared. Jealousy can almost always be prevented if the older child is taken fully into the family's confidence and told that with the coming of a little brother or sister his own position will be one of new importance and responsibility. Great care must be taken to reassure him that his claim on his parents' affection is undiminished. If ways can be found for enlisting the coöperation of the older child in the care of the new baby, he or she will be helped to learn the necessary lesson of ceding privileges to others. If any untoward symptoms appear, they indicate that the older child is endeavoring to recapture the mother's attention, and, far from punishing him, greater efforts must be made to reassure.[3]

THE DIFFERENTIAL TREATMENT OF BOYS AND GIRLS

Artificial Sex Differences Due to Early Nurture. Almost universally, different standards are set for boys and girls from an early age, and they are accorded very different treatment. Positive ideals of health and fitness are not inculcated in the same way with girls as they are with boys: girls are allowed to be more emotional, are not encouraged in the same way to be

---

[1] *The Practice and Theory of Individual Psychology* (1924), pp. 321–322.

[2] The influence of economic and cultural status is indicated by Levy's study of 576 clinic cases in Chicago and of 209 maladjusted children in the schools of a wealthy suburb. Only children showed a greater tendency to be maladjusted in the socially superior group, while first-born showed such a tendency only among the clinic cases. See H. E. Jones, "Order of Birth," *Handbook of Child Psychology*, p. 581.

[3] Pathological behavior may result where the coming of a new baby is not satisfactorily explained. For a case of this kind see H. T. Woolley "Personality Studies of Three-year-olds," *Journal of Experimental Psychology*, Vol. V, pp. 381–392.

independent and responsible and to make a success of what they do. While deprived of as wholesome and free outlets for their energies as are open to boys, girls are allowed, on the other hand, to become overconscious of their appearance. Altogether, far less is expected of girls: a state of affairs natural enough in a society which makes no equivalent demands for self-support on women and on men.[1]

Moreover, the fatal tendency, already alluded to, of evaluating all differences quantitatively rather than qualitatively, in terms of superior and inferior, is nowhere more evident than in the veiled, but none the less real, disparagement of "feminine" qualities. As Olga Knopf points out, even to-day a girl, "from the moment of her birth . . . , is treated, however subtly and delicately, with whatever compensations in the way of help and affection, as belonging to an inferior species. . . . Women have been curtailed, limited and discouraged from the beginning of their lives. They have had to contend against the inferiority feelings of all mankind and in addition there has been put upon them the burden of belonging to a sex which everyone—themselves included—considered as inferior."[2]

While this is less universally true to-day than earlier, its essential accuracy is born witness to by the fact that while girls do not mind being called tomboys or told, "you ought to have been a boy," boys are insulted if called sissies or if any suggestion is made of their possession of what are considered feminine qualities. No wonder, since energy, courage, initiative, active and forceful intelligence are labeled masculine, while—in addition to charm, patience, and tenderness which are considered feminine— "all that is childish, sentimental, timid and a trifle silly has become hopelessly identified with the idea of being a woman in many minds."[3]

Effects of Differential Treatment. Although it is hard to find children young enough to have escaped the influence of conven-

---

[1] In her autobiography, Lady Rhondda points out that being a girl is treated as an excuse for failure. "A boy is educated all along with a view to having to take up responsibility. A girl is not. . . . A girl in innumerable, subtle, indirect ways is taught to mistrust herself. . . . Every woman of my generation was brought up from her babyhood to believe in her very bones that in every department outside the home, and even in the really important things inside the home . . . , she must submit to Authority." *This Was My World* (1933), pp. 231–233.

[2] *The Art of Being a Woman,* p. 79. She points out that Otto Weininger's famous book, *Sex and Character* (1906), in which, in keeping with masculine tradition, all truly admirable qualities are labeled masculine, had great influence in crystalizing the common attitude to masculinity and femininity.

[3] Mary Chadwick, *Adolescent Girlhood* (1932), p. 107.

tional beliefs, yet up till four the play interests of boys and girls are much the same. Studies show that, even before one year old, more girls play with dolls, the appropriate feminine plaything, although boys also enjoy dolls and would almost certainly enjoy them longer if older children did not tease them.[1] And little girls like toy trains, and "boys' toys and games," just as much as do little boys. But very soon divergencies appear; girls continue to like dolls, and play house, store, school, and games of family life, while boys, after a stage in which they still play these games but assume an aggressive masculine rôle, give them up in favor of cowboys, Indians, wagons, and mechanical toys.

The effects of differential treatment become most evident from about four or five on, and certain data gathered by a White House Conference study are of particular interest in this connection. This study agrees with all others that have been made of jealousy among children, in finding girls more jealous than boys. But in consulting the figures a significant fact appears. It is not till *between four and five* that girls become consistently more jealous than boys, and they continue so at later ages! [2] The same study confirms the usual impression that girls are more timid and fearful than boys, but the difference is less in the early years and boys begin to get rid of fears *earlier* and particularly from five on get rid of them more rapidly. Such data confirm the impression that boys are held to ideals of conduct befitting the sex destined to play the superior rôle in life.[3]

Although it is not until puberty that sex differences become pronounced, long before then boys and girls have adopted their fundamental attitudes towards life and towards the opposite sex, under the influence of pervasive social pressure, which differentiates between the interests and activities appropriate respectively to boys and girls. Girls are apt to find restrictions closing round them as they grow older, until they are driven to a reluctant acceptance of an inferior rôle, or to a morbid aggressiveness which may take several forms.

The exact rôle assumed by a girl is determined by many factors: her aptitudes, physical and mental, her parents' treat-

---

[1] Blanche Weill "Is It for a Boy or for a Girl?" *Child Study*, Vol. X (Dec., 1932), pp. 75–76.

[2] *The Young Child in the Home*, pp. 230–231.

[3] The jealousy of girls may be due in part not only to the continually implied superiority of boys, but also to the fact that boys are allowed greater freedom and a wider range of activities. Boys, too, are often allowed to be domineering, disorderly, even bad tempered and lacking in self-control, in a way which would be far more censured in a girl.

ment, and her relations with brothers and sisters.[1] An only girl with brothers responds typically in one of two ways. She may become a spoiled darling with an accentuation of feminine traits, or she may become the companion of her brothers and interest herself in their "masculine" activities. The valuations implied in the family pattern are also of great importance. Where the mother plays the traditional subordinate rôle of deference to masculine authority, both sons and daughters are profoundly influenced. The girls may be pampered and petted, but this is actually symptomatic of their inferior status.

The adoption of an ultra-feminine rôle is one of two ways in which girls will endeavor to assert their superiority, to dominate and get the better of men, by being helpless, seemingly soft, and submissive. In reality, "no one is tougher, more selfish and obstinate than the weak and clinging woman who thrusts on others the responsibility for making her happy and fulfilling her aims."[2]

The other typical attitude of girls who resent the implied inferiority of their sex is the so-called "masculine protest." This may take exaggerated forms, such as resentment at female physiological processes, or an intense and jealous antagonism to men. Not only the athletic type of girl, but the very feminine type, may manifest such symptoms, usually if she has become aware of the fact that her birth, as "only a girl," was a disappointment to her parents. In many cases, of course, what is apt to be called a masculine protest may be simply the wholesome refusal of a girl to be bound by artificial restrictions. This is particularly true of gifted girls, because of their frequent preference for activities hard to follow on account of their sex.[3]

[1] This is, of course, equally true of boys: for example, where there are one boy and several girls in a family, he is apt to develop an attitude of superiority, unless indeed one of the girls is more able than he intellectually, when the results may be most unfortunate. He usually develops, however, an attitude of responsibility for those he considers weaker. A boy with several older sisters is often tempted to remain dependent, and in later life may compensate by demanding exaggerated respect from women.

[2] Knopf, op. cit., p. 77. Significant of the way in which patterns of dependence on men are fostered in girls is the Lynds study of the sources of spending money among high school boys and girls: 53% of the girls as against 15% of the boys were dependent for all their spending money upon asking their parents for it or upon gifts. Over half the boys were learning habits of independence by earning and managing at least a part of their money, while over half the girls were learning the habits of money dependence characteristic of Middletown wives. One senior girl remarked: "Some of us don't want an allowance, you can get more without one." Middletown, p. 142.

[3] When Terman contrived a "masculinity" index, on the basis of a preference for certain types of games, he found gifted girls more "masculine" than the control group. Terman's findings bear witness to the obstacles put in the way of the full development

Constructive Parental Attitudes. It should, as we saw, be made quite clear to little boys and girls that they will some day be fathers and mothers respectively.[1] But *both* from the first should be given every encouragement and full opportunity to develop special capacities as responsible human beings. Girls and boys should also be encouraged to accept the unique value and significance of their respective rôles of motherhood and fatherhood. After all, as Knopf says, "the problems of life are the same for both sexes. The best attitude towards life is also the same for both sexes; and it is only the circumstances in which this attitude must be worked out that make the difference."[2] "As soon as coöperation between the sexes has been started . . . mothers will change in their attitudes towards their children. They will bring up boys and girls without measuring them against each other; they will consider the individualities of their children without regard to sex. Interests and capacities will be allowed to develop freely, without any limit except the welfare of others. It is the parent's part to guide and encourage, not to restrict or compel. Of course a mother cannot overlook the sex of her children or even bring them up to the same tasks: but there should be no valuation in any difference made. . . . It is only where there is a difference in valuation that a girl will envy the tasks of a boy."[3]

Any difference in treatment between boys and girls should be constructive rather than restrictive. They should be allowed to follow any interests they choose without any suggestion that they are unsuitable on account of sex.[4] One point, however, is of great importance as puberty approaches. Girls should develop positive ideals of health as a matter of supreme significance from the standpoint of future motherhood. Parents must bear in mind dangers of overstrain either physical or mental, in the years between ten and fifteen, but girls should be encouraged to think of menstruation as a normal function which need not in-

of girls. In his follow-up of 1,000 gifted boys and girls he found that gifted boys maintain their level of intellectual superiority to a greater extent than gifted girls. B. S. Burks, D. W. Jensen, and L. M. Terman. *Genetic Studies of Genius*, Vol. III (1930).

[1] Where it is not clearly understood by children that they must remain either boys or girls, it is sometimes found that little girls imagine that, if they cut their hair short or wear boy's clothes, they may become boys.

[2] *Op. cit.*, p. 87.   [3] *Op. cit.*, pp. 288–289.

[4] When sharing in the work of the household, for example, there is not the slightest reason why girls alone should make beds, wash dishes, sweep, dust, sew, or help with cooking, while boys alone mow the lawn, pull weeds, clean the car, and do odd carpentry jobs. If girls like mechanics and carpentry, they should by all means be encouraged to become skilful craftsmen, and to be of use in making small repairs, while a boy who enjoys cooking may be most useful in the kitchen.

capacitate or even greatly inconvenience. For individual happiness and for social well-being it is essential that girls, as well as boys, should accept their rôle in life as full of positive significance, and that both be given equal opportunities from earliest infancy for full individual development.

THE USE OF MONEY

Principles of Financial Education. Money plays so large a part in contemporary life that the financial training of children involves far more than skill in the management of money. In experience with money, children are introduced to vital problems, and develop emotional, social, and moral attitudes of determining influence in later life. Children should, in the first place, be brought to realize that money is a medium of exchange, a means for providing satisfaction of needs; and that the real sources of wealth are natural resources and human effort. Emphasis must be shifted from money and possessions as ends-in-themselves to the satisfactions they provide. The central principle of family education with regard to money is to use it always as a means only, and subject always to a further consideration of the values to be obtained through its use. It should then become apparent that questions of money are largely irrelevant in connection with the deepest and most enduring of life's values.

Such lessons can be best learned in a coöperative family, for here, in the midst of a competitive society, we have a small group where goods and services are given and shared without any consideration of pay. Yet the family, as we saw, is intimately involved in the financial organization of society, and the well-being of the group and its constituent members is largely conditioned by the sufficiency and wise use of its income. Children may, therefore, combine experience of intrinsic non-pecuniary values with learning, through supervised practice, how to handle the potent instrument of money. Just as each child receives as a matter of course his share in the goods and services provided in the family circle, so too should he be given his appropriate share of the family income. Experience in the free use of an allowance, as well as with saving and earning, is necessary, if young people are to have sufficient opportunity for developing skill and discrimination in the management of money.[1]

[1] In view of this fact, studies of prevalent custom are of interest. In the Lynds' study, 3% of the boys and 11% of the girls received all spending money in the form of an allowance; 9% of the boys and 5% of the girls both had allowances and

Children's Allowances. The allowance, even in its earliest form of a stated amount of pocket money, should be received by the child *regularly* and *unconditionally;* it should be exclusively his to control, and in no way dependent on good behavior. *Spending money* must be supplied to the little child as soon as he becomes interested in money: 5¢ a week is sufficient at the age of five to enable the child to begin learning the principle of exchange and the importance of choice. In general, at any age, the child's financial resources should never be so great as to render consideration of relative values unnecessary, nor so small as to make choice and planning impossible. In general, too, the amount of the allowance should be decided between parents and child, and determined according to the child's needs and the family income. It should grow according to need, and may be made monthly, rather than weekly, with increasing skill in management; and be extended gradually to cover items other than spending money proper. For instance, it may cover the fixed amounts necessary for car fare and lunch, and also that part of the expenditure for clothing in which freedom of choice seems advisable. From about fourteen on, young people become capable of managing a comprehensive allowance which covers all costs except those for board, lodging, and educational expenditures.

Exclusive control of an allowance, by the child, does not, of course, mean that parents may not offer unobtrusive help. But in the earlier stages, at least, much may be learnt through making mistakes. As the allowance grows and comes to include items other than spending money, budgeting may be introduced and the value of written accounts becomes evident. Planning for the future and saving for some desired object also develop naturally as part of the child's experience of spending.

Practice in Saving and Earning. Early saving must not be made into a ritual. To hoard money is contrary to the central principle of its effective use. The real value of saving is best learnt if the child chooses to put away small sums for a short period for some concrete object. It is then discovered that the

earned; 37% of the boys and 9% of the girls earned all their spending money. *Middletown*, p. 142. According to the study reported in *The Adolescent in the Family*, p. 38 and Table 35, p. 349, 26% urban, 19% small city, and 12% rural children received regular allowances. In the study of younger children reported in *The Young Child in the Home*, pp. 206–209, a quarter of the children six to twelve were given allowances, the practice being more common in families of higher socio-economic status. Two studies reported in *The Home and the Child*, pp. 131 *et seq.*, gave higher percentages for allowances, 42% girls and 28% boys, in grades six to nine, in a Rochester study; and 77% girls and 65% boys, in grades five to eight, in a Brookline study.

power of money may either be used immediately or conserved for future use. Only later on, with much larger sums, can saving be intelligently adopted as a forward-looking policy. As the child learns the possibilities of planning and saving, he will be introduced to the further possibilities of borrowing and lending. For purchases which admit of no postponement, money may be borrowed, to be paid back in instalments from the allowance.

One important lesson cannot be learnt from an allowance: what money really costs in terms of effort, time, and skill. Therefore young people should also have direct experience of earning. But the earning should be genuine not fictitious: a fact which raises difficult problems. Few really suitable opportunities now exist outside the home for young people to earn in return for work; and within the home they should be expected to share in the family work with no question of payment. It is possible, however, to agree upon certain definite extra jobs which the child is free to undertake or not. According to the Gruenbergs "the one positive rule that seems applicable is this: children may be paid for doing only that for which somebody else would otherwise be hired."[1] For children who live in the country more opportunities present themselves; productive enterprises are possible, such as raising garden produce or poultry-keeping.

The relation between earning and an allowance presents still another problem which requires careful adjustment in each individual case. With younger children, where possible, earnings should supplement an undiminished allowance. Never, while children are dependent, should earnings be demanded by parents.[2] And where prolonged preparation for a profession postpones self-support, it is most important that parental subsidies should be provided with no hint of reproach for prolonged dependence, and no assumption of a right to control their grownup sons' and daughters' lives.

All family problems involving the use and distribution of money may be most amicably and justly settled by means of a family council, in which all the children participate. Exact knowledge of family resources and mutual consideration of individual needs form the surest basis for an apportionment of income satisfactory to all. Children learn far more than the management of money from such a council; they learn participa-

---

[1] *Parents, Children, and Money* (1933), p. 117.

[2] Sons and daughters who are supporting themselves should, as we saw, not only be expected to pay their personal expenses, but, if living at home, to contribute their share of household expenses.

tion with others in the service of the group, and absorb standards for choice based on discrimination of values. "In the whole business of homemaking," Abel says, "there is perhaps nothing more important than the open discussion of comparative values of that for which the family spends its money." [1]

THE USES OF LEISURE

The Significance of the New Leisure. With the transition from an economy of scarcity to an economy of abundance, it is becoming apparent that "for the first time in history . . . we stand on the threshold of a democratic age of leisure." [2]   To those who realize the significant relationship between leisure and human happiness, the "new leisure" appears as a stirring challenge. [3] "It is only with leisure," says Pack, "that we are able to measure in any human terms at all the value of living. . . . Leisure stands out as the great opportunity for America, because it provides an indispensable means of leavening our social fabric on a workable and human basis." [4]

Only the few can find ample means for individual development and self-expression in their work; for the many full contentment can be found only through interests developed in leisure time. Nor is this all, according to Pack. Leisure-time activities furnish outlets, not alone for those deprived of other opportunities, but also for the excess energies and competitive urges of those who combine keener minds with the "fundamental human urge to exercise superiority." [5] Our modern intensive civilization tends to divert the urge to adventure and to control of material energies into the pursuit of wealth; to divert human creative impulses into channels that are essentially predatory. A new emphasis on the inherent values of leisure-time activities, which turns attention from exclusive preoccupation with production to "doing for its own sake," may, Pack hopes, be "a vital factor in solving our fundamental socio-economic problem." [6]

Tendencies in Leisure-time Activities. Mechanical inventions have led not only to an industrial revolution, an economy of

[1] *Successful Family Life on the Moderate Income*, p. 185.

[2] H. O. Overstreet, "The Great and Growing Problem of Leisure," *New York Times Magazine*, April 21, 1935.

[3] "If the day of physical pioneering is done," says Hambidge, "the day of mental and spiritual pioneering is far from done." *Time to Live* (1933), p. 17.

[4] From *The Challenge of Leisure* (1934), pp. 16, 17. By permission of The Macmillan Company, publishers.

[5] *Ibid.*, p. 36.   [6] *Ibid.*, p. 48.

abundance, and increasing leisure time, but also to a revolution in the use of leisure.[1] It is, therefore, not at all surprising that the development of far-sighted policies for utilization of new recreational facilities has failed to keep pace with their amazingly rapid expansion. Many opportunities have been neglected, others have been misused.[2] And emphasis has fallen on expensive automobiles, radios, and other forms of equipment for sport or recreation, as conferring social prestige. Finally, a major trend to-day is towards the widespread development of commercialized facilities for passive amusements. Too much leisure is occupied with merely looking at and listening to ready-made entertainment. And because this second-hand play cannot take the place of first-hand activities, still further thrills are sought in gambling, which, as Pack says, is the "*sauce piquante* which may be added to almost anything or nothing."[3] And, indeed, the less scope there is for adventure in everyday life, in what has been called our "push-button" civilization, the more craving there is for thrills, for more speed for the sake of speed, for the vicarious thrills experienced by spectators at sports or the movies. A real purpose is served by many passive forms of entertainment: release from tension and escape from the routine of everyday life. Refreshment may be had from change of occupation, but to serve as outlets for creative urges, for surplus energies, and the spirit of adventure, leisure-time activities must provide for the *active* participation of muscles, senses, imagination, and thought.

Accordingly, it is to be hoped that the trend towards passive amusement may be increasingly offset by the other major trend of to-day, the rapid growth of private and public facilities for a variety of active forms of recreation. Participation in sports is becoming an accepted part of life for more and more people. Another wholesome trend is towards outdoor life and contact

[1] Delisle Burns, by means of a suggestive diagram, makes evident the fact that all the new machinery for leisure first came into general use within the lifetime of those now 80: railways, bicycles, phonographs, automobiles and, within the latter half of that period, airplanes, cinemas, and radio. *Leisure in the Modern World* (1932), p. 134.

[2] Automobiles, for example, which make possible the refreshment and enrichment of experience which comes with travel, particularly travel away from the crowded life of cities, to sea-shore, forests, and mountains, are used very largely for aimless and restless wandering, or for the thrills to be obtained from reckless speed. The marvelous potentialities of the latest means of conquering space, the radio, are beginning to be realized; but, for the most part, radio is used to broadcast to the farthest corners of the earth the trivial banalities of popular entertainers and the impassioned appeals of high-pressure advertising.

[3] *Op. cit.*, p. 137.

with nature through hiking and camping.[1] Outdoor life brings opportunity for physical exercise and appreciation of natural beauties, and also serves to foster interests such as photography and the observation and collection of various natural objects.[2]

Of recent years there has been greatly increased interest in art. Keppel sees "a definite trend towards the belief that beauty, its creation, reproduction and its . . . enjoyment has an essential place in normal human life."[3] More and more emphasis is being placed on art in the schools.[4] There is growing interest in good music, in classes in arts and crafts, and in community theaters.

Some of the most interesting and stimulating forms of social life are found in connection with shared interests: poetry, painting, music, drama, collecting, gardening, reading, or discussion. With further development of such groups it is to be hoped that they will supersede much of the conventional so-called social life of to-day, with its trivial gossip, and competition in clothes, or in meaningless elaborations of entertainment: a poor imitation at best of the companionship which is possible through shared interests.

Leisure and Family Life. In the creation of a beautiful environment for family life ample opportunity is found for artistic expression. In gardening, physical exercise is combined with mental adventure and the creation of beauty. Education in the handicrafts is making possible the construction of beautiful things for home use; pottery, metal work, textiles, even furni-

[1] Existing facilities as yet serve only the few. The White House Conference report on *Summer Vacation Activities of the School Child* (1933) found that only one-fourth of urban children and very few rural children have summer playground privileges. During some part of the summer, an estimated 500,000 go with parents on camping tours, while a few travel or have constructive home life in the country, in the mountains, or at the sea-shore. Vacation activities offer unparalleled opportunities for educational experiments, and the improvement of vacation schools is urged by Eugene T. Lies, *The New Leisure Challenges the Schools* (1933). Brief descriptions of the vacation programs of a number of organizations may be found in *Child Study*, Vol. XII (April, 1935), pp. 199–212.

[2] Collecting may take innumerable forms in which it becomes a veritable mental adventure and an absorbing hobby. "Hobbies," Pack says, "may be said to fall into three more or less overlapping fields. One is the acquiring of knowledge, which is, after all, the collection and integration of facts. Another is the collection of objects, and still another is the creating of things." *Op. cit.*, p. 154.

[3] "The Arts in Social Life," *Recent Social Trends*, Vol. II, p. 1003.

[4] In February, 1936, a Music and Art High School was opened as part of the New York City school system. Gifted students are given an opportunity to develop their talent while receiving a regular high school education. At the end of its first year, 700 were enrolled, and 250 more will be admitted each semester until a maximum of 1,800 is reached. *New York Times*, Apr. 11, 1937.

ture.[1] Already, in families whose chief concern is the development of the family members, many possibilities for the cultivation of varied interests and the use of leisure are being explored. Parents may encourage the development of skill in sports, interest in arts and crafts, or in collections and hobbies. And many ways may be discovered in which the family group may share their leisure hours.

Some of the happiest hours of home life are spent where father or mother reads aloud to the family group. The tiniest children love to have nursery rhymes or little illustrated books read to them; as they grow older, the time will soon come when they will enjoy books which appeal also to older members of the family. There are growing numbers of excellent children's books which entertain and enrich the child's experience, while they introduce him to the inexhaustible joys of reading to himself. [2]

Resources offered by libraries, museums, playgrounds, parks, theaters, and concerts may be fully used by the family whose interests center in the home; and parents and children may share many an outing together. Where parents supervise their children's earlier contacts with the outside world and also provide substitutes for ready-made amusements, there is less inducement later to follow the crowd and spend all leisure time away from home. At present, only the exceptional family makes adequate provision for home recreation.[3] Nevertheless, Pack holds:

[1] A survey of the leisure-time activities of 5,000 urban people, made recently by the National Recreation Association, showed that in those families which retained a reasonable degree of employment, though adversely affected by the depression, leisure-time activities tended to re-center about the home. Gardening, sewing, or cooking, taken up at first as tasks, had become transformed into worthwhile pursuits in themselves. More leisure was reported for reading, conversation, playing of musical instruments, and home dancing or card parties.

[2] Children whose interest in reading is stimulated and guided will learn to consult books in pursuit of their interests. The instructive features of the *Book of Knowledge*, for example, are often as eagerly absorbed as any fairy tale. The White House Conference report on *Children's Reading* (1932) found that normal children will read good books and periodicals if they are accessible. In all the better libraries there are now special services for children, all the more necessary because of the few good books to be found in the average home. Over half of the children in the study reported in *The Young Child in the Home* grew up in homes where there were *less than fifty books*, and three-fourths in homes where there were fewer than 100! Many lists of children's books are available, and there are also a number of recent surveys of children's literature. Some of these are *A Better Beginning in Reading for Young Children* (Association for Childhood Education, 1932); N. Beust, *Graded List of Books for Children* (1930); B. E. Mahoney and E. Whitney, *Realms of Gold in Children's Books* (1929).

[3] "Family recreations are not well provided for, in either country or city, and there is particular neglect of recreation within the home." *The Adolescent in the Family*, p. 163, and see pp. 162–169, and Tables 63–69, pp. 371–377.

"If there is any meaning at all to the principles and ideals of home life that we all profess to accept, then the home can and will become the irradiating center for the New Leisure and for a fuller living."[1] Shared interests, sports, hobbies all "possess potentialities of human relationship in addition to their directly creative functions. . . . The curious fact in the spiritual essence of human relationship seems to be that each smallest human service or interest in helping a fellow man offers a thrill of creation . . . , epitomizing whatever it is that makes the individual human life happy, contented and complete."[2]

RELIGION

Children's Need for a Philosophy of Life. The task of parents is incomplete if they have not helped their children to formulate for themselves a philosophy of life, a vision of spiritual values which sustain, integrate, and give direction to the life of the individual. Young people need the stability, security, and purpose which can be derived only from a sense of the significance of their lives as responsible participants in a mysterious but inspiring adventure. The earliest opportunities for cultivating a sense of the spiritual occur in answer to the little child's questions about who made the world, and about death. Interest in these matters is at first fleeting, and rarely urgent when a child feels secure in the affection of his parents. With the young child, moreover, interest in these matters is at first objective. Only with the emotional and intellectual development of adolescence, is there fully awakened longing to discover the meaning of life and the individual's place in the scheme of things.

Dangers of Dogmatism. Religious education is taken as a matter of course by orthodox adherents of churches, particularly by Catholics who make religion a part of the daily life of the child. But dogmatic religious instruction in childhood may have a number of unfortunate consequences: grotesque images and ideas, emotional maladjustments, and fear complexes. Moreover, for the well-educated and intelligent, doubt is inescapable in adolescence and leads to confusion and conflict. Feelings of futility, pessimism, and cynicism frequently result from the loss of previously accepted religious belief and a sense of the illusory character of human hopes and aspirations. Despair may even lead to suicide. If, on the other hand, the adolescent continues to accept orthodox answers to the enigmas of existence, his religious experience may be lacking in mystical quality and less

[1] *Op. cit.*, p. 210.   [2] *Ibid.*, pp. 211, 210.

effective on conduct, and he is very likely to become zealous and intolerant and to feel himself superior to those who differ with him. Where environmental pressure stifles the normal impulses of curiosity and inquiry, the adolescent is deprived of his opportunity for working out his own solution. "The automatic acceptance of a scheme of belief is as poor a substitute for actual spiritual experience as is the refusal to consider any belief at all."[1]

Constructive Parental Attitudes. Many parents neglect or evade any form of religious instruction, either because they are agnostics and wish their children kept free from indoctrination, or because they are confused, or simply indifferent. But little children cannot be left "free" to choose for themselves, and to "do nothing" is to do something, namely, to reveal the uncertainty or indifference of the parents. Contact with the religious beliefs and usages of friends add to bewilderment where there is no home guidance. In this age of criticism and reconstruction there is but one way in which parents can help their children to develop a coherent and sustaining philosophy of life. They must themselves discover the good life; the values of greatest worth and ways of belief and aspiration which make life significant. Family life may thus provide the child with a spiritual climate which permeates all subsequent moral and religious attitudes.

Little children who are given loving and understanding care feel at home in the world, and need nothing more until they become in some degree aware of the mysteries of life and death. There should be no dragging in of abstract religious concepts, even when children's questions have genuine religious quality, being concerned with the values, meanings, and purposes of life. Parents may then answer in the light of their own faith; and may also bring to the child something of the religious heritage of humanity, a sense of an enduring spiritual quest, and knowledge of the lives and work of the great religious and moral leaders of mankind.[2]

Little children must not be shielded from the knowledge of death; they will, in any case, soon discover the fact of death and

[1] Sidney I. Schwab and Borden S. Veeder, *The Adolescent: His Conflicts and Escapes* (1929), p. 329. They believe that "it seems logical to blame a good deal of the intolerance of the adolescent upon religion [which is] warped in its method of presentation. . . . Intolerance has its basis . . . in uncertainty. . . . From indecision and the feeling that what is held to be true is uncertain there is a tendency to shut the door upon the intrusion of new and uncomfortable ideas."

[2] If parents have no faith of any kind, they can at least communicate the substance of their hope. If hope fails, and life seems without significance, they should bring no more children into the world.

question their parents. The first need is for calm information as to the inevitability of death as part of the normal cycle of all living beings, and it is wise to admit that we have no certain knowledge beyond present experience. When the child begins to sense the sorrow brought by death, or experiences the loss of a pet animal, parents may bring reassurance on the basis of their deepest convictions; that the dead are sleeping, or at peace, or, perhaps, that they are happy somewhere. The need for such reassurance is great when a child loses brother or sister or parent, and the utmost care must be taken to protect him from fear, shock, or morbid imaginings which may be derived from the emotional behavior of others. Under no circumstances should young children be present at funerals. They must if possible be saved from being overwhelmed by the death of one they love, and there is no excuse for allowing them to acquire a horror of death as a mysterious and terrible calamity.

Parents best help their children if they lead them to face reality courageously while living in the light of ideals; if they are fortified to meet changes and insecurity through a sense of a sustaining spiritual whole. Family life may foster this sense when it becomes a center for a widening idealism; a realization of kinship with humanity, past, present, and future, and with the encompassing whole of which humanity's adventure forms an integral part.

"We possess only that which we set free," according to a Chinese proverb. The quality of parenthood may be judged in the last analysis by the measure in which parents have endowed their children with effective freedom; freedom fully to live their own lives, to think their own thoughts, and to seek for an individual interpretation of and reconciliation with the mystery of life.

SUGGESTED READING

Arlitt, A. H., *Adolescent Psychology*, 1933.
Averill, L. A., *Adolescence*, 1936.
Children's Bureau, *Publication 225*, "Guiding the Adolescent," 1933.
Conklin, E. A., *Principles of Adolescent Psychology*, 1935.
Elliott, G. L., *Understanding the Adolescent Girl*, 1930.
Gruenberg, S. M. and B. C., *Parents, Children, and Money*, 1933.
Hollingworth, L. S., *The Psychology of the Adolescent*, 1928.
Office of Education, *Bulletin 18*, 1936: II, "Leisure for Living."
Pack, A. N., *The Challenge of Leisure*, 1934.
Pruette, L., *Parents and the Happy Child*, 1932.
Richmond, W., *The Adolescent Boy*, 1933.

Schwab, S. I., and Veeder, B. S., *The Adolescent, His Conflicts and Escapes*, 1929.

Seabury, D., *Growing into Life*, 1928.

Steiner, J. F., "Recreation and Leisure-time Activities," *Recent Social Trends*, 2 vols., 1933, Vol. II, Ch. XVIII.

Thom, D. A., *Normal Youth and Its Everyday Problems*, 1932.

Weill, B., *The Behavior of Young Children of the Same Family*, 1928.

White House Conference, *The Adolescent in the Family*, 1934.

——, *Children's Reading*, 1932.

——, *Summer Vacation Activities of the School Child*, 1933.

——, *The Young Child in the Home*, 1936.

EPILOGUE

CHAPTER XXV

NEW HORIZONS FOR THE FAMILY

The family endures through the ages as the nuclear process within which the future of humanity is wrought. The mating of man with woman determines the specific biological heritage of the new lives springing from their union: as father and mother, they protect, sustain, and nurture their children, selecting, as they do so, the influences which condition development of body, mind, and character. The underlying pattern of the family is rooted deep in human needs; its vital strands being the intangible bonds which unite men and women and children in the most intimate of all interrelationships. Nevertheless, strong and enduring as are these vital strands, they are also flexible and liable to distortion; and they have repeatedly become entangled with strands irrelevant to the underlying pattern.

The family has survived through its ability to adjust itself to changing social conditions, and to perform many functions in addition to those essential functions which it alone can combine and harmonize: procreation and nurture of the young; stable satisfaction of the sexual needs of the parents; the provision of home, the physical, social, and spiritual environment of family life. But the recent acceleration of social change has subjected the traditional pattern of the family to such unprecedented strain that its fabric has been torn asunder. From this disruption has emerged a new appreciation of the potential values of family life, a new awareness of its essential functions: an appreciation and an awareness stimulated by the development of social psychology. For, with the discovery that human nature is profoundly modifiable, it becomes evident that, within the family, lie potent means for its progressive amelioration.

For the first time, then, it becomes possible to view the family from a scientific and experimental point of view; deliberately to plan a family pattern designed to facilitate the performance of the family's essential functions, while remaining always alert to modify this pattern on the basis of results and in the light of newer knowledge. Present knowledge of the conditions of optimum development already indicates the supreme significance of enlightened and voluntary parenthood, and of the possibilities inherent in coöperative family life. It would appear that family influences may provide the necessary leaven for the development of a more fully coöperative society: they may promote individual development and foster social disposition and at the same time prevent the warping of character which is so potent a source of social ills. With progress in scientific understanding, there should be correlative advance in the discovery of methods and techniques more fully effective in achieving these ends.

But the family requires to be sustained by society and re-enforced in innumerable ways if it is to fulfill its essential functions. Legal reforms, economic reorganization, educational and other social developments are all necessary. Given progress along these lines, however, we may confidently rely on the potentialities for social betterment immanent in family life. For they derive their force from the most powerful of all human motives, the love of parents for their children.

Even so, misgivings arise. Are not we, to-day, faced with what Wells envisages as a race between education and catastrophe; may we not all be engulfed in an impending cataclysm in human affairs, in a storm whose ominous shadows already envelop us? Wars and rumors of wars, struggles between classes and nations suggest the imminence of a terrestrial day of judgment.

The primary human problem of maintenance still permeates both the struggle for economic reorganization within national boundaries and the rivalries between nations. The original problem of securing sufficient sustenance has been solved, but the immediate result has been the mad scramble for power and economic advancement which characterize what Tawney calls our *acquisitive* society; and an intense preoccupation in economic problems which Tawney compares to that of a hypochondriac, "absorbed in the processes of his own digestion." The economic problem, according to John Meynard Keynes, is "nothing but a frightful muddle, a transitory and unnecessary muddle. For the Western world already has the resources and the techniques, if we would create the organization to use them, capable of reducing the economic problem which now absorbs our moral and material energies to a position of secondary importance."[1] If such a change were brought about, human beings would at last be free to occupy themselves with their real and permanent problems: problems of human relations, of creation, of religion, of living "wisely, agreeably, and well." The obstacles to eco-

[1] Quoted by Harold Callender, "Critic of Britain's Muddling Through," *New York Times Magazine*, Sept. 17, 1933.

nomic reorganization lie "in the state of knowledge, judgment, and opinion of those who sit in the seats of authority." But these, in turn, are due to prevailing attitudes and the patterning of human nature in an acquisitive society. To avoid the control of the economic order by *coercive* power, every effort must be bent on the cultivation of socialized disposition and coöperative attitudes. For in this way alone may be generated what Mary Follett describes as *coactive* power, emergent from an integration of human interests.[1]

America is still animated with the vigor and hopefulness of youth; and certain of its faults are faults of immaturity. Yet there is grave danger in the continuance of a shallow philosophy of getting and spending, which brings no content, but only feverish restlessness. The Lynds' most recent report on Middletown justifies misgivings for the future of the American dream already expressed by James Truslow Adams.[2] Middletown has learnt little from the critical events of recent years. The depression was regarded as "just a bad bump on the road," a temporary deviation from normal, and was "the fault of some individuals (or, collectively of human nature) rather than anything amiss with the organization and functioning of culture."[3] Indeed, all efforts to change institutions constitute a "misguided assault on the one source of strength and progress within a nation, namely, the personal drive within the individual to accumulate wealth and to 'better himself.' 'Progress' . . . is a by-product of the pursuit of wealth."[4]

Below the surface, however, latent conflicts grow more insistent; above all, there is a widening gap between the ruthless realities of a pecuniary culture, the power-dominance-aggressive values of the business world, and the old traditions of friendly neighborliness. The very emphases laid on community spirit, loyalty, on being a "joiner," and spending leisure with others, all point to the substitution of a spurious counterfeit for genuine coöperation. A sentimentality which sugar-coats the actual facts must be the recourse of a social order which negates the very values it extols most highly. Moreover, in this community, bound into service to money making, "if personal and community security continue to be in serious jeopardy; not only the

---

[1] Mary P. Follett, *Creative Experience* (1924).
[2] *Our Business Civilization* (1929), and articles in the *New York Times Magazine*, May 14, 1933, and Oct. 18, 1936.
[3] *Middletown in Transition* (1937), pp. 493–495.   [4] *Ibid.*, pp. 493–495.

gentler values but values fertile to growth . . . may find themselves held in the iron grip of 'practical' need."[1] The Lynds thus find, in Middletown, "the possible seeds of an eventual coercive control which in Europe to-day goes under the name of fascism."[2]

The disconcerting features of Middletown are due in part to local peculiarities, but they are also representative of America, and in some degree of the whole of Western civilization. Ortega y Gasset, Carrel, and others have deplored the dearth of superior individuals, and the fact that intensive specialization debars those there are from positions of leadership, based on knowledge at once inclusive and expert.[3] At the same time, the masses, made the beneficiaries of the superior intelligence and social idealism of the few, are coming prematurely to power. The term masses is here used to denote, not necessarily the working classes, but all those who are standardized and commonplace, devoid of aspiration and distrustful of the rare and excellent.[4] It is such as these who, if comfort and security are threatened, become resentful, seeking a scapegoat to blame for their misfortunes, and a leader powerful enough to enforce his will through direct action and violence. Through identification with such a leader and a common cause, what were hitherto the inferiorities of innumerable weak and undeveloped human beings become merged in the formidable superiority of a "many-headed multitude." Modern facilities of communication have vastly increased the power of propaganda to reach the masses, and to weld them together in fanatical zeal through appealing to their emotions and antagonisms.

The methods of dictatorship are everywhere alike, whether in Communist Russia, Fascist Italy, or Nazi Germany. Fanatical idealism is the surest source of ruthlessness: ruthless cruelty in the crushing out of human lives; ruthless suppression of freedom of speech; ruthless terrorism as a means for imposing conformity and compliance. Even Russia's many and real achievements have been secured only at a terrible cost. Nevertheless, the dictators

---

[1] *Ibid.*, p. 428.   [2] *Ibid.*, p. 387.
[3] Ortega y Gasset, *The Revolt of the Masses* (1932), and Alexis Carrel, *Man the Unknown* (1935). At the Harvard Tercentenary Conference of Arts and Sciences central emphasis was laid on the pressing need for an organization of scientific intelligence in the interests of human well-being. Undoubtedly a large proportion of the world's potential leaders, in the sciences, arts, and in statesmanship, died in the World War.
[4] It is "characteristic of our time," says Ortega y Gasset, "that the vulgar proclaims and imposes the rights of vulgarity, or vulgarity as a right." *Op. cit.*, p. 77.

have been able to delude themselves and their peoples with their perverted ideologies. For they offer a way of escape from futility, and bring meaning into existence. In these new religions of the Communist, German, and Roman states, individuals lose themselves in the service of all-embracing ends. Most sinister of all is the zealous indoctrination of children. From the age of six in Italy, and ten in Germany, armies of little boys wear uniforms symbolic of their mental and spiritual regimentation. And little Bolsheviki and little Nazis alike are being taught from their nursery days to *hate* the enemy. What will all these marching children, bred to violence and hatred, mean to the future of humanity?

Long centuries of unjust exploitation of the weak by the strong have eventuated in a situation full of menace for the future: a situation which makes evident the spiritual starvation of the West, the restless search of modern man for an enduring and sustaining whole which shall endow the individual life with significance and bring peace and reassurance. The triumphant progress of a materialistic and mechanistic philosophy of life proclaimed human ideals to be illusory, and human aspirations doomed to frustration.[1]

Many, of course, all along refused to face the contradiction between "truths felt and truths thought," as Unamuno puts it.[2] They have remained within the fold of traditional religion, or else have deliberately found assuagement of "the tragic sense of life," in acceptance of fictions *as if* they possessed validity beyond their function as guides to practical experience.[3] Fortunately for the cause of social reform the full implications of mechanism, its utter fatalism and devaluation of human values, have usually been ignored or evaded. But in the post-war period of disillusionment there came for many a despairing sense of the futility and triviality of human life.[4]

[1] "We see," said Bertrand Russell, "surrounding the narrow raft illuminated by the flickering light of human comradeship, the dark ocean on whose rolling waves we toss for a brief hour. . . . All the loneliness of humanity amid hostile forces is concentrated upon the individual soul, which must struggle alone with what courage it can command, against the whole weight of a universe which cares nothing for its hopes and fears." "A Free Man's Worship," *Mysticism and Logic* (1918), p. 54.

[2] Miguel de Unamuno, *The Tragic Sense of Life* (1926).

[3] H. Vaihinger, *The Philosophy of "As If"* (1924). "Being," Nietzsche said, "is a fiction invented by those who suffer from becoming." *The Birth of Tragedy* (1870).

[4] Faiths and philosophies represent, according to Joseph Woods Krutch, "the successive and increasingly desperate expedients by which man, the ambitious animal, endeavors to postpone the inevitable realization that living is merely a physiological

What, then, of humanism? What of the undoubted fact that never before have so many, inspired by ideals of social justice, sought to make humanitarian attitudes effective through social and economic reform? It is a noteworthy fact that the philosophy of the greatest of contemporary humanists, John Dewey, escapes entirely from the stranglehold of mechanism. Science discloses the fact that "nature *has* a mechanism sufficiently constant to permit of calculation, inference and foresight." But, Dewey points out, this does not imply that "nature *is* a mechanism and only a mechanism."[1] Human life is a part of nature and "the intelligent activity of man is . . . nature realizing its own potentialities in behalf of a fuller and richer issue of events."[2] Values are genuine elements of nature, giving a clue to the inherent possibilities of experience and providing imagination with ideal ends. How, then, may the precious things of human life be made less insecure, more enduring; how may all human beings be given full participation in the joys of human association, of art and knowledge? For, while certain physical and social conditions lend support, others thwart and frustrate. To have faith in intelligence means realization of the fact that it is we, "looking to what the world and life might become," who must deliberately construct the future.[3]

Faith in the ideal possibilities of experience, that they may through our efforts be brought into existence, is *moral* faith, freed through experimental idealism from entanglement with intellectual beliefs about the ultimate inner nature of reality, such as are adhered to by orthodox religions. But the quality of such moral faith may be genuinely religious where its ends are sufficiently inclusive to arouse emotion, to evoke a passionate allegiance, and to impart unity and perspective to life. Vivid realization of our common human predicament, that we are a link in the human community, that all we have and are we owe to those who came before us, and that we are responsible for those who come after, brings with it a religious " sense of community and

process with only a physiological meaning and that it is most satisfactorily conducted by creatures who never feel the need to attempt to give it any other." *The Modern Temper* (1924), p. 235. This is but one step removed from Spengler's insistence that man is "a beast of prey" and "conflict is the original fact of life." Spengler prophesies with enthusiasm the coming to an end of the "domination of the rootless urban intellect," and with it democracy and the "dreary train of world-improvers." *The Hour of Decision* (1934).

[1] *The Quest for Certainty*, p. 248. Recent physical theory substantiates Dewey's argument.

[2] *Ibid.*, pp. 214–215.

[3] *Ibid.*, p. 285.

one's place in it."[1] Moreover, "the community of causes and consequences in which we, together with those not born, are enmeshed, is the widest and deepest symbol of the mysterious totality of being the imagination calls the universe."[2] Hence, "even in the midst of conflict, struggle and defeat, a consciousness is possible of the enduring and comprehending whole. . . . Within the flickering unconsequential acts of separate selves dwells a sense of the whole which claims and dignifies them. In its presence we put off mortality and live in the universal."[3] In the following passage, more clearly than anywhere else, Dewey reveals his faith.[4]

Fidelity to the nature to which we belong, as parts however weak, demands that we cherish our desires and ideals till we have converted them into intelligence, revised them in terms of the ways and means which nature makes possible. When we have used our thought to its utmost and have thrown into the moving unbalanced balance of things our puny strength, we know that though the universe slay us, still we may trust, for our lot is one with whatever is good in existence. We know that such thought and effort is one condition of the coming into existence of the better. As far as we are concerned it is the only condition, for it alone is in our power. To ask more than this is childish; but to ask less is a recreance no less egotistic, involving no less a cutting of ourselves from the universe than does the expectation that it meet and satisfy our every wish. To ask in good faith as much as this from ourselves is to stir into motion every capacity of imagination, and to exact from action every skill and bravery.

To ask that nature conform wholly to our desires would, indeed, be childish egoism; but we may surely *hope* for more than is explicitly offered by Dewey's faith in nature and the possibilities of experience. We may hope that what Montague calls the "momentous possibility" is an *actuality:* "the possibility that what is highest in spirit is also deepest in nature, that the ideal and the real are at least to some extent identified, not merely evanescently in our own lives, but enduringly in the universe itself."[5] Presumably even from Dewey's point of view this actuality may be eventually disclosed through experience.[6] For

[1] Dewey, *Human Nature and Conduct*, p. 330.
[2] Dewey, *A Common Faith* (1934), p. 85.
[3] Dewey, *Human Nature and Conduct*, pp. 330–332.
[4] *Experience and Nature* (Open Court Publishing Company, 1926), pp. 420–421.
[5] W. P. Montague, *Belief Unbound* (1930), p. 6.
[6] We may, Dewey says "have faith in experience when intelligently used . . . as a means for penetrating continually further into the heart of nature . . . , as a growing progressive self-disclosure of nature itself." *A Common Faith*, p. 86.

here is none of that isolation of man from nature, that setting over of the supernatural as opposed to the natural which has been influential throughout history in turning attention away from the betterment of human life here on earth.[1]

Now, more than ever before, is it essential that human aspiration be not deflected from realization of present social responsibilities. Not only has "intelligence after millions of years of errancy . . . found itself as a method," but this discovery has been made at a time when there is no alternative to dependence on intelligence save "drift and casual improvisation, or the use of coercive force stimulated by unintelligent emotion and fanatical dogmatism."[2]   Moral and intellectual integrity demand that we accept the full implications of scientific method in theory and in practice; that we face the fact that our lives are hedged in by the unknown and mysterious, and are beset with tragic uncertainty. But, as William James said, "the most useful investigator, because the most sensitive observer, is always he whose eager interest in one side of the question is balanced by an equally keen nervousness lest he be deceived."[3]   Without relinquishing reliance on science, without demanding certainty, may we not encourage ourselves with a hope, a faith even, in possibilities which lie beyond earthly experience?

Were social justice to reign more fully on the earth, would not human beings still be afflicted with the "incurable sadness and loneliness" of which Montague speaks? Why do sensitive and highly developed human beings long for personal survival and hope for evidence of a spiritual principle in nature? Not at all from fear of annihilation. Who could fear dreamless sleep? Nor from desire for perpetuation of their limited individual lives. But rather that they may outgrow these limitations; perceive new beauty, understand more fully. And most of all they desire survival, not so much for themselves, as for others whose personalities are of such unique value that the thought of their annihilation is intolerable.[4]   The most utterly disinterested and spiritual

---

[1] See T. V. Smith's discussion of religion as "humanity's institutionalized shortcut," *The Philosophic Way of Life* (1929).

[2] Dewey, *Liberalism and Social Action* (1935), p. 93.

[3] *The Will to Believe* (1896), p. 21.

[4] "Passed from themselves and far from me, their light
   Lost in an unimaginable Light
   Or sunken to dark flame, I might not know
   Nor soul nor body. But save Death restore
   Those heaven-climbers I had known when young
   Life has been vain."

                                        A. E., "How?" in *Vale and Other Poems.*

of human motives are those which most forcefully actuate a hope for survival.

The present age is characterized by new scientific discoveries which may have epoch-making results in allowing fuller understanding of the course and destiny of human life. There is, moreover, a significant convergence of individual thinkers, in different fields, upon a common emphasis: a vivid realization both for thought and social action of the full implications of our mutual and reciprocal relationships with all other human beings. There is a growing sense that we are approaching an end of an era, and that in the confusion and darkness of the present there are signs which presage the dawn: not only of a new age, but perhaps of a new level of human life.[1]

Human beings, Heard points out, represent the culminating embodiment of "the principle that life evolves by sensitiveness and awareness, by being exposed and not protected. . . . The creature which ascends is a creature who somehow chooses sensitiveness, awareness, a constantly widening focus and new experiences."[2] In the evolutionary process, power and protection, security, certainty, and comfort have been bought repeatedly at the cost of continuing sensitiveness, more intense consciousness, and the path of ascending life. Defensive violence and parasitic cunning may succeed for the day, but lead at last to arrested development or destruction. The easiest way, relapse into violence, has been taken again and again in the history of civilization. It is, indeed, the inevitable course, whenever material discoveries, economic mastery, and self-conscious individualism are not balanced by psychological discoveries which allow human beings to recapture their sense of the larger life which they share with all other human beings.

Reunion with the larger life has in all ages been sought through religion. Already by 3400 B.C., in Egypt, moral aspiration was beginning to develop, and there was conscious realization that violence brought sin and strife, and made righteousness and peace impossible.[3] And more than a thousand years later,

---

[1] See, for example, Henry M. Bernard, *Some Neglected Factors in Evolution* (1911), a book which Sir J. Arthur Thompson said was at least forty years in advance of its time; Cora L. Williams, *Creative Involution* (1916); William Patten, *The Grand Strategy of Evolution* (1920); Gerald Heard, *The Source of Civilization* (1935) and *The Third Morality* (1937).

[2] *The Source of Civilization*, p. 70.

[3] See Breasted, *The Dawn of Conscience.* In this fascinating account of the earliest recorded discussions of right and wrong, Breasted shows that social judgments were already being made in 3400 B.C. But the oldest historical monument in the world,

in 2000 B.C., the records tell of an age of disillusionment, scepticism, and pessimism, when the ruins of the "sixty-mile rampart of Pyramids, sweeping along the margin of the Western desert," were already ancient.[1] "None cometh from thence to tell us how they fare." Moreover, "the gentle man perishes, the bold-faced goes everywhere."[2]

Also, from time to time, and more especially in the East, there have arisen exponents of new ways of life: mystics and sages, seemingly possessed of psychological insight beyond what humanity has yet attained. It has been suggested that men such as Buddha, Socrates, and Christ presage the emergence of a new level of conscious life, higher than is ours at present.

But, in spite of religious aspiration and the teaching of sages and the visions of the mystics, little progress has been made in eliminating violence. To-day, through scientific invention, the world becomes more and more closely knit together, and humanity is beginning to assume the aspect of some vast unwieldy organism deprived as yet of the spirit which might integrate and harmonize its warring impulses. It grows more and more obvious that stability and enduring peace can never be won by violence, for "as the means are so are the ends achieved," and force breeds counter-force.[3] As yet, however, the minds and emotions of men are too undeveloped, too undisciplined, for the task of working out the peaceful interrelationships without which the world seems doomed to disintegration and chaos.

Authorities on the human brain believe it to be in its early youth; but man's manifest lack of control over human nature causes self-inflicted catastrophes which act as a brake on its development. Few brains, indeed, ever reach the maturity of which they are even now capable. Such considerations render of first importance the discovery of F. Matthias Alexander of methods for the coördination of psycho-physical activities through conscious control; and give added significance to his contention that progress from the pre-civilized state to civilization demands a concomitant change from a subconscious to a

also dating from the same century, shows a Pharoah about to crush the skull of an Asiatic captive; and is therefore a monument to brute force and to possession, by right of conquest, of the neighboring copper and turquoise mines. Breasted emphasizes the recency of the beginnings of the Age of Character, not five thousand years ago, as contrasted with the Age of Violence, holding sway from time immemorial. Heard, on the other hand, holds it probable that an age of organized violence supervened, with the beginnings of civilization, on a more primitive age of *spontaneous coöperation*.

[1] *Ibid.*, p. 161. [2] *Ibid.*, p. 172.

[3] Dewey, *Liberalism and Social Action*, p. 86.

conscious plane of control.[1] He has shown that individuals may be educated or reëducated in the direction and control of their psycho-physical mechanism, so as to bring about positive health, emotional stability, confidence, and happiness. Perhaps, were human beings thus given fuller control of themselves and their emotions, they might find effective coöperation possible. Heard believes that to achieve this end there will have to be a development of psycho-physical techniques designed to "enlarge" consciousness and give the individual direct awareness of his kinship with other human beings and with all life.[2] The scientific and experimental development of such methods has been made possible, he holds, by the development of psychology.

A point has undoubtedly been reached where all facts and possibilities of human experience should be investigated, so far as possible, by scientific methods. The time is ripe for the open-minded research into metapsychological phenomena.[3] This is all the more essential because of the widespread preoccupation with occultism.[4] While there are undoubted dangers in the influx of Eastern influences into Western lands, yet the West with its one-sided absorption in material progress cannot lightly dismiss the spiritual experience of the older civilizations of the East. Jung has expressed the hope that, if a bridge of psychological understanding can be built between East and West, the West may be helped to find its own way in what he calls "the tremendous experiment of becoming conscious."[5]

[1] See F. Matthias Alexander, *Man's Supreme Inheritance, Constructive Conscious Control of the Individual*, and *The Use of the Self* (1932). In an introduction to the second of these volumes Dewey says that Alexander has demonstrated "a new scientific principle with respect to the control of human behavior, as important as any principle which has ever been discovered in the realm of external nature."

[2] In the concluding chapter of *The Third Morality* (1937), Heard describes such a technique. In this connection we may also note a suggestion of profound and far-reaching importance made by Trigant Burrow, *The Social Basis of Consciousness* (1927). He believes that the usual methods of praise and blame, suggesting as they do from the outset of life that the right and good will be rewarded and the wrong and bad will bring penalty, inevitably lead to a contraction of the child's "universe of feeling," until it comprises but his own ego and egoistic advantage and self-interest, and excludes a third factor essential to a fully rounded consciousness: namely, a sense of interrelationship with others, "of the organic continuity of consciousness that unites the individuals of the species into a confluent whole." P. 60; and see Chapter III.

[3] Intolerance is only permissible, as T. V. Smith points out, "in defense of tolerance," *Creative Sceptics* (1934), p. 260. In the last few years, telepathy, clairvoyance, prevision and the techniques of Yoga have been subjected to scientific investigation. See, I. B. Rhine, *Extra-Sensory Perception* (1934), and Kovoor Behanan, *Yoga, a Scientific Evaluation* (1937).

[4] Jung says that, in comparison with these movements to-day, the interest in scientific psychology is negligible. *Modern Man in Search of a Soul* (1933), pp. 138 *et seq.*

[5] In his introduction to the translation of an ancient Chinese manuscript, *The Secret of the Golden Flower* (Eng. tr. 1932).

In recent years earlier scientific concepts of matter, life, and mind have been revolutionized. All is apparently dissolved into electrical energy, and modern theoretical physics no longer studies a universe existing in its own right in space and time, but is concerned rather to reduce to law and order the impressions the universe makes on human senses. We, who perceive, and all that we perceive are interrelated and interacting parts of a vast system of rhythmic forces. From among these our sense organs select and transmit to the brain those to which we can respond. Our world is thus a construct of our psycho-physical being.

So far as present knowledge goes, the individual appears as a center of experience, a focus of interrelationships, dependent on cosmic energies and yet in some sense independent. "We do not know," Carrel says, "how he is bound to *other* beings, where his spatial and temporal frontiers are."[1] The significance of time for an understanding of consciousness and life has been increasingly stressed since Bergson developed his philosophy of creative evolution, which sees in duration, or *experienced and lived time*, the fundamental reality, not only of human life but of the universe. Bergson's theory of duration involves the probability "that in man, though perhaps in man alone, consciousness pursues its path beyond this earthly life."[2] One investigator, Dunne, has actually been able to develop a technique for experiencing the future, and has, on this basis, made a mathematical analysis of time, which also seems to give assurance of the survival of consciousness.[3] Further developments may well bring to light discoveries of immense significance, revolutionizing our whole outlook on life.[4]

A wide perspective must thus include a realization of the precarious situation in which humanity finds itself to-day, and also consideration of possibilities for the future of humanity, beyond our present power to imagine. We must view the life of to-day in the light of man's enduring quest for the ideal and the eternal, his pursuit of truth, his love of beauty, and his sense of justice

[1] *Op. cit.*, p. 258.

[2] "Life and Consciousness," *The Hibbert Journal*, Vol. X (Oct., 1911), p. 43.

[3] *Experiment with Time* (1927) and *A Serial Universe* (1934). In the first of these books Dunne describes his experiences in dreaming of the future, and the experiences of friends whom he had induced to adopt his technique. The second volume presents the highly technical development of a theory of time to explain such experiences.

[4] In his most recent book, Bergson speaks of the "joy . . . which would automatically follow a vision of the life beyond attained through the furtherance of scientific experiment." *The Two Sources of Morality and Religion* (Eng. tr. 1935), p. 274.

and of the moral responsibilities inherent in human association.[1] Levels of consciousness, higher than those of contemporary humanity, have already been attained by individuals of genius, not only by mystics and sages, but by others in different lines of endeavor, poets, composers, mathematicians. These lead the way in bringing to lesser human beings new revelations of beauty, new perceptions of meaning and of the possibilities immanent in shared experience.[2] It may be a dream that we are on the upward path to a new and higher level of human life. Nevertheless,

> The mind of man urged on
> By an invincible passion, never will cease
> To ask. What is beyond? . . .[3]

And this very passion and our dreams of the beyond, provided they remain deep-rooted in present fact, provide inspiration to present effort.

Family life must be placed in the perspective of considerations such as these, if we are to discern its full potential significance for the future of humanity. If we would have peace and progress, we must develop social institutions which liberate capacity, promote good habits of thinking, and, above all, foster sentiments and attitudes necessary to effective coöperation. And of all social institutions, none possesses a fraction of the potential power of the family.

Once more, then, in the course of human evolution it appears probable that a turning point in human affairs may be largely dependent on significant developments in family life. The prolongation of infancy and the consequent long association between mother and offspring were concomitant with the development of specific human characteristics, community living, speech, and intelligence. The attachment of the male to his mate and offspring was conducive to greater security, better nurture, and social development. It seems highly probable, therefore, that

[1] Bertrand Russell has said: "Those who best promote life . . . aim . . . at what seems like a gradual incarnation, a bringing into our human existence of something eternal, something that appears to imagination to live in a heaven remote from strife and failure and the devouring jaws of time." *Why Men Fight* (1917), p. 268.

[2] The growing appreciation of great music is a phenomenon of the utmost social importance. Every human mood and aspiration can become shared experience through music. The influences of martial music and dance rhythms are familiar. The soothing, healing, cleansing, enhancing, and enlightening influence of music on human emotion and thought has not been sufficiently realized.

[3] Alfred Noyes, *The Torchbearers* (1930), Vol. III, p. 149.

the mutual coöperation which made human evolution possible had its roots in family relationships.

And, once again, the earliest surviving records of human thought furnish "conclusive *historical* evidence that moral discernment had its roots in the life of the family."[1] Egyptian tomb reliefs and inscriptions, dating from five thousand years ago, "unmistakably . . . disclose the family as the primary influence in the rise and development of moral ideas . . . , the most important fundamental step in the evolution of civilization."[2]

May we not hope for still further advance, this time through the *deliberate* enlightenment and enhancement of family life? In the five thousand years that are gone, physical force and violence have permeated human relationships and molded institutions. The patriarchal family has been both a result and a cause of this *man*-made social order.[3] The antagonism so often noted between family interests and wider social interests readily obtains in the typical self-centered patriarchal family, with the arrested development of the woman, and the one-sided specialization of the man for aggression and the exercise of power.

In a family which is genuinely coöperative, the relationships between father, mother, and their children may once again become a radiating source of sympathy and understanding, in widening circles of social relationship. For the *care of life*, which in all ages has been the central preoccupation of women, is now recognized as the most vital concern of society. The spirit of motherliness, utterly opposed to force and violence, is found invaluable in human affairs. As more women become emancipated from ignorance, idleness, and the bonds of tradition, we may hope for fuller integration of scientific knowledge in the interests of human relationships, and for the shaping of new instrumentalities of social control.

[1] Breasted, *The Dawn of Conscience*, p. 121.

[2] *Ibid.*, pp. 116–117. "It was the sunshine and the atmosphere of the earliest human homes that created ideals of conduct and revealed the beauty of self-forgetfulness. . . . There is one supreme human relationship, that which has created the home and made the family fireside the source out of which man's highest qualities have grown up to transform the world. As historical fact, it is to family life that we owe the greatest debt which the mind of man can conceive." Pp. 410–411.

[3] Investigations undertaken by the Institut für Socialforschung reveal that the patterns of nurture characteristic of the patriarchal family prepare individuals for the acceptance of authority in society, and are thus in large measure responsible for the present growth of authority, as manifested in totalitarian states. A first report of these investigations was published in 1936 under the title of *Studien über Autorität und Familie*.

But, as the spirit of motherliness is needed in the life of the world, so is there need for a fuller participation of men in family life—for a more intensive fatherliness. Manliness with its emphasis on protective strength, reliability, and courage is the correlative of womanliness, from which all trace of immature dependence has gone, but where the emphasis is still upon the qualities conducive to the care of life. Where manly men and womanly women also become developed human beings, the coöperative family will more fully emerge as the prevailing pattern of family life. Only then will its consequences for individual happiness and social well-being become apparent.

The White House Conference fittingly and prophetically dedicated its volumes to the children, "whose faces are turned toward the light of a new day and who must be prepared to meet a great adventure." In the measure in which all men and women likewise dedicate themselves, humanity will become aware of what lies beyond the new horizons which, in our day, are opening for the family.